THE ASSASSINATIONS

THE ASSASSINATIONS

DALLAS AND BEYOND—
A GUIDE TO COVER-UPS
AND INVESTIGATIONS

edited by Peter Dale Scott,
Paul L. Hoch and Russell Stetler

 Vintage Books / A Division of Random House / New York

FIRST VINTAGE BOOKS EDITION, February 1976

Copyright © 1976 by Peter Dale Scott, Paul L. Hoch and Russell Stetler

All rights reserved under International and Pan-American Copyright Conventions. Published in the United States by Random House, Inc., New York, and simultaneously in Canada by Random House of Canada Limited, Toronto. Originally published by Random House, Inc., in 1976.

Library of Congress Cataloging in Publication Data

Main entry under title:
The Assassinations.

  Bibliography: p.
  Includes index.
    1. Kennedy, John Fitzgerald, Pres. U.S., 1917–1963—
Assassination.   2.   United States. Warren Commission.
Report of the President's Commission on the Assassination
of President John F. Kennedy.   3.   Kennedy, Robert,
1925–1968—Assassination.   4.   King, Martin Luther—
Assassination.   5.   United States. Commission on CIA
Activities within the United States.   I.   Scott, Peter
Dale.   II.   Hoch, Paul.   III.   Stetler, Russell.
[E842.9.A8 1976b]   364.1′524′0973   75-40621
ISBN: 0-394-71650-7

Manufactured in the United States of America

9 8 7 6 5 4 3 2

First Edition

ACKNOWLEDGMENTS

We wish to express our personal gratitude to all the contributors whose cooperation made this book possible. We are also indebted to a much wider community of critics who have selflessly pursued the truth about assassinations in America. These critics endured a long period in which their views were scorned, their labor went unrewarded, and their reputations were smeared with invective and abuse.

Our agent, the late Cyrilly Abels, was of great help in transforming this manuscript into a book.

In the headnotes which introduce the book's four main sections, we explain our reasons for choosing the particular selections. Our editorial role has for the most part been confined to selection, excerption, and in a small number of instances emendation. We resisted the temptation to add footnotes to question the accuracy of a given interpretation or to update hypotheses. As much as possible, the texts are published as they originally appeared, without editorial insertions, in the belief that the adversary style of the collection will leave few erroneous statements unchallenged. The index will permit interested readers to compare the varying points of view on specific issues.

Finally, we want to acknowledge that the political murders which are the focus of this book are no worse, nor more worthy of study, than the killings at Kent State or Jackson State, or the death by napalm of an anonymous peasant apparently more remote from our lives. To speak of the politics of assassination is to imply a range of questions that is beyond the scope of this volume even to enumerate. Readers who are moved by this anthology to inquire more deeply into the politics of assassination should not forget the wider setting.

INTRODUCTION

If a nation decides to live by lies, it has chosen a course of intellectual stagnation, and ultimately of political decay. Lies and murders frequently go together, for both are customary instruments of political forces that cannot secure their ends by other means.

In 1966 a Gallup poll indicated that a majority of American citizens doubted the findings of the Warren Commission, yet a majority also did not wish to see the issue of the John F. Kennedy assassination reopened. In those days many sophisticated observers would argue privately that to insist on the truth would put too great a strain on the American political process. Liberals who could recall the McCarthyite witch hunts for conspirators in the 1950s were only too happy not to encourage the so-called "paranoid style" in American politics. The consequences of these accommodations to unreason are much more evident a decade later. The invocation of "national security interests," which helped to suppress the issue in the mid-sixties, is precisely the ground on which to reopen it today.

In 1976, as we look back at our last three presidential elections, we see that the outcomes of all three have been profoundly affected, if not determined, by the bullets which killed the two Kennedy brothers and wounded Governor George Wallace. In each case we have been offered the stereotype, by now almost comic, of the demented loner who lays a self-incriminating trail of evidence. In theory, of course, all these shootings could be unrelated; but they have all met with the same bizarre official response. Time after time disinterested observers have pointed to serious flaws in the official accounts. These critics have been answered not by serious counterarguments, but with silence, ridicule, harassment and misrepresentation in the most powerful segments of the national media. According to a member of the Warren Commission, the late Representative Hale Boggs, the FBI leaked information intended to discredit critics, including "photographs of sexual activity and reports of alleged Communist affiliations of some authors of articles and books on the assassination."* And as this went on, Martin Luther King and many other leaders—particularly in the black community—have been shot in circumstances which more than once suggest official collusion.

The official deafness to the objections of the critics does not of course prove that all these critics are right. Pioneers on any intellectual frontier must often use rough tools. Some critics have, by careless and imprecise charges, unintentionally made it easier for the national media to treat all of the so-called assassination buffs with condescension or even abuse. This has obscured the existence of a growing and, as yet, unanswered body of painstaking, scholarly research which challenges most of the key official "lone assassin" theories. To retrieve this research from such journals as *Modern Medicine* and the *Texas Observer* is one of the main purposes of this anthology. Another is to let readers see and judge for themselves how the serious work of Sylvia Meagher, to take one example, has been "answered" by a combination of cheap insults and a one-sided press.

It is beyond our ambition to solve the mysteries or even to reconcile the differing interpretations of many of the critics. In some cases, there are even factual errors which have become evident in the light of new disclosures or investigation, but we have not attempted to remove from these generally valuable pieces all of those claims with which we disagree. Our main goal is simply to reflect the range of serious criticism and to suggest starting points for new investigations.

Since 1963, other factors have fostered a growing cynicism and distaste for the current style of our national life: most notably the Indochina war, official lying, the abuse of power and high-level criminal conspiracies surrounding Watergate. Some of the essays

---

* See Ron Kessler, "FBI Data on Critics to Boggs," *Washington Post*, January 21, 1975, p. 1.

in this collection will argue that these factors are themselves consequences of the bullet politics which has so influenced the White
House succession since November 1963. Not all readers will agree.
Some indeed may be so disillusioned with the traditional political
alternatives in this country as to see little more than a symbolic
importance in the national habit of shooting leaders and
dissenters.

Either way, whether the politics of assassination is a determining reality or a mere symptom of larger problems, the failure to
discuss it has degraded the normal political context of rational
discourse. More than one figure in the Democratic Party, which so
far has been the chief party of the victims, will admit privately,
if not in public, that they fear death as the reward for a successful
presidential campaign. The national silence about this fear indicates how deeply it is felt—not that it is ignored.*

This collection begins with excerpts from the criticism of the
Warren Report by the courageous first generation of assassination
researchers—people like Mark Lane, Harold Weisberg and Sylvia
Meagher. Their appeal to reason won them only a popular, unofficial audience, even though most of their objections, far more than
could be printed here, remain unanswered and perhaps unan-
swerable today.

The first wave of negative criticism has since been expanded
and supplemented in two directions. On the one hand there has
been expert research into physical details, such as Dr. Cyril Wecht's
painstaking demonstration that the Warren Commission's theory
of a single assassin cannot be reconciled with the available physical
evidence (see pages 228–242). Other critics have transferred their
attention from the events of the assassination to their sociopolitical
context, such as the intelligence connections of Lee Harvey Oswald
and his Cuban contacts, and the police and underworld connections of Jack Ruby. Such researchers contend that in the long run
one cannot understand the working of a throttle without studying
the working of the whole engine: it is the same with assassination
politics.

Since we began to put this book together, events have moved

---

* A related problem is the neglect of the consequences of the assassinations on
policy—both domestically and in foreign affairs. All too little has been written on
these important matters.

very rapidly. The tide of disbelief in the multiple-lone-assassins theory has risen dramatically, moving from the underground press into the national media. We suspect it is no accident that those in the highest authority have proven to be most resistant to a reopening of the search for truth. The Presidency is itself in crisis, for the normal pattern of succession simply has not been followed since 1963. Kennedy's assassination, Johnson's failure to seek a second term, Nixon's dirty tricks, the Agnew-Nixon resignations —these events show the Presidency's dysfunction. In this context, to raise questions about the politics of assassination is to touch a raw nerve. This would be true even if the present incumbent were not one of the survivors (and most vocal defenders) of the original Warren Commission.

We expect that the next few months will see the rise of many new stories, as well as the revival of old ones, not all of which will be aimed at disclosing the truth. We have already seen the reemergence of one such old allegation: that Oswald was an agent of Fidel Castro. The dubious sources for this same story in 1963 (see pp. 360 and 361) incline us to view it with extreme skepticism.

In general we are not confident that the current revival of interest in political murders will lead to their rapid solution. Too much is at stake: to raise questions about Dallas is ultimately to raise questions about the whole structure of political manipulation and control in this country. But that is precisely why we consider the subject matter of this book to be important. Although the ensuing articles will do little to identify the true assassins, they will, we believe, tell alert readers more about important covert processes of politics in America. And such knowledge will be necessary if the role of these covert processes is ever to be diminished.

Every true act of skepticism presupposes an act of faith. The questions raised in this book presuppose an act of faith in the people of America, in their ability to demand, discern, and ultimately settle for no less than an adequate accounting of the truth.

July 30, 1975
Peter Dale Scott
Paul L. Hoch
Russell Stetler

CONTENTS

WHAT HAPPENED IN DEALEY PLAZA?

THE COMMISSION, THE CRITICS AND THE PRESS

OTHER ASSASSINATIONS

INTRODUCTION

MARTIN LUTHER KING

ROBERT F. KENNEDY

FROM DALLAS TO WATERGATE: THE POLITICS OF ASSASSINATION

THE ROCKEFELLER COMMISSION AND ITS UNANSWERED QUESTIONS

KEY TO SYMBOLS

Citations referring to the *Report of the President's Commission on the Assassination of President Kennedy (The Warren Report*; Washington: U.S. Government Printing Office, 1964) are notated by the symbol "WR," or simply "R," followed by page numbers. References to testimony from the *Hearings Before the President's Commission on the Assassination of President Kennedy (Hearings and Exhibits*; Washington: U.S. Government Printing Office, 1964) are indicated by the volume number of the Hearings, followed by the page number (for example, 2H 301 designates Volume II of the Hearings, page 301). References to the Exhibits indicate the name and/or number of the Exhibit (for example, Kantor Exhibit No. 3; or CE 150). Page numbers which follow Exhibit designations may refer either to the pages of the Exhibit itself, or to the pages of the volume in which it appears. Notations such as *"Archives,* CD 80" refer to the vast store of unpublished documents in the National Archives, in this case, Warren Commission Document No. 80.

THE ASSASSINATION OF PRESIDENT JOHN F. KENNEDY

INTRODUCTION

The assassination of President John F. Kennedy, closely followed by the nationally televised murder of his alleged assassin Lee Harvey Oswald, stunned and paralyzed America in a way that is difficult to recapture as we look back. There was a seemingly universal sense of wanting this shocking event to be over, wanting the case to be closed. The Dallas police and the FBI could compensate for their failure to prevent the crime of assassination by reassuring us that at least the mystery was promptly solved and justice was speedily rendered when Jack Ruby took the law into his own hands. A broad body of liberal opinion was likewise uncomfortable that Oswald's alleged leftist affiliations might touch off another wave of McCarthyism. It was reassuring to learn that Lee Oswald was a loner, not a joiner. There would be no invidious chain reaction of guilt by association with him. Thus, a national consensus arose very quickly—a consensus both relieved by the Dallas authorities' explanation of things and reluctant to pursue the matter any further.

Less than a month after the assassination, attorney Mark Lane had put together a journalistic defense brief, pointing out that Oswald should have enjoyed the presumption of innocence in the press and that an adversary proceeding would have certainly raised a host of conflicts in the eyewitness testimony recorded by the media. The only publication that would touch Lane's brief was the National Guardian, a rather eclectic paper of the left wh

*then described itself as a progressive newsweekly. A pattern
had already begun. While the leading journals of anti-McCarthy
liberalism showed little sustained interest in disputing the official
theory, the writers who questioned the "lone deranged assassin"
hypothesis were given the support they deserved by courageous
but relatively obscure publications such as M. S. Arnoni's* Minority of One *and* Liberation.

*The Warren Report, published in September 1964, provided a
definitive statement of the official explanation of the events in
Dallas. It basically confirmed the conclusions of the Dallas police
and the FBI (which those two agencies made available to the public respectively a few days and a few weeks after the assassination)
that the assassination was the work of one man, Lee Harvey
Oswald, with no evidence of a conspiracy. Among those who had
studied the early critiques of the Dallas police–FBI hypothesis,
the Warren Report did little to establish the case against Oswald.*

*The earliest criticisms focused on internal inconsistencies in the
pre–Warren Commission case. Some of the points made in the
writings of these earliest critics, including Joachim Joesten and
Thomas Buchanan, were rebutted in the Warren Report; other
points were misrepresented or ignored. The most prominent of
the early critics was Mark Lane, who appeared before the Commission on behalf of Oswald's mother. He holds the distinction
of being singled out by President Gerald Ford, a member of the
Commission, in his book* Portrait of the Assassin *(New York:
Simon and Schuster, 1965, written with John R. Stiles). Ford
noted that Lane "stumped Europe, peddling his questions" about
the assassination and "harassed the work of the Commission by
innuendo and inference."*

*Upon its publication, the Warren Report was attacked as a
prosecutor's brief rather than an impartial study. The Commission also published twenty-six volumes of hearings and exhibits—
quickly prompting critics to argue that the Report did not fairly
represent the evidence published in support of its conclusions.
This wave of criticism was led by Harold Weisberg in* Whitewash:
The Report on the Warren Report *and by Lane in* Rush to
Judgment.

One different approach was that of Edward J. Epstein, whose
Inquest *(published in 1966) attempted to understand the*

workings of the Warren Commission and established that (even by the Commissioners' own standards) the investigation was restrained by the pressures of time and the complexity of the Commission's relationship with its investigative arms—primarily the FBI and CIA. Epstein's analysis was based on interviews with members of the Commission and its staff (and limited access to their papers). It also brought out new evidence about conflicting official reports of the basic facts of the shooting which had been suppressed from the twenty-six volumes and the Warren Report, such as the FBI's assertion in its Summary Report (contrary to the Warren Report) that the first bullet to hit Kennedy did not pass through his body. After Watergate, Epstein's approach appears quite tame, but his book had a substantial impact at the time of its publication.

The critics then proceeded with their analysis of the evidence in the twenty-six volumes. The Commission hadn't bothered to index this material, but critic Sylvia Meagher produced a subject index to the Report and the Hearings. In 1967 her definitive work on the twenty-six volumes and the integrity of the Commission's work appeared under the title Accessories after the Fact. We have chosen to represent the early critical books only by excerpts from Meagher, whose own work includes a distillation of much of the best analysis done by her colleagues. We have deliberately chosen to reprint her work in an area that is less well known, the killing of Dallas police officer J. D. Tippit, in part because this narrowly focused chapter demonstrates the depth and range of the first wave of criticism and also because the Tippit killing has emerged as a central concern of one of the most outspoken defenders of the Report, former Commission counsel David Belin. (We also include a brief exchange between Meagher and Belin.) The critics progressed from an essentially negative critique to an attempt to analyze the evidence with the fairmindedness and thoroughness which the Commission itself had failed to show.

To round out the defense-brief approach, we are including a selection on Oswald's alibi for the assassination from a newly published book by Howard Roffman. Critics now hold differing views on whether Oswald was actually involved in the assassination or in a related conspiracy, but Roffman shows how a competent defense lawyer would have approached the problem of raising reasonable doubt in the minds of a jury as to whether Oswald was guilty as charged. Our collection does not attempt to resolve the question of Oswald's guilt or innocence, or to reconcile the differing views of even the critics among our contributors. It is wrong to lay the burden of resolving such questions upon those who lack the powers and resources of an official investigation.

Whether or not Oswald was involved, there was serious evidence of a conspiracy to implicate him. Meagher's treatment of some of this material in "The Proof of the Plot" shows that one of the most important leads in the Commission's evidence had not been properly pursued.

As the Commission's files in the National Archives gradually became available, the case against the Warren Commission became overwhelming. Even Albert Newman, perhaps the only serious critic to endorse the Report's lone-assassin conclusion, faulted most of the Commission's work. Some critics moved into a more positive, but more difficult and risky, undertaking—to try to understand what had actually taken place in Dallas's Dealey Plaza. Harold Weisberg was among the first of the researchers to explore the files in the Archives. His 1967 book Photographic White-wash: Suppressed Kennedy Assassination Pictures documents how the Commission failed to gather some of the most basic evidence for a reconstruction of the crime. Richard Sprague collected and studied the photographic evidence. As some of our selections in the section on Dealey Plaza show, a significant part of the critics' effort went into developing and applying technical expertise to do what the Commission had failed to do.

Sylvia Meagher eloquently points out that the most basic and spectacular evidence in regard to the physical details of the assassination, the 8-mm home movie taken by a spectator to the President's motorcade, Abraham Zapruder, raises serious questions not resolved by the Warren Report. That much is beyond doubt. What the film and the physical evidence do show is still subject to debate among responsible critics. Two of our contributors, David Lifton and David Welsh, argue, for example, that President Kennedy was hit from the front as well as the rear, whereas two others, Cyril Wecht and Robert Smith, argue that the medical evidence does not show a shot from the front. But both arguments establish that the Warren Commission's conclusions discount much evidence which would ordinarily be taken very seriously.

Six Seconds in Dallas, by Josiah Thompson, was the first book (1967) to attempt a systematic reconstruction of the details of the shooting. We have selected an excerpt from Thompson's case against the famous single-bullet hypothesis. The critics had no difficulty showing that the Commission failed to make appropriate scientific studies of alternatives to the single-bullet theory, but they were denied access to crucial evidence themselves for many years. The Kennedy autopsy material was unavailable to independent experts until 1972. The articles by Wecht and Smith reflect the first examination of this material by a non-government-sponsored pathologist. (For contrary medical interpretations, see the writings of Dr. John Lattimer.) Their case against the lone-assassin hypothesis is cautious, factually conservative and compelling. Stronger allegations, based on the Zapruder film's indication of the timing of shots and of the movements of the President's head (as summarized by David Lifton), cannot be established with comparable certainty at present.

In the meantime, newly available evidence and new investigative tools and methods have permitted the critics to extend the scope of their understanding. The executive session transcript of the Warren Commission's meeting of January 27, 1964—released as a result of a Freedom of Information suit filed by Harold Weisberg—provides an insight into the mechanism of the cover-up in the important matter of Oswald's alleged informant relationship with the FBI. FBI reports on apparent threats against Kennedy and Martin Luther King were also rescued from obscurity in the Archives by Weisberg. These reports (the so-called Milteer documents) provide striking confirmation of earlier evidence of the Commission's failure to give serious attention to hypotheses other than the "lone nut" theory.

Some key evidence remains unavailable. Attorney Jim Lesar's account of his legal efforts to obtain spectrographic test results—basic scientific test data—under a Freedom of Information Act suit reveals how strongly the government continues to resist disclosure.

George O'Toole, meanwhile, has used a new "truth detector" —the polygraph-like Psychological Stress Evaluator—to argue fr *a scientific point of view what Lane and others argued as lawyers: that Oswald was innocent.*

Our concluding section on the Kennedy assassination contains the observations of the last three Presidents, who backed the Warren Report. The exchange between Sylvia Meagher and David Belin exposes the lack of factual support for his defense of his work on the Commission staff. The latest major defense of the Report—by two of the Commission's staff lawyers, W. David Slawson and Richard Mosk—has a new concession. Though they support the Commission's conclusions and oppose a full reopening of the inquiry, they argue that everything on the assassination in the National Archives should be made available to the public "unless its disclosure can be shown to be definitely detrimental to the national security." Though this proposal may still limit disclosure, it is far from the attitude shown by the government to date.

Although there have been indications that our national media may make a large contribution to the mounting public pressure to reopen the investigation of the JFK assassination, certain pitfalls remain. One problem is that sensational charges are often more newsworthy—and more easily understood and communicated— than the subtle discoveries of long-term research. The only way the press will appreciate the significance of the less sensational research is through its own sustained investigation, and it is to be hoped that long-term investigative assignments in this area will be made. Beside this hope is the reminder that powerful sections of the press have tangled with the critics to the point where both sides maintain distrust of one another. We include a recent article by Jerry Policoff which chronicles this negative side of press treatment of the assassination critics.

Finally, we report the greatest controversy suffered thus far by the critics. From the peak of public interest in early 1967 until the case against Clay Shaw faded into nothing some two years later, public attention was focused on New Orleans District Attorney Jim Garrison. Critics disagree sharply and intensely on the significance of Garrison's investigation, and the definitive study of this phenomenon has yet to be done. It would have to take into account both the strength of the case made by various critics for a conspiracy touching on Oswald's activities in New Orleans and the weight of the forces stacked against Garrison, in the media as well as in the government. *But it would also have to examine the factual weaknesses in his case and particularly the seemingly indefensible prosecution of Clay Shaw. Bill Turner's 1968 pro-Garrison article establishes the factual context in which the Garrison investigation operated (as does Harold Weisberg's book* Oswald in New Orleans). *The selections by Peter Noyes and Sylvia Meagher illustrate the kind of criticism that has been directed at Garrison from within the critical community. The Garrison investigation is a sobering reminder of how difficult it is to get the whole truth about the assassination with anything less than the full powers and resources of the federal government on the side of an open and honest inquiry.*

THE WARREN REPORT AND ITS PROBLEMS

A MOST URGENT TASK
Lyndon B. Johnson

The Vantage Point / 1971

One of the most urgent tasks facing me after I assumed office was to assure the country that everything possible was being done to uncover the truth surrounding the assassination of President Kennedy. John Kennedy had been murdered, and a troubled, puzzled, and outraged nation wanted to know the facts.

Led by the Attorney General [Robert F. Kennedy], who wanted no stone unturned, the FBI was working on the case twenty-four hours a day and Director J. Edgar Hoover was in constant communication with me. Some very disturbing facts about Lee Harvey Oswald were coming to light—notably, that he considered himself a Communist, that he had once given up his citizenship to live in Russia, and that when he finally returned to the United States, with a Russian wife, he immediately hoisted the banner of Fidel Castro.

Reprinted from *The Vantage Point* by Lyndon Baines Johnson, pages 25–27. Copyright © 1971 by HEC Public Affairs Foundation. Reprinted by permission of Holt, Rinehart and Winston, Publishers.

What did all this mean? Was Oswald the killer? If so, was he carrying out orders from someone else? Did he have accomplices or did he act alone? There was hope, at least, that Oswald would supply the answers. But on Sunday, November 24, with millions of people watching on their television sets, Jack Ruby, a previously anonymous nightclub operator, walked calmly into the garage of the Dallas jail and shot Lee Harvey Oswald to death. The answers were lost, perhaps for all time.

With that single shot the outrage of a nation turned to skepticism and doubt. The atmosphere was poisonous and had to be cleared. I was aware of some of the implications that grew out of that skepticism and doubt. Russia was not immune to them. Neither was Cuba. Neither was the State of Texas. Neither was the new President of the United States.

Lady Bird had told me a story when I finally arrived at our home in northwest Washington on the night of November 22. She and Liz Carpenter had driven home immediately after our arrival at the White House, while I stayed on to work. On their way to our house, Liz had commented: "It's a terrible thing to say, but the salvation of Texas is that the Governor was hit."

And Lady Bird replied: "Don't think I haven't thought of that. I only wish it could have been me."

Now, with Oswald dead, even a wounded Governor could not quell the doubts. In addition, we were aware of stories that Castro, still smarting over the Bay of Pigs and only lately accusing us of sending CIA agents into the country to assassinate him, was the perpetrator of the Oswald assassination plot. These rumors were another compelling reason that a thorough study had to be made of the Dallas tragedy at once. Out of the nation's suspicions, out of the nation's need for facts, the Warren Commission was born.

The idea of a national commission was first mentioned to me by Eugene Rostow of the Yale Law School. He called the White House the day Oswald was shot and suggested that with the prime suspect now dead, a blue-ribbon commission was needed to ascertain the facts. Dean Rusk and columnist Joseph Alsop soon made the same recommendation to me.

While I was considering what sort of investigative body to commission for this task, two facts became abundantly clear. First, this could not be an agency of the Executive branch. The commissio had to be composed of men who were known to be beyond pressure and above suspicion. Second, this represented too large an issue for the Texas authorities to handle alone. Several columnists reported that a "Texas commission" would be set up. Waggoner Carr, the Attorney General of Texas, considered setting up a board of inquiry. I urged him to examine every possible aspect and to explore all avenues fully, but I also told him that I hoped he would sit in on the national commission, and that is what he wisely did.

The commission had to be bipartisan, and I felt that we needed a Republican chairman whose judicial ability and fairness were unquestioned. I don't believe I ever considered anyone but Chief Justice Earl Warren for chairman. I was not an intimate of the Chief Justice. We had never spent ten minutes alone together, but to me he was the personification of justice and fairness in this country.

I knew it was not a good precedent to involve the Supreme Court in such an investigation. Chief Justice Warren knew this too and was vigorously opposed to it. I called him in anyway. Before he came, he sent word through a third party that he would not accept the assignment. He opposed serving on constitutional grounds. He said that if asked, he would refuse. He thought the President should be informed of that.

Early in my life I learned that doing the impossible frequently was necessary to get the job done. There was no doubt in my mind that the Chief Justice had to be convinced that it was his duty to accept the chairmanship of the commission. We had to bring the nation through that bloody tragedy, and Warren's personal integrity was a key element in assuring that all the facts would be unearthed and that the conclusions would be credible.

When the Chief Justice came into my office and sat down, I told him that I knew what he was going to say to me but that there was one thing no one else had said to him: In World War I he had put a rifle to his shoulder and offered to give his life, if necessary, to save his country. I said I didn't care who brought me a message about how opposed he was to this assignment. When the country is confronted with threatening divisions and suspicions, I said, and its foundation is being rocked, and the President of the

United States says that you are the only man who can handle the matter, you won't say "no," will you?

He swallowed hard and said, "No, sir."

I had always had great respect for Chief Justice Warren. From that moment on I became his great advocate as well.

As for the makeup of the rest of the commission, I appointed the two men Bobby Kennedy asked me to put on it—Allen Dulles and John McCloy—immediately. Then I called each of the prospective members personally and obtained his agreement to serve. The final roster of the commission members included Chief Justice Warren, Senator Richard Russell of Georgia, Senator John Sherman Cooper of Kentucky, Representative Hale Boggs of Louisiana, Representative Gerald Ford of Michigan, former CIA Director Allen W. Dulles of Washington, and former U.S. High Commissioner of Germany John J. McCloy of New York. They all served with great distinction and great sacrifice.

The Warren Commission brought us through a very critical time in our history. I believe it fair to say that the commission was dispassionate and just.

REPORT OF THE WARREN COMMISSION: SUMMARY AND CONCLUSIONS

Report of the President's Commission on the Assassination of President Kennedy / September 24, 1964

PRESIDENT'S COMMISSION
ON THE
ASSASSINATION OF PRESIDENT KENNEDY

CHIEF JUSTICE EARL WARREN, *Chairman*

SENATOR RICHARD B. RUSSELL
SENATOR JOHN SHERMAN COOPER
REPRESENTATIVE HALE BOGGS
REPRESENTATTIVE GERALD R. FORD
MR. ALLEN W. DULLES
MR. JOHN J. McCLOY

J. LEE RANKIN, *General Counsel*

Assistant Counsel

FRANCIS W. H. ADAMS
JOSEPH A. BALL
DAVID W. BELIN
WILLIAM T. COLEMAN, JR.
MELVIN ARON EISENBERG
BURT W. GRIFFIN
LEON D. HUBERT, JR.

ALBERT E. JENNER, JR.
WESLEY J. LIEBELER
NORMAN REDLICH
W. DAVID SLAWSON
ARLEN SPECTER
SAMUEL A. STERN
HOWARD P. WILLENS*

Staff Members

PHILLIP BARSON
EDWARD A. CONROY
JOHN HART ELY
ALFRED GOLDBERG
MURRAY J. LAULICHT
ARTHUR MARMOR

RICHARD M. MOSK
JOHN J. O'BRIEN
STUART POLLAK
ALFREDDA SCOBEY
CHARLES N. SHAFFER, JR.
LLOYD L. WEINREB

* Mr. Willens also acted as liaison between the Commission and the Department of Justice.

The assassination of John Fitzgerald Kennedy on November 22, 1963, was a cruel and shocking act of violence directed against a man, a family, a nation, and against all mankind. A young and vigorous leader whose years of public and private life stretched before him was the victim of the fourth Presidential assassination in the history of a country dedicated to the concepts of reasoned argument and peaceful political change. This Commission was created on November 29, 1963, in recognition of the right of people everywhere to full and truthful knowledge concerning these events. This report endeavors to fulfill that right and to appraise this tragedy by the light of reason and the standard of fairness. It has been prepared with a deep awareness of the Commission's responsibility to present to the American people an objective report of the facts relating to the assassination.

NARRATIVE OF EVENTS

At 11:40 a.m., c.s.t., on Friday, November 22, 1963, President John F. Kennedy, Mrs. Kennedy, and their party arrived at Love Field, Dallas, Tex. Behind them was the first day of a Texas trip planned 5 months before by the President, Vice President Lyndon B. Johnson, and John B. Connally, Jr., Governor of Texas. After leaving the White House on Thursday morning, the President had flown initially to San Antonio where Vice President Lyndon B. Johnson joined the party and the President dedicated new research facilities at the U.S. Air Force School of Aerospace Medicine. Following a testimonial dinner in Houston for U.S. Representative Albert Thomas, the President flew to Fort Worth where he spent the night and spoke at a large breakfast gathering on Friday.

Planned for later that day were a motorcade through downtown Dallas, a luncheon speech at the Trade Mart, and a flight to Austin where the President would attend a reception and speak at a Democratic fund-raising dinner. From Austin he would proceed to the Texas ranch of the Vice President. Evident on this trip were the varied roles which an American President performs—Head of State, Chief Executive, party leader, and, in this instance, prospective candidate for reelection.

The Dallas motorcade, it was hoped, would evoke a demonstration of the President's personal popularity in a city which he had lost in the 1960 election. Once it had been decided that the trip to Texas would span 2 days, those responsible for planning, primarily Governor Connally and Kenneth O'Donnell, a special assistant to the President, agreed that a motorcade through Dallas would be desirable. The Secret Service was told on November 8 that 45 minutes had been allotted to a motorcade procession from Love Field to the site of a luncheon planned by Dallas business and civic leaders in honor of the President. After considering the facilities and security problems of several buildings, the Trade Mart was chosen as the luncheon site. Given this selection, and in accordance with the customary practice of affording the greatest number of people an opportunity to see the President, the motorcade route selected was a natural one. The route was approved by the local host committee and White House representatives on November 18 and publicized in the local papers starting on November 19. This advance publicity made it clear that the motorcade would leave Main Street and pass the intersection of Elm and Houston Streets as it proceeded to the Trade Mart by way of the Stemmons Freeway.

By midmorning of November 22, clearing skies in Dallas dispelled the threat of rain and the President greeted the crowds from his open limousine without the "bubbletop," which was at that time a plastic shield furnishing protection only against inclement weather. To the left of the President in the rear seat was Mrs. Kennedy. In the jump seats were Governor Connally, who was in front of the President, and Mrs. Connally at the Governor's left. Agent William R. Greer of the Secret Service was driving, and Agent Roy H. Kellerman was sitting to his right.

Directly behind the Presidential limousine was an open "followup" car with eight Secret Service agents, two in the front seat, two in the rear, and two on each running board. These agents, in accordance with normal Secret Service procedures, were instructed to scan the crowds, the roofs, and windows of buildings, overpasses, and crossings for signs of trouble. Behind the "followup" car was the Vice-Presidential car carrying the Vice President and Mrs. Johnson and Senator Ralph W. Yarborough. Next were a

Vice-Presidential "followup" car and several cars and buses for additional dignitaries, press representatives, and others.

The motorcade left Love Field shortly after 11:50 a.m., and proceeded through residential neighborhoods, stopping twice at the President's request to greet well-wishers among the friendly crowds. Each time the President's car halted, Secret Service agents from the "followup" car moved forward to assume a protective stance near the President and Mrs. Kennedy. As the motorcade reached Main Street, a principal east-west artery in downtown Dallas, the welcome became tumultuous. At the extreme west end of Main Street the motorcade turned right on Houston Street and proceeded north for one block in order to make a left turn on Elm Street, the most direct and convenient approach to the Stemmons Freeway and the Trade Mart. As the President's car approached the intersection of Houston and Elm Streets, there loomed directly ahead on the intersection's northwest corner a seven-story, orange brick warehouse and office building, the Texas School Book Depository. Riding in the Vice President's car, Agent Rufus W. Youngblood of the Secret Service noticed that the clock atop the building indicated 12:30 p.m., the scheduled arrival time at the Trade Mart.

The President's car which had been going north made a sharp turn toward the southwest onto Elm Street. At a speed of about 11 miles per hour, it started down the gradual descent toward a railroad overpass under which the motorcade would proceed before reaching the Stemmons Freeway. The front of the Texas School Book Depository was now on the President's right, and he waved to the crowd assembled there as he passed the building. Dealey Plaza—an open, landscaped area marking the western end of downtown Dallas—stretched out to the President's left. A Secret Service agent riding in the motorcade radioed the Trade Mart that the President would arrive in 5 minutes.

Seconds later shots resounded in rapid succession. The President's hands moved to his neck. He appeared to stiffen momentarily and lurch slightly forward in his seat. A bullet had entered the base of the back of his neck slightly to the right of the spine. It traveled downward and exited from the front of the neck, causing a nick in the lower portion of the knot in the President's necktie. Before the shooting started, Governor Connally had been facing toward the crowd on the right. He started to turn toward the left and suddenly felt a blow on his back. The Governor had been hit by a bullet which entered at the extreme right side of his back at a point below his right armpit. The bullet traveled through his chest in a downward and forward direction, exited below his right nipple, passed through his right wrist which had been in his lap, and then caused a wound to his left thigh. The force of the bullet's impact appeared to spin the Governor to his right, and Mrs. Connally pulled him down into her lap. Another bullet then struck President Kennedy in the rear portion of his head, causing a massive and fatal wound. The President fell to the left into Mrs. Kennedy's lap.

Secret Service Agent Clinton J. Hill, riding on the left running board of the "followup" car, heard a noise which sounded like a firecracker and saw the President suddenly lean forward and to the left. Hill jumped off the car and raced toward the President's limousine. In the front seat of the Vice-Presidential car, Agent Youngblood heard an explosion and noticed unusual movements in the crowd. He vaulted into the rear seat and sat on the Vice President in order to protect him. At the same time Agent Kellerman in the front seat of the Presidential limousine turned to observe the President. Seeing that the President was struck, Kellerman instructed the driver, "Let's get out of here; we are hit." He radioed ahead to the lead car, "Get us to the hospital immediately." Agent Greer immediately accelerated the Presidential car. As it gained speed, Agent Hill managed to pull himself onto the back of the car where Mrs. Kennedy had climbed. Hill pushed her back into the rear seat and shielded the stricken President and Mrs. Kennedy as the President's car proceeded at high speed to Parkland Memorial Hospital, 4 miles away.

At Parkland, the President was immediately treated by a team of physicians who had been alerted for the President's arrival by the Dallas Police Department as the result of a radio message from the motorcade after the shooting. The doctors noted irregular breathing movements and a possible heartbeat, although they could not detect a pulsebeat. They observed the extensive wound in the President's head and a small wound approximately one-fourth inch in diameter in the lower third of his neck. In an effort to facilitate breathing, the physicians performed a tracheotomy by enlarging the throat wound and inserting a tube. Totally absorbed in the immediate task of trying to preserve the President's life, the attending doctors never turned the President over for an examination of his back. At 1 p.m., after all heart activity ceased and the Last Rites were administered by a priest, President Kennedy was pronounced dead. Governor Connally underwent surgery and ultimately recovered from his serious wounds.

Upon learning of the President's death, Vice President Johnson left Parkland Hospital under close guard and proceeded to the Presidential plane at Love Field. Mrs. Kennedy, accompanying her husband's body, boarded the plane shortly thereafter. At 2:38 p.m., in the central compartment of the plane, Lyndon B. Johnson was sworn in as the 36th President of the United States by Federal District Court Judge Sarah T. Hughes. The plane left immediately for Washington, D.C., arriving at Andrews AFB, Md., at 5:58 p.m., e.s.t. The President's body was taken to the National Naval Medical Center, Bethesda, Md., where it was given a complete pathological examination. The autopsy disclosed the large head wound observed at Parkland and the wound in the front of the neck which had been enlarged by the Parkland doctors when they performed the tracheotomy. Both of these wounds were described in the autopsy report as being "presumably of exit." In addition the autopsy revealed a small wound of entry in the rear of the President's skull and another wound of entry near the base of the back of the neck. The autopsy report stated the cause of death as "Gunshot wound, head," and the bullets which struck the President were described as having been fired "from a point behind and somewhat above the level of the deceased."

At the scene of the shooting, there was evident confusion at the outset concerning the point of origin of the shots. Witnesses differed in their accounts of the direction from which the sound of the shots emanated. Within a few minutes, however, attention centered on the Texas School Book Depository Building as the source of the shots. The building was occupied by a private corporation, the Texas School Book Depository Co., which distributed school textbooks of several publishers and leased space to representatives of the publishers. Most of the employees in the building worked for these publishers. The balance, including a 15-man warehousing crew, were employees of the Texas School Book Depository Co. itself.

Several eyewitnesses in front of the building reported that they saw a rifle being fired from the southeast corner window on the sixth floor of the Texas School Book Depository. One eyewitness, Howard L. Brennan, had been watching the parade from a point on Elm Street directly opposite and facing the building. He promptly told a policeman that he had seen a slender man, about 5 feet 10 inches, in his early thirties, take deliberate aim from the sixth-floor corner window and fire a rifle in the direction of the President's car. Brennan thought he might be able to identify the man since he had noticed him in the window a few minutes before the motorcade made the turn onto Elm Street. At 12:34 p.m., the Dallas police radio mentioned the Depository Building as a possible source of the shots, and at 12:45 p.m., the police radio broadcast a description of the suspected assassin based primarily on Brennan's observations.

When the shots were fired, a Dallas motorcycle patrolman, Marrion L. Baker, was riding in the motorcade at a point several cars behind the President. He had turned right from Main Street onto Houston Street and was about 200 feet south of Elm Street when he heard a shot. Baker, having recently returned from a week of deer hunting, was certain the shot came from a high-powered rifle. He looked up and saw pigeons scattering in the air from their perches on the Texas School Book Depository Building. He raced his motorcycle to the building, dismounted, scanned the area to the west and pushed his way through the spectators toward the entrance. There he encountered Roy Truly, the building superintendent, who offered Baker his help. They entered the building, and ran toward the two elevators in the rear. Finding that both elevators were on an upper floor, they dashed up the stairs. Not more than 2 minutes had elapsed since the shooting.

When they reached the second-floor landing on their way up to the top of the building, Patrolman Baker thought he caught a glimpse of someone through the small glass window in the door separating the hall area near the stairs from the small vestibule leading into the lunchroom. Gun in hand, he rushed to the door and saw a man about 20 feet away walking toward the other end of the lunchroom. The man was empty-handed. At Baker's command, the man turned and approached him. Truly, who had started up the stairs to the third floor ahead of Baker, returned to see what had delayed the patrolman. Baker asked Truly whether he knew the man in the lunchroom. Truly replied that the man worked in the building, whereupon Baker turned from the man and proceeded, with Truly, up the stairs. The man they encountered had started working in the Texas School Book Depository Building on October 16, 1963. His fellow workers described him as very quiet—a "loner." His name was Lee Harvey Oswald.

Within about 1 minute after his encounter with Baker and Truly, Oswald was seen passing through the second-floor offices. In his hand was a full "Coke" bottle which he had purchased from a vending machine in the lunchroom. He was walking toward the front of the building where a passenger elevator and a short flight of stairs provided access to the main entrance of the building on the first floor. Approximately 7 minutes later, at about 12:40 p.m., Oswald boarded a bus at a point on Elm Street seven short blocks east of the Depository Building. The bus was traveling west toward the very building from which Oswald had come. Its route lay through the Oak Cliff section in southwest Dallas, where it would pass seven blocks east of the roominghouse in which Oswald was living, at 1026 North Beckley Avenue. On the bus was Mrs. Mary Bledsoe, one of Oswald's former landladies who immediately recognized him. Oswald stayed on the bus approximately 3 or 4 minutes, during which time it proceeded only two blocks because of the traffic jam created by the motorcade and the assassination. Oswald then left the bus.

A few minutes later he entered a vacant taxi four blocks away and asked the driver to take him to a point on North Beckley Avenue several blocks beyond his roominghouse. The trip required 5 or 6 minutes. At about 1 p.m. Oswald arrived at the roominghouse. The housekeeper, Mrs. Earlene Roberts, was surprised to see Oswald at midday and remarked to him that he seemed to be in quite a hurry. He made no reply. A few minutes later Oswald emerged from his room zipping up his jacket and rushed out of the house.

Approximately 14 minutes later, and just 45 minutes after the assassination, another violent shooting occurred in Dallas. The victim was Patrolman J. D. Tippit of the Dallas police, an officer with a good record during his more than 11 years with the police force. He was shot near the intersection of 10th Street and Patton Avenue, about nine-tenths of a mile from Oswald's roominghouse. At the time of the assassination, Tippit was alone in his patrol car, the routine practice for most police patrol cars at this time of day. He had been ordered by radio at 12:45 p.m. to proceed to the central Oak Cliff area as part of a concentration of patrol car activity around the center of the city following the assassination. At 12:45 Tippit radioed that he had moved as directed and would be available for any emergency. By this time the police radio had broadcast several messages alerting the police to the suspect described by Brennan at the scene of the assassination—a slender white male, about 30 years old, 5 feet 10 inches and weighing about 165 pounds.

At approximately 1:15 p.m., Tippit was driving slowly in an easterly direction on East 10th Street in Oak Cliff. About 100 feet past the intersection of 10th Street and Patton Avenue, Tippit pulled up alongside a man walking in the same direction. The man met the general description of the suspect wanted in connection with the assassination. He walked over to Tippit's car, rested his arms on the door on the right-hand side of the car, and apparently exchanged words with Tippit through the window. Tippit opened the door on the left side and started to walk around the front of his car. As he reached the front wheel on the driver's side, the man on the sidewalk drew a revolver and fired several shots in rapid succession, hitting Tippit four times and killing him instantly. An automobile repairman, Domingo Benavides, heard the shots and stopped his pickup truck on the opposite side of the street about 25 feet in front of Tippit's car. He observed the gunman start back toward Patton Avenue, removing the empty cartridge cases from the gun as he went. Benavides rushed to Tippit's side. The patrolman, apparently dead, was lying on his revolver, which was out of its holster. Benavides promptly reported the shooting to police headquarters over the radio in Tippit's car. The message was received shortly after 1:16 p.m.

As the gunman left the scene, he walked hurriedly back toward Patton Avenue and turned left, heading south. Standing on the northwest corner of 10th Street and Patton Avenue was Helen Markham, who had been walking south on Patton Avenue and had seen both the killer and Tippit cross the intersection in front of her as she waited on the curb for traffic to pass. She witnessed the shooting and then saw the man with a gun in his hand walk back toward the corner and cut across the lawn of the corner house as he started south on Patton Avenue.

In the corner house itself, Mrs. Barbara Jeanette Davis and her sister-in-law, Mrs. Virginia Davis, heard the shots and rushed to the door in time to see the man walk rapidly across the lawn shaking a revolver as if he were emptying it of cartridge cases. Later that day each woman found a cartridge case near the house. As the gunman turned the corner he passed alongside a taxicab which was parked on Patton Avenue, a few feet from 10th Street. The driver, William W. Scoggins, had seen the slaying and was now crouched behind his cab on the street side. As the gunman cut through the shrubbery on the lawn, Scoggins looked up and saw the man approximately 12 feet away. In his hand was a pistol and he muttered words which sounded to Scoggins like "poor dumb cop" or "poor damn cop."

After passing Scoggins, the gunman crossed to the west side of Patton Avenue and ran south toward Jefferson Boulevard, a main Oak Cliff thoroughfare. On the east side of Patton, between 10th Street and Jefferson Boulevard, Ted Callaway, a used car salesman, heard the shots and ran to the sidewalk. As the man with the gun rushed past, Callaway shouted "What's going on?" The man merely shrugged, ran on to Jefferson Boulevard and turned right. On the next corner was a gas station with a parking lot in the rear. The assailant ran into the lot, discarded his jacket and then continued his flight west on Jefferson.

In a shoe store a few blocks farther west on Jefferson, the manager, Johnny Calvin Brewer, heard the siren of a police car moments after the radio in his store announced the shooting of the police officer in Oak Cliff. Brewer saw a man step quickly into the entranceway of the store and stand there with his back toward the street. When the police car made a U-turn and headed back in the direction of the Tippit shooting, the man left and Brewer followed him. He saw the man enter the Texas Theatre, a motion picture house about 60 feet away, without buying a ticket. Brewer pointed this out to the cashier, Mrs. Julia Postal, who called the police. The time was shortly after 1:40 p.m.

At 1:29 p.m., the police radio had noted the similarity in the descriptions of the suspects in the Tippit shooting and the assassination. At 1:45 p.m., in response to Mrs. Postal's call, the police radio sounded the alarm: "Have information a suspect just went in the Texas Theatre on West Jefferson." Within minutes the theater was surrounded. The house lights were then turned up. Patrolman M. N. McDonald and several other policemen approached the man, who had been pointed out to them by Brewer.

McDonald ordered the man to his feet and heard him say, "Well, it's all over now." The man drew a gun from his waist with one hand and struck the officer with the other. McDonald struck out with his right hand and grabbed the gun with his left hand. After a brief struggle McDonald and several other police officers disarmed and handcuffed the suspect and drove him to police headquarters, arriving at approximately 2 p.m.

Following the assassination, police cars had rushed to the Texas School Book Depository in response to the many radio messages reporting that the shots had been fired from the Depository Building. Inspector J. Herbert Sawyer of the Dallas Police Department arrived at the scene shortly after hearing the first of these police radio messages at 12:34 p.m. Some of the officers who had been assigned to the area of Elm and Houston Streets for the motorcade were talking to witnesses and watching the building when Sawyer arrived. Sawyer entered the building and rode a passenger elevator to the fourth floor, which was the top floor for this elevator. He conducted a quick search, returned to the main floor and, between approximately 12:37 and 12:40 p.m., ordered that no one be permitted to leave the building.

Shortly before 1 p.m., Capt. J. Will Fritz, chief of the homicide and robbery bureau of the Dallas Police Department, arrived to take charge of the investigation. Searching the sixth floor, Deputy Sheriff Luke Mooney noticed a pile of cartons in the southeast corner. He squeezed through the boxes and realized immediately that he had discovered the point from which the shots had been fired. On the floor were three empty cartridge cases. A carton had apparently been placed on the floor at the side of the window so that a person sitting on the carton could look down Elm Street toward the overpass and scarcely be noticed from the outside. Between this carton and the half-open window were three additional cartons arranged at such an angle that a rifle resting on the top carton would be aimed directly at the motorcade as it moved away from the building. The high stack of boxes, which first attracted Mooney's attention, effectively screened a person at the window from the view of anyone else on the floor.

Mooney's discovery intensified the search for additional evidence on the sixth floor, and at 1:22 p.m., approximately 10 minutes after the cartridge cases were found, Deputy Sheriff Eugene Boone turned his flashlight in the direction of two rows of boxes in the northwest corner near the staircase. Stuffed between the two rows was a bolt-action rifle with a telescopic sight. The rifle was not touched until it could be photographed. When Lt. J. C. Day of the police identification bureau decided that the wooden stock and the metal knob at the end of the bolt contained no prints, he held the rifle by the stock while Captain Fritz ejected a live shell by operating the bolt. Lieutenant Day promptly noted that stamped on the rifle itself was the serial number "C2766" as well as the markings "1940" "MADE ITALY" and "CAL. 6.5." The rifle was about 40 inches long and when disassembled it could fit into a handmade paper sack which, after the assassination, was found in the southeast corner of the building within a few feet of the cartridge cases.

As Fritz and Day were completing their examination of this rifle on the sixth floor, Roy Truly, the building superintendent, approached with information which he felt should be brought to the attention of the police. Earlier, while the police were questioning the employees, Truly had observed that Lee Harvey Oswald, 1 of the 15 men who worked in the warehouse, was missing. After Truly provided Oswald's name, address, and general description, Fritz left for police headquarters. He arrived at headquarters shortly after 2 p.m. and asked two detectives to pick up the employee who was missing from the Texas School Book Depository. Standing nearby were the police officers who had just arrived with the man arrested in the Texas Theatre. When Fritz mentioned the name of the missing employee, he learned that the man was already in the interrogation room. The missing School

Book Depository employee and the suspect who had been apprehended in the Texas Theatre were one and the same—Lee Harvey
Oswald.

The suspect Fritz was about to question in connection with the
assassination of the President and the murder of a policeman was
born in New Orleans on October 18, 1939, 2 months after the
death of his father. His mother, Marguerite Claverie Oswald, had
two older children. One, John Pic, was a half-brother to Lee from
an earlier marriage which had ended in divorce. The other was
Robert Oswald, a full brother to Lee and 5 years older. When Lee
Oswald was 3, Mrs. Oswald placed him in an orphanage where his
brother and half-brother were already living, primarily because
she had to work.

In January 1944, when Lee was 4, he was taken out of the
orphanage, and shortly thereafter his mother moved with him to
Dallas, Tex., where the older boys joined them at the end of the
school year. In May of 1945 Marguerite Oswald married her third
husband, Edwin A. Ekdahl. While the two older boys attended a
military boarding school, Lee lived at home and developed a
warm attachment to Ekdahl, occasionally accompanying his
mother and stepfather on business trips around the country. Lee
started school in Benbrook, Tex., but in the fall of 1946, after a
separation from Ekdahl, Marguerite Oswald reentered Lee in the
first grade in Covington, La. In January 1947, while Lee was still
in the first grade, the family moved to Fort Worth, Tex., as the
result of an attempted reconciliation between Ekdahl and Lee's
mother. A year and a half later, before Lee was 9, his mother
was divorced from her third husband as the result of a divorce
action instituted by Ekdahl. Lee's school record during the next
5½ years in Fort Worth was average, although generally it grew
poorer each year. The comments of teachers and others who knew
him at that time do not reveal any unusual personality traits or
characteristics.

Another change for Lee Oswald occurred in August 1952, a few
months after he completed the sixth grade. Marguerite Oswald
and her 12-year-old son moved to New York City where Marguerite's oldest son, John Pic, was stationed with the Coast Guard.
The ensuing year and one-half in New York was marked by Lee's
refusals to attend school and by emotional and psychological prob-

lems of a seemingly serious nature. Because he had become a chronic school truant, Lee underwent psychiatric study at Youth House, an institution in New York for juveniles who have had truancy problems or difficulties with the law, and who appear to require psychiatric observation, or other types of guidance. The social worker assigned to his case described him as "seriously detached" and "withdrawn" and noted "a rather pleasant, appealing quality about this emotionally starved, affectionless youngster." Lee expressed the feeling to the social worker that his mother did not care for him and regarded him as a burden. He experienced fantasies about being all powerful and hurting people, but during his stay at Youth House he was apparently not a behavior problem. He appeared withdrawn and evasive, a boy who preferred to spend his time alone, reading and watching television. His tests indicated that he was above average in intelligence for his age group. The chief psychiatrist of Youth House diagnosed Lee's problem as a "personality pattern disturbance with schizoid features and passive-aggressive tendencies." He concluded that the boy was "an emotionally, quite disturbed youngster" and recommended psychiatric treatment.

In May 1953, after having been at Youth House for 3 weeks, Lee Oswald returned to school where his attendance and grades temporarily improved. By the following fall, however, the probation officer reported that virtually every teacher complained about the boy's behavior. His mother insisted that he did not need psychiatric assistance. Although there was apparently some improvement in Lee's behavior during the next few months, the court recommended further treatment. In January 1954, while Lee's case was still pending, Marguerite and Lee left for New Orleans, the city of Lee's birth.

Upon his return to New Orleans, Lee maintained mediocre grades but had no obvious behavior problems. Neighbors and others who knew him outside of school remembered him as a quiet, solitary and introverted boy who read a great deal and whose vocabulary made him quite articulate. About 1 month after he started the 10th grade and 11 days before his 16th birthday in October 1955, he brought to school a note purportedly written by his mother, stating that the family was moving to California. The note was written by Lee. A few days later he dropped out of school and almost immediately tried to join the Marine Corps. Because he was only 16, he was rejected.

After leaving school Lee worked for the next 10 months at several jobs in New Orleans as an office messenger or clerk. It was during this period that he started to read communist literature. Occasionally, in conversations with others, he praised communism and expressed to his fellow employees a desire to join the Communist Party. At about this time, when he was not yet 17, he wrote to the Socialist Party of America, professing his belief in Marxism.

Another move followed in July 1956 when Lee and his mother returned to Fort Worth. He reentered high school but again dropped out after a few weeks and enlisted in the Marine Corps on October 24, 1956, 6 days after his 17th birthday. On December 21, 1956, during boot camp in San Diego, Oswald fired a score of 212 for record with the M–1 rifle—2 points over the minimum for a rating of "sharpshooter" on a marksman/sharpshooter/expert scale. After his basic training, Oswald received training in aviation fundamentals and then in radar scanning.

Most people who knew Oswald in the Marines described him as a "loner" who resented the exercise of authority by others. He spent much of his free time reading. He was court-martialed once for possessing an unregistered privately owned weapon and, on another occasion, for using provocative language to a noncommissioned officer. He was, however, generally able to comply with Marine discipline, even though his experiences in the Marine Corps did not live up to his expectations.

Oswald served 15 months overseas until November 1958, most of it in Japan. During his final year in the Marine Corps he was stationed for the most part in Santa Ana, Calif., where he showed a marked interest in the Soviet Union and sometimes expressed politically radical views with dogmatic conviction. Oswald again fired the M–1 rifle for record on May 6, 1959, and this time he shot a score of 191 on a shorter course than before, only 1 point over the minimum required to be a "marksman." According to one of his fellow marines, Oswald was not particularly interested in his rifle performance, and his unit was not expected to exhibit the usual rifle proficiency. During this period he expressed strong admiration for Fidel Castro and an interest in joining the Cuban army. He tried to impress those around him as an intellectual, but his thinking appeared to some as shallow and rigid.

Oswald's Marine service terminated on September 11, 1959, when at his own request he was released from active service a few months ahead of his scheduled release. He offered as the reason for his release the ill health and economic plight of his mother. He returned to Fort Worth, remained with his mother only 3 days and left for New Orleans, telling his mother he planned to get work there in the shipping or import-export business. In New Orleans he booked passage on the freighter SS *Marion Lykes*, which sailed from New Orleans to Le Havre, France, on September 20, 1959.

Lee Harvey Oswald had presumably planned this step in his life for quite some time. In March of 1959 he had applied to the Albert Schweitzer College in Switzerland for admission to the spring 1960 term. His letter of application contained many blatant falsehoods concerning his qualifications and background. A few weeks before his discharge he had applied for and obtained a passport, listing the Soviet Union as one of the countries which he planned to visit. During his service in the Marines he had saved a comparatively large sum of money, possibly as much as $1,500, which would appear to have been accomplished by considerable frugality and apparently for a specific purpose.

The purpose of the accumulated fund soon became known. On October 16, 1959, Oswald arrived in Moscow by train after crossing the border from Finland, where he had secured a visa for a 6-day stay in the Soviet Union. He immediately applied for Soviet citizenship. On the afternoon of October 21, 1959, Oswald was ordered to leave the Soviet Union by 8 p.m. that evening. That same afternoon in his hotel room, Oswald, in an apparent suicide attempt, slashed his left wrist. He was hospitalized immediately. On October 31, 3 days after his release from the hospital, Oswald appeared at the American Embassy, announced that he wished to renounce his U.S. citizenship and become a Russian citizen, and handed the Embassy officer a written statement he had prepared for the occasion. When asked his reasons, Oswald replied, "I am a Marxist." Oswald never formally complied with the legal steps necessary to renounce his American citizenship. The Soviet Government did not grant his request for citizenship, but in January 1960 he was given permission to remain in the Soviet Union on a year-to-year basis. At the same time Oswald was sent to Minsk where he worked in a radio factory as an unskilled laborer. In January 1961 his permission to remain in the Soviet Union was extended for another year. A few weeks later, in February 1961, he wrote to the American Embassy in Moscow expressing a desire to return to the United States.

The following month Oswald met a 19-year-old Russian girl, Marina Nikolaevna Prusakova, a pharmacist, who had been brought up in Leningrad but was then living with an aunt and uncle in Minsk. They were married on April 30, 1961. Throughout the following year he carried on a correspondence with American and Soviet authorities seeking approval for the departure of himself and his wife to the United States. In the course of this effort, Oswald and his wife visited the U.S. Embassy in Moscow in July of 1961. Primarily on the basis of an interview and questionnaire completed there, the Embassy concluded that Oswald had not lost his citizenship, a decision subsequently ratified by the Department of State in Washington, D.C. Upon their return to Minsk, Oswald and his wife filed with the Soviet authorities for permission to leave together. Their formal application was made in July 1961, and on December 25, 1961, Marina Oswald was advised it would be granted.

A daughter was born to the Oswalds in February 1962. In the months that followed they prepared for their return to the United States. On May 9, 1962, the U.S. Immigration and Naturalization Service, at the request of the Department of State, agreed to waive a restriction under the law which would have prevented the issuance of a United States visa to Oswald's Russian wife until she had left the Soviet Union. They finally left Moscow on June 1, 1962, and were assisted in meeting their travel expenses by a loan of $435.71 from the U.S. Department of State. Two weeks later they arrived in Fort Worth, Tex.

For a few weeks Oswald, his wife and child lived with Oswald's brother Robert. After a similar stay with Oswald's mother, they moved into their own apartment in early August. Oswald obtained a job on July 16 as a sheet metal worker. During this period in Fort Worth, Oswald was interviewed twice by agents of the FBI.

The report of the first interview, which occurred on June 26, described him as arrogant and unwilling to discuss the reasons why he had gone to the Soviet Union. Oswald denied that he was involved in Soviet intelligence activities and promised to advise the FBI if Soviet representatives ever communicated with him. He was interviewed again on August 16, when he displayed a less belligerent attitude and once again agreed to inform the FBI of any attempt to enlist him in intelligence activities.

In early October 1962 Oswald quit his job at the sheet metal plant and moved to Dallas. While living in Fort Worth the Oswalds had been introduced to a group of Russian-speaking people in the Dallas-Fort Worth area. Many of them assisted the Oswalds by providing small amounts of food, clothing, and household items. Oswald himself was disliked by almost all of this group whose help to the family was prompted primarily by sympathy for Marina Oswald and the child. Despite the fact that he had left the Soviet Union, disillusioned with its Government, Oswald seemed more firmly committed than ever to his concepts of Marxism. He showed disdain for democracy, capitalism, and American society in general. He was highly critical of the Russian-speaking group because they seemed devoted to American concepts of democracy and capitalism and were ambitious to improve themselves economically.

In February 1963 the Oswalds met Ruth Paine at a social gathering. Ruth Paine was temporarily separated from her husband and living with her two children in their home in Irving, Tex., a suburb of Dallas. Because of an interest in the Russian language and sympathy for Marina Oswald, who spoke no English and had little funds, Ruth Paine befriended Marina and, during the next 2 months, visited her on several occasions.

On April 6, 1963, Oswald lost his job with a photography firm. A few days later, on April 10, he attempted to kill Maj. Gen. Edwin A. Walker (Resigned, U. S. Army), using a rifle which he had ordered by mail 1 month previously under an assumed name. Marina Oswald learned of her husband's act when she confronted him with a note which he had left, giving her instructions in the event he did not return. That incident and their general economic difficulties impelled Marina Oswald to suggest that her husband leave Dallas and go to New Orleans to look for work.

Oswald left for New Orleans on April 24, 1963. Ruth Paine, who knew nothing of the Walker shooting, invited Marina Oswald and the baby to stay with her in the Paines' modest home while Oswald sought work in New Orleans. Early in May, upon receiving word from Oswald that he had found a job, Ruth Paine drove Marina Oswald and the baby to New Orleans to rejoin Oswald.

During the stay in New Orleans, Oswald formed a fictitious New Orleans Chapter of the Fair Play for Cuba Committee. He posed as secretary of this organization and represented that the president was A. J. Hidell. In reality, Hidell was a completely fictitious person created by Oswald, the organization's only member. Oswald was arrested on August 9 in connection with a scuffle which occurred while he was distributing pro-Castro leaflets. The next day, while at the police station, he was interviewed by an FBI agent after Oswald requested the police to arrange such an interview. Oswald gave the agent false information about his own background and was evasive in his replies concerning Fair Play for Cuba activities. During the next 2 weeks Oswald appeared on radio programs twice, claiming to be the spokesman for the Fair Play for Cuba Committee in New Orleans.

On July 19, 1963, Oswald lost his job as a greaser of coffee processing machinery. In September, after an exchange of correspondence with Marina Oswald, Ruth Paine drove to New Orleans and on September 23, transported Marina, the child, and the family belongings to Irving, Tex. Ruth Paine suggested that Marina Oswald, who was expecting her second child in October, live at the Paine house until after the baby was born. Oswald remained behind, ostensibly to find work either in Houston or some other city. Instead, he departed by bus for Mexico, arriving in Mexico City on September 27, where he promptly visited the Cuban and Russian Embassies. His stated objective was to obtain official permission to visit Cuba, on his way to the Soviet Union. The Cuban Government would not grant his visa unless the Soviet Government would also issue a visa permitting his entry into Russia. Oswald's efforts to secure these visas failed, and he left for Dallas, where he arrived on October 3, 1963.

When he saw his wife the next day, it was decided that Oswald would rent a room in Dallas and visit his family on weekends. For 1 week he rented a room from Mrs. Bledsoe, the woman who later saw him on the bus shortly after the assassination. On October 14, 1963, he rented the Beckley Avenue room and listed his name as O. H. Lee. On the same day, at the suggestion of a neighbor, Mrs. Paine phoned the Texas School Book Depository and was told that there was a job opening. She informed Oswald who was interviewed the following day at the Depository and started to work there on October 16, 1963.

On October 20 the Oswalds' second daughter was born. During October and November Oswald established a general pattern of weekend visits to Irving, arriving on Friday afternoon and returning to Dallas Monday morning with a fellow employee, Buell Wesley Frazier, who lived near the Paines. On Friday, November 15, Oswald remained in Dallas at the suggestion of his wife who told him that the house would be crowded because of a birthday party for Ruth Paine's daughter. On Monday, November 18, Oswald and his wife quarreled bitterly during a telephone conversation, because she learned for the first time that he was living at the roominghouse under an assumed name. On Thursday, November 21, Oswald told Frazier that he would like to drive to Irving to pick up some curtain rods for an apartment in Dallas. His wife and Mrs. Paine were quite surprised to see him since it was a Thursday night. They thought he had returned to make up after Monday's quarrel. He was conciliatory, but Marina Oswald was still angry.

Later that evening, when Mrs. Paine had finished cleaning the kitchen, she went into the garage and noticed that the light was burning. She was certain that she had not left it on, although the incident appeared unimportant at the time. In the garage were most of the Oswalds' personal possessions. The following morning Oswald left while his wife was still in bed feeding the baby. She did not see him leave the house, nor did Ruth Paine. On the dresser in their room he left his wedding ring which he had never done before. His wallet containing $170 was left intact in a dresser-drawer.

Oswald walked to Frazier's house about half a block away and placed a long bulky package, made out of wrapping paper and tape, into the rear seat of the car. He told Frazier that the package contained curtain rods. When they reached the Depository parking lot, Oswald walked quickly ahead. Frazier followed and saw

Oswald enter the Depository Building carrying the long bulky package with him.

During the morning of November 22, Marina Oswald followed President Kennedy's activities on television. She and Ruth Paine cried when they heard that the President had been shot. Ruth Paine translated the news of the shooting to Marina Oswald as it came over television, including the report that the shots were probably fired from the building where Oswald worked. When Marina Oswald heard this, she recalled the Walker episode and the fact that her husband still owned the rifle. She went quietly to the Paine's [sic] garage where the rifle had been concealed in a blanket among their other belongings. It appeared to her that the rifle was still there, although she did not actually open the blanket.

At about 3 p.m. the police arrived at the Paine house and asked Marina Oswald whether her husband owned a rifle. She said that he did and then led them into the garage and pointed to the rolled up blanket. As a police officer lifted it, the blanket hung limply over either side of his arm. The rifle was not there.

Meanwhile, at police headquarters, Captain Fritz had begun questioning Oswald. Soon after the start of the first interrogation, agents of the FBI and the U.S. Secret Service arrived and participated in the questioning. Oswald denied having anything to do with the assassination of President Kennedy or the murder of Patrolman Tippit. He claimed that he was eating lunch at the time of the assassination, and that he then spoke with his foreman for 5 to 10 minutes before going home. He denied that he owned a rifle and when confronted, in a subsequent interview, with a picture showing him holding a rifle and pistol, he claimed that his face had been superimposed on someone else's body. He refused to answer any questions about the presence in his wallet of a selective service card with his picture and the name "Alek J. Hidell."

During the questioning of Oswald on the third floor of the police department, more than 100 representatives of the press, radio, and television were crowded into the hallway through which Oswald had to pass when being taken from his cell to Captain Fritz' office for interrogation. Reporters tried to interview Oswald during these trips. Between Friday afternoon and Sunday morning he appeared in the hallway at least 16 times. The generally confused conditions outside and inside Captain Fritz' office increased the difficulty of police questioning. Advised by the police that he could communicate with an attorney, Oswald made several telephone calls on Saturday in an effort to procure representation of his own choice and discussed the matter with the president of the local bar association, who offered to obtain counsel. Oswald declined the offer saying that he would first try to obtain counsel by himself. By Sunday morning he had not yet engaged an attorney.

At 7:10 p.m. on November 22, 1963, Lee Harvey Oswald was formally advised that he had been charged with the murder of Patrolman J. D. Tippit. Several witnesses to the Tippit slaying and to the subsequent flight of the gunman had positively identified Oswald in police lineups. While positive firearm identification evidence was not available at the time, the revolver in Oswald's possession at the time of his arrest was of a type which could have fired the shots that killed Tippit.

The formal charge against Oswald for the assassination of President Kennedy was lodged shortly after 1:30 a.m., on Saturday, November 23. By 10 p.m. of the day of the assassination, the FBI had traced the rifle found on the sixth floor of the Texas School Book Depository to a mailorder house in Chicago which had purchased it from a distributor in New York. Approximately 6 hours later the Chicago firm advised that this rifle had been ordered in March 1963 by an A. Hidel for shipment to post office box 2915, in Dallas, Tex., a box rented by Oswald. Payment for the rifle was remitted by a money order signed by A. Hidell. By 6:45 p.m. on November 23, the FBI was able to advise the Dallas police that, as a result of handwriting analysis of the documents used to purchase the rifle, it had concluded that the rifle had been ordered by Lee Harvey Oswald.

Throughout Friday and Saturday, the Dallas police released to the public many of the details concerning the alleged evidence against Oswald. Police officials discussed important aspects of the case, usually in the course of impromptu and confused press conferences in the third-floor corridor. Some of the information divulged was erroneous. Efforts by the news media representatives to reconstruct the crime and promptly report details frequently led to erroneous and often conflicting reports. At the urgings of the newsmen, Chief of Police Jesse E. Curry, brought Oswald to a press conference in the police assembly room shortly after midnight of the day Oswald was arrested. The assembly room was crowded with newsmen who had come to Dallas from all over the country. They shouted questions at Oswald and flashed cameras at him. Among this group was a 52-year-old Dallas nightclub operator —Jack Ruby.

On Sunday morning, November 24, arrangements were made for Oswald's transfer from the city jail to the Dallas County jail, about 1 mile away. The news media had been informed on Saturday night that the transfer of Oswald would not take place until after 10 a.m. on Sunday. Earlier on Sunday, between 2:30 and 3 a.m., anonymous telephone calls threatening Oswald's life had been received by the Dallas office of the FBI and by the office of the county sheriff. Nevertheless, on Sunday morning, television, radio, and newspaper representatives crowded into the basement to record the transfer. As viewed through television cameras, Oswald would emerge from a door in front of the cameras and proceed to the transfer vehicle. To the right of the cameras was a "down" ramp from Main Street on the north. To the left was an "up" ramp leading to Commerce Street on the south.

The armored truck in which Oswald was to be transferred arrived shortly after 11 a.m. Police officials then decided, however, that an unmarked police car would be preferable for the trip because of its greater speed and maneuverability. At approximately 11:20 a.m. Oswald emerged from the basement jail office flanked by detectives on either side and at his rear. He took a few steps toward the car and was in the glaring light of the television cameras when a man suddenly darted out from an area on the right of the cameras where newsmen had been assembled. The man was carrying a Colt .38 revolver in his right hand and, while millions watched on television, he moved quickly to within a few feet of Oswald and fired one shot into Oswald's abdomen. Oswald groaned with pain as he fell to the ground and quickly lost consciousness. Within 7 minutes Oswald was at Parkland Hospital where, without having regained consciousness, he was pronounced dead at 1:07 p.m.

The man who killed Oswald was Jack Ruby. He was instantly arrested and, minutes later, confined in a cell on the fifth floor of the Dallas police jail. Under interrogation, he denied that the killing of Oswald was in any way connected with a conspiracy involving the assassination of President Kennedy. He maintained that he had killed Oswald in a temporary fit of depression and rage over the President's death. Ruby was transferred the following day to the county jail without notice to the press or to police officers not directly involved in the transfer. Indicted for the murder of Oswald by the State of Texas on November 26, 1963, Ruby was found guilty on March 14, 1964, and sentenced to death. As of September 1964, his case was pending on appeal.

CONCLUSIONS

This Commission was created to ascertain the facts relating to the preceding summary of events and to consider the important questions which they raised. The Commission has addressed itself to this task and has reached certain conclusions based on all the available evidence. No limitations have been placed on the Commission's inquiry; it has conducted its own investigation, and all Government agencies have fully discharged their responsibility to cooperate with the Commission in its investigation. These conclusions represent the reasoned judgment of all members of the Commission and are presented after an investigation which has satisfied the Commission that it has ascertained the truth concerning the assassination of President Kennedy to the extent that a prolonged and thorough search makes this possible.

1. The shots which killed President Kennedy and wounded Governor Connally were fired from the sixth floor window at the southeast corner of the Texas School Book Depository. This determination is based upon the following:

(a) Witnesses at the scene of the assassination saw a rifle being fired from the sixth floor window of the Depository Building, and some witnesses saw a rifle in the window immediately after the shots were fired.

(b) The nearly whole bullet found on Governor Connally's stretcher at Parkland Memorial Hospital and the two bullet fragments found in the front seat of the Presidential limousine were fired from the 6.5-millimeter Mannlicher-Carcano rifle found on the sixth floor of the Depository Building to the exclusion of all other weapons.

(c) The three used cartridge cases found near the window on the sixth floor at the southeast corner of the building were fired from the same rifle which fired the above-described bullet and fragments, to the exclusion of all other weapons.

(d) The windshield in the Presidential limousine was struck by a bullet fragment on the inside surface of the glass, but was not penetrated.

(e) The nature of the bullet wounds suffered by President Kennedy and Governor Connally and the location of the car at the time of the shots establish that the bullets were fired from above and behind the Presidential limousine, striking the President and the Governor as follows:

(1) President Kennedy was first struck by a bullet which entered at the back of his neck, causing a wound which would not necessarily have been lethal. The President was struck a second time by a bullet which entered the right-rear portion of his head, causing a massive and fatal wound.

(2) Governor Connally was struck by a bullet which entered on the right side of his back and traveled downward through the right side of his chest, exiting below his right nipple. This bullet then passed through his right wrist and entered his left thigh where it caused a superficial wound.

(f) There is no credible evidence that the shots were fired from the Triple Underpass, ahead of the motorcade, or from any other location.

2. The weight of the evidence indicates that there were three shots fired.

3. Although it is not necessary to any essential findings of the Commission to determine just which shot hit Governor Connally, there is very persuasive evidence from the experts to indicate that the same bullet which pierced the President's throat also caused Governor Connally's wounds. However, Governor Connally's testimony and certain other factors have given rise to some difference of opinion as to this probability but there is no question in the mind of any member of the Commission that all the shots which caused the President's and Governor Connally's wounds were fired from the sixth floor window of the Texas School Book Depository.

4. The shots which killed President Kennedy and wounded Governor Connally were fired by Lee Harvey Oswald. This conclusion is based upon the following:

(a) The Mannlicher-Carcano 6.5-millimeter Italian rifle from which the shots were fired was owned by and in the possession of Oswald.

(b) Oswald carried this rifle into the Depository Building on the morning of November 22, 1963.

(c) Oswald, at the time of the assassination, was present at the window from which the shots were fired.

(d) Shortly after the assassination, the Mannlicher-Carcano rifle belonging to Oswald was found partially hidden between some cartons on the sixth floor and the improvised paper bag in which Oswald brought the rifle to the Depository was found close by the window from which the shots were fired.

(e) Based on testimony of the experts and their analysis of films of the assassination, the Commission has concluded that a rifleman of Lee Harvey Oswald's capabilities could have fired the shots from the rifle used in the assassination within the elapsed time of the shooting. The Commission has concluded further that Oswald possessed the capability with a rifle which enabled him to commit the assassination.

(f) Oswald lied to the police after his arrest concerning important substantive matters.

(g) Oswald had attempted to kill Maj. Gen. Edwin A. Walker (Resigned, U.S. Army) on April 10, 1963, thereby demonstrating his disposition to take human life.

5. Oswald killed Dallas Police Patrolman J. D. Tippit approximately 45 minutes after the assassination. This conclusion upholds the finding that Oswald fired the shots which killed President Kennedy and wounded Governor Connally and is supported by the following:

(a) Two eyewitnesses saw the Tippit shooting and seven eyewitnesses heard the shots and saw the gunman leave the scene with revolver in hand. These nine eyewitnesses positively identified Lee Harvey Oswald as the man they saw.

(b) The cartridge cases found at the scene of the shooting were fired from the revolver in the possession of Oswald at the time of his arrest to the exclusion of all other weapons.

(c) The revolver in Oswald's possession at the time of his arrest was purchased by and belonged to Oswald.

(d) Oswald's jacket was found along the path of flight taken by the gunman as he fled from the scene of the killing.

6. Within 80 minutes of the assassination and 35 minutes of the Tippit killing Oswald resisted arrest at the theatre by attempting to shoot another Dallas police officer.

7. The Commission has reached the following conclusions concerning Oswald's interrogation and detention by the Dallas police:

(a) Except for the force required to effect his arrest, Oswald was not subjected to any physical coercion by any law enforcement officials. He was advised that he could not be compelled to give any information and that any statements made by him might be used against him in court. He was advised of his right to counsel of his own choice and was offered legal assistance by the Dallas Bar Association, which he rejected at that time.

(b) Newspaper, radio, and television reporters were allowed uninhibited access to the area through which Oswald had to pass when he was moved from his cell to the interrogation room and other sections of the building, thereby subjecting Oswald to harassment and creating chaotic conditions which were not conducive to orderly interrogation or the protection of the rights of the prisoner.

(c) The numerous statements, sometimes erroneous, made to the press by various local law enforcement officials, during this period of confusion and disorder in the police station, would have presented serious obstacles to the obtaining of a fair trial for Oswald. To the extent that the information was erroneous or misleading, it helped to create doubts, speculations, and fears in the mind of the public which might otherwise not have arisen.

8. The Commission has reached the following conclusions concerning the killing of Oswald by Jack Ruby on November 24, 1963:

(a) Ruby entered the basement of the Dallas Police Department shortly after 11:17 a.m. and killed Lee Harvey Oswald at 11:21 a.m.

(b) Although the evidence on Ruby's means of entry is not

conclusive, the weight of the evidence indicates that he walked down the ramp leading from Main Street to the basement of the police department.

(c) There is no evidence to support the rumor that Ruby may have been assisted by any members of the Dallas Police Department in the killing of Oswald.

(d) The Dallas Police Department's decision to transfer Oswald to the county jail in full public view was unsound. The arrangements made by the police department on Sunday morning, only a few hours before the attempted transfer, were inadequate. Of critical importance was the fact that news media representatives and others were not excluded from the basement even after the police were notified of threats to Oswald's life. These deficiencies contributed to the death of Lee Harvey Oswald.

9. The Commission has found no evidence that either Lee Harvey Oswald or Jack Ruby was part of any conspiracy, domestic or foreign, to assassinate President Kennedy. The reasons for this conclusion are:

(a) The Commission has found no evidence that anyone assisted Oswald in planning or carrying out the assassination. In this connection it has thoroughly investigated, among other factors, the circumstances surrounding the planning of the motorcade route through Dallas, the hiring of Oswald by the Texas School Book Depository Co. on October 15, 1963, the method by which the rifle was brought into the building, the placing of cartons of books at the window, Oswald's escape from the building, and the testimony of eyewitnesses to the shooting.

(b) The Commission has found no evidence that Oswald was involved with any person or group in a conspiracy to assassinate the President, although it has thoroughly investigated, in addition to other possible leads, all facets of Oswald's associations, finances, and personal habits, particularly during the period following his return from the Soviet Union in June 1962.

(c) The Commission has found no evidence to show that Oswald was employed, persuaded, or encouraged by any foreign government to assassinate President Kennedy or that he was an agent of any foreign government, although the Commission has reviewed the circumstances surrounding Oswald's defection to the Soviet Union, his life there from October of 1959 to June of 1962 so far as it can be reconstructed, his known contacts with the Fair Play for Cuba Committee, and his visits to the Cuban and Soviet Embassies in Mexico City during his trip to Mexico from September 26 to October 3, 1963, and his known contacts with the Soviet Embassy in the United States.

(d) The Commission has explored all attempts of Oswald to identify himself with various political groups, including the Communist Party, U.S.A., the Fair Play for Cuba Committee, and the Socialist Workers Party, and has been unable to find any evidence that the contacts which he initiated were related to Oswald's subsequent assassination of the President.

(e) All of the evidence before the Commission established that there was nothing to support the speculation that Oswald was an agent, employee, or informant of the FBI, the CIA, or any other governmental agency. It has thoroughly investigated Oswald's relationships prior to the assassination with all agencies of the U. S. Government. All contacts with Oswald by any of these agencies were made in the regular exercise of their different responsibilities.

(f) No direct or indirect relationship between Lee Harvey Oswald and Jack Ruby has been discovered by the Commission, nor has it been able to find any credible evidence that either knew the other, although a thorough investigation was made of the many rumors and speculations of such a relationship.

(g) The Commission has found no evidence that Jack Ruby acted with any other person in the killing of Lee Harvey Oswald.

(h) After careful investigation the Commission has found no credible evidence either that Ruby and Officer Tippit, who was killed by Oswald, knew each other or that Oswald and Tippit knew each other.

Because of the difficulty of proving negatives to a certainty the possibility of others being involved with either Oswald or Ruby cannot be established [sic] categorically, but if there is any such evidence it has been beyond the reach of all the investigative agencies and resources of the United States and has not come to the attention of this Commission.

10. In its entire investigation the Commission has found no

evidence of conspiracy, subversion, or disloyalty to the U.S. Government by any Federal, State, or local official.

11. On the basis of the evidence before the Commission it concludes that Oswald acted alone. Therefore, to determine the motives for the assassination of President Kennedy, one must look to the assassin himself. Clues to Oswald's motives can be found in his family history, his education or lack of it, his acts, his writings, and the recollections of those who had close contacts with him throughout his life. The Commission has presented with this report all of the background information bearing on motivation which it could discover. Thus, others may study Lee Oswald's life and arrive at their own conclusions as to his possible motives.

The Commission could not make any definitive determination of Oswald's motives. It has endeavored to isolate factors which contributed to his character and which might have influenced his decision to assassinate President Kennedy. These factors were:

(a) His deep-rooted resentment of all authority which was expressed in a hostility toward every society in which he lived;

(b) His inability to enter into meaningful relationships with people, and a continuous pattern of rejecting his environment in favor of new surroundings;

(c) His urge to try to find a place in history and despair at times over failures in his various undertakings;

(d) His capacity for violence as evidenced by his attempt to kill General Walker;

(e) His avowed commitment to Marxism and communism, as he understood the terms and developed his own interpretation of them; this was expressed by his antagonism toward the United States, by his defection to the Soviet Union, by his failure to be reconciled with life in the United States even after his disenchantment with the Soviet Union, and by his efforts, though frustrated, to go to Cuba.

Each of these contributed to his capacity to risk all in cruel and irresponsible actions.

12. The Commission recognizes that the varied responsibilities of the President require that he make frequent trips to all parts of the United States and abroad. Consistent with their high responsibilities Presidents can never be protected from every potential threat. The Secret Service's difficulty in meeting its pro-

tective responsibility varies with the activities and the nature of the occupant of the Office of President and his willingness to conform to plans for his safety. In appraising the performance of the Secret Service it should be understood that it has to do its work within such limitations. Nevertheless, the Commission believes that recommendations for improvements in Presidential protection are compelled by the facts disclosed in this investigation.

(a) The complexities of the Presidency have increased so rapidly in recent years that the Secret Service has not been able to develop or to secure adequate resources of personnel and facilities to fulfill its important assignment. This situation should be promptly remedied.

(b) The Commission has concluded that the criteria and procedures of the Secret Service designed to identify and protect against persons considered threats to the President, were not adequate prior to the assassination.

(1) The Protective Research Section of the Secret Service, which is responsible for its preventive work, lacked sufficient trained personnel and the mechanical and technical assistance needed to fufill its responsibility.

(2) Prior to the assassination the Secret Service's criteria dealt with direct threats against the President. Although the Secret Service treated the direct threats against the President adequately, it failed to recognize the necessity of identifying other potential sources of danger to his security. The Secret Service did not develop adequate and specific criteria defining those persons or groups who might present a danger to the President. In effect, the Secret Service largely relied upon other Federal or State agencies to supply the information necessary for it to fulfill its preventive responsibilities, although it did ask for information about direct threats to the President.

(c) The Commission has concluded that there was insufficient liaison and coordination of information between the Secret Service and other Federal agencies necessarily concerned with Presidential protection. Although the FBI, in the normal exercise of its responsibility, had secured considerable information about Lee Harvey Oswald, it had no official responsibility, under the Secret Service criteria existing at the time of the

President's trip to Dallas, to refer to the Secret Service the information it had about Oswald. The Commission has concluded, however, that the FBI took an unduly restrictive view of its role in preventive intelligence work prior to the assassination. A more carefully coordinated treatment of the Oswald case by the FBI might well have resulted in bringing Oswald's activities to the attention of the Secret Service.

(d) The Commission has concluded that some of the advance preparations in Dallas made by the Secret Service, such as the detailed security measures taken at Love Field and the Trade Mart, were thorough and well executed. In other respects, however, the Commission has concluded that the advance preparations for the President's trip were deficient.

(1) Although the Secret Service is compelled to rely to a great extent on local law enforcement officials, its procedures at the time of the Dallas trip did not call for well-defined instructions as to the respective responsibilities of the police officials and others assisting in the protection of the President.

(2) The procedures relied upon by the Secret Service for detecting the presence of an assassin located in a building along a motorcade route were inadequate. At the time of the trip to Dallas, the Secret Service as a matter of practice did not investigate, or cause to be checked, any building located along the motorcade route to be taken by the President. The responsibility for observing windows in these buildings during the motorcade was divided between local police personnel stationed on the streets to regulate crowds and Secret Service agents riding in the motorcade. Based on its investigation the Commission has concluded that these arrangements during the trip to Dallas were clearly not sufficient.

(e) The configuration of the Presidential car and the seating arrangements of the Secret Service agents in the car did not afford the Secret Service agents the opportunity they should have had to be of immediate assistance to the President at the first sign of danger.

(f) Within these limitations, however, the Commission finds that the agents most immediately responsible for the President's safety reacted promptly at the time the shots were fired from the Texas School Book Depository Building.

RECOMMENDATIONS

Prompted by the assassination of President Kennedy, the Secret Service has initiated a comprehensive and critical review of its total operations. As a result of studies conducted during the past several months, and in cooperation with this Commission, the Secret Service has prepared a planning document dated August 27, 1964, which recommends various programs considered necessary by the Service to improve its techniques and enlarge its resources. The Commission is encouraged by the efforts taken by the Secret Service since the assassination and suggests the following recommendations.

1. A committee of Cabinet members including the Secretary of the Treasury and the Attorney General, or the National Security Council, should be assigned the responsibility of reviewing and overseeing the protective activities of the Secret Service and the other Federal agencies that assist in safeguarding the President. Once given this responsibility, such a committee would insure that the maximum resources of the Federal Government are fully engaged in the task of protecting the President, and would provide guidance in defining the general nature of domestic and foreign dangers to Presidential security.

2. Suggestions have been advanced to the Commission for the transfer of all or parts of the Presidential protective responsibilities of the Secret Service to some other department or agency. The Commission believes that if there is to be any determination of whether or not to relocate these responsibilities and functions, it ought to be made by the Executive and the Congress, perhaps upon recommendations based on studies by the previously suggested committee.

3. Meanwhile, in order to improve daily supervision of the Secret Service within the Department of the Treasury, the Commission recommends that the Secretary of the Treasury appoint a special assistant with the responsibility of supervising the Secret Service. This special assistant should have sufficient stature and experience in law enforcement, intelligence, and allied fields to provide effective continuing supervision, and to keep the Secretary fully informed regarding the performance of the Secret Service. One of the initial assignments of this special assistant

should be the supervision of the current effort by the Secret Service
to revise and modernize its basic operating procedures.

4. The Commission recommends that the Secret Service completely overhaul its facilities devoted to the advance detection of
potential threats against the President. The Commission suggests the following measures.

(a) The Secret Service should develop as quickly as possible
more useful and precise criteria defining those potential threats
to the President which should be brought to its attention by
other agencies. The criteria should, among other additions,
provide for prompt notice to the Secret Service of all returned
defectors.

(b) The Secret Service should expedite its current plans to
utilize the most efficient data-processing techniques.

(c) Once the Secret Service has formulated new criteria
delineating the information it desires, it should enter into agreements with each Federal agency to insure its receipt of such
information.

5. The Commission recommends that the Secret Service
improve the protective measures followed in the planning, and
conducting of Presidential motorcades. In particular, the Secret
Service should continue its current efforts to increase the precau-
tionary attention given to buildings along the motorcade route.

6. The Commission recommends that the Secret Service continue its recent efforts to improve and formalize its relationships
with local police departments in areas to be visited by the
President.

7. The Commission believes that when the new criteria and
procedures are established, the Secret Service will not have sufficient personnel or adequate facilities. The Commission recommends that the Secret Service be provided with the personnel and
resources which the Service and the Department of the Treasury
may be able to demonstrate are needed to fulfill its important
mission.

8. Even with an increase in Secret Service personnel, the protection of the President will continue to require the resources and
cooperation of many Federal agencies. The Commission recommends that these agencies, specifically the FBI, continue the practice as it has developed, particularly since the assassination, of

assisting the Secret Service upon request by providing personnel or other aid, and that there be a closer association and liaison between the Secret Service and all Federal agencies.

9. The Commission recommends that the President's physician always accompany him during his travels and occupy a position near the President where he can be immediately available in case of any emergency.

10. The Commission recommends to Congress that it adopt legislation which would make the assassination of the President and Vice President a Federal crime. A state of affairs where U.S. authorities have no clearly defined jurisdiction to investigate the assassination of a President is anomalous.

11. The Commission has examined the Department of State's handling of the Oswald matters and finds that it followed the law throughout. However, the Commission believes that the Department in accordance with its own regulations should in all cases exercise great care in the return to this country of defectors who have evidenced disloyalty or hostility to this country or who have expressed a desire to renounce their American citizenship and that when such persons are so returned, procedures should be adopted for the better dissemination of information concerning them to the intelligence agencies of the Government.

12. The Commission recommends that the representatives of the bar, law enforcement associations, and the news media work together to establish ethical standards concerning the collection and presentation of information to the public so that there will be no interference with pending criminal investigations, court proceedings, or the right of individuals to a fair trial.

A DEFENSE BRIEF FOR LEE HARVEY OSWALD
Mark Lane

National Guardian / *December 19, 1963*

In all likelihood there does not exist a single American community where reside 12 men or women, good and true, who presume that Lee Harvey Oswald did not assassinate President Kennedy. No more savage comment can be made in reference to the breakdown of the Anglo-Saxon system of jurisprudence. At the very foundation of our judicial operation lies a cornerstone which shelters the innocent and guilty alike against group hysteria, manufactured evidence, overzealous law enforcement officials, in short, against those factors which militate for an automated, prejudged, neatly packaged verdict of guilty. It is the sacred right of every citizen accused of committing a crime to the presumption of innocence.

This presumption, it has been written, is a cloak donned by the accused when the initial charge is made, and worn by him continuously. It is worn throughout the entire case presented against him, and not taken from the defendant until after he has had an opportunity to cross-examine hostile witnesses, present his own witnesses and to testify himself.

Oswald did not testify. Indeed, there will be no case, no trial, and Oswald, murdered while in police custody, still has no lawyer. Under such circumstances the development of a possible defense is difficult, almost impossible. Under such circumstances, the development of such a defense is obligatory.

There will be an investigation. No investigation, however soundly motivated, can serve as an adequate substitute for trial. Law enforcement officials investigate every criminal case before it is presented to a jury. The investigation in almost all such cases

Reprinted from *National Guardian*, December 19, 1963, by permission of the publisher, Guardian, Independent Radical Newsweekly.

results in the firm conviction by the investigator that the accused is guilty. A jury often finds the defendant innocent, notwithstanding.

That which intervenes between the zealous investigator and the jury is due process of law, developed at great cost in human life and liberty over the years. It is the right to have irrelevant testimony barred. It is the right to have facts, not hopes or thoughts or wishes or prejudicial opinions, presented. It is the right to test by cross-examination the veracity of every witness and the value of his testimony. It is, perhaps above all, the right to counsel of one's own choice, so that all the other rights may be protected. In this defense, Oswald has forfeited all rights along with his life.

The reader, inundated at the outset with 48 solid television, radio and newspaper hours devoted to proving the guilt of the accused and much additional "evidence" since then, cannot now examine this case without bringing to it certain preconceived ideas. We ask, instead, only for a temporary suspension of certainty. . . .

[Discussion of case against Oswald omitted—Eds.]

THE INVESTIGATION

The FBI, having completed its investigation, has submitted what amounts to its findings and conclusions as well. The verdict, deftly and covertly divulged to the press, and then blared forth throughout the world, is impressively simple: "Oswald is the assassin. He acted alone." This remarkable law enforcement and investigatory agency, unable to solve a single one of the more than 40 Birmingham bombings, is now able to function as investigator, prosecutor, judge and jury. No other American agency has presumed to occupy so many positions of trust at one time.

The essential problem is that no investigating agency can fairly evaluate the fruits of its own work. Were the FBI certain of its conclusions it seems likely it would not be so reluctant to permit witnesses to talk with the press. It might not feel the need continually to leak information favorable to its verdict to the press. Most disquieting of all, however, is that the FBI, once wedded to a conclusion conceived before investigation, might be motivated to discover evidence which supports that conclusion. Within a few hours after Oswald was arrested the Dallas police, with the FBI at its side, announced the very same verdict now reinforced by the latest FBI discoveries. Under such circumstances, we fear that evidence tending to prove Oswald innocent might be discarded and evidence proving him guilty might be developed out of proportion or even created.

The Justice Department has already privately expressed "disappointment" with the FBI report, fearing that it "has left too many questions unanswered."

THE STAKES ARE BIG

The FBI investment in a Warren Commission finding identical with its own cannot be emphasized too boldly. Should the Warren Commission reach and publish a conclusion substantially different from the one submitted so publicly by the FBI, public confidence in the FBI would be so shaken as, in all likelihood, to render the FBI as it is now constituted almost absolutely useless. One can assume that the FBI wishes to avoid that result.

It may be argued on many different levels of governmental life that a finding by the commission that an American lynched in a Dallas courthouse might be innocent would result in the further destruction of the American image abroad.

It will be extremely difficult for any commission, in these circumstances, to bear the responsibility imposed upon it. For the sake of our country let us hope that Justice Earl Warren, a fair and great American, may successfully guide his commission through the sea of hatred and malice surrounding this case in its search for the truth.

AN ERA OF UNDERSTANDING?

There are those who have said much good may come from this assassination, that a new era of understanding and unity may result. I doubt this. From hate comes hate. From murder—as we have already seen—murder. And from hysteria—rejection of the great Anglo-Saxon tradition of justice. But if it is possible to leave behind us the America of violence and malice, our national renaissance must begin with a respect for law and disdain for the hysteria that has thus far made fair consideration of this case impossible.

Our national conscience must reject the massive media conviction of Oswald—presumed to be innocent—and begin to examine and to analyze the evidence. We must recognize that the same reckless disregard for human life and decency that resulted in the death of our President resulted also in the death of Oswald while in police custody. And, before that, it resulted in the destruction of every right belonging to an American accused of a crime. The press, the radio and the television stations share that guilt.

The law enforcement officials, however, beginning with District Attorney Wade, who falsely stated evidence to the entire world repeatedly and who gave leadership to the development of a carnival atmosphere, must bear history's harshest judgment.

You are the jury. You are the only jury that Lee Harvey Oswald will ever have.

A terrible crime has been committed. A young, vital and energetic leader of perhaps the world's most powerful nation has been killed by the cowardly act of a hidden assassin. The murderer or murderers were motivated by diseased minds or by such depths of malice as to approach that state. We will perhaps never know their motives. We must, however, know and approve of our own conduct and our own motives.

We begin with a return to an old American tradition—the presumption of innocence. We begin with you.

Let those who would deny a fair consideration of the evidence to Oswald because of a rage inspired, they say, by their devotion to the late President, ponder this thought: If Oswald is innocent —and that is a possibility that cannot now be denied—then the assassin of President Kennedy remains at large.

THE MURDER OF TIPPIT
Sylvia Meagher

Accessories after the Fact / *1967*

Although the Warren Report inundates the reader with biographical material on Oswald, the so-called lone assassin remains essentially a mysterious personality, motivated by commitments or convictions which in the last analysis leave even the Warren Commission in fumbling uncertainty. Indeed, the Commission's preoccupation with Oswald's history is out of balance with its somewhat cursory attention to the crimes of which he was accused. If Oswald did not commit those crimes, his life history has very limited relevance. Although the Commission did not quite succeed in inadvertently proving his outright innocence, it certainly failed to prove his guilt. This might be more obvious if Oswald's biography, distracting attention from the evidence and scarcely calculated to arouse sympathy, did not appear three times—in capsule form, then expanded, and finally in an appendix in full detail—between the covers of the Warren Report.

The Report also gives generous attention to the biography of Jack Ruby.

When we turn to J. D. Tippit, we find no biographical excesses but extreme reticence. Tippit, the policeman and the man, is a one-dimensional and insubstantial figure—unknown and unknowable. The Commission was not interested in Tippit's life, and apparently interested in his death only to the extent that it could be ascribed to Oswald, despite massive defects in the evidence against him.

The Commission's profound lack of interest in Tippit may be measured by its failure to take testimony from his widow, who probably saw him less than two hours before his death (*CE 2985*), or from his brothers and sisters (their names appeared in the obituary columns of the Dallas newspapers), or from any of his friends or neighbors. We know strangely little about Tippit. According to an FBI report (*CE 2985*), he led the most ordinary of lives. He had been on the Dallas police force ten years (without promotion), and at the time of his death he had a weekend job at Austin's Barbecue, to supplement his salary. The owner, Austin Cook, said that he and Tippit never discussed politics. (Yet as a self-proclaimed member of the John Birch Society, wouldn't Cook have had an occasional impulse to proselytize?) Tippit's bank balance was very modest; his standard of living was consistent with his station in life and his known income. He was a devoted family man and church-goer.

There are only a few tiny discordant notes in that exemplary record—fragmentary hints which rouse curiosity. . . .

. . . a question to Chief of Police Jesse Curry from Commissioner Allen Dulles: Is there any truth to the rumor that Tippit was involved in narcotics? No, Curry never heard such a rumor, knew nothing about anything like that. (*4H 177–178*) Where did the Commission hear that rumor? Was Curry's disclaimer sufficient to dispose of it or was it investigated as it should have been? The documents do not disclose these answers.

Missing also from the documents is an autopsy report on Tippit. The ambulance attendants who removed him to the hospital were never questioned; the doctor who performed the post-mortem examination was not a Commission witness. A Dallas police captain told the American Society of Newspaper Editors, months after the murder, that Tippit had been shot three times (*King Exhibit 4*); the Commission says four times. (*WR 165*)

Nor are we on firm ground when we come to the one segment of Tippit's life to which the Commission devoted such energies as it reserved for him: the hour of his death.

As I shall show later, the Commission's version of the circumstances that took Tippit to the street where he died is completely at odds with the evidence, which the Commission has examined hastily, superficially, and incompletely in its anxiety to determine an "innocent" reason for his presence in a strange district of Dallas where nothing was happening—until he himself was murdered.

The time of the shooting remains uncertain. The key witness, Helen Louise Markham, said in her affidavit of November 22 that the shooting took place at 1:06 p.m.; when she testified in March 1964, she reiterated the time was 1:06 or 1:07 p.m. (*CE 2003*, p. 37; *3H 306*) But as her testimony reveals, she is not a person in whom reasonable men would place implicit trust—for she appears to be given to extreme confusion or even, at times, estrangement from reality.

Another citizen, a Mr. T. F. Bowley, also put the time of the shooting earlier than the Commission, which claims it was at approximately 1:15 p.m. (*WR 165*) Bowley was in his car on his way to call for his wife when he saw Tippit's body lying on the street; he got out of the car and looked at his watch, which said 1:10 p.m. (*CE 2003*, p. 11) Of course, Bowley's watch may have been slow, or fast. He was never interviewed by the Commission or its servant agencies.

Bowley is the only known witness who deliberately checked the time. Other witnesses on whom the Commission relied were not certain of the exact time, or were not asked about it. Three said that it was about one o'clock; one said that it was shortly after; one said that it was about 1:20 p.m.; and one said 1:30 p.m.

The exact time of the shooting is of great importance in the context of Oswald's alleged timetable after the shooting of the President. If the shooting of Tippit took place at 1:06 or 1:10 p.m., Oswald would have to be exonerated on the grounds that he could not possibly have walked the nine-tenths of a mile from his rooming house, from which he departed a few minutes after 1 p.m., in time to reach the scene. The Commission has estimated Oswald's other walks (from the Book Depository to the bus and from the bus to the taxi) at one minute per block. At that rate, Oswald would have required 18 minutes to walk from his rooming house to the spot where Tippit was shot.[1] Therefore, if Tippit was shot at 1:15 p.m. as the Commission asserts, Oswald should have left his rooming house a few minutes before, not after 1 p.m.—and that does not even allow for the fact that he was last seen by Earlene Roberts standing motionless at a bus stop near the rooming house. Not one witness has come forward who saw Oswald walking from the house to the Tippit scene. The

---

[1] Commission Counsel David Belin reenacted the walk, stopwatch in hand, in 17 minutes, 45 seconds. (*6H 434*)

Commission assumes that he took the shortest route (after all, didn't he get there in time to shoot Tippit at 1:15?) but offers no evidence. Indeed, the Commission has ignored the question of where Oswald was heading—if it *was* Oswald—when he was stopped by Tippit. He had no known social or business contacts in that immediate area, but, as many critics of the Report have pointed out, Jack Ruby's apartment was in the direction in which "Oswald" was walking and only a few short blocks from the scene of the Tippit shooting. Another "irrelevancy" in this "most exacting and detailed investigation in the history of crime."

Oswald did not have time to reach the Tippit scene on foot even if the shooting took place at 1:15 p.m.; if it was earlier by seven or ten minutes Oswald must be ruled out.

But, the Commission points out, two eyewitnesses to the shooting identified Oswald as the killer, and seven eyewitnesses identified him as the man who was seen fleeing the scene holding a revolver (*WR 157*); at least 12 persons, the Commission says, saw the man with the revolver immediately after the shooting. (*WR 166*) The Commission also provides a photo chart showing "the location of eyewitnesses to the movements of Lee Harvey Oswald in the vicinity of the Tippit killing" (*WR 164*) which mixes indiscriminately the names of those who did *not* identify Oswald with those who did.

The two eyewitnesses to the shooting who identified Oswald as the killer were, according to the Commission, Helen Markham and William Scoggins. Scoggins, a taxi-driver, was not really an eyewitness because a bush obstructed his view of the actual shooting. The second eyewitness to the shooting was really Domingo Benavides, a truck-driver, who was in fact the closest person to the policeman and the killer at the moment of the murder—he was about 15 feet away, according to his testimony (*6H 447*), although the report says 25 feet. (*WR 166*) He told the police that he did not feel able to identify the killer. The police evidently took him at his word and did not take him to view Oswald in a line-up.

Benavides, the man who had the closest view of the murder, did not identify Oswald at that time or even when he was shown a photograph of Oswald months later during his testimony for the Commission. This should be borne in mind when the other identifications are evaluated, whether on the basis of a line-up or photographs.

The testimony of Helen Markham, the other eyewitness to the shooting, has been denounced sufficiently by critics of the Warren Report. I do not wish to further belabor the point that she lacks any semblance of credibility. She said that she was alone with Tippit for 20 minutes before an ambulance arrived, and that Tippit—who is said to have died instantaneously—tried to talk to her; she was in hysterics and somehow managed to leave her shoes on top of Tippit's car (*CE 1974*); sedatives had to be administered before she was taken to view the line-up at about 4:30 p.m. on Friday.

Mrs. Markham identified Oswald as the man who shot Tippit, just as the Commission claims, but here is how she described it in her testimony, which the Commission contends has "probative value."

BALL: Now when you went into the room you looked these people over, these four men?

MRS. MARKHAM: Yes, sir.

BALL: Did you recognize anyone in the line-up?

MRS. MARKHAM: No, sir.

BALL: You did not? Did you see anybody—I have asked you that question before—did you recognize anybody from their face?

MRS. MARKHAM: From their face, no.

BALL: Did you identify anybody in these four people?

MRS. MARKHAM: I didn't know anybody . . . I had never seen none of them, none of these men.

BALL: No one of the four?

MRS. MARKHAM: No one of them.

BALL: No one of all four?

MRS. MARKHAM: No, sir.

BALL: Was there a number two man in there?

MRS. MARKHAM: Number two is the one I picked. . . . Number two was the man I saw shoot the policeman. . . . I looked at him. When I saw this man I wasn't sure, but I had cold chills just run all over me. . . .

(*3H 310-311*)

Reading this testimony about the "identification" on which the Commission relied, I feel a few cold chills too.

But the Commission has a third witness—the taxi-driver, Scoggins, whom it classifies as an eyewitness to the shooting although there was a bush which obstructed his view of the gunman in the act of firing. But Scoggins identified Oswald as the man who came toward him right after the shots, gun in hand, escaping from the scene. The identification took place at a line-up on Saturday at about midday. William Whaley, another taxi-driver, came with Scoggins to view the line-up. Whaley testified:

. . . me and this other taxi-driver who was with me, sir, we sat in the room awhile and directly they brought in six men, young teen-agers, and they were all handcuffed together . . . you could have picked [Oswald] out without identifying him by just listening to him because he was bawling out the policeman, telling them it wasn't right to put him in line with these teen-agers. . . . He showed no respect for the policemen, he told them what he thought about them . . . they were trying to railroad him and he wanted his lawyer. . . . Anybody who wasn't sure could have picked out the right one just for that. . . .

(2H 260-261)

If Scoggins or the other witnesses who picked Oswald out of the line-up could not tag him by his protests of a frame-up, or by his conspicuous bruises and black eye, they had the added advantage of hearing him state his name and place of work—the Book Depository, which the whole country believed to be the site of the assassination. The three men who appeared in the line-ups with Oswald on Friday were all Dallas police employees—W. E. Perry and Richard Clark, detectives, and Don Ables, jail clerk. Each of those men testified that he was asked his name and occupation and that he gave fictitious answers. Oswald also responded when he was asked his name and occupation—information which was saturating all the news media—but his replies were factual, not fictitious. (7H 234, 237-239, 241-42) The same question-and-answer routine was followed at the Saturday line-up, according to one of the participants. (7H 245-246) How, then, could anyone fail to "identify" Oswald?

The Warren Commission saw nothing wrong with the composition or management of the line-ups. It was "satisfied that the line-ups were conducted fairly." (*WR 169*) In my view neither the line-ups nor the Commission were "fair," and I would insist that all the identifications of Oswald by witnesses to the Tippit murder be discarded as utterly valueless.

The witnesses who saw a man fleeing the scene are numerous.[2] Four of them (Barbara Jeanette Davis, Virginia Davis, Ted Callaway, and Sam Guinyard) identified Oswald after viewing a line-up on Friday. I discount those four identifications for the reasons already given. Moreover, there is reason to question whether Callaway really saw a man fleeing the scene, as he claimed, as may be seen from the testimony of Domingo Benavides (Callaway's employee).

. . . when Ted Callaway got around there, he opened the car door and picked up the phone and called in and told them there was an officer that had been killed. . . . Then he jumped out and ran around and asked me did I see what happened, and I said yes. And he said let's

---

[2] There have been reports of at least four more eyewitnesses who are never mentioned in the Warren Report. A B.B.C. broadcast includes an interview with a Mrs. Ann McCravey (phonetic spelling), who witnessed the shooting from her window. George and Patricia Nash, in an article "The Other Witnesses" in the *New Leader* of October 12, 1964, revealed the existence of three additional witnesses—Frank Wright and his wife, and Acquilla Clemons. None of those four witnesses was summoned by the Warren Commission or, apparently, even interviewed by its servant agencies.

Still another witness at the Tippit scene comes to light in the testimony of a Dallas Police Reserve, Kenneth Hudson Croy. (*12H 186-206*) Croy told Commission Counsel Burt Griffin (the same Griffin as the one who cited as evidence for Oswald's presence in the Book Depository window the fact that Oswald had shot Tippit) that he had been driving to a restaurant where he had a lunch date when he came to the Tippit scene, just as the body was being loaded into the ambulance. He had talked to several of the known eyewitnesses and also to "a man that was standing there in the yard." (*12H 202*) The man had seen "Oswald" walk up the street "some blocks to where he got to before he got to Tippit's car."

Croy testified that he had turned this witness over to some other officers "and they talked to him"; he did not remember the man's name. Nor is there anything in the record about this man, without or with a name, although he had witnessed the Tippit killer's walk along East Tenth Street and might well have had important information and at least a description to contribute. The fact that the Dallas police (other than Reserve Officer Croy) have mentioned nothing about this unnamed man cannot justify the assumption that his observations were unimportant or unnecessary; they may in fact justify the opposite inference.

Mr. Griffin seems not to have followed up Croy's interesting testimony about a hitherto unknown Tippit witness.

chase him, and I said no. . . . So he then turned around and went to the cab that was sitting on the corner. . . . And so Ted then got in the taxicab and the taxicab came to a halt and he asked me which way [the killer] went. I told him he went down Patton Street toward the office, and come to find out later Ted had already seen him go by there.   (6H 452)

Indeed, it is paradoxical that Callaway, who supposedly had seen the killer after he turned the corner and was out of Benavides' range of vision, should have asked him "which way he went." The lawyers for the Commission seem to have been immune to discrepancies of this kind; predictably, they did not pay attention to this contradiction.

Other witnesses who saw a man fleeing the scene were never contacted until the end of January 1964, two months after their fleeting glimpse of an unknown man. Several of them identified Oswald from a photograph as the man they had seen two months before—however, they did not select his photograph from a group, according to standard practice, because they were shown only Oswald's picture. That such "identifications" are worthless is, of course, self-evident. The Commission makes itself ridiculous by asking us to regard them as serious evidence.

Some of the witnesses who were contacted at the end of January did not identify Oswald. One of them, Warren Reynolds, was shot in the head the next day.* He recovered and conveniently reversed himself, in July 1964, and at that time identified Oswald from a photograph shown him during his Commission testimony. L. J. Lewis, on the other hand, maintained that he had been too distant from the man to identify him—an obstacle that did not deter two witnesses in the same location as Lewis from identifying Oswald from a photograph, on January 22, 1964.

The eyewitness identifications are highly vulnerable and would have been torn to shreds in a courtroom. What other evidence, then, remains to incriminate Oswald? A jacket discarded near the Tippit scene, which will be discussed in detail later, and the fact that four discarded shells matched the revolver which Oswald is

* This incident and the deaths of many assassination-related figures have been examined by the courageous Texas newspaper editor Penn Jones in his series of books, Forgive My Grief.—Eds.

said to have had on his person when he was arrested in the Texas Theater. As we shall see, the four shells do not correspond exactly with the four bullets recovered from Tippit's body, and the bullets themselves were too mangled to be identified as having been fired from any specific weapon. Consequently, the ballistics evidence does not provide conclusive proof of Oswald's culpability.

Finally, one more point must be taken into account. It involves a signed, first-person story by Dallas Police Officer N. M. McDonald, in which he gives an account of the arrest of Oswald in the Texas Theater. The story appeared in the *Dallas Morning News* of November 24, 1963.[3] McDonald wrote that while he was cruising toward Oak Cliff the police got a tip that a "man acting funny was holed up in the balcony of the Texas Theater. . . . The cashier at the picture show was the one who called in to say this guy was acting suspicious and hidden out in the balcony." There were ten to fifteen people in the theater, "spread out good" (only two of whom gave evidence, the others remaining unknown to this day). "A man sitting near the front, and I still don't know who it was, tipped me the man I wanted was sitting in the third row from the rear, not in the balcony" (this is not the story as told in the Warren Report or in the testimony of Johnny Calvin Brewer, the shoe salesman who supposedly pointed Oswald out).

"I went up the aisle, and talked to two people sitting about in the middle. I was crouching low and *holding my gun* in case any trouble came." McDonald, according to his published story, then approached Oswald, who muttered that it was all over now and hit him a "pretty good one" in the face with his fist. "I saw him going for his gun and I grabbed him around the waist." They struggled; McDonald got his hand on the butt of the pistol but Oswald had his hand on the trigger. McDonald pulled the gun toward him and heard the hammer click. "The primer was dented and it didn't fire."

There are many discrepancies between McDonald's newspaper story and the final version of the arrest. For example, here is a passage from the testimony of FBI firearms expert Cortlandt Cunningham.

---

[3] N. M. McDonald, "Officer Recalls Oswald Capture," *Dallas Morning News*, November 24, 1963, p. 13.

EISENBERG: Now, Officer McDonald's statement that the primer of one round was dented on misfire: as far as you can tell, could this statement be confirmed?

CUNNINGHAM: No, sir; we found nothing to indicate that this weapon's firing pin had struck the primer of any of these cartridges. (3H 463)

Did an experienced police officer really make so gross an error as to see a dent where there was none?

Even more intriguing is McDonald's statement that he was crouching low and *holding his gun* as he approached Oswald. Here is a truly sensational admission, one which undermines the whole official version of the arrest—for no one of sound mind can possibly believe that Oswald punched McDonald, or tried to draw his own gun, while the policeman's gun was already pointing at him.

After the story of November 24, McDonald never suggested in his testimony or reports that he had his revolver in his hand as he approached Oswald, but that is what he wrote right after the event, when the predispositions of the case were not yet clear.

The Warren Commission undoubtedly studied the contents of the Dallas newspapers which appeared both before and after the assassination. Surely the Commission did not overlook McDonald's signed story, with its startling implications. Yet when McDonald testified before the Commission, he was not questioned about or confronted with his published statement and its crucial discrepancies.

A question of such importance must not be allowed to remain unresolved, for historians to grapple with many years from now. It is not too late: McDonald should be allowed to speak now—to the American people, if the Warren Commission has not the dignity to clarify this and a host of similar defects in its case against Oswald.

TIPPIT'S MOVEMENTS

First news flashes out of Dallas on the Tippit shooting said that he had been shot to death when he and another policeman pursued a suspect in the assassination into the Texas Theater following a tip. The suspect—Lee Harvey Oswald—had shot Tippit. He was subdued and arrested by other policemen.

By the next day, newspapers reported that Tippit actually had been shot and killed some blocks away from the theater and that Oswald had been arrested for Tippit's murder, not for the assassination of the President. The new version of the Tippit shooting raised a puzzling question: What was Tippit doing outside of his assigned district, at the location where he was shot? This remained a mystery until the Warren Report was published, leading to the various conspiracy theories predicated on Tippit's complicity in the assassination.

The Warren Report seemed to dispose of the question, telling us that at 12:45 p.m. the police dispatcher had ordered No. 78 (Tippit) to "move into central Oak Cliff area" (*WR 165*) and assuring us that that instruction appeared on the police radio log. (*WR 651*) But study of the radio log and scrutiny of the testimony of various police witnesses suggest that the pronouncements in the Warren Report, far from clearing up the mystery of Tippit's whereabouts, are untenable and illusory.

The Warren Commission received three different transcripts of the police radio log. The first transcript was an edited one prepared by the Dallas police on December 3, 1963. (*Sawyer Exhibits No. A and No. B*) An explanatory covering note indicated that it covered only messages relating to the assassination and to the shooting of Tippit but not routine police business. But this transcript did not include an instruction to Tippit at 12:45 to move into central Oak Cliff, although such an instruction was indisputably relevant to the Tippit murder and could not be classified as "routine police business." If the instruction was on the tape record, it should have been transcribed in the edited transcript.

In early April 1964, the Warren Commission was still seeking to determine the reason for Tippit's presence on the street where he was shot. A number of Dallas police officers were asked why, in their opinion, Tippit had left his assigned district and moved to the scene of the shooting.

Sergeant Calvin Bud Owens (*7H 81*), Lieutenant Rio S. Pierce (*7H 77*), and Sergeant James A. Putnam (*7H 75*) speculated about what Tippit's reasoning might have been under the circumstances that prevailed immediately after the police broadcast that shots had been fired at the President at Dealey Plaza. They postulated that Tippit, exercising proper discretion in the light of the prevailing emergency, had started in the direction of the downtown area where the attack on the motorcade had occurred, and that his route to that destination had taken him to the vicinity where his body was found. Not one of the witnesses suggested that Tippit had been sent out of his own district by the police dispatcher. Apparently talk and speculation within the Dallas Police Department during the five months which had elapsed since the Tippit murder had not elicited any reference to the alleged 12:45 instruction to Tippit, at least in the hearing of Owens, Pierce, or Putnam.

The suggestion which they had put forward—that Tippit had proceeded on his own initiative to the district where he was killed—is weak. Had Tippit decided by himself to move to the scene of the assassination, he would have arrived there within 15 or 20 minutes at most (the Commission asserts that it took Oswald only six minutes to make a somewhat shorter trip in reverse). But Tippit was cruising slowly on East Tenth Street at 1:15 p.m., that location being some four miles from Dealey Plaza. Obviously he was not en route to the Book Depository area, as the three witnesses speculated. The lawyer who had solicited their opinions did not pose this self-evident objection to their rationalization.

At the end of April, the Warren Commission—still without an acceptable explanation of Tippit's movements—requested and received a verbatim transcript of the radio log, again prepared by the Dallas police, in which the personnel reporting to the dispatcher were designated by number and not by name. (CE 705) (Still later, the Commission requested the FBI to prepare a transcript in verbatim form, setting forth the names as well as the numbers of the personnel (CE 1974); the FBI verbatim transcript was completed in August 1964.)

Although a number of police witnesses had suggested that Tippit's departure from his own district was a normal procedure under the existing circumstances, the Dallas police verbatim transcript of the radio log (CE 705) now included an instruction—issued simultaneously to No. 78 (Tippit) and No. 87 (Nelson)—to move into central Oak Cliff, transmitted at 12:45 p.m.

This was the first indication of the alleged instruction, and it immediately raised the question of why it had not appeared in

the edited transcript of December 1963. That question was posed
to Police Chief Jesse Curry when he appeared before the Commission on April 22, 1964. His reply was confused and incoherent.
Curry, one of the key officials responsible for the President's
safety in Dallas, was distraught and seemed merely to improvise
his answers—at one point seeming to suggest that Tippit had
moved out of his assigned district to search for his own murderer.
(4H 192)

Curry said first that the 12:45 instruction to Tippit had been
omitted from the December edited transcript because it was difficult to hear everything clearly; his men had spent many hours
replaying the recording and copying down the conversations; he
himself had heard the recording and could vouch for the correctness of the verbatim transcript. (4H 186) A dubious reply, for if
the instruction to Tippit was audible when the verbatim transcript was prepared, it must have been equally audible when the
edited transcript was made.

J. Lee Rankin vindicated Curry by asking if the instruction
might not have been omitted from the first transcript for reasons
of brevity, as other routine messages had been omitted. Curry
hastened to agree. (4H 185-186) But it has already been pointed
out that the instruction to Tippit was fundamental to the events
leading to his murder and could not be regarded as "routine" by
any standard.

The omission of the message in the first transcript of the radio
log, its sudden appearance in the second transcript, and the lame
or absurd explanations given by Curry and other police witnesses
inevitably raise suspicion about the authenticity of the message.
That suspicion is intensified by further study of the radio log.

If the instruction to Tippit—and Nelson—is authentic, we must
ask why the dispatcher singled out those two officers for special
and quite curious treatment. They were the *only* officers contacted by the dispatcher with instructions unrelated to the assassination and lacking any other apparent purpose. During the half-
hour after the President was shot there was no breach of law and
order in central Oak Cliff, and no strategic reason for sending
reinforcements there. The assassination took place at a point
some four or more miles from central Oak Cliff. As it turned out,
a Book Depository employee who was missing and under suspicion

was en route to his furnished room in Oak Cliff at 12:45 p.m.—
but there was no way for the dispatcher or Tippit to know that.
Oswald's absence had not yet been noticed at 12:45; his Oak Cliff
address was not known to his wife or his employers, much less to
the Dallas police. If the dispatcher nonetheless sent two policemen closer to the vicinity of Oswald's rooming house, at random,
or if Tippit went there on his initiative, it would have been an
incredible coincidence.

The order to Tippit and Nelson was given 15 minutes after the
President was shot, in a setting of unprecedented emergency. A
frenzy of police activity centered at the Book Depository and at
Parkland Hospital. So much traffic jammed police communications lines that officers had to wait their turn to get through with
urgent information.

The dispatcher had sent out a general order for all downtown
squads to proceed to the Book Depository. Aside from Tippit and
Nelson, the dispatcher did not contact any specific squad cars, nor
did he give any general order to men in the outlying districts to
move elsewhere. We are asked to believe that, in the midst of this
consternation, the dispatcher took the time to call Tippit and
Nelson and give them instructions which make no sense.

The Warren Commission saw nothing curious in this. The
Commission did not question the dispatcher about his reason for
giving the alleged instruction, although there was already a peculiar aura about the radio log. Such questioning was all the more
necessary because, according to the transcript, policemen from the
outermost districts of Dallas who called the dispatcher to ask if
there was anything they could do in the emergency were told to
report to the Book Depository—even though in some instances
they were far more distant from that location than Tippit or
Nelson.

Even stranger is the fact that Nelson, supposedly told simultaneously with Tippit to move in to central Oak Cliff, is not heard
from until 45 minutes later, at about 1:30 p.m., *at the Book
Depository*, as if he had never received or acknowledged the
12:45 instruction. When Nelson reported from the Book Depository, the dispatcher raised no question about his seeming disregard for an explicit order to proceed to a different location. In
itself this suggests that Nelson never received such an order, nor

did Tippit; the force of this inference is strengthened by a police report on a different matter (*CE 2645*), stating that after the assassination, Nelson was dispatched to the Book Depository, where he remained on guard in front of the building for the remainder of the afternoon!

If the 12:45 instruction to Nelson to proceed to central Oak Cliff was fabricated, as his actions at the time and the later report (*CE 2645*) suggest, was the 12:45 instruction to Tippit—never mentioned until some five months later—authentic?

According to the radio log, Tippit not only was sent to central Oak Cliff, but he remained the subject of extraordinary solicitude. At 12:45, nine minutes after the alleged instruction, the dispatcher signaled Tippit again and asked his location. Tippit replied that he was in Oak Cliff, as instructed, at Lancaster and Eighth Streets. The dispatcher then told Tippit to "be at large for any emergency that comes in." In the prevailing atmosphere of crisis and intense police activity, such an axiomatic reminder is certainly bizarre.

The next relevant entry in the radio log creates still more confusion and perplexity. At 1 p.m. the same dispatcher who supposedly heard Tippit report at 12:45 that he was at Lancaster and Eighth signaled Tippit again—this time, it would appear, in search of a squad car to pick up blood and rush it to Parkland Hospital. The exchange of messages between the dispatcher and various cruising policemen indicates that the dispatcher was seeking the squad car nearest to the blood bank.

But the blood bank was located in the 2000 block of Commerce Street, about five miles distant from Lancaster and Eighth. If the 12:45 and 12:54 messages were authentic, the dispatcher would have known that Tippit was nowhere near the blood bank. If he did not signal Tippit at 1 p.m. in connection with the delivery of blood to the hospital, what else was he calling about? This question, too, remained unasked by the Warren Commission and unanswered by the dispatcher.

Tippit did not reply to the 1 p.m. signal. Where was he? Why didn't he answer?

Let us look at the testimony of Dallas policeman Harry Olsen, who was a casual friend of Jack Ruby and boy friend of Kay Coleman, a stripper at Ruby's Carousel Club. Olsen's account of his whereabouts at the time of the assassination is extremely interesting. He told Commission Counsel Arlen Specter, who deposed him on August 6, 1964, that he had been off duty on the day of the assassination and had agreed to substitute on a moonlighting job for a motorcycle policeman assigned to the motorcade. The job was to guard an estate in the absence of its owners. Olsen did not remember the name of the motorcycle policeman; there is no indication that the Commission attempted to establish his identity. Where was the estate? Olsen said it was on Eighth Street in Oak Cliff, about two blocks from the freeway—that is, at or very near Lancaster and Eighth, the location from which Tippit supposedly had reported at 12:54.

Where was Olsen at that hour? He testified that he had learned that the President had been shot when he answered a phone call for the absent owner of the estate; he had then gone outside and exchanged comments about the tragedy with passersby. (*14H 629*)

Olsen, then, was in the right place at the right time to encounter Tippit—with whom he admittedly was acquainted—if Tippit was actually at Lancaster and Eighth. Arlen Specter seemed unaware of the import of Olsen's testimony. He did not ask Olsen if he had seen or spoken to Tippit, perhaps at one o'clock (when Tippit failed to answer the dispatcher's signal).

But perhaps Olsen never saw Tippit; there seems to have been another reason for Tippit's silence at 1 p.m. At that very time, a police car pulled up to the rooming house on North Beckley Street where Oswald was a tenant, sounded its horn, and slowly drove away, according to Earlene Roberts, the housekeeper there. (*6H 443-444*) Mrs. Roberts said that there were two police officers in the car; she was confused about the number on the vehicle and gave several different versions. In some of the three-digit combinations she suggested, the first two figures were a 1 and a 0; Tippit's car was "No. 10."

Investigation failed to turn up any squad car that stopped in front of Oswald's boarding house at 1 p.m. or any officer who admitted stopping there. Tippit, who did not reply to a one-o'clock signal, cannot be questioned, of course.

According to the police verbatim transcript of the radio log (*CE 705*), Tippit twice signaled the dispatcher at 1:08 p.m., but the dispatcher did not acknowledge or reply to the signal. In the corresponding part of the FBI verbatim transcript (*CE 1974*,

p. 48) Tippit's call number ("No. 78") is missing, and the signal is attributed to "No. 488," with a notation that the sound was garbled. No. 488 is not identified by name, and no other listing for No. 488 appears anywhere in the radio log.

Between 12:45 and 1:08 p.m. there was a total of four signals involving Tippit—three calls by the dispatcher in a 15-minute interval, the last call unanswered, and an unanswered call from Tippit to the dispatcher at 1:08 p.m. The Warren Commission sees nothing strange in the fact that an inconsequential patrolman, stationed far from the scene of the assassination, is called repeatedly by the dispatcher for no apparent reason, at a time of unparalleled traffic on the police radio.

Finally we come to the most extraordinary of the Tippit signals to be found in the radio log. At about 1:16 p.m. a citizen broke in on the police radio, to report the shooting of a policeman at 404 East Tenth Street (which lies in District 91). According to all three transcripts of the radio log, the dispatcher's immediate reaction was to call No. 78 (Tippit) again—and, according to two of the transcripts, before there was any reason for the dispatcher to link the officer who was shot with Tippit.

The police verbatim transcript interpolates a parenthetical reference to background noises in which No. 78 and Car No. 10 could be heard, giving the impression that the dispatcher heard Tippit's code number and car number before signaling him. (CE 705, p. 408) But the indication of background noises is *not* found in the FBI verbatim transcript, which, like the edited transcript (*Sawyer Exhibit A*, p. 394), indicates that the dispatcher began to signal Tippit immediately after the citizen's intrusion and before the mention of any numbers by which Tippit might be identified. (CE 1974, p. 858) The reference to background noises, which is found only in the police verbatim transcript, is all the more suspect for the fact that no one at the scene of the shooting could have known that the murdered policeman was No. 78.

Tippit, ostensibly pulled out of his own district, No. 78, reported at 12:54 from a location inside District 109.[4] Some 20 minutes later he was shot to death on a street inside District 91,

---

[4] Identification of district numbers is based on the official Dallas Police Radio Patrol District Map (*Putnam Exhibit No. 1*) and on a street map of Dallas.

where the assigned officer, No. 91 (Mentzel), was present on duty in his squad car. The dispatcher, on receiving a citizen's report of a shooting on East Tenth Street, did not signal No. 91 (Mentzel) —he signaled Tippit, without any reason to believe that Tippit was the victim of the shooting or that he was the closest officer to the scene. Only after calling Tippit did the dispatcher signal and reach Mentzel, who, according to an FBI report: "Was eating lunch at 430 West Jefferson at time of assassination. Left restaurant to answer shooting call in 400 block East Tenth Street, Oak Cliff." (CE 2645)

The transcripts of the radio log are studded with aberrations and inconsistencies, both in absolute terms and in divergence from each other. None of the many warning signals in the transcripts indicating that something more than meets the eye was transpiring in the hour of Tippit's death has been acknowledged or investigated by the Warren Commission. The assurances in the Warren Report that everything was innocent and routine are misleading. The radio log suggests irresistibly that Tippit was on something other than routine business, on his own behalf or under instructions, and that the truth of the circumstances which led him to the quiet street where he was shot to death has either not been ferreted out, or has been carefully concealed.

I cannot accept the assertion in the Warren Report that Tippit was instructed as a matter of normal police routine to move into central Oak Cliff, for the following reasons:

(1) The first transcript of the radio log did not include the 12:45 instruction to Tippit, and five months later police witnesses were still unaware of such a transaction and were venturing the opinion that Tippit must have acted on his own initiative in leaving his assigned district.

(2) Officers from the outermost districts were sent to the Book Depository.

(3) No other districts received orders such as those allegedly given to No. 78 (Tippit) and No. 87 (Nelson).

(4) Nelson's actual movements suggest that he never received a 12:45 instruction to move into central Oak Cliff; another Commission exhibit establishes the fact that Nelson was actually assigned to the Book Depository.

(5) The dispatcher tried to contact Tippit at 1 p.m. for an

apparent purpose which is completely inconsistent with the authenticity of the 12:45 and 12:54 messages.

(6) Tippit's failure to respond to signals at 1 p.m. remains unexplained; his 1:08 call to the dispatcher comes after too long an interval to be regarded as a response to the 1 p.m. signal, if Tippit was merely cruising at a leisurely speed on quiet streets where there was no incident requiring police action until he himself was shot.

(7) The dispatcher's signals to Tippit after a citizen's report of a shooting—without reason to believe that Tippit was in the district and before any indication that Tippit was the victim—remain unexplained and may point to clandestine activities on Tippit's part which would nullify the official theory of his murder.

TIPPIT AND THE PEDESTRIAN

In the early days of the case police spokesmen maintained that Tippit had heard the police radio description of the suspect in the assassination and on that basis had halted the pedestrian who shot him. Skeptics ridiculed this as being utterly inconsistent with the facts and with an eyewitness description of the encounter. Rumors circulated that Tippit and Oswald were known to each other, and published speculations suggested that the two men were involved in a plot to assassinate the President.

The Warren Report later asserted that there was no evidence that Oswald and Tippit were acquainted, had ever seen each other, or had any mutual acquaintances. There was no way to determine with certainty whether Tippit had recognized Oswald from the description broadcast on the police radio, but it was "conceivable, even probable," that Tippit had done so. (WR 651)

Information in the Hearings and Exhibits provides cause for serious reservations about the Commission's assertions and reasoning. I have already pointed out that the radio log throws grave doubt on the official explanation of Tippit's movements and that at 1 p.m. he was mysteriously absent from his car, or refused for other reasons to reply to the dispatcher's signal. We do not know what Tippit was doing between 12:54 p.m. and the time he was shot, but there is nothing to suggest that he was stopping pedestrians who fit the description of the assassination suspect, an "unknown white male, approximately thirty, slender build, height five feet ten inches, weight 165 pounds, reported to be armed with a .30 caliber rifle." (*CE 705*) It would be amazing if Tippit saw no male pedestrian on the streets of Oak Cliff between 12:45 and the time he was shot who fit that vague description. Did Oswald, viewed from behind, fit the description? He was younger than thirty by six years; was not armed with a rifle. It would be even more remarkable, then, if Tippit stopped him and no one else.

Were the actions of Tippit and the pedestrian whom he stopped consistent with the theory that the man was stopped because he resembled the description broadcast on the police radio? Only one witness claims to have seen what happened: Mrs. Helen Markham.

BALL: Where was the police car when you first saw it?

MRS. MARKHAM: He was driving real slow, almost up to this man, well, say this man, and he kept, this man kept walking, you know, and the police car going real slow now, real slow, and they just kept coming into the curb, and finally they got way up there a little ways up, well, it stopped.

BALL: The police car stopped?

MRS. MARKHAM: Yes, sir.

BALL: What about the man? Was he still walking?

MRS. MARKHAM: The man stopped. . . . I saw the man come over to the car very slow, leaned and put his arms just like this, he leaned over in this window and looked in this window. . . . The window was down. . . . Well, I didn't think nothing about it; you know, the police are nice and friendly and I thought friendly conversation. Well, I looked, and there was cars coming, so I had to wait. . . . This man, like I told you, put his arms up, leaned over, he—just a minute, and he drew back and he stepped back about two steps. . . . The policeman calmly opened the door, very slowly, wasn't angry or nothing, he calmly crawled out of his car, and I still just thought a friendly conversation. . . . (*3H 307*)

The encounter as Mrs. Markham has described it is compatible with any number of causes. Tippit might have stopped the man to ask for a match, and they might have exchanged comments about the shooting of the President less than an hour before. Tippit might have stopped an acquaintance and stopped to ask how his sick mother was feeling. The scene sketched by Mrs. Markham suggests that the pedestrian made no attempt to avoid the policeman and that he exhibited no signs of alarm or tension. This hardly suggests a man unnerved by fear and guilt or a man who had spent the preceding 45 minutes darting about on foot and by vehicle in an "escape." Tippit's behavior is even less compatible with the Commission's theory. He should have known better than to leave the car had he been suspicious of the man he stopped. He should have summoned reinforcements on the police radio, just as another officer did who was working alone and found a man whom he wished to arrest, as shown in the radio log. (CE 1974, pp. 48-51) He might have told the man to get into the car to be taken to the police station for questioning. But why should Tippit leave the car under the circumstances which the Commission considers "conceivable, even probable"? He did not leave the car in order to search the pedestrian for a concealed rifle. He did not leave the car to subdue by force a suspect who had made no gesture of resistance and didn't try to run away. If Tippit had stopped the pedestrian—whether Oswald or someone else—on suspicion that he was the Presidential assassin, it was reckless and probably against regulations for him to leave his car. It seems to me that a solitary policeman seeking to apprehend a dangerous criminal would first have called on the police radio to give information, ask instructions, and seek help.[5] That is what was done by other officers. Unfortunately the Commission did not inquire into the rules that were applicable in the "conceivable, even probable" circumstances which it postulated. Unfortunately the Commission did not ponder the strangeness of Tippit's actions under such a hypothesis.

These considerations suggest that it was not probable, perhaps not even conceivable, that Tippit stopped the pedestrian who shot him because of the description broadcast on the police radio. The facts indicate that Tippit was up to something different which, if

[5] Perhaps that was the purpose of Tippit's unanswered signal at 1:08 p.m. If so, the suspect could not have been Oswald, who could not have walked from his rooming house to the scene of the shooting in time.

uncovered, might place his death and the other events of those three days in a completely new perspective. We do not know what was in Tippit's mind during his last hours. There was a clue, but the Commission did not follow it up, as seen in the testimony of Sergeant W. E. Barnes of the police laboratory. Barnes, who had taken photographs at the scene of the Tippit shooting, was questioned about those photographs on April 7, 1964.

BELIN: Inside the window there appears to be some kind of paper or document. Do you remember what that is at all, or not?

BARNES: That is a board, a clipboard that is installed on the dash of all squad cars for the officers to take notes on and keep their wanted persons names on.

BELIN: Were there any notes on there that you saw that had been made on this clipboard?

BARNES: Yes, we never read his clipboard. . . . I couldn't tell you what was on the clipboard.   (7H 274)

Perhaps the Commission found it plausible that the Dallas police did not bother to examine the clipboard of a murdered officer, seeking a clue to his murder. Be that as it may, why did the Commission not obtain and examine it? There might have been notations on the clipboard which might have cast light on Tippit's activities before he was shot—notations which might have strengthened the basis for the Commission's speculations, or shown them to be mistaken.

If neither the police nor the Commission took the trouble to examine Tippit's clipboard, they were poorly qualified to undertake a murder investigation. If the clipboard was examined, the findings have been concealed and must be assumed to be incompatible with the official theory.

We revert now to the Commission's assertion that there was no evidence that Oswald and Tippit were acquainted or had ever seen each other.

In the early days there was considerable speculation, some of which was irresponsible, that Oswald and Tippit might have been fellow conspirators in a plot with other unknown persons to assassinate the President. The theory of a clandestine or criminal association between Oswald and Tippit was unaccompanied by serious evidence. Apparently it sprang from an effort of the imagination to invest logic and credibility in the implausible and naïve version of the Tippit murder which issued from official sources. The proposition that Tippit had stopped an unknown pedestrian on the strength of a vague description on the police radio satisfies few students of the case and offends those who seek meaning in human affairs and do not conceive of history as governed by random, irrational, and incessant coincidence.

The theorists and their theories of sinister links between Oswald and Tippit were coldly dismissed by the Warren Commission. The Commission said flatly that there was "no evidence that Oswald and Tippit were acquainted, had ever seen each other, or had any mutual acquaintances." (*WR 651*)

Like many other assertions in the Report, this pronouncement collides head-on with the Commission's own exhibits. In this case, the exhibit concerns an FBI investigation of possible links between Oswald and Ruby which led the FBI to Dobbs House, a restaurant reputedly patronized by both men. According to the FBI report, one of the waitresses who was interviewed, Mary Dowling, said that she

. . . recalled the person now recognized as Oswald was last seen by her in the restaurant at about 10 a.m. Wednesday, November 20, at which time he was "nasty" and used curse words in connection with his order. She went on to relate that Officer *J. D. Tippit was in the restaurant, as was his habit at about that time each morning, and "shot a glance at Oswald.*" She said there was no indication, however, that they knew each other. [Italics added] (*CE 3001*)

The interview with Mary Dowling took place in December 1963. Her report of a link between Oswald and Tippit, however tenuous and impersonal the link might be, obviously was of potential importance and demanded further investigation.

For unknown reasons, the FBI did not immediately inform the Warren Commission of the results of the interview with Mary Dowling in December. For equally inscrutable reasons, the FBI waited some six months before interviewing another waitress at Dobbs House, Mrs. Dolores Harrison, who was a party to the incident reported by Mary Dowling. The FBI report on the interview with Mrs. Harrison indicates:

Mrs. Dolores Harrison advised she had been employed as a waitress at the Dobbs House for approximately six years.

She stated that during the latter months of 1963, specific dates unrecalled, Lee Harvey Oswald came into the Dobbs House numerous times. Mrs. Harrison related that on November 21, 1963 she recalls Oswald having been in the Dobbs House for breakfast, specific time unrecalled. She stated she recalls this particular occasion, inasmuch as Oswald had ordered "eggs over light" and, when served, made a complaint that the eggs were "cooked too hard."

Mrs. Harrison advised [that] she prepared Oswald's eggs and Mary Dowling, a waitress, served same to him. She related that, although Oswald complained of the eggs, he accepted them.

She related [that] although she saw Oswald at the Dobbs House a number of times, she did not know his identity until seeing his picture in the newspaper as being the accused assassin of President Kennedy. Mrs. Harrison advised she has never seen Jack L. Ruby at the Dobbs House [or] at any other location; she has no knowledge of the assassination of President John F. Kennedy, or of any connections between Ruby and Oswald. (CE 3001)

Surely Mrs. Harrison was describing the same incident as Mary Dowling. Nevertheless, the FBI did not ask her if J. D. Tippit had been present during the episode of Oswald's eggs. The information that Tippit had regularly patronized the same restaurant that Oswald had visited numerous times during the months preceding the assassination only stirred further questions addressed to possible contacts between Oswald and *Ruby*, not Oswald and Tippit and certainly not Tippit and Ruby.

The FBI reported the results of these interviews with the two waitresses in a letter to the Warren Commission dated July 31, 1964 (CE 3001), apparently for the first time, more than seven months after receiving a report that Oswald and Tippit were both present in the same restaurant two days at most before the assassination. After reporting the interview with Mary Dowling, the FBI letter explains why her information was ignored: information previously obtained from the Book Depository indicated that Oswald had worked from 8 a.m. to 4:45 p.m. daily, with a lunch period at noon. The record indicated that he had worked eight hours on Wednesday, November 20; therefore, the reasoning seems to go, Oswald could not have been in Dobbs House at 10 a.m. as Mary Dowling claimed.[6]

Apparently the possibility that Mary Dowling might have been mistaken about the hour, or that time-keeping at the Book Depository was lax (as Oswald claimed), seemed to the Commission as well as the FBI to merit no inquiry. The possibility that Oswald and Tippit may have patronized the restaurant at the same time on other occasions was not investigated. Against this background of indifference to evidence of potential importance, the Report suavely asserts that Oswald and Tippit had never seen each other before the fatal encounter on the streets of Oak Cliff.

The treatment of this matter is part of a well-defined pattern in the Commission's "fact finding"; first, to discount information inimical to the thesis that Oswald was the lone assassin, and, second, to proclaim that such information does not even exist. Time and again, the Commission's own documents give the lie to its Report and outrage the handful of students who have ventured into the neglected pages of exhibits and testimony. In the light of Mary Dowling's report and the total deafness with which it was greeted, the Commission's disclaimer of any link between Oswald and Tippit and its apocryphal version of the encounter in which Tippit was shot to death can hardly be regarded as the last word.

DESCRIPTION OF THE KILLER

The Warren Report informs us that at 1:22 p.m. the Dallas Police radio broadcast a description of the man wanted for the murder of Tippit, and that "according to Patrolman Poe this description came from Mrs. Markham and Mrs. Barbara Jeanette Davis." (*WR 175*) According to the Report, Mrs. Markham told patrolman J. M. Poe that the killer was a white male, about twenty-five, about five feet eight inches tall, brown hair, wearing a white jacket; Mrs. Davis gave Poe the same general description,

---

[6] By that token, it is nonsense to believe that Oswald was arrested and incarcerated by the police on the afternoon of the assassination. According to Book Depository records, he worked a full eight-hour day on November 22. (*CE 1949*, p. 6)

also saying that the killer was wearing a white jacket. (*WR 175*)

This passage in the Report is almost wholly inaccurate and misleading. First, let us examine the statement that Poe obtained the description from the two women and then broadcast it over the police radio (the Report does not say that explicitly but it is the only possible inference which can be drawn). Poe did testify that when he arrived at the scene of the Tippit murder Mrs. Markham gave him a description of the killer, but he added:

POE: We gave the description to several of the officers at the scene. You couldn't get on the radio . . . and then I talked to several more witnesses around there.

BALL: Did you ever put that description on the radio?

POE: I believe we did. But I couldn't swear to it. . . .   (*7H 68*)

BALL: At 1:22 p.m. on the transcript of the radio log, I note it says, "Have a description of suspect on Jefferson. Last seen about 300 block of East Jefferson. White male, thirties, five feet eight inches, black hair, slender built, wearing white shirt black slacks." Do you know whether you gave Walker that description?

POE: I remember giving Walker a description. My partner got in the car with Walker.

BALL: Did you give Walker a description similar to that?

POE: Yes, sir.   (*7H 69*)

No wonder the Commission carefully avoided stating that Poe put the description on the police radio, but left the reader to infer just that: Poe was not at all certain that he had broadcast the description and "couldn't swear to it." Hence, Mr. Ball proceeded to ask if Poe had given the description to his fellow officer, C. T. Walker—for, according to the verbatim transcript of the police radio log, it was "85 (Walker)" who called in the description of the Tippit suspect at 1:22 p.m. (*CE 1974*, p. 59) But this is what C. T. Walker testified:

BELIN: You were not the one that put out the first description of the suspect they sought?

C. T. WALKER: I didn't.   (*7H 36*)

If Ball and Belin had examined the radio log with greater care, they would have seen that it was not C. T. Walker who called in the description at 1:22 p.m., but R. W. Walker, a patrolman who was not a witness before the Commission. Indeed, they would have seen that immediately after R. W. Walker phoned in the description, Officer Poe reported to the police radio dispatcher that he and his partner, Patrolman L. E. Jez, had just arrived at the Tippit scene. (*CE 1974*, p. 59)

The Commission has labored to create the impression that the 1:22 p.m. description originated with Mrs. Markham and Mrs. Barbara Jeanette Davis, via officer Poe. That description actually originated with patrolman R. W. Walker, who called in saying:

R. W. WALKER: We have a description on this suspect over here on Jefferson. Last seen about the 300 East Jefferson. He's a white male, about thirty, five feet eight inches, black hair, slender, wearing a white jacket and dark slacks.

DISPATCHER: Armed with what?

R. W. WALKER: Unknown. (*CE 1974*, p. 59)

Walker had no known contact with Mrs. Markham and Mrs. Davis and it is obvious from the contents of his message that he obtained the description from a person whose identity has never been established.

Not only is there no known contact between R. W. Walker and the two women, but the description he transmitted does not correspond with the description attributed to the women in the Report. (*WR 175*) The age is thirty, not twenty-five; the hair is black, not brown; and while the two women saw the suspect with a revolver in his hand, R. W. Walker did not know if the man was armed, or with what.

Moreover, there is reason to question the description that is said to have been given to Poe by Mrs. Markham and Mrs. Davis. FBI Agent Odum reported that on the afternoon of the Tippit murder Mrs. Markham told him that the killer was a white male, about eighteen, black hair, red complexion, wearing black shoes, tan jacket, and dark trousers (*3H 319*)—a description seriously in conflict with the one she is said to have given to Poe.

Mrs. Davis is said to have given Poe the same general description (of a man wearing a white jacket) as the one given by

Mrs. Markham; but here is what Mrs. Davis told the Warren Commission:

BALL: Was he dressed the same in the line-up as he was when you saw him running across the lawn?

MRS. DAVIS: All except he didn't have a black coat on when I saw him in the line-up.

BALL: Did he have a coat on when you saw him?

MRS. DAVIS: Yes, sir . . . a dark coat.   (3H 347)

Despite all this contrary evidence, the Report tries to persuade the reader that the 1:22 p.m. description came from the two women and that Poe called it in over the police radio—assertions which are absolutely false and misleading. As if that were not enough, the Report then suppresses completely the important fact that between 1:33 and 1:40 p.m. the dispatcher received the following message from "221 (H. W. Summers)":

Might can give you some additional information. I got an eyeball witness to the getaway man; that suspect in this shooting. He is a white male, twenty-seven, five feet eleven inches, 165, black wavy hair, fair complected, wearing light gray Eisenhower-type jacket, dark trousers and a white shirt and but last seen running on the north side of the street from Patton on Jefferson, and was apparently armed with a .32, dark finish, automatic pistol which he had in his right hand.

(CE 1974, p. 74)

There are a number of elements in Summers' message which should have occasioned careful investigation by the Commission. The identity of the "eyeball witness to the getaway man" should have been determined, and his testimony obtained and evaluated, since his observations as transmitted by Summers seem clearly incompatible with the Commission's conclusion that Oswald was the "getaway man." That any witness should have described Oswald as having "black wavy hair" is inconceivable.

Even more startling is the report, presumably by the same unknown "eyeball" witness, that the suspect was armed with a .32 automatic pistol, when the Tippit murder weapon is said to have been a .38 Smith & Wesson revolver—the ancestor, so to speak, of the automatic pistol. Anyone who was sufficiently familiar with firearms to describe a weapon as a .32 automatic pistol almost certainly would be too knowledgable to make such an error if the weapon were really a .38 revolver. That inference, in itself, is hardly sufficient to warrant a conclusion that the suspect actually was holding a .32 automatic pistol, but there is strong supporting evidence from another source.

Only a few minutes after Summers transmitted the description of the suspect, Sergeant Gerald Hill signaled the dispatcher with the following message: "The shell at the scene indicates that the suspect is armed with an automatic .38 rather than a pistol." (*CE 1974*, p. 78)

Sergeant Hill testified on April 8, 1964 that when he returned to the Tippit scene after an abortive search of two vacant houses toward which the killer had run, according to a citizen's report, he encountered Officer Poe. Hill said:

And Poe showed me a Winston cigarette package that contained three spent jackets from shells that he said a citizen had pointed out to him where the suspect had reloaded his gun and dropped these in the grass, and the citizen had picked them up and put them in the Winston package. (*7H 48-49*)

Here is still more surprising news: not only did this trained police officer identify a shell at the scene as that of an automatic rather than a revolver, but he testified that there were three cartridge cases in the empty cigarette box, instead of two. Domingo Benavides testified that he had picked up and placed two shells in a cigarette box, which he then turned over to a policeman. (*6H 450*) Did the policeman then find or receive from someone else a third shell, as Hill's testimony suggests? Or did Hill mistake the number of shells as well as the type?

When we deal with the ammunition for the revolver in the Tippit shooting, discussed later in this chapter, we will find new discrepancies—involving the number and brand of the shells and the bullets—which the Commission was unable to resolve. Those discrepancies made it all the more important for the Commission to investigate the radio log messages from Summers and Hill, which create grave new doubt about the identity of the killer and the weapon. Instead, the Commission ignored the Summers description and turned a deaf ear to the startling discrepancy in Hill's testimony.

The passage in the Warren Report purporting to explain the origin of the 1:22 p.m. description of the Tippit suspect (*WR 175*) consists of sentences each of which is literally true, but which in the aggregate are completely misleading. Misrepresentation piled on misrepresentation cannot be ascribed to inadequate work alone since it manifests a constant and premeditated motif: the incrimination of a man who received even less justice and mercy from the Warren Commission after his death than he got from the Dallas police when he was alive.

THE ABANDONED JACKET

Commission Exhibit 162 is a light-weight gray zipper jacket. In the view of the Warren Commission, it is a key item of evidence in the Tippit murder. The Commission contends that the gray jacket (1) belonged to Lee Harvey Oswald, (2) was worn by Oswald at the time of the Tippit shooting, (3) was described and identified by eyewitnesses at or near the scene, and (4) was discarded by Oswald during his flight and discovered minutes later under a parked car by Captain W. R. Westbrook of the Dallas Police. These, in substance, are the explicit or implicit claims made in the Warren Report. (*WR 175-176, 653*)

A close examination of the testimony and documents discloses (1) that the ownership of the jacket is not established beyond reasonable doubt, (2) that the eyewitnesses' descriptions of the killer's jacket do not match the gray jacket and in some cases are completely inconsistent with it, (3) that some of those eyewitnesses were unable to identify the gray jacket when it was displayed to them, and (4) that the jacket was not found by Captain Westbrook, as the Report asserts, but by a man whose identity the Commission did not even try to establish.

If the evidence is evaluated objectively in its entirety, the only facts that remain solid are (a) that at about one o'clock Oswald donned a zipper jacket which did not correspond with the gray zipper jacket (*CE 162*), according to the only person who saw him at the time; and (b) that when Oswald was arrested inside the Texas Theater less than an hour later, he no longer wore any jacket nor, apparently, had a jacket in his possession. This, by itself, hardly incriminates Oswald in the Tippit murder. (The radio log and other documents reveal that a jacket was found during the same general time period on Industrial Boulevard; apparently an unidentified man discarded it there, yet he did not come under suspicion as a result.)

In the preceding pages, I have discussed the origin of the 1:22 p.m. description of the Tippit suspect in which he was said to be dressed in a white jacket, and Poe's testimony that both Helen Markham and Barbara Jeanette Davis had told him at the scene that the killer wore a white jacket. More significantly, the jacket discovered under a parked car near the Tippit scene was called a white jacket by the finder when he told the dispatcher over the police radio of the discovery. The Commission, on the other hand, tells us that the jacket under the car was the gray zipper jacket pictured in Commission Exhibit 162.

Are we to assume that the witnesses, including a police officer trained in accurate observation, saw a gray jacket but mistakenly called it white? Or did they call it white because it was in fact white?

The Commission does not offer any guidance—perhaps wisely, for while a weathered white garment might well be described as light gray or ivory, the reverse is far less likely.

That Mrs. Markham actually said that the killer wore a white jacket is doubtful, since she is a generally unreliable witness. That Mrs. Davis did so is even more doubtful, since she testified that the suspect wore a black or dark jacket. But if we eliminate those two references to a white jacket, we must still account for the fact that the unknown police officer who found the jacket and picked it up called it a *white* jacket; in addition, we must still account for the white jacket mentioned in the 1:22 p.m. description called in by Officer R. W. Walker on the basis of a report by a witness whose identity has not been established.

How did the known eyewitnesses describe the jacket worn by Tippit's killer? Mrs. Markham, when she testified before the Warren Commission, said that "it was a short jacket, open in the front, kind of grayish tan" (*3H 311*); however, when the light gray zipper jacket was displayed (*CE 162*) she said that she had never seen it before, that it was too light to be the jacket worn by the killer. (*3H 312*)

Domingo Benavides, the second if not the sole eyewitness to the shooting, testified that the killer wore a light beige zipper-type jacket. (*6H 450*) A few minutes later, Mr. Belin excused himself in order to obtain some exhibits for identification. He returned with a jacket which Benavides promptly identified as the jacket worn by Tippit's killer. But in his haste Belin had brought the wrong jacket—not the gray one (*CE 162*), but a blue zipper jacket (*CE 163*), also said to belong to Oswald, which had been discovered in the Book Depository about ten days after the assassination. (*6H 453*) Obviously, Mr. Benavides, much as he wished to be of assistance, was anything but helpful to the Committee.

William Scoggins, whom the Commission inaccurately designates as an eyewitness to the shooting, did not give an independent description of the killer's jacket; he wasn't asked for it by the lawyer who took his testimony. But when the gray zipper jacket was displayed (*CE 162*), Scoggins failed to identify it, saying, "I thought it was a little darker" (*3H 328*); he did not remember whether the killer's jacket had a zipper or buttons.

Barbara Jeanette Davis said, as mentioned already, that the suspect wore "a dark coat. . . . It was dark and to me it looked like it was maybe a wool fabric, it looked sort of rough. Like more of a sporting jacket." (*3H 347*) Shown the gray zipper jacket (*CE 162*) and asked if it was the one worn by Tippit's killer, Mrs. Davis said, "No." (*3H 347*)

William Arthur Smith, like Mrs. Davis, thought that the killer wore "a sport coat of some kind. . . . I can't really remember very well." Shown the gray zipper jacket (*CE 162*), Smith said, "Yes, sir; that looks like what he had on. A jacket." (*7H 85*)

The Commission paid no attention to the fact that two witnesses remembered a light gray zipper jacket as a sport coat or sport jacket, although for anyone to confuse the one with the other despite wide differences in style, fabric, and general appearance seems almost impossible.

Virginia Davis testified that the killer "had on a light-brown-tan jacket" (*6H 457*), but no jacket was displayed to her for identification—not even the wrong one—perhaps because she nearly disoriented Mr. Belin by swinging like a pendulum between two versions of the time at which she first saw the killer.

Ted Callaway said that the man he saw wore "a light tannish gray windbreaker jacket"; when he was shown the gray zipper jacket (*CE 162*), he said that it was the same *type* jacket but "actually, I thought it had a little more tan to it." (*3H 356*)

Sam Guinyard was the only witness who described the gray zipper jacket accurately and then identified it without question. Guinyard testified that the suspect "had on a pair of black britches and a brown shirt and a little sort of light-gray-looking jacket . . . and a white T-shirt"; when he was shown the gray jacket (*CE 162*), he said, "That's the jacket." (*7H 401*)

The other seven witnesses either did not describe the gray zipper jacket accurately, or failed to identify it as the one worn by the suspect, or identified the wrong jacket. Because of the witnesses' wildly divergent and inconsistent testimony, the Commission was forced to acknowledge that "the eyewitnesses vary in their identification of the jacket." (*WR 175-176*) Mentioning some of the less glaring variations (but not of course the sport jackets, or the rough fabric, or the dark color described by some of the witnesses), the Commission salvages what it can and asserts that "there is no doubt, however . . . that the man who killed Tippit was wearing a light-colored jacket." (*WR 176*)

Needless to say, the Report does not call attention to the fact that the same group of witnesses failed to identify the brown long-sleeved shirt (*CE 150*) which Oswald supposedly was wearing under his jacket—not because they could not see the shirt but because they did not recognize it.

Three witnesses who were not present at the Tippit scene were also asked to identify the gray zipper jacket. (*CE 162*) Taxi-driver William Whaley identified it as the jacket Oswald was wearing in his taxi *before* visiting his furnished room and, according to the Commission, putting the jacket on. (*2H 260*) The Report considers that Whaley was mistaken, since, according to the Commission's reconstruction, Oswald was without any jacket during the taxi-ride. (*WR 163*)

Earlene Roberts, housekeeper at the rooming house, failed to identify the gray zipper jacket (*CE 162*) as the one Oswald wore when he left the premises a few minutes before the Tippit murder. Shown the jacket, Mrs. Roberts said, "I don't remember it," adding that Oswald's jacket was darker. (*6H 439*)

Finally, Wesley Frazier, who worked with Oswald and chauffeured him between Dallas and Irving on weekends, was unable to recognize the gray zipper jacket. (*2H 238*)

Turning to the discovery of the gray zipper jacket, we find again a wide gulf between the facts and the corresponding assertions in the Report. According to the Report:

Police Captain W. R. Westbrook . . . walked through the parking lot behind the service station and found a light-colored jacket lying under the rear of one of the cars. Westbrook identified Commission Exhibit No. 162 as the light-colored jacket which he discovered underneath the automobile. (*WR 175*)

But Westbrook himself denied that he had discovered the jacket, as may be seen from his testimony.

BALL: Did you ever find some clothing?
WESTBROOK: Actually, I didn't find it—it was pointed out to me by either some officer that—that was while we were going over the scene in the close area where the shooting was concerned, someone pointed out a jacket to me that was lying under a car and I got the jacket and told the officer to take the license number.
BALL: Was that before you went to the scene of the Tippit shooting?
WESTBROOK: Yes sir. . . . I got out of the car and walked through the parking lot.
BALL: What parking lot?
WESTBROOK: I don't know—it may have been a used car lot. . . .
BALL: Why did you get out of the car at this time?
WESTBROOK: Just more or less searching—just no particular reason—just searching the area— . . . Some officer, I feel sure it was an officer, I still can't be positive—pointed this jacket out to me. . . .
BALL: What was the name of the officer?
WESTBROOK: I couldn't tell you that, sir. (*7H 115-117*)

No wonder Westbrook could not identify the policeman who pointed the jacket out to him—no wonder he was vague about the location of the parking lot, and at such a loss to explain why he had even left his car: according to the verbatim transcript of the police radio log, Westbrook set out to search for the jacket said to have been discarded by the suspect *about fifteen minutes after the jacket had already been found and reported.* The radio log contains the following entries, logged at about 1:25 p.m.

CALLER	CONVERSATION
279 (Unknown):	279 . . . 279 (Unknown)
Dispatcher:	279 (Unknown)
279 (Unknown):	We believe we've got that suspect on shooting this officer out here. Got his white jacket. Believe he dumped it on this parking lot behind this service station at 400 block East Jefferson, across from Dudley Hughes [funeral parlor], and he had a white jacket on. We believe this is it.
Dispatcher:	You do not have the suspect, is that correct?
279 (Unknown):	No, just the jacket laying on the ground.
	(About 1:39 p.m.)
550 (Capt. W. R. Westbrook):	We got a witness that saw him go up North Jefferson and he shed his jacket—let's check that vicinity, toward Tyler. (*CE 1974*, pp. 62-77)

Westbrook, then, was *not* present when the jacket was discovered by the mysterious "279 (Unknown)" and Westbrook cannot be used, as the Commission uses him, to authenticate the jacket or the circumstances in which it was found. The witness misrepresented the facts, and the Report then misrepresented his misrepresentation.

The Report does not mention another police officer, T. A. Hutson, who testified also that he witnessed the discovery of the jacket. Hutson said:

. . . while we were searching the rear of the house in the 400 block of East Jefferson . . . a white jacket was picked up by another officer. I observed him as he picked it up, and it was stated that this is probably the suspect's jacket. . . .

BELIN: Do you know the name of the officer that found it?

HUTSON: No, sir; I don't know.   (*7H 30-33*)

I am not prepared to consider Hutson's account sufficient to authenticate the jacket, since his testimony, like Westbrook's, has defects. In his written report to his superiors dated December 3, 1963, Hutson described his activities in connection with the Tippit murder but failed to mention anything about the discovery of a gray zipper jacket (which he termed white in his testimony) (*CE 2003*, pp. 89-90); Westbrook, in his similar report (*CE 2003*, pp. 102-103) also failed to mention the jacket. There is no report from any police officer who claims to have been present when the jacket was found or claims that he found it.

"No. 279 (Unknown)" obviously made no written report of the discovery which, the radio log indicates, was made by him. In an investigation that was merely adequate, it would have been elementary to establish the identity of No. 279, to take evidence from him, and to determine the chain of possession of the jacket from the moment it came under police custody. The Warren Commission did none of those things, although it is easy enough, simply by studying its own exhibits, to determine that No. 279 was J. T. Griffin of the second platoon, Traffic Division, Dallas Police. (*Lawrence Exhibit 2*, p. 2; *Batchelor Exhibit 5002*, p. 14)

The second platoon consists of 12 three-wheel motorcycle officers, including not only J. T. Griffin but also T. A. Hutson, who testified that he could not identify the officer who picked up the jacket. How could Hutson fail to recognize a fellow officer assigned to the same 12-man platoon, if Hutson was really present when the jacket was found?

If the Warren Commission had been interested in finding the truth, it should have conducted an inquiry to determine:

(a) the identity of No. 279, who was not recognized by his fellow officer Hutson or by Captain Westbrook;

(b) whether Westbrook was actually present when the jacket was found, despite the entries in the radio log, and if he was not present, why he lied, and in complicity with whom;

(c) why both Griffin (No. 279) and Hutson described a gray jacket as white, if it was in fact the gray jacket (*CE 162*) that Griffin found; and

(d) whether a gray zipper garment was really found near the Tippit scene, or any jacket—or whether evidence was fabricated to strengthen the case against Oswald.

If the gray zipper jacket (*CE 162*) is legitimate, it was in the hands of the police before Oswald was arrested. The police never confronted him with the jacket or gave him the opportunity to confirm or deny that it was his property. That singular omission becomes even stranger when we read that "Oswald complained of a line-up wherein he had not been granted a request to put on a jacket" like the other men in the line-up. (*WR 625*) If the police really had in their hands a gray zipper jacket which they believed to belong to Oswald and which they thought he had worn at the Tippit scene, why didn't they let him wear that jacket in the sight of witnesses for whose benefit Oswald was being displayed in the line-ups? Clearly it would have been to their own advantage and would have facilitated the identification of their suspect. Conversely, Oswald seemed not to realize that wearing a jacket might make it easier for the Tippit witnesses to identify him, although he had a fine appreciation of what was or was not incriminating, and complained loudly for a jacket to wear in the line-up.

When Captain Fritz interrogated Oswald about his visit to his rented room at one o'clock, Oswald stated that he had "changed both his shirt and trousers before going to the show." (*WR 604-605*) Fritz, with the gray zipper jacket (or a white jacket) presumably in his possession, did not even ask Oswald if he had put on any garment over his shirt. In short, both at the line-ups and the interrogations, the police acted as though there were no jacket, gray or white.

The claim that the gray zipper jacket was the property of Lee Harvey Oswald rests solely on the word of his wife. The Report says:

This jacket belonged to Lee Harvey Oswald. Marina Oswald stated that her husband owned only two jackets, one blue and the other gray. The blue jacket was found in the Texas School Book Depository and was identified by Marina Oswald as her husband's. Marina Oswald also identified Commission Exhibit No. 162, the jacket found by Captain Westbrook, as her husband's second jacket.   (*WR 175*)

I have already shown that the jacket was not found by Westbrook; now, let us determine whether the whole of this passage from the Report is more reliable than one of its parts, which indisputably is false.

According to the list of items of evidence turned over to the FBI by the Dallas police on November 28, 1963, the gray zipper jacket bore a laundry tag with the number "B 9738." (*CE 2003*, p. 117) There is no indication of any attempt by the police or the FBI to trace the laundry tag, in accordance with what seems to be standard police procedure. An unsupported identification by Marina Oswald, who changed her testimony on other matters, is scarcely enough to establish ownership. Moreover, Marina Oswald told the FBI in an interview on April 1, 1964 that:

. . . she cannot recall that Oswald ever sent either of these jackets to any laundry or cleaners anywhere. She said she can recall washing them herself. She advised to her knowledge Oswald possessed both of these jackets at Dallas on November 22, 1963.   (*CE 1843*)

The FBI, which might have traced the laundry tag as a matter of routine when it received the gray zipper jacket on November 28, 1963, heard from Marina Oswald on the first of April that Oswald had never sent the jacket to any laundry or cleaners anywhere. How, then, did his jacket acquire a laundry tag? At this point, if not before, the FBI was obliged to trace the laundry tag and to determine whether Oswald, *or some other person*, had taken that jacket to be laundered or cleaned.

Why didn't the FBI trace that tag, and why didn't the Warren Commission ask the FBI to trace it? The reason seems obvious, for each serious probe into the so-called evidence against Oswald diminishes it, or destroys it outright.

THE REVOLVER AMMUNITION

ACCORDING TO THE WARREN REPORT

The Report (*WR 559-560*) states that when Oswald was arrested, 6 live cartridges were found in the revolver—3 Western .38 Specials and 3 Remington-Peters .38 Specials. Five live cartridges were found in his pocket, all Western .38s. Four expended cartridge cases were found near the Tippit scene—2 Western .38s and 2 Remington-Peters .38s. Four bullets were recovered from Tippit's body—3 Western-Winchesters and 1 Remington-Peters.

The Report offers several possible explanations for the discrepancy between the shells (2 Westerns and 2 Remington-Peters) and the corresponding bullets (3 Westerns and 1 Remington-Peters):

(a) The killer fired 5 bullets—3 Westerns and 2 Remington-Peters; 1 Remington-Peters bullet missed Tippit; that bullet and one Western cartridge case were "simply not found."

(b) The killer fired only 4 bullets—3 Westerns and 1 Remington-Peters—but prior to shooting Tippit he had an expended Remington-Peters shell in the revolver which was ejected with the other 4 shells, including a Western which "was not found."

(c) That he used hand-loaded bullets to save money; this is extremely unlikely because there is no evidence that the 4 recovered shells have been resized.

APPRAISAL

In one respect, the ammunition for the revolver presents the same kind of problem as that presented by the ammunition for the rifle. Although two different brands of .38 Specials are found (11 Westerns and 4 Remington-Peters bullets, live or expended, and 2 shells of each brand), no bullets of either kind were found in Oswald's room in Dallas or in the Paine home at Irving. Presumably at some point in time Oswald purchased at least one box of Western .38s and one box of Remington-Peters .38s. His purchase of such ammunition has not, however, been established. Again we are presented with the paradox that Oswald must have exhausted his supply of both brands of ammunition except for 11 bullets of one brand and 4 of the other at the time of the Tippit killing.

How could he have used up most of two boxes of ammunition? There is nothing whatever to suggest that he ever fired the .38 Smith & Wesson revolver at any time before November 22. If he did *not* purchase two boxes of ammunition, how did he acquire the 11 Western and the 4 Remington-Peters .38s? If he *did* purchase supplies of each brand, there is no evidence of the transaction, no evidence of use, and no left-over ammunition among his possessions.

The Warren Commission has offered no answers to these ques-

tions in attempting to explain why the bullets recovered from
Tippit's body failed to match the corresponding shells. Explanation (c) is a mere space-filler. The Commission had ruled out
hand-loading long before, on the basis of the cost and bulk of
the required equipment. Explanation (b) fails to present the
slightest evidence that Oswald had ever fired a Remington-
Peters bullet, leaving the shell in the gun, and is on the same
level of probability as hand-loading. Explanation (a) requires
the killer to fire five shots at point-blank range and miss one—
inconsistent with the marksmanship of the sniper who hit Kennedy and Connally under vastly more difficult circumstances.
Moreover, (a) ignores the fact that most of the Tippit witnesses
heard only two to four shots. Even if one shot had missed, it is
difficult to believe a claim that it went unnoticed and that the
shell remained undiscovered.

The Commission's "explanations" explain nothing. The problem of reconciling 2 Brand A and 2 Brand B shells with 3 Brand
A and 1 Brand B bullets awaits a serious and credible solution.

A related puzzle which the Commission has not acknowledged
is the arresting fact that Captain Glen King—in an address in
April 1964 to the American Society of Newspaper Editors—said
that Tippit had been shot *three* times. (*King Exhibit No. 5*, Vol.
XX, p. 465) It is surely strange that a senior police official
should have made such an error six months after the murder, if
error it was. We cannot be certain because the autopsy report on
Tippit is not to be found in the 26 volumes of Hearings and
Exhibits—a strange and unexplained omission.

To compound the puzzle, there is the peculiar manner in
which three of the four bullets allegedly recovered from Tippit's
body were presented to the FBI laboratory for examination *four
months* after the murder. According to the testimony of FBI
Expert Cunningham (*3H 474*), the FBI originally received only
one bullet, on November 23, 1963. The Dallas police said it was
the only bullet recovered or obtained. The matter rested there
until March 1964, when the Warren Commission (to its credit)
asked the FBI to determine where the other three bullets were.
They were discovered in the dead files of the Dallas police!

It was only at that stage that the mismatching of bullets and
shells became apparent, presumably too late to undertake a

search for a missing bullet or a missing shell under explanation (a). The Report does not even mention the belated debut of the three bullets ostensibly recovered from Tippit's body, perhaps in order to spare us uneasiness about their authenticity.

But misgivings are unavoidable when one is confronted by an alleged assassin who shot the President when he was down to his last four rifle bullets, and the police officer when he was down to his last 15 revolver bullets out of a supply of two boxes. Misgivings are inevitable when bullets fail to match their shells and only contrived and irresponsible "explanations" are suggested. The Warren Commission, despite the unparalleled investigatory resources at its disposal, has left the case cluttered with mysteries like this—neither acknowledging their existence nor offering acceptable explanations.

These lacunae undermine the Commission's conclusions about the Tippit murder and, in turn, about Oswald's role during the fateful weekend of the assassination.

THE ALIBI: OSWALD'S ACTIONS AFTER THE SHOTS
Howard Roffman

Presumed Guilty / *1975*

The first person to see Oswald after the assassination was Dallas Patrolman Marrion Baker, who had been riding a motorcycle behind the last camera car in the motorcade. As he reached a position some 60 to 80 feet past the turn from Main Street onto

"The Alibi: Oswald's Actions after the Shots" by Howard Roffman. Reprinted from *Presumed Guilty* by Howard Roffman, by permission of the publisher, Fairleigh Dickinson University Press.

Houston, Baker heard the first shot (3H246). Immediately after the last shot, he "revved up that motorcycle" and drove it to a point near a signal light on the northwest corner of Elm and Houston (3H247). From here Baker ran 45 feet to the main entrance of the Book Depository, pushing through people and quickly scanning the area. At the main entrance, Baker's shouts for the stairs were spontaneously answered by building manager Roy Truly as both men continued across the first floor to the northwest corner, where Truly hollered up twice for an elevator. When an elevator failed to descend, Truly led Baker up the adjacent steps to the second floor. From the second floor, Truly continued up the steps to the third; Baker, however, did not. The Report describes the situation:

On the second floor landing there is a small open area with a door at the east end. This door leads into a small vestibule, and another door leads from the vestibule into the second-floor lunchroom. The lunchroom door is usually open, but the first door is kept shut by a closing mechanism on the door. This vestibule door is solid except for a small glass window in the upper part of the door. As Baker reached the second floor, he was about 20 feet from the vestibule door. He intended to continue around to his left toward the stairway going up but through the window in the door he caught a fleeting glimpse of a man walking in the vestibule toward the lunchroom. (R151)

Baker ran into the vestibule with his pistol drawn and stopped the man, who turned out to be Lee Harvey Oswald. Truly, realizing that Baker was no longer following him, came down to the second floor and identified Oswald as one of his employees. The two men then continued up the stairs toward the Depository roof.

"In an effort to determine whether Oswald could have descended to the lunchroom from the sixth floor by the time Baker and Truly arrived," the Commission staged a timed reconstruction of events. The Commission knew that this encounter in the lunchroom such a short time after the shots could have provided Oswald with an alibi, thus exculpating him from involvement in the shooting. The reconstruction could not establish whether Oswald was at the sixth-floor window; it could, however, tell whether he was *not*. In the interest of determining the truth, it was vital that this reenactment be faithfully conducted, simulating the proper actions to the most accurate degree possible.

From beginning to end, the execution of the reconstruction was in disregard of the known actions of the participants, stretching—if not by intent, certainly in effect—the time consumed for Baker to have arrived on the second floor and shrinking the time for the "assassin's" descent.[1] . . .

If we take the Commission's minimum time of one minute, 14 seconds (giving the advantage to the official story) and add the additional six or seven seconds needed just to evacuate the immediate area of the window, plus the 15 to 20 seconds more for hiding the rifle, we find that it would have taken *at least* a minute and 35 seconds to a minute and 41 seconds for a sixth-floor gunman to have reached the second-floor lunchroom, *had all his maneuvers been planned in advance*. Had Oswald been the assassin, he would have arrived in the lunchroom *at least* five to eleven seconds *after* Baker reached the second floor, even if Baker took the *longest* time obtainable for his ascent—a minute, 30 seconds. Had Baker ascended in 70 seconds—as he easily could have—he would have arrived at least 25 seconds before Oswald. Either case removes the possibility that Oswald descended from the sixth floor, for on November 22 he had unquestionably arrived in the lunchroom *before* Baker.

The circumstances surrounding the lunchroom encounter indicate that Oswald entered the lunchroom *not* by the vestibule door from without, as he would have had he descended from the sixth floor, but through a hallway leading into the vestibule. The outer vestibule door is closed automatically by a closing mechanism on the door (7H591). When Truly arrived on the second floor, he did not see Oswald entering the vestibule (R151). For the Commission's case to be valid, Oswald must have entered the vestibule through the first door before Truly arrived. Baker reached the second floor immediately after Truly and caught a fleeting glimpse of Oswald in the vestibule through a small window in the outer door. Although Baker said the

---

[1] The first critical analysis of these reconstructions appeared in [Harold Weisberg,] *Whitewash*, pp. 36–38.

vestibule door "might have been, you know, closing and almost shut at that time" (3H255), it is dubious that he could have distinguished whether the door was fully or "almost" closed.

Baker's and Truly's observations are not at all consistent with Oswald's having entered the vestibule through the first door. Had Oswald done this, he could have been inside the lunchroom well before the automatic mechanism closed the vestibule door. Truly's testimony that he saw no one entering the vestibule indicates either that Oswald was already in the vestibule at this time or was approaching it from another source. However, had Oswald already entered the vestibule when Truly arrived on the second floor, it is doubtful that he would have remained there long enough for Baker to see him seconds later. Likewise, the fact that neither man saw the mechanically closed door in motion is cogent evidence that Oswald did not enter the vestibule through that door.

One of the crucial aspects of Baker's story is his position at the time he caught a "fleeting glimpse" of a man in the vestibule. Baker marked this position during his testimony as having been immediately adjacent to the stairs at the northwest corner of the building (3H256; CE 497). "I was just stepping out on to the second floor when I caught this glimpse of this man through this doorway," said Baker.

It should be noted that the Report never mentions Baker's position at the time he saw Oswald in the *vestibule* (R149-51). Instead, it prints a floor plan of the second floor and notes Baker's position "when he observed Oswald in *lunchroom*" (R150). This location, as indicated in the Report, was immediately outside the vestibule door (see CE 1118). The reader of the Report is left with the impression that Baker saw Oswald in the vestibule as well from this position. However, Baker testified explicitly that he first caught a glimpse of the man in the vestibule from the stairs and, upon running to the vestibule door, saw Oswald in the lunchroom (3H256). The Report's failure to point out Baker's position is significant.

Had Oswald descended from the sixth floor, his path through the vestibule into the lunchroom would have been confined to the north wall of the vestibule. Yet the line of sight from Baker's position at the steps does not include any area near the north wall. From the steps, Baker could have seen only one area in the vestibule—the southeast portion. The only way Oswald could have been in this area on his way to the lunchroom is if he entered the vestibule through the southernmost door, as the previously cited testimony indicates he did.

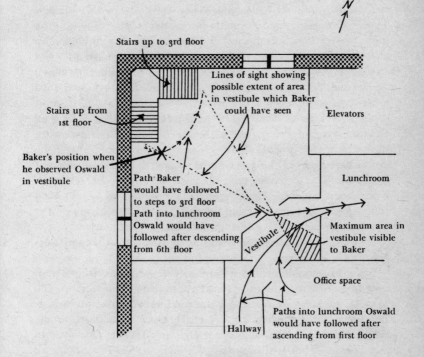

Shown above is a detail of the northwest portion of the second floor. The line of sight from Baker's position at the stairs through the window in the vestibule door shows that he could not have seen a significant portion of the north area of the vestibule. Had Baker continued to the third-floor stairs before looking into the vestibule (i.e., he did not catch a glimpse of Oswald as soon as he arrived on the second floor), his field of view in the vestibule would have moved further south.

Had Oswald entered the vestibule after descending from the sixth floor, he would have followed a path into the lunchroom that would have put him out of Baker's view. The only way Oswald could have been in the area of the vestibule visible to Baker is if he entered through the south door, accessible to him only had he come up from the first floor. To do this, he would have gone the reverse of his "escape route" (as illustrated in CE 1118).

Oswald could not have entered the vestibule in this manner had he just descended from the sixth floor. The only way he could have gotten to the southern door is from the first floor up through either a large office space or an adjacent corridor. As the Report concedes, Oswald told police he had eaten his lunch on the first floor and gone up to the second to purchase a coke when he encountered an officer (R182).

Thus, Oswald had an alibi. Had he been the sixth-floor gunman, he would have arrived at the lunchroom *at least* 5 seconds *after* Baker did, probably more. It is extremely doubtful that he could have entered the vestibule through the first door without Baker's or Truly's having seen the door in motion. Oswald's position in the vestibule when seen by Baker was consistent only with his having come up from the first floor as he told the police.

Oswald *could not* have been the assassin.

The Commission had great difficulty with facts, for none supported the ultimate conclusions. Instead, it found comfort and security in intangibles that usually had no bearing on the actual evidence. Amateur psychology seems to have been one of the Commission's favorite sciences, approached with the predisposition that Oswald was a murderer. This was manifested in the Report's lengthy chapter, "Lee Harvey Oswald: Background and Possible Motives" (R375-424).

To lend credibility to its otherwise incredible conclusion that Oswald was the assassin, the Commission accused Oswald of yet another assassination attempt—a shot fired at right-wing Maj. Gen. Edwin Walker on April 10, 1963 (R183-87). Thus, Oswald officially was not a newcomer to the "game" of political assassination. Although I am not in accord with the conclusion that Oswald shot at Walker, I find it illuminating that the Commission did not follow its inclination for psychology in its comparison of Oswald as the Walker assailant to Oswald as the Kennedy assailant.

Having just torn open the head of the President of the United States, as the Commission asserts, how did Oswald react when stopped by a policeman with a drawn gun? Roy Truly was first asked about Oswald's reaction to the encounter with Baker:

MR. BELIN: Did you see any expression on his face? Or weren't you paying attention?

MR. TRULY: He didn't seem to be excited or overly afraid or anything. He might have been a little startled, like I might have been if someone confronted me. But I cannot recall any change in expression of any kind on his face. (3H225)

Officer Baker was more explicit under similar questioning:

REP. BOGGS: When you saw him [Oswald]. . . ., was he out of breath, did he appear to have been running or what?

MR. BAKER: It didn't appear that to me. He appeared normal you know.

REP. BOGGS: Was he calm and collected?

MR. BAKER: Yes, sir. He never did say a word or nothing. In fact, he didn't change his expression one bit.

MR. BELIN: Did he flinch in anyway when you put the gun up. . . .?

MR. BAKER: No, sir. (3H252)

SEN. COOPER: He did not show any evidence of any emotion?

MR. BAKER: No, sir. (3H263)

This "calm and collected" "assassin" proceeded to buy himself a coke and at his normal "very slow pace," was then observed by Depository employee Mrs. Robert Reid walking through the office space on the second floor on his way down to the first floor (3H279). Presumably he finished his coke on the first floor. Documents in the Commission's files (but omitted from the Report, which assumes Oswald made an immediate get-away) indicate very strongly that, at the main entrance after the shots, Oswald directed two newsmen to the Depository phones (CD354).

According to the evidence credited by the Commission, Oswald was not such a cool cucumber after his first assassination attempt. Here the source of the Commission's information was

Oswald's wife, Marina, and his once close "friends," George and Jeanne De Mohrenschildt. The incident in question is described in the Report as follows:

The De Mohrenschildts came to Oswald's apartment on Neely Street for the first time on the evening of April 13, 1963 (three days after the Walker incident), apparently to bring an Easter gift for the Oswald child. Mrs. De Mohrenschildt then told her husband, in the presence of the Oswalds, that there was a rifle in the closet. Mrs. De Mohrenschildt testified that "George, of course, with his sense of humor—Walker was shot at a few days ago, within that time. He said, 'Did you take a pot shot at Walker by any chance?'" At that point, Mr. De Mohrenschildt testified, Oswald "sort of shriveled, you see, when I asked this question . . . made a peculiar face . . . (and) changed the expression on his face" and remarked that he did target-shooting. Marina Oswald testified that the De Mohrenschildts came to visit a few days after the Walker incident and that when De Mohrenschildt made his reference to Oswald's possibly shooting at Walker, Oswald's "face changed, . . . he almost became speechless." According to the De Mohrenschildts, Mr. De Mohrenschildt's remark was intended as a joke, and he had no knowledge of Oswald's involvement in the attack on Walker. Nonetheless, the remark appears to have created an uncomfortable silence, and the De Mohrenschildts left "very soon afterwards." (R282-83)

De Mohrenschildt further testified that his "joking" remark "had an effect on" Oswald, making him "very, very uncomfortable" (9H249-50). In another section, the Report adds that Oswald "was visibly shaken" by the remark (R274).

The Commission certainly chose a paradoxical assassin. We are asked to believe, according to the Commission, that Oswald was guilty of attacking both Walker and Kennedy. Yet, this man who officially became markedly upset when jokingly confronted with his attempt to kill Walker did not even flinch when a policeman put a gun to his stomach immediately after he murdered the President!

The Commission begged for the charge of being ludicrous in drawing its conclusions relevant to Oswald and the assassination; it insulted common sense and intelligence when it asked that those conclusions be accepted and believed.

THE PROOF OF THE PLOT
Sylvia Meagher

Accessories after the Fact / 1967

When the radio flashed the news that the President had been shot while riding in a motorcade in Dallas, a young woman who heard the bulletin fainted and had to be removed by ambulance to a hospital in Irving [a Dallas suburb].

She was Sylvia Odio, a twenty-six-year-old Cuban *émigrée* who was active in the anti-Castro movement. The shock that sent her into unconsciousness was the recollection of three men who had visited her apartment in Dallas at the end of September 1963 and the realization that it was "very possible that they might have been responsible, as one had mentioned that night that President Kennedy should have been killed by the Cubans." (*CE 3147*)

The three men who had called on Mrs. Odio on or about the twenty-sixth or twenty-seventh of September 1963 had identified themselves as members of an anti-Castro organization and as friends of Mrs. Odio's father, a political prisoner in Cuba, with whom they displayed personal familiarity. Two of the men appeared to be Cuban or Mexican. One called himself "Leopoldo" and the other had a name "something like Angelo." (*11H 370*) The third man was an American who was introduced as "Leon Oswald." (*11H 369*)

When Mrs. Odio saw Lee Harvey Oswald on television after his arrest, she recognized him immediately as "Leon Oswald." Her sister, Annie Laurie Odio, who had seen the three visitors briefly, independently recognized Oswald as one of the three men as soon as she saw him on television. (*11H 382*)

Mrs. Odio did not inform the authorities of her encounter with "Oswald" in September, perhaps because she "feared that the Cuban exiles might be accused of the President's death" (*CE 3147*); but a woman friend in whom Mrs. Odio had confided notified the FBI, on or before November 29, 1963 (*11H 379*, *CE 3108*).

In reporting Mrs. Odio's experience (*WR 321-324*), the Warren Commission does not question that three men visited her, as she alleged, but gives apparently forceful reasons for concluding that Oswald was not one of those men. The main argument is that Oswald's known movements ruled out his presence in Dallas at the time of the visit, on Thursday, September 26 or Friday, September 27, 1963.

The Commission points out that Oswald crossed the border into Mexico between 6 a.m. and 2 p.m. on Thursday, September 26. On Wednesday, he had cashed an unemployment check at a store in New Orleans which did not open until 8 a.m.; "therefore, it appeared that Oswald's presence in New Orleans until sometime between 8 a.m. and 1 p.m. on September 25 was quite firmly established." (*WR 323*)

The Commission acknowledges that there is no firm evidence of the means by which Oswald traveled to Houston on the first leg of his trip from New Orleans to Mexico but claims that his only time which is unaccounted for was between the morning of Wednesday the twenty-fifth (when his presence in New Orleans was "quite firmly established") and 2:35 a.m. on Thursday the twenty-sixth, when he boarded a bus in Houston headed for Laredo. The only way Oswald could have gone to Dallas, visited Mrs. Odio, and still arrived in Houston in time to catch the 2:35 bus to Laredo on Thursday the twenty-sixth was to fly, and investigation disclosed no indication that Oswald had traveled between those points by air.

IMPORTANT PROBLEMS

In the Commission's own words:

In spite of the fact that it appeared almost certain that Oswald could not have been in Dallas at the time Mrs. Odio thought he was, the Commission requested the FBI to conduct further investigation to determine the validity of Mrs. Odio's testimony. The Commission considered the problems raised by that testimony as important in view of the possibility it raised that Oswald may have had companions on his trip to Mexico.   (*WR 324*)

Note should be taken of the stipulation that Mrs. Odio's testimony was important, although the Commission somewhat understates the reasons. If Oswald had companions on his trip to Mexico, it would point to an organized, covert activity almost certainly related in some way to the Castro regime. Such mysterious associations and activities in September would demolish any November proposition that Oswald was a *lone* assassin and would pose overwhelmingly the outlines of a plot, implicating Cubans of some denomination, perhaps with non-Cuban backers, joined in a conspiracy against the life of the President of the United States.

If any aspect of the investigation was more crucial in its implications, it is not readily apparent. The Commission itself recognized the importance of Mrs. Odio's testimony. It is to be expected, then, that her story was the subject of extremely thorough and exacting scrutiny—scrutiny that enabled the Commission to satisfy itself and to assure the American people that there was no "Cuban plot" behind the assassination of President Kennedy but only a lone deranged assassin without political motive.

Just how thorough and exacting was the Commission's investigation?

UNFINISHED BUSINESS

The answer is that the Commission sent its Report to press without even completing the investigation into Mrs. Odio's story. This unbelievable denouement is acknowledged in the Report.

The Commission specifically requested the FBI to attempt to locate and identify the two men who Mrs. Odio stated were with the man she thought was Oswald.[1]

On September 16, 1964, the FBI located Loran Eugene Hall in Johnsandale, Calif. Hall has been identified as a participant in numerous anti-Castro activities. He told the FBI that in September 1963 he was in Dallas, soliciting aid in connection with anti-Castro activities. He said he had visited Mrs. Odio. He was accompanied by Lawrence Howard, a Mexican-American from East Los Angeles, and one William Seymour from Arizona. He stated that Seymour is similar in appear-

[1] In a letter to J. Edgar Hoover dated August 28, 1964. (*CE 3045*)

ance to Lee Harvey Oswald; he speaks only a few words of Spanish, as Mrs. Odio had testified one of the men who visited her did.

While the FBI had not yet completed its investigation into this matter at the time the report went to press, the Commission has concluded that Lee Harvey Oswald was not at Mrs. Odio's apartment in September 1963. [Italics added] (WR 324)

Considerable complacency is necessary to join the Warren Commission in assuming, on the basis of an unfinished investigation and an incomplete record, that William Seymour was the "Oswald" at Mrs. Odio's door. We are entitled to proof, not supposition. We are entitled to sworn testimony from Seymour, Hall, and Howard and to further testimony from Mrs. Odio and her sister after they are confronted with those three men.

However, even if the Commission had made a thorough investigation to prove that Hall, Howard, and Seymour were the three men who visited Mrs. Odio and that she and her sister mistakenly had identified Seymour as Oswald, the episode would still constitute strong evidence of conspiracy—but one directed against Oswald as well as the President.

Is there any other way to explain Seymour's introduction as "Leon Oswald"[2] or the telephone call that Mrs. Odio received from "Leopoldo" the next day (*11H 377*) when he carefully told her (1) that "Leon Oswald" was a former Marine; (2) that "Oswald" was a crack marksman; (3) that "Oswald" felt that President Kennedy should have been assassinated after the Bay of Pigs; and (4) that "Oswald" was "loco" and the kind of man who could do anything, like "getting" the Cuban underground or killing Castro.

Whether the visitor was Oswald himself, or Seymour impersonating Oswald, "Leopoldo" took pains to plant seeds which inevitably would incriminate Oswald in the assassination carried out on November 22, so that an anonymous phone call would be enough to send the police straight after him even if he had not been arrested within the hour. In itself, this setting-the-stage

---

[2] The FBI was not unaware of this stumbling block, but it seems unnecessary to take seriously its suggestion that "the name Loran Hall bears some phonetic resemblance to the name Leon Oswald" (*CE 3146*), an "explanation" that the Commission prudently omitted from the Report—without, however, offering a better one, or, for that matter, confronting the difficulty at all.

made it imperative for the Commission to press the investigation
to the limits and to consider Loran Hall, Lawrence Howard, and
William Seymour as prime suspects in the assassination, if they
proved to be the men who had visited Mrs. Odio, unless an
innocent and incontrovertible explanation for their antics was
established.

The Commission's failure to get to the bottom of this affair,
with its inescapable implications, is inexcusable. If the Commission could leave such business unfinished, we are entitled to ask
whether its members were ever determined to uncover the truth.
Indeed, the Commission did not even give an honest account of
such facts as *were* established. Its own Exhibits expose the "evidence" presented in the Report as a tissue of evasion and deception which discredits more than it justifies the conclusion that
Oswald could not have visited Mrs. Odio.

A CREDIBLE WITNESS

Before documenting the charge of deception by the Commission,
we should examine the possibility of deception by Mrs. Odio in
her testimony about a visit at the end of September 1963 by three
men who represented themselves as members of the anti-Castro
underground. Several points speak in favor of her credibility,
including the fact that the Commission itself concedes the reality
of the visit and questions only the identity of one member of the
trio.

Mrs. Odio's sister corroborates the visit and recognizes Oswald
as one of the men. A letter from Mrs. Odio's father (*Odio
Exhibit 1*) corroborates her testimony (*11H 368*) that she had
written to him to inquire whether the three men were his friends,
as they claimed.

Moreover, Mrs. Odio related the incident to her psychiatrist a
few days after the event (*11H 373, 381*); representatives of the
Warren Commission had a discussion lasting more than an hour
with the psychiatrist, Dr. Einspruch, which apparently satisfied
them that Mrs. Odio was trustworthy (*11H 381*). (The official
record does not include a transcript or summary of that discussion,
perhaps in deference to the confidential nature of the doctor/
patient relationship.)

Finally, Mrs. Odio's collapse upon hearing the news of the assassination adds force to her story.[3]

AN ACCURATE WITNESS?

The accuracy of Mrs. Odio's identification of "Oswald" must be evaluated also. The following facts suggest that it is very unlikely that this was a case of mistaken identity:

(1) The use of the name "Leon Oswald";

(2) The immediate recognition of Oswald on television;

(3) The assertion by the three men that they had just come to Dallas from New Orleans (*11H 372*), the city which Oswald is said to have left on September 25;

(4) The assertion by the three men that they were "leaving for a trip" (*11H 372*), just as Oswald embarked on a trip to Mexico City; and

(5) "Leopoldo's" statement that he might attempt to introduce "Leon Oswald" into the underground in Cuba, shortly before Oswald actually attempted to obtain a visa for travel to Cuba.

This series of parallels may not constitute conclusive evidence that Mrs. Odio's identification of "Oswald" was correct, but if they are not in the realm of the supernatural, they are persuasive manifestations of the authentic Oswald. If the Commission nevertheless wishes to substitute William Seymour, it might at least explain the means by which the image of Oswald was projected with such fidelity—and why.

THE WAYWARD BUS-RIDER

Although the prima-facie evidence for Mrs. Odio's encounter with the real Oswald is strong, the constraints postulated by the Commission against Oswald's presence in Dallas at the appropriate time cannot be ignored. According to the Report, Mrs. Odio fixed the time of the visit as Thursday the twenty-sixth or Friday the twenty-seventh of September. Mrs. Odio actually told the FBI that the visit might have been on Wednesday the twenty-fifth,

---

[3] Edward Jay Epstein's book *Inquest* (p. 102) throws additional light on Mrs. Odio's credibility, revealing that Counsel Wesley J. Liebeler "found that a number of details in the woman's story coincided with facts she could not possibly have known."

"although she considered the Thursday date to be the most probable." (*CE 3147*)

While the Report does not make it clear that the visit *might* have taken place on Wednesday the twenty-fifth, it does concede the absence of firm evidence as to the means by which Oswald traveled on that date from New Orleans to Houston. Somewhat murkily, the Commission then suggests that Oswald's presence on a Continental Trailways bus that left New Orleans at 12:30 p.m. on Wednesday the twenty-fifth "would be consistent with other evidence." (*WR 323*) In Appendix XIII, the Commission becomes bolder, and asserts that "he left New Orleans by bus, probably on Continental Trailways Bus No. 5121, departing New Orleans at 12:20 p.m. on September 25 and scheduled to arrive in Houston at 10:50 p.m." (*WR 731*)

That assertion is arbitrary, lacking positive evidence and overcoming negative evidence by the simple expedient of disregarding it. As will be shown, the Commission did not even convince itself that Oswald left New Orleans on that bus. There is no documentary trace of his presence; the driver did not remember "ever seeing Oswald in person at any time" (*CE 2134*); and not one passenger has turned up who recalled seeing Oswald on Bus No. 5121. Since the bus ride from New Orleans to Houston takes almost 12 hours (*CE 2962*), the lack of witnesses to Oswald's presence on a bus between those two points is evidence of a sort against the Commission's supposition. Other dates or other modes of travel must therefore be considered.

Mrs. Odio's callers were traveling in a car, with "Leopoldo" driving (*11H 372*), a detail which the Report neglects to mention. The authors, arguing against a stopover in Dallas en route to Houston, say laconically that "automobile travel in the time available, though perhaps possible, would have been difficult." (*WR 323*)

Even under the Commission's restrictions on "the time available," and in the admitted absence of firm evidence of the way in which Oswald traveled the 358 miles from New Orleans to Houston (*CE 3090*), it appears that he *could* have traveled from New Orleans to Dallas (503 miles) in "Leopoldo's" car, and from Dallas to Houston (244 miles) in the same vehicle, or by private airplane for all we know.

Under the Commission's constraints, Oswald had to cover those distances between 8 a.m. Wednesday, September 25, and 2:35 a.m. Thursday, September 26. But if the basic facts are disentangled from the Report, extracted from the Hearings and Exhibits, and reassembled, the constraints begin to appear dubious, if not artificial. The evidence that Oswald boarded "Bus No. 5133 in Houston and departed at 2:35 a.m." on Thursday, September 26 (*WR 732*) is unclear. A ticket agent in the Houston bus terminal sold a ticket to Laredo to a man who could have been Oswald (*WR 323*); but the man's clothes (brown and white sweater, white dungarees, and white canvas shoes) did not correspond with any of Oswald's garments, and none of the other 11 employees on duty in the bus terminal at the time had any recollection of seeing Oswald (*CE 2191*). A married couple who were passengers on Bus No. 5133 stated, in a brief affidavit, that they believed that they first saw Oswald on the bus shortly after they awoke at 6 a.m. (*11H 214*); however, they were not pressed to be more precise, and it cannot be said that their testimony is sufficient to place Oswald on the bus at 2:35 a.m. at Houston.

The other constraint imposed by the Commission is even shakier. Oswald was seen leaving his apartment in New Orleans, carrying two suitcases, on Tuesday evening, September 24, according to a neighbor. (*WR 730*) After that time, there is no definite trace of him in that city. But the Report insists that Oswald was in New Orleans at least until 8 a.m. on Wednesday because he cashed a check at a New Orleans store sometime after 8 a.m. that day. The citation for that statement is an FBI memorandum dated April 7, 1964, which reports:

The Winn-Dixie Store, #1425, 4303 Magazine Street, New Orleans, Louisiana, the place where the warrant dated September 23, 1963 was cashed, was not open to the public on September 25, 1963 until 8 a.m. J. D. Fuchs, Manager . . . approved the warrant for cashing. . . . Mrs. Thelma F. Fisher, Cashier #3 . . . actually cashed the warrant. . . .

(*CE 2131*)

Usually, when the Commission discusses a specific check issued to and cashed by Oswald, the footnotes refer to reports of interviews with the cashiers (*see, for example, CE 1165, 1167*) and photocopies of the face and back of the check (*see CE 1173-1175, 3121*). But when the Commission discusses the $33 check which is claimed to fix Oswald's presence in New Orleans until a specific hour on a specific day, only the FBI memorandum (*CE 2131*) is cited—no interviews with Mr. Fuchs or Mrs. Fisher and no photocopy of the specific check.

In this instance the Commission itself was not satisfied with the evidence. The direction of the Commission's thinking less than a month before its Report was released is graphically revealed in a letter signed by J. Lee Rankin, addressed to J. Edgar Hoover, dated August 28, 1964. Rankin states:

We are also concerned about the possibility that *Oswald may have left New Orleans on September 24, 1963 instead of September 25, 1963 as has been previously thought.* In that connection, Marina Oswald has recently advised us that her husband told her he intended to leave New Orleans the very next day following her departure on September 23, 1963. She has also indicated that he told her an unemployment check would be forwarded to Mrs. Ruth Paine's address in Irving from his post office box in New Orleans. We also have testimony that Oswald left his apartment on the evening of September 24, 1963 carrying two suitcases.

It also seems *impossible to us that Oswald would have gone all the way back to the Winn-Dixie Store at 4303 Magazine Street to cash the unemployment check* which he supposedly picked up at the Lafayette Branch of the Post Office when he could have cashed it at Martin's Restaurant, where he had previously cashed many of his Reily checks and one unemployment check. That is particularly true if he received the check on September 25, 1963, as previously thought, and had left his apartment with his suitcases the evening before. [Italics added]

(*CE 3045*)

No new evidence on these points was turned up after Rankin's letter to the FBI on August 28, 1964; the possibility that Oswald had left New Orleans on Tuesday, September 24 instead of Wednesday, September 25 was not ruled out. Nonetheless, when the Warren Report was published less than a month later, the very same allegations which Rankin had questioned sharply were now incorporated as "facts."

It is imprudent to overlook the alacrity with which the FBI

produced Loran Eugene Hall on September 16, 1964 following on Rankin's request of August 28 to "determine who it was that Mrs. Odio saw in or about late September." (*CE 3045*) The FBI had been investigating Mrs. Odio's story without locating the three men since December 18, 1963, when she was interviewed by FBI agents James Hosty and Bardwell Odum. (*11H 369*) For reasons unknown, the FBI report on that interview has been omitted from the exhibits; also missing are about ten FBI reports mentioned in Rankin's letter to Hoover (*CE 3045*).[4]

It's amazing how efficiently the FBI found Loran Hall after Rankin's letter, following an unsuccessful investigation during the preceding nine months; unfortunately, there is no interview report on Loran Hall, no address, no physical description, no indication of his age, nor any details which might permit a comparison with "Leopoldo."

Another footnote to Rankin's letter of August 28, 1964, in which he suggested that Oswald might have left New Orleans a day earlier than believed previously, is the press leak that appeared a few days later. The *New York Post* of August 31, 1964 reported:[5]

Investigative agencies have spent many hours and interviewed hundreds of witnesses since the Nov. 22 assassination trying to trace Oswald's steps on the Mexico trip.

It is known, for instance, that *he was seen in a Dallas bus station at 6 p.m. Sept. 25* and that he crossed the border at Nuevo Laredo next day. [Italics added]

That is the first and last we hear of witnesses who saw Oswald in a Dallas bus station at six o'clock Wednesday; the Report does not dignify that rumor with a refutation.

At the end of this trail of uncertain and shifting evidence, there seem to be strong but not conclusive grounds for believing that Mrs. Odio's identification of Oswald was correct. However, the

[4] Reports of Gemberling, December 23, 1963; O'Connor, December 31, 1963; Clements, December 14, 1963; Callendar, December 24, 1963, April 16, 1964; Kemmy, December 23, 1963; letterhead memorandum, April 15, 1964. The reports covered investigations in Dallas, Miami, New Orleans, Houston, and San Antonio.

[5] "Bus Stub Traces Oswald in Mexico," *New York Post*, August 31, 1964, p. 4.

Commission's failure to press its investigation to completion leaves open at least a possibility that "Leon Oswald" was really William Seymour; and that—in complicity with Loran Hall and Lawrence Howard—Seymour was possibly engaged in a deliberate impersonation of Oswald.

But such a hypothesis requires a link between Oswald and his impersonator through which the latter acquired sufficient familiarity with Oswald's history and circumstances to permit successful impersonation.*

THE INGREDIENTS OF CONSPIRACY

In the vein of pure speculation, it is possible to postulate a series of threads connecting persons known and unknown which would satisfy the conditions for successful impersonation. The starting point is the summer of 1963, when Oswald came into contact with Carlos Bringuier and others who were active in the organized anti-Castro movement at New Orleans. (*WR 407-408, 728-729*)

Oswald sought out Bringuier under circumstances which suggest a calculated attempt to infiltrate the anti-Castro movement, perhaps in the hope of acquiring "credentials" for a future defection to Cuba. That is how Bringuier regarded the incident. (*10H 32-43*)

Bringuier alerted other anti-Castroites against Oswald. One of Bringuier's cohorts went on an infiltration mission of his own, after consulting Bringuier. He went to Oswald's house "posing as a pro-Castro" to "try to get as much information as possible from Oswald." (*10H 41*) Bringuier also informed Edward Butler, an anti-Communist propagandist (*10H 42; 11H 166, 168*), who tried "to contact some person, somebody in Washington, to get more [on] the background of Oswald" (*10H 42*), and apparently did obtain information on Oswald from the House Un-American Activities Committee (*11H 168*).

It is a reasonable assumption that a warning against Oswald went out also to the right wing of the anti-Castro movement in other cities, Dallas included, and to their American sponsors and supporters, both official (CIA and perhaps FBI) and unofficial

* The theme of impersonation was developed in *The Second Oswald* by Richard Popkin (New York, 1966).—Eds.

(various ultra-reactionary groups). The anti-Castro movement is composed of many competing factions, ranging from the Batistianos and far-rightists (DRF, for example[6]) who seek the restoration of a regime like Batista's (under which Cuba was an American colony in everything but name), to liberal and reform groups (like Manolo Ray's MRP or later his JURE,[7] which is considered leftist and tantamount to "Castroism without Castro"). The reactionary wing of the movement and the CIA have cordial and close relations, whereas the moderate and progressive factions do not enjoy the CIA's confidence and were systematically excluded from the CIA's planning of the Bay of Pigs adventure (see, for example, *Bay of Pigs* by Haynes Johnson,[8] or *A Thousand Days* by Arthur M. Schlesinger, Jr.[9]).

The right-wing Cuban *émigrés* were bitter and infuriated by the humiliating defeat at the Bay of Pigs, blaming President Kennedy for refusing to permit direct American military participation in the invasion. The CIA, whose conduct of the whole affair brought the agency into disgrace and jeopardy, had made arrangements to overrule President Kennedy if he canceled the invasion at the last minute, so that the landing at the Bay of Pigs would go ahead regardless of Presidential orders. The revelation that the CIA had contemplated countermanding the White House, on top of its incredible bungling of the invasion from beginning to end, suggested an early end to what has been called "the invisible government,"[10] and a threat to their Cuban protégés.

Dallas, with its hospitable political climate and its plentiful money, inevitably was an outpost of the anti-Castro right wing. Mrs. Odio testified that the Crestwood Apartments, where she lived at the time of the visit by "Leon Oswald," was "full of Cubans." (*11H 374*) Fund-raising meetings were held in a Dallas bank, by Cuban exiles and their American sympathizers. (*CE 2390*) Mrs. Odio said that all the Cubans knew that she was a

[6] DRF [*Frente Revolucionario Democratico*]

[7] MRP [*Movimiento Revolucionario del Pueblo*]; JURE [*Junta Revolucionaria*]

[8] *The Bay of Pigs* (Dell Books, New York, 1964).

[9] *A Thousand Days* (Houghton Mifflin, Boston, 1965).

[10] According to *The New York Times* of April 25, 1966 (p. 20, col. 3), President Kennedy told one of the highest officials of his Administration after the Bay of Pigs disaster that he wanted "to splinter the C.I.A. in a thousand pieces and scatter it to the winds."

member of JURE, "but it did not have a lot of sympathy in Dallas and I was criticized because of that." (*11H 370*)

Father Walter J. McChann, who was active in a Cuban Catholic committee concerned with the welfare and relief of Cuban refugees in Dallas, told the Secret Service about a Colonel Caster who was associated with the committee. Father McChann said that Colonel Caster was a retired Army officer who seemed to be "playing the role of an intelligence officer in his contacts with the Cubans" and that he seemed to be "more interested in their political beliefs than in their economic plight or their social problems in the new country." (*CE 2943*)

Mrs. C. L. Connell, a volunteer worker in the committee, also mentioned the Colonel. She told the FBI on November 29, 1963 that "General Walker and Colonel (FNU) Caster, a close acquaintance of Walker, have been trying to arouse the feelings of the Cuban refugees in Dallas against the Kennedy administration" in speeches before Cuban groups in the Dallas area "in recent months." (*CE 3108*) (Neither the FBI nor the Warren Commission found that news of sufficient interest to warrant an interview with the Colonel.)

At this point, a hypothetical series of links connects Oswald to Bringuier—Bringuier to the anti-Castro movement in Dallas— the anti-Castro movement to Colonel Caster—and Colonel Caster to General Walker. Walker's right-hand man is Robert Allan Surrey.[11] According to Surrey's own statement in the *Midlothian* (Tex.) *Mirror*, he and FBI agent James Hosty are bridge-playing companions.[12]

Another thread leads from the Walker establishment to Jack Ruby. A former employee of the General's, William McEwan Duff, believed that he had seen Ruby visiting the Walker residence. (*CE 2981*) There is strong evidence from Robert McKeown (*CE 1688-1689, CE 3066*) and testimony from Nancy Perrin Rich (*14H 345-353*) that Ruby was involved in the illegal supply of arms to the Cuban underground.

Mrs. Rich testified that she had attended a meeting in Dallas to

[11] Surrey, apparently, "closely resembled" Oswald (*CEs 1836, 2473*).
[12] "Reopen the Warren Commission," *Midlothian* (Tex.) *Mirror*, March 31, 1966, p. 2, col. 3.

discuss an offer to her husband of a large sum of money for running guns to Cuba and bringing refugees out to Miami. The head of the group that tried to enlist her husband was an army colonel; another member present at the meeting was Jack Ruby, whom Mrs. Rich recognized at once as her former employer at the Carousel Club, where she had worked briefly as a cocktail waitress.

Ruby, of course, had close links to the Dallas police, some of whom had independent links to the ultra-right in Dallas. J. D. Tippit, for example, had a moonlighting job at Austin's Barbecue; the man who was his boss, Austin Cook, is an acknowledged member of the John Birch Society. (*CE 2985*)

All these threads can be combined in a web that covers the terrible and unfathomed events of November 22-24, 1963. The nucleus consists of reactionary Cuban exiles who have compiled a record of violence in their new country, ranging from attacks with bicycle chains and Molotov cocktails on peacefully assembled American citizens, to a bazooka attack on the United Nations building; these Cuban counter-revolutionaries are linked to the American ultra-right by many mutual interests, not the least of which was a hatred for President Kennedy, kept at the boiling point by systematic propaganda from, among others, former American army officers.

Is it farfetched to postulate the formation of a plot among members of those circles to revenge themselves not only against the President whom they considered a Communist and a traitor but also against a Marxist and suspected double-agent who had tried to infiltrate the anti-Castro movement?

This hypothesis is, of course, purely theoretical, a mere exercise in speculation attempting to explain the possible rationale for an impersonation of Oswald, in the context of Mrs. Odio's experience and of other stories that pose the possibility of deliberate and informed impersonation.

I am not arguing that such a plot existed, but I do suggest that the Warren Commission's job was to consider and check out all possible theories, however far-out, and not to dispose of disturbing evidence like that lingering in the Odio story by illusory "facts."

Congressman Gerald Ford, one of the members of the Commission, has said that "the monumental record of the President's Commission will stand like a Gibraltar of factual literature through the ages to come."[13] The Commission's unfinished business may not disturb the Commission's self-satisfaction or its self-imposed silence; but for those who are haunted by sentience of a frightful miscarriage of justice, and troubled by the loose ends in the "monumental record," that complacency remains incomprehensible.

EPILOGUE TO THE ODIO STORY

Senator John Sherman Cooper never replied to this author's letter of January 21, 1966, requesting information on the results of the investigation of Loran Eugene Hall and his friends, which was still in progress when the Warren Report was published.

In July 1966 researcher Paul Hoch was kind enough to make available excerpts from Commission Document 1553 which he had obtained at the National Archives, consisting of an FBI report dated October 2, 1964. That FBI report indicates that only two days after the original locating of Loran Eugene Hall on September 16, 1964, an interview with William Seymour (the FBI did not say whether Seymour in fact resembled Lee Harvey Oswald) elicited a denial that he was even in Dallas in September 1963 or had ever had any contacts with Sylvia Odio. Subsequent interviews with Loran Hall, Lawrence Howard, Sylvia Odio, and Annie Laurie Odio resulted in the collapse of the assumption that Hall, Howard, and Seymour were the men who had visited Mrs. Odio, representing one of their number as "Leon Oswald."

The FBI report of October 2, 1964 was transmitted to the allegedly disbanded Warren Commission well before the release of the Hearings and Exhibits at the end of November 1964. The document was not included among the Exhibits, and if it ever came to the attention of Senator Cooper, he was not prepared to communicate the fact that the possibility of an innocent mistake in identity had disintegrated.

That denouement throws wide open again the whole Odio story with all its implications. We know from Warren Commission Counsel Liebeler that details in Mrs. Odio's story coincided with facts to which she had no access and that the possibility of fabrica-

[13] *Portrait of the Assassin*, (Simon & Schuster, New York, 1965), pp. 451–452.

tion is thus virtually destroyed. That leaves two possibilities open: that the real Oswald visited Mrs. Odio with two companions, one of whom deliberately planted highly incriminating information about him without his knowledge; or that a mock-Oswald visited her, to accomplish the same purpose.

If there is a re-investigation of the assassination—as there must be if we are not to become the permanent accomplices in the degradation of justice which has taken place—the Odio affair should be high on the agenda.

NEW LIGHT

THE MILTEER DOCUMENTS
Harold Weisberg

Frame-Up / 1971

On February 2, 1967, reporter Bill Barry broke a sensational
story in the Miami News. It began, "Two weeks before John
Fitzgerald Kennedy was assassinated in Dallas, a man sat in a Miami
apartment and described how it could be done. The man was an
organizer for a States Rights party. And his conversation was
being taped by the Intelligence Division of the Miami Police
Department. The man said that a plan to kill the President was
in the works. He said Kennedy would be shot with a high-
powered rifle from an office building, and he said the gun would
be disassembled, taken into the building, assembled, and then
used for murder." Author Harold Weisberg was the first of the
assassination critics to draw attention to this report, which he
quoted in his book Oswald in New Orleans (New York: Canyon
Books, 1967), p. 383.

  Although this serious threat was made known to the Secret

"The Milteer Documents" by Harold Weisberg. Reprinted from *Frame-Up* by
Harold Weisberg, by permission of the author/publisher, Route 12, Frederick, Md.

*Service and FBI prior to the assassination, it received no attention
in the Warren Report, and the right-wing organizer who
described the assassination scenario in Miami—Joseph Milteer—
got off with only a little questioning from the FBI. The FBI's
version of the Miami warning was given to the Commission near
the end of its investigation and then lay buried among myriad
documents—only to be rediscovered by Harold Weisberg. Here
Weisberg introduces the transcript of an interview between an
unnamed Miami Police Department informant and (subject)
Joseph Milteer.—Eds.*

In the final chapter of my book *Oswald in New Orleans* ("Preliminary
Postscript from Miami"), I reported what was then (winter of 1966–
1967) known of an intercepted threat against President Kennedy two
weeks before his assassination. That threat was taped by the Miami
police, who gave copies to both the FBI and the Secret Service on
November 10, 1963. Stringent measures were taken to protect the
President in Miami, including elimination of a planned motorcade.
The files of the Warren Commission contain neither the tape nor a
transcript, nor, in fact, any reference to either—which surely makes
sense, considering that they were investigating his assassination and
this material amounted to a blueprint of what is officially alleged to
have happened. The National Archives also assured me that its files
contained no reference to Joseph Adams Milteer . . . who discussed
the threat and the man who was planning that assassination and was
doing more—attempting to kill [Martin Luther] King. The manner of
King's murder—not by that man, who died before he could pull it—is
exactly as set forth in the tape, which is printed here for the first time
(in toto, with no changes made in the transcription, and with the addition of some necesary background material). With some effort, I did
obtain at least some of the "non-existent" FBI Milteer reports. This
also is the first publication of those that I could obtain. . . . [—H. W.]

INFORMANT: Now we are going to, you are going to have to take,
Kenney, what do you call his last name?

SUBJECT: Kenneth Adams. [Adams has had his own share of
headlines and heroics. . . . [In 1961,] he was implicated in
the burning of a "Freedom Riders" bus. He was found not guilty
by a directed verdict. . . . After deliberating 11 hours, an all-white

jury, on November 21, 1966, acquitted him of a charge of receiving Army explosives. The stolen items included blocks and sticks of explosives, phosphorus bombs, hand grenades, and three boxes of .50-caliber ammunition, which is not for handguns. Because of Adams's acquittal, the judge said he would not jail the man who had already confessed the theft.—H.W.]

INFORMANT: Yeah, you are going to take him in, he is supposed to be one of the hard core of the underground, are you going to invite him into that, too? What about Brown, now, are you going to invite Brown in? You are going to have Brown in it? [Believed to be Jack H. Brown who, like Adams, had been extremely active in the Klans. He operated a gas station in a Chattanooga suburb. He has been reported to be "contact man" for the United White Party; to have arranged for the Klan to be entered in the Chattanooga softball series; to have been an NSRP presidential elector; to believe the Klan needed a flag and to have offered to design it; to have died of a heart attack in 1965, leaving chips off the old block to continue his good works.—H.W.]

SUBJECT: Yeah.

INFORMANT: Now, I will tell you between me and you, because we are talking, we aren't going to talk to everybody like we are talking here. Now, you know this, I like Brown, he is a good fellow, you know him, now here is something, when we was in his house, now, he knows me and you, but he didn't know Lee McCloud, well I think he done too much talking in front of a man he didn't know. Brown trusts a lot of people, he figures everybody is good.

SUBJECT: Yeah.

INFORMANT: And you know when he was telling her [or him, not legible] about blowing up all those churches and, you know, I don't think he should have said all that in front of McCloud.

SUBJECT: That is exactly the way I feel about it, too. And I didn't talk about it any more after we left there.

INFORMANT: No, I see you didn't, you see, these things come to my mind, I don't know McCloud well, and Brown never seen him before in his life, that I know of, now you seen this boy, Jackie, didn't open his mouth, he just sit there and listened. Jack Caulk [phonetic] he is a very quiet boy, Brown it just seems, well, he, I guess he has gotten by with so much he just don't care. He come out with all that about going over to Atlanta carrying that stuff, and showing them how to operate, I didn't want to say anything to him, but I don't think it is a good idea for people to discuss thinks like that in front of strangers. What do you think about it?

SUBJECT: No, I—He should operate that, the same as he does the rest of it.

INFORMANT: That's right, damn right that is right. Now you take like the Birmingham . . . [Subject breaks in]

SUBJECT: Any conclusion they come up with, that's them, not him.

INFORMANT: That is true.

SUBJECT: He didn't give them anything.

INFORMANT: Well, he didn't give them nothing.

SUBJECT: Just like me at home there folks want to know, "Joe, where do you get all of your information?" "Well, I get it, that is all you are interested in," and that is as far as it goes, see. And the same guy will turn around and give me some information, but he doesn't know where I am getting my information. The same guy who asks me where I get my information, will turn around and give me information.

INFORMANT: Well, sure, of course, I realize that.

SUBJECT: That is the way you have got to operate.

INFORMANT: Well, that is what I say, if you are going to take Brown in, and Brown is going to be one of the head men, the man behind you, then you have got to talk to Brown a little bit, and tell him, you know, "You have got to be a little more conscientious, especially on these bombings, and killings," after all he comes right out with it.

SUBJECT: We have got to let him understand, that, that is his operation, and not ours.

INFORMANT: Yeah, that is true. We don't care, if he wants to go to Birmingham and blow up a church, let him.

SUBJECT: If he wants to blow up the National Capital, that is alright with me. I will go with him, but not as a party though, as an individual.

INFORMANT: Well, if you want to go with him and help him blow it up, that is not the party, it is an individual, you are going to have to make him understand that.

SUBJECT: There is a party movement, and there is also an individual movement.

INFORMANT: Yeah, that is right.

SUBJECT: And they are distinct and separate.

INFORMANT: Well, you are going to have to make him understand that, right there, he didn't exactly admit it, but Jesus Christ, he intimated, he indicated right there, he backed the bombings of killing the negroes in Birmingham, well, you know damn well we don't want anybody talking like that.

SUBJECT: Can't afford it.

INFORMANT: Well, you know damn well that is bad talk especially to somebody he don't know. He could have said that to me, and you would have been alright, it would have been between you and me then.

SUBJECT: That is true.

INFORMANT: But to go ahead and say it in front of Lee McCloud, what that [sic] hell [Subject breaks in]

SUBJECT: Well, I think he thought that he would [not] have been with us, if he had not have been alright. But that is still not enough.

INFORMANT: No, hell no, that is no good, at least before he made all those statements, he should have called you outside, or consulted about this man a little bit.

SUBJECT: You have to have reservations, you know.

INFORMANT: That is right. Hell, he didn't say these things in any way to try to get us in trouble, because the only one who could be in trouble would be him, he was confessing on his damn self, he wasn't confessing on us, because we hadn't done a damn thing.

SUBJECT: You and I would not get up there on the stand and say that he told us a cotton picking thing either.

INFORMANT: Well, he knows that, but how about the other man.

SUBJECT: Well, that is what I say.

INFORMANT: Yeah, hell yes. I tell you something, you take Kenneth Adams over there, he is a mean damn man, like Brown was saying, the guy he was sending him to, well Kenneth is real mean, and the way Brown indicated they [not legible] the negroes, well, we don't care anything about that. I would rather he wouldn't tell us those stories.

SUBJECT: You sure can't repeat them.

INFORMANT: Yeah. That is the set-up we are in now, I mean, we have to work with them, but let them operate their grollings [phonetic], like you say, if you want to go with them, that is your opinion, you go with him up to Washington and blow with him, if you want to go [Subject breaks in].

SUBJECT: I have a man who is the head of his underground of his own up there in Delaware, and since I worked on the Supreme Court, he wanted me to give him the lay-out there so they could go over there and do some things there, you know. But he called it off, I don't know why, I didn't even ask him why. That was his affair, but he called it off. But I was ready to go with him. I gave him the damn information he wanted.

INFORMANT: You worked on the Supreme Court.

SUBJECT: Yeah, three and a half years.

INFORMANT: Well, that is why he wanted you to go, then, well, them things have got to be done, but outside the Party, we have got to be mighty careful who the hell we let know anything. Now, here is one thing you have got to realize, transporting dynamite across the state line is a federal offense, well you better let them know that.

SUBJECT: Well, there is a way to beat that, you know. All you have to do is pull up to the state line, unload it there, slide it across the line, get in the car and load it again, and they can't accuse you of transporting it then, because you didn't do it. I have done the same thing with a woman. I had one, then I had a woman frame me on it. I got to the state line, and I said, "Listen, Toots, this is the state line, get out, and I will meet you over there," she got out, walked across the line, got in my car in the other state, I didn't transport her, there wasn't a fucking thing she could do about it, I had her ass for a long time.

INFORMANT: I was talking to a boy yesterday, and he was in Athens, Georgia, and he told me, that they had two colored people working in that drug store, and that them, uh, they went into the basement, and tapped them small pipes, I guess that they are copper together, and let that thing accumulate, and blowed that drug store up. He told me that yesterday, do you think that is right?

SUBJECT: It could have happened that way.

INFORMANT: Well, that is what he told me, and he is in town right now.

SUBJECT: Does he know who did it? Do they think these negroes did it?

INFORMANT: Oh, no, they killed the negroes, because they had two negroes working in the place, that is what he told me. He is in town now, he is from Chattanooga. He knows Brown, he knows all of them, his uncle is in the Klan there. He is a young boy, he has been in the Marines, and he really knows his business. He went there, he went down and looked, and he told me that is what happened. So he has been involved in quite a little bit of stuff, according to his story about Nashville, Chattanooga, and Georgia. I have no reason not to believe him, because he told me too much about Brown's operation, that is the reason I [not legible].

SUBJECT: Yeah. You take this boy, Connor McGintis [phonetic] [reference is probably to an old-time northern racist, Conde McGinley—H.W.], boy up there in Union, N.J., of course he doesn't go to anything like that, but he is on our side, he is the one that puts out that *Common Sense*. He is an ex-Marine. He is all man, too.

INFORMANT: Now, you see, we will talk to these other people, you have made up your mind that you are going to use the Constitutional Party as a front.

SUBJECT: Yeah, Constitutional Party States Rights.

INFORMANT: Yeah, and it will [be] strictly secret, and nobody will be exposed except you.

SUBJECT: Yeah.

INFORMANT: Because when we talk to them today, you want to know exactly what to tell them, how it operates.

SUBJECT: Yeah, and we have got to set up a little fund there to get it operating.

INFORMANT: Oh, yeah, sure.

SUBJECT: And I am going to devote my time to it, I don't have any idea of getting elected to that City Commission, but I am just making it cost them bastards it cost them as it is, it cost them between $1,500 and $2,000 to beat me before, so I want to make it cost them another couple of thousand dollars. If they want to get rid of me, they can buy my fucking property, and I will get out of the damn town. In other words, they will save money. I am going to put that out in one of the damn bulletins there, see. We put, the way I operate, put out these little bulletins, like a typewriter page, eight and a half by eleven, and brother don't you think they ain't waiting for them, when I don't put them out, "Joe, where is the bulletin?" Bill, that could go all over the country the same way. That was just a trial proposition, if it will work in a little stinking town like that, it will work anywhere.

INFORMANT: I don't know, I think Kennedy is coming here on the 18th, or something like that to make some kind of speech, I don't know what it is, but I imagine it will be on the TV, and you can be on the look for that, I think it is the 18th that he is suppose to be here. I don't know what it is suppose to be about.

SUBJECT: You can bet your bottom dollar he is going to have a lot to say about the Cubans, there are so many of them here.

INFORMANT: Yeah, well he will have a thousand bodyguards, don't worry about that.

SUBJECT: The more bodyguards he has, the easier it is to get him.

INFORMANT: What?

SUBJECT: The more bodyguards he has the more easier it is to get him.

INFORMANT: Well how in the hell do you figure would be the best way to get him?

SUBJECT: From an office building with a high powered rifle, how many people [room noise—tape not legible] does he have going around who look just like him? Do you know about that?

INFORMANT: No, I never heard that he had anybody.

SUBJECT: He has got them.

INFORMANT: He has?

SUBJECT: He has about fifteen. Whenever he goes any place they [not legible] he knows he is a marked man.

INFORMANT: You think he knows he is a marked man?

SUBJECT: Sure he does.

INFORMANT: They are really going to try to kill him?

SUBJECT: Oh, yeah, it is in the working. Brown himself, Brown is just as likely to get him as anybody. He hasn't said so, but he tried to get Martin Luther King.

INFORMANT: He did.

SUBJECT: Oh yes, he followed him for miles and miles, and couldn't get close enough to him.

INFORMANT: You know exactly where it is in Atlanta don't you?

SUBJECT: Martin Luther King, yeah.

INFORMANT: Bustus Street [phonetic].

SUBJECT: Yeah 530.

INFORMANT: Oh Brown tried to get him huh?

SUBJECT: Yeah.

INFORMANT: Well, he will damn sure do it, I will tell you that. Well, that is why, look, you see, well, that is why we have to be so careful, you know that Brown is operating strong.

SUBJECT: He ain't going for play you know.

INFORMANT: That is right.

SUBJECT: He is going for broke.

INFORMANT: I never asked Brown about his business or anything, you know just what he told me, told us, you know. But after the conversation, and the way he talked to us, there is no question in my mind about who knocked the church off in Birmingham, you can believe that, that is the way I figured it.

SUBJECT: That is right, it is about the only way you can figure it.

INFORMANT: That is right.

SUBJECT: Not being there, not knowing anything.

INFORMANT: But just from his conversation, as you and me know him, but if they did, it is their business, like you say [Subject breaks in].

SUBJECT: It is up to the individual.

INFORMANT: That is right. They are individual operators, we don't want that within the party. Hitting this Kennedy is going to be a, a hard proposition, I tell you, I believe, you may have figured out a way to get him, you may have figured out the office building, and all that. I don't know how them Secret Service agents cover all them office buildings, or anywhere he is going, do you know whether they do that or not?

SUBJECT: Well, if they have any suspicion they do that of course. But without suspicion chances are that they wouldn't. You take there in Washington, of course it is the wrong time of the year, but you take pleasant weather, he comes out on the veranda, and somebody could be in a hotel room across the way there, and pick him off just like [fades out].

INFORMANT: Is that right?

SUBJECT: Sure, disassemble a gun, you don't have to take a gun up there, you can take it up in pieces, all those guns come knock down, you can take them apart.

INFORMANT: They have got a damn, this boy was telling me yesterday about, they have got an explosive that you get out of the army, it is suppose to be like putty or something, you stick it up, and use a small fuse, you just stick it like that, he told me, and I think that is what happened in the church in Birmingham, they stuck this stuff, somebody stuck it under the steps with a short fuse, and went on home.

INFORMANT: This boy is pretty smart, demolition is that what you call it?

SUBJECT: Demolition, that is right.

INFORMANT: I am going to talk with him some more.

SUBJECT: Yeah I would.

INFORMANT: I am going to talk with him some more, and find out a lot more about his operation, because he knows a hell of a lot.

SUBJECT: You need a guy like that around, too. Where we can put our finger on him, when we want him.

INFORMANT: Yeah. Well, you have got somebody up there in that country now, if you need him.

SUBJECT: Well, we are going to have to get nasty first [not legible].

INFORMANT: Yeah, get nasty.

SUBJECT: We have got to be ready, we have got to be sitting on go, too.

INFORMANT: Yeah, that is right.

SUBJECT: There ain't any count down to it, we have just got to be sitting on go. Count down they can move in on you, and on go they can't. Count down is alright for a slow prepared operation, but in an emergency operation, you have got to be sitting on go.

INFORMANT: Boy, if that Kennedy gets shot, we have got to know where we are at. Because you know that will be a real shake, if they do that.

SUBJECT: They wouldn't leave any stone unturned there no way. They will pick up somebody within hours afterwards, if anything like that would happen just to throw the public off.

INFORMANT: Oh, somebody is going to have to go to jail, if he gets killed.

SUBJECT: Just like that Bruno Hauptmann in the Lindbergh case you know. [Dials telephone.]

INFORMANT: "Hello, is Jim there?" "Has he gone to the office?" "Uh, huh, well, is he coming back home?" "Alright, I will do that, thank you." He has gone out to one of his apartment houses, and he will be back later. We will go see *whatamacallit*, he closes at 1:00 o'clock. We will go up and see Andrew, and we will double back to Jim's [room noise].

SUBJECT: Actually the only man we are interested in up at that place [room noise—not legible—door closes].

MM 89-35
FPG:ggr/ds
1
—

Re: Threat to Kill President
      KENNEDY by J. A. MILTEER,
      Miami, Florida
      November 9, 1963
      _____

On November 10, 1963, a source who has furnished reliable information in the past and in addition has furnished some
information that could not be verified or corroborated, advised
SA LEONARD C. PETERSON that J. A. MILTEER on Novem-
ber 9, 1963, at Miami, Florida, made a statement that plans were in
the making to kill President JOHN F. KENNEDY at some future
date; that MILTEER suggested one JACK BROWN of Chattanooga, Tennessee, as the man who could do the job and that he
(MILTEER) would be willing to help. MILTEER reportedly
said that he was familiar with Washington and that the job could
be done from an office or hotel in the vicinity of the White House
using a high-powered rifle.

U.S. Secret Service was advised of the foregoing information.

[FBI Report, CD 1347, p. 119]

_____

The FBI's titling of this report, page 119 of Warren Commission File (CD) 1347,
is unequivocal. It is a *serious* "Threat to Kill President KENNEDY," by one Joseph
Adams Milteer, . . . These reports exactly coincide with the Miami tape,
here also reproduced, and with the cancellation of the scheduled motorcade when
the President addressed the Inter-American Press Association, in Miami. The "source
who has furnished reliable information in the past" may be the informant or the
Miami police, which gave dubs of the tape to both the FBI and the Secret Service.
(The man had also been an FBI informant.) [—H. W.]

MM 89-35

1.

Re: Threat to Kill President
    KENNEDY by J. A. MILTEER,
    Miami, Florida
    November 9, 1963

On November 26, 1963, a source who has furnished reliable information in the past and in addition has furnished some information that could not be verified or corroborated, advised SA PETERSON as follows:

On November 23, 1963, J. A. MILTEER was in the Union Train Station, Jacksonville, Florida, and at about 4:25 p.m. on that date stated he was very jubilant over the death of President KENNEDY. MILTEER stated, "Everything ran true to form. I guess you thought I was kidding you when I said he would be killed from a window with a high-powered rifle." When questioned as to whether he was guessing when he originally made the threat regarding President KENNEDY, MILTEER is quoted as saying, "I don't do any guessing."

On the evening of November 23, 1963, MILTEER departed Jacksonville, Florida, by automobile en route to Columbia, South Carolina. During this trip, MILTEER stated that he had been in Houston, Ft. Worth, and Dallas, Texas, as well as New Orleans, Louisiana, Biloxi and Jackson, Mississippi, and Tuscaloosa, Alabama. MILTEER said he was acquainted with one R. E. DAVIS of Dallas, Texas, whom he described as a "good man," but did not indicate he was personally acquainted with DAVIS. MILTEER did not indicate on what dates he was in the above cities, except for Tuscaloosa, Alabama.

MILTEER related that he was in Tuscaloosa,
Alabama, and contacted ROBERT SHELTON of the United
Klans of America, Inc., Knights of the Ku Klux Klan
(United Klans), on the evening prior to the bombing of the

[FBI Report, CD 1347, p. 120]

Having blueprinted the JFK assassination in advance, . . . Milteer here took
credit for it. What better reason for total suppression—*after* Oswald was officially
ordained assassin? R. E. Davis also figures in an also-suppressed Secret Service investigation (the copies of which I have) of a suspected Minuteman involvement. Neither
investigative agency made this correlation for the Commission. [H. W.]

The Federal Bureau of Investigation has requested that
certain pages of this document not be disclosed. This
request was incorporated in a letter of August 13, 1965,
to Dr. Wayne C. Grover, Archivist of the United States
from Norbert A. Schlei, Assistant Attorney General,
Office of Legal Counsel, Department of Justice.

Commission Document Number: 1347

Pages Withheld: 121

From the file index (the FBI slipped up, not editing their indexes to hide what
they were suppressing), it is apparent that [some of] what is suppressed here deals
(like the Miami tape, pp. 118–127) with the November 15, 1963 bombing of a
Birmingham, Alabama, church in which innocent black children were murdered.
(Names mentioned on the suppressed page are: "Association of South Carolina Klans;
Baptist Church, Birmingham, Alabama; Bolen, A. O.; Hendricks, Jack; Kennedy,
Robert; King, Martin Luther; Knights of Ku Klux Klan [United Klans]; Mims,
Belton; Ulmer, Will; United Klans of America, Inc.; Wade Hampton Hotel, Columbia, S.C.") This National Archives form proves the FBI is directly responsible for the
suppressions—not, as Hoover, pretends, the Department of Justice. (In almost every
case that I have been able to check—by getting what was suppressed by the FBI—
what is withheld deals with the extreme of the radical right or is designed to prevent embarrassment to the government. *Defamatory* material *should* be withheld,
but I have found *no single case* where defamations of those even slightly liberal or
anti-war were withheld.) [H. W.]

MM 89-35
3.

A characterization of the Association of South Carolina Klans follows. Sources therein have furnished reliable information in the past.

After their arrival, MILTEER stated that there was no point in discussing President KENNEDY, and again stated, "We must now concentrate on the Jews." MILTEER advised that he was preparing a pamphlet which he wanted to disseminate throughout the country. Prior to concluding their discussion, information was received that JACK RUBY had killed LEE HARVEY OSWALD. In view of this, MILTEER said he would have to alter the information he was setting out in his pamphlet.

The source advised that based on his contact with MILTEER, he could not definitely state whether MILTEER was acquainted with either RUBY or OSWALD.

[FBI Report, CD 1347, p. 122]

MM 89-35
FPG:ggr
1

Re: Threat to Kill President
      KENNEDY by J. A. MILTEER,
      Miami, Florida,
      November 9, 1963

J. A. MILTEER is also known as JOSEPH ADAMS MILTEER. He was born February 26, 1902, at Quitman, Georgia, and lives at Quitman and Valdosta, Georgia. He reportedly is a wealthy bachelor who inherited an estimated $200,000 from his father. He is reported to have no family, no employment and to spend a great deal of time traveling throughout the Southeastern United States. He has been unsuccessful in city politics in Quitman and publishes a weekly pamphlet critizing [sic] the operation of the Quitman City Government. MILTEER has associated himself with the Constitution Party of the United States and attended a convention of this party held at Indianapolis, Indiana, during October, 1963. He was reprimanded by this party for describing himself as being the party regional chairman for the Southeastern states. MILTEER reportedly became disillusioned with the Constitution Party of the United States and has attempted to form a party known as the Constitutional American Parties of the United States. MILTEER allegedly intends to use the Constitutional American Parties of the United States as a front to form a hard core underground for possible violence in combating integration.

[FBI Report, CD 1347, p. 123]

1
—
DL 89-43
PEW/ds

The interview of JOSEPH ADAMS MILTEER, as well as additional information regarding him, is contained on pages 24-26 of the report of Special Agent CHARLES S. HARDING, Atlanta, Georgia, dated December 1, 1963, in the case entitled "LEE HARVEY OSWALD; INTERNAL SECURITY-RUSSIA." [CD 20]

[Pp. 125 and 126 are withheld from research.]
[FBI Report, CD 1347, p. 124]

What a filing system, what FBI logic: reports on a murderous native fascist under "Oswald" and "Russia"! The note on withholding is by the Archives staff. [—H. W.]

FD-302 (Rev. 1-23-60)

FEDERAL BUREAU OF INVESTIGATION

Date___December 1, 1963___

JOSEPH ADAMS MILTEER, Quitman, Georgia, was interviewed November 27, 1963, at which time he advised that during April, 1963, he attended a national meeting of the Congress of Freedom, New Orleans, Louisiana. He described this organization as one that believed in Americanism and he attended this meeting as the result of an invitation by a Mr. THOMAS, Chairman of the organization, Omaha, Nebraska. He stated during this meeting neither he nor anyone in his presence discussed the assassination of President KENNEDY.

MILTEER stated further that in June, 1963, he went to Dallas, Texas, to attempt to persuade DAN SMOOT, author of the "Dan Smoot Report" to run as Vice-President on the Constitution Party ticket in the election in November, 1964. He stated he had no other business in Dallas.

MILTEER further stated that on October 18-20, 1963, he traveled to Indianapolis, Indiana, with BILL SOMERSETT of Miami, Florida, and LEE McCLOUD of Atlanta, Georgia. They attended the National Convention of the Constitution Party. He stated he attended this meeting as the result of an invitation by CURTIS B. DALL, former son-in-law of the late President FRANKLIN D. ROOSEVELT.

MILTEER described himself as a non-dues-paying member of the White Citizens Council of Atlanta, Georgia, the Congress of Freedom and the Constitution Party.

MILTEER emphatically denies ever making threats to assassinate President KENNEDY or participating in any such assassination. He stated he has never heard anyone make such threats. He also denied making threats against anyone subsequent to the assassination of President KENNEDY. He stated he does not know, nor has he ever been in the presence of LEE HARVEY OSWALD or JACK RUBY to his knowledge.

MILTEER denied any knowledge of the bombing of the Sixteenth Street Baptist Church in Birmingham, Alabama, on November 15, 1963.

On ___11/27/63___ at ___Quitman, Georgia___ File # ___Atlanta 105-3193___

by ___SAs KENNETH A. WILLIAMS and DONALD A. ADAMS___ :cb Date dictated ___12/1/63___

This document contains neither recommendations nor conclusions of the FBI. It is the property of the FBI and is loaned to your agency; it and its contents are not to be distributed outside your agency.

[FBI Report, CD 20, p. 24]

With Milteer's voice on tape blueprinting the assassination for which he later took credit, the FBI here reports his denial dead-pan, and keeps secret the fact that it had a dub of precisely these threats in Milteer's own voice! The last sentence of this page pretty clearly relates to the suppressed page of the FBI report printed on pp. 129–132. [—H. W.]

FORD, JAWORSKI, AND THE NATIONAL SECURITY COVER-UP
Paul L. Hoch

August 1974

Ten years ago, Gerald Ford and his colleagues on the Warren Commission led the official investigation of the assassination of President Kennedy. In August 1972, Attorney General Kleindienst suggested, with unintended irony, that the original Watergate investigation would match the Warren Commission's work in extent and thoroughness. The cloak of national security in which Richard Nixon tried to wrap himself was successfully used to impress the investigators (up to and including Earl Warren) with the delicacy of their job—which was not to find the truth, but to reassure the nation that the truth had been found.

A contribution to this reassurance was a book published in 1965 by Ford, with his assistant, John R. Stiles, titled *Portrait of the Assassin*. Ford testified at his vice-presidential confirmation hearing that his intention was to make the conclusions of the Commission more readable; to that end, excerpts from witnesses' testimony make up most of the book. The book also revealed for the first time how the Commission reacted to a report that Lee Harvey Oswald had been an FBI informant. Ford reported with pride the Commission's determination to get to the bottom of the story, but not their failure to do so.

Ford described a "tense and hushed" emergency executive session on January 22, 1964, after Texas Attorney General Waggoner Carr had reported the rumor. Two days later, Carr presented the allegation in Washington, accompanied by Dallas District Attorney Henry Wade, his Assistant D.A. Bill Alexander, and the two lawyers who were assisting Carr as Special Counsel for the Texas Court of Inquiry, Robert Storey and Leon Jaworski. On January 27, the Commission met to consider its response.

There was no question about the serious import of the allegation about Oswald and the FBI. Although efforts were made to suggest that overzealous reporters had generated it, it is clear that various police sources were encouraging the allegation, and that the Texans had reasons of their own for spreading it. One predictable effect was to take the heat off Texas, where the President had been shot and Oswald had been murdered while in police custody, and to put it on the federal government. If Oswald had been an FBI informant, the argument went, naturally the FBI would not have considered him dangerous, and that would be why the FBI and the Secret Service did not warn the Dallas Police about him.

Ford testified that he and Stiles "did not use in that book any material other than material that was in the 26 volumes of testimony and sold to the public generally." That statement is incorrect. His description of the January 27, 1964, Commission meeting (which he had not attended) consists mainly of excerpts from a transcript which was classified Top Secret until this year. It was declassified in June in response to a suit by author and Warren Commission critic Harold Weisberg. The cover page of the transcript alleges that it contains "information affecting the national defense of the United States" and that its disclosure to an unauthorized person was "prohibited by law." Ford's use (presumably not authorized) was a violation of the security-classification system, but (like the publication of the Pentagon Papers) probably not illegal.

The full transcript shows that Ford edited it as badly as Nixon edited the Watergate transcripts. His biggest distortion was to present this discussion in support of the false claim that the Commission investigated the allegation "with an intensity of purpose that left no stone unturned." The Commissioners were well aware of the obstacles to a proper investigation of the FBI-Oswald story, and of other issues. They knew the inadequacy of what they would end up doing. The Warren Report ultimately relied on statements by the FBI and the CIA that Oswald had not been an informant. The Commission never even saw all of the FBI's files on Oswald. Although the factual situation is complicated, there is very strong evidence that the FBI did have a special relationship with Oswald which was not revealed to the

Commission. The FBI apparently did not respond to Oswald's leftist activities with authentic concern.

The Commission members clearly understood the worthlessness of a categorical denial from an intelligence agency. As a matter of policy, they were told, the CIA would lie to protect an informant or agent, unless otherwise instructed by the President:

REP. [HALE] BOGGS: Let's say [U-2 pilot Francis Gary] Powers did not have a signed contract but he was recruited by someone in CIA. The man who recruited him would know, wouldn't he?

MR. [ALLEN W.] DULLES [FORMER CIA DIRECTOR]: Yes, but he wouldn't tell.

THE CHAIRMAN [EARL WARREN]: Wouldn't tell it under oath?

MR. DULLES: I wouldn't think he would tell it under oath, no.

THE CHAIRMAN: Why?

MR. DULLES: He ought not tell it under oath. Maybe not tell it to his own government but wouldn't tell it any other way. [sic]

MR. [JOHN J.] MCCLOY: Wouldn't he tell it to his own chief?

MR. DULLES: He might or might not. If he was a bad one then he wouldn't. . . . I would tell the President of the United States anything, yes, I am under his control. He is my boss. I wouldn't necessarily tell anybody else, unless the President authorized me to do it. We had that come up at times.

The obligatory approach to the FBI was recognized as delicate as well as substantively inadequate. The Commission's General Counsel, J. Lee Rankin, explained:

We thought, first, about approaching the Department [of Justice] with a request that the Attorney General [Robert Kennedy] inform us as to the situation, not only as to what he would say about whether Oswald was or was not an undercover agent, but also with the supporting data that the commission could rely upon, and there is some difficulty about doing that. As the head of the department [sic] the FBI, of course, is under the Attorney General, but I think we must frankly recognize amongst ourselves that there is a daily relationship there involved in the handling of the problems of the Department and the work of the FBI for the Department, and that we wouldn't want to make that more difficult.

We were informed by Mr. [Howard P.] Willens, the liaison with the Department . . . that it is the feeling of the Department . . . that such a request might be embarrassing, and at least would be difficult for the Attorney General, and might, if urged, while we would get the information we desired, make [it] very much more difficult for him to carry on the work of the Department for the balance of his term.

The Commission understandably chose not to involve Robert Kennedy in this problem; he had little to do with any of the investigation. Nevertheless, the Commission and its defenders were eager to interpret Robert Kennedy's silence as an endorsement of the Warren Report.

In this closed session, the Commissioners admitted the problems raised by the FBI's prior conclusion that Oswald was the lone assassin. This concern was never admitted later in such unguarded terms (no doubt in deference to the FBI's claim that it reports only facts, not conclusions), but it governed the work of the Commission throughout. Rankin responded to the idea of questioning the FBI about their investigation:

MR. RANKIN: Part of our difficulty in regard to it is that they [the FBI] have no problem. They have decided that it is Oswald who committed the assassination, they have decided that no one else was involved, they have decided—

SEN. [RICHARD B.] RUSSELL: They have tried the case and reached a verdict on every aspect.

REP. BOGGS: You have put your finger on it. . . .

MR. RANKIN: . . . They have decided the case, and we are going to have maybe a thousand further inquiries that we say the Commission has to know all these things before it can pass on this. And I think their reaction probably would be, "Why do you want all that? It is clear."

SEN. RUSSELL: "You have our statement, what else do you need?"

MR. McCLOY: Yes, "We know who killed cock robin." That is the point. It isn't only who killed cock robin. Under the terms of reference we have to go beyond that.

The immediate problem—the allegation that Oswald had been an FBI (or CIA) informant—was discussed in the context of these obstacles. Two distinct approaches were presented. Warren wanted to start by having the Commission get information directly from the sources of the rumor, notably *Houston Post* reporter Lonnie Hudkins. Rankin recommended first going to Hoover for his explanation and the expected *pro forma* denial. The real issue was how to avoid the unavoidable implication that they were investigating Hoover. After considerable discussion, the members voted without dissent to let Rankin proceed as he thought best.

Warren hoped that direct inquiries by the Commission would avoid a clash with Hoover. As he put it, "I am not going to be thin-skinned about what Mr. Hoover might think, but I am sure if we indicated to Mr. Hoover that we were investigating him he would be just as angry at us as he was, or would be at the Attorney General for investigating him." Warren was right about Hoover's reaction, but it was too late to avoid it. In a letter of January 27, received the day after the meeting, Hoover angrily denied that Oswald had been an informant. He said (erroneously) that the FBI had "previously made available to the Commission full information concerning our contacts with Oswald." Hoover mentioned that he had learned of the Texans' January 24 visit; it came out only later that the FBI had interviewed Assistant D.A. Alexander the following day. After reviewing the FBI's relations with Oswald "so that there may be no doubt" about them, Hoover said, "In the event you have any further questions concerning the activities of the FBI in this case, we would appreciate being contacted *directly*." [Emphasis added.]

Most of the Commission's subsequent investigation was done as Hoover wanted: in effect, by asking the FBI to investigate itself. The possible primary sources (Hudkins, Alexander and Dallas Deputy Sheriff Allen Sweatt) were not witnesses before the Commission or its staff. Hoover cleverly undercut the Commission. For example, although Rankin said on January 27 that he did not intend to let the FBI interview Hudkins, the Bureau had already done so. After obtaining information about an official source for the allegation from Joseph Goulden (then reporting for the *Philadelphia Inquirer*), the FBI hid that lead from the Commission by reporting a single interview of Goulden about two reports from that source in two separate documents. The Commission ultimately relied upon the testimony of Hoover and other FBI personnel, and on an incomplete and inadequate set of affidavits asserting that Oswald had never been an informant.

This transcript reflects poorly on practically all of the parties involved, not just the FBI. J. Lee Rankin, for example, gave a presentation to the Commission which was at variance even with a memo he had prepared for the record. He referred to a Secret Service interview of the reporter Hudkins as an interview of Sheriff Sweatt, contributing to the incorrect consensus that "this all stems back to" Hudkins and not to the Texas officials. The Texans themselves told contradictory stories, and (as the Commission recognized) their motives were suspect.

Comparison of the transcript with the first chapter of Ford's book reveals serious distortion of the nature of the discussion, resulting from unindicated omissions and other heavy editing. The Robert Kennedy problem, for example, is not even mentioned, and the essence of the disagreement between Warren and Rankin is obscured. A rational discussion of strategy is made directionless. For example, the Ford and Stiles book omits (without indication) the italicized words in this suggestion by Rankin:

MR. RANKIN: "Would it be acceptable *to go to Mr. Hoover and tell him about the situation and that we would like* to go ahead and find out what we could about these—[allegations, by going to the sources]. . . ."

With this change, Warren's response does not make sense:

THE CHAIRMAN: Well, Lee, I wouldn't be in favor of going to any agency and saying, "We would like to do this." I think we ought to know what we are going to do, and do it, and take our chances one way or the other.

Ford then quotes Warren's determination ("I don't believe we should apologize or make it look that we are in any way reticent about making any investigation that comes to the Commission") but not the equivocating next sentence: "But on the other hand, I don't want to be unfriendly or unfair to him [Hoover]."

Like Rankin and the FBI, Ford plays down the role of Texas police officials as sources for the allegation, and overemphasizes the role of the press (Hudkins, Goulden and Harold Feldman, who wrote an article in *The Nation*). Sheriff Sweatt, who was named by Hudkins as a source, is not mentioned in Ford's book; three references to him were deleted. For example, where Senator John Sherman Cooper referred to the Commission's duty "to see what Hudkins and Sweatt say about it, where [did (?)] you get that information," he is quoted by Ford as saying "to see what Hudkins says about it, where he got that information."

We now know that a national security classification of Top Secret was used for ten years to suppress material which is sensitive only politically. The classification was even applied to a status report at the end of the meeting, where various investigative problems (some still unresolved) were discussed. On the other hand, the transcript contains a number of points which it is surprising to see released even now: a discourse by Dulles on how intelligence agencies can incriminate informants and tie them to their employers by getting receipts; a discussion of the FBI's responsibility to infiltrate the Fair Play for Cuba Committee, followed by McCloy's remark that he had "run into some very limited mentalities both in the CIA and the FBI (Laughter)"; and the revelation that during World War II D.A. Henry Wade (then with the FBI) had paid the head of the Ecuadorean police "more than his salary each month," without submitting full records to Washington, "so that they got better service than the local government did."

Since this transcript supplements what critics have known for years about how bad the Commission's investigation was, why has it been declassified now? The government claims that it was cleared for release by the National Archives, the FBI and the CIA after a review prompted by Harold Weisberg's suit under the Freedom of Information Act. (Executive Order 11652 provides for such a review of certain Top Secret material which is more than ten years old.) Weisberg argued persuasively that the Top Secret classification was unjustified by the subject of the discussion, was technically unauthorized, and had been made routinely. On May 3, 1974, Judge Gerhard Gesell ruled against Weisberg, not because of the classification but on an unsubstantiated government claim that the transcript was withholdable under the exemption granted to certain investigatory files. The subsequent release may have reflected a desire to avoid a bad precedent, and an awareness that Gesell's decision should have been reversed on appeal. The full 86-page transcript, with annotations and a commentary on the legal and factual issues, is being privately published by Weisberg.*

The disclosure of damaging material about the Commission and the FBI, and the revelation of Ford's Nixonian editing skills, may be just a coincidence. It is also possible that the release had something to do with the evidence that Hoover was looked upon as a possible obstruction. John Erlichman has made a parallel argument in justifying the Plumbers' operations; other material embarrassing to the FBI has been released in the counterintelligence program (COINTELPRO) and Kissinger wiretap cases. In any event, whatever use may have been intended, the transcript supports the case for strengthening the Freedom of Information Act.

The most charitable interpretation of the Commissioners' position at and after this January 27 meeting is that, assuming the allegation that Oswald was an FBI informant was false, their concern was to establish its falsity in a way which appeared thorough but which did not offend the FBI. President Johnson had convinced Warren to serve on the Commission only by arguing that squelching various (unspecified) rumors was essential to the nation's security. Warren passed on to the Commission staff Johnson's estimate that 40 million deaths would result from a nuclear war. At best the Commission never recognized just how much its concern about national security and national tranquility precluded its professed commitment to finding the truth.

The details of the Commission's failure to check out Oswald's relationship with the FBI reveal much about how a successful cover-up materializes. One minor aspect of that complicated story is noteworthy now: Leon Jaworski unfairly deprecated Hudkins's report. Apparently he was asked to check it out informally; he spoke not to the reporter but to his editor. Jaworski reported back to Rankin, noting that Hudkins's story did not say that Oswald was an informant but raised that question based on the "speculations" of others. Jaworski pointed out that the Commission already had the testimony of the FBI agents (but

---

* *Whitewash IV*, $6.25, published by Weisberg and available from him at Route 12, Frederick, Md. 21701.

only some of those involved, as Jaworski should have realized) and of Oswald's mother (who was being emphasized as the source of the rumor, to discredit it). He concluded, "I am wondering if it is really worth your effort to follow up on Hudkins." The Commission evidently agreed that the effort was not worthwhile. In their own final report, Carr, Jaworski and Storey endorsed the Commission's investigation, claiming that they knew of "no untapped sources" of relevant information, while repeating the implication that the Federal authorities should have warned the Texans about Oswald.

In the few days after Nixon's resignation, the country was reportedly eager to forget Watergate—a mood cultivated if not created by the media. Ford and Jaworski were in the key positions to decide how and whether the still-unexplained crimes of the last few years would be investigated. Ford's prolonged support of Nixon on issues from Vietnam to Watergate, and his work on the Warren Commission, are reminders that a reputation for integrity and candor among his colleagues in the government does not mean that he will serve the interests of the people. Jaworski's contacts with the Warren Commission's investigation show that he at least knows how to go along with a cover-up when the supposed perpetrator of the crime is out of the way and broader national interests are thought to be involved.

We do not need a second cover-up in the guise of amnesty and a desire to forget the past. At the very least, some of the roots of Watergate go back to before the Kennedy assassination —for example, "the whole Bay of Pigs thing" in which E. Howard Hunt was involved and which Nixon wanted to keep under wraps. (It may be that Nixon was euphemistically referring to Hunt's involvement in attempts to assassinate Fidel Castro; such attempts, it is widely speculated, had some connection with Kennedy's murder. [See, for example, Victor Marchetti and John Marks, *The CIA and the Cult of Intelligence*, p. 306; E. Howard Hunt, *Give Us This Day*, p. 38.]) As Representative Henry Gonzalez has suggested, a congressional committee should reexamine and reopen the investigation of the assassination. One of the lessons of Watergate is that the country wants, and can learn from, the truth.

Unpublished manuscript. © 1974 Paul L. Hoch.

THE SPECTRO EVIDENCE
James Lesar

Whitewash IV / 1974

The FBI performed spectrographic comparisons on certain bullet fragments found in the wounds of President Kennedy and Governor Connally, and on larger fragments found in the limousine floor and on a hospital stretcher. Critics of the Warren Commission were struck by the limited claims expressed in the language of the Hearings and of supporting FBI statements. An FBI report to the Dallas police, for example, notes that the tests show the lead in the fragments in question is "similar"—not that all components of the core are present in identical amounts. In a letter to the Commission's General Counsel, J. Lee Rankin, FBI Director J. Edgar Hoover referred to the more sensitive neutron activation analyses which supplemented the spectro tests. He indicated that it was not possible to tell which of the larger fragments any particular minute fragment came from, since there was no significant difference between the larger fragments. But Hoover failed to comment on the more important question of whether any of the minute fragments did not come from the larger ones.

The technique of spectrographic analysis is to induce the chemical elements of a sample to emit a spectrum, which is then photographed. Analysis of the spectrum reveals which elements are present and in what percentages. Two fragments cannot originate from one source unless their spectra are identical in the elements revealed and in the percentages of each element. Identity under such analysis is necessary, but not sufficient, to establish the common origin of two fragments. Thus, one set of findings in the FBI tests would be consistent with the Warren Report's finding of a lone gunman, without establishing the cer-

Reprinted from *Whitewash IV* by Harold Weisberg and James Lesar, by permission of the author and the publisher, Harold Weisberg, Route 12, Frederick, Md.

tainty that all the fragments came from one gun. But any other findings would conclusively disprove the Report's conclusion.

In the case of the spectro tests, the Commission did not follow its usual procedure of introducing each report into evidence as a Commission exhibit. Instead, an FBI ballistics expert was asked to describe the results of the tests and to confirm that the report would remain in the permanent files of the FBI. The absence of the data from the Commission's files and the peculiar wording of all references to the tests heightened critics' curiosity and prompted a number of attempts to obtain the test results. Author Harold Weisberg ultimately filed a suit under the Freedom of Information Act. His lawyer, Jim Lesar, describes the resulting legal battle.—Eds.

The government had always maintained that the Warren Commission *Report* had stated the truth about the assassination, and that the evidence supported its conclusions. If so, then why not make the evidence public?

The government and its apologists answered that the critics of the Warren Commission were sensationalists and commercializers who wanted to exhibit the gory details of the assassination to the public or obtain information that invaded someone's personal privacy. Actually, the government itself was the chief violator of responsible standards of conduct. For example, it shamefully invaded the personal privacy of Marina Oswald by making public some forty pages of properly exempt medical records pertaining to her pregnancy.

The spectro suit cut through the fog of government obfuscation and deception. This was a request for hard evidence. It is obvious that if the spectrographic results do support the findings of the Warren Commission, the Department of Justice would have long ago released them voluntarily, even begged the press to print them on page one.

This was the political strength of the spectro suit. It made clear one ineluctable fact: the truth about the assassination *had* been covered up. And *continued* to be covered up. This was social and political dynamite. Under the right combination of circumstances, spectro could do what seemed impossible: force a new and entirely open and public official investigation into President Kennedy's assassination.

From the standpoint of winning a victory in court, the strength of the spectro suit was also its weakness. If the courts concluded that the Department of Justice was suppressing the spectrographic reports because it knew they discredited the official version of the assassination, the courts could be so frightened by the implications that they would sanction the suppression, regardless of what the law provided.

Aside from this one drawback, which had its own compensations, the case for disclosure of the spectrographic analyses was legally quite solid. There was only one conceivable legal justification which the Department of Justice could invoke, its old favorite, the exemption for "investigatory files compiled for law enforcement purposes."

But the purpose of the investigatory files exemption was to prevent premature discovery which "could harm the government's case in court." Unless the government would admit to conspiracy, the only possible law enforcement action had expired on November 24, 1963, when Jack Ruby gunned down Lee Harvey Oswald, the government's only suspect.

Moreover, the analyses had been done as part of an investigation the FBI made for the Warren Commission. Where the assassination was concerned, neither the FBI nor the Warren Commission had law enforcement powers. Indeed, FBI Director J. Edgar Hoover testified before the Warren Commission that his agency had no jurisdiction to investigate the crime. (5H98)

The Warren Commission did have authority to investigate the assassination, but *not* for the purpose of prosecuting law violators. Its purpose was to establish the truth and report it to the President. The Foreword to the Commission's *Report* expressly abjured any law enforcement functions:

The Commission has functioned neither as a court presiding over an adversary proceeding nor as a prosecutor determined to prove a case, but as a factfinding agency committed to the ascertainment of truth. (R. xiv)

At the time the spectro suit was filed, the case law in the District of Columbia Circuit was favorable to Weisberg's right to have access to the spectrographic results. The Court of Appeals had just decided *Bristol-Myers Company v. F.T.C.*, and this quickly became the leading case on the interpretation of the investigatory files exemption.

In *Bristol-Myers* the Court of Appeals said that when the government invokes the investigatory files exemption, "the threshhold question . . . is whether the files sought . . . relate to anything that can fairly be characterized as an enforcement proceeding." Specifically, the Court of Appeals held that "the District Court must determine whether the prospect of enforcement proceedings is concrete enough to bring into operation the exemption for investigatory files, and if so whether the particular documents sought . . . are nevertheless discoverable."

Because there had been no "concrete prospect of enforcement proceedings" since the day Oswald was shot, *Bristol-Myers* clearly supported Weisberg's right of access to the spectrographic results.

This put the Department of Justice in a tight bind. It was committed to a bitter-end fight to suppress the spectrographic analyses but its chances of winning an open and honest court battle were slim, if not nonexistent. Consequently, it resorted to the only tools at hand: trickery, deception, obfuscation, and intimidation.

The Department's first trick was to sneak an affidavit by an FBI agent into the record under conditions that effectively precluded Weisberg from filing a written opposition to it before the case was heard. Weisberg's complaint was filed on August 3, 1970. Two months later, on October 6, 1970, the Department filed a motion to dismiss, or, in the alternative, for summary judgment. No affidavit was attached to the Department's October 6th motion, where it belonged.

On October 16th Weisberg filed an answer to the Justice Department's motion to dismiss. A hearing was set for November 9, 1970. On November 3, however, the Department moved *ex parte* for a postponement until November 16, 1970. It was granted.

On November 9, the Department filed a supplemental motion to dismiss, which contained only an attached affidavit by FBI agent Marion Williams. The xerox of a carbon copy of the Williams affidavit which was served on counsel for Weisberg was unsigned and undated. Three years later, while reviewing the record of the case, I became suspicious of the Williams affidavit and made a special trip to court to examine the original. I learned, too late, that Williams had sworn to the affidavit on August 19, 1970, two and a half months *before* it was filed in court. It had been withheld for filing at the last possible moment as part of a successful attempt to prevent Weisberg from filing a written response to it.

The Williams affidavit was an absurd document. It contained at least one provably false statement; mischaracterized Weisberg's request for the results obtained from the spectrographic tests as a request for the release of "raw data"; and recited a catalogue of speculative horrors which Williams said might ensue court-ordered release of the analyses:

It could lead, for example, to exposure of confidential informants; the disclosure out of context of the names of suspected persons on whom criminal justice action is not yet complete; possible blackmail; and, in general, do irreparable harm.

The Williams affidavit was clearly preposterous. There is no way that releasing the spectrographic results could lead to the exposure of confidential informants or any of the other harms Williams imagined.

At oral argument before Judge [John] Sirica on November 16, [Attorney Bernard] Fensterwald attacked the Williams affidavit and asked for an evidentiary hearing at which Williams and other witnesses could be put on the stand and cross-examined. But the government, through Assistant United States Attorney Robert Werdig, effectively diverted the judge from the Williams affidavit by a couple of tricks.

The hearing was set for 9:30. Werdig, however, did not show up on time. When he did arrive, Judge Sirica announced that the hearing would have to be short because he had an appointment to keep. Then Werdig pulled a tactical ploy which wrongly shifted the government's burden to justify its suppression to Weisberg:

I would preliminarily state, your Honor, the motion as you recognize is for Summary Judgment or to dismiss for failure to state a claim upon which relief can be granted. Ordinarily, inasmuch as the government filed the motion we would ask that we argue first; however, under these circumstances I believe we can reserve our comments more in the nature of rebuttal and I would like to ask Your Honor if I might have the privilege of having the last word as if I had the opening argument.

Caught by surprise, Fensterwald agreed to this proposal. Unfortunately, however, this device enabled Werdig to divert attention from the Williams affidavit. Werdig answered none of the questions about that affidavit which were raised by counsel for Weisberg. And by getting Fensterwald to address the court first, Werdig had created the impression that Weisberg had the burden of justifying disclosure. This is, of course, contrary to the Freedom of Information law, which places the burden of proof on the agency withholding the information.

Werdig had another and dirtier trick up his sleeve, one which also helped divert attention from the spurious Williams affidavit. He told Judge Sirica that: "In this instance the Attorney General of the United States has determined that it is not in the national interest to divulge these spectrographic analyses."

Because Congress had expressly rejected "national interest" as a grounds for withholding information, Werdig's assertion was at best irrelevant and irresponsible. I now believe that it was worse than that [. . .] I believe that [. . .] no Attorney General has ever made any such determination. No such "determination" has been produced. In a later case, the government refused to answer an interrogatory I addressed to it about this "determination."

All of this also detracted from the failure of the Department of Justice to justify its legal position. For example, when pressed to say what law was being enforced by the FBI's investigation for the non-law enforcing Warren Commission, Werdig could do no better than to argue that there just had to be *some* law, "natural or human."

At the conclusion of oral argument Judge Sirica, ruling from the bench, granted the government's motion to dismiss. He delivered no opinion and made no findings of fact.

Weisberg appealed the decision. Oral argument was heard on April 14, 1971, before a panel of the Court of Appeals. A long and exasperating wait for the panel decision followed.

Then, nearly two years later, the decision came down. By a

2-1 vote, we won. The opinion was written by District Judge Frank Kaufman, who had been specially designated to sit on the panel, and concurred in by Chief Judge David Bazelon. It focused squarely on the affidavit of FBI agent Marion Williams:

The Court below granted the Government's motion to dismiss, not its motion for summary judgment. Thus, it seemingly accorded no weight to the affidavit of Agent Williams. But even if that affidavit is given full consideration, it is a document which is most general and conclusory and which in no way explains *how* the disclosure of the records sought is likely to reveal the identity of confidential informants, or to subject persons to blackmail, or to disclose the names of criminal suspects, or in any other way hinder F.B.I. efficiency. The conclusions that the disclosure Weisberg seeks will cause any of those harms is neither compelled nor readily apparent, and therefore does not satisfy the Department's burden of proving under 5 U.S.C. §552 (b) (7), as the Department must, some basis for fearing such harm. Neither the F.B.I. nor any other governmental agency can shoulder that burden by simply stating as a matter of fact that it has so done, or by simply labelling as investigatory a file which it neither intends to use, nor contemplates making use of, in the near future for law enforcement purposes, at least not without establishing the nature of some harm which is likely to result from public disclosure of the file. Something more than mere edict or labelling is required if the Freedom of Information Act is to accomplish its "primary purpose, i.e., 'to increase the citizen's access to government records.' " [Citation deleted] This would be just as true in a case in which the public appetite for further information has been fully met as it is in this case in which the disclosure sought relates to a national tragedy concerning which discussion and debate continue.

The case was remanded to the district court for proceedings in accordance with the opinion. In a footnote the Court of Appeals emphasized its doubt about the relevance and honesty of the Williams affidavit by directing Judge Sirica to let Weisberg explore his objections to it.

Judge Kaufman has a reputation for writing careful opinions which are rarely overturned on appeal. In our view, he lived up to that reputation in the spectro decision. And the decision itself helped restore some of our lost faith in the ability of the judiciary to handle controversial cases according to law.

Our satisfaction and renewed hope was marred, however, by the dissenting opinion filed by Senior Circuit Judge John A. Danaher. His dissent was emotional, error-laden, and illogical, couched in contemptuous language rarely found in an appellate opinion. It also provides a frightening look at an authoritarian mind dressed in judicial robes:

To me, it is unthinkable that the criminal investigatory files of the Federal Bureau of Investigation are to be thrown open to the rummaging writers of some television crime series, or, *at the instance of some "party" off the street,* that a court may by order impose a burden upon the Department of Justice to justify to some judge the reasons for Executive action involving Government policy in the area here involved. [Emphasis in the original]

Dragging in old newspaper clippings on the assassination of President Kennedy, and other irrelevancies, Judge Danaher worked up to a highly emotional conclusion:

I suggest that . . . the law, as to the issue before us, forfends against this appellant's proposed further inquiry into the assassination of President Kennedy.

REQUIESCAT IN PACE.

Although the conclusion, like the rest of the dissent, was undeniably authoritarian, I did not take it seriously. Apparently Judge Danaher thought of the "Freedom of Information" law as a sort of prior restraint on any further discussion of the President's assassination. It was at once pathetic and ridiculous.

I should not have been so cavalier. Judge Danaher, too, was soon to be proven prophet.

The Department of Justice filed a petition for a rehearing *en banc*. Although appellate rules state that such petitions are looked upon with disfavor, this one was granted. Weisberg was denied the customary opportunity to oppose it.

The Court of Appeals next consolidated *Weisberg v. Department of Justice*, the spectro suit, with another Freedom of Information case, one which had not yet been decided by the panel assigned to it and which presented entirely different legal and factual issues.

The Court of Appeals, sitting *en banc*, heard oral argument on the two cases in July, 1973. On October 24, 1973, it overruled the panel by a 9-1 vote. Only Chief Judge Bazelon dissented. The majority opinion was written by the Court's ex officio member, Senior Circuit Judge Danaher, who had dissented from the panel decision.

Judge Danaher's opinion is basically the same as his dissent. He did tidy the language up a bit. The embarrassing "REQUIESCAT IN PACE" is dropped, and the opinion no longer contains the insulting reference to Weisberg as "some 'party' off the street." But the same authoritarian ideas are still there:

It may to some appear *unthinkable* that the criminal investigatory files of the Bureau of Investigation, compiled for law enforcement purposes, are to be thrown open to some "person" as defined in 5 U.S.C. §551 (2) who asserts entitlement in reliance upon §552 (a) (3) . [Emphasis in the original]

The opinion also repeats the same factual errors so obvious in Danaher's dissent. For example, Judge Danaher asserts that:

It was speedily developed that the rifle from which the assassin's bullets had been fired had been shipped to one Lee Harvey Oswald.

Had Danaher not been the victim of the Department of Justice's disinformation policy which he was bent upon sustaining, he might have known that:

1. The rifle alleged to be the murder weapon was not shipped to Lee Harvey Oswald but to one "Alex J. Hidell." Although postal regulations require that the Post Office retain a signed receipt, it produced none.

2. This rifle was *never* placed in Oswald's possession. His wife told the Secret Service that it was not his rifle.

3. *At least two other rifles were placed at the scene of the crime.* Oswald himself, and *only* Oswald, reported them to the police.

4. No bullets fired from this rifle have been connected with the crime except by inference. The only intact bullet which can be connected with this rifle is CE 399 which fell from under the

mattress on a rolling stretcher in the hospital hallway. The man who found it protested he could not sleep nights if he swore to what was demanded of him, that he state who had been on that stretcher.

Danaher's conclusion assumes that this bullet and various fragments were used in the crime. He had no evidence on this. The analyses could hold this missing evidence. Danaher invented proof, exactly the suppressed proof sought in this suit.

Other aspects of Danaher's opinion are more disturbing than these factual errors. The Department of Justice was not able to and never did specify what the law enforcement purpose of the spectrographic analyses was, except to argue, as Werdig had, that there must be some law, "natural or human." Judge Danaher was more imaginative. He simply invented a law enforcement purpose—"collaboration with Texas authorities"—and then decreed it was fact.

Of course, there was no evidence in the record to support this fact. Indeed, the only evidence disputes it. Even the Department of Justice had not been bold enough to make this claim. For the truth is that the federal agencies did *not* collaborate with the Texas authorities but instead kidnapped the corpse and confiscated the most important evidence, including the alleged murder weapon and the empty shells, and never returned them. Even Dallas Police Chief Jesse Curry complained of this.

But the most ominous feature of the Court of Appeals decision in *Weisberg v. Department of Justice* is its holding on the legal issue which the case presents:

We deem it demonstrated beyond peradventure that the Department's files: (1) were investigatory in nature; and (2) were compiled for law enforcement purposes. When that much shall have been established, as is so clearly the situation on the record, and the district judge shall so determine, such files are exempt from compelled disclosure.

The effect of this decision is to convert the Freedom of Information law into a withholding statute. As a result the vast majority of government records could now be suppressed merely by labeling them "investigatory files." All that is needed to suppress a document is a government official willing to execute an obfuscatory or perjurious affidavit claiming the document is part of an "investigatory file compiled for law enforcement purposes." The government need not cite a specific statute or law to be enforced, nor need the district court subject the affiant to cross-examination. The court can merely take the government's untested word. . . .

In response to Executive Branch obstructionism in this and other cases, in November 1974 Congress amended the Freedom of Information Act to limit the use of the exemptions. In April 1975, the FBI released seventy-three pages of raw data from the spectrographic tests to Harold Weisberg. Another researcher who has been seeking access to the physical evidence, Dr. John Nichols, claims that the evidence which has been released "is incomplete, contains errors, and has essential factors missing." On May 5, Dr. Cyril Wecht declared that "it is too early to draw conclusions as to [the data's] significance." At this writing, Weisberg is persisting in his court case to achieve (and certify) full disclosure.—Eds.

LEE HARVEY OSWALD WAS INNOCENT
George O'Toole

Penthouse / April 1975

The assassination of Napoleon Bonaparte was a perfect crime: It went undiscovered for 140 years. There had been rumors and suspicions, of course. Napoleon himself wrote, just three weeks before his death, "My death is premature. I have been assassinated by the English oligarchy." But the official autopsy report stated that Napoleon died from natural causes, and there the matter rested for nearly a century and a half.

In 1961 two Swedish researchers decided to investigate the death of Napoleon through the use of one of the newest weapons in the arsenal of forensic science, a technique known as neutron activation analysis. They obtained some strands of hair taken from the head of the exiled emperor immediately after his death. With the help of a scientist at the University of Glasgow, the Swedes placed these hairs in a nuclear reactor at Britain's Harwell atomic-research laboratory and subjected them to a beam of neutrons. After twenty-four hours the specimens were sent to Glasgow for analysis.

The irradiated hairs yielded up their secret. They contained over ten times the normal amount of arsenic. Additional samples of Napoleon's hair were then obtained, and the experiment was repeated. This time the hair was cut into segments, each corresponding to two weeks' growth. The distribution of arsenic in the segments showed that the exile of St. Helena had received regular doses of the poison during the last year of his life. The Swedish and Scots researchers were convinced: Napoleon Bonaparte had been slowly poisoned to death by his jailers.

There is, of course, no doubt that the death of President John F. Kennedy in Dallas was an assassination; yet, like the death of Napoleon, the event has been obscured by questions and doubts. During the ten years since the assassination, the facts have been sifted again and again, first by the Warren Commission and then by a host of independent investigators. Few of the latter have been able to agree with the official conclusions of the commission, but none has offered a satisfactory account of what really happened on that November afternoon in Dallas. With the passage of time, the details of the controversy have dimmed in our minds, leaving a dull residue of doubt and a despair of ever learning the truth. And yet we may hope that, as with the assassination of Napoleon Bonaparte, new scientific discoveries will perhaps someday shed some light on the murder of John Kennedy. It was just this hope that I began to cherish when I first heard of a remarkable device called the Psychological Stress Evaluator.

There is no simple way of stating accurately in lay terms what the Psychological Stress Evaluator (or PSE) is or what it does. But if the precision of scientific language can be abandoned for a moment, it can be said that the PSE is a new type of lie detector that works through the medium of the voice.

I first heard of the Psychological Stress Evaluator in 1972, when I met two of its inventors, Allan D. Bell, Jr. and Charles R. McQuiston. Bell and McQuiston, both former lieutenant colonels, retired from army intelligence several years ago to form a company called Dektor Counterintelligence and Security, Inc. It was a logical second career for the two men. Both are experts in the technology of espionage and either one could pick the lock on your front door in less time than it takes you to find your key. Colonel Bell wears a Black Belt in karate, is an accomplished swordsman and small-arms expert, and has a dozen inventions to his credit, from antibugging devices to a miniaturized microdot camera. McQuiston is one of the foremost polygraph experts in the U.S., a specialist in radio and audio surveillance, and a qualified locksmith.

The PSE grew from an effort to improve the polygraph. Standard polygraphs measure four variables: pulse, blood pressure, respiration, and perspiration. Some also measure additional physiological variables. The more variables measured, the more reliable the polygraph.

Bell and McQuiston discovered that the frequencies composing the human voice are not fixed; they shift very slightly from eight to fourteen times every second. But when the speaker is under stress, this normal frequency modulation disappears. What remains are the pure component frequencies of the voice. And a strong indication that the speaker is lying.

The two men developed a device to detect this phenomenon and planned to use it as an additional "channel" on the polygraph. Then they discovered that the new variable was so reliable and accurate a measure of psychological stress there was really no need to measure the other polygraph variables.

Freed from the necessity of strapping the subject into a chair, stretching a pneumographic tube across his chest, gluing electrodes to his palms, and clamping his arm with a blood-pressure cuff, Bell and McQuiston found the PSE to be much more versatile than the polygraph. Because it can work from a telephone or tape recorder, the PSE can be used without the knowledge or even the physical presence of the subject.

Sound-recording technology is almost a century old (Edison invented the phonograph in 1877), and an enormous amount of history is stored away in the sound archives of the world. There are scores of mysteries from the past hundred years that could be cleared up once and for all if the related interviews, public pronouncements, and press conferences could be retrieved from the archives and subjected to the scrutiny of the PSE. But none of these mysteries can compare in terms of sinister murkiness, frustrating paradox, or sheer historical impact to the question of what really happened in Dealey Plaza at 12:30 P.M., central standard time, November 22, 1963.

Throughout the long afternoon and evening of that November 22, the reporters poured into Dallas. Nearly every major newspaper, wire service, and television network was represented. In the homicide and robbery bureau on the third floor of Dallas police headquarters, a police captain and agents of the FBI and Secret Service were questioning Lee Harvey Oswald. Outside in the corridor, television cameramen were setting up their equipment and newsmen were beginning to assemble. As the evening wore on, more than one hundred reporters jammed into the narrow third-floor hallway.

Inside the homicide and robbery bureau—according to reports by the Dallas police, the FBI, and the Secret Service—Oswald was advised of his rights to legal representation and to remain silent, and that any statement he made could be used against him in a court of law. Sometime during that night, Oswald was asked about the shootings, and he emphatically denied killing either President Kennedy or Dallas police officer J. D. Tippit. He refused to discuss the assassination with the FBI agents until he was represented by an attorney. When he was asked to submit to a polygraph examination, he refused to do so until he had had an opportunity to consult a lawyer.

Several times during the evening, Oswald was taken under guard from the third-floor office to appear in lineups and to be arraigned for the murder of Officer Tippit. At midnight he was taken to the basement for a brief and confused "press conference." Whenever Oswald was brought out of the third-floor office, the reporters elbowed forward, vying with each other to get a statement from the prisoner. In answer to their shouted questions, Oswald expressed bewilderment at his situation and protested that he had not been allowed legal representation. When asked if he had killed the president, Oswald replied that he had not. Although nothing he said in the police interrogation room was recorded, the newsmen's microphones captured Oswald's statements in the corridor and at the press conference. At least two of his claims to innocence were recorded on tape.

He couldn't have known it at the time, but when Oswald spoke those words, he was taking a test. Seven years would pass before the lie detector would be invented that could actually test for the subtle and inaudible vocal clues that are evidence of truth or deception. Another three years would elapse before anyone used the Psychological Stress Evaluator to test Oswald's denials that he killed President Kennedy. In 1973, I obtained copies of those recordings and processed them with the PSE.

The CBS tapes contained this brief exchange between Oswald and the newsmen, recorded at the midnight press conference in the basement of police headquarters.

OSWALD: I positively know nothing about this situation here. I would like to have legal representation.

REPORTER: (unintelligible)

OSWALD: Well, I was questioned by a judge. However, I protested at that time that I was not allowed legal representation during that very short and sweet hearing. I really don't know what this situation is about. Nobody has told me anything, except that I'm accused of murdering a policeman. I know nothing more than that. I do request someone to come forward to give me legal assistance.

REPORTER: Did you kill the president?

OSWALD: No, I have not been charged with that. In fact, nobody has said that to me yet. The first thing I heard about it was when the newspaper reporters in the hall asked me that question.

The press conference was held under circumstances very unfavorable for stress-deception analysis. Oswald was shackled between two policemen. He had been brought into the basement lineup room to face a battery of television lights and cameras and a surging mob of newsmen. Each reporter was trying to out-shout his fellows in the competition for a statement. I expected to find a uniform level of hard stress in both relevant and irrelevant statements, but I discovered that this was not the case.*

The first statement, "I positively know nothing about this situation here," showed good-to-hard stress. The stress was moderate-to-good in, "I would like to have legal representation." It remained at that level until he said, "I protested at that time," when it went back up to hard. The stress dropped back to good, then moderate-to-good in the phrase, "I really don't know what this situation is about." It continued good until he said, "I know nothing more than that," at which time it turned hard again. "I do request someone to come forward to give me legal assistance" was moderate-to-good, except for the word "someone," which was hard.

The statement, "No, I have not been charged with that" showed an unusual range of stress. It began with almost no stress, but there was hard stress on the word "that." On listening repeatedly to the recording, I noticed that Oswald ran the words "no" and "I" together, producing the same phonetic effect as "know why." Electronically, it was a single, two-syllable word, and it produced a single waveform on the PSE chart. The wave-form began with almost no stress but ended with good stress. Obviously, it was important to discover how much of the stress had been present during the "no" part of the utterance.

I played the tape several times at a reduced speed until I was able to identify the point at which the *o* vowel ended and the *i* sound began. I made a small visible mark on the tape at this point, then switched the recorder to the even slower speed required by the PSE. I backed up the tape, switched on the PSE, and played the statement again. When the mark on the tape reached the recorder's playback head, I switched off the machine. The PSE stylus dropped back to the zero line. I looked at the waveform.

The stress was none-to-moderate.

I asked Mike Kradz, Dektor's director of training, to look at

---

* In this article, stress is ranked on a scale of low, moderate, good, and hard.— Eds.

the charts. I told him that the speaker was a young man accused of murdering a policeman and an executive, who had been interviewed by reporters under chaotic conditions in a police station. I showed Kradz the transcript of the tape, but I had altered the question, "Did you kill the president?" to read, "Did you kill him?" As Kradz inspected the charts, he had no way of knowing that the speaker was Lee Harvey Oswald or that the murdered executive was John Kennedy.

Kradz studied the charts carefully and said it seemed the speaker was telling the truth when he denied the murder. While he was impressed with the low level of stress in the "no," which I had separated electronically from the rest of the statement, he felt that even considering the increased stress that appears later in the sentence there was a strong indication that the young man wasn't lying. Kradz pointed out that the stress, although considerable, was not equal to the consistently hard stress shown in the phrases, "I positively know nothing about this situation here," and "I know nothing more than that." The young man may have been lying when he made these statements, or there may have been some other reason for the stress. But whatever the case, Kradz pointed out, that subject seemed to mean a great deal more to the speaker than the matter of murdering the executive. The indication was that he didn't do it.

After he announced his conclusion, I told Kradz that the speaker was Lee Harvey Oswald and the murdered executive President Kennedy. The ex-cop stared at me for a moment, then picked up the charts again and examined them minutely. Finally he put them down and shook his head in disbelief. "I wonder who he thought he killed," he said.

Kradz's incredulity was only natural; the charge that Lee Harvey Oswald killed President Kennedy has gained widespread acceptance, even in the face of public doubts about the Warren Report. During the first few years after the assassination, Oswald was described in the press as "the alleged assassin," an implicit reference to the fact that he had not lived to be convicted of the crime in a court of law. But, as propagandists have often demonstrated, repetition of a charge gradually leads to its public acceptance. Ten years after the event, even most skeptics doubted no more than that "Oswald acted alone."

I was too familiar with the weaknesses in the case against Oswald and I had seen too many indications of deception in the recorded statements of the witnesses against him to be very surprised at this new discovery. I remembered the words of ex-FBI agent William Turner in his book, *Invisible Witness*: "While in police custody Oswald's demeanor was not that of a wanton assassin. He steadfastly denied the crime and some newsmen were struck by the appearance of genuine shock when he was told he was accused of the assassination."

But Mike Kradz's skepticism led him to think further about the chart and transcript I had shown him, and he finally raised a point which, I was forced to agree, made the PSE results less than 100 percent conclusive—this is that it's not completely clear what Oswald meant when he responded to the question, "Did you kill the president?" The Warren Report contains the following transcription of his reply: "No. I have not been charged with that." If the statement is read as two distinct sentences, Oswald seems to be denying his guilt and then adding that he has not been charged with the crime (which, at the time of the midnight press conference, was the case). But, as I knew from listening to the tape, Oswald sounded as though he were saying, "No, I have not been charged with that," in one sentence, not two. Was "no" a specific denial of guilt, or merely a rejection of the question, a way of saying, in effect, "Don't ask me that; even the police haven't accused me of that"?

Of course, if Oswald had been the man who killed the president only hours earlier, he might be expected to show hard stress while making any reference to the shooting, no matter how oblique; and it certainly should have been a more stressful subject than what he knew about the circumstances of his arrest. But Oswald's denial seemed ambiguous, and the PSE results, however interesting, could not be called absolutely conclusive. It seemed likely, however, that Oswald was asked the crucial question by newsmen again during the night of November 22, and his answer was probably recorded on tape somewhere. So I set out to find a recording of a categorical denial, and several weeks later I succeeded.

Ironically, my search ended in Dallas. I was visiting Al Chapman, one of the hundreds of private citizens who do not believe the Warren Report and continue to investigate the case. Chapman has compiled a small library of materials relating to the assassination, including some sound recordings. Among these I found a long-playing record called *Probe*, which was released several years ago by Columbia Records. *Probe* is an audio documentary on the assassination (and one of the bitterest attacks on the critics of the Warren Report), and it contains many excerpts from news recordings that were made during the weekend of the assassination.

Oswald speaks only once on the record, apparently while being led along the crowded third-floor corridor of the police station:

OSWALD: These people have given me a hearing without legal representation or anything.

REPORTER: Did you shoot the president?

OSWALD: I didn't shoot anybody, no sir.

I transferred the segment to tape. Later, I processed the recording with the PSE.

Oswald's protest that he has been given a hearing without legal representation shows good-to-hard stress. His categorical denial that he shot anyone contains almost no stress at all. Stress is a necessary, but not sufficient, condition of lying; it must be interpreted, and therein lies the margin of error. But the absence of stress is a sufficient condition of truthfulness. If someone is talking about a matter of real importance to himself and shows absolutely no stress, then he must be telling the truth.

Oswald denied shooting *anybody*—the president, the policeman, anybody. The psychological stress evaluator said he was telling the truth.

But, despite the many other indications that Oswald was innocent, the almost complete absence of stress in his voice is still remarkable, in view of the circumstances of his conversation with the press. The recording sounded clear and was of excellent technical quality, and hard stress was apparent in Oswald's voice when he protested that he had been denied legal representation. Still, I wondered if some yet unknown recording phenomenon had managed to eradicate the stress in his statement of innocence. This didn't seem very likely, but I was uncomfortable with the fact that the tape had been made from a phonograph record, which, in turn, had been cut from another recording. None of my other results had come from phonograph records. Did something about this medium sometimes erase stress? I decided that I would have to obtain another tape of the statement, one that was not the result of a re-recording chain involving a phonograph record. Otherwise, I couldn't be certain.

The John F. Kennedy Library in Waltham, Massachusetts, has a stack of audio tapes that had been recorded from the television network coverage of the events of November 22-25, 1963. After two days of listening, I found what I was looking for. This copy sounded the same as the recording I had found in Dallas—with one exception. On the Dallas recording Oswald says, "I didn't shoot anybody, no sir." On the Waltham recording he can be heard to say, "No, I didn't shoot anybody, no sir." The two recordings were probably made from two different microphones, and indeed many photographs of Oswald in custody show several newsmen holding up microphones in front of him. The reporter who asked him, "Did you shoot the president?" was probably at Oswald's side, and Oswald may have been turning to face the man as he answered. Thus, some of the microphones would have been likely to miss the "no."

I ran the Waltham recording on the PSE. The initial "no" showed moderate stress. The PSE waveforms for the rest of Oswald's statements were virtually identical to the ones I made from the Dallas tape. There was good-to-hard stress on, "These people have given me a hearing without legal representation or anything," and almost no stress on, "I didn't shoot anybody, no sir." There was no longer any question of distortion from the phonograph record. The evidence that the Waltham tape had been recorded from a different microphone from the Dallas tape established that the two tapes were the end points of two completely separate transmission and recording chains. And both tapes yielded identical PSE results. It was not some strange sound-recording fluke; quite clearly Lee Harvey Oswald was telling the truth.

I returned from Waltham and visited Mike Kradz at Dektor. I showed him the second set of transcripts and charts. No prolonged examination was necessary; the utter lack of stress in

Oswald's statement was immediately obvious. It was hard to accept, but Kradz had run too many criminal cases on the PSE to have any doubts about the meaning of the PSE charts I showed him. There was no other possible explanation than that Oswald was telling the truth.

Kradz asked me if I would object to his showing the charts to someone else. I said that I wouldn't, and he stepped out of his office and returned in a few minutes with a wiry, middle-aged man whom he introduced as Rusty Hitchcock.

L. H. "Rusty" Hitchcock is a former army intelligence agent and one of the most experienced polygraph examiners in the country. Since he graduated from the army's polygraph school at Fort Gordon in 1954, lie detection has been his specialty. Besides conducting thousands of polygraph investigations, he has also carried out basic research in lie detection and is an expert on the phenomenon of the galvanic skin response and the effect of hypnosis on polygraph results. He is the author of many training manuals and procedural guides used by army polygraph examiners. Hitchcock is, of course, well-known in professional polygraph circles and, although he now embraces the heretical Psychological Stress Evaluator, he is still held in high regard by most of his fellow members of the American Polygraph Association. He is retired and spends most of his time raising cattle on his Georgia ranch, but he occasionally serves as a consultant to law-enforcement agencies and private security firms.

Rusty Hitchcock was incredulous when Kradz showed him the PSE charts I had run on Oswald. He questioned me closely to assure himself that I had not made some procedural mistake in operating the PSE equipment. Convinced that I had not, he speculated that there might be a defect in the equipment I was using, and he also pointed out that I had run Oswald in only one of the PSE modes and at only one tape speed (varying the speed of the tape recorder or chart drive mechanism can sometimes reveal low-level stress which would otherwise go unnoticed). This was true, but the combination of mode and tape speed I had used was the one most often used in criminal cases, since it is completely sensitive to the levels of stress likely to be produced in such matters. Oswald had shown hard stress on the irrelevant issue and almost none on his claim of innocence.

I was certain the PSE and recorder I had used were working properly, and I was confident I would get the same results no matter what equipment, PSE mode, or tape speed I used. I offered Hitchcock a copy of the recording and suggested he check my findings with his own instruments. He replied by inviting me to his ranch, suggesting that we review the tape together. Several weeks later, I accepted his invitation.

We spent most of a morning and a roll of chart paper on the test. I watched over his shoulder as Rusty tried each combination of PSE mode and recorder speed in turn. The answer was always the same. In the end he too was convinced. Rusty is no student of assassinations, but he is a specialist in the natural history of lying. Perhaps better than anyone, Rusty could read the message written over and over again that day by the stylus of his PSE. He had the courage of his convictions, and he gave me his findings in the form of a signed statement. It reads as follows:

Dear Mr. O'Toole:

As you requested, I have analyzed with the Psychological Stress Evaluator the tape recordings you provided of the voice of Lee Harvey Oswald. Oswald's comments regarding the circumstances of his arrest and his statements that he had been denied legal representation show considerable situation stress. When he is asked, "Did you kill the president?" his reply, "No, I have not been charged with that," shows no harder stress than that found in his earlier comments. In replying to the question, "Did you shoot the president?" his reply, "No, I didn't shoot anybody, no sir," contains much less stress than I found in his earlier statement regarding legal representation, made only moments before this.

My PSE analysis of these recordings indicates very clearly that Oswald believed he was telling the truth when he denied killing the president. Assuming that he was not suffering from a psychopathological condition that made him ignorant of his own actions, I can state, beyond reasonable doubt, that Lee Harvey Oswald did not kill President Kennedy and did not shoot anyone else.

(signed)
Lloyd H. Hitchcock

Was Oswald a madman? The Warren Commission reported that it could reach no definite conclusion regarding Oswald's sanity in the legal sense of the word. The commission included in its report a lengthy and detailed biography of Oswald, and the report of a psychiatrist who examined Oswald when he was arrested for truancy as a thirteen-year-old. The psychiatrist found Oswald to be withdrawn and insecure, but not psychotic. Nothing in the commission's detailed record of Oswald's childhood and adult life suggests that he was, in any sense, insane.

Rusty Hitchcock explained that he was not concerned about the possibility that Oswald was a pathological liar; the hard stress evident in some of his statements shows that he was responding normally to the situation in which he found himself. Rusty was allowing for the possibility that, for some reason such as temporary amnesia, Oswald was unaware of his recent actions. However, there is absolutely nothing in the official accounts of Oswald's statements while in custody that suggests he ever said that he couldn't remember what he had been doing on the afternoon of November 22. There is no other plausible interpretation of the Oswald PSE charts than the explanation that Oswald was simply telling the truth.

But after ten years of repetition in books, magazines, newspapers, and the broadcast media, it is difficult to abandon the official doctrine that Lee Harvey Oswald was an assassin. Even the serious student of the Warren Report who is completely familiar with the defects in the commission's case against Oswald may be unable to resist the cumulative effect of a "well-known fact." The problems raised by skeptics with the testimony and evidence against Oswald tend to focus on the negative, to argue that the commission failed to prove its case. In debating the ballistic, photographic, and medical evidence, one has a tendency to ignore the substantial positive arguments in favor of Oswald's innocence. . . .

Oswald is one of the most hated figures in American history, and his guilt has been largely unquestioned. While critics of the Warren Commission sometimes find receptive and sympathetic audiences to hear their arguments, one proclaims Oswald innocent at his own peril. To offer a professional opinion in support of this thesis takes great courage. Those who have done so have earned my gratitude and admiration.

But there is more than a professional reputation to be risked in considering the PSE evidence of Oswald's innocence. There is one's peace of mind, and all who have dared to look over my shoulder have lost it. I remember vividly the emotions I felt during the afternoon and evening of November 22, as the reports came in from Dallas. During those tragic hours there was some small consolation in knowing that the murderer had been captured. But whatever comfort there was in that belief, it is now gone. The president was killed by a person or persons unknown. Until the murderers are found, until the truth is known, until justice is done, there can be no rest and no peace. None for John Kennedy, none for Lee Oswald, and none for the rest of us.

WHAT HAPPENED IN DEALEY PLAZA?

THE ZAPRUDER FILM
Sylvia Meagher

Accessories after the Fact / *1967*

Without daring to state it as a conclusive finding, the Warren Report makes a prodigious effort to persuade us that a single shot struck the President in the neck and proceeded on to strike the Governor, causing all of his wounds. The authors state that there is "very persuasive evidence from the experts to indicate that the same bullet which pierced the President's throat also caused Governor Connally's wounds." They acknowledge that there is a difference of opinion about that hypothesis (including the firm dissent of the Governor himself), but they claim that "it is not necessary to any essential findings of the Commission to determine just which shot hit Governor Connally." (*WR 19*)

Surely that is one of the most misleading statements in the whole Report. The Commission insists that all the shots came from the Book Depository. If the Governor was wounded by a pristine bullet and not by either of the two missiles which struck

the President, it is self-evident under the Commission's reconstruction of the crime that the assassin made three hits in three
tries, in a span of five and one-half seconds. Not one of the
sharpshooters who tested their skill with the Mannlicher-Carcano
rifle (the alleged murder weapon) achieved such accuracy, even
though the experiments utilized stationary rather than moving
targets. It is therefore impossible to make a serious claim that
the Commission's essential findings do not hinge upon a determination of the shot that struck the Governor—if, indeed, only one
bullet inflicted all of his wounds.

One might expect the Zapruder film to establish the moment
at which the Governor was hit in relation to the shot that struck
the President in the neck. Unfortunately, neither the film nor
the color slides made for the Commission by the *Life* magazine
photo laboratory (now available for examination at the National
Archives) enable the viewer to pinpoint this moment. Nevertheless, careful study of the color slides has other rewards.

A significant fact recorded on the slides is that several persons
are seen to move abruptly, as if reacting to a stimulus such as the
sound of a shot, before the earliest point at which the Commission believes the President could have been hit by the first bullet.
Mrs. Kennedy makes a sudden sharp turn toward the President,
bending her head as if to look at him, in Frame 204. Howard
Brennan is seen sitting on a wall and looking over his left shoulder at the Presidential car until Frame 207, when he turns his
head suddenly to look at the right. The Secret Service agent
riding on the front right running board of the follow-up car,
directly behind the Presidential limousine, also looks sharply to
his right in Frame 207.

If the interpretation of those movements is valid, it implies
strongly that the first shot was fired before Frame 204, during
the sequence in which the President was concealed from the
Book Depository window by tree foliage (Frames 166 to 210)
and when a sniper positioned in that window could not have
seen or aimed at him. That was the decisive factor to a Commission predisposed to "find" that all the shots came from that window. Thus the Commission says:

. . . the evidence indicated that the President was not hit until at least
Frame 210 and that he was probably hit by Frame 225. The possibility

of variations in reaction time in addition to *the obstruction of Zapruder's view by the sign precluded a more specific determination* than that the President was probably shot through the neck between Frames 210 and 225. . . . (Italics added)   (*WR 105*)

The Commission has stated, in effect, that Zapruder did not see the President at the moment that he was first shot because of the intervention of the traffic sign. This is a contradiction of Zapruder's testimony: *"I heard the first shot and I saw the President lean over and grab himself like this* [holding his left chest area]." (*7H 571*) (Italics added) As Harold Weisberg has pointed out in his book *Whitewash,* Zapruder's testimony in itself strongly suggests that the President was hit before he disappeared behind the sign at Frame 210 and while he was still invisible to a rifleman in the sixth-floor window. The lawyer who took Zapruder's testimony failed to appreciate or explore this important observation, and the Warren Report, ignoring the Zapruder testimony, inaccurately asserts that he did not see what he so inconveniently saw.

At Frame 225 the President is reacting to the bullet in the back but the Governor shows absolutely no evidence of being shot. Students of the Zapruder film and color slides differ with each other in identifying the frame or approximate frame at which the Governor was shot. The earliest point suggested is Frame 228; the Governor himself designates Frames 231-234; others believe that he was not struck until considerably later—some on the basis of his unperturbed appearance, and others reasoning that his right hand appears to grip a metal bar at the side of the car as late as Frame 233 and that his hand must still have been uninjured at that point by the bullet that ultimately smashed the right wristbone.

It is frustrating and ironic that the Zapruder film does not enable the viewer to pinpoint the exact moment of impact of the bullet in the President's back or of the bullet (or bullets) that struck the Governor.[1] But the film does establish a definite

[1] The article "A Matter of Reasonable Doubt" in *Life* magazine of November 25, 1966 (p. 48) reviewed the Zapruder color frames and reported an interview with Governor Connally in which he reiterated his absolute certainty that he was hit by a separate bullet, in Frame 234. (Ray Marcus of Los Angeles has concluded from his expert analysis of the Zapruder frames that Connally was hit in Frame 238.)

delay between the wounding of the two men—a delay too short for the Carcano rifle to be fired twice by one man, and too long to leave the single-missile hypothesis with credibility.[2] That time lapse therefore compromises the single-bullet theory and destroys the Commission's pretense that a determination of just which shot hit Governor Connally was "not necessary to any essential findings" (as even Lord Devlin, supremely uncritical partisan of the Warren Report, belatedly conceded in the London *Observer* of September 25, 1966).[3]

The problem posed by the time lapse between the wounding of the two men is discussed in the following passage from the testimony:

DULLES: But you would then have the problem you would think if Connally had been hit at the same time, [he] would have reacted in the same way, and not reacted *much later* as these pictures show. [Italics added]

SHANEYFELT: That is right.

DULLES: Because the wounds would have been inflicted.

McCLOY: That is what puzzles me.

DULLES: That is what puzzles me. (5H 155)

[2] Senator Richard B. Russell joined Governor Connally in rejecting the single-bullet theory, in the wake of the *Life* article, as did Malcolm Kilduff (*The New York Times*, November 22, 1966, p. 1).

[3] Apologists for the Warren Report such as Professor Alexander M. Bickel of Yale and former Assistant Counsel Wesley J. Liebeler have tried to validate the Commission's untenable pronouncement by suggesting that Oswald could have fired the first shot and struck Kennedy earlier, at Frame 185 of the Zapruder film, when there was a break in the foliage of an obstructing oak tree for one-eighteenth of a second. That improvisation can be discarded immediately, for an earlier shot would have meant a steeper downward trajectory, leaving the so-called exit wound in the anterior neck unaccounted for and thus reintroducing at least one more assassin.

Liebeler developed the theme of a first shot that hit the President "while the limousine was partly obscured from the window by the tree" during a public discussion at the Theater for Ideas in New York City on September 30, 1966. After pronouncing himself at some length on the plausibility of that theory, he was asked where that bullet would have wound up. Liebeler replied:

"Where did that bullet end up? Well, that was the bullet—that was the bullet that came into the President's back, and then—and then, came out his throat. [Pause] Well, that raises a problem, doesn't it? [Laughter] Wait a minute, just a minute [Mixed voices of audience and panel]. . . . And that is why, Mr. Popkin, I think it *did* go through the President first and hit the Governor. . . ." (WBAI radio, New York City, broadcast December 30, 1966)

The Commission tried to dispose of the puzzlement by suggesting that the Governor had experienced a delayed reaction to his wounds. (*WR 112-113*) In presenting this proposition, the Commission does not cite supporting medical testimony. However, the records show that the Commission in fact did solicit medical opinion on the possibility of a delayed reaction by the Governor to a bullet that smashed his rib, collapsed his lung, and fractured his wrist.

SPECTER: Could that missile have traversed Governor Connally's chest without having him know it immediately or instantaneously?

DR. HUMES: I believe so. I have heard reports, and have been told by my professional associates, of any number of instances where people received penetrating wounds in various portions of the body and have only the sensation of a slight discomfort or slight slap or some other minor difficulty from such a missile wound. *I am sure that he would be aware that something happened to him*, but that he was shot, I am not certain. [Italics added]

FORD: Would that have been the potential reaction of the President when first hit, as shown in [CE] 385?

DR. HUMES: It could very easily be one of some type of an injury— I mean the awareness that he had been struck by a missile, I don't know, but people have been drilled through with a missile and didn't know it.   (*2H 376*)

SPECTER: Dr. Dziemian, Governor Connally testified that he experienced the sensation of a striking blow on his back which he described as being similar to a hard punch from a doubled-up fist. Do you have an opinion as to whether that sensation would necessarily occur immediately upon impact of a wound such as that received by Governor Connally, or could there be a delayed reaction in sensing that feeling?

DR. DZIEMIAN: I don't have too much of an opinion on that. All I can say is that some people are struck by bullets and do not even know they are hit. This happens in wartime. But I don't know about that.

SPECTER: So that it is possible in some situations there is some delay in reaction?

DR. DZIEMIAN: I couldn't say.

SPECTER: Is it a highly individual matter as to the reaction of an individual on that subject?

DR. DZIEMIAN: I don't know.

DULLES: But take a wrist wound like the wound of Governor Connally. He couldn't get that without knowing it, could he?

DZIEMIAN: I think he said that he didn't know he had a wrist wound until much later.

(*Discussion off the record*)

SPECTER: I have no further questions of Dr. Dziemian. (*5H 93-94*)

McCLOY: Let me ask you this, Doctor, in your experience with gunshot wounds, is it possible for a man to be hit some time before he realizes it?

DR. SHAW: Yes. There can be a delay in the sensory reaction.

McCLOY: Yes; so that a man can think as of a given instant he was not hit, and when actually he could have been hit.

DR. SHAW: There can be an extending sensation and then just a gradual building up of a feeling of severe injury.

McCLOY: But there could be a delay in any appreciable reaction between the time of the impact of the bullet and the occurrence?

DR. SHAW: Yes; but in the case of a wound which strikes a bony substance such as a rib, usually the reaction is quite prompt.

(*4H 115-116*)

The Commission was wise to omit reference to the doctors' testimony, even in a footnote. It would be hard to argue that they supported the farfetched conjecture of a delayed reaction, despite the pressure of leading questions. It is true, as Dr. Arthur J. Dziemian said, that the Governor was not aware of his wrist wound until much later; yet it seems obvious from the Governor's own account that severe pain from the chest wound blocked out awareness of lesser pain. Perhaps that point was clarified during the off-the-record discussion.

The net effect of the medical testimony is hardly favorable to the proposition of a delayed reaction, and it would be idle to pretend that this further vitiation of the single-missile thesis is immaterial to the Commission's "essential findings."

The Commission is far more persuasive when it discusses the relative positions of the President and the Governor as evidence for the single-missile theory, but its arguments are by no means conclusive so long as the time of the Governor's shot and his posture at that time remain uncertain. Moreover, there is a cutoff point after which the Governor could not have received his injuries from a shot that came from the Book Depository window, whether or not that shot first struck the President. The Warren Report states that "at some point between Frames 235 and 240 is the last occasion when Governor Connally could have received his injuries, since in the frames following 240 he remained too far to his right." (*WR 106*) A footnote to that statement cites the testimony of FBI Expert Robert Frazier. (*5H 170*) However, Frazier's actual testimony (*5H 170-171*) is misrepresented in the Report, since he places the cut-off point at Frame 225. He states repeatedly that the Governor could have been struck between Frames 207 and 225 and sustained his actual wounds; and he specifically excludes Frames 235 and 240.[4]

Both Frazier and the Commission predicate the cut-off point on a shot that came from the Book Depository window, refusing to confront the possibility that he might have been shot from another location—a possibility that must be examined in the light of the Governor's lack of reaction before or at the cut-off time. Instead of examining all the possibilities in an impartial and scientific spirit, the Commission resorted to pure conjecture and, as laymen, posed the highly implausible and obviously dubious "delayed reaction" sub-hypothesis. The argument that the bullet that passed through the President's neck must have struck the Governor because it did not strike the car or any other occupants or objects (and it had to go *somewhere*) seems compelling at first glance. Against that argument one may cite the repeated published reports after the assassination that a bullet had lodged in the President's body and testimony indicating that a bullet had hit the pavement near the Presidential car during the shooting.[5]

[4] Frazier testified that "there is only one position beyond Frame 225 at which the Governor could have been struck" (*5H 170*) but he did not specify that position, nor was he asked by examining counsel to do so.

[5] The *Washington Post* reported on December 18, 1963—and *The New York Times* on January 26, 1964—that the bullet that hit the President in the right shoulder several inches below the collar-line had lodged in the body. The *Washington Post* said on May 29, 1966 (page A3, column 4) that "on December 18, 1963, the *Washington Post* and other newspapers reported on the basis of rumors from Dallas that the first bullet to strike the President 'was found deep in his shoulder.' *This report was confirmed prior to publication by the FBI.*" (Italics added)

LIEBELER: So, you were standing directly in front of the Depository and on the same side of Elm Street that the Depository is located?

MRS. BAKER: Yes.

LIEBELER: Tell me what you saw.

MRS. BAKER: Well, after he passed us, then we heard a noise and I thought it was firecrackers, because I saw a shot or something hit the pavement.

LIEBELER: And you heard that immediately after the first noise; is that right?

MRS. BAKER: Yes . . . I saw the bullet hit on down this way, I guess, right at the sign, angling out.   (7H 508-509)

Thanks to the initiative of another witness, Royce Skelton, we know that he too saw a bullet hit the pavement. He volunteered, when counsel had already thanked and dismissed him, that he had seen a bullet hit the pavement at the left front of the Presidential car. (6H 238) In addition to the observations of Skelton and Mrs. Baker, there is the fact (discussed earlier) that a bystander was cut on the cheek and a curbstone was hit by a bullet or bullet fragment. Taken as a whole, this evidence scarcely permits the Commission to postulate that the first bullet that struck the President must have hit the Governor because it did not hit anything else.

Other anomalies cannot be ignored in an evaluation of the single-missile thesis—the trajectory of the shots, for example. Arlen Specter, the assistant counsel who was primarily responsible for the medical and ballistics evidence, repeatedly posed to witnesses a hypothetical set of circumstances in which the shots that struck Kennedy and Connally followed a 45° angle of descent. (See 3H 362; 3H 373; 5H 92; and 6H 110) Dr. J. J. Humes testified that the trajectory of the wounds sustained by both men was about 45°. (2H 370) In his autopsy report, however, Dr. Humes said that the shots came from a point "behind and somewhat above the level of the deceased" (WR 543), which does not seem to agree with a sixth-story window or a 45° trajectory.

The 45° trajectory postulated repeatedly by Specter and others was abandoned abruptly when Dr. Robert Shaw told the Commission that its diagram of the Governor's wounds gave an incorrect position for the exit wound in the chest. He corrected the diagram by raising the exit wound (*4H 105, 112*), thus reducing the trajectory to 25°, the figure quoted in the Report. (*WR 93*)

The Report, however, does not base the trajectory of the bullets that hit the President on medical or physical findings; it utilizes other data. (*WR 106-107*) The trajectory from the Book Depository window to the car in Frames 210-225 (the interval during which the President was shot in the back, according to the Commission) ranged from 21°34′ to 20°11′, somewhat less than that of the bullets that hit the Governor. In absolute terms, that might suggest that the Governor was hit before Frame 210, when the car was closer to the Book Depository (but concealed from the sixth-floor window by thick tree foliage); on the other hand, if the 45° trajectory for the President's non-fatal wounds put forward by Dr. Humes and by Specter was maintained after the trajectory for Connally was corrected, it might have compelled the conclusion that the Governor was shot considerably later than the President.

How did the Commission establish the trajectory? According to the testimony (*5H 153, 162*) and the Report (*WR 106*), it was established by taking an average of the angle from the window to the car between Frames 210 and 225, which (after adjustment to allow for the 3° slope of the street) came to 17°43′30″; and by "piercing" stand-ins for Kennedy and Connally with a rod held at that angle of descent. (*CE 903*) Thus, it is hardly surprising that the rod went through the stand-ins at points "approximating" the sites of the wounds actually sustained by the victims. The disparity of almost 8° in the trajectory of Connally's wounds is written off to either a slight deflection of the bullet or a slight shift in the Governor's posture. (*WR 107*)

Thus, by virtue of those ingenious calculations, approximations, and speculations, a trajectory of 45° is reduced to one of about 17°, without regard for the physical law stating that the line between two fixed points (the Book Depository window and the car positioned at the Stemmons Freeway sign) is a constant.

The Warren Commission has formulated a new law: The shots came from the Book Depository window and no other point in the universe; everything else is mutable.

To regard such capriciously fluctuating "evidence" as authoritative or authentic would be folly, all the more so when the testimony of the groundskeeper at Dealey Plaza, Emmett Hudson, reveals that one of the two fixed points—the Stemmons sign—had been shifted from its place after the assassination and removed completely by early in 1965. (7H 562-563) Nevertheless, Liebeler, the counsel who examined Hudson, failed to ask a single question about the removal of the sign or to take the slightest interest in this provocative information. Consequently, we do not know if the sign was moved before or after the FBI re-enactment tests of May 24, 1964 or, for that matter, before or after the Secret Service re-enactments of December 5, 1963.

The repositioning and ultimate disappearance of the Stemmons sign is a mystery with ominous undertones. Having no interest in evidence which did not incriminate Oswald, the Warren Commission took not the slightest interest in the Stemmons sign and, needless to say, made no investigation into when and why it was moved.

Before leaving the subject of the Zapruder film, it is apropos to quote from a report written by Thomas Stamm after seeing a screening of the film at the National Archives in September 1965. Stamm wrote, in an unpublished manuscript:

Of greatest importance in the film is the sequence of the fatal shot and its aftermath. This sequence shows President Kennedy thrust violently back against the rear seat, from which he bounces forward and spins off to his left into Mrs. Kennedy's arms. Almost immediately he begins to fall away from Mrs. Kennedy as she rises in obvious shock, revulsion, and horror and climbs onto the back of the limousine from which she is thrust back into the car by Secret Service Agent Hill.

The sudden explosive violence with which President Kennedy is slammed back against the rear seat is unmistakable. It is within the realm of speculative possibility that the violent backward thrust of the President was caused by the sudden acceleration of the limousine, as Secret Service Agents Kellerman and Greer, in the front seats, made their effort to escape the murder site and obtain medical help at Parkland Hospital. Against that thesis is the fact that Mrs. Kennedy is obviously not thrust back but maintains her position while the President gyrates back, forward, and into her arms.

Against that thesis, also, is the testimony of Governor and Mrs. Connally, as noted in the Report: "Mrs. Connally heard a second shot fired and pulled her husband down into her lap. . . . The Governor was lying with his head on his wife's lap when he heard a shot hit the President. At that point, both Governor and Mrs. Connally observed brain tissue splatter over the interior of the car. According to Governor and Mrs. Connally, it was after this shot that Kellerman issued his emergency instruction and the car accelerated." (*WR 50*) No other testimony relating to this point is adduced in the Report, and the Commission apparently accepted the testimony of the Governor and his wife as accurate and factual.

The violent backward thrust of President Kennedy occurs, to the eye, at the instant of impact of the fatal shot. The two events appear to be simultaneous and to have the obvious relationship of cause and effect. The service of truth requires no other explanation.

That President Kennedy could have been thrust back violently against the rear seat in consequence of a bullet fired from above and behind him seems a manifest impossibility. This sequence in the Zapruder film, occupying a mere fraction of a second, invalidates the official autopsy finding and demolishes the Commission's thesis and findings of a lone gunman firing from the southeast corner sixth-floor window of the Depository. It makes of the Report a monstrous fabrication erected to obscure the truth which must now be disinterred despite the official verdict.

Subsequently other researchers have viewed the Zapruder film (thanks to the courtesy of Mr. Edward Kern of *Life* magazine, I was able to view some 25 screenings of the film and excellent color transparencies of the individual frames). Without exception or hesitation, each of the viewers has corroborated the dramatic thrust of the President's body back and to the left in reaction to the bullet that hits his head in Frame 313. Vincent J. Salandria and Gaeton Fonzi conclusively demonstrated the backward recoil by tracing the position of the body in successive frames, using two projectors and projecting one slide upon the other. The resultant diagram[6] constitutes conclusive and irrefutable proof that the bullet that sent the President violently backward and to his left was fired in front of and to the right of the car and not from the Book Depository. Some six months after that diagram was published no spokesman for the Warren Commission has challenged the data or the accompanying conclusion that the fatal shot came from somewhere on the grassy knoll.

The Zapruder film was screened many times for viewing by "Commission representatives and representatives of the FBI and Secret Service" in the Commission's building. (5H 138) The film was viewed also by doctors who had operated on Governor Connally, and by the Governor. To the critic who has seen the Zapruder film and gasped at this graphic proof of a conspiracy to kill the President—for there must have been a gunman in front of the car as well as behind it—one thing arouses even more alarm and anguish than the sight of his exploding head: the silence of the Warren Commission (and its lawyers, investigators, and witnesses) in regard to this visible evidence clearly implicating at least two riflemen in the crime.

That silence, as much as any other single abuse of logic or misrepresentation of evidence in the Warren Report, convicts the Commission of dishonesty and calculated deception. The Commission did not acknowledge the slam of the body against the back of the seat; it did not solicit opinion from experts as to whether that body recoil conceivably could be reconciled with a shot from behind the car; and it did not inform the public—the vast majority of whom will never view the Zapruder film at the National Archives—that the camera had recorded events central to the establishment of the truth and utterly inconsistent with the lone-assassin thesis.[7]

[6] *The Greater Philadelphia Magazine*, August 1966, p. 44.

[7] In January 1967 *Ramparts* published the results of a study conducted for the magazine by Dr. R. A. J. Riddle, assistant professor of physics at UCLA. After studying the relevant segment of the Zapruder film, Dr. Riddle pointed out that the law of conservation of momentum governs the movement of an object hit by a projectile and gives the object a motion in the same direction as the motion of the projectile. After applying that principle to Frames 310–323, Dr. Riddle reached a conclusion that "contradicts the findings of the Warren Commission"—that is, that the shot came from the front and right of the car.

THE CASE FOR THREE ASSASSINS
David S. Lifton and David Welsh

Ramparts / January 1967

THE WOUND IN THE THROAT

The Commission's contention that the bullet which entered President Kennedy's back went on to exit at his throat . . . is not supported by the evidence.

Left unanswered in [the previous] discussion, however, was the question: If the throat wound was not caused by the exit of the back bullet, how *was* it caused?

One theory is that a piece of bone or a metallic fragment pierced the President's throat at the time of the fatal head shot. The head shot, however, was not inflicted until Zapruder frame 313, and the President appeared to be grabbing at his throat at least as early as frame 225,[1] about five seconds before being hit in the head. It is therefore reasonable to assume that the throat wound was not caused by a fragment of bone or metal exiting from the fatal head wound.

The most likely possibility—that the throat wound was caused by a shot fired from the front—is consistent with the statements of Parkland Hospital doctors, the only medical personnel to see the wound. Their statements were reported in press accounts and in testimony before the Commission.

[1] WR 98.

A "How Could the President Have Been Shot in the Front from the Back?"

Veteran reporter Tom Wicker talked with doctors on the day of the assassination:

. . . Dr. Malcolm Perry, an attending surgeon, and Dr. Kemp Clark, chief of neurosurgery at Parkland Hospital, gave more details. Mr. Kennedy was *hit by a bullet in the throat*, just below the Adam's apple, they said. This wound had the appearance of a bullet's entry. . . .[2]

Early news reports are not always accurate, and it is possible that accounts written in the hectic hours immediately after the assassination might contain errors. It was four days after the assassination, however, when another veteran reporter, John Herbers, supported his colleague:

Dallas. Nov. 26 . . . Dr. Kemp Clark, who pronounced Mr. Kennedy dead, said one [bullet] *struck him about the necktie knot.* "It ranged downward in his chest and did not exit," the surgeon said.[3]

In the same issue of the New York Times that carried Herbers' story another item appeared. It cited "informed sources" explaining the frontal entry wound in terms of Oswald firing on the motorcade while it was still on Houston Street, before it made the better-than-90-degree turn onto Elm.[4]

The "informed sources" quoted by the Times four days after the assassination and the autopsy, explained the Parkland doctors' analysis of an entry wound in the throat by concluding that it was inflicted while the motorcade was still on Houston Street. At that time, of course, the Presidential car was *facing* the Texas School Book Depository, where the alleged sole assassin was firing.

But Life magazine, which had bought the original Zapruder film, soon knew better. The film showed that the President's car had already turned onto Elm and was over 100 feet past the Book Depository (and approaching the Grassy Knoll) when the

[2] New York Times, Nov. 23, 1963; italics added.
[3] New York Times, Nov. 27, 1963; italics added.
[4] New York Times, Nov. 27, 1963; italics added.

first wound was inflicted. (Life at first attempted an awkward explanation to support the Oswald-firing-from-the-rear thesis of the Commission,[5] but has now joined with earlier critics in asking for a reopening of the investigation.)

Nine days after the assassination, the St. Louis Post-Dispatch carried a story by renowned reporter Richard Dudman under the headline, "Uncertainties Remain Despite Police View of Kennedy Death." The subhead was, "Position of Wound Is Puzzling —Did Assailant Have an Accomplice?"

Dudman wrote:

The strangest circumstance of the shooting, in this reporter's opinion, is the position of the throat wound, thought to have been caused by the first of two shots that struck Mr. Kennedy. Surgeons who attended him at Parkland Hospital described it as an entrance wound. . . . The question that suggests itself is: *How could the President have been shot in the front from the back?* Dr. Perry described the bullet hole as an entrance wound. Dr. McClelland told the Post-Dispatch: "It certainly did look like an entrance wound." He explained that a bullet from a low velocity rifle like the one thought to have been used characteristically makes a small entrance wound, sets up shock waves inside the body and tears a big opening when it passes out the other side.

Dr. McClelland conceded that it was possible that the throat wound marked the exit of a bullet fired into the back of the President's neck . . . "but we are familiar with wounds," he said. "We see them every day—sometimes several a day. This did appear to be an entrance wound."[6]

The problem of resolving an entry wound in the throat with the proposition that a lone assassin was firing from the rear, hadn't gone away by the following week. The New York Times

[5] Life undertook to explain the contradiction in its issue of Nov. 29, 1963; "But the 8-mm. film shows the President *turning his body far around to the right as he waves to someone in the crowd. His throat is exposed—toward the sniper's nest—* just before he clutches it." (italics added)

Unfortunately for Life's explanation, the Zapruder film shows no such thing. One had only to look at the film frames published in that same issue—and more recently republished in Life for November, 1966—to see that the President was clearly facing forward and turned slightly to the right when he was shot.

[6] St. Louis Post-Dispatch, Dec. 1, 1963; italics added.

reported: ". . . Thirteen days after the assassination of President Kennedy, federal investigators were still reconstructing the crime on film today. . . . One question was *how the President could have received a bullet in the front of the throat* from a rifle in the Texas School Book Depository after his car had passed the building and was turning a gentle curve away from it. One explanation from a competent source was that the President had turned to his right to wave, and was struck at that moment."[7]

If the FBI, in reconstructing the event 13 days later, had access to the conclusion of the autopsy—that the throat wound was a wound of exit—it might not have puzzled over this problem. According to Dr. Humes, the autopsy report was written and transmitted to "higher authority" by Sunday, November 24. Why was the FBI reconstructing the crime the "wrong" way on December 5? Did it have the final autopsy report? Did it have another, earlier version? The next lines from the same Times story are not reassuring: "The best authority presumably on the *exact angle of entry* of the bullet is the man who conducted the autopsy. He is Dr. J. J. Humes of the Naval Medical Center, Bethesda, Md. Dr. Humes said he has been forbidden to talk."[8]

On the following March 16, Dr. Humes was indeed an authority, before the Warren Commission—on the angle of *exit*. Yet if we are to accept the findings of the Commission—then we must also accept the spectacle of the FBI reconstructing the crime *as though the front neck wound were one of entrance inflicted by a lone assassin firing from behind,* and doing so two weeks after the autopsy, apparently without access to authoritative medical evidence as to the origin of the shots. J. Edgar Hoover disclosed that the FBI and the Warren Commission did not receive *official* copies of the autopsy report until December 23, 1963, from the Secret Service.[9]

. . . on December 18, the Post-Dispatch carried the headline, "Secret Service Gets Revision on Kennedy Wound," with the subhead, "After Visit by Agent, Doctors Say Shot was from the Rear." The story read, in part:

[7] New York Times, Dec. 6, 1963; italics added.
[8] New York Times, Dec. 6, 1963; italics added.
[9] New York Times, Nov. 26, 1966.

Two Secret Service agents called last week on Dallas surgeons who attended President Kennedy and obtained a reversal of their original view that the bullet in his neck entered from the front.

The investigators did so by showing the surgeons a document described as an autopsy report from the United States Naval Hospital at Bethesda. The surgeons changed their original view to conform with the report they were shown.

"There was no coercion at all," Dr. Robert N. McClelland told the Post-Dispatch. "They didn't say anything like 'This is what you think, isn't it?' "

The surgeons' earlier description of a wound in the front of the President's throat as an entry wound had cast doubt on the official belief that Lee Harvey Oswald was the only assassin. . . . The surgeons now support the official view that both bullets that struck the President were from behind. . . . They now believe that the bullet in the neck entered from the back . . . and passed out through the hole in front, about two inches below the Adam's apple.[10]

B THE PARKLAND DOCTORS' TESTIMONY

Because the outlines of the frontal throat wound were destroyed by an emergency tracheotomy performed in an attempt to revive the President, the only persons able to see the original throat wound were the staff at Parkland Hospital.

Let us examine their testimony:

DR. MALCOLM PERRY: "The wound was roughly spherical to oval in shape, not a punched-out wound, actually, nor was it particularly ragged. It was rather clean cut, but the blood obscured any detail about the edges of the wound exactly."[11]

DR. ROBERT MCCLELLAND: ". . . if I saw the wound in its state in which Dr. Perry described it to me, I would probably initially think this were an entrance wound. . . ."[12]

DR. RONALD JONES: "The hole was very small and relatively clean

[10] St. Louis Post-Dispatch, Dec. 18, 1963.
[11] VI, 9.
[12] VI, 37.

cut, as you would see in a bullet that is entering rather than exiting from a patient."[13]

DR. CHARLES BAXTER: "Judging from the caliber of the rifle that we later found or became acquainted with, this would more resemble a wound of entry."[14]

REGISTERED NURSE MARGARET HENCHLIFFE also thought is was an entrance wound. She testified that she had never seen an exit bullet hole that looked like that one.[15]

The Parkland staff clearly showed, by their testimony, that they observed the throat puncture to have all the characteristics of an entrance wound (small, clean cut) and none of the characteristics of the usual type of exit wound (large, jagged edges). But Commission Counsel Specter was not content to hear testimony on what the only doctors who had seen it *observed* of the wound. In his questioning, he asked each of them to *assume* that the bullet had traversed from back to front through the President via a "fascia channel" (fascia are thin tissue membranes that connect muscle), undeflected, without wobble or yaw. The doctors were then asked to express an opinion, based on that type of passage, as to whether the throat puncture was consistent with an exit wound.

Typical was Specter's questioning of Dr. James Carrico:

Permit me to add some facts which I shall ask you to assume as being true for purposes of having you express an opinion. First of all, assume that the President is struck by a . . . bullet from a rifle . . . at a time when the President was approximately 160 to 250 feet from the weapon [Oswald's range], with the President being struck from the rear at a downward angle of approximately 45 degrees [Specter here seems to accept the angle cited in the FBI Summary Report, instead of the angle of about 15 degrees shown in the artist's drawing—Commission Exhibit 385—which accompanies the autopsy report; this 45 degree angle would render the pass-through theory just that much more ridiculous], being struck on the upper right posterior thorax [near the base of the neck]. . . . Assume further that the missile passed through the

[13] VI, 55.
[14] VI, 42.
[15] VI, 141.

body of the President striking no bones, traversing the neck and sliding between the large muscles in the posterior aspect of the President's body through a fascia channel . . . then exiting precisely at the point where you observe the *puncture wound* to exist. Now based on those facts, was the appearance of the wound in your opinion consistent with being an exit wound?[17]

Dr. Carrico responded: *"With those facts, and the fact as I understand it no other bullet was found, this would be . . . I believe . . . an exit wound."*[18]

Dr. Perry, who had given the vivid description of an entry-type wound quoted above, responded to similar questioning ". . . with the facts which you have made available and with these assumptions, I believe that it was an exit wound."[19]

It is obvious that such yanked-from-mouth testimony cannot be taken seriously as independent medical opinion—when, questioned on whether the wound was caused by an entry or an exit, the doctors are asked to assume the wound to be an exit to begin with. Norman Redlich, who wrote chapter three of the Warren Report, made liberal use of such testimony, safely out of context, to support the conclusion that the throat puncture was an exit wound.

Some of the Parkland doctors, however, gave more argumentative answers to Specter's leading questions.

Dr. Charles Baxter testified:

Although it would be *unusual* for a high velocity missile of this type to cause a wound as you have described, the passage through tissue planes . . . could have well resulted in the sequence which you outline; namely, that the anterior wound does represent a wound of exit. . . . It would be *unlikely* because . . . the further it went, the more jagged would be the damage that it created; so that ordinarily there would have been a rather large wound of exit.[20]

Dr. Ronald Jones was highly dubious of the Commission's thesis, but assented with one important condition:

[17] III, 362; italics added.
[18] III, 362; WR 92.
[19] III, 373; WR 92.
[20] VI, 42; italics added.

DR. JONES: If this were an exit wound, you would think that it exited at a very low velocity to produce no more damage than this had done, and if this were a missile of high velocity, you would expect more of an explosive type of exit wound, with more tissue destruction than this appeared to have on superficial examination.

SPECTER: Would it be consistent, then, with an exit wound but of low velocity, as you put it?

DR. JONES: Yes: of very low velocity to the point that you might think that this bullet barely made it through the soft tissues and just enough to drop out of the skin on the opposite side.[21]

Dr. Jones' testimony is of singular importance. His condition for conceding that the throat wound may have been a wound of exit—that the bullet had to be traveling so slowly as to "barely make it through"—precludes the possibility that it subsequently went through Connally. It could not, then, be the same bullet that hit Connally and smashed ten centimeters of his fifth rib, fractured his right wrist, and went on to wound his thigh. By this criterion, even if the bullet defied all the evidence and passed through Kennedy it would not have possessed sufficient energy to cause *any* of Connally's wounds.

The Zapruder film shows that the President had his back to the Texas School Book Depository throughout the assassination sequence, and that at the time the throat wound was believed to have been inflicted, he was facing slightly to his right. This position is consistent with the strong evidence that the throat puncture was a wound of entry.

There was at least one gunman firing from the front. There were at least three assassins.

THE 64 WITNESSES INDICATING FIRING FROM THE GRASSY KNOLL AREA

An estimated 32 known witnesses indicated that shots were fired from the Book Depository,[22] an observation consistent with the strong evidence that at least two gunmen were firing from somewhere to the rear of the motorcade.

[21] VI, 55.
[22] Harold Feldman, Minority of One, March 1965.

By the same token 64 known witnesses indicated that shots originated from forward of the motorcade, from the vicinity of the Grassy Knoll, lending further credence to the physical evidence that President Kennedy was hit from the right front. At least four persons saw smoke in the Knoll area, several smelled smoke there, and a healthy majority of witnesses heard the sound of shots coming from the Knoll. Yet the Commission was able to conclude: ". . . There is no question in the mind of any member of the Commission that all the shots . . . were fired from the sixth floor window of the Texas School Book Depository . . . There is *no credible evidence* that the shots were fired . . . from any other location."[23]

One reason for the Commission's apparent ignorance of this impressive body of evidence is their consistent failure to call witnesses who indicated, in statements to sheriff's deputies or the FBI, that they thought shots came from the Knoll. For example, photographs show approximately 20 persons standing with their backs to the Knoll, facing the Presidential motorcade, at the time of the assassination. Of these, 12 were interviewed by the sheriff's department or the FBI, 10 of whom thought the shots had come from the Knoll directly behind them. Only two were called to testify before the Commission.

Photographs and documents show more than 100 more witnesses to the event than were interviewed by any investigative agency, let alone the Commission. To call them all, said one member of the Commission staff, would have been "redundant."

A. Witnesses Standing on the Triple Overpass:

A1. Sam Holland, railroad signal supervisor for the Union Terminal, was standing on the Triple Overpass inspecting signals and switches when he stopped to watch the parade. He said in a sworn affidavit on the day of the assassination:

. . . The President's car was . . . just about to the arcade [when] I heard what I thought for the moment was a firecracker . . . and I looked over towards the arcade and trees and saw a puff of smoke come

[23] WR 19.

from the trees. . . . The puff of smoke I saw definitely came from be-hind the arcade and through the trees.[24]

What Holland calls the "arcade"—also called by other witnesses the "monument"—is a structure on the Grassy Knoll.

Testifying later before the Commission, Holland reiterated:

I have no doubt about seeing that puff of smoke come out from under those trees. . . . I definitely saw the puff of smoke and heard the re-port from under those trees.[25]

In his lengthy and detailed testimony, Holland tells about "two policemen that were riding in that motorcade and one of them throwed the motorcycle down right in the middle of the street and run towards that location with his gun in his hand." They were heading, he said, toward "where I saw the puff of smoke. And another one tried to ride up the hill on his motorcycle and got halfway up there and he run up the rest of the way on foot."[26]

Holland advised the Commission that he immediately ran to the corner of the fence near the arcade and that by the time he arrived there were 12 or 15 policemen and people he surmised to be plainclothesmen. He said that among the other cars backed up to the fence was a station wagon with mud on the bumper "as if someone had cleaned their foot, or stood up on the bumper to see over the fence." On the grass by the station wagon was "a spot, I'd say three foot by two foot, looked to me like somebody had been standing there for a long period. I guess if you could count them about a hundred foottracks in that little spot and also mud up on the bumper of that station wagon."[27]

A2. Frank Reilly, electrician for the Union Terminal, standing with Holland on the Overpass, told the Commission: "It seemed to me like the shots come out of the trees. . . . On the north side of Elm Street at the corner up there. . . . at that park where all the shrubs is up there . . . up the slope."[28]

[24] XXIV, 212.
[25] VI, 244.
[26] VI, 247.
[27] VI, 244-6.
[28] VI, 230.

A3. James Simmons, railroad employee standing on the Triple Overpass, was interviewed by the FBI. An FBI report states:

Simmons said he thought he saw exhaust fumes of smoke near the embankment. . . .[29]

A4. Clemon Johnson, machinist for the railroad, standing on the Triple Overpass, was interviewed by the FBI (never by the Commission). An FBI report says: "Mr. Johnson stated that white smoke was observed near the pavilion."[30]

A5. Austin L. Miller, mail clerk and tariff compiler for the Texas-Louisiana Freight Bureau located in Union Terminal, was standing on the railroad overpass. He testified:

I turned and looked toward the—there is a little plaza sitting on the hill. I looked over there to see if anything was there, who threw the firecracker or whatever it was. . . .[31]

Miller also swears in a sheriff's department affidavit: "One shot apparently hit the street past the car. I saw something which I thought was smoke or steam coming from a group of trees north of Elm off the railroad tracks."[32]

B. WITNESSES STANDING ON THE GRASSY KNOLL

B6. Abraham Zapruder, who was filming the assassination sequence from a concrete abutment extending from the pavilion, testified to Assistant Commission Counsel Wesley Liebeler:

LIEBELER: . . . you say the police ran over behind the concrete structure behind you and down the railroad track behind that, is that right?

ZAPRUDER: . . . yes, some of them were motorcycle cops—I guess they left their motorcycles running and they were running right behind me, of course, in the line of the shooting. I guess they thought it came from right behind me.[33]

[29] XXII, 833.
[30] XXII, 836.
[31] VI, 225.
[32] XIX, 485.
[33] VII, 571.

Zapruder said his initial impression was that "it came from back of me," but he added that he could not be positive because "there was too much reverberation. There was an echo which gave me a sound all over."[34] Later in his testimony the following exchange took place:

ZAPRUDER: . . . they claim it was proven it could be done by one man. You know there was an indication there were two?

LIEBELER: Your films were extremely helpful to the work of the Commission, Mr. Zapruder.[35]

B7. Mary Woodward, Maggie Brown, Aurelia Lorenzo and Ann Donaldson, four newspaperwomen watching the motorcade from the sidewalk near the east end of the pavilion, said they heard ". . . a horrible, ear-shattering noise coming from behind us and a little to the right."[36]

B8. Jean Newman, who was standing halfway between the Stemmons Freeway sign (about halfway down the Elm Street slope) and the Depository, facing the motorcade, said in a sheriff's department affidavit: ". . . the shots came from my right"[37] (the Depository was to her left).[38]

B9. John Arthur Chism swore in his sheriff's department affidavit: "I was standing with my wife and three year old boy, we were directly in front of the Stemmons Freeway sign. . . . At this point [just after the second shot was fired], I looked behind me, to see whether it was a fireworks display or something."[39] Behind Chism was the Grassy Knoll.

B10. Marion Faye Chism, his wife, said in her affidavit: "It came from what I thought was behind us."[40] The Chisms were not called to testify before the Commission.

B11 and B12. Mr. and Mrs. William Newman were standing near the curb with their two children, further down from the Stemmons Freeway sign, directly in front of the concrete wall on

[34] VII, 571-2.
[35] VII, 576.
[36] Dallas Morning News, Nov. 23, 1963; Feldman, Minority of One, March, 1965.
[37] XXIV, 218.
[38] XXII, 843.
[39] XXIV, 204.
[40] XXIV, 205.

the Grassy Knoll. In William Newman's sheriff's department affidavit, filed within hours after the shooting, he swears:

I was looking directly at him when he was *hit in the side of the head.* . . . Then we fell down on the grass as it seemed that we were in direct path of fire. . . . I thought the shot had come from the garden directly behind me, that was on an elevation from where I was right on the curb. I do not recall looking towards the Texas School Book Depository. I looked back in the vicinity of the garden.[41]

Mrs. Gayle Newman supported her husband's testimony. Neither was called by the Commission.

B13. Emmett Hudson, caretaker of Dealey Plaza, was a few feet past the Newmans, standing on the steps that ascend the Grassy Knoll. In his sheriff's department affidavit filed that afternoon, he swears: ". . . I was sitting on the front steps of the sloping area and about half way down the steps. . . . The shots that I heard definitely came from behind and above me."[42][43]

B14. A. J. Millican, standing on the north side of Elm Street, about halfway between Houston Street and the underpass on the Grassy Knoll, states in his deposition:

Just after the President's car passed, I heard three shots come from up towards Houston and Elm right by the Book Depository Building and then immediately I heard two more shots come from the Arcade between the Book Store and the underpass, and then three more shots came from the same direction only sounded further back. It sounded approximately like a .45 automatic, or a high powered rifle. Then everybody started running up the hill.[44]

C. WITNESSES STANDING IN DEALEY PLAZA

C15. Ronald B. Fisher, standing on the curb at the southwest corner of Houston and Elm (the Texas School Book Depository is on the northwest corner; the Presidential car was heading west) during the assassination, was questioned by Commission Counsel David W. Belin:

[41] XXIV, 219; italics added.
[42] XXIV, 213.
[43] VII, 560; italics added.
[44] XIX, 486.

BELIN: Where did the shots appear to be coming from?

FISHER: . . . from just west of the School Book Depository Building. There were some railroad tracks and there were some railroad cars back in there.

BELIN: And they appeared to be coming from those railroad cars?

FISHER: Well, that area somewhere. . . . We ran up to the top of the hill there where all the Secret Service men had run, thinking that that's where the bullets had come from since they seemed to be searching that area over there.[45]

c16. Mrs. Jean Hill, school teacher and companion of Mrs. Mary Moorman, was standing on the curb of Dealey Plaza directly opposite the concrete wall on the Knoll—as close to the Presidential limousine as any other witness before the Commission. She testified:

We were standing on the curb and I jumped to the edge of the street and yelled. "Hey, we want to take your picture!" . . . The shot rang out. Mary took the picture and fell to the ground and I . . . grabbed my slacks and said, "Get down, they're shooting. . . ." I have always said there were some four to six shots. There were three shots—one right after the other, and a distinct pause . . . and then I heard more. . . . They were rather rapidly fired. . . . I think there were at least four or five shots and perhaps six. . . .[46]

I frankly thought they were coming from the Knoll. . . . I thought it was just people shooting from the Knoll. . . . I did think there was more than one person shooting . . . the way the gun report sounded . . . the timing. . . .[47]

The [first] three were fired as though one person were firing . . . just like you could reload and fire again. . . . I thought they [the rest of the shots] were different—I thought the sequence was quicker . . . more automatic.[48]

Mrs. Hill testified that she had talked to a Secret Service man on the afternoon of the assassination, and that she had asked him, "Am I a kook or what's wrong with me? . . . They keep saying

[45] VI, 195 -6.
[46] VI, 206-7.
[47] VI, 212-3.
[48] VI, 207.

three shots—three shots . . . I know I heard more. I heard from four to six shots anyway." She testified that the Secret Service man replied, "Mrs. Hill, we were standing at the window and we heard more shots also, but we have three wounds and we have three bullets [an apparent reference to the three spent shells found on the sixth floor of the Depository], three shots is all that we are willing to say right now."[49]

As soon as the motorcade passed, Mrs. Hill testified, she saw:

. . . a man up there running, or getting away . . . at the tip of the slope. . . .[50]

Commission Counsel Arlen Specter had Mrs. Hill indicate the location of the running man on a hand-drawn sketch. The sketch appears in the hearings as "Hill Exhibit 5." It is stamped with the notation, "TOP SECRET."[51] Nobody knows why.

Within hours of the shooting, a local newsman, James Featherstone, instructed Mrs. Hill not to mention that she had seen the running man. She testified:

He said, "You know you were wrong about seeing a man running." He said, "You didn't . . ." and I said, "But I did," and he said, "No, don't say that any more on the air." . . . He said . . . that the shots had come from a window up in the Depository and for me not to say that any more, that I was wrong about it. . . .[52]

c17. Charles Brehm told police reporter George Carter of the Dallas Times-Herald that he was standing on the curb approximately ten feet from the Presidential limousine when the shots struck. Carter wrote: "Brehm seemed to think the shots came from in front of or beside the President. He explained the President did not slump forward as he would have after being shot from the rear."[53]

[49] VI, 220-1.
[50] VI, 210-3.
[51] XX, 158.
[52] VI, 222.
[53] Dallas Times-Herald, Nov. 22, 1963.

D. WITNESSES IN OR IMMEDIATELY OUTSIDE THE DEPOSITORY

D18. William Shelley, manager of the Depository, testified that he was on the top landing of the entrance watching the motorcade when he heard the shots:

BALL: What seemed to be the direction or source of the sound?

SHELLEY: Sounded like it came from the west.[54]

The Oswald "nest," of course, was directly over Shelley's head. To the west of his position is the Grassy Knoll area.

D19. Roy S. Truly, superintendent of the Depository, was standing in front of the building at the time of the shots. He joined a policeman, Marrion Baker, and showed him the way to the top of the Depository.

[Commission Counsel David] BELIN: Where did you think the shots came from?

TRULY: I thought the shots came from the vicinity [of] the railroad or the WPA project, behind the WPA project west of the building [the reference is to the pavilion on the Knoll].

BELIN: Did you have any conversation with the officer . . . about where you thought the shots came from?

TRULY: I said, ". . . I think we are wasting our time up here," or words to that effect, "I don't believe these shots came from the building."[55]

D20. Ochus Virgil Campbell, vice president of the Depository, was standing next to Truly in front of the building. He gave an affidavit to the FBI:

. . . I heard shots being fired from a point which I thought was near the railroad tracks located over the viaduct on Elm Street.[56]

D21. Steven F. Wilson, vice president of a textbook publishing company, watched the motorcade from his corner office on the

[54] VI, 328-9.
[55] III, 227.
[56] XXII, 638.

third floor of the Depository—three floors directly beneath the Oswald "nest." Wilson said in an FBI affidavit:

At that time it seemed the shots came from the west end of the building or from the colonnade located on Elm Street across from the west end of our building. The shots really did not sound like they came from above me.[57]

D22. Mrs. Alvin Hopson was looking out of a fourth floor window on the south side of the Depository, facing on Elm Street, during the assassination. Although she was never called by the Warren Commission, she was questioned by the FBI, which reported:

She stated that it did not sound to her like the sounds were coming from her building. . . . She stated she thought they had been set off on the street below, and she saw people on the street running toward the underpass and the railroad tracks.[58]

D23. Mrs. Charles Thomas (Avery) Davis was standing on the steps of the Depository, where she worked, when she heard "three explosions." She told the FBI, "I did not know from which direction the shots had come, but thought they were from the direction of the viaduct which crosses Elm Street west from where I was standing."[59]

D24. Dorothy Ann Garner was watching the motorcade from a fourth floor window in the Depository when she heard the shots. She said in an FBI affidavit, "I thought at the time the shots or reports came from a point to the west of the building."[60]

D25. Mrs. George Andrew (Dolores Arlene) Kounas was outside the Depository, her place of employment, when she heard gunfire. She told the FBI:

Although I was across the street from the Depository building and was looking in the direction of the building as the motorcade passed and

[57] XXII, 685.
[58] XXIV, 521.
[59] XXII, 642.
[60] XXII, 648.

following the shots, I did not look up at the building as I had thought the shots came from a westerly direction in the vicinity of the viaduct.[61]

D26. Otis Neville Williams, a bookkeeping supervisor at the Depository, who was standing on the steps of the building when the assassination occurred, told the FBI that he heard "three loud blasts" and that "I thought these blasts or shots came from the direction of the viaduct which crosses Elm Street."[62]

D27. Victoria Adams was watching from a pair of windows on the fourth floor of the Book Depository, where she worked. The alleged assassin's window was two floors above her and to her left; the Grassy Knoll was below and to her right. Testifying about the source of the shots, she said, ". . . It seemed as if it came from the right below rather than from the left above."[63]

D28. Billy Lovelady, an employee of the Depository who at the time of the assassination was standing on the steps at the entrance to the building, was questioned by Commission Counsel Joseph Ball:

BALL: Where was the direction of the sound?

LOVELADY: Right there around that concrete little deal on that knoll. . . .

BALL: How did you happen to go down there?

LOVELADY: . . . because everybody was running . . . toward that way; everybody thought it was coming from that direction.[64]

Lovelady told the FBI, "I did not at any time believe the shots had come from the Texas School Book Depository Building."[65]

D29. Danny Arce, who was standing in front of the Depository, where he worked, testified: "I thought [the shots] came from the railroad tracks to the west" of the Depository.[66]

D30. Wesley Frazier, the Depository employee who had driven

[61] XXII, 659.
[62] XXII, 683.
[63] VI, 388.
[64] VI, 338-9.
[65] XXII, 662.
[66] VI, 365.

Oswald to work that morning, was standing on the steps of the Depository building. He testified:

Well, to be frank with you I thought it come from down there, you know, where that underpass is. There is a series, quite a few number, of them railroad tracks running together and from where I was standing it sounded like it was coming from down the railroad tracks there.[67]

D31. Joseph Molina was standing on the steps of the Depository building. He was interviewed by the Commission:

BALL: Where—what was the source of this sound?

MOLINA: . . . sort of kind of came from the west side. . . . I didn't want to think what was happening . . . but I wanted to find out so I went down to where the grassy slope is. . . .[68]

D32. Mrs. Donald Baker, who had been standing at the southwestern corner of the Depository—at the end of the building nearest the Grassy Knoll—testified that she heard shots after the President's car passed the building.

LIEBELER: Did you have any idea where they were coming from?

MRS. BAKER: Well, the way it sounded . . . there was a railroad track that runs behind the building . . . so I guess it would be by the underpass . . . as well as I can remember now, back there, and we all ran to the plaza. . . .

LIEBELER: And you say there are some railroad tracks back in there . . . immediately behind Dealey Plaza away from Elm Street . . . and is that where you thought the shots came from?

MRS. BAKER: Yes.[69]

D33. James Jarman Jr., a Depository employee, was on the fifth floor of the building watching the motorcade from the southeast windows. He thought the shots came from below, near the motorcade.[70]

[67] II, 234.
[68] VI, 371-2.
[69] VII, 510-1.
[70] III, 204.

Jarman was standing with two other employees, Bonnie Ray Williams and Harold Norman, both of whom testified that they heard shots from above them. Upon hearing the shots, however, the immediate reaction of all three men was to run to the west side of the building, not upstairs. "We saw the policemen and people running. . . . There are some tracks on the west side of the building, railroad tracks. They were running towards that way and so we all ran that way."[71]

Williams was later questioned by Commissioner Gerald Ford:

FORD: Why didn't you go up to the sixth floor?
WILLIAMS: I really don't know. We just never did think about it.[72]

E. MEMBERS OF THE DALLAS COUNTY SHERIFF'S DEPARTMENT

Because law enforcement officers are trained observers and familiar with firearms, the following sheriff's deputies, as well as Secret Service agents and Dallas police officers in the sections to follow, are being treated separately.

E34. E. L. Boone was standing in front of the sheriff's office on Main Street at Houston, a block south of Elm. He raced across Houston Street when he heard shots coming from the vicinity of the President's car (only Dealey Plaza separated him from the car).

"Some of the bystanders said the shots came from the overpass," Boone said. "I ran across the street [Elm] and up the imbankment [sic] over the retaining wall and into the freight yard. . . .[73]

E35. Harry Weatherford, standing in the same place as Boone, said in his sworn affidavit:

. . . I heard a loud report which I thought was a railroad torpedo, as it sounded as if it came from the railroad yard. . . . By this time I was running towards the railroad yards where the sound seemed to come from.[74]

[71] III, 175.
[72] III, 177.
[73] XIX, 508.
[74] XIX, 502.

E36. Harold E. Elkins, who was also standing in front of the sheriff's office at the time of the shooting, declared in an investigation report:

I immediately ran to the area from which it sounded like the shots had been fired. This is an area between the railroads and the Texas School Book Depository. . . . There were several other officers in this area, and we secured it from the public. . . . Later a City of Dallas policeman came to our office with three prisoners who he had arrested on the railroad yards. I took these three to the city jail and turned them over to Captain Fritz.[75]

There is no mention in the Warren Report of who these men were, why they were arrested, or the disposition of their cases.

E37. Seymour Weitzman was questioned by Commission Counsel Ball:

WEITZMAN: I immediately ran toward the President's car. Of course, it was speeding away and somebody said the shots or the firecracker, whatever it was at that time, we still didn't know the President was shot, came from the wall. I immediately scaled that wall.

BALL: What is the location of that wall?

WEITZMAN: It would be between the railroad overpass and I can't remember the name of that little street that runs off Elm; it's cater-corner—the section there between the—what do you call it?—the monument section?[76]

BALL: Didn't you, when you went over to the railroad yard, talk to some yardman?

WEITZMAN: I asked a yardman if he had seen or heard anything during the passing of the President. He said that he thought he saw somebody throw something through a bush. . . .

BALL: Did the yardman tell you where he thought the noise came from?

WEITZMAN: Yes, sir; he pointed out the wall section where there was a bunch of shrubbery. . . .[77]

[75] XIX, 540.
[76] VII, 106.
[77] VII, 109.

E38. Roger Craig was standing in front of the sheriff's office. "At the retort [sic] of the first shot," he stated, "I started running . . . up the terrace on Elm Street, and into the railroad yards."[78]

E39. A. D. McCurley was also standing at the front entrance of the sheriff's office when the shots were fired. He said:

I rushed towards the park and saw people running towards the railroad yards . . . and I ran over and jumped a fence and a railroad worker stated to me that he believed the smoke from the bullets came from the vicinity of a stockade fence which surrounds the park area.[79]

E40. J. E. Decker is the sheriff of Dallas County. He was riding in a car immediately ahead of the President's car.

I noted motorcycle officers coming off their cycles and running up the embankment. . . . I took the microphone and requested the [Dallas Police Department dispatcher] to notify all officers in my department to immediately get over to the area where shooting occurred and saturate the area of the park. . . .[80]

The "park" referred to by Sheriff Decker is the Grassy Knoll.

E41. J. L. Oxford reported that shots rang out as the end of the motorcade passed in front of him. He declared:

Officer McCurley [E39, above] and myself ran across Houston Street on across Elm and down to the underpass. When we got there, everyone was looking toward the railroad yards. . . . When we got over there, there was a man who told us that he had seen smoke up in the corner of the fence. We went on up to the corner of the fence to see what we could find. . . .[81]

E42. Luke Mooney was another deputy who was standing in front of the sheriff's office when he heard the shots. "I started running across Houston Street and down across the lawn to the

[78] XIX, 524.
[79] XIX, 514.
[80] XIX, 458.
[81] XIX, 530.

triple underpass," he stated, "and up the terrace to the railroad yards. I searched, along with many other officers, this area. . . ."[82]

E43. Jack Falkner, a deputy who later helped to search the Depository, said in his investigative report:

When we got down to the third floor, we talked to office workers who told us they were looking out of the third floor window when the shots were fired from the street near the concrete arcade.[83]

E44. I. C. Todd, watching the motorcade from Houston Street, said that after hearing the shots he "immediately recognized them as being gunfire. I ran across the street and went behind the railroad tracks. . . ."[84]

E45. James N. Crawford, deputy district clerk at the Dallas County Courthouse, watched the motorcade from the corner of Houston and Elm. He was questioned by Commission Counsel Joseph Ball:

BALL: Did you have any impression as to the source of the sound, from what direction the sound came, the sound of the explosion?
CRAWFORD: Yes; I do . . . I thought it was a backfire in the cavalcade from down the hill, down the hill toward the underpass.[85]

F. SECRET SERVICE AGENTS

F46. Roy Kellerman was the Secret Service agent for the President. He was riding in the right front seat of the President's car. He testified before the Commission:

. . . there was a sign on the side of the road which I don't recall what it was or what it said, but we no more than passed that and you are in the open. . . .[86]

[82] XIX, 528.
[83] XIX, 511.
[84] XIX, 543.
[85] VI, 173.
[86] II, 73.

SPECTER: You say that you turned to your right immediately after you heard a shot?

KELLERMAN: Yes, sir.

SPECTER: What was the reason for your reacting to your right?

KELLERMAN: That was the direction I heard this noise, pop.[87]

The sign to which Kellerman referred was probably the Stemmons Freeway sign mentioned in other testimony and shown in the Zapruder film. Directly to Kellerman's right at the moment the gunfire sounded was the Grassy Knoll.

F47. Clinton Hill was riding in the Presidential follow-up car with fellow Secret Service agent Emory Roberts. At the time of the shooting, the Depository was to the rear of their vehicle; the Grassy Knoll was on the right. Hill was also questioned by Commission Counsel Specter:

SPECTER: And did you have a reaction or impression as to the source or point of origin of the second shot that you described?

HILL: It was right, but I cannot say for sure that it was rear, because when I mounted the car it was—it had a different sound, first of all, than the first sound that I heard. The second one had almost a double sound. . . .[88]

F48. Emory Roberts was riding in the front seat of the follow-up car directly behind the President. He stated, "I could not determine from what direction the shots came, but felt they had come from the right side."[89]

F49. Paul Landis Jr. was riding in the right rear of the follow-up car. He recalled: ". . . I heard what sounded like the report of a high powered rifle from behind me, over my right shoulder." An estimated two or three seconds later, Landis heard another shot. "I still was not certain from which direction the second shot came," he related, "but my reaction at this time was that the shot came from somewhere towards the front, right-hand side of the road."[90]

[87] II, 74.
[88] II, 144.
[89] XVIII, 739.
[90] XVIII, 754-5.

F50. Forrest Sorrels, head of the Dallas office of the Secret Service, was riding in the lead car of the motorcade. Almost at the Triple Underpass when the shots rang out, he testified that he ". . . turned around to look up on this terrace part there, because the sound sounded like it came from the back and up in that direction."[91]

G. DALLAS POLICE OFFICERS

G51. Jesse Curry, the chief of police, spoke over the police radio at 12:30 p.m.:

Notify station five to move all men available out of my department back into the railroad yards and try to determine what happened and hold everything secure until Homicide and other investigators can get in there.[92]

G52. Robert Hargis, the motorcycle patrolman riding escort at the left rear of the Presidential car:

. . . At the time it sounded like the shots were right next to me. . . . There was something in my head that said that they probably could have been coming from the railroad overpass, because I thought since I had got splattered, with blood—I was just a little back and left of . . . Mrs. Kennedy, but I didn't know. . . . I ran up to this kind of a little wall, brick wall up there to see if I could get a better look on the bridge, and, of course, I was looking all around that place by that time.

Hargis then jumped back on his motorcycle and "rode underneath the first underpass to look on the opposite side in order to see if I could see anyone running away from the scene. . . ."[93]

G53. Clyde Haygood, the motorcycle policeman riding to the right rear of the Presidential car, was just turning the corner from Houston onto Elm when he heard shots:

[91] VII, 345.
[92] XXI, 390-1.
[93] VI, 294-6.

... I could see all these people laying on the ground there on Elm. Some of them were pointing back up to the railroad yard, and a couple of people were headed back up that way. . . . And I left my motor on the street and ran to the railroad yard.[94]

G54. E. L. Smith, who at the time of the shots was standing catercorner from the Depository, testified to the Commission:

I thought when it came to my mind that there were shots, and I was pretty sure there were when I saw his [President Kennedy's] car because they were leaving in such a hurry, I thought they were coming from this area here [the Grassy Knoll area], and I ran over there and checked back of it. . . .[95]

G55. J. M. Smith was standing at Houston and Main when he heard the shots. He testified, ". . . This woman came up to me and she was just in hysterics. She told me, 'They are shooting the President from the bushes.' "[96] Smith said he ran past the Depository, up the Grassy Knoll and into the parking lot behind. In a newspaper interview he said that he smelled gunpowder there, a "faint smell of it—I could tell it was in the air."[97]

G56. Earle Brown, on duty at a railroad overpass directly behind the railroad yards, testified, "I heard these shots and then I smelled this gunpowder."[98]

H. Witnesses Riding in the Motorcade

H57. Robert Jackson, a staff photographer for the Dallas Times-Herald who rode in the motorcade, testified:

It did sound like it came from ahead of us or from that general vicinity but I could not tell whether it was high up or on the ground. . . . It did sound as though it came from somewhere around the head of the motorcade.[99]

[94] VI, 298.
[95] VII, 568-9.
[96] VII, 535.
[97] The Texas Observer, Dec. 13, 1963.
[98] VI, 233.
[99] II, 162.

Jackson also saw a rifle being withdrawn from a window of the Depository.

H58. Mrs. John Connally, wife of the Governor and a passenger in the Presidential limousine, testified, "I had not thought of whether they were high or low or where. *They just came from the right*; sounded like they were to my right."[100] Directly to Mrs. Connally's right was the Grassy Knoll.

H59. Malcolm Couch, Dallas TV news cameraman who rode in the motorcade, was questioned by Commission Counsel David Belin:

BELIN: Is there any particular reason, Mr. Couch, why you didn't take your first pictures of the School Book Depository Building itself when you say you saw a rifle being withdrawn?

COUCH: . . . The excitement on the ground . . . the activity on the ground kept my attention. . . . All the policemen had their pistols pulled. And people were pointing back around those shrubs. . . . You would think there was a chase going on in that direction.[101]

H60. David Powers, a Presidential aide in the right side jump seat of the follow-up car, said in an affidavit:

My first impression was that the shots came from the right and overhead, but I also found a fleeting impression that the noise appeared to come from the front in the area of the Triple Overpass. This may have resulted from my feeling, when I looked forward toward the overpass, that we might have ridden into an ambush.[102]

I. OTHER WITNESSES

161. Lee Bowers, towerman for the Union Terminal Company, was at work in a railroad tower 14 feet high, located just north of the Grassy Knoll behind the curving railroad tracks. He tells of three cars that slowly cruised the area during the half hour before the shooting.

Two had out-of-state plates, he said, and a third, a 1957 black Ford, had "one male in it that seemed to have a mike or telephone. . . . He was very close to the tower. I could see him. . . ."

[100] IV, 149; italics added.
[101] VI, 159-60.
[102] VII, 473.

The last Bowers saw of another of the cars, ". . . he was pausing . . . just above the assassination site. . . . At the moment I heard the sound, I was looking directly towards the area. . . . At the time of the shooting there seemed to be some commotion. . . . I just am unable to describe rather than it was something out of the ordinary, a sort of milling around, but something occurred in this particular spot which was out of the ordinary, which attracted my eye for some reason, which I could not identify."[103]

162. James Tague, an automobile salesman standing on the south side of Main Street near the mouth of the Triple Underpass watching the parade, was wounded in the cheek after a bullet struck the curb near him. He told the Commission:

My first impression was that up by the, whatever you call the monument . . . somebody was throwing firecrackers up there. . . . When I saw the people throwing themselves on the ground is when I realized there was serious trouble. . . .[104]

163. J. C. Price had been standing on the roof of the Terminal Annex Building. He said in a sheriff's deposition:

. . . There was a volley of shots, I think five. . . . I saw one man run towards the passenger cars on the railroad siding after the volley of shots. . . . He had something in his hand. I couldn't be sure but it may have been a head piece.[105]

164. Arnold Rowland, who at the time of the shooting was standing with his wife in front of the Dallas Courthouse, about 150 feet from the corner of Main and Houston Streets, gave his impression of the point of origin of the first shot:

I didn't look at the building mainly, and as practically any of the police officers that were there then will tell you, the echo effect was such that it sounded like it came from the railroad yards. That is where I looked, that is where all the policemen, everyone, converged on the railroads. . . .

[103] VI, 286-8.
[104] VII, 557.
[105] XIX, 492.

SPECTER: Why did you not look back at the Texas School Book Depository Building in view of the fact that you had seen a man with a rifle up there [earlier] in the day?

ROWLAND: . . . It was mostly due to . . . the fact that it sounded like it came from this area [indicating the Triple Underpass on Commission Exhibit 354] and that all the officers, enforcement officers, were converging on that area and I just didn't pay any attention to it at that time.[106]

A NOTE ON THE FATAL SHOT
David S. Lifton

August 1975

The belated and limited availability of additional medical evidence (from the autopsy photos and X-rays) is summarized in this comment by David Lifton. For many people, this new material does not resolve questions raised by the other major piece of "hard" evidence (the Zapruder film), and by much of the "soft" evidence (such as the doctors' opinions on the validity of the single-bullet theory).—Eds.

Published writings on the Kennedy assassination reflect a divergence of opinion regarding the proper interpretation of the movement of President Kennedy's head in response to the fatal shot, as shown in the Zapruder film. On this point, there is disagreement among the critics themselves, as well as between critics and defenders of the Warren Report. The purpose of this note is not to evaluate this controversy, but to trace its evolution.

When projected at camera speed, the Zapruder film appears to show that the President's head and upper body are thrown violently backward and to his left. There is no indication that this

[106] II, 180-1.
"A Note on the Fatal Shot, as Depicted on the Zapruder Film" by David S. Lifton. Printed by permission of the author. © David S. Lifton, 1975.

motion was ever noticed by anyone on the Warren Commission or its staff, despite the fact that the film was closely studied in connection with the analysis of time intervals between the shots. On the basis of other evidence (medical and ballistic), the Commission concluded that the shots came from the Texas School Book Depository, located to the rear.

After the Warren Report was published, the Commission's records (along with its copy of the Zapruder film) were deposited at the National Archives. Black and white stills were published in the twenty-six volumes in November 1964, and a few color frames appeared in *Life*. The critics, notably Vincent Salandria in *Liberation* (Jan. and Mar. 1965) and Ray Marcus, noted that the backward motion indicated a shot from the front, as did some of the eyewitness and medical reports. By fall 1965, the film itself was available for screenings, and the first assassination researchers to view it (notably Thomas Stamm and Vincent Salandria) were astounded by the head-shot sequence.

The issue became more complex when the film was closely examined on a frame-by-frame basis. It was then discovered that while the head does not go forward *after* frame 313, there *is* a small forward motion between frames 312 and 313 (i.e., between the last frame before the visible impact of the fatal shot and the first frame after it).* Taking this into account, three general schools of thought emerged:

(1) *Double head hit.* Based (in part) on this 312/313 forward motion, the theory was put forward that the President was hit twice, almost simultaneously, in the head. The first shot, from the rear, is presumed responsible for the forward motion observed between frames 312 and 313. The second shot, from the front, is

---

* One of the earliest students of the film, Ray Marcus, found that two frames of the film immediately following the head shot—frames 314 and 315—were printed in reverse sequence in the Commission's hearings (18H70-71). In response to a query from the author, J. Edgar Hoover wrote that this frame reversal was "a printing error." The reversal has been given a sinister interpretation by some, who argue that it was deliberately done to mislead the investigators and/or the public about the head-snap issue. However, no attempt was made to conceal the reversal, by (for example) removing the visible section of adjacent frames. Furthermore, since the Commission had the film (on which there is no frame reversal) and left it at the Archives, the only confusion the reversal could have caused was among those analyzing the black and white published reproductions in volume 18.

presumed responsible for the backward movement after frame 313. (This theory is presented, in considerable detail, in *Six Seconds in Dallas* by Josiah Thompson.)

(2) *Single shot from the front.* Proponents of this theory have focused on the backward movement of the President's head, following frame 313, and offered alternate explanations—other than a shot from the rear—to explain the small forward motion between frames 312 and 313. For example, it has been suggested that the President is already sagging before frame 313, and that there is no reason to interpret the forward motion between 312 and 313 as anything more than a continuation of that same sagging motion. Another hypothesis (one put forward by the author) is that the 312/313 motion, while previously described as "forward," is in fact a clockwise turning motion of the head about the neck (clockwise in the plane of the Zapruder film)—the result of a bullet impacting from the front at an angle of about 25 degrees or more above the horizontal.

(3) *Single shot from the rear.* Proponents of this viewpoint employ physics to argue that the 312/313 forward movement was caused by a hit from the rear. To explain the subsequent backward motion, they postulate a neuromuscular reaction and/or a "jet recoil effect." The occurrence of a strong neuromuscular spasm has been suggested speculatively by many people, but to date there are no published studies which explore this possibility scientifically. The term "jet effect" refers to a situation in which some energy transfer mechanism exists to cause fragments of bone to fly forward fast enough so that (conserving momentum) the rest of the head moves backward. (Any target which does *not* fragment must, as expected, move away from the gun.)

The above discussion has been limited to the Zapruder film. Interpretations of what the film shows, however, cannot be made in that isolated context: the medical evidence must be taken into account. Indeed, were this a routine homicide that was accidentally recorded on film, then one would rely on the medical evidence to draw conclusions about the trajectories of the shots—not on the film of the shooting.

In this regard, any interpretation of the head-shot sequence which postulates a hit from the front is in direct disagreement with the Kennedy autopsy report and the related medical and ballistic evidence as set forth by the Warren Commission. It is also in conflict with the autopsy X-rays and photographs which—although unexamined by the Warren Commission—were examined after the Kennedy family deposited them at the National Archives in October 1966. Under the agreement between the family and the Archives, the materials could only be seen by government pathologists for a five-year period. In February 1968, Attorney General Ramsey Clark convened a panel of distinguished experts to review them. (Neither the existence of the Clark panel nor its findings were disclosed until January 17, 1969.) As regards the fatal shot, the panel found that the President was hit only once, from behind. The panel did not address the issue posed by the movement of the President's head on the Zapruder film. After the five-year period, a number of nongovernmental doctors examined the photos and X-rays; none has found any support for a shot from the front.

The issue first reached a mass audience in early 1975, when Robert Groden, a New York photo technician, went on television with an extraordinarily clear print of the film, including close-up and slow-motion sequences of the head snap. As a result, the Rockefeller Commission on the CIA undertook to review the Zapruder film as well as the medical evidence and to specifically address the question of why the President appeared to move backward in response to the fatal hit.

Another panel of experts was convened. The Commission gave official endorsement to the third explanation outlined above for the President's motion: a single shot from the rear. Some of the Commission's experts attributed the rearward motion to a neuromuscular reaction; others cited the "jet effect." (The Rockefeller Report noted, but drew no explicit conclusion from, the forward head motion between frames 312 and 313.) Without publishing any underlying documentation, the Rockefeller Commission reported that its panel of experts was "unanimous" in finding that the backward motion was not caused by a shot from the front, and expressed its belief that the motion is "fully consistent with" a shot from the direction of the School Book Depository.

PHYSICAL EVIDENCE
Josiah Thompson

Six Seconds in Dallas / 1967

My initial feeling was that if this was a simple assassination, as the Commission claimed, with one assassin firing three shots from one vantage point, the facts would come together very neatly. If there were more than one assassin the details would not fit.—Vincent J. Salandria, *The Greater Philadelphia Magazine*, August, 1966.

THE CARTRIDGE CASES

[*Three 6.5-millimeter cartridge cases were found on the sixth floor of the Depository shortly after the assassination. Thompson argued from an analysis of the trajectories that only two shots were fired from this location. How, he then asked, do we account for the third, or extra, cartridge case?Eds.*]

On the face of it, the presence of one, two, or three cartridge cases does not establish that any particular number of shots was fired from a location. More shots could have been fired and some of the cases retrieved. Fewer shots could have been fired and an extra case dropped. Moreover, when we consider the condition of the rifle and the cartridges when they were discovered, it becomes even harder to draw clear inferences from them.

Although the rifle clip can hold six rounds (and an extra in the chamber), only four bullet casings were found—a live round in the chamber and three cartridge cases on the floor. No fingerprints were found on any of the cases or on the rifle clip (4H253, 258-260). In fact, the only print on the rifle was found after disassembly on a portion of the barrel ordinarily covered by the front stock.[1] Whoever fired this rifle curiously loaded it with only four rounds when it would hold six or seven, and then was careful to remove all fingerprints from it and from the cases fired.

These considerations merely point up certain oddities about the condition in which the rifle and cases were found. It is only when we begin examining the three cases themselves that our suspicions are aroused. In this examination Lieutenant J. C. Day of the Dallas Police is a central figure.

Two and One

On November 22, 1963, Lieutenant Day headed the crime scene search section of the Dallas Police. In company with his assistant, R. L. Studebaker, he arrived at the Depository about 1:12 P.M. and went immediately to the sixth floor (4H249). Learning that some cartridge cases had been found near a southeast-corner window, he instructed Studebaker to photograph them from various angles, and then he dusted them for fingerprints (4H250). Studebaker's photos show two cases lying next to the window wall and a third some 5 feet away to the northwest.

It would be interesting to know which of the three cartridges had been thrown so oddly distant from the other two. Lieutenant Day, however, scooped up all three cartridges and placed them in an envelope before they were marked with respect to their location of discovery (4H253, 7H162-163). So today, no one has any idea which of the three cases was the one lying 5 feet down the wall. This is unfortunate in light of certain disparities between one of the cases and the other two and particularly in view of what next happened to the envelope.

Detective Richard H. Sims helped Lieutenant Day pick up the cartridge cases. He then took the envelope containing the cases and turned it over to Captain Will Fritz at police headquarters (7H183). When Lieutenant Day was given the enve-

[1] 4H260-263. Sylvia Meagher describes the curious way in which this palm print was handled by the Dallas Police. See Sylvia Meagher, *Accessories after the Fact* (New York: The Bobbs-Merrill Company, Inc., 1967), pp. 120-127.

lope later that evening, it contained only two cases—the third had been removed by Captain Fritz and was being held by him (4H254). Day now marked the two cases with his initials and forwarded them to the FBI lab with other evidence (4H254). These two cases were subsequently given FBI designations C7 and C38 and Commission Exhibit Numbers 544 and 545 (4H254-255).

Both of these cases had marks "identified as having been produced by the chamber of Oswald's rifle" (26H449-450). One of them had a "set of marks identified as having been produced by the magazine follower" [the spring-tensioned lever that presses up the last cartridge in the clip] of Oswald's rifle (26H450), while the other showed marks that could have come only from the bolt of Oswald's rifle (24H449). Both of these cases showed marks indicating that each had been loaded into a weapon (not necessarily Oswald's) at least twice (24H449-450).

The remaining cartridge case (designated C6 and CE 543) differed from the other two in a number of respects. It was kept by the Dallas Police until the FBI demanded it from Captain Fritz in the early morning hours of November 28 (7H404). Its most astonishing characteristic is a sharp dent in its lip of sufficient magnitude to prevent the fitting of a projectile in the opening. In its present condition it could not have been fired in any rifle on November 22.

The crucial question arises as to when this dent was incurred. Could it have happened after it was fired but before it was photographed and retrieved by Lieutenant Day? Perhaps it was dented in striking the wall or floor during the ejection process? This suggestion must be immediately ruled out—the case is made of rigid brass and would not dent under any such impact.[2] Could it have been stepped on? Two facts work against this possibility. First, the dent itself is sharply defined—it resembles what happens when an empty case is "dry loaded" in the breech and strikes some sharp metal projection. It does not have the gentler contours that would be the expected result of contact

[2] I have thrown hundreds of similar cases against a wall and never succeeded in denting one.

with a person's shoe. Second, it was discovered and guarded by Sheriff's Officer Luke Mooney, who tells of the care he took in moving in the area and his anxiety that no evidence be disturbed (3H284). If anyone stepped on the cartridge it would have had to have been Mooney, yet, in May, 1967, Mooney assured me in no uncertain terms that neither he nor anyone else stepped on any of the cases before they were picked up by the Dallas Police.[3]

Thus, it seems extremely unlikely that CE 543 was dented after being ejected from Oswald's rifle. But in its present condition it could not have been fired in any rifle—its lip will not receive a projectile. The possibility suggests itself that CE 543 was never fired on November 22 but was dropped by one of the assassins, either inadvertently or as a means of throwing the subsequent investigation off the track. Certain other features of CE 543 urge such a conclusion even more strongly.

Marks found on the dented case indicated that it had been loaded in and extracted from a weapon at least three times (26H449). In addition, it had "three sets of marks on the base" that were not found on the others or on any of the numerous test cartridges obtained from Oswald's rifle (26H449). A ballistics expert testified that these anomalous marks were possibly caused by a "dry firing" run—that is, by inserting the empty cartridge case in the breech while practicing with the rifle (3H510). Of all the various marks discovered on this case, only one set links it to Oswald's rifle, and this set was identified as having come from the magazine follower. Yet the magazine follower marks only the last cartridge in the clip, a position that must have been occupied on November 22 not by the dented case but by the live round subsequently found in the chamber. Thus, unlike the other two cases that bear marks from the chamber and bolt of Oswald's rifle, the only mark borne by the dented case, linking it to Oswald's rifle, could not have been incurred on November 22.[4]

[3] Author's interview with Luke Mooney, May, 31, 1967.
[4] This conclusion emerges from J. Edgar Hoover's June 2, 1964, letter to the Commission, a letter in which he recounts the results of FBI examinations on the cartridge cases (26H449-450). His letter conflicts with earlier testimony furnished by FBI firearms expert Robert Frazier (3H390-441). On Mar. 31 Frazier testified that

All this excites our suspicion with respect to CE 543, the dented cartridge case. What is most surprising—perhaps conclusive—about this cartridge case is that it lacks a characteristic impression along the side exhibited in one form or other by all the other cartridges we know to have been seated in the chamber of Oswald's rifle. I first noticed this characteristic mark while supervising the photographing of the cartridges for *Life*. I observed on two of the cartridge cases (CE's 544, 545) an impression on the side in the same relative position on each. I examined the third and saw that no such impression was apparent. The anomaly did not excite my interest until I noticed that the live round found in the chamber of Oswald's rifle (CE 141) exhibited a similar impression in the same place. On the live round the mark was not as pronounced—perhaps due to the fact that it had not been fired. The pressure of firing would tend to accentuate any indentation caused by contact with the chamber. I now had three cartridge cases, all of which ostensibly were at one time or other in the chamber of Oswald's rifle and all of which evidenced a characteristic mark. If this mark was caused by a characteristic of the chamber of Oswald's rifle, then the lack of it on CE 543 might indicate that it had never been fired in Oswald's rifle. One way to test my hypothesis was to examine CE 577—two cartridge cases from test rounds fired in Oswald's rifle. Both of these cases displayed the characteristic mark in the

---

microphotographs of the base of the cartridge cases showed up points of similarity with the bolt of Oswald's rifle. Frazier concluded from this similarity that all the cases at one time or another had been in contact with the bolt of Oswald's rifle (3H414-419). This conclusion is in direct conflict with Hoover's later letter. In it the Director of the FBI explicitly states that *only* one cartridge case, C7, had a set of marks "identified as having been produced by contact with the bolt of C14" (26H449-450).

My own opinion is that CE 543 was most likely "dry loaded" in Oswald's rifle at some earlier time. Such a "dry loading" would account for (1) the magazine follower marks noted in Hoover's letter (26H449), (2) the microscopic bolt similarities noted in Frazier's testimony (3H519), and (3) the sharp dent in the lip. If we suppose that the lip of CE 543 was dented in such a "dry loading" operation, this also accounts for the missing chambering mark—because 543 was lighter than a loaded cartridge, its lip struck the metal projection rather than the cartridge body, as was the case with the other exhibits. Another reason for believing in the existence of such a "dry loading" operation with respect to CE 543 is the conviction that a would-be assassin would take this minimal precaution with respect to evidence destined to be left at the scene of the crime.

same spot.[5] Thus the cartridge case that had an extra dent in the lip seemed to lack a mark exhibited by every other case we know to have been in the breech of Oswald's rifle.

The combination of these factors—the peculiar treatment accorded CE 543 by the Dallas Police, its inexplicably dented lip, the three sets of marks on the base absent on the other cases while present on 543, and finally its lack of the characteristic chambering mark—suggests that although two of the cartridge cases may have been ejected from Oswald's rifle, the third, CE 543, is most likely an extra, unfired shell and possibly a deliberate fake. Such a conclusion would mate perfectly with the description of events earlier laid down, namely, that only two of the shots fired that day in Dealey Plaza came from the Depository.

SUPERBULLET: COMMISSION EXHIBIT 399

Deep in the recesses of the National Archives, carefully packed in cotton and enclosed in a small plastic case marked Commission Exhibit Number 399, rests a copper-jacketed 6.5-millimeter bullet. Along its straight sides can be seen the spiral channels of rifling grooves. Although the bullet's tail is somewhat squeezed, its nose and midsection are perfectly preserved. Given such a perfect projectile, experts had no difficulty in matching it to Oswald's rifle to the exclusion of all other weapons (3H429, 499–500).

No piece of physical evidence has excited more controversy than CE 399. Basically, the controversy turns on the Commission's contention that "all the evidence indicated that the bullet found on the Governor's stretcher could have caused all his wounds" (R95). As succeeding pages will show, "all the evidence" indicates precisely the opposite; not only does it appear extremely unlikely that this bullet could have caused all the Governor's wounds, but subsequent investigation at Parkland Hospi-

[5] Although quite obvious on one of the cases, the mark was more difficult to discern on the other. Since these two cases were selected from some thirty or more test firings (3H402, 426), the difference between the two marks may very well reflect a difference in firing order—the more pronounced mark suggesting a case early in the firing series, the less pronounced mark suggesting a case later in the series.

tal has disclosed that bullet 399 was most likely found on a stretcher unconnected with the care of either Governor Connally or President Kennedy.

A PERFECT BULLET

According to the Commission's "single-bullet" theory, the missile that wounded the Governor had first transited the President's neck. Following this transit, it entered the Governor's back, making a 1.5 centimeter hole before shattering his fifth rib and blowing out an exit hole 5 centimeters wide. The bullet continued on to smash Connally's forearm and wrist, splintering the radius bone at its largest point and leaving along its path a trail of bone and metal fragments. This bullet finally embedded itself in the Governor's thigh, leaving behind two small fragments before falling out on the stretcher. According to the Commission, the bullet that accomplished all this—that shattered two bones and caused seven separate wounds in two people—was Commission Exhibit 399 (R95).[6]

Critics of the *Report* have argued against this conclusion on two grounds. First, they point to the minuscule loss of CE 399's substance and to the conviction of two of the autopsy surgeons that 399 could not have caused the Governor's wounds for the simple reason that more metal was found in his wrist than was missing from 399. Second, they point to 399's undeformed state as evidence that it could not have caused the damage ascribed to it. The second argument is much stronger than the first. . . .

Although the argument from weight loss fails, the more critical argument from deformation succeeds. The nearly pristine character of CE 399 precludes its being the bullet that injured the Governor. Still, there is one additional piece of evidence that should not be overlooked—where it was found.

WHICH STRETCHER?

An investigation at Parkland Hospital, including the reenactment of the bullet's discovery in the presence of the principal

[6] There are a multitude of reasons for believing that no bullet at all transited the President's neck. We restrict ourselves only to one part of the Commission's thesis, namely, that CE 399 caused all the Governor's wounds.

witnesses, has disclosed that 399 was actually found on a stretcher unrelated to the care of either Connally or Kennedy. The history of 399 is complex. Before attempting to offer a plausible account of how it came to be discovered on a stretcher in Parkland Hospital, it is imperative that we understand clearly what is known and unknown about both its discovery and subsequent transmission to Washington. The place to begin is at the FBI Crime Laboratory in Washington on the night of November 22.

We know that Robert Frazier of the FBI Crime Lab received 399 on the evening of November 22 from another FBI agent, Elmer Todd (3H428, 24H412). They both marked the bullet with their initials (24H412). Todd, in turn, had received it a few minutes earlier from Chief Rowley of the Secret Service, who had been given it by one of his agents, Richard Johnsen (24H412). When Johnsen turned the bullet over to Rowley he attached a short note of explanation which reads as follows:

The attached expended bullet was received by me about 5 minutes prior to Mrs. Kennedy's departure from the hospital. It was found on one of the stretchers located in the emergency ward of the hospital. Also on this same stretcher was [sic] rubber gloves, a stethoscope and other doctors' paraphernalia. It could not be determined who had used this stretcher or if President Kennedy had occupied it. No further information was obtained. Name of person from whom I received this bullet

        Mr. O. P. Wright
        Personnel Director of Security
        Dallas County Hospital District

By

        Richard E. Johnsen
        Special Agent
        7:30 p.m.
        Nov. 22, 1963   (18H800)

Since the presidential party departed from Parkland Hospital at approximately 2:00 P.M. (18H726, 744, 756-757), we infer that Agent Johnsen received the bullet from Mr. Wright at approximately 1:55 P.M. Wright first learned of its existence when hospital engineer Darrell Tomlinson came to him and told him of its discovery on a hospital stretcher. Together they went to a vestibule where the bullet was seen to lie on a stretcher blocking the corner entrance to the men's room. The bullet lay exposed between the stretcher mat and its rim. Wright examined it and then went to find a federal officer who would take custody of the bullet. After one refusal from an FBI agent, he found Agent Johnsen, who agreed to accept the bullet. From this information we can draw the very important conclusion that *Tomlinson found the bullet between 1:45 P.M. and 1:50 P.M. on November 22*. Much later Tomlinson and Wright were shown CE 399 and both declined to identify it as the bullet they each handled on November 22 (24H412).[7]

In a report dated November 30 Richard Johnsen reiterates what his note of November 22 had affirmed, namely, that Mr. Wright had told him that the stretcher on which the bullet was discovered also carried "rubber gloves, a stethoscope, and other doctors' paraphernalia" (18H799). Again in November, 1966,

[7] In the report of the FBI agent who showed Tomlinson and Wright CE 399 we learn that although neither could positively identify 399 as the bullet they handled on November 22, nevertheless they thought it bore a general resemblance to 399. This makes all the more strange what Wright told me in November, 1966.

I asked him what the bullet looked like, and he replied that it had a pointed tip like the one I held in my hand (earlier he had procured a .30 caliber unfired projectile that we had placed on the stretcher cart in our reenactment). I then drew three bullet shapes: one pointed like the .30 caliber; another long with rounded tip—like 399; still another squat and rounded, like a .38 caliber. Wright picked the pointed tip as the one that most resembled the bullet found on the stretcher. I then showed him photographs of CE's 399, 572 (the two ballistics comparison rounds from Oswald's rifle), and 606 (revolver bullets), and he rejected all of these as resembling the bullet Tomlinson found on the stretcher. Half an hour later in the presence of two witnesses, he once again rejected the picture of 399 as resembling the bullet found on the stretcher. Sometime later he asked me if one of the pictures I had shown him was supposed to be the bullet found on the stretcher. I replied, "Yes," and he seemed quite prepared to stick by his story. As a professional law-enforcement officer, Wright has an educated eye for bullet shapes. Tomlinson's recollection of bullet shapes was not very clear, and he could say only that the bullet found resembled either CE 572 (the ballistics comparison rounds) or the pointed, .30 caliber bullet Wright had procured for us.

This is an appalling piece of information, for if Wright's recollection is accurate, then CE 399 must have been switched for the real bullet sometime later in the transmission chain. This could have been done only by some federal officer, since it was in government possession from that time on. If this is true, then the assassination conspiracy would have to have involved members of the federal government and been an "inside" job.

Mr. Wright told me that this was the case. He also verified that the stretcher on which the bullet rested was the one in the corner—the one blocking the men's room door. All these seemingly trivial details become important when we turn to the testimony of Darrell Tomlinson, the man who first discovered the bullet.

Tomlinson was interviewed by Assistant Counsel Specter on Mar. 20, 1964. To aid in his testimony, Tomlinson drew a small sketch of the vestibule area. He had come to the vestibule shortly after 1:00 P.M. in answer to a call for someone to operate the elevator (6H129):

SPECTER: Was there anything on the elevator at that time?

TOMLINSON: There was one stretcher.

SPECTER: And describe the appearance of that stretcher, if you will, please.

TOMLINSON: I believe that stretcher had sheets on it and had a white covering on the pad.

SPECTER: What did you say about the covering on the pad, excuse me?

TOMLINSON: I believe it was a white sheet that was on the pad.

SPECTER: And was there anything else on that?

TOMLINSON: I don't believe there was on that one, I'm not sure, but I don't believe there was.

SPECTER: What, if anything, did you do with that stretcher?

TOMLINSON: I took it off of the elevator and put it over against the south wall....

SPECTER: Was there any other stretcher in that area at that time?

TOMLINSON: There was a stretcher about 2 feet from the wall already there (6H129-130).

Assistant Counsel Specter then asked Tomlinson: "Will you mark with a 'B' the stretcher which was present at the time you pushed stretcher 'A' off the elevator?" (6H130). Tomlinson complied and then went on to explain how he made several trips up and down on the elevator. Sometime later he noticed that stretcher "B"—the vestibule stretcher—had been pushed out from the wall by someone entering the men's room:

TOMLINSON: Well, he pushed the stretcher out from the wall to get in, and then when he came out he just walked off and didn't push the stretcher back up against the wall, so I pushed it out of the way where we would have a clear area in front of the elevator.

SPECTER: And where did you push it to?

TOMLINSON: I pushed it back up against the wall.

SPECTER: What, if anything, happened then?

TOMLINSON: I bumped the wall and a spent cartridge or bullet rolled out that apparently had been lodged under the edge of the mat.[8]

SPECTER: And that was from which stretcher?

TOMLINSON: I believe it was "B."

SPECTER: And what was on "B" if you recall; if anything?

TOMLINSON: Well, at one end they had one or two sheets rolled up; I didn't examine them. They were bloody. They were rolled up on the east end of it and there were a few surgical instruments on the opposite end and a sterile pack or so (6H130-131).

Could it have been President Kennedy's stretcher on which Tomlinson found the bullet? Almost certainly not. The President was taken to Trauma Room 1, where he was pronounced dead at 1:00 P.M. His body remained on this stretcher in Trauma Room 1 until the casket arrived at 1:40 P.M. (18H814). It was then lifted up and placed in the casket while the stretcher was stripped of sheets and rolled across the hall into Trauma Room 2 (6H138, 142, 146). There is every reason to believe that the President's stretcher was still in Trauma Room 2 when the presidential party departed at 2:00 P.M. But Tomlinson found the bullet at approximately 1:45 P.M. Thus, the Kennedy stretcher could not have been the one on which the bullet was found

[8] Tomlinson's observation that the bullet "had been lodged under the edge of the mat" has fed attacks on the Commission's *Report*. For how, critics ask, could a bullet fall out of the Governor's thigh and manage to get *"under* the edge of the mat"? The record should be set straight on this detail. At no time did Tomlinson see the bullet roll out from under the mat. He told me that he pushed the stretcher against the wall and then heard a clink of metal on metal. He walked over and saw the bullet lying between the pad and the rim of the stretcher. It could have been lying there all along, and taken a roll only when he pushed the stretcher. Or it could have rolled out from under the pad. Tomlinson agreed that neither he nor anyone else will *ever* be able to judge with certainty which one of these two possibilities was in fact the case.

because (1) it was stripped of linen while Tomlinson's stretcher carried both sheets and equipment, and (2) its movements are accounted for until after the time the bullet was found.

Could it have been Governor Connally's stretcher? No again, and here we differ with the Commission. When the presidential limousine arrived at Parkland Hospital, two stretchers were brought out to accommodate the wounded men, one from Major Surgery, the other from OB/GYN (6H135). The President and the Governor were placed on these stretchers, which, after pausing at the Triage Desk, were taken into Trauma Rooms 1 and 2.

In Trauma Room 2 Governor Connally's clothes were removed,[9] a bandage was applied to his chest wound, and a drainage tube inserted (6H84, 116). Before the Governor's clothing had been completely removed, Dr. Shaw (the thoracic surgeon) arrived and said the Governor could be taken up to Surgery (6H84). His stretcher was wheeled out of Trauma Room 2 into the emergency elevator, and carried up to the second-floor operating suite (6H117).

When the elevator reached the second floor, the stretcher was wheeled into the operating suite to a point just outside Operating Room 5 (6H121). The Governor was then lifted up and placed on an operating room table (6H121, 126). Jane Wester, R.N., pushed the stretcher some 20 or 30 feet in the direction of the elevator, removed "several glassine packets of hypodermic needles . . . some alcohol sponges, and a roll of 1 inch tape," and then turned the stretcher over to Orderly R. J. Jimison (6H122).[10] Jimison rolled it the remaining distance into the

[9] I talked to Rosa Majors, a nurse's aide at Parkland, who removed the Governor's trousers, shoes, and socks. She told me that after removing his trousers, she held them up and went through the pockets for valuables. Had a bullet fallen out of the Governor's thigh, it would have been trapped in his trousers. When Rosa Majors held them up, any such bullet should have fallen out and been discovered at that time. She told me she never saw any bullet while she was caring for Governor Connally. Much later she heard that a bullet was supposed to have been found on his stretcher. She can't conceive where such a bullet could have come from.

[10] Miss Wester also mentioned that she believed she had rolled up the sheets on this stretcher, a detail that is in conflict with the testimony of Jimison (6H126) and Tomlinson (6H129). I asked her about this in May, 1967. She pointed out that she couldn't be certain she had rolled up the sheets since this was not standard hospital procedure—"sometimes you do, sometimes you don't." She continued in this vein: "You have to take into consideration the fact that the operating room at that time

elevator and closed the door (6H126). Since anesthesia was started on the Governor at 1:00 P.M. (*Archives*, CD 379), and since Jimison testified that the stretcher was put on the elevator "less than 10 minutes" after Governor Connally entered the Operating Room (6H127), we can conclude that the Governor's stretcher was put on the elevator in the interval 1:00-1:05 P.M.

It was at just this time, we recall, that Darrell Tomlinson found stretcher "A" on the elevator and wheeled it off into the vestibule. According to Tomlinson, this stretcher had "a white sheet that was on the pad" (6H129). When asked by Specter if there was anything else on the stretcher, he replied: "I don't believe there was on that one" (6H129). Jimison last remembered the Connally stretcher as empty except for the sheets:

SPECTER: What was on the stretcher at that time?

JIMISON: I noticed nothing more than a little flat mattress and two sheets as usual.

SPECTER: And what was the position of the sheets?

JIMISON: Of course, them sheets was, of course, as usual, flat out on the bed.

SPECTER: Had they been rolled up?

JIMISON: More or less, not rolled, which yes, usually they is, the mattress and sheets are all just throwed, one of them about halfway, it would be just throwed about halfway.

SPECTER: Were the sheets flat or just turned over?

JIMISON: Well, just turned over (6H126).

Jimison went on to testify that there were no other stretchers placed on the elevator from the second floor up until 3:00 P.M. (6H127). Subsequent inquiries at Parkland Hospital disclosed that in the interval 12:30-2:30 P.M. no patients besides Governor Connally were treated in Surgery (second floor) or in the Delivery Rooms (third floor). Since any stretcher found in the elevator must have come from one of these two floors,[11] it seems

---

was not anywhere near the normal state that it usually is. And when you have something like 15 or 30 people standing very close trying to get into the OR and us trying to keep them out, you have a problem. It was mass confusion. So like I say, that is the best I can remember. I . . . maybe, I remembered wrong. I don't know."

[11] On November 22 this elevator operated only from the basement to the third floor, with floors one through three being patient treatment areas.

virtually a certainty that the stretcher found in the elevator by Tomlinson at approximately 1:00 o'clock belonged to Governor Connally. The description of the Governor's stretcher given by Jimison matches Tomlinson's description of the stretcher he found in the elevator.

Yet Tomlinson maintains that the bullet was not found on the elevator stretcher (stretcher "A") but on the vestibule stretcher (stretcher "B"). This stretcher, which he found already present in the vestibule at 1:00 P.M., carried two rolled-up bloody sheets, doctors' equipment, some gauze pads, and rubber gloves. It would seem that the stretcher on which the bullet was found was used neither in the care of Governor Connally nor President Kennedy, but in the treatment of some other patient unconnected with the assassination. But if so, which patient? And how did it get its bloody sheets (rolled up at one end) and its medical equipment?

RONALD FULLER

In the Emergency Room Admission Records for November 22 we find Governor Connally admitted at 12:40 P.M.; his chief complaint was listed as "gunshot wound" and he was given admission number 24744 (21H156). The next admission number, 24745, was given to Ronald Fuller, age two and one-half, chief complaint: "fell" (21H156). Ronnie Fuller was admitted 14 minutes after the Governor at 12:54 P.M. (21H156). It is one of history's final ironies that Commission Exhibit 399—the bullet that supposedly struck both President Kennedy and Governor Connally—was very likely found on a stretcher used for a cut and bleeding two-and-one-half-year-old child.

Triage Orderly Joe Richards reported that he helped lift Governor Connally out of the presidential limousine. After pushing the Governor into Trauma Room 2, he helped some Secret Service men find telephones. Then:

Minutes later, a lady brought her child to the Registration Desk [Triage Desk] with a cut chin, and I carried him back, placed him on a carriage [stretcher] in the hallway near the Nurses' Station. After the mother calmed down enough to register the child in, I escorted her to where he was (21H226).

The "hallway near the Nurses' Station" is in Major Surgery not far from Trauma Rooms 1 and 2. Aide Shirley Randall corroborates Richards' account:

Just as I got out there, a lady brought her little boy in who had been cut on the jaw. Blood was all over he [sic] and the child. She started to faint and the triage orderly [Richards] grabbed the child and I grabbed the mother and took her to the nearest chair. Miss Lozano watched her while I went right across from the desk to the Blood Bank and got some ammonia for the mother to smell; she got alright [sic] then. I led her to the Emergency Room and found a booth in [Major] Medicine for the doctor to suture the baby. That is when he told me and some more aides that the President was dead (21H218).

The little boy with the bloody cut is undoubtedly Ronnie Fuller. But when did all this occur? The admissions list places his admission at 12:54 P.M.[12] Was he put on the stretcher and removed from it in time for Tomlinson to find it empty shortly after 1:00 P.M.? The statement of Aide Era Lumpkin furnishes some assistance:

The doctors got ready to take Gov. Connally up to second floor to Surgery. I left out of trauma II and went back into Maj. Surg. near the nurses' station.

Someone brought in this baby that was all bloody. Mrs. Nelson said, "Rosa, you and Era take the baby and put him on a cart." We got the baby's clothes off, trying to determine from where the blood was coming. I spotted the cut on the cheek. I asked about the mother. No one knew where she was. I went out to the desk and was told the mother was on her way inside the Emergency Room.

When I got back into the Emergency Room, the mother had arrived. A doctor said, "Put the child in a booth." So we put the child in a booth. The child was crying so loud, someone asked us to carry the baby in major medicine and set up a booth for suturing (21H208-209).[13]

[12] Ronnie Fuller most likely arrived at the hospital Emergency Room some minutes before this. This time was recorded by a time clock after the admission slip was filled out. As Shirley Randall indicated, the mother fainted upon arrival in the Emergency Room. Since she had to be revived before the admission slip could be filled out, 12:54 gives a very late time for the child's arrival; 12:45 to 12:50 would be a more accurate estimate.

[13] Due to a new hospital rule prohibiting interviews with Parkland personnel, I was unable to interview Shirley Randall, Joe Richards, or Era Lumpkin. Before this

Ronnie Fuller arrived at Parkland Hospital shortly before the Governor was taken up to Surgery. Bleeding profusely, the little boy was placed on a stretcher "in the hallway near the Nurses' Station." He stayed there for only a brief time before being picked up and carried into Major Medicine. He left behind a stretcher whose sheets were soiled with blood. This is as far as we can trace Ronnie Fuller's stretcher. We cannot know for certain that it was then rolled some 30 feet into the elevator vestibule where, shortly after 1:00 P.M., it was seen by Tomlinson. Certain facts, however, indicate that this is what happened.

It was standard hospital procedure to shift used stretchers into the elevator vestibule. The bloody sheets clearly would label this stretcher as "used," and the crowded conditions in Major Surgery would necessitate its speedy removal. Then, too, there was the equipment found on the vestibule stretcher—gauze pads, rubber gloves, stethoscope, and "other doctors' paraphernalia." Rosa Majors told me that she and Era Lumpkin had used gauze pads to clean the child, that either she or Era had been wearing rubber gloves, and that Era had had a stethoscope.[14] She cannot remember what happened to this equipment—the events of that afternoon were so confusing. But it is possible that it was left behind on the stretcher when the two aides carried Ronnie Fuller into Major Medicine.

---

rule went into effect I had the good fortune to interview Rosa Majors, who cleared up two points of possible confusion in Era Lumpkin's statement: 1) Richards and Randall stated that Richards placed the child on a stretcher while Era Lumpkin leaves the impression that she and Rosa Majors did this. Rosa Majors told me that Richards took the child and placed him on a stretcher near the Nurses' Station in Major Surgery. 2) Era Lumpkin states that "someone asked us to carry the baby in major medicine." Does this mean "carry in the arms" or "carry on the stretcher"? I asked Rosa Majors this:

THOMPSON: So you took the child in your arms?

MAJORS: We carried it and laid it in there on the carriage.

THOMPSON: Now where was the carriage?

MAJORS: It was in the Major Medicine area.

[14] It seemed strange to me that nurses' aides would be equipped with stethoscopes. I was told that this was to enable them to monitor frequently the blood pressure of Emergency Room patients.

We do not know for certain that it was Ronnie Fuller's stretcher on which CE 399 subsequently was found. We know his stretcher was empty and 30 feet from the vestibule at approximately 1:00 P.M. We know that standard hospital procedure would require its movement into that vestibule. We know that it carried bloody sheets and that gauze pads, rubber gloves, and a stethoscope were used in the treatment of its last patient. All this only establishes the likelihood that Ronnie Fuller's stretcher was the one in question. As with most aspects of this case, final certainty again eludes us.

Yet if we cannot know with certainty the identity of the stretcher on which the bullet was found, we can know a far more important fact with something approaching certainty: Whatever stretcher the bullet was found on, it was *not* a stretcher used in the care of either President Kennedy or Governor Connally. On this one fact hangs a considerable mystery. . . .

PATHOLOGIST'S VIEW OF JFK AUTOPSY: AN UNSOLVED CASE
Cyril H. Wecht

Modern Medicine / *November 27, 1972*

The assassination of President John F. Kennedy in Dallas nine years ago last week simply did not happen the way the Warren Commission said it did. I state this because it is clear to me, from a strictly scientific point of view, based on my examination of available records, that the commission failed to make its case.

Moreover, it is my judgment that more than one person was involved in the shooting of President Kennedy. And I also believe that it is still possible to unravel the mystery—at least the scientific aspects of it.

The end of the thread is to be found in the assassination evidence in the National Archives, Washington, D.C. I was the first forensic pathologist—in fact, the first pathologist of any sort—outside the government to be permitted to inspect this evidence. I did so on August 23 and 24 of this year. Previous examinations were made only by the autopsy pathologists and a government-appointed panel in 1968.

However, I must emphasize at the outset that much of the autopsy evidence, including some of the most important material from the forensic standpoint, is not at the National Archives. For example, we know that the President's brain was preserved and that several sections were prepared for microscopic examination. Moreover, certain sections were taken through the skin at the supposed wounds of entry in the scalp and the upper back of the President. The preserved brain and these various brain and skin tissue sections were examined by the autopsy team about two weeks after the original autopsy, and additional photographs were then made. We know this because these items are described in the supplemental autopsy report included in volume 16 of the Warren Commission Exhibits. Yet, these items—the brain, the microscopic sections, and the supplemental photographs—are all missing from the National Archives.

Further, we know from testimony of Commander James J. Humes of the government autopsy team that color photographs were taken of the interior of the President's chest. These photos are crucial to a determination of the path of the bullet that purportedly entered the President's upper back. They are missing.

All these items were supposed to have been turned over to the National Archives on April 26, 1965, by Admiral George Burkley, but they are not included in the inventory of items officially given by Mrs. John F. Kennedy to the United States government on October 29, 1966. There has been no accounting for this discrepancy, and I have received no reply to my written inquiries addressed to the official representative of the Kennedy family.

Yet, even without these vanished materials, the remaining evidence specifically discredits the "single bullet" theory of the Warren Commission Report. This evidence also underscores certain procedural discrepancies and omissions in the way the entire investigation was handled from a *scientific, medical* point of view.

In light of the available evidence, as scrutinized by a forensic pathologist, there are at least three reasons why the single bullet theory is implausible and scientifically untenable:

1. The bullet that is said to have struck both President Kennedy and Governor John B. Connally weighed, in its found state, approximately 159 gr. Such a 6.5 mm bullet in its pristine state weighs from 161 to 161.5 gr. Thus, the loss of substance in the found bullet was about 2 to 2.5 gr. or about 1.5 percent.

Yet this is the bullet that is alleged to have entered the right side of the President's back, coursing through the uppermost portions of the thorax and mediastinum and exiting from the midline of the anterior neck region at about the level of the knot of the tie. Thereafter, this same bullet is supposed to have entered the right side of Governor Connally's back, breaking his right fifth rib. It then exited from the anterior aspect of his right chest and entered his dorsal right wrist region, where it shattered the distal radius. Finally, it exited from the volar aspect of the wrist and entered his left thigh.

Now, an experienced forensic pathologist would expect a bullet that had done all this to have had a loss of substance much in excess of 1.5 percent.

Also, x-rays of the President's chest and the Governor's chest, right wrist, and left thigh show visible particles of material that everybody has agreed are metallic fragments from the bullet. Admittedly, these are quite small, but they are visible to the naked eye. It is my contention that it is simply not possible for a bullet to have left grossly visible, radiographically evident particles in four different anatomic locations in two human beings and to have emerged with a loss of substance of only approximately 2 gr. out of a total of 161.

2. The bullet is fully jacketed in copper and measures about 3 cm. in length. The upper 2 cm. toward the nose of the bullet and the midportion of the bullet show no grossly visible deformities, areas of mutilation, loss of substance, or any other kind of significant scathing.

There is one small piece that was removed from the jacket by an FBI agent for spectrographic analysis, and the agent noted this in the records.

Otherwise, there is no deformity of the upper two-thirds of the bullet. The lower one-third shows minimal flattening, giving the impression that there was a slight squeezing of the bullet and a very minimal outpouring of the inner metallic core onto focal portions of the copper rim at the base of the bullet.

(If one can picture a volcano that has erupted slightly, with some of the lava coming up to the rim and congealing at certain points there, that is the general appearance of the bullet at its base.)

This is *not* the appearance of a bullet that has struck and fractured two bones, particularly the wrist bone. I say "particularly" because of that bone's thickness and density and the extensive fracturing that occurred.

A bullet that had caused such damage would have been more deformed and more mutilated (in a technical sense) and would have shown more markings and more loss of substance. Moreover, visual examination of this bullet shows that its copper jacket is completely intact. None of its weight loss, small as it is, could have come from any part of the bullet other than its *base*—that portion of the bullet that in normal flight is least exposed to fracture or impact forces during penetration of tissues. The nose of the bullet, the portion most exposed to such forces, is entirely smooth, except for the notch made by the FBI in taking a sample for spectrographic examination.

3. This single bullet, according to the Warren Report, came from the sixth floor window of the Texas School Book Depository Building. It therefore came on a definite angle of about 10 degrees from the right, as well as from above and behind the President. It entered the upper right side of the President's back and, again according to the Warren Commission, exited in the

midline of the anterior neck, grazing the knot of the President's tie on the left side as it came out.

Also, traveling at this significant angle from right to left, states the report, the bullet struck no bone in the President's body and was not deflected by any kind of firm or rigid object either inside or outside the body.

However, Governor Connally, who was sitting directly in front of the President, as can be seen in the Zapruder film at the National Archives, was also supposedly struck by this same bullet. He was struck in the back near the right axilla, as all the testimony and exhibits show.

This means that the bullet, moving from right to left, entering the right side of the President's back and exiting from the midline of the neck anteriorly, had to have done a rather phenomenal thing: Just after exit, it would have had to make a fairly acute angular turn around the knot of the President's tie in midair, back toward the right, to enter the far right side of Governor Connally's back!

A diagramming of the course of the bullet clearly indicates that without this impossible turn, it would have passed the Governor on the left side.

If we take great liberties with the assumed position of Governor Connally, the bullet might have entered his back somewhere to the left of his vertebral column, but certainly not to the right of the midline.

I am surprised that only a very few people, even among the critics of the Warren Commission Report, have referred to this matter. And, of course, the commission's protagonists, defenders and apologists simply ignore it. It is the kind of thing that the commission never addressed itself to, never answered, never evaluated.

If confronted with the question, the commission people say: "Well, you can't be sure exactly what the President and Governor Connally were doing at the time; maybe the car lurched, and maybe somebody was thrown," and so on.

But there is no evidence that these things did happen, and much evidence that they did *not*.

These "maybe" defenses of the Warren Commission's conclusions are motivated by the same feeling of necessity that led to the single bullet theory itself. The fact that the alleged murder weapon, a sluggish, bolt-action, war-surplus rifle, could not be reloaded, re-aimed and fired a second time in less than two and one-half seconds, plus the fact that Governor Connally was known to have been wounded less than two seconds after the President's first wounding, forced the commission to postulate that both men were hit by the same bullet.

That is the only way that one person, whether Lee Harvey Oswald or anyone else, could have done all the shooting, and the commission needed that conclusion very badly. Because if one person could not have done the shooting, and there were two or more people involved, we have by legal definition a conspiracy —something much more sinister than the Warren Commission would have us believe.

I believe that there was a second assassin, most likely firing from the rear, but not necessarily from the Texas School Book Depository Building. So far as the available materials show, there might even have been shots fired from the front and right, from the so-called grassy knoll area.

The reason for this equivocation is that the bullet hole in the President's neck was described by physicians who observed it when they worked on him in Dallas as circular, symmetrical, small, uniform, etc. This led several of them who had seen a fair number of gunshot wounds to conclude that it was a wound of entrance, not exit.

Once it was determined that the bullet had ripped through the trachea, that wound was utilized, and understandably so, as the site of a tracheostomy. The pathologists who did the autopsy some seven to eight hours later at Bethesda Naval Hospital did not report having made any attempt to reconstruct the wound by pulling its edges together. As a matter of fact, they did not even realize at the time they did the autopsy that the tracheostomy had been superimposed upon a preexisting bullet hole!

Because of the missing autopsy materials, the autopsy findings do not stand on their own as scientific proof of a rear source of the shots. Instead, external data such as witness reports from Dealey Plaza had to be relied on to justify this conclusion.

Indeed, a newspaper story is cited in the official autopsy report!

Likewise, because the microscopic autopsy slides were not available to me at the National Archives, I cannot determine whether all the shots were fired from the rear, or whether some were fired from the right front.

The missing slides could show microscopic characteristics of the epidermis and dermis that one sees with wounds of entrance and that are not found in wounds of exit. A forensic pathologist reviewing such a case as this should see such slides, if they exist. I find it rather disturbing that people who have previously reviewed the evidence have not commented on the absence of the slides and did not state that their unavailability seriously compromised any conclusions they reached.

As to the missing brain, photographs in the National Archives of the superior portions of the brain reveal a dark gray-brown object, generally parallelogram-shaped and measuring roughly 1/2 by 3/4 in. It has a slight focal shimmering effect in some pictures that could just be photographic artifacts or could be due to some light reflection caused by materials contained in the object.

Now, what the object is, I don't know. It could be a fragment of a bullet, or a brain tumor, or a vascular malformation. But, most amazing to me is that the autopsy pathologists, who could not have missed seeing it, never mentioned it! The review panel in 1968 did mention its presence and went on to say they could not tell what it was, but that was all.

Isn't such an item obviously significant in a case of gunshot wound(s) of the head?

The autopsy pathologists properly decided not to examine the brain in its "fresh," hemorrhagic state at the time of autopsy, but fixed it in formalin and went back to it for a supplemental examination exactly two weeks later.

However, at this time, they *still* didn't examine the brain, but simply took a few sections from the edges, stating in their report that "coronal sections of the brain are not made in order to preserve the specimen."

Especially in a case like this, coronal sections—parallel cuts spaced every 3/4 in. or closer from one side of the brain to the other—are the proper and routinely uniform way to examine a brain. In this manner, you can follow the bullet track(s), locate foreign objects, and so on. If you do not do this, you cannot know what the full extent of the pathology is in the brain.

To voluntarily omit such an examination is to be incompetent or a fool, and I do not believe the autopsy pathologists were either. I believe that they were *instructed* not to do a complete examination of the brain. The decision was not theirs.

So, without engaging in wild speculation, I think we can say that it is very clear that the brain should have been sectioned but was not, and that the brain was available at the time of autopsy but is not now.

Also, I think it is very clear that the autopsy pathologists did not comment on that object in the brain because, again, they were *instructed* not to.

I am disappointed that the review panel, which did see the object and did comment on it, but then passed it over, did not say in their conclusions: "We have to see the brain; we have to see the microscopic tissue slides. Unless we can examine these items of physical evidence, it is scientifically impossible for us to corroborate the conclusions of the Warren Commission Report."

I have requested from the official representative of the Kennedy family in this matter, in addition to his help in locating these missing materials, that they be made available, with the items already at the National Archives, to an independent team of experts.

I have specifically asked for the opportunity to go back to the Archives as a forensic pathologist with a group of specialists in neurosurgery, radiology, criminalistics, firearms investigation, and questioned document examination.

With all these people involved from a scientific viewpoint with this case, along with all the materials previously made available, and with several other tests that could be done, I think we would find the *real* answer to President Kennedy's assassination.

It is important to note here that two tests would answer some of the most urgent questions. Although spectrographic analysis was ordered—and presumably done—the results have never been made available. Also, neutron activation analysis—a test that was not performed—would enable us to match fragments of infinitesimal size with a known object.* This could be done

* c.f. pp. 144–154—Eds.

with the bullet (Exhibit 399) and the fragments still in the Archives. All this is vital information.

However, I am still waiting for a reply to my requests, which were made three months ago. In light of the obvious scientific inconsistencies and incomplete examinations, it is indeed most puzzling why the government and representatives of the Kennedy family would not be eager to cooperate in a bona fide attempt to resolve these critical problems in a sound, objective and impartial medical fashion.

THE MEDICAL EVIDENCE IN THE ASSASSINATION OF PRESIDENT JOHN F. KENNEDY
Cyril H. Wecht and Robert P. Smith

Forensic Science / 1974

EVALUATION AND JUDGMENT

Commission Exhibit 399, the bullet which was believed by the Commission to have caused all the non-fatal wounds in President Kennedy and Governor Connally, shattering two bones in the process, shows no deformity (other than an FBI artifact), on its

"The Medical Evidence in the Assassination of President John F. Kennedy" by Cyril H. Wecht and Robert P. Smith. Reprinted from *Forensic Science* 3, 1974, pages 124–128. Reprinted by permission of the publisher, Elsevier Sequoia S.A. and the authors.

nose or anywhere in the upper two-thirds of its length. The lower third, though it shows some flattening and a small loss of lead at the base, has no impact marks on its surface. Moreover, the completely intact copper jacket of the bullet is entirely inconsistent with the observation that all four wound sites show depositions of metallic fragments. This is not the appearance of a bullet which has struck and fractured two bones, particularly Governor Connally's right radius. A bullet that had caused such damage would have been much more deformed and mutilated, would have shown clearly visible surface markings, and would have lost substantially more substance than the 2 to 2½ grains estimated by the FBI.

On these grounds, we reject the Commission's hypothesis as incompatible with experience. It should be pointed out, however, that these grounds do not entirely eliminate the possibility that some lesser combination of wounds (not including the wrist wound of Governor Connally) might have been caused by the bullet in question, or that some different bullet (not recovered or possibly not recognized among the fragments) may have caused them.

When we examine the indicated trajectories of the wounds and the bullet flight paths required by the Commission's hypothesis, other major obstacles arise. According to the Commission's theory, a bullet entered the upper right side of the President's back and emerged at the midline of the anterior throat, grazing the left side of the knot of the President's tie as it emerged. Thereafter, this bullet is said to have entered the far right side of Governor Connally's back near the axilla and then to have traversed his chest, exiting just below the right nipple.

Governor Connally was seated directly in front of the President. Motion pictures and still photographs taken at the time or just before these body wounds were inflicted show no indication that either man's body was appreciably turned, tilted, or displaced relative to the car or each other.[1] The lateral angle of the

[1] The Governor's body *is* turned when he first emerges from behind a sign as seen in the Zapruder film, and he makes further turns in subsequent frames, exactly as he testified to the Commission. But by this time the film clearly shows that the President has already been hit and is making *voluntary* movements in response to his wounds.

wounds, relative to the longitudinal axis of the car as the men were seated, is approximately the same for both men, 17½ degrees for President Kennedy and 20 degrees for Governor Connally, the bullet moving from right to left as it traversed forward. The Commission's theory therefore requires that the bullet, just after leaving the President's throat and grazing the *left* side of the knot of his tie, make an acute angular turn to the right in mid-air in order to enter the far right side of Governor Connally's back. Bullets have been known to take inexplicable pathways in bodies, but they do not make spontaneous sharp turns in mid-air. The theory that one bullet caused both the President's back/neck wound and the Governor's chest wound is therefore untenable.

It should also be pointed out that the indicated pathways of these wounds are in considerable disagreement with the calculated trajectories from the postulated firing position of the assassin. The supposed assassin's site looked down on the car at an angle which varied from 22 to 20 degrees in the vertical plane and from 12 to about 8 degrees (right to left) in the horizontal plane, during the time interval over which these wounds might have been inflicted. The slope of the street, about 3 degrees, might perhaps be deducted from the vertical angle if we assume that the men's seating posture was determined by the slope of the car rather than their own sense of balance. (The Warren Commission made this correction although it is open to some question.) However, the vertical angle through the President's back/neck wound measures only about 11½ degrees, while that through the Governor's chest is larger, namely about 25 degrees. The indicated lateral angles (right to left in the horizontal plane) are about the same for both men, namely about 20 degrees.[2] While these angular measurements are subject to error of a few degrees either way, the discrepancies seem too large to explain away in this fashion.

We now have three major objections to the Commission's "single-bullet theory," namely the near-pristine condition of Exhibit 399, the impossibility of the bullet flight path from the President's throat to the right side of the Governor's back, and

[2] The fact that both wounds were inflicted at substantial lateral angles is also supported by the horizontal elongation of the President's back wound and of the hole in the back of Governor Connally's suit coat.

the large discrepancies between the wound angles and the postulated firing trajectories. To these could be added the visible difference in the times of reaction by the two men as seen in the Zapruder film and Governor Connally's own testimony that he believes he was hit by a separate shot.

However, it is clear that both men were hit within a very short time interval, not over 1½ seconds. Since the rifle found at the scene could not be fired twice consecutively in less than 2.3 seconds, another rifle is required to account for one of the shots. Presumably the ballistic evidence from that other rifle was not recovered, nor was the rifle itself. This is not at all implausible, considering the confusion that ensued at the scene immediately after the assassination. The Warren Commission itself, having concluded that three shots were fired, was forced to concede that one whole bullet was lost, since the bullet and bullet fragments recovered aggregated only 1½ bullets altogether. The Commission postulated that the missing bullet missed the Presidential car and its occupants entirely. In the absence of that bullet, there can be no microballistic examination to determine what rifle fired it.

The wound angle data from the President's back/neck wound and Governor Connally's chest would suggest very strongly that both guns were fired from a position considerably further west in the Texas School Book Depository than was thought to be the location of the assassin. The size and position of this building, relative to the Presidential car at the time of the assassination, is entirely compatible with this judgment. Moreover, the angles of the wounds in the *vertical* plane suggest that President Kennedy's wound was inflicted by a bullet fired from a low or intermediate floor, while Governor Connally's was inflicted by a bullet fired from a high floor or possibly the roof.

The available evidence, assuming it to be valid, gives no support to theories which postulate gunmen to the front or right-front of the Presidential car. The wound in the President's head, as evidenced in the autopsy photographs and X-rays, can only have been fired from somewhere to the rear of the President. However, it cannot be determined whether this shot was fired from the same location or locations as the shots which caused the non-fatal wounds. If any other bullet struck the President's head, whether before, after, or simultaneously with the known shot, there is no evidence for it in the available autopsy materials.

The absence or unavailability of certain evidence in this case leaves a number of residual doubts and unexplained mysteries. The missing evidence includes several autopsy items—the preserved brain tissue slides, including sections of brain and of skin at the wounds of supposed entry, and several photographs of the chest cavity—and the analytical data from the FBI's laboratory examination of the bullet and bullet fragments. All of these items are known to exist, or to have existed at one time. Their continued withholding leaves important questions unanswered and is a disservice to the nation.

For example, the detailed data from the spectrographic analysis and from the neutron activation analysis of the bullet, Commission Exhibit 399, and the various bullet fragments and lead particles recovered, could settle a number of questions important in reconstructing the shooting. For example, is the lead fragment removed from Governor Connally's wrist of the same composition as the lead in Commission Exhibit 399 or is it not? Does its composition match that of any other fragment recovered, e.g., one of the large fragments found in the front of the car? Is the copper in the two large fragments found in the front of the car from the same bullet or from two different bullets? From what bullet or fragment did the lead found on the inside of the windshield originate? Or the lead smear found on the street curb in the vicinity? Are there any fragments or particles whose composition indicates a different manufacturer from the others? Such questions *can* be answered by good analytical work, and in a case so fraught with difficulties in explaining the shooting, there can be no legitimate excuse for not providing the results of the tests already performed and for not conducting other appropriate scientific tests which might well resolve these questions conclusively.

SUMMARY AND CONCLUSIONS

Autopsy Conditions and Procedures

The autopsy of President Kennedy was deficient in failing to report a number of important facts about the nature of the President's wounds and in neglecting to make accurate measurements of the locations of the wounds. At least one serious oversight occurred[3] in respect to a wound in the President's throat, which oversight was not corrected until the following day, after belated consultation with doctors who treated the President in Dallas.

The autopsy was completely dominated by military personnel under military orders. Instructions were given to the autopsy doctors which prevented the performance of important procedures, such as dissection of an observed wound in the upper back and the sectioning of the brain.

Too many extraneous personnel were in attendance, while highly qualified civilian forensic pathologists, who might have ensured a thorough autopsy, were deliberately not invited.

GOVERNMENTAL HANDLING AND DISCLOSURE OF EVIDENCE

The Government's handling of the evidence in the case created much unnecessary confusion and skepticism. The FBI itself was unaware, for almost two months as reflected in their official reports, that the autopsy team had corrected itself the day after the autopsy and concluded that a bullet had exited from the President's throat. Photographs and X-rays of the President's body were not examined by the Warren Commission, and instead reliance was placed on artist's sketches and verbal descriptions which were later found to be in error.

After the Warren Report was published, the Government continued to withhold fundamental medical and other evidence. The autopsy photographs and X-rays have been kept secret from the public and, until recently, they have even been withheld from qualified, independent, non-government pathologists.

Important analytical data concerning the bullet and bullet fragments continue to be withheld. The data could settle a number of critical questions about the details of the shooting; the data are

[3] During the autopsy examination, the missile wound in the anterior neck was not recognized as such because of the tracheotomy incision. It was discovered only through a telephone call the following day to one of the attending physicians in Dallas. While the failure to recognize the presence of the wound may be rationalized on the basis of the surgical incision, the failure to consult the Dallas physicians before or during the autopsy cannot.—CHW

known to have been acquired by the FBI laboratory, but there is no indication that the Warren Commission ever saw them or even asked for them.

Certain important autopsy materials, including the preserved brain, certain tissue and skin sections, and several photographs are unavailable and unaccounted for.

Present State of Knowledge of the Details of the Shooting

The Warren Commission's "single-bullet theory" is untenable, and the Commission's conclusion that there was only one assassin cannot be reconciled with available evidence. Medical and photographic data, including measurements of wound angles and calculations of bullet trajectories, strongly suggest that there were two rifles used. The indicated locations are in the same building concluded by the Warren Commission to be the site of a lone assassin, but at points further west in this building and on two different floors.

So far as the available medical evidence shows, all shots were fired from the rear. No support can be found for theories which postulate gunmen to the front or right-front of the Presidential car. The medical evidence indicates that the President's back was hit by one bullet and that his head was hit by one other bullet only.

Residual doubts exist about the details of the shooting. At least some of these can be cleared up by making all of the autopsy materials available, and by releasing the detailed FBI laboratory data on the spectrographic and neutron activation analyses of the bullet and bullet fragments recovered.

THE COMMISSION, THE CRITICS AND THE PRESS

In August 1971 the Texas Observer, *a small but influential liberal weekly, published the following exchange between critic Sylvia Meagher and Commission lawyer David Belin focusing on the testimony of one of Oswald's co-workers at the Texas School Book Depository. Meagher later sent copies of the exchange to* The New York Times *in the hope of securing wider coverage of the debate. On the eighth anniversary of the assassination the* Times *published a slightly rewritten version of Belin's side of the controversy on its Op-Ed page, under the title "The Warren Commission Was Right."—Eds.*

THE CURIOUS TESTIMONY OF MR. GIVENS
Sylvia Meagher

Texas Observer / *August 13, 1971*

New York City

One witness who helped to incriminate Lee Harvey Oswald in the assassination of President John F. Kennedy was a Book Depository porter named Charles Givens. The Warren Commission gave prominence to his testimony that he had forgotten his cigarettes on the sixth floor and that when he went to retrieve them just before noon he had encountered Oswald near the southeast corner window.

In a book published in 1967 (*Accessories after the Fact*, Bobbs-Merrill Co., Inc.), I discussed the discrepancies between the Givens story as set forth in the Warren Report and the corresponding testimony and exhibits, and the grounds for concluding that the story suggested perjury and collusion. It was logically inconsistent with a genuine encounter at about 11:45 between Oswald and a group of employees who were racing two elevators from the sixth to the first floor, when Oswald had called to them to send one elevator back so that he could go down too. Ten minutes later, if one accepted Givens' testimony, Oswald declined to go down for the lunch break. Moreover, while Givens supposedly exchanged a few words with Oswald on the sixth floor, other witnesses observed him on the first floor. Most of all, Givens' testimony was suspect because in his affidavit to the Dallas police later that afternoon he said nothing about forgetting his cigarettes, returning to the sixth floor, or meeting Oswald there—an omission that was incomprehensible, if the encounter was authentic.

That is how the situation appeared back in 1967. Some months ago, I obtained from the National Archives a collection of unpublished Warren Commission documents ("CD's") concerning Charles Givens. Reading them was a shock not soon to be forgotten. I had half-expected that the CD's would reconcile and dispose of the contradictions that earlier had forced me to question the legitimacy of the Givens testimony. Instead, these new documents raise even stronger questions about Givens' testimony and the role of two or more Warren Commission lawyers in extracting that testimony.

Here is a chronological reconstruction of the Givens affair from which anyone easily can judge for himself whether or not there are sufficient grounds for an accusation of perjury, collusion, and falsification of evidence with the clear purpose of incriminating Oswald as the assassin of President Kennedy. (The citations in each case refer to both published transcripts and exhibits and to unpublished commission documents or internal reports and papers.)

NOVEMBER 22, 1963

At 1:46 p.m. Inspector Sawyer of the Dallas police issued an alert on the police radio for Charles Givens, a porter at the Book Depository, because he had "a police record and he left" (CE 705 page 30). It was known at that hour that Oswald, too, had left the scene but no alert for him was issued—Captain Will Fritz and two detectives intended to proceed to Irving personally, in search of Oswald.

Within an hour or two, Givens was escorted to the police head-quarters, where he was questioned and where he executed an affidavit stating that he had left the sixth floor at about 11:30 a.m., had gone to the washroom, at noon had taken his lunch period, had gone to a parking lot to visit with a friend employed there (CE 2003 page 27). Givens' affidavit said nothing about a return to the sixth floor for cigarettes or an encounter there with Oswald.

Later that day Givens was interviewed by FBI agents Griffen and Odum. He gave them the same story as in the affidavit but added one additional piece of information—*that at 11:50 a.m. he had seen Oswald reading a paper in the "domino room" on the first floor* (CD 5 page 329).

NOVEMBER 23, 1963

Bonnie Ray Williams, another Book Depository employee, in an interview by FBI agents Griffen and Odum described a race between two elevators on November 22nd at about 11:30 a.m. in which he, Givens, and others participated. On the way down, they had seen Oswald on the fifth floor. Williams had returned to the sixth floor at about noon and had seen no one there (CD 5 page 330).

DECEMBER 2, 1963

Givens, interviewed by the Secret Service, said that he had seen Oswald with a clipboard on the sixth floor at about 11:45 a.m., shortly after which he and some fellow-workers had boarded the two elevators. While racing to the first floor, Oswald had called to them to send one elevator back up (Ball/Belin Report No. 1, dated Feb. 25, 1964). Again Givens said nothing about a return to the sixth floor for his cigarettes at any time after the elevator race.

DECEMBER 9, 1963

The FBI Summary Report (withheld from the public until mid-1966, when certain excerpts were published in the book *Inquest*, raising a furor of doubt about the Warren Report) to President Johnson stated that Oswald had been observed on the fifth floor between 11:30 a.m. and noon and that during that period of time he had asked Givens, who was in an elevator, to close the gates when he got off so that the elevator could be summoned (CD 1 page 6). The FBI Summary Report *omits* Givens' statement to two FBI agents on the day of the assassination that he had seen Oswald reading a paper in the domino room at 11:50.

FEBRUARY 13, 1964

Lt. Jack Revill of the Dallas police was interviewed by FBI agent Robert Gemberling about press rumors of a Negro being held in protective custody. Revill "stated that Givens had been previously handled by the Special Services Bureau on a marijuana charge and he believes that *Givens would change his story for money.*" (Emphasis added.) Gemberling's report repeats the story of the elevator race during which Oswald yelled to Givens to close the gates when he got off (CD 735 pages 296-297). Almost three months after the "fact," there is still no hint from Givens, Revill, or the FBI of cigarettes forgotten by Givens or his return to the sixth floor and encounter there with Oswald. But in another context, Revill volunteers the opinion that Givens would give false information "for money."

FEBRUARY 25, 1964

Warren Commission lawyers Joseph Ball and David Belin complete a first joint report, summarizing the evidence known by that date, and note discrepancies as to the time of Givens' departure (and elevator race) from the sixth floor—11:35 as against 11:40 or 11:45 a.m. Ball and Belin also note that Givens saw Oswald at 11:50 a.m. in the domino room and that three other witnesses also place Oswald on the first floor—William Shelley, at about 11:50 a.m.; Eddie Piper, at noon; and Mrs. Carolyn Arnold, who believed she had seen Oswald near the front door of the Book

Depository at about 12:15 p.m. (Ball/Belin memorandum of Feb. 25, 1964, pages 101, 105-107, 110).

MARCH 18, 1964

Givens, in an affidavit furnished by him to FBI agents Trettis and Robertson, states that when President Kennedy was shot, he was standing at the corner of Record and Elm Streets. "I returned to the Depository Building, and was told by a Dallas policeman that I could not enter the building. About an hour later I went to the Dallas Police Department and was questioned by the police for about 45 minutes." (CE 1381 page 36) Wearisome though it is, it must again be pointed out that there was no mention during the 45-minute interrogation of the cigarettes left and retrieved or of seeing Oswald on the sixth floor, nor were these alleged circumstances hinted at in the March, 1964, affidavit to the FBI, four months after the assassination.

APRIL 8, 1964

Charles Givens gives sworn testimony to the Warren Commission in a deposition taken by lawyer David Belin, with no one else present except the court reporter. Now, for the *first time*, Givens tells the story (later embodied in the Warren Report) about the cigarettes forgotten on the sixth floor and the encounter with Oswald (6H 345-356, WR 143). Belin should have been fully aware that Givens had told a completely different story to the FBI and the police on the day of the assassination, and subsequently to the Secret Service and the FBI, since Belin had co-authored the report which discussed Givens' accounts of his movements in considerable detail. But Belin did not challenge Givens' *new* story nor place on record that on several earlier occasions Givens had sworn to a completely different account of his movements and actions on the day of the assassination. Indeed, in one oblique question, he asked, "Did you ever tell anyone that you saw Lee Oswald reading a newspaper in the domino room around 11:50 . . . that morning?" (6H 354). Givens replied, "No, sir," which meant either that he was giving Belin a false response or that the two FBI agents who had interviewed him on Nov. 22 had invented Givens' reported statement that he had seen Oswald in the domino room at 11:50 a.m. Yet neither Givens nor the FBI agents were challenged or even queried in an attempt to determine which story was true and which was false.

APRIL 8, 1964

Lawyer Belin took the testimony of Inspector Herbert Sawyer on the same day as he questioned Givens. Sawyer stated that he had sent out an alarm for Givens an hour after the shooting on Dealey Plaza because "he was supposed to have some information about the man that did the shooting" (6H 315-325). Belin apparently accepted that statement, despite the fact that Givens when he was picked up did not produce information "about the man who did the shooting" and despite the language of the alert broadcast on the police radio, which shows clearly that Givens was wanted because he had a police record and was missing from the Book Depository.

Why did Sawyer (and later, Revill, as discussed below) attempt retroactively to authenticate a story which Givens articulated for the first time in April? Was this testimony part and parcel of a deliberate, planned collusion among police officials, commission lawyers, and a witness who was a man with a police record and who was appraised as a man who would change his story for money?

MAY 13, 1964

Lt. Revill testified before the Warren Commission, J. Lee Rankin conducting the examination in the presence of Warren, Gerald Ford, Allen Dulles, Norman Redlich, Arlen Specter, and Charles Murray, ABA observer. Revill stated that at about 2:30 or 3 p.m. on the day of the assassination he knew only that someone named Lee had been arrested and that "this was told to him by a colored employee of the Depository." Revill continued, "I asked him if he had been on the sixth floor . . . he said, yes, that he had observed Mr. Lee, over by this window. . . . So I turned this Givens individual over to one of our Negro detectives and told him to take him to Captain Fritz for interrogation" (5H 35-36).

This testimony is patently false, for the obvious reason that Givens on arrival at the police department did not state that he had seen Oswald "over by this window" and never said so until April, 1964. Chief Curry, when he was questioned on June 2, 1964, by FBI agent Vincent Drain, gave a different version than Revill of what had transpired: "Givens told Revill that he had been in the . . . Depository . . . with Oswald on the morning of Nov. 22, 1963, but was on the street during the . . . motorcade . . . Chief Curry related that everyone who might have any knowledge of Oswald, known as Lee to Givens, was being questioned" (CD 1245 page 181). *This* seems to be the authentic story —that Givens was questioned not because he had any special information but because he was employed at the Book Depository.

June 2, 1964

Police Chief Curry was interviewed by FBI agent Drain, as reported in the preceding paragraph.

June 3, 1964

The FBI promptly re-interviewed Givens, who told FBI agents Switzer and Petraskis that he *now recalled* that he had returned to the sixth floor at about 11:45 a.m. to get his cigarettes, etc. (CD 1245 page 182). The FBI did not even raise an eyebrow at Givens' sudden recovery from sustained amnesia.

September 20, 1964

The Warren Report was released, with its "forgotten cigarettes" version of Givens' activities. It contained no indication, explicit or implicit, of Givens' original story, which had placed Oswald in the domino room at 11:50, nor did it mention that another witness had also seen Oswald on the first floor at precisely that time while still other witnesses saw him still on the first floor at noon and at about 12:15 p.m.

The report also "cleared up" some of the confusion about items of evidence which had arisen because of fragmentary or misleading press reports out of Dallas in the first frantic hours after the assassination. For example, news stories about the chicken remains and a cigarette package had created the impression of a sniper who had concealed himself for a prolonged time on the sixth floor, awaiting the President's appearance. The report explained that the chicken remains were discarded innocently by one of the Book Depository employees who had eaten his lunch on the sixth floor. But it said nothing about the cigarette package mentioned in the initial press stories but then completely forgotten by the news media. Oswald, after all, did not smoke.

But Charles Givens *did* smoke. If he really left his package of cigarettes on the sixth floor, it may have been picked up together with the chicken bones since the burden of the unpublished documents is that he never returned there to retrieve anything. Certainly it is curious that the elusive cigarette pack is not mentioned anywhere in the 26 volumes of testimony and exhibits nor in the hundreds of pages of unpublished documents which deal in great detail with the crime search and the laboratory tests of materials and objects found on the sixth floor.

APRIL 1971

Relying solely on the official documents and papers of the Warren Commission, I have assembled a chronological account of the conflicting statements and testimony in the matter of Charles Givens and suggested why they raise profound misgivings about the commission's findings. I am confident that no spokesman for the Warren Commission will come forward with clarifications that effectively reconcile the contradictions in the evidence or that can justify the embodiment in the Warren Report of a version of Givens' story that is incompatible with all his earlier statements, without acknowledgment that there had been previous, different versions by the same witness.

TRUTH WAS MY ONLY GOAL
David W. Belin

Texas Observer / *August 13, 1971*

Des Moines

Like the proverbial person who is so close to the forest that he cannot see the trees, the assassination sensationalists have talked about cigarette packages, fictitious puffs of smoke from smokeless gunpowder and chicken bones. What they have not talked about is the heart of the physical evidence and key witnesses such as Johnny Calvin Brewer, whose testimony I took before a court reporter in Dallas on April 2, 1964. (Vol. VII, pp. 1-8)

Mr. Brewer was the assistant manager of a shoe store located near the Texas Theatre in the Oak Cliff section of Dallas. He became suspicious of the way Oswald ducked into his store early in the afternoon of Nov. 22, 1963, when police sirens were heard coming down the street. After the police sirens subsided, Oswald left the front of the shoe store and Brewer followed him into the Texas Theatre and then had the theatre cashier call the police. When they arrived at the theatre, Brewer pointed out Oswald, who pulled out a revolver which he had in his possession as the police approached him.

Carrying a concealed weapon is a crime, and the very fact that Oswald had such a weapon in his possession on November 22, 1963, surely cannot be ignored. Moreover, the act of pulling out a revolver as a police officer approaches is somewhat suspicious, to say the least. Documentary evidence proved that this very revolver had been purchased by Oswald under an alias. Finally, irrefutable scientific evidence proved that this revolver to the exclusion of all other weapons in the world was the weapon which discharged the cartridge cases which witnesses saw the murderer of Officer J. D. Tippit toss away as he was leaving the scene of the Tippit murder. (The bullet slugs themselves in Tippit's body were too mutilated to avail themselves of conclusive ballistic testi-

"Truth Was My Only Goal" by David W. Belin. Reprinted from *The Texas Observer*, August 13, 1971, by permission of the publisher.

mony, but cartridge cases can be individually traced to a particular weapon, just as unmutilated bullet slugs can.)

In addition to the physical evidence of the gun and the cartridge cases, there were several witnesses including William Scoggins, Ted Callaway and Barbara Jeanette Davis who saw the gunman at or near the scene of the Tippit murder and who identified Oswald as the gunman in police lineups.

The silence of the assassination sensationalists is very telling—they cannot seriously challenge the conclusion that Oswald killed Tippit, in light of the weapon found in his possession, the ballistic evidence of the cartridge cases and the combined effect of this with the eye witness testimony of independent witnesses near the murder scene plus the testimony of Johnny Calvin Brewer.

In the case of the murder of President Kennedy, two of the bullet fragments found in the presidential limousine were large enough for ballistic identification. In addition, a nearly whole bullet was found at Parkland Memorial Hospital. Less than an hour after the assassination, a Mannlicher-Carcano rifle, No. C2766, was found stuffed between some cartons near the back stairway on the sixth floor of the Texas School Book Depository Building. Irrefutable scientific evidence proved that these bullets came from that particular weapon to the exclusion of all other weapons in the world. I, myself, examined these bullet slugs with test bullets from the rifle with a comparison microscope.

In addition to the bullet and two large portions of a bullet(s), three cartridge cases were discovered shortly after the assassination at the southeast corner window of the sixth floor of the Texas School Book Depository Building. Scientific evidence proved that these cartridge cases, like the bullets, came from that particular rifle to the exclusion of all other weapons in the world.

I personally took the testimony of the executive officer of Klein Sporting Goods, which was the company that sold and shipped the rifle to Lee Harvey Oswald's post office box in Dallas under his assumed alias, A. Hidell. I personally saw the copy of the order form that Oswald sent in for the rifle.

The only persons who testified they saw a rifle at the time of the assassination testified they saw that rifle in the southeast corner of the Texas School Book Depository Building. There are myriads of other facts, all of which are summarized in our official report of the Warren Commission which conclusively show that Lee Harvey Oswald was the assassin of President Kennedy.

Through the past several years, I have marveled how easily the world has been deceived by assassination sensationalists like Sylvia Meagher. The device used has been relatively simple: Distortion by commission, coupled with distortion by omission and often the use of innuendo.

Perhaps I, too, would have been misled by some of the writings of the sensationalists if I had not personally worked with the Warren Commission as one of the two lawyers who concentrated in what we called "Area II: The determination of who was the assassin of President Kennedy." My partner was the distinguished California attorney, Joseph A. Ball. By the time we had completed our work, we had more first-hand knowledge of the evidence pertaining to who was the assassin of President Kennedy and who murdered Dallas Police Officer J. D. Tippit than any other people in the world.

When Kaye Northcott, editor of *The Texas Observer*, wrote me that she was considering for publication the contrived article by Sylvia Meagher, I replied on December 10, 1970, that ". . . all of the allegations in the article of Sylvia Meagher are false. . . . If one takes the time to read and study the basic report of the Warren Commission, the evidence as a whole conclusively shows that Lee Harvey Oswald killed John F. Kennedy and also killed Officer J. D. Tippit. Moreover, as one of the lawyers who was intimately involved in the interrogation of the key witnesses to the assassination, I know that the evidence was impartially and objectively gathered with the one goal that we all had in mind: the truth, the whole truth, and nothing but the truth. As an independent lawyer, I am beholden to no one and there is not a person in the world who could have made me sign any report concluding that Oswald murdered President Kennedy and Officer Tippit if I did not believe that the evidence as a whole showed that the murderer of Officer Tippit and the murderer of John F. Kennedy beyond a reasonable doubt was Lee Harvey Oswald."

One inherent problem in defending the Warren Commission report is that a lie can be uttered in a relatively few sentences. In contrast, in order to give a true picture of the entire facts, several paragraphs, or more, may be necessary. Yet, space limitations do not permit such a complete reply.

For instance, Sylvia Meagher writes about references to Charles Givens on pages 101, 105-107 and 110 of what she refers to as the "Ball/Belin Memorandum of February 25, 1964." She omits vital portions of this document (the correct name of which was "Ball-Belin Report #1"), including the following from the initial three paragraphs of this 238-page document:

. . . Our report contains a summary of tentative conclusions reached on the basis of the thousands of pages of material examined thus far, but these conclusions are subject to change depending upon the results of further materials examined, the taking of evidence and additional information received from crime laboratory reports.

We should also point out that the tentative memorandum of Jan. 23 substantially differs from the original outline of our work in this area which had as its subject, "Lee Harvey Oswald as the Assassin of President Kennedy," and which examined the evidence from that standpoint. *At no time have we assumed that Lee Harvey Oswald was the assassin of President Kennedy. Rather, our entire study has been based on an independent examination of all of the evidence in an effort to determine who was the assassin of President Kennedy.* (Emphasis added.)

A primary purpose of this report is its adaptability for our own use in making further investigation. We have not attempted to make an exhaustive analysis of the interviews with the various persons involved. Rather, we have tried to pinpoint the most important facts and problems which appear from the data which has been examined thus far.

As an experienced trial lawyer, I know that whenever there are two or more witnesses to an event, you most likely find contradictions in the testimony between and among witnesses, and you often find contradictions within the testimony of a single witness. I also know that the best source of testimony is from the witness, himself, rather than from hearsay reports of that third party, such as police officers or FBI or secret service agents might write down. Included in our Ball-Belin Report #1 were comments on a number of contradictions within the hearsay statements of third parties, including inconsistencies in the testimony of Mr. Givens.

I also noted in one of the written reports the observation of an officer that Mr. Givens might be readily subject to influence.

When I went to Dallas to take the testimony of various witnesses, including Mr. Givens, I did not go as a participant in an adversary proceeding—either a prosecuting attorney or a defense attorney—but rather I went as an attorney trying to ascertain the facts in a manner that would avoid leading any of the witnesses into giving preconceived or any type of "desired" testimony. Mr. Givens is a perfect example of this, for in a portion of his testimony which Sylvia Meagher did not quote, I asked Mr. Givens:

MR. BELIN: Is there anything else you can think of, whether I have asked it or not, that in any way is relevant to the assassination?

MR. GIVENS: No, sir.

MR. BELIN: Anything else you can think of about Lee Oswald, whether I have asked it or not, that might in any way be helpful?

MR. GIVENS: No, sir. Other than he is just a peculiar fellow. He is just a loner. Don't have much to say to anybody. Stayed by himself most of the time. (Vol. VI, p. 355)

Any experienced trial lawyer knows you do not ask questions such as this if you are trying to hide any facts. Mrs. Meagher writes such garbage as, "Was the testimony part and parcel of a deliberate, planned collusion among police officials, commission lawyers and a witness who was a man with a police record and was appraised as a man who would change his story for money?" Not only do the foregoing portions of my interrogation of Mr. Givens show the utter falsity of such an allegation, but a minute or two later in the interrogation of Mr. Givens I asked a similar series of questions once again and then concluded with a statement in the record showing how my interrogation of witnesses was conducted:

MR. BELIN: Anything else you can think of?

MR. GIVENS: No, sir; that is about it.

MR. BELIN: Well, Mr. Givens, we surely appreciate your cooperation in coming down here. Now you and I didn't talk about this at all until we started taking this deposition, did we?

MR. GIVENS: No, sir.

MR. BELIN: You walked into the room and you raised your right hand and we started taking your testimony. Is that correct?

MR. GIVENS: Yes, sir.

MR. BELIN: Have I ever met you before?

MR. GIVENS: I don't believe so. I don't believe I have. (Vol. VI, pp. 355, 356)

In light of this record which Sylvia Meagher no doubt read, her use of the innuendo of "planned collusion" is an outright prostitution of the truth. At all times while I was with the Warren Commission, my sole concern was to get at all of the facts, letting the chips fall where they may, without trying to arrive at any preconceived result.

With this as a frame of reference, let us further examine the testimony of Givens with reference to the various discrepancies in police and FBI reports of interviews with him. Givens testified that around 8:30 a.m., on Nov. 22, he saw Lee Harvey Oswald on the first floor of the School Book Depository Building. The record shows the following:

MR. BELIN: All right. You saw him at 8:30 on the first floor?

MR. GIVENS: Yes, sir.

MR. BELIN: Then what did you do?

MR. GIVENS: Well, we went back upstairs and started to work.

MR. BELIN: You went back up to the sixth floor to continue laying the floor?

MR. GIVENS: Yes, sir.

MR. BELIN: When did you see Lee Harvey Oswald next?

MR. GIVENS: Next?

MR. BELIN: Yes.

MR. GIVENS: Well, it was about a quarter till twelve, we were on our way downstairs, and we passed him, and he was standing at the gate on the fifth floor. I came downstairs, and I discovered I left my cigarettes in my jacket upstairs, and I took the elevator back upstairs to get my jacket with my cigarettes in it. When I got back upstairs, he was on the sixth floor in that vicinity, coming from that way.

MR. BELIN: Coming from what way?

MR. GIVENS: Toward the window up front where the shots were fired from. (Vol. VI, pp. 347, 348)

Givens testified that Oswald was walking with a clipboard in his hand, from the southeast corner of the sixth floor. After the assassination, Oswald's clipboard was found on the sixth floor, not too far from the place where the assassination weapon was discovered stuck between some book cartons near the back stairway.

After Givens' testimony about returning to the sixth floor, I specifically asked him about the domino room because of early written reports of third parties in our possession. Mrs. Meagher refers to one area of questioning which occurred on page 354 of Volume VI:

MR. BELIN: Did you ever tell anyone that you saw Lee Oswald reading a newspaper in the domino room around 11:50, 10 minutes to 12 on that morning on November 22nd?

MR. GIVENS: No, sir. (Vol. VI, p. 352)

However, she conveniently omits the following testimony which appears on page 352 of Volume VI:

MR. BELIN: Now you said you saw Lee Oswald on the sixth floor around 11:55?

MR. GIVENS: Right.

MR. BELIN: Did you see Lee Oswald anywhere else in the building between 11:55 and the time you left the building?

MR. GIVENS: No, sir.

MR. BELIN: On November 22nd?

MR. GIVENS: No, sir.

MR. BELIN: Did you see him in the domino room at all around anywhere between 11:30 and 12 or 12:30?

MR. GIVENS: No, sir. (Vol. VI, p. 352)

The foregoing omissions of Sylvia Meagher are typical of all of the assassination sensationalists who have picked at extracts from an overall record with the Joseph McCarthy-like technique of innuendo of conspiracy. Moreover, in concentrating on innuendo and minute particles of an overall mass of evidence, there has been a most significant silence concerning the crux of the physical evidence and the overwhelming weight of testimony from the record. A full reading of the Warren Commission Report and the underlying published documentary evidence and testimony of witnesses conclusively shows that within a one-hour period, Lee Harvey Oswald killed two men in Dallas, Tex., on November 22, 1963: President John F. Kennedy and Dallas Police Officer J. D. Tippit.

Perhaps some day I shall take the time to write a book and expose the Sylvia Meaghers and the Mark Lanes and others for the inaccurate sensationalists that they have been. Yet, although I know that they have deceived the public, surely their sins of deception are not that great when compared with the kind of deception that has plagued America this past decade, Number One on the list, of course, being the Vietnam War.

When a Gulf of Tonkin resolution can pass both Houses of Congress and lead a President of the United States to commit over a half million American men and One Hundred Billion Dollars to fight a land war in Southeast Asia with all of the terrible consequences of such a war on both the American people as well as the Vietnamese, I do not get so worked up about the utter falsity of the writings about the Warren Commission by people such as Sylvia Meagher. After all, what is most important is not what others say that I did but rather what I know actually took place and that is very simple:

Like all of the other lawyers working with the Warren Commission, truth was my only goal. On the basis of the overall record as I investigated the two murders of Nov. 22, beyond a reasonable doubt, the man who killed President John F. Kennedy and Dallas Police Officer J. D. Tippit was Lee Harvey Oswald.

THE WARREN COMMISSION WAS RIGHT
David W. Belin

The New York Times / *November 22, 1971*

DES MOINES, Iowa—The susceptibility of human nature to the mystique of conspiracy has afforded a fertile field for the assassination sensationalists. Through misrepresentation, omission and innuendo they have been successful in deceiving a large body of world public opinion into questioning the validity and veracity of the Warren Commission conclusion that Lee Harvey Oswald on Nov. 22, 1963, murdered President John F. Kennedy and Dallas police officer J. D. Tippit.

I served as an independent lawyer with the Warren Commission in 1964 and together with the distinguished California attorney, Joseph A. Ball, concentrated in what we called, "Area II: The determination of who was the assassin of President Kennedy."

In a sense, the Rosetta Stone to the solution of President Kennedy's murder is the murder of officer Tippit. It strikes at the heart of the claims of the assassination sensationalists who seek to prove that Oswald was in some way "framed." They allege that Oswald was innocent of the murders of both Kennedy and Tippit and that the reason for his arrest had nothing to do with either killing.

For instance, Prof. Hugh Trevor-Roper in an introduction to one of the best-selling books attacking the Warren Commission Report wrote: "The plain fact is that there was no evidence at all to explain how or why the Dallas police instantly pounced on Oswald. . . ."

"The plain fact" is that the Warren Commission Report accurately shows why Oswald was arrested. An alert citizen, Johnny Calvin Brewer, is the key witness.

Brewer managed a shoe store in the vicinity of the place where Tippit was killed. I took his testimony in Dallas on April 2, 1964.

Shortly after Brewer learned from radio newscasts about the shooting of Tippit in his neighborhood, he became suspicious of the way a man first ducked into the entryway of his shoe store when police sirens were heard coming down the street and then left the front of the store soon after the police sirens subsided.

Brewer followed the man down the street into the Texas Theater and then had the cashier call the police. When the police arrived at the theater, Brewer pointed out the man, who was Lee Harvey Oswald. As a policeman approached, Oswald pulled out a revolver.

Carrying a concealed gun is a crime. The fact that Oswald had such a weapon in his possession and drew it is highly suspicious. Subsequent evidence proved that this very revolver had been purchased through the mail by Oswald under the same alias he used to acquire the rifle used in the assassination of President Kennedy.

Finally, irrefutable scientific evidence proved that this revolver to the exclusion of all other weapons in the world was the weapon which discharged the cartridge cases which witnesses saw the murderer of officer Tippit toss away as he left the scene of the crime.

Several eyewitnesses including William Scoggins, Ted Callaway and Barbara Jeanette Davis who saw the gunman at close range unequivocally identified Oswald.

We also found that the overall record showed that beyond a reasonable doubt Lee Harvey Oswald was the assassin of President Kennedy. In addition to the Tippit murder, that record included (1) ballistic testimony which absolutely identified through both cartridge cases and bullets Oswald's rifle as the assassination weapon, (2) overwhelming evidence which specifically proved that the shots came from the southeast corner of the sixth-floor window of the Texas School Book Depository Building where Oswald worked, (3) Oswald's palmprint on the rifle barrel, (4) Oswald's purchase and ownership of the rifle, (5) Oswald's activities both before and after the assassination including the long and bulky package containing the rifle that he carried into the School Book Depository Building on the morning of the assassination,

(6) Oswald's palmprint and fingerprint located on cartons stacked near the window from which the shots were fired, (7) the similarity of Oswald's appearance with the description of the assassin by the key eyewitness, Howard Brennan, (8) the time sequences I personally checked out in retracing Oswald's steps from the time of the assassination to the scene of the Tippit murder, (9) the physical evidence of the clothing of President Kennedy which shows the shots came from the rear, (10) objective expert witness testimony, (11) moving pictures and still pictures taken by both amateur and professional photographers, (12) the relative ease of the "line-type" shots, the first bullet striking President Kennedy when he was approximately sixty yards from the assassination window, which with a four-power scope made it appear as if he were only approximately fifteen yards away from the gunman, and the fatal shot striking the President when he was only 265 feet away from the assassination window, which with the four-power scope translates into approximately 22 yards, and (13) the discovery of the assassination weapon and Oswald's clipboard near the back stairway of the sixth floor of the depository building.

In my work with the Warren Commission, I served as an independent lawyer from Des Moines, beholden to no one. There is not a person in the world who could have made me write any portion of any report if I disagreed with its ultimate conclusion.

I know that truth was my only goal, regardless of political consequences, just as it was the goal of all of the other independent lawyers working with the Warren Commission.

I also know that despite the success of the assassination sensationalists in deceiving a large body of world opinion, the Warren Commission Report will stand the test of history for one simple reason: The ultimate truth beyond a reasonable doubt is that Lee Harvey Oswald killed both John F. Kennedy and J. D. Tippit on that tragic afternoon of Nov. 22, 1963.

THE MEDIA AND THE MURDER OF JOHN KENNEDY
Jerry Policoff

New Times / *August 8, 1975*

". . . It happens to be to our interest, as well as the interest of the Commission and of the country, to obtain as wide a distribution of this document as we can. . . ."

> Letter from then-Assistant Managing
> Editor of the New York *Times*, Clifton
> Daniel, to J. Lee Rankin, Chief Counsel
> to the Warren Commission, dated May
> 21, 1964 (four months prior to the
> publication of the Warren Report)

It has been nearly 12 years since John Fitzgerald Kennedy, the 35th President of the United States, was felled by a hail of bullets as he rode through Dallas. The case was officially closed with the issuance of the Warren Commission's Report, which found that Lee Harvey Oswald was the lone assassin. Those findings have recently come under renewed attack as the controversy has reemerged after a rather lengthy period of hibernation. Once again, charges of omission and distortion by commission detractors and similar counter-charges by commission defenders are filling the air, leaving many confused and befuddled.

In this atmosphere, one might expect the press to clarify the facts—to delve into the story, follow up the leads and unmask the cover-up, if one existed. Unfortunately, the story of the Kennedy assassination controversy is one of continuous government manipulation of a press that seems only too willing to be manipulated. With conspiracy rumors raging anew, the press shows few signs of change on this issue.

The press could learn a good deal about the assassination, and about its own failure to pursue the story independently, by reviewing its own initial reporting out of Dallas. Those early reports stand in stark contrast to what is officially alleged to have transpired. The infamous "grassy knoll," for example, was no concoction of the Warren Commission critics. "The shots apparently came from a grassy knoll in the area," reported the Associated Press in its initial dispatches.

Word of shots from the front dominated early reports from the site (witnesses interviewed by the press seemed to be nearly unanimous on this point), but these reports were forgotten by the press within several hours, as Dallas authorities began to make it clear that a local "communist" by the name of Lee Harvey Oswald had fired all of the shots from a sniper's nest constructed on the sixth floor of the Texas School Book Depository to the rear of the presidential limousine.

Leaked biographical data depicting the "erratic" nature of the "political malcontent" Oswald began to flood the media almost immediately. . . .

By the time Oswald himself was assassinated, all pretense had disappeared. The press had found Oswald guilty without benefit of trial. "President's Assassin Shot. . . ," proclaimed the New York *Times*. *Life* profiled the "Assassin: The Man Held—And Killed—For Murder." *Time*'s combination biography/obituary was titled simply "The Man Who Killed Kennedy."

Successive leaks from Dallas authorities, the FBI (whose report on the assassination was summarized in the press before it was received by the Warren Commission) and the Warren Commission itself continued to implicate Oswald as the sole perpetrator of a deranged act. The press, by its uncritical reporting, was allowing itself to be set up to the point at which official findings, regardless of what they might be, would have to be accepted, applauded and defended. Thus, the press' curiosity was not aroused when a 7.65 caliber German Mauser mutated into a 6.5 caliber Italian Mannlicher-Carcano; or when the grassy knoll receded into oblivion; or when an entrance wound in the President's throat became an exit wound (first for a fragment from the head wound and then for a bullet from the back wound); or when a wound six inches below the President's shoulder became a wound at the base of the neck. The press was thereby weaving a web that would inevitably commit it to the official findings.

For some, the ultimate publication of those findings was anticlimactic. The New York *Times*, for example, published a Page 1 exclusive on June 1, 1964, by then-Supreme Court correspondent Anthony Lewis: "Panel to Reject Theories of Plot in Kennedy Death." The story amounted to a detailed preview of the Warren Report three months before the commission completed taking testimony and nearly four months before the report was released.

The release of the Warren Report on September 27, 1964, was greeted with near-unanimous praise by the press, led by the New York *Times*, which went to the enormous expense of publishing the entire report as a 48-page supplement to the September 28 editions. The *Times* also collaborated with The Book of the Month Club and Bantam Books to publish hard-bound and soft-cover editions of the Warren Report. . . .

By late 1966 the Kennedy assassination became a major issue as Gallup and Harris polls revealed that few Americans were satisfied that the truth was known and Mark Lane's critical book *Rush to Judgment* climbed to the top of the best seller list. Such pillars of the establishment as *The London Times*, former Kennedy aides Arthur Schlesinger Jr. and Richard Goodwin, *The Saturday Evening Post*, the Vatican newspaper *L'Osservatore*, William F. Buckley, Walter Lippmann, Cardinal Cushing and The American Academy of Forensic Sciences began to call for a reopening of the case.

Under this setting, the New York *Times* quietly undertook an investigation of its own in early November 1966 under the direction of Harrison Salisbury, who had recently called for a new investigation in the pages of *Progressive* magazine, acknowledging that questions of major importance remained unanswered. Salisbury, an early ardent defender of the Warren Report, clarified his limited objectives in *Newsweek:* "We will go over all the areas of doubt," he said, "and hope to eliminate them."

Later that month the *Times*, in a carefully worded editorial, "Unanswered Questions," called for an end to official silence, saying that thoughtful citizens had articulated enough solid doubts to require official answers.

Rather than attempting to answer those questions itself, however, the *Times* investigation ended as abruptly as it began. It was "temporarily" suspended in December, when Salisbury received permission to visit Hanoi. It was never completed—nor would the New York *Times* ever again question the findings of the Warren Commission. Some added perspective into the *Times* inquiry was provided recently by the *Times* Houston bureau chief, Martin Waldron, in an interview with *Rolling Stone*. Waldron, a member of the 1966 team, said that he and others came up with "a lot of unanswered questions" that the *Times* didn't bother to pursue. "I'd be off on a good lead and then somebody'd call me off and send me out to California on another story or something. We never really detached anyone for this. We weren't really serious."

The *Times*'s return to the fold is amply illustrated by its relationship with David W. Belin, a junior counsel for the Warren Commission who recently has gained a degree of prominence as executive director for the Rockefeller Commission on the CIA.

The story of Belin and the *Times* begins in August 1971, when an article by Warren Commission critic Sylvia Meagher implicating Belin in subornation of perjury appeared in *The Texas Observer*, a liberal Texas weekly with a small but influential national circulation. Meagher's 1967 book, *Accessories after the Fact*, is generally considered by those familiar with Kennedy assassination literature to be the most scholarly, objective and definitive critique of the Warren Report.

Meagher took Belin to task for his treatment of the testimony of an Oswald co-worker named Charles Givens. In a deposition taken by Belin, Givens testified that he had left the sixth floor of the Depository at about 11:30 a.m. on the day of the assassination, but that he had forgotten his cigarettes and returned about 15 minutes later to retrieve them. There, on an otherwise empty sixth floor, he encountered Oswald. Belin did not challenge Givens' testimony and it was given great weight by the Warren Commission in its efforts to establish Oswald's presence on the sixth floor during the period leading up to the assassination.

But on the day of the assassination, Meagher pointed out,

Givens had told authorities that he had last seen Oswald on the *first* floor of the Depository reading a newspaper. Neither then nor in subsequent affidavits prior to his Warren Commission testimony had Givens ever mentioned a sixth floor encounter. However, a document found in the National Archives by Mrs. Meagher placed Givens' later testimony in a rather sinister light. The document, an FBI report, quoted Lt. Jack Revill of the Dallas Police Department to the effect that Givens, who had once been arrested on a marijuana charge, "would probably change his testimony for money."

Belin replied in the same issue of the *Observer*; he ignored the charges while viciously attacking the "assassination sensationalists" and proclaiming his own integrity. The *Observer*, in an editorial, branded this "the slick irrelevant reply of a lawyer who doesn't have much of a defense to present."

Meagher sent a copy of the Belin exchange to several media people including Harrison Salisbury, who was then editor of the *Times* Op-Ed page. The result: On November 22, 1971, the eighth anniversary of the assassination, the *Times* Op-Ed page featured a condensed version of Belin's *Texas Observer* attack upon the critics of the Warren Report. "The Warren Commission Was Right," proclaimed the headline.

An angry letter from Sylvia Meagher to the Op-Ed page received a form card reply. An angrier letter to Salisbury received the following verbatim reply from Salisbury: "Do forgive the form card which went back to you. That was a product of our bureaucracy, I'm afraid. I hadn't seen your letter, alas, having been out of the office for a few days."

Belin, in his foray against the critics, had threatened to write a book that would answer the wild charges once and for all. In 1973 Quadrangle Books, the publishing company of the New York *Times*, published *November 22, 1963: You Are The Jury*, by David W. Belin. Harrison Salisbury provided a laudatory introduction, and Belin, for his part, expressed special thanks to Salisbury, "who was the catalyst in my undertaking to write this book."

It is difficult to understand why the *Times* published this work, for it is literally little more than a rewrite of the Warren Report accompanied by excerpts of testimony from the 26 volumes. The "definitive" reply to the critics addresses only two of them; Sylvia Meagher is not even relegated to footnote status. The testimony of Charles Givens is cited as if its veracity had never been challenged. Predictably, the book sold few copies.

Belin's book was reviewed in *The New York Times Book Review* on November 18, 1973, by George and Priscilla McMillan, a remarkable choice of reviewers. George McMillan, who is writing a biography of James Earl Ray that is yet to be completed seven years after its undertaking, told the *Times* in a 1969 interview: "This guy is a loner." "I have never investigated any aspect of conspiracy," he said, "which left me free to work on his biography." George's wife, Priscilla, has long been one of the most vocal and intriguing defenders of the Warren Report. As Moscow correspondent for The North American Newspaper Alliance, she had interviewed a young defector in 1959—Lee Harvey Oswald—and [discussed that meeting with the American Consul, at whose suggestion she had conducted the interview]. Following the CIA-engineered defection of Svetlana Alliluyeva to the United States, it was Priscilla McMillan who translated her book. An unpublished Warren Commission document includes her name among "employees of the State Department" who had contacted Oswald in Moscow.* On the day of the assassination, she filed a story with the Boston *Globe*, "The Stuff of Which Fanatics Are Made." This and other articles in *Harper's* and *The Christian Science Monitor* published in the weeks and months following the assassination were widely quoted and helped bolster the public image of a hapless fanatic who had murdered the President. Still later, Priscilla became a confidante of Marina Oswald and was designated her official biographer (like her husband's, the book is unfinished after 11 years). Nor was Priscilla any stranger to the *Times*. Her Freudian pieces on Oswald had twice graced the Op-Ed page. Four days after the Belin review, she informed *Times* readers that the reason people cling

---

* This document is an FBI report of a phone conversation with the State Department on November 23, 1963, when the FBI was apparently trying to locate people who had known Oswald (CD 49.24). On the same day, the former Consul described her as a correspondent for the North American Newspaper Alliance (CD 49.26). She so identified herself in her testimony (11H 442) and has denied that she was a State Department employee.—Eds.

to conspiracy theories is that Oswald had committed symbolic patricide and since we all subconsciously want to kill our fathers we believe in conspiracy "as a defense, a screen, a barrier, against having to hold those feelings in ourselves."

But the best illustration of *Times* policy involves another book review that dared to be critical of the Warren Report. Between early and late editions the title of the review changed from "Who Killed John F. Kennedy?" to "The Shaw-Garrison Affair." A paragraph headed "MYSTERIES PERSIST" vanished, along with the last 30 lines of the review, which were critical of the official version of events. Readers of the *Times* were thus spared the confusing and disquieting questions of a reviewer who did not, apparently, know better. That reviewer, John Leonard, later became editor of *The New York Times Book Review*, where he continued the *Times* policy of selecting hostile reviewers for conspiracy books.

The 1966 flood of criticism aimed at the Warren Report also left its mark at *Life*. As the controversy grew, Richard Billings, then *Life*'s associate editor in charge of investigative reporting, assigned his staff to look into controversial aspects of the Kennedy case. The objective was to produce several articles on the Warren Report controversy.

On November 25, 1966, what was to be the first article of the series appeared. The cover of *Life* carried a frame from the Zapruder film with the caption: "Did Oswald Act Alone? A Matter of Reasonable Doubt." Billings and his staff examined the single bullet theory: The Warren Commission had theorized that one bullet had inflicted both of Kennedy's non-fatal wounds and had gone on to inflict each of the five wounds suffered by Connally (including shattering a rib and a wrist) while emerging virtually unscathed. The bullet in question had been discovered on a stretcher by an orderly at Parkland Hospital. Although the commission had alleged otherwise, the single bullet theory was absolutely essential to the lone assassin theory because the rifle allegedly used by Oswald had been proved incapable of firing two shots rapidly enough to hit both men.

Life concluded, based upon its examination of the Zapruder film, that the single bullet theory was wrong and that the lone assassin theory was thus in doubt. A *Life* editorial called for a new investigation.

Time magazine's November 25 issue, on the other hand, editorially attacked the "phantasmagoria" and concluded that "there seems little valid excuse for so dramatic a development as another full-scale inquiry."

Questioned about the conflicting editorial postures, Hedley Donovan, editor-in-chief of both *Time* and *Life*, said: "Time and Life agree that valid doubts and discussions about the Warren Report will continue. Life advocated a new special investigation, while Time questioned whether a full-scale inquiry would achieve anything without new evidence. We would like to see our magazines arrive at consistent positions on major issues, and I am sure in due course we will on this one."

Due course was not long in coming. In January Billings was told by a superior, "It is not *Life*'s function to investigate the Kennedy assassination." The first article on the Kennedy case became the last, and the investigation by Billings' staff was terminated. After that, neither *Time* nor *Life* again questioned or criticized the Warren Report.

For all their efforts, the New York *Times* and Time Inc. could not approach CBS' performance in a four-part documentary, *The Warren Report*, broadcast in June 1967. The documentary was produced by Les Midgely and reported by Walter Cronkite, Dan Rather and Eddie Barker, news director for CBS' Dallas affiliate, KRLD. This same quartet had collaborated on a two-hour special broadcast on the eve of the release of the Warren Report—a program that had echoed the rest of the media in heaping praise upon the Warren Commission.

CBS designed spurious tests to support the Warren Report. When these loaded tests disproved the report, they were interpreted to support it anyway. Eleven master marksmen were supplied with a rifle capable of firing faster than Oswald's, were allowed to practice with the rifle and then fired 37 firing runs of three shots each at a target simulating the President. CBS eliminated 17 of these runs "because of trouble with the rifle," which actually meant that the marksman took more than 7.5 seconds to get off three shots. The average for the remaining firing runs was identical to the *maximum* time available to Oswald, a poor marksman who owned a slower gun. CBS' masters averaged only 1.2 hits compared to Oswald's two hits. Cronkite's conclusion: "It seems reasonable to say that an expert could fire that rifle in five seconds. It seems equally reasonable to say that Oswald, under normal circumstances, would take longer. But these were not normal circumstances. Oswald was shooting at a President."

To clear up the location of the back wound, CBS called upon Commander Humes, the pathologist who had directed the autopsy and had subsequently burned his notes. Humes confirmed for CBS that the wound was indeed in the neck (indicating that four Secret Service agents, a Dallas motorcycle policeman and two FBI agents were all mistaken about the location of the wound below the shoulder, as were the President's shirt and jacket, which displayed holes 5½ inches below the collar).

To test the single bullet theory, CBS called upon the same "expert" utilized by the Warren Commission (and more recently by the Rockefeller Commission). Blocks of gelatin and masonite were set up to simulate most, but not all, of the tissue and bone supposedly traversed by the missile. (Connally's rib, which was shattered and would have slowed the bullet down considerably, was *not* simulated.) None of the bullets test-fired into the gelatin was able to do what the Warren Commission's magic bullet had done, but CBS said that it would have taken "very little more velocity." CBS thus interpreted this test as proving "that a single bullet could indeed have wounded both men." Using these and other equally dubious tests, CBS concluded that "Oswald was the sole assassin."

Robert Richter, formerly a producer for *CBS Reports* and an associate producer on the Warren Commission project, was dismayed by what had finally appeared on the air. "From the material gathered for the program," he told me, "someone could have taken the same raw footage and utilized the same tests, chosen different excerpts from the same interviews, and given the audience a completely different, more objective impression of what the facts added up to." . . .

The Kennedy assassination cover-up has survived so long only because the press, confronted with the choice of believing what it was told or examining the facts independently, chose the former. Unless and until the press repudiates that choice, it is unlikely that we shall ever know the truth.

KENNEDY CONSPIRACY DISCOUNTED
W. David Slawson and Richard M. Mosk

Los Angeles Times / *May 11, 1975*

There were always those who believed there was a conspiracy to assassinate President Kennedy, and many of these persons brushed aside the report of the Warren Commission, which found no evidence to support the conspiracy theory and concluded that Lee Harvey Oswald acted alone.

Recently, talk of plots to assassinate foreign leaders, and investigations into what role, if any, the American CIA may have had in such plots, has revived speculation over the Kennedy assassination.

The conspiracy theory persists partly because some persons find it difficult to believe that such a momentous act could be done so capriciously, and by such an insignificant, hapless man as Lee Harvey Oswald.

"Kennedy Conspiracy Discounted" by W. David Slawson and Richard M. Mosk. Reprinted from the *Los Angeles Times*, May 11, 1975, by permission of the publisher and the authors.

Few persons not familiar with the Warren Report realize the large number of chance occurrences underlying the assassination. It is very unlikely that Oswald would ever have killed Kennedy had the President not gone to Dallas when he did and passed the building in which Oswald was working. At the time Oswald took his job, there was no way of knowing that the presidential parade route would go right by the building in which he worked, or that there would be a presidential parade at all in the foreseeable future in Dallas.

The night before the assassination, Oswald hitched a ride with a friend out to a suburb to see his wife, Marina, from whom he was then separated. He begged her to come back and live with him. He offered to rent an apartment in Dallas for the two of them *the next day*. She refused. The next morning Oswald left his wedding ring and almost all his money on the dresser, and departed with the same friend for work, with the rifle dismantled and concealed in a package. Kennedy might be alive today had Marina relented.

Allegations concerning CIA activities in the late 1950s and the 1960s have created added doubts, because the CIA assisted the commission in its investigation. However, the CIA was only one such outside source of assistance, and it was not the most important one. (The most important was the FBI.) Moreover, the commission double-checked and cross-checked all significant information among a variety of sources—governmental and private.

The principal reason for the criticisms and conspiracy theories, however, is the breadth of the Warren Report. The published materials comprise 27 volumes. The National Archives contain additional material, which has for the most part been made public. Critics of the report, by selective and inaccurate citations, have turned this vast amount of material against the commission.

The commission took testimony from over 500 people. Thousands more were interviewed or gave affidavits. The FBI alone conducted approximately 25,000 interviews. As is true with even the simplest accident case, some people's reactions, memories, observations and actions were imperfect.

For example, critics have claimed that one of the doctors who worked to save the President's life said the wound on the President's throat was an entry wound, which if true would prove that there was a second gunman since Oswald was behind the President.

What these critics fail to disclose is that the doctor, at a raucous news conference right after the President died, said that it was possible that a bullet had entered the throat. He later testified that at the time he made the remark, he had not seen the wounds on the back of the President. Although the throat wound could not thereafter be definitely analyzed, because of a tracheotomy which this doctor, among others, had performed, other doctors later said the wound probably was an exit wound.

The commission, on the basis of this and other expert testimony, fiber analysis of the clothes, the location of bullets and other evidence concluded that the hole in the throat was an exit wound, which would demonstrate that the bullet came from the rear where Oswald was located.

Quite apart from eyewitnesses, the evidence supporting Oswald's guilt is overwhelming. Ballistics evidence demonstrated that Oswald's rifle was the murder weapon; Oswald's prints were on the rifle; handwriting analysis of order forms and pictures of Oswald with the rifle demonstrated that the rifle was his; the rifle was found in the building where Oswald worked and where Oswald was seen shortly before the shooting; his prints were located in the part of the room where the rifle and spent cartridges were found and from which witnesses saw the rifle protruding at the time of the assassination; X-rays, photographs and the autopsy show that the bullet came from the area where Oswald was located; after the shooting, Oswald promptly left the premises and resisted apprehension by killing a policeman. Finally, he lied about a number of facts during his interrogation.

Thus, the claims that the rifle was inaccurate, that the shot was difficult, that Oswald was a poor shot and that stress analysis tests of Oswald's voice allegedly show him to have been telling the truth when he denied his guilt are all unpersuasive in light of so much uncontroverted evidence. These claims, even in isolation, are misleading: Oswald was a former Marine and hunter. He practiced with the rifle when he was a civilian. Tests showed that his rifle was sufficiently accurate. The shot was not particularly difficult. It was from a stable, prepared position at a target moving 11 m.p.h. almost straight away at a range of 177 to 266 feet. The rifle had a telescopic sight. The voice stress analysis has not achieved general acceptance as a reliable lie detector test.

Most critical commentaries focus on suggestions that there had to be at least two gunmen.

One of the oldest claims is that Oswald could not have fired three shots in the time he had and have two of them hit the President. The commission utilized the film of the event by Abraham Zapruder to determine that the interval between the two hits was between 4.8 and 5.6 seconds (the exact time is not determinable since the first shot hit the President while a road sign was between him and Zapruder's camera).

Some have said that 4.8 to 5.6 seconds is too short a time for three shots to be fired and two of them to hit. But the time interval is between two shots—the two that hit—not three. The commission found the evidence inconclusive as to whether, of the three shots fired, it was the first, second or third that missed. Since the time interval is that *between* the two shots which hit, Oswald had all the time he needed to fire the first shot. A period of 4.8 to 5.6 seconds is ample time for aiming and firing one shot —the second one that hit.

The evidence concerning the wounds conclusively dispels the idea of shots from the front, another part of the conspiracy theory. The wounds both slanted *downward* from Kennedy's back. This is clear beyond doubt from the autopsy and from the photographs and X-rays of the body. The photographs and X-rays are still not open to public view, because of Jacqueline Kennedy Onassis' wishes, but to doubt the evidence of the wounds is to label as liars the doctors who examined the body, the pictures and the X-rays for the commission. The inward pointing of the threads of the back of Kennedy's clothing and the outward pointing of the threads in the front of his clothing demonstrate that the bullet which first hit him entered from the rear and exited from the front. Since the car was in a low underpass, a bullet from any direction would have to have been going downward, and would have hit the car after leaving Kennedy.

All the bullet damage to the car was in front of Kennedy, which is consistent with a bullet entering from the rear.

A great deal of publicity has been given recently to the claim that Kennedy must have been hit from the front because the Zapruder film shows his head jerking back.

In fact, the head jerks back not when the bullet hits it but slightly later. Actually, at the time of the hit, the President's head appears to move slightly forward and the sprayed flesh also moves forward. The jerk, therefore, cannot have been a momentum reaction. It must have been a neural or muscular reaction caused by either bullet or by a reaction to some other stimulus.

Many critics have pointed to a rough sketch of the location of the neck wound and to the location of the bullet hole in the President's shirt and suit jacket as proving that the rear wound was lower on the President's body than the wound in front. From this it follows, supposedly, that some other gunman must have been firing in a downward direction from the front.

But the best evidence of the wound's location are the autopsy records and the photos and X-rays of the body itself. These unambiguously show the rear wounds higher than the wound at the front. The rough sketch was just that: rough. The holes in the shirt and jacket seem to indicate a low wound on the body only because the clothing, when photographed, was laid flat and because, presumably, when the President was sitting in the car his clothing was slightly bunched up his back.

Critics have criticized the "single-bullet theory," which is the commission's conclusion that the first bullet passed through the President and also hit, and eventually came to a stop in, Gov. Connally. Why anyone should think it unlikely that a rifle bullet should go through one man and hit another, when the men were sitting close together, escapes us.

Of course, it was difficult for the commission to reconstruct exactly what the path through both men was, but a reconstruction proved possible, and the conclusion that it was a single bullet which hit both men makes, by far, the most sense in the context of all the other evidence. No bullet was left inside the President; the nature of the President's wound shows that the bullet that made it was hardly slowed down and so must have been stopped by something else, but there was no appreciable damage to the car in front of the President; the films show Connally to have been hit at or near the same time as the President; the nature of Connally's wounds show that he, too, was hit from the rear.

The fact that the recovered bullet that apparently went through both Kennedy and Connally was not greatly distorted itself actually supports the single-bullet theory. In order that a bullet be recovered without being greatly distorted, it must be brought to a slow and gentle stop. By going through two men, and by tumbling end over end through flesh and muscle and by glancing off, rather than penetrating, large bones, the bullet was brought to a slow and gentle stop and so was able to emerge in a relatively unscathed condition.

The photographs supposedly showing shadowy outlines of gunmen in the bushes of trees actually show this only to someone with a wild imagination. What they really show are only shadows such as can be seen on almost any photograph taken from a distance of trees and shrubbery.

There has been speculation recently that various people masqueraded before the assassination as Oswald and, thus, there must have been a conspiracy.

Just as thousands of people claim to have seen Patty Hearst in various places at the same time, many people reported seeing Oswald. The Oswald "identifications" were even more doubtful because many of them allegedly took place months and years before the assassination. If there was a conspiracy, what possible purpose would have been served by sending fake "Oswalds" around the country?

The recent surge in speculation about purported CIA or FBI connections with, or cover-up of, the assassination is not a result of any newly discovered link between those agencies and the assassination. It is a result of the revelations of alleged unsavory practices in other matters by these agencies.

In October, 1963, the CIA's Mexican department sent a message and a photograph to the FBI saying, in effect, that the man in the photograph was thought to be Lee Harvey Oswald. The photograph was not of Oswald, but it was not until shortly after the assassination that this fact was established. These events have led to the speculation that either the man in the photograph was a CIA agent masquerading as Oswald or that Oswald was a CIA agent.

This happened because the CIA had several secret sources of information operating in Mexico and, as is frequently the case in this kind of work, the central headquarters had difficulty in putting the bits of information from the different sources together properly. One source reported that a man calling himself Oswald had visited the Soviet Embassy in Mexico City. Another source obtained a photograph of a man who probably visited the same embassy about the same time. No source was able to get a photograph of Oswald in Mexico City, and no source was able to obtain the name of the man in the photograph who visited the Embassy. Someone in the CIA who was responsible for putting bits of information together guessed, mistakenly it turned out, that the two men were the same.

With all of this confusion, the time has come for everything on the assassination in the National Archives to be made available to the public, unless its disclosure can be shown to be definitely detrimental to the national security.

We do not believe that a reopening of the inquiry, in the sense of establishing a new commission to carry on its own investigation or to hear argument from private investigators, would serve any useful purpose.

The legitimate interest of the American people in knowing as surely as possible that they have found out the whole truth can be served, we think, by the creation of special, limited new investigations if and when a need for one of them arises. Currently, for example, the news media has reported that the White House commission on the CIA is investigating the allegation that the CIA may not have fully disclosed all relevant information to the Warren Commission in an effort to cover up its own involvement with an assassination attempt on Castro. Such an issue should be investigated and apparently it is.

THE GARRISON COMMISSION
William Turner

Ramparts / January 1968

THE FBI CLEARS A SUSPECT

On the morning after the assassination, as the nation lay stunned by grief, [Jim] Garrison summoned his staff to the office for a "brain-storming session" to explore the possibility that Lee Harvey Oswald had accomplices in New Orleans, where the previous summer he had stumped the streets advocating Fair Play for Cuba.

The DA's men put out feelers into the city's netherworld, and it was First Assistant DA Frank Klein who registered the first feedback. A slight, furtive, sometime private eye named Jack S. Martin confided that a David William Ferrie had taken off on a sudden trip to Texas the afternoon of the assassination. The tipster knew Ferrie well, although there was bad blood between them. Both had worked intermittently for the same detective firm, W. Guy Banister & Associates, and were affiliated with the Apostolic Orthodox Old Catholic Church, a sect steeped in theological anti-communism. An exceptionally skilled pilot, Ferrie had been dismissed from Eastern Air Lines in 1962 due to publicity over alleged homosexual activities.

According to Martin, Ferrie had commanded a Civil Air Patrol squadron of which Oswald had once been a member. He had taught Oswald to shoot with a telescopic sight, and had become involved with his protégé in an assassination plot. Less than two weeks before the target date, Ferrie had made a trip to Dallas. His assigned role in the assassination, Martin said, was to fly the escaping conspirators to Matamoros, Mexico, near Brownsville, Texas.

When Ferrie returned to New Orleans on the Monday following President Kennedy's death, he was interrogated by the DA's office. He said his trip had been arranged "on the spur of the moment." With two companions, Alvin Beauboeuf and Melvin Coffey, he had driven straight through to Houston Friday night. On Saturday afternoon, the three skated at an ice rink; that evening they made the short jog to Galveston and hunted geese Sunday morning. Sunday afternoon they headed back to New Orleans, but detoured to Alexandria, Louisiana, to visit relatives of Beauboeuf.

Garrison was unconvinced by Ferrie's account. An all-night dash through the worst rainstorm in years to start a mercurial junket of over 1000 miles in three days for recreational purposes was too much to swallow. "It was a curious trip to a curious place at a curious time," the DA recalls. He booked Ferrie as a "fugitive from Texas" and handed him over to the FBI. The G-men questioned him intensively, then released him.

Since the 40-odd pages recording the FBI interrogation of Ferrie are still classified in the National Archives, one can only surmise the reasons the Bureau stamped its file on him "closed."*

Apparently the FBI did not take the pilot too seriously. A short Bureau document in the National Archives reveals Ferrie had admitted being "publicly and privately" critical of Kennedy for withholding air cover at the Bay of Pigs, and had used expressions like "he ought to be shot," but agents agreed he did not mean the threat literally.

Most convincing at the time, the fact that Ferrie did not leave New Orleans until hours after the assassination seemed to rule out his role as a getaway pilot. Moreover, the Stinson monoplane he then owned was sitting at Lakefront Airport in unflyable condition.

Accepting the FBI's judgment, Garrison dropped his investigation. "I had full confidence in the FBI then," he explains. "There was no reason to try and second guess them."

For three years the DA's faith in the Bureau's prowess remained unshaken. Then in November 1966, squeezed into a tourist-class seat on an Eastern jet headed for New York, his inter-

---

* Many pages on Ferrie were released in 1970—Eds.

est in the possibility of a conspiracy was rekindled. Flanking
him were Senator Russell B. Long of Louisiana and Joseph Rault
Jr, a New Orleans oilman. The previous week, Long had remarked
in the course of a press conference that he doubted the findings
of the Warren Commission. It was at the height of the controversy stirred by publications ripping at the Commission's methods and conclusions.

Garrison bombarded the senator with questions in the manner, he reminisces, "of a prosecutor cross-examining a witness."
Long maintained that there were grievous flaws and unexplored
territory in the Warren Report. He considered it highly implausible that a gunman of Oswald's "mediocre skill" could have fired
with pinpoint accuracy within a time constraint barely sufficient
"for a man to get off two shots from a bolt-action rifle, much
less three."

The DA's mind reverted to the strange trip of pilot David
Ferrie, and he began to wonder how perceptive the FBI had
really been in dismissing the whole thing. When he returned to
New Orleans, he went into virtual seclusion in his study at home,
lucubrating over the volumes of the Warren Report. When he
became convinced that Oswald could not have acted alone, and
that at least a phase of the conspiracy had been centered in New
Orleans, he committed his office to a full-scale probe. He
launched it quietly, preferring to work more efficiently in the
dark.

The probe refocused on Ferrie, and on December 15 he was
brought in for further questioning. Asked pertinent details of the
whirlwind Texas trip in 1963, he begged lack of memory and
referred his questioners to the FBI. What about the goose hunting? "We did in fact get to where the geese were and there
were thousands," he recounted. "But you couldn't approach
them. They were a wise bunch of birds." Pressed for details of
what took place at the ice rink, Ferrie became irritated. "Ice
skate—what do you think?" he snapped.

It didn't take the DA's men long to poke holes in Ferrie's story.
Melvin Coffey, one of his companions on the 1963 Texas trip,
deposed that it was not a sudden inspiration:

Q. The trip was arranged before?
A. Yes.

Q. How long before?

A. A couple of days.

The probers also determined that no one had taken along any shotguns on the "goose-hunting" trip.

In Houston, the ice skating alibi was similarly discredited. In 1963, the FBI had interviewed Chuck Rolland, proprietor of the Winterland Skating Rink. "FERRIE contacted him by telephone November 22, 1963, and asked for the skating schedule," a Bureau report, one of the few unclassified documents on Ferrie, reveals. "Mr. FERRIE stated that he was coming in from out of town and desired to do some skating while in Houston. On November 23, 1963, between 3:30 and 5:30 PM, Mr. FERRIE and two companions came to the rink and talked to Mr. ROLLAND." The report continues that Ferrie and Rolland had a short general conversation, and that Ferrie remarked that "he and his companions would be in and out of the skating rink during the weekend" (Commission Document 301). When Garrison's men recently talked to Rolland, they obtained pertinent facts that the FBI had either missed or failed to report in 1963. Rolland was certain that none of the three men in Ferrie's party had ice skated; Ferrie had spent the entire two hours he was at the rink standing by a pay telephone—and finally received a call.

At Houston International Airport, more information was gleaned. Air service personnel seemed to recall that in 1963 Ferrie had access to an airplane based in Houston. In this craft, the flight to Matamoros would take little more than an hour.

Ferrie had patently lied about the purpose of the trip. One of the standard tactics of bank robbers is to escape from the scene of the crime in a "hot car" that cannot be traced to them, then switch to a "cold car" of their own to complete the getaway. Garrison considers it possible that Ferrie may have been the pilot of a second craft in a two-stage escape of the Dallas assassins to south of the border, or may have been slated to be a backup pilot in the event contingency plans were activated.

Did Ferrie know Oswald? The pilot denied it, but the evidence mounts that he did. For example, there is now in Garrison's hands information that when Oswald was arrested by Dallas police, he had in his possession a *current* New Orleans library card issued to David Ferrie. Reinforcing the validity of this information is a Secret Service report on the questioning of Ferrie by that agency when he was in federal custody in 1963. During an otherwise mild interrogation, Ferrie was asked, strangely enough, if he lent his library card to Oswald. No, he replied, producing a card from the New Orleans public library in the name of Dr. David Ferrie. That card had expired.

When he realized he was a suspect in Garrison's current investigation, Ferrie seemed to deteriorate. By the time he died on February 22, 1967, he was a nervous wreck, subsisting on endless cigarettes and cups of coffee and enough tranquilizers to pacify an army. He had sought out the press only days before his death, labeling the probe a "fraud" and complaining that he was the victim of a "witch hunt." "I suppose he has me pegged as a getaway pilot," he remarked bitterly.

When Garrison delivered his epitaph of Ferrie as "one of history's most important individuals," most of the press winked knowingly. The probe was, after all, a publicity stunt, and the DA had had his headlines. Now that his prime suspect had conveniently passed away, he had the perfect excuse to inter his probe alongside the deceased pilot.

But for DA Jim Garrison, it was not the end but the beginning.

544 CAMP STREET, NEW ORLEANS

"While the legend '544 Camp St., NEW ORLEANS, LA.' was stamped on some of the literature that Oswald had in his possession at the time of his arrest [for "disturbing the peace"] in New Orleans, extensive investigation was not able to connect Oswald with that address" (Warren Report, p. 408). So said the Commission. But Garrison *has* connected Oswald with that address. His investigation shows that Oswald functioned in a paramilitary right-wing milieu of which 544 Camp Street was a nerve center, and that Oswald's ostentatious "Fair Play for Cuba" advocacy was nothing more than a facade.

The dilapidated building at 544 Camp Street is on the corner of Lafayette Place. Shortly after news of Garrison's investigation broke, I went to 531 Lafayette Place, an address given me by Minutemen defector Jerry Milton Brooks as the office of W. Guy

Banister, a former FBI official who ran a private detective agency. According to Brooks, who had been a trusted Minutemen aide, Banister was a member of the Minutemen and head of the Anti-Communism League of the Caribbean, assertedly an intermediary between the CIA and Caribbean insurgency movements. Brooks said he had worked for Banister on "anti-Communist" research in 1961–1962, and had known David Ferrie as a frequent visitor to Banister's office.

Banister had died of an apparent heart attack in the summer of 1964. But Brooks had told me of two associates whom I hoped to find. One was Hugh F. Ward, a young investigator for Banister who also belonged to the Minutemen and the Anti-Communism League. Then I learned that Ward, too, was dead. Reportedly taught to fly by David Ferrie, he was at the controls of a Piper Aztec when it plunged to earth near Ciudad Victoria, Mexico, May 23, 1965.

The other associate was Maurice Brooks Gatlin Sr, legal counsel to the Anti-Communism League of the Caribbean. Jerry Brooks said he had once been a sort of protégé of Gatlin and was in his confidence. Brooks believed Gatlin's frequent world travels were as a "transporter" for the CIA. As an example, he said, Gatlin remarked about 1962, in a self-important manner, that he had $100,000 of CIA money earmarked for a French right-wing clique that was going to attempt to assassinate General de Gaulle; shortly afterward Gatlin flew to Paris. The search for Gatlin, however, was likewise futile: in 1964 he fell or was pushed from the sixth floor of the El Panama Hotel in Panama during the early morning, and was killed instantly.

But the trip to 531 Lafayette Place was not entirely fruitless. The address, I discovered, was a side entrance to 544 Camp Street. Entering either at the front or the side, one arrives via a walkup staircase at the same second floor space. That second floor once housed the Cuban Democratic Revolutionary Front and W. Guy Banister & Associates.

Guy Banister had been in charge of the Chicago FBI office before retiring in 1955 and becoming New Orleans deputy superintendent of police for several years. He was regarded as one of the city's most vocal anti-Castroites, and published the racist Louisiana Intelligence Digest, which depicted integration as a communist conspiracy. Evidence of his relationship with the federal intelligence *apparat* has recently surfaced. A man who knew Banister well has told Garrison that Banister became associated with the Office of Naval Intelligence through the recommendation of Guy Johnson, an ONI reserve officer and the first attorney for Clay Shaw when he was arrested by Garrison.

A copyrighted story in the New Orleans States-Item, April 25, 1967, further illuminates the Camp Street scene. The newspaper, which at the time had an investigative team working parallel to the Garrison probe, reported that a reliable source close to Banister said he had seen 50 to 100 boxes marked "Schlumberger" in Banister's office-storeroom early in 1961 before the Bay of Pigs. The boxes contained rifle grenades, land mines and unique "little missiles." Banister explained that "the stuff would just be there overnight . . . a bunch of fellows connected with the Cuban deal asked to leave it there overnight." It was all right, assured Banister, "I have approval from somebody."

The "somebody," one can surmise from the Gordon Novel episode which follows, was the CIA. Novel is wanted by the DA as a material witness in the 1961 burglary of the Schlumberger Well Co. munitions dump near New Orleans. Subpoenaed by the grand jury last March, Novel fled to McLean, Virginia, next door to the CIA complex at Langley, and took a lie detector test administered by a former Army intelligence officer which, he boasted to the press, proved Garrison's probe was a fraud. He then skipped first to Montreal and then to Columbus, Ohio, from where Governor James Rhodes, in one of the most absurd stipulations ever attached to a normally routine procedure, refuses to extradite him unless Garrison agrees not to question him on the assassination.

From his Ohio sanctuary the fugitive cryptically asserted that the munitions caper was one of "the most patriotic burglaries in history." When an enterprising reporter took him to a marathon party, Novel's indiscreet tongue loosened further. According to the States-Item article, Novel's oft-repeated account was that the munitions bunker was a CIA staging point for war matériel destined for use in the impending Bay of Pigs invasion. He is quoted as saying that on the day the munitions were picked up, he "was called by his CIA contact and told to join a group which was ordered to transport munitions from the bunker to New Orleans." The key to the bunker was provided by his CIA contact. Novel reportedly said the others in the CIA group at the bunker were David Ferrie, Sergio Arcacha Smith—New Orleans delegate to the Cuban Democratic Revolutionary Front—and several Cubans. The munitions, according to his account, were dropped in Novel's office, Ferrie's home and Banister's office-storeroom.

Ferrie worked on and off for Banister as an investigator, and the mutual affinity was such that in 1962, when Eastern Air Lines was in the process of dismissing Ferrie for publicity over alleged homosexual acts, Banister appeared at a Miami hearing and delivered an impassioned plea on his behalf. When Banister suddenly died, the ex-pilot evidently acquired part of his files. When he realized he was a prime suspect in Garrison's probe, Ferrie systematically disposed of his papers and documents for the years 1962 and 1963. But in photocopying the bibliography of a cancer paper he had written (at one time he had caged mice in his home on which he experimented with cancer implants), he inadvertently overlapped the bottom portion of notes recording the dispositions. Included is the notation: "Copies of B's [presumably Banister's] microfilm files to Atlanta rite-wingers [sic]."

The Banister files were reputed to be the largest collection of "anti-communist intelligence" in Louisiana, and part were sold by his widow to the Sovereignty Commission, a sort of state HUAC, where a Garrison investigator was able to examine them. Banister's filing system was modeled after the FBI's, and contained files on both friends and foes. The "10" and "23" classification dealt with Cuban matters; 23-5, for example, was labeled Cuban Democratic Revolutionary Front and 10-209 simply Cuban File. There was a main file, 23-14, labeled Shaw File, but someone had completely stripped it before Garrison's man got there.

The Cuban Democratic Revolutionary Front, which occupied what was grandiosely called Suite 6 at 544 Camp Street, was the coalition of Cuban exile "liberation" groups operating under CIA aegis that mounted the Bay of Pigs invasion. Arcacha, the New Orleans delegate of the Miami-based organization, is a dapper, moustachioed man who had served in Batista's diplomatic corps. There are numerous witnesses who attest that he was a confidant of Banister and Ferrie, and that his office was a way station for the mixed bag of Cuban exiles and American adventurers involved in the "liberation" movement. Late in 1962, the Front closed up shop, at which time Arcacha became a founder of the Crusade to Free Cuba, a paramilitary group of militant right wingers. In March 1963, he moved to Houston, Texas. Early in his investigation, Garrison charged Arcacha with being a party to the munitions burglary with Novel and Ferrie, but by this time he was living in Dallas, where he refused to talk to the DA's men without Dallas police and assistant DA Bill Alexander present. When Garrison obtained an arrest warrant and sought to extradite him, Texas Governor John Connally would not sign the papers.

As for Oswald and 544 Camp Street, Garrison declares that "we have several witnesses who can testify they observed Oswald there on a number of occasions." One witness is David L. Lewis, another in Banister's stable of investigators. In late 1962, Lewis says, he was drinking coffee in the restaurant next to 544 Camp Street when Cuban exile Carlos Quiroga, who was close to Arcacha, came in with a young man he introduced as Leon Oswald. A few days later, Lewis saw Quiroga, Oswald and Ferrie together at 544 Camp Street. A few days after that, he barged into Banister's office and interrupted a meeting between Banister, Quiroga, Ferrie and Leon Oswald. It was not until he was interviewed by Garrison that Lewis concluded that Leon Oswald was probably Lee Harvey Oswald. Noting that the "natural deaths of Banister and Ferrie were strikingly similar," Lewis has slipped into seclusion.

CIA: THE COMMON DENOMINATOR

On or about the night of September 16, 1963, a nondescript Leon Oswald, the brilliant, erratic David Ferrie, and a courtly executive-type man named Clem Bertrand discussed a guerrilla ambush of President Kennedy in Ferrie's apartment. There was talk of "triangulation of fire . . . the availability of exit . . . one man had to be sacrificed to give the other one or two gunmen time to escape." Escape out of the country would be by a plane flown by Ferrie. This was the nub of the testimony of Perry Raymond Russo at a preliminary hearing for Clay Shaw, accused by Garrison of conspiracy in the assassination. Russo identified Leon Oswald as Lee Harvey Oswald, and Clem Bertrand as Clay Shaw.

What would bring three such widely disparate men together in the first place? One possible answer: the CIA.

On the fringe of downtown New Orleans, the building at 544 Camp Street is across the street from the government building which in 1963 housed the local CIA headquarters. One block away, at 640 Magazine Street, is the William B. Reily Co., a coffee firm where Oswald was employed that pivotal summer. He worked from May 10 to July 19, earning a total of $548.41 (Commission Exhibit 1154). Despite this, he did not seem hard put to support Marina and their child. Nor did he seem particularly concerned about being fired. The personnel manager of the Reily Co. told the Secret Service that "there would be times when Oswald would be gone for periods of an hour or longer and when questioned he could not furnish a plausible explanation as to where he had been . . ." (CE 1154).

Next door is the Crescent City Garage, whose owner, Adrian T. Alba, testified that Oswald spent hours on end in his waiting room buried in gun magazines (Warren Report, Vol. 10, p. 226). Shortly before leaving the coffee firm, Oswald mentioned to Alba that his employment application was about to be accepted "out there where the gold is"—the NASA Saturn missile plant at Gentilly, a suburb (Vol. 10, p. 226).

On the face of it, the idea that Oswald could get a job at a space agency installation requiring security clearance seems preposterous. He was a self-avowed Marxist who had tried to renounce his American citizenship in Moscow, married the niece of a Soviet KGB colonel, openly engaged in "Fair Play For Cuba" activity, and attempted to join the Communist Party, U.S.A. But Garrison points out that it is an open secret that the CIA uses the NASA facility as a cover for clandestine operations. And it is his contention that Oswald was a "witting" agent of the CIA.

There is a surfeit of indications of Oswald's status. One is the story of Donald P. Norton, who claims he was impressed into the Agency's service in 1957 . . . In September 1962, Norton related, he was dispatched from Atlanta to Mexico with $50,000 for an anti-Castro group. He had no sooner registered in the Yamajel Hotel in Monterrey, Mexico, per instructions, than he was contacted by one Harvey Lee, a dead ringer for Oswald except that his hair seemed slightly thicker. In exchange for the money, Lee gave him a briefcase containing documents in manila envelopes. According to plan, Norton delivered the briefcase to an employee of an American oil firm in Calgary, Alberta, who repeated the pass phrase, "The weather is very warm in Tulsa."

Norton also contends he met David Ferrie earlier in his CIA career. In early 1958, he was tapped for a courier trip to Cuba and told to meet his contact at the Eastern Air Lines counter at the Atlanta airport. The contact was a singular-appearing man who called himself Hugh Pharris or Ferris; Norton now states it was Ferrie. "Here are your samples," Ferrie remarked, handing Norton a phonograph record. "It is in the jacket." "It" was $150,000, which Norton duly delivered to a Cuban television performer in Havana. Norton asserts he went to Freeport, Grand Bahamas, on an Agency assignment late in 1966, and upon his return to Miami his contact instructed that "something was happening in New Orleans, and that I [Norton] should take a long, quiet vacation."

He did, and started to fret about the "people who have died in recent months—like Ferrie." Then he decided to contact Garrison. Norton was given a lie detector test, and there were no indications of deception.

Garrison believes that Oswald was schooled in covert operations by the CIA while in the Marine Corps at the Atsugi Naval Station in Japan, a U-2 facility (interestingly, two possibly relevant documents, "Oswald's access to information about the U-2" [CD 931] and "Reproduction of CIA official dossier on Oswald" [CD 692] are still classified in the National Archives).* Curiously the miscast Marine who was constantly in hot water had a Crypto clearance on top of a Top Secret clearance, and was

* Mostly now released.—Eds.

given two electronics courses. "Isn't it odd," prods Garrison, "that even though he supposedly defected to the Soviet Union with Top Secret data on our radar nets, no action was taken against him when he came back to the United States?"

Equally odd is Oswald's acquisition of Russian language ability. Although the Warren Report spread the fiction that he was self-taught, and Oswald himself falsely told a New Orleans acquaintance that he had studied Russian at Tulane University, the likelihood is that he was tutored at the CIA's Atsugi station. Marine Corps records reflect that on February 25, 1959, at the conclusion of his Atsugi tour of duty, he was given a Russian language proficiency test (Folsom Exhibit No. 1, p. 7). A former Marine comrade, Kerry Thornley, deposed to Garrison that Oswald conversed in Russian with John Rene Heindel every morning at muster.

Oswald's "defection" to the Soviet Union also smacks of being CIA-initiated. In retrospect, the clearance of U.S. departure and reentry formalities seems unduly expeditious. When the Marine Corps *post facto* downgraded his discharge to less than honorable, Oswald indignantly wrote Secretary of the Navy John B. Connally, "I have and allways [sic] had the full sanction of the U.S. Embassy, Moscow USSR and hence the U.S. government" (Warren Report, p. 710). When an interviewer on a New Orleans radio station asked him on August 21, 1963, if he had had a government subsidy during his three years in Russia, the normally articulate Oswald stammered badly: "Well, as I er, well, I will answer that question directly then as you will not rest until you get your answer er, I worked in Russia, er, I was er under the protection er, of the er, that is to say I was not under protection of the American government but I was at all times er, considered an American citizen . . ." (This is the original version as disseminated by the Associated Press. The version released by the Warren Commission has been edited to delete the hemming and hawing and the apparent slip of the tongue, "I *was* under the protection . . ." [Vol. 21, p. 639].)

Possibly the most cogent suggestion of Oswald's mission in the Soviet Union can be found in the testimony of Dennis H. Ofstein, a fellow-employee at Jaggars-Chiles-Stovall Co. in Dallas (this is the photographic/graphic arts firm where Oswald worked

upon his return from Russia; it receives many classified government contracts). Ofstein's smattering of Russian evidently set
the usually phlegmatic Oswald to talking. "All the time I was in
Minsk I never saw a vapor trail," Ofstein quotes him. "He also
mentioned about the disbursement [dispersement?] of military
units," Ofstein continued, "saying they didn't intermingle their
armored divisions and infantry divisions and various units the
way we do in the United States, and they would have all of
their aircraft in one geographical location and their tanks in
another geographical location, and their infantry in another . . ."
On one occasion, Oswald asked Ofstein to enlarge a photograph
taken in Russia which, he explained, represented "some military
headquarters and that the guards stationed there were armed
with weapons and ammunition and had orders to shoot any
trespassers . . ." (Vol. 10, p. 202). Oswald's inordinate interest in
the contrails of high flying aircraft, Soviet military deployment
and a military facility involving an element of risk to photograph
hardly seems the natural curiosity of a hapless ex-Marine private.

An intriguing entry in Oswald's address book is the word
"microdots" appearing on the page on which he has notated
the address and phone number of Jaggers-Chiles-Stovall (CE
18, p. 45). Microdots are a clandestine means of communication
developed by German intelligence during World War II and still
in general use among espionage agencies. The technique is to
photograph the document to be transmitted and vastly reduce
the negative to a size that will fit inside a period. The microdot
can be inserted in an innocuous letter or magazine and mailed,
or left in a "dead drop"—a prearranged location for the deposit
and pickup of messages.

Thus it may be significant that Oswald obtained library cards
in Dallas and New Orleans, and usually visited the libraries on
Thursday. The possible implication of his visits was not overlooked by the FBI, which confiscated every book he ever
charged out, and never returned them. A piece that may fit into
the puzzle is the discovery by Garrison of an adult borrower's
card issued by the New Orleans public library in the name Clem
Bertrand. The business address shown is the International Trade
Mart [Shaw's former place of employment], and the home
address 3100 Louisiana Avenue Parkway, a wrong number, but

conspicuously close to that of David Ferrie at 3330 Louisiana Avenue Parkway. There may be a pattern here, since Oswald supposedly carried a card issued to Ferrie when arrested in Dallas.

Still another hint of Oswald's intelligence status is the inventory of his property seized by Dallas police after the assassination. Included is such sophisticated optical equipment as a Sterio Realist camera, a Hanza camera timer, filters, a small German camera, a Wollensak 15 power telescope, Micron 6X binoculars and a variety of film—hardly the usual accouterments of a lowly warehouseman (Stovall Exhibits).

Upon his return from Russia, the man who subscribed to Pravda in the Marine Corps and lectured his fellow Marines on Marxist dialectics set about institutionalizing his leftist facade. He wrote ingratiating letters to the national headquarters of the Communist Party, Fair Play for Cuba Committee and Socialist Workers Party (a copy of the famous snapshot of Oswald with a revolver on his hip, a rifle in one hand and the Party organ, the Militant, in the other was mailed to the SWP office in New York in April 1963). Garrison believes the facade was intended to facilitate his entry into communist countries for special missions.

Ferrie's involvement with the CIA seems to stem mainly from his anti-Castro paramilitary activity, although there is a suggestion that he was at one time a pilot for the Agency. In the late 1940s and early 1950s he flew light planes commercially in the Cleveland, Ohio area, and was rated by his colleagues as an outstanding pilot. In the middle 1950s there is an untraceable gap in his career. Then he turns up as an Eastern Air Lines pilot. Although he supposedly obtained an instrument rating at the Sunnyside Flying School in Tampa, Florida, there is no record that any such school ever existed.

A clue to Ferrie's activities may lie in the loss of hair he suffered. A fellow employee at Eastern recalls that when Ferrie first joined the line he was "handsome and friendly," but in the end became "moody and paranoiac—afraid the communists were out to get him." The personality change coincided with a gradual loss of hair. First a bald spot appeared, which Ferrie explained was caused by acid dripping from a plane battery. Then the hair began falling out in clumps—Ferrie desperately studied medicine to try to halt the process—until his body was entirely devoid of hair. One speculation is that he was moonlighting and suffered a physiological reaction to exposure to the extreme altitudes required for clandestine flights. Chinese Nationalist U-2 pilots reportedly have suffered the same hair-loss phenomenon.

One of Ferrie's covert tasks in the New Orleans area was to drill small teams in guerrilla warfare. One of his young protégés has revealed that he trained some of his Civil Air Patrol cadets and Cubans and formed them into five-man small weapons units, this under the auspices of the Marine Corps and State Department. Coupled with this is the information from another former protégé that Ferrie confided "he was working for the CIA rescuing Cubans out of Castro prisons," and on one occasion was called to Miami so that the CIA could "test him to see if he was the type of person who told his business to anybody." In a speech before the Military Order of World Wars in New Orleans in late 1961, Ferrie related that he had trained pilots in Guatemala for the Bay of Pigs, and professed bitter disappointment that they were not used.

Clay Shaw, an international trade official with top-level contacts in Latin America and Europe, would have been a natural target for CIA recruitment. Gordon Novel, who was acquainted with Shaw, was quoted by the States-Item as venturing that Shaw may have been asked by the CIA to observe the traffic of foreign commerce through New Orleans. More persuasive is Shaw's membership on the board of directors of a firm called *Centro Mondiale Commerciale* in Rome. According to the newspapers Paese Sera of Rome and Le Devoir of Montreal, among others of the foreign press, CMC was an obscure but well-financed firm that was ousted from Italy by the police because it was suspected of being a CIA front. It transplanted its operation to the more friendly climate of Johannesburg, South Africa, where it still functions.

The same group that incorporated CMC also set up a firm called Permidex Corporation in Switzerland, but that company was dissolved by the Swiss government when it was proved to be a conduit for funds destined for the Secret Army Organization (OAS), a group of right-wing French officers dedicated to "keeping Algeria French" by force of arms. The composition of the CMC group with which Shaw was associated is of more than cursory interest, since it includes a former U.S. intelligence officer, now an executive of the Bank of Montreal; the publisher of the neo-Nazi National-Zeitung of Germany; Prince Guitere de Spadaforo, an Italian industrialist related by marriage to Hitler finance minister Hjalmar Schacht; and the lawyer to the Italian royal family and secretary of the Italian neo-Fascist Party. Through his attorney, Shaw has stated he joined the CMC board of directors in 1958 at the insistence of his own board of directors of the International Trade Mart of New Orleans. . . .

WHERE IT ALL BEGAN
Peter Noyes

Legacy of Doubt / *1973*

On February 16, 1967, reporter Rosemary James of the *New Orleans States-Item* disclosed the first details of Jim Garrison's investigation into the assassination of President Kennedy and, in so doing, touched off a tidal wave of curiosity. Newspaper, radio, and television reporters from all over the world swarmed into New Orleans, bracing themselves for sensational disclosures. And at first, they were not to be disappointed.

After all, hadn't Lee Harvey Oswald lived in New Orleans prior to the JFK assassination? And hadn't this one-time defector to the Soviet Union taken part in the Communist-inspired activities of the Fair Play for Cuba Committee? It had all begun in the land of the Mardi Gras, so why shouldn't it end there?

The Gallup Poll showed that the majority of the American peo-

"Where It All Began" by Peter Noyes. Reprinted from *Legacy of Doubt* by Peter Noyes. Copyright © 1973 by Peter Noyes. Reprinted by permission of Pinnacle Books, Inc.

ple desperately wanted to believe in Jim Garrison, a hulking figure of a man who had whetted their appetite with the advancement of a conspiracy theory in the JFK assassination. At first glance, the towering Garrison seemed to have the credibility of a Lincoln. He had a reputation for taking on all comers in New Orleans, including Criminal Court judges, and usually winning. Newsmen checking into New Orleans were advised never to underestimate "Big Jim."

In a series of interviews Garrison speculated about the possible forces behind the assassination, singling out such diverse groups as right-wing extremists, anti-Castro Cubans, Cubans in general, the FBI, the CIA, the "military-industrial complex," and "other."

Gradually word about the D.A.'s probe leaked out and the plot thickened. Garrison identified the major culprits as socialite-businessman Clay Shaw, the retired director of the International Trade Mart, a nonprofit corporation formed to promote world trade through the Port of New Orleans, and David William Ferrie, a brilliant but extremely odd individual and a notorious homosexual. At the time Shaw was fifty-four; Ferrie forty-nine.

Ferrie was considered Garrison's most significant catch. Shortly after the JFK assassination he was questioned about a possible relationship with Oswald by both the FBI and Secret Service, then cleared of any complicity in the crime. Ferrie had been an outstanding pilot for Eastern Airlines for ten years but had been fired because of his homosexual activities.

But more significant than all the folderol about Ferrie's past, which Garrison played up so prominently, is the fact that on the day John Kennedy's blood was shed in Dealey Plaza, Ferrie's name was mentioned almost immediately.

At that time David Ferrie was [working as an] investigator for [a lawyer who represented] Carlos Marcello, a squat Mafia chieftain who ruled his territory in the southeastern United States with an iron hand. If any man had reason for wanting the Kennedy brothers killed, it was Carlos Marcello, who claimed he had been kidnapped at their instigation and flown out of the country.

Not once during the New Orleans investigation did Jim Garrison allude to Ferrie's ties to Marcello and the possibility that organized crime could have masterminded the assassination. Instead Garrison chose to depict Ferrie as a "right-wing radical" who plotted with anti-Castro Cuban extremists. That very well may have been an accurate description of one side of Ferrie. But the other side was a man who served the Brotherhood and served it well. David Ferrie worked for the Mafia by his own admission.

So it seems strange that Carlos Marcello let his most trusted investigator fall into Jim Garrison's legal staitjacket. It is no secret in New Orleans that Garrison and Marcello are friends. So if the investigation was a sham, as United States Attorney General Ramsey Clark and countless others contended, why didn't Marcello try to intervene on Ferrie's behalf? Marcello had once tried to intervene with a bribe on behalf of his good friend Jimmy Hoffa. And Ferrie had done much more for Marcello than Hoffa.

Perhaps David Ferrie had become expendable? He knew more about Marcello than anyone else in the organization. And as a homosexual, Ferrie was extremely vulnerable. He had been showing increasing symptoms of instability, and perhaps David Ferrie was a marked man.

In the early stages of the investigation Garrison made no mention of Edgar Eugene Bradley.* But he frequently made sinister references to unnamed coconspirators, some of whom, he alleged, were present in Dealey Plaza when John Kennedy was murdered.

The sensational nature of the D.A.'s probe struck like a rapier. Garrison's investigators marched into Clay Shaw's baroque dwelling and emerged triumphantly with an assortment of whips, robes, and other bizarre playthings that implied that the silver-haired businessman had a certain demoniacal quality.

There was nothing much in the body of evidence that could link Clay Shaw to Lee Harvey Oswald, despite Garrison's contention that the killer of the President knew Shaw under the name of "Clay Bertrand." The chief witness against Shaw was Vernon Bundy, a twenty-seven-year-old black who happened to be a narcotics addict. Bundy admitted he took four "caps" of heroin daily.

---

* On December 20, 1967, Garrison charged Bradley with conspiring to murder President Kennedy. Bradley denied Garrison's allegation that he had been in Dallas on the day of the assassination and successfully fought extradition from California. Noyes raises the possibility that Garrison somehow confused Bradley with Eugene Hale Brading (also known as Jim Braden), a man who allegedly had Mafia contacts, and whose presence at the scene of the assassination was recorded at the time.—Eds.

Bundy said that one morning in the summer of 1963 he was about to take a "pop" on the shore of Lake Pontchartrain, near New Orleans, when he saw Clay Shaw hand Oswald a "wad" of money.

Asked by Shaw's lawyer how he supported his expensive heroin habit, Bundy answered, "I steal sometimes."

Other witnesses produced by Garrison were equally dubious. According to Garrison, one of his critical witnesses was a twenty-five-year-old insurance salesman named Perry Raymond Russo. According to the D.A., Russo knew Ferrie well and had once heard him say that President Kennedy should have been killed for bungling the Bay of Pigs invasion. Also, according to Garrison, Russo had knowledge of a conspiracy meeting in Ferrie's apartment attended by both Shaw and Oswald.

But Garrison's credibility suffered a setback when James Phalen, a writer for the *Saturday Evening Post*, discovered documents in the D.A.'s own office that showed Russo had had no knowledge of an assassination plot or of a meeting at Ferrie's apartment until the time he was given sodium pentothal, the so-called truth serum. Phalen reported that Dr. Esmond Fatter put Russo in a hypnotic state—at Garrison's direction—and told him to picture a television screen on which he would see "Bertrand, Ferrie, and Oswald . . . and they are talking about assassinating someone." At first Phalen's story seemed incredible. District Attorneys just don't behave that way. But then it was confirmed that Russo had indeed been hypnotized—just a few hours before a scheduled pretrial appearance called by Garrison.

Garrison was wrong about Clay Shaw and Edgar Eugene Bradley. The case against them was a monumental fraud. [Shaw was acquitted and Bradley was never tried.] But both were convenient for Garrison's purposes—Shaw because of his personal vulnerability, Bradley perhaps because of his name and physical characteristics.

Although there was positive evidence that David Ferrie had known Oswald, despite the disclaimers of Warren Commission investigators, it didn't make much difference. On February 22, 1967, six days after the *New Orleans States-Item* disclosed what Garrison was up to, Ferrie's body was found in his apartment, which was littered with newspaper clippings, magazine articles, and diagrams relating to the JFK assassination.

The coroner of New Orleans, Dr. Nicholas Chetta, said Ferrie died of a ruptured blood vessel in his brain. At first, Garrison said it was murder. Then he pronounced that Ferrie had killed himself because his involvement in the JFK assassination was known at last. At this point, a sort of mass hysteria was starting to build once more among the American people. It was symbolized by an editorial cartoon by Paul Conrad, the Pulitzer Prize winner, which showed persons dropping dead all over New Orleans, just as they had in Dallas after the JFK assassination.

That may have been the zenith of Garrison's career. His credibility was never better. He seemed to be beaming when he called a news conference in New Orleans and told reporters:

The apparent suicide of David Ferrie ends the life of a man who, in my judgment, was one of history's most important individuals. Evidence developed by our office has long since confirmed that he was involved in events culminating in the assassination of President Kennedy. Apparently, we waited too long.

Although Ferrie was dead, Garrison gave the impression that he was intensifying his investigation. He maintained that Ferrie was the man selected to fly the getaway plane for Lee Harvey Oswald and his coconspirators. It was simply a matter of tying up the loose ends. Clay Shaw would have his day in court, and so would Edgar Eugene Bradley.

Then Garrison started talking about his "new evidence." He maintained that Edgar Eugene Bradley had been active in New Orleans, plotting the assassination with Shaw, Ferrie, and Oswald, and the D.A. obtained a Grand Jury indictment to that effect.

I called Garrison's office and asked an aide about the language of the indictment. Did it specify the date on which the conspiracy allegedly took place?

"Yes it did," the Garrison aide told me. "The indictment says the meeting took place in the middle of September in 1963." It was difficult for me to believe that the indictment was not more precise. If there was such a meeting and witnesses were present, wasn't it logical that the exact date would be spelled out in the indictment? Wouldn't the witnesses at least know what day of the week the meeting took place?

"No," the Garrison aide said. "We don't do things that way down here."

Every time Garrison opened his mouth in the days after Ferrie's death, his appearance of credibility appeared to be giving way to one of lunacy. Perhaps the most perceptive observer of the circus in New Orleans was Hugh Aynesworth, of *Newsweek* magazine. Writing in the May 15, 1967, edition of *Newsweek*, Aynesworth had this to say about the Garrison investigation:

Jim Garrison is right. There has been a conspiracy in New Orleans— but it is a plot of Garrison's own making. It is a scheme to concoct a fantastic "solution" to the death of John F. Kennedy, and to make it stick; in this cause the district attorney and his staff have been parties to the death of one man and have humiliated, harassed and financially gutted several others.

Aynesworth accused Garrison of offering $3,000 and a job with an airline to [Alvin] Beauboeuf, a supposed friend of Ferrie, to testify that he overheard the planning of the JFK assassination. And Aynesworth continued:

I also know that when the D.A.'s office learned this entire bribery attempt had been tape-recorded, two of Garrison's men returned to the "witness" [Beauboeuf], and he says, threatened him with physical harm. Another man who spent many hours with the District Attorney in a vain attempt to dissuade him from his assassination-conspiracy theory has twice been threatened—once by the D.A.'s own "witnesses," the second time by Garrison himself.

That was one view of the Garrison investigation. Hugh Aynesworth may have been right in stating that there was a "plot" of Garrison's own making, but the reasons for it may have been far more subtle than they appeared on the surface.

From the start, Garrison was prepared for the role of martyr if he got caught in his own crossfire. In an interview with *Playboy* magazine he said, "I was perfectly aware that I might have signed my political death warrant the moment I launched this case—but I couldn't care less as long as I could shed some light on John Kennedy's assassination."

Despite what Garrison said, his moves against David Ferrie appeared designed to create an element of doubt. He set up a straw man, destroyed him, then walked away from the macabre scene. Why was Jim Garrison the architect of his own political downfall? Why had he picked David Ferrie as the instrument of that self-destruction?

Ferrie was a strange individual, a New Orleans curiosity. He was bald and had no eyebrows (reportedly because of burns), so he covered up his hairless spots with pasted-on mohair. In his youth Ferrie had studied to be a Catholic priest. He read Latin and Greek and spoke fluent Spanish. He was listed in the New Orleans city directory as a psychiatrist, although he had no degree nor any formal education in that field. His real skill was that of a hypnotist. His powers of persuasion were said to be uncanny.

One CIA agent who was assigned to Lee Harvey Oswald for a time was convinced that Ferrie placed the President's assassin in a hypnotic trance; that Oswald actually had no idea of the tragedy he had brought about when he walked out of the Texas Book Depository on November 22, 1963. At best that would appear to be a highly doubtful theory, despite Ferrie's ability as a hypnotist.

Ferrie feared death. After Garrison's investigators started staking out his apartment, he was observed pacing back and forth in his living room hour after hour. Carlos Marcello made no attempt to shield him, even though a mere whistle from the Mafia boss would have called off the wolves.

Shortly before Garrison planned to charge him with murder, friends reported that Ferrie was terrified and that he had no idea why he was under constant surveillance. They said he went to the D.A. and asked for physical protection against unnamed persons. After several days in protective custody he returned to his apartment, where he was found dead seventy-two hours later.

In his apartment, police found an unsigned, undated note which said, "To leave this life is, for me, a sweet prospect. I find nothing in it that is desirable and on the other hand everything that is loathsome."

About a week after Ferrie's death, *Newsweek* writer Aynesworth interviewed Garrison at his home. He quoted the D.A. as admitting to him: "Yeah, we killed the son of a bitch."

Since Ferrie was dead and Governor Reagan refused to extradite Edgar Eugene Bradley from California to stand trial on the conspiracy charges, Clay Shaw was the only sitting duck left in Garrison's shooting gallery.

The trial was a sham; it was perhaps the most disgraceful legal event of the twentieth century. The jury wasted no time in finding Shaw not guilty. Many of Garrison's colleagues in the legal profession demanded that he be impeached. Yet in 1969, shortly after the trial, he was elected for a third term as District Attorney of New Orleans. . . .

SERIOUS MISGIVINGS
Sylvia Meagher

Accessories after the Fact / *1967*

Because of the nature of the investigation, it is probable that the assassins who shot down President John F. Kennedy have gone free, undetected. The Warren Report has served merely to delay their identification and the process of justice.

No more time need be devoted to denouncing those who are responsible for this frustration of justice. They have destroyed their own case, and conceivably their reputations. What must now be done is to set about finding the assassins. Such a new investigation, if it is undertaken, must be performed by a competent and impartial body, and in the light of the bitter lesson learned from the Warren Report, the new investigation must be in the framework of an adversary proceeding.

The new investigative body should first attack the evidence against Oswald presented in the Warren Report and the Hearings and Exhibits, and present an objective and scientific evaluation of that evidence so that the ambiguity about his role in the assassination will, if possible, be dispelled. The new body must also be given access to the suppressed documents of the Warren Commission. The 75-year time vault must be opened and its contents must be put before the new body—and, at the appropriate moment, before the public, *within* our lifetime. The leads and clues which were not followed up by the Warren Commission, or which were incompletely investigated, now must be pursued with vigor, by *independent investigators* and not by the governmental agencies compromised by their role in the protection of the murdered President.

A scrupulous and disinterested investigation—even now at this late stage and despite the death of several key witnesses during the past three years—must once and for all resolve the question of Oswald's guilt or innocence and establish whether or not he was even implicated in the crimes of which he stands accused and, for all purposes, convicted and punished. It must almost inevitably point also to the identity of those who are guilty of the assassination and the collateral murders.

In advocating a new investigation, I do not have in mind the inquiry in progress in New Orleans—even though it will not have escaped notice that District Attorney Jim Garrison of the Parish of Orleans, in accusing anti-Castro Cuban exiles and CIA agents of complicity in the assassination, has postulated a theory which has much in common with the hypothetical construct elaborated in [pages 101–116 of this volume].

Since February 1967, when it was first revealed that Mr. Garrison was conducting his own investigation of the assassination and that he considered the Warren Report to be mistaken, his activities and pronouncements have been much in the headlines. I must admit that at the beginning, Mr. Garrison's rhetoric was disarming—"Let justice be done, though the heavens fall,"[1] for example, and "I have no reason to believe at this point that Lee Harvey Oswald killed anybody in Dallas that day."[2] For the first time, a public official armed with subpoena power and ready to use it had openly repudiated the conclusions of the Warren Commission and had pledged to expose the guilty parties and bring them to justice. At a preliminary court hearing in the arrest by

[1] CBS Television Network newscast, Channel 2, New York, February 18, 1967.
[2] "Figure in Oswald Inquiry Is Dead in New Orleans," *The New York Times,* February 23, 1967, page 22, col. 5.

District Attorney Garrison of an individual whom he charged with conspiring to assassinate President Kennedy, three presiding judges rejected a motion to admit the Warren Report into evidence, on the ground that it was a compound of hearsay and error.[3]

But as the Garrison investigation continued to unfold, it gave cause for increasingly serious misgivings about the validity of his evidence, the credibility of his witnesses, and the scrupulousness of his methods. The fact that many critics of the Warren Report have remained passionate advocates of the Garrison investigation, even condoning tactics which they might not condone on the part of others, is a matter for regret and disappointment. Nothing less than strict factual accuracy and absolute moral integrity must be deemed permissible, if justice is, indeed, to be served.

June 1967

[3] *The New York Times,* March 16, 1967, page 39, col. 2.

PRESIDENTIAL DOUBTS: COMMENTS FROM PRESS CONFERENCES AND INTERVIEWS OF LYNDON JOHNSON, RICHARD NIXON AND GERALD FORD

What have John Kennedy's successors in the White House really *thought about his assassination? Have they believed in private the conclusions of the Warren Commission which they have affirmed in public? Lyndon Johnson's doubts have been revealed posthumously, first in an interview with Leo Janos published in the* Atlantic Monthly *in July 1973.* Johnson reportedly told*

* "The Last Days of the President," p. 39.

Janos, "I never believed that Oswald acted alone, although I can accept that he pulled the trigger." According to Janos, Johnson discovered upon taking office in November 1963 that "we had been operating a damned Murder, Inc. in the Caribbean." Noting that a CIA-backed assassination team had been picked up in Havana a year or so before Kennedy was shot, Johnson reportedly speculated to Janos that Dallas had been a retaliation for this "thwarted attempt." The late President told Janos he had no proof and asked Attorney General Ramsey Clark to look into it, but Clark reported back in two weeks that he had found nothing new.

Columnist Marianne Means of the King Features Syndicate responded to what she called "current speculation that the Central Intelligence Agency might somehow have been involved in the Kennedy assassination" April 24, 1975, by revealing a confidential interview with Johnson a year before he died which she felt "debunked" the speculations about the CIA. She reported that Johnson told her that Oswald had acted alone but was "either under the influence or the orders" of Cuban Premier Fidel Castro.

The following night, Walter Cronkite of CBS News broadcast a 1969 interview with Johnson in which the late President admitted, "I can't honestly say that I've ever been completely relieved of the fact that there might have been international connections" in the JFK assassination. Johnson went on to defend the Warren Commission as competent, judicious and bipartisan men who "did the best they could." But he added, "I don't think they, or me, or anyone else, is always absolutely sure of everything that might have motivated Oswald or others that could have been involved." Cronkite asked Johnson directly whether his lingering suspicions pointed to Cuba. Johnson replied:

"Oh, I don't think we ought to discuss suspicions because there's not any hard evidence that would lead me to the conclusion that Oswald was directed by a foreign government or that his sympathies for other governments could have spurred him on this effort.

"But he was quite a mysterious fellow, and he did have a connection that bore examination, and the extent of the influence of those connections on him I think history will deal with more than we're able to now."

When he was questioned closely about wiretapping in a press conference August 22, 1973, President Richard M. Nixon also appeared to many observers to reveal doubts that Oswald had acted alone. He defended his own wiretaps by pointing out that Presidents Kennedy and Johnson had also sanctioned such surveillance:

". . . I should also point out that when you ladies and gentlemen indicate your great interest in wiretaps—and I understand that—that the height of the wiretap was when Robert Kennedy was attorney general in 1963. I don't criticize it, however. He had over two hundred and fifty in 1963 and of course the average in the Eisenhower administration and in the Nixon administration is about a hundred and ten. But if he had ten more, and as a result of wiretaps had been able to discover the—discover the Oswald plan [*Emphasis in original—Eds.*], *it would have been worth it. . . ."*

A later questioner returned to the problem of how "Oswald's plan" could have been discovered by wiretaps. Nixon responded:

"No, what I said—let me, let me correct you, sir. I want to be sure that the assumption is correct. I said if ten more wiretaps could have found, er, the conspiracy, if it was a conspiracy, or the individual, then it would have been worth it. As far as I'm concerned, I'm no more of an expert on that assassination than anybody else; but my point is that wiretaps in the national security area were very high in the Kennedy administration, for very good reasons: because there were many threats on the President's life; because there were national security problems, and that is why that in that period on [sic] 1961 to '63 there were wiretaps on news organizations, on news people, on civil rights leaders, and on other people. And I think they were perfectly justified, and I'm sure that President Kennedy and his brother Robert Kennedy would never have authorized them, as I would never have authorized them, unless he thought they were in the national interest."

President Nixon was then asked whether assassination threats merit more national security wiretaps. He responded:

"No. No, as far as I'm concerned, I was only suggesting that in terms of those times—of those times—that to have the Oswald thing happen just seemed . . . so unbelievable, with his record . . . with everything that everybody had on him, that this fellow could

*have been where he was, in a position to shoot the President of
the United States, seems to me to be—to have been a terrible
breakdown in our . . . protective, security areas."*

*President Gerald Ford has been most consistent in his defense
of the Warren Report. As late as April 3, 1975, Ford engaged in
this exchange with reporters:*

Q. Mr. President, in light of current concerns regarding the assassination of President Kennedy and the recent showings of the Zapruder film, do you still have the same confidence in the finding of the Warren Commission that you had as a member of that commission?

A. I think you'd have to read very carefully what the Warren Commission said and I as a member of the Warren Commission helped to participate in the drafting of the language. We said that Lee Harvey Oswald was the assassin. We said that the commission had found no evidence of a conspiracy, foreign or domestic. Those words were very carefully drafted.

And so far I have seen no evidence that would dispute the conclusions to which we came. We were most careful because in 1963 and '64, when we most carefully analyzed all the evidence available there was none of the involvement of anybody or anybody as a group in the assassination. It's my understanding that the Rockefeller Commission may if the facts seem to justify it, take a look at it—the problems—and I suspect that the House and Senate Committees that are currently investigating C.I.A. history may do the same.

But the commission was right when it made its determination and it was accurate at least to this point and i want to re-emphasize that as to the evidence that we saw.

OTHER
ASSASSINATIONS

INTRODUCTION

There are many other assassinations which it might have been appropriate to discuss in this section of our collection, but we have limited the consideration to the killings of two figures of national prominence, Robert Francis Kennedy and Martin Luther King, Jr. To have opened the discussion to the problem of assassinations abroad—even to that large subcategory in which CIA involvement has been suspected or alleged—would have so widened the scope of the inquiry as to make it impossible to maintain the same level of concreteness as for domestic assassinations.

Recent interest in CIA activities has focused on the assassinations of Anastasio Somoza (Nicaragua, 1956), Carlos Castillo Armas (Guatemala, 1957), Rafael Trujillo Molina (Dominican Republic, 1961) and Ngo Dinh Diem (South Vietnam, 1963). Comparatively little has been written about the rather high incidence of assassinations in postcolonial Africa, from Patrice Lumumba (Congo, 1961) to Herbert Chitepo (Rhodesia, 1975). The forces behind these killings deserve closer examination.

Restricting consideration to assassinations inside the United States, we might have included the killings of other black leaders, such as NAACP field secretary Medgar Evers in Jackson, Mississippi, in 1963; Malcolm X in New York in 1965; and Black Panther Fred Hampton in Chicago in 1969. These deaths also merit serious scrutiny, and it is to be hoped that our examination of the assassinations covered here will help to stimulate a wider interest.

Even in the cases of Robert Kennedy and King it was difficult to overcome the widespread reticence about assassinations. Former Congressman Allard K. Lowenstein, who is now writing a book on the assassination of Robert F. Kennedy, recently described his own reluctance to examine the assassination issues. Writing in the Washington Star, *May 4, 1975, attorney Lowenstein disclosed:*

Like many others, I tried for a long time afterward to avoid anything connected with the assassination of [Robert] Kennedy. The loss was too staggering, and it was hard enough to move ahead without making matters even more difficult by picking at a scar too close to the heart. Furthermore, the facts seemed obvious, and in the context of those times there seemed no reason to question the obvious.

During my term in Congress, I continued to refuse to listen to questions about any of the assassinations. I believe we all are indebted to those people who researched these questions and kept them alive during that long period before revelations about other matters finally made some of us realize how closed-minded we had been about the assassinations.

Lowenstein went on to summarize the evidence that finally convinced him the RFK case (in which Sirhan Sirhan was convicted as the "lone assassin") should be reopened: (1) The autopsy proved the fatal bullet was fired from a shorter distance than eyewitness testimony establishes for Sirhan's position. (2) Some ballistics experts say the bullets from Robert Kennedy and a wounded bystander don't match. (3) Sound paneling removed from the ceiling of the scene of the crime has not been analyzed to see whether the bullet holes in it are entrance or exit holes, indicating a richochet—a crucial determination which could establish whether more shots were fired than the eight which were known to have come from Sirhan's gun. (It was later learned that the ceiling panels were destroyed before they could be analyzed.)

We include here two quite different pieces on the Robert Kennedy assassination. A 1975 article by Betsy Langman and Alexander Cockburn describes the ballistics problems surrounding Sirhan's gun. An excerpt from Robert Blair Kaiser's book

"R.F.K. Must Die!" analyzes the evidence that Sirhan may have been under posthypnotic suggestion when he shot at Kennedy. Kaiser's study of Sirhan's diary finds strong evidence that Sirhan associated a monetary reward with the killing. A former Time *correspondent, Kaiser spent nearly two hundred hours interviewing Sirhan, who later tried to block publication of Kaiser's book when he found he couldn't censor it.*

On the Martin Luther King killing we have a list of the key questions pointing to a conspiracy, as summarized by Harold Weisberg in his 1971 book on the case, Frame-Up. *We also include an article by Wayne Chastain, the only metropolitan newspaper reporter who has ever had an in-depth interview with convicted assassin James Earl Ray. In addition, for contextual purposes, we are reprinting an excerpt from J. Edgar Hoover's COINTELPRO documents on the FBI Counterintelligence Program to prevent the rise of a black "Messiah." Our point is not to imply that the FBI had a hand in King's killing, but to establish the context in which a cover-up was less difficult and King's protection—despite his international stature—was virtually unthinkable. As other reports have shown, the FBI was more concerned with tapping King's telephone and spying on his sex life.**

California Congressman Ronald V. Dellums has recently termed Hoover's concern about a "black Messiah" in the COINTELPRO documents a "morbid preoccupation" deserving extensive investigation. Dellums, co-sponsor of a bill to reopen investigation of the Kennedy and King shootings, also recently told a reporter, "I have never for one moment believed these were isolated acts. I have always believed that they were a conspiracy." (San Francisco Bay Guardian, July 12, 1975, p. 7.) He concluded that the killings may involve unrelated conspiracies, or "there may be a thread running through all of them."

---

* See Victor S. Navasky, *Kennedy Justice* (New York: Atheneum, 1971).

MARTIN LUTHER KING

COINTELPRO
J. Edgar Hoover

March 4, 1968

Date: 3/4/68

[Transmit the] following in _____

(Type in plaintext or code)

[via] AIRTEL

_____   _____

(Priority)

- -

To: SAC, Albany   <u>PERSONAL ATTENTION</u>

From: Director, FBI ✗✗✗✗✗✗✗

COUNTERINTELLIGENCE PROGRAM
BLACK NATIONALIST-HATE GROUPS
RACIAL INTELLIGENCE

[Deletion and omission—Eds.]

GOALS

For maximum effectiveness of the Counterintelligence Program, and to prevent wasted effort, long-range goals are being set.

1. Prevent the *coalition* of militant black nationalist groups. In unity there is strength; a truism that is no less valid for all its triteness. An effective coalition of black nationalist groups might be the first step toward a real "Mau Mau" in America, the beginning of a true black revolution.

2. Prevent the *rise of a "messiah"* who could unify, and electrify, the militant black nationalist movement. xxxxxxxxx might have been such a "messiah;" he is the martyr of the movement today. xxxxxxxxxxxx xxxxxxxxxxxxxxxxxxxxxxxxxxxxxxx xxxxxxxxxxxxxxxxx all aspire to this position. xxxxxxxxxxxx xxxxxxxx is less of a threat because of his age. xxxxxxxxxxxx be a very real contender for this position should he abandon his supposed "obedience" to "white, liberal doctrines" (nonviolence) and embrace black nationalism. xxxxxxxxxxxxxxxx x has the necessary charisma to be a real threat in this way.

3. Prevent *violence* on the part of black nationalist groups. This is of primary importance, and is, of course, a goal of our investigative activity; it should also be a goal of the Counterintelligence Program. Through counterintelligence it should be possible to pinpoint potential troublemakers and neutralize them before they exercise their potential for violence.

4. Prevent militant black nationalist groups and leaders from gaining *respectability*, by discrediting them

to three separate segments of the community. The goal of discrediting black nationalists must be handled tactically in three ways. You must discredit these groups and individuals to, first, the responsible Negro community. Second, they must be discredited to the white community, both the responsible community and to "liberals" who have vestiges of sympathy for militant black nationalists simply because they are Negroes. Third, these groups must be discredited in the eyes of Negro radicals, the followers of the movement. This last area requires entirely different tactics from the first two. Publicity about violent tendencies and radical statements merely enhances black nationalists to the last group; it adds "respectability" in a different way.

5. A final goal should be to prevent the long-range *growth* of militant black nationalist organizations, especially among youth. Specific tactics to prevent these groups from converting young people must be developed.

Besides these five goals counterintelligence is a valuable part of our regular investigative program as it often produces positive information.

TARGETS

Primary targets of the Counterintelligence Program, Black Nationalist-Hate Groups, should be the most violent and radical groups and their leaders. We should emphasize those leaders and organizations that are nationwide in scope and are most capable of disrupting this country. These targets should include the radical and violence-prone leaders, members, and followers of the: [FBI deletion—Eds.]

RAY SAYS GUILTY PLEA COERCED
Wayne Chastain, Jr.

Pacific News Service | *October 20, 1974*

MEMPHIS, Tenn.—The world may get a flashback glimpse into history at 9 a.m. Tuesday when U.S. Judge Robert McRae taps his gavel in a Memphis courtroom to begin what could be the longest proceeding of its kind in legal history.

The case: A habeas corpus proceeding into the case of James Earl Ray vs. Tennessee.

Ray, 47, is the man history has already recorded—and probably forgotten—as the assassin who shot and killed Dr. Martin Luther King Jr. as he stood on a balcony of a Memphis motel at 6:01 p.m. on April 4, 1968.

Memphis police, the FBI and the state of Tennessee contend that Ray fired the shot from the bathroom window at the back of a dingy rooming house next to the motel.

If the authorities and historians are in error, Ray must share the blame, because he pled guilty to King's murder on March 10, 1969, in exchange for a 99-year sentence.

However, Ray attempted to reverse his guilty plea less than 24 hours later.

In a letter he wrote shortly after arriving in the Tennessee State Prison in Nashville, Ray pled his innocence, fired his attorney, Percy Foreman of Houston, and contended Foreman had coerced him into making the guilty plea. He sent his letter to Judge Preston Battle, who had approved the negotiated guilty plea. Battle received the letter five days after the hearing, and dropped dead of a heart attack after conferring with a Shelby County assistant prosecutor most of the day over the matter.

"Ray Says Guilty Plea Coerced" by Wayne Chastain, Jr. Reprinted from *St. Paul Sunday Pioneer Press* (Pacific News Service Dispatch) by permission of Pacific News Service and the author.

Today, Ray still maintains he is innocent.

This writer talked to Ray in a four-hour interview at the Tennessee State Prison last May—one of only two interviews Ray has granted to newsmen in his six years in prison.

Ray says he was "set up as a patsy" for King's murder by a mysterious French Canadian named Raoul, a husky and swarthy underworld character enmeshed in profitable narcotics and gun smuggling activities.

He said he met Raoul on the Montreal docks in the summer of 1967—some three months after Ray escaped from the Missouri State Prison where he was serving a 30-year sentence for armed robbery.

Raoul, Ray says, brought him to Memphis in 1968. Ray thought they were to meet an international gunrunner and work out details of a gun smuggling scheme in South America—an operation that Raoul said would make Ray rich.

Ray says he had no knowledge of a conspiracy to murder King. Looking back, however, he says he now realizes it was a murder conspiracy hatched by professionals. At least one other man than Raoul was involved—the purported gunrunner, whom Ray said he never formally met.

This writer has been investigating King's assassination since the night it occurred. I showed Ray some photographs of the man believed by Ray's attorney to be the "international gunrunner" and the trigger man.

Ray believes he saw this man twice the afternoon of King's murder—once in a beer lounge two blocks from the rooming house, later in a cafe downstairs from the rooming house. "I had the feeling the man was following me," he says.

Ray ran several errands for Raoul, then met him in a room that had been rented that afternoon. (Ray earlier admitted renting the room, he said, to protect Raoul—but the rooming house manager, Bessie Brewer, said Ray was not the man who rented the room.)

"Raoul told me he was going to meet this gunrunner at 6 p.m. and that the gunrunner would speak more freely if I was not there," Ray said. "Raoul gave me $200 and told me to go downtown and see a picture show."

Raoul, Ray said, also instructed him to leave the white Mustang parked at the curb on the street below, only a few feet from the foot of the stairwell.

"He said the other man and he might want to use the Mustang later in the evening," Ray said. "It was about 5:20 when I reached the street below because I remembered looking at my watch. I saw a low tire on the Mustang and I saw I had plenty of time to have the tire filled and be back at the rooming house by 6."

Ray said a feeling of relief passed through him as he pulled away from the curb. At first he had thought that the man he had seen in the beer lounge—whom he vaguely recalled seeing before —might have been a federal investigator of some sort, but now he was convinced that this man was the gunrunner Raoul was supposed to meet.

He drove the Mustang to a service station about three blocks away, waiting a long time for service because attendants were very busy. While a black attendant was filling the low tire, Ray said, he recalled seeing an ambulance go by. He looked at his watch and saw that it was about 6:05.

"I drove back, but when I got to the rooming house, the entire block was sealed off," Ray said. "Police were swarming all over the place.

"There was a policeman standing in the middle of the street. He yelled 'Get out of here' as I tried to drive and park somewhere in front of the rooming house."

Ray said he asked the policeman if he could make a U-turn (illegal under traffic ordinances) and proceed north on South Main Street. Ray quoted the policeman as saying:

"I don't care what you do, just get out of here."

Ray said he made the U-turn and proceeded to drive south out of Memphis toward Mississippi.

"It wasn't until I almost got to Grenada, Miss., (about 100 miles away) that I turned on the radio and heard what had happened," Ray said. "The radio broadcast mentioned 422½ South Main Street (address of the rooming house) and it wasn't until then I learned I had been associated with the men who killed Dr. King."

If Ray had no knowledge of King's death, then why did he flee Memphis to Mississippi via back roads?

"I was afraid that the man whom I suspected of following me had turned out to be a federal investigator after all, and had led a raid on the rooming house to arrest Raoul and the gunrunner," Ray said.

"Also, I didn't want to get caught—no matter what kind of scheme they were involved in—because I still owed the state of Missouri 30 years."

Witnesses for the state in the evidentiary hearing will be: Ray's former attorney, Percy Foreman, and William Bradford Huie, author of a book, "He Slew the Dreamer," and numerous magazine articles on the King assassination. Both have testified in depositions that Ray acted alone and that Ray killed King.

The hearing will examine Ray's charges that:

• Ray did not make his guilty plea "voluntarily."

• Ray's former attorney, Percy Foreman, deliberately compromised Ray's right to a fair trial in order to further Huie's and his own financial successes (Foreman and Huie had an agreement that Foreman's legal fees would be paid by sales of Huie's books and income from a film to which both had film rights).

• Foreman withheld exculpatory evidence proving Ray's innocence from both Ray and the state, and insisted to Ray that the state had an "air-tight case" against him and that he would die in the electric chair if he went to trial.

Foreman continued to deal with Huie even after telling Ray that Huie had compromised Ray's rights to a fair trial by an article published in Look magazine. Huie's dealings with Ray's first attorney, Arthur Hanes of Birmingham, Ala., were "legally and ethically improper," Ray quotes Foreman as saying.

Huie wrote him in December 1968, saying it would be in Ray's financial interest to plead guilty, because this would insure financial success of "He Slew the Dreamer." A book about the man who did not kill Dr. King would not sell, Ray quotes Huie as saying.

Foreman assured Ray he would get a new trial after he pled guilty and accepted a negotiated sentence, and promised that if he did not get a new trial, Foreman would see to it that he got a pardon when John Jay Hooker Jr., son of Foreman's law associate, was elected governor of Tennessee.

"I was browbeaten, badgered and bribed into pleading guilty," Ray told this reporter. "My mental state bordered on insanity as I was kept awake by lights on at all times in my cell—for 24 hours at a time. I only managed to grab a few minutes of sleep at a time, and my nervous and irritable state prevented me from making any rational decisions about my fate."

Foreman denies these allegations. In an unsigned deposition taken by the state attorney general, Foreman says Ray is the assassin, calling him a "racist who wanted recognition and praise from his old inmates back at Jefferson City (site of Missouri State Prison)."

However, Foreman announced on Oct. 2 that he will not be able to appear at the Memphis hearing because of a heavy court docket in Houston, Tex.

Judge McRae has ruled that Foreman cannot be compelled to appear, on grounds that habeas corpus is technically a civil proceeding.

Ray's attorneys think that Foreman's failure to appear voluntarily will help Ray win a new trial in the Tennessee courts.

McRae has granted Ray's attorneys access to Foreman's file in the Ray case; Huie's financial records on the sales of his book; and the state's records of evidence it had planned to present if Ray had gone to trial in 1969.

Asst. Atty. Gen. Henry Haille, who opposed the broad discovery powers McRae granted to Ray's attorneys, said Ray's hearing will probably be the longest evidentiary hearing in legal history.

"It will be a matter of retrying an entire state criminal case in federal court—under the guise of an evidentiary hearing."

McRae replies that a full review of the evidence is called for.

"The appellate court ordered a full and fair hearing on all matters pertaining to whether Ray's plea was voluntary," McRae said. "The very issue the high court asked to be decided lies at the heart of the evidence Ray's attorneys are seeking to discover."

As this book goes to press, Ray's pleas for a new trial have all been turned back.—Eds.

KEY QUESTIONS, MAJOR DOUBTS
Harold Weisberg

Frame-Up / *1971*

. . . the basic question is not, really, whether or not Ray is guilty, important as that is, but whether the oft-quoted requirement of the law, "beyond reasonable doubt and to a moral certainty," was met. Because of the *public* official posture that there was no conspiracy (now privately altered as a consequence of the work represented by this book), this means that the proof must be:

that Ray, *alone*, fired a single, fatal shot;

and that he was *not, in any way*, helped by *anybody*. . . .

Is there any proof that Ray, in person, was at the scene of the crime, particularly at the moment it was committed?

Does a single credible eyewitness place him there?

Does fingerprint evidence place him there, even at another time?

Why was the fact of the extreme drunkenness of the only claimed eyewitness suppressed from all official records, including his own sworn statement? And why was the more credible but contradictory word of his sober and lucid common-law wife suppressed? Can her mysterious sequestration, which made her unavailable to the defense, be no more than an inexplicable coincidence?

Is there *any* proof the so-called Ray rifle was used in the crime?

Even if there were, as there now is not, is there any proof Ray used it? Or that it was ever in his possession at any time after purchase?

Does the exchanging of the rifle as soon as it was bought make

"Key Questions, Major Doubts" by Harold Weisberg. Reprinted from *Frame-Up* by Harold Weisberg, by permission of the author/publisher, Route 12, Frederick, Md.

any sense at all, except as another means of leaving a clear and obvious trail leading to Ray?

Is there, in fact, *any* ballistics proof identifying *any* rifle or rifles used in the crime?

In the official, minitrial evidence:

Why did the prosecution and the federal government suppress and misrepresent the medical evidence, hiding the existence of another and major wound?

Why was not the eyewitness testimony of known police-spy observers from the "red" squad placed in the record? And why was the *existence* of these police eyewitnesses hidden—suppressed?

Why is there no picture of the corpse as found by the police in the evidence? (If no police photographer was present, a professional photographer was and he did take pictures.)

Were any FBI agents present? If so (as seems likely), why is this also hidden?

Is there *any* established connection between the finding of Ray's property near the scene of the crime and the crime itself? If there is not, is not the finding of this Ray property at that point and at that time indicative that it was planted to be found, to link him with the crime?

Is *either* of the official and contradictory accounts of the finding of this property credible?

Is it true, as he swore, that Inspector Zachary found it? . . .

Can a fleeing assassin—even an insane one—have detoured and tossed such incriminating clues [the rifle and a radio which was traced to Ray] *into the entrance of Canipe's store*, as shown in the suppressed picture I had to sue to get?

[. . .] Could that bundle, not tied and with its imputed career and contents, have stayed intact after being tossed into the entrance? Could the radio, magically, have escaped it and, undamaged, just happened to stand upright, while the longer, heavier rifle did not show?

If this is not a faked picture (with the bundle itself faked), is not the evidence relating to it perjurious?

Is there any proof that Ray, personally and alone, drove that Mustang, *to* or *from* Memphis?

Why does the disappearance at Memphis of an Atlanta-to-Chicago ticketed airline passenger—and at just the right time—remain an official mystery, suppressed from the official evidence?

Is there any proof that on the way to Memphis Ray, personally, checked the car into the New Rebel Motel?

Why, whether or not innocent, was knowledge of the presence of handwriting other than Ray's on the motel registration suppressed from the evidence and thus from all publicly available records?

Why was there official suppression of the existence of other, identical white Mustangs?

When Ray is alleged to have driven that Mustang, sleepless and entirely alone, for almost 400 miles through the night, why is there no evidence of a single one of his fingerprints anywhere in or on it? After he drove it for more than a year? Is this within possibility?

If he had been entirely alone, why was property other than his found in that car? Why is its owner not identified? Were there no other fingerprints in or on the car—*none* of *anyone*—after that spectacular dash?

Whose fingerprints are on the cigarette butts? Ray is a non-smoker.

Why would even a lunatic drive *400 miles in the wrong direction* escaping such a crime if he were entirely alone and planned flight to Canada?

Why would the entirely alone Ray have marked up that map of Atlanta and then not have committed the crime there?

How did he do it without leaving a single fingerprint on the map?

Were any *other* fingerprints on it or on any of the other maps, other property?

Why would the entirely alone Ray have ordered such specialized camera equipment, so ideally suited for spying, in a way that needlessly left so clear a record, when he could have gotten it locally in any good camera shop?

Could an entirely alone Ray, traveling aimlessly, have known as accurately and in advance when he would be where and for how long?

Could Ray, entirely alone and unassisted, have financed and planned all the traveling, including the adoption of false identities? Could he have seen the *signature* of the *adult* Eric St. Vincent Galt [in which the middle name, "St. V." resembles "Starvo," the middle name in the Galt alias used by Ray] in the newspaper notice of the *birth* of the *infant* Eric St. Vincent Galt [said in the official explanation to be Ray's source of the alias]?

Did the government make *any real* investigation of *any* of Ray's connections, especially in New Orleans, particularly where there was credible proof of their existence?

Or, was the investigation made and its results suppressed? How can government, honorably and honestly, have sought and obtained an indictment for conspiracy in Birmingham, then claim in court in London that there was no conspiracy, and then claim again in the Memphis minitrial that there was no conspiracy?

Further, how can it now suppress evidence to which Ray is entitled under conditions which can mean only that it believes there was a conspiracy and in that preserves a "prosecutive interest"?

Were the requirements of British extradition law met?

Were they thereafter also violated?

Why did the government confiscate the only official affidavit evidence publicly accessible, with the complicity of the British government; then deny its existence and access to it?

Is there, in fact, another case in history when the public record of the public trial of an American citizen was confiscated?

Why did the Department of Justice always lie to me about this evidence and, ultimately, lie to the federal judge, under oath?

Can all this official wrongdoing be considered but the behavioral and legal norm of the "law and order" Nixon-Agnew-Mitchell administration, or was another, sinister purpose served?

With a crime of this magnitude, is it possible that no more than official carelessness caused the always automatic all-points police alert not to be issued?

Why does the prosecution refuse access to the evidence it withheld from the minitrial evidence—thereby suppressing it? And even to that part of it that is, by stipulation, part of the official record?

Why did the prosecution edit and misrepresent the evidence?

Why did Foreman agree to this?

Did the prosecution, in fact, violate the canons of legal ethics?

Was this not also true of the entire deal—and the participation in and domination of it by the judge?

Did not these things:

Deny Ray any possibility of a fair trial?

Condition his mind and thinking so that he could make no free choice?

Assure that he had to agree to the deal, "cop" the plea to a more severe penalty than any jury could have been expected to agree to?

Did Ray, within the meaning of the Constitution and the law, ever have "effective" counsel?

Did either Hanes or Foreman and Stanton ever make any *real* investigation of the merits of the case against Ray? If they did not, was any effective defense possible?

Were his lawyers ridden with conflicts of interests, where their possibilities of financial reward were opposed to Ray's and justice's legal interests and minimal needs?

Did Hanes and Foreman also not contract to violate the bar's canons of ethics?

To these questions, I would add two more, not directly related to Ray's guilt or innocence:

Can American justice survive such intrusions into and corruptions of the judicial processes and the workings of the law as these by the Huie-Hanes-Foreman "defense"?

Does an assassin or assassins roam free, set free by the official frustration of justice in the King/Ray case?

ROBERT F. KENNEDY

THE CASE IS STILL OPEN
Robert Blair Kaiser

"R.F.K. Must Die!" / 1970

I did not believe that Sirhan killed Kennedy in order to strike a blow for his side in the Arab-Israeli conflict. A bona fide avenging Arab hero would have shouted something like *"sic semper tyrannis"* or "no more jets to Israel" when he was seized in the Ambassador Hotel pantry. He would have poured forth his story to the police when he submitted to questioning during the early-morning hours after his arrest. Instead, he worked out his role as Arab hero little by little, as the months rolled by after the assassination. I still wondered why Sirhan said nothing in the pantry, why he was a "Silent Sam" with the police, why he hid so many details about himself and his crime from his own attorneys. I wasn't satisfied with the prosecution theory that Sirhan told his Arab hero story on the stand to save his life, for it got him (as he was warned it would) a verdict of first-degree murder and a sentence of death.

"The Case Is Still Open" by Robert Blair Kaiser. Reprinted from *"R.F.K. Must Die!"* by Robert Blair Kaiser (E. P. Dutton & Co., Inc., 1970). Reprinted by permission of the author and his agent, Maximilian Becker.

I had an easier time accepting Dr. Bernard Diamond's theory that Sirhan had—by his automatic writing—"programmed himself exactly like a computer is programmed by its magnetic tape . . . for the coming assassination." Dr. Diamond's theory implied that Sirhan had no conscious plan of action when he went to the Ambassador. On the stand, Dr. Diamond admitted that this theory was absurd and preposterous, but I admired his courage in propounding it. Dr. Diamond was an expert in the law, in psychiatry and criminology, and he had a great deal of clinical experience. Though I knew that Dr. Diamond might be inclined toward evidence supporting a legal defense he had helped pioneer, the defense of diminished capacity, I also knew he didn't have to make Sirhan into an unconscious assassin to prove diminished capacity. It would have been sufficient to say, as Dr. Eric Marcus did, that Sirhan's premeditation was not the product of a healthy mind and let it go at that. Dr. Diamond would not let go. He had to find a theory into which he could fit *all* the facts. And he was the only one on either side of the case who seemed to bother doing that.

After the trial, I discovered further evidence to corroborate Dr. Diamond's hypothesis.

I found, first of all, new evidence that Sirhan appeared to be in a trance the night he killed. In a police report, I read that at 10:30 P.M. or so on June 4, Mrs. Mary Grohs, a teletype operator for Western Union who was working in the Colonial Room of the Ambassador Hotel, saw Sirhan "staring fixedly" at her teletype machine. The report was a brief one, and so I phoned to ask her what she had seen on the night of June 4.

She was very defensive. "I certainly didn't smell any alcohol," she said.

"Well, okay," I said. "But what did you see?"

After some hesitation, Mrs. Grohs gave this report. "Well, he came over to my machine and started staring at it. Just staring. I'll never forget his eyes. I asked him what he wanted. He didn't answer. He just kept staring. I asked him again. No answer. I said that if he wanted the latest figures on Senator Kennedy he'd have to check the other machine. He still didn't answer. He just kept staring."

"In retrospect," I asked, "do you think that he might have been in some kind of trance?"

"Oh, no!" she said. "He wasn't under hypnosis." I hadn't mentioned the word "hypnosis," but perhaps Mrs. Grohs had read the newspapers during the trial when the possibility was discussed. Or perhaps she had been coached. I didn't ask her if she'd ever seen anyone under hypnosis before. I did ask her why Sirhan didn't respond to her. "I just assumed," she said, "that he couldn't speak English."

"But he could, couldn't he?"

"What?"

"Speak English."

"Huh?"

"He spoke pretty good English at the trial, didn't he?"

"Yes."

"Then why do you think he didn't answer you?"

"What was your name again?" asked Mrs. Grohs. "I want to talk to the police about you. They told me not to say anything about this."

I asked Dr. Diamond for his assessment of this exchange. He was angry. He and the prosecution psychiatrist—and the jury—should have heard the testimony of Mrs. Grohs. But he was pleased to know that there was one eyewitness, at least, who, however reluctantly, could support his theory that Sirhan was in some kind of dissociated state on the night of the murder.

Ten thirty P.M. was earlier than Dr. Diamond had suspected Sirhan "went under." Perhaps, Dr. Diamond conjectured, Sirhan was in a trance through much of that evening. This supposition might even better account, he said, for Sirhan's only half-plausible explanations of why he went to Los Angeles that night, why he first went to the Ambassador without his gun and then returned to get it from the back seat of his car, and how he ended up in the Ambassador pantry at midnight. As Dr. Diamond had proved in experiments with Sirhan, Sirhan could easily be programmed to climb his cell bars or sing an Arab tune; afterward, he would present half-plausible (but false) reasons of his own for each action. Sirhan's "reasons" for his action before the shooting were like that: only half-plausible.

After the crime, Sirhan's pupils were dilated—evidence that he was under some alien influence. And he was unbelievably detached when the police led him through an all-night interrogation, a most unusual posture for a young man who had just gunned down one who he later said was "a god to me." I thought it likely that Sirhan was then in a kind of twilight state and that he didn't start coming out of it until 9:00 A.M. on June 5, when Dr. Marcus Crahan found Sirhan shivering in his cell. Sirhan had similar chills in his cell each and every time he came out of his hypnotic trances with Dr. Diamond.

To explain this behavior, Dr. Diamond had posited his theory: Sirhan, already hypnosis-prone from his experiments with the occult, went into a spontaneous trance at the Ambassador. Triggered by the drinks he had had and the bright lights and the mirrors in the lobby, he went out to his car, got his gun and, programmed by his instructions to himself in the notebook but with no knowledge then that Kennedy would move through the pantry, just happened to be there when Kennedy appeared. It was a million-to-one shot. Dr. Diamond didn't believe Jesus Perez, the busboy witness, who reported that Sirhan asked him whether Kennedy was coming through the pantry. And neither did I. I think he confused Sirhan with another young man in the pantry named Michael Wayne who looked like Sirhan. Wayne did ask several people in the pantry, including Perez, which way Kennedy was coming.

Dr. Diamond's theory, as he admitted on the stand, was only a theory, a hypothetical framework to help explain the facts. After the trial, however, I discovered new information (also withheld from the defense) that clashed with Dr. Diamond's theory.

On May 20, 1968, a bartender named Albert LeBeau, a husky blond fellow, had been set to guard a stairway leading to the second-floor banquet room of Robbie's Restaurant in Pomona during an appearance there by Senator Kennedy. At 12:30 P.M., a young man who LeBeau believed was Sirhan started to force his way up the stairs. It was an abnormally hot day, and Sirhan had a heavy jacket hooked over his right arm. In retrospect, LeBeau thought, the coat, which was draped over Sirhan's right elbow and completely obscured his right hand, would have concealed a gun very nicely. There was a girl with him, five feet, four inches, twenty-five to thirty years old, light brown hair, fairly attractive, no bangs, satin blouse. She did all the talking, insisting she and her young man were with the Kennedy party, until finally LeBeau let both of them through. A few minutes later, LeBeau, found the pair inside, toward the back of the room, the young man standing in a suspicious crouch, the coat still over his arm. LeBeau challenged them: if they were with the Kennedy party, what were they doing in the back of the room? The young man turned on him savagely and demanded: "What the hell is it to you?"

The records show that Detective Sergeants Sandlin and Strong of the LAPD questioned LeBeau about his story. Yes, LeBeau said, he was fairly sure the young man was Sirhan. Would he swear it under oath? No, he couldn't swear under oath. End of investigation. The district attorney didn't need to put Sirhan in Pomona on May 20 to get a conviction. And the detectives certainly didn't need to go back to headquarters with more talk of a mystery girl. Headquarters was sick of having to tell the press they couldn't find the "girl in the polka-dot dress," and the LAPD had knocked itself out persuading witnesses at the Ambassador that they'd never seen such a girl.

I believed LeBeau. His account was corroborated in part by two others at the restaurant and he had no apparent reason for making up such a story. The police, never anxious to confess their own incompetence, had reason to cover it up. For if LeBeau was right, then Sirhan had a female accomplice. *And the police couldn't find her.*

I also believed Dr. Joseph Sheehan, a professor of psychology at the University of California at Los Angeles, and his wife Margaret, who told police they were sure they had seen Sirhan after a Kennedy rally at the L.A. Sports Arena on May 24. He was dark and sinister-looking, and he hung around afterward on the fringes of the obviously more affluent groups who lingered at the arena, as if he were looking for someone. They made a special note of him at the time because he had looked so malevolent, and Dr. Sheehan remarked that it was too bad the Senator "had to run the gauntlet of people like that."

It was becoming clearer to me that Sirhan stalked Kennedy and that he wasn't necessarily alone. I believed he did so on

May 20 and May 24, and I believed he tried again at the Ambassador at a Kennedy rally on Sunday, June 2. At the trial, Sirhan maintained that his presence at that Sunday rally was innocent of any ill intent, but the fact was that he tried at first to deny that he was even there. Shortly after his arrest he had told his brother Adel to tell the police he was home all day that Sunday; and he also denied being at the Ambassador on Sunday when I first asked him about it. Only later, having reflected on my report to him that the LAPD might have some movie footage which would prove he was in the crowd, did Sirhan admit to his attorney, Russell Parsons, that he was there.

And if Sirhan was after Kennedy on May 20 and May 24 and June 2, why not also on June 3? Sirhan changed his story three times about his movements on June 3. First, he said he was home all day. Then he admitted to me that he'd gone to Corona. Later still, he told me it wasn't Corona at all, but "someplace in that direction." And still later, he told Investigator Michael McCowan with some satisfaction that he'd put 350 miles on his car June 3 and no one knew where he'd gone. In this context, his sneering judgment of the FBI made more sense: "The FBI doesn't know everything." Maybe, as McCowan speculated, Sirhan drove to San Diego that afternoon. Driving from Pasadena to San Diego and back might explain the 350 miles. Why San Diego? That night at the El Cortez Hotel in San Diego, one of the candidates was scheduled to speak, but he begged off, overcome with exhaustion. The candidate was Senator Robert F. Kennedy.

But if Sirhan had deliberately stalked Kennedy for two weeks, why was he in a trance on June 4 (as some evidence seemed to show)?

I thought the new evidence would indicate that Sirhan's "trance" was no accident but a by-product, rather, of his intense resolve. His moves that night had a far more specific finality than any revealed in his notebook. In the notebook Sirhan said he would kill Kennedy, but in no place did Sirhan indicate how he thought he would do the deed. In fact, Sirhan went out of the Ambassador to get his gun, got it, came back and worked his way through a crowd and past some guards, took up a stand in the pantry, waited for Kennedy, recognized him, walked up and shot, point-blank. When he did so, according to the best eyewitness in the pantry, Freddy Plimpton, Sirhan had a look on his face of "intense concentration." That figured. Sirhan had resolved to kill Kennedy, had already failed on more than one occasion. On this night, he focused, oblivious to all distraction, ready to reach Kennedy no matter what the obstacles.

How did he come to be so focused? As late as May 5, 1969, Sirhan himself was still groping for an answer; he told me then in his cell that he may have been like the original assassins, the *hashshashin*, members of a secret Mohammedan cult who drugged themselves before they committed their appointed murders. "It must have been something like that with me," he said.

I believed him. "Something like that. . . ." I had sat in on most of the hypnotic sessions Sirhan had had with Dr. Diamond. Although those sessions produced far less information than Dr. Diamond had hoped they would, they convinced me that— although Sirhan didn't tell the whole truth while hypnotized— he was not faking when he said he couldn't remember the details of the assassination. But why couldn't he?

If he had programmed himself to kill Kennedy, he should have had some recollection, if not of the killing, at least of the programming. He didn't remember that either.

It had been my guess, during the weeks that Dr. Diamond was making his investigations, that Sirhan programmed himself during his autohypnotic sessions at home. Dr. Diamond tested that theory and concluded on February 1, after he put Sirhan through some experiments in automatic writing, that that was precisely what Sirhan had done.

But there were those (myself and Dr. Diamond included) who asked how it happened that Sirhan had learned such occult arts. Sirhan was evasive about this. Before the trial, he told me his friend, Tom Rathke, the groom, had introduced him to the occult. During Dr. Diamond's probe, he said he'd learned it all from a book called *Cyclomancy*. Where did he get the book? It was recommended to him by Tom Rathke.

Was it possible that one of the friends with whom he had studied the occult had put Sirhan up to killing Kennedy, possibly without his knowledge? Sirhan didn't like that suggestion. Nor did I. It was a farfetched theory, fetched in fact from Richard Condon's novel, *The Manchurian Candidate*. There, Raymond Shaw, the antihero who had been brainwashed in North Korea, was moved by the phrase, "Why don't you pass the time by playing a little solitaire?" to riffle through a deck of playing cards until he came to the queen of hearts and then wait for further instructions, then kill without knowing why he had killed or even that he had killed. But a good investigator looks into every possibility, no matter how fantastic. And Sirhan had played around with mind-bending exercises. . . . I thought the line was worth pursuing. And so, marvel of marvels, did Sirhan. He finally asked me, on December 31, to investigate further. Could anyone have had such an influence over his mind?

I did some research on crime and hypnosis and discovered interesting real-life examples of murder-by-proxy, through hypnosis. In 1951, in Copenhagen, Bjorn Nielsen had programmed Palle Hardrup to go into a trance at the sight of the letter X, rob a bank and kill anyone who got in his way, almost completely unaware that he had been used. Unlike the fictional Raymond Shaw, Hardrup had some notion of what had happened. In jail, he recalled enough about his former associations with Nielsen to suspect that he had been used. And he was moved to confide his suspicions to a psychiatrist who, as I have reported earlier, spent almost a year cracking the "locking mechanism" that obscured Hardrup's recollections.

On February 8, 1969, during the trial, Dr. Diamond programmed Sirhan, under hypnosis, to climb the bars of his cell. Sirhan had no idea what he was doing up on the top of the bars. When he finally discovered that climbing was not his own idea, but Dr. Diamond's, he was struck with the plausibility of the idea that perhaps he had been programmed by someone else, in like manner, to kill Kennedy.

In this, Sirhan seemed sincere enough, but the idea was too much for Dr. Diamond. To him, that was "a crackpot theory." It was, unless I could find a Kennedy-hater with hypnotic skills who used them on Sirhan. And I couldn't find such a man.

I sought out some of those persons who had played occult games with Sirhan. One of them admitted that he had written a menacing letter to Chief Justice Earl Warren which brought investigators from the FBI. And he told a somewhat different version of his recent association with Sirhan than Sirhan had told me. But this didn't argue to his complicity in a plot, and I found no reason to believe that any of those I talked to were involved in the assassination.

But I still had a feeling that somewhere in Sirhan's recent past there was a shadowy someone. So did Roger LaJeunesse, the FBI agent in charge of the Sirhan investigation, who confided to me: "The case is still open. I'm not rejecting the Manchurian Candidate aspect of it." LaJeunesse had attended the trial, he heard Dr. Diamond's testimony and he seemed convinced that Sirhan was indeed in a trance on the night of June 4. And he knew, better than I, that Robert Kennedy had enemies who could have chosen Sirhan, with his antiauthority feelings and his inert paranoia, as a possible tool. Sirhan was a man with nothing to lose, with enough conscious and unconscious hatred within him to draw the attention of anyone looking for a likely gunman.

Who would have wanted to use Sirhan? I didn't know. But the police and the FBI now had evidence that Sirhan associated with extremists from both the Right and the Left and that he had some connections with the so-called underworld. The police and the FBI were the agencies with the legal mandate and the resources to investigate these ties, if they would. I could only hope they would, that, secretly, they were applying wit and imagination even then while PR-minded spokesmen continued to force the facts or reveal only those that enhanced their own image—as Robert Houghton, the LAPD's assistant chief, did in his report on the assassination (*Special Unit Senator*, Random House, 1970).

We looked for a conspiracy, Houghton said, and we didn't find one. He looked the other way when his own detectives browbeat [assassination witness] Thomas Vincent DiPierro, until DiPierro reneged on his story of seeing "the girl in the polka-dot dress" [shortly before the shooting, apparently talking with Sirhan]. His suspicions were not aroused by the story of the Pomona bartender who saw Sirhan stalking Kennedy on May 20 in the company of a pretty girl. He overlooked the insurance executive who saw Sirhan at target practice in May at Rancho California, again with a pretty girl (his detectives told him the eyewitness failed to pick Sirhan's face out of a picture file of Sirhan and some look-alikes, but that would have been pretty difficult, seeing that the detectives interviewed the man by telephone). He brushed aside the puzzle of Edward Van Antwerp, who mysteriously disappeared from Corona twelve hours before RFK was shot and reappeared two weeks later in Eureka, California. Van Antwerp had told the FBI he never knew Sirhan when, as a matter of fact, he had roomed with Sirhan for five months. Houghton did not find it strange that the FBI and his own operatives took ten months to find the man who brought Sirhan to Corona in the first place, Frank Donnarauma, alias Henry Donald Ramistella of New Jersey. He overlooked the direct, naïve approaches which investigators made to Jimmy Hoffa and the likes of Hoffa who were not above suspicion: ("Tell us about your contract to have Senator Kennedy killed, Jimmy. No? No contract? Oh. Well, sorry to have bothered you, Jimmy.") And he approved the facile dumb-cop analysis that anyone who had facts running counter to their lone-assassin theory was "psycho."

It wasn't easy for Houghton to ignore the evidence in Sirhan's notebook that Sirhan associated the killing of Robert Kennedy with some kind of payoff to himself. Whenever the name of Kennedy appeared there, it was always accompanied by "please pay to the order of Sirhan" and that phrase appeared nowhere else in the notebook—only on "kill" or "Kennedy" pages. That should have aroused the suspicions of anyone over eight, much more of a cop who was always ready to expect the worst. But Houghton made the supreme effort. He ignored that, too, in part because he assumed that Sirhan had to have the money in hand before he struck, and Houghton couldn't find any extra money.

It was entirely possible that Sirhan was gunning for Kennedy on a simple promise of money, sweetened by a small down payment. He could have bet that at the track, or stashed it, or, indeed, given it to his family. But if he had, they certainly wouldn't tell the police about it. The Sirhan family did not go out of their way to help the police. But then, the police were naïve to expect help from the Sirhans.

Grant Cooper once asked Sirhan about the money angle, and Sirhan answered Cooper's question with another question: "If I got the money, where is it?"

Here, Sirhan seemed genuinely evasive. But it was clear that in his notebook he was repeating instructions to forget any promises of money: "I have never heard please pay to the order of of of of of of of of of of of this or that 8oooo."

Sirhan never could explain the references in his notebook to money. But where did the instructions come from? Sirhan or another?

It was possible that they came from another; and that then Sirhan drummed them into himself. But no one could say with certainty. It would take a psychoanalyst as skilled as Dr. Diamond perhaps another year of interviews with Sirhan to test this theory thoroughly—to put Sirhan through more hypnotic sessions in an effort to see if, indeed, his memory had been blocked by some kind of locking mechanism; and, further, to explore with Sirhan the significance of his assertions that he could, for instance, "blow the top off this case" if he chose to say what he knew, to see what was prompting his successive stories that Lyndon Johnson or Richard Nixon or James Hoffa had put him up to killing Kennedy, to find out why he thought that "the FBI did a lousy job of investigation" and "didn't know everything." And it would take me another year to run down all the investigative avenues that still intrigued me.

That would have been another book. And, in the chaotic summer of 1970, two years after the death of the man we now realized we needed more than we had known, I was having enough trouble getting this book published. Sirhan had fired Cooper and Russell Parsons because they couldn't force me to let Sirhan censor my book. And he found new attorneys who promised they would try. They asked courts in California and New York to enjoin publication. New legal battles began. Finally, the California court denied their petition. As Judge Richard Schauer put it when he turned them down in Los Angeles, "Now the cat is out of the bag." Sirhan was very unhappy.

SIRHAN'S GUN
Betsy Langman and
Alexander Cockburn

Harper's / *January 1975*

Until recently the only assassination that seemed beyond question was that of Robert F. Kennedy, killed by Sirhan Sirhan in the Ambassador Hotel in Los Angeles on June 5, 1968. Nearly 100 people were in the pantry when the fatal shots were fired. Many eyewitnesses saw Sirhan spring forward, raise his gun, and fire. Many saw Kennedy fall, mortally wounded. There was no hurried autopsy, or whisking away of the body, as occurred in Dallas. There was an enormous investigation, conducted by the FBI and the Los Angeles Police Department.

The police were aware that their investigation would be subjected to the closest of scrutinies. Robert Houghton, chief of detectives of the LAPD and author of *Special Unit Senator*, the unofficial record of the investigation, understood that he was faced with a crime "that would be examined everywhere in the world, possibly for decades to come. . . . There were the clever people, as usual, standing by to profit from the cry of conspiracy, hooking their theories to journalistic wagons before the Arlington soil was tamped." No one wanted another Dallas and another tidal wave of speculation—so injurious to the self-esteem and reputation of investigative agencies. So the police took enormous pains, and just over a year after the assassination the Special Investigating Unit headed by Houghton reduced its vast researches into ten illustrated volumes entitled *An Investigation and Summary of the Senator Robert F. Kennedy Assassination*. This report has not been made public, but Houghton summarized its main conclusions as follows: that Sirhan fired the shots which killed Kennedy and wounded five others; that his act was premeditated; that he was not under the influence of any drug or intoxicant; that he was legally sane; and that there was no evidence of conspiracy.

Despite the conviction of Sirhan on a charge of first-degree murder and the proclaimed intensity of police investigation, doubts were raised almost within the year. The most popular area of speculation—as always in such cases—centered around the problem of whether Sirhan had been involved in a conspiracy. Although many theories have been advanced, starting with the famous girl in the polka-dot dress and stretching forward through Sirhan's possible connection with Al Fatah or other Arab groups, no hard evidence has yet been found to support any one of them. And if one considers the Manchurian Candidate theory (that Sirhan was the hypnotized agent of conspirators), then it becomes impossible to arrive at any conclusions without the discovery of other conspirators. But if Sirhan was hypnotized to do the murder, he could have been hypnotized into amnesia about his instructions to perform it. Investigators following this line must mount a treadmill of speculation.

About two years after the assassination, what one might call the conspiracy-minded sections of the community began to speculate along very different lines. Much of this questioning was stimulated by *The Second Gun*, a film made by Theodore Charach in 1970. This film—shown around New York in late 1972 and 1973 —tilted the whole RFK assassination industry in an entirely new direction.

Charach's film raised questions surrounding the physical circumstances of Kennedy's death: the gun fired by Sirhan and the bullets that struck Kennedy and five others. Charach's film suggested that a second gun had been fired, that ballistic evidence seemed to show that all the bullets could not have come only from Sirhan's gun, and that the autopsy evidence of where the bullets hit Kennedy could not be reconciled with eyewitness testimony.

In all this there was something both disturbing and bizarre. After all, Kennedy had been shot in front of many eyewitnesses, who, unlike some of the participants in the Dallas drama, are still alive. It seemed a little like saying that there were "questions" as to whether Jack Ruby really killed Oswald, despite his committing the deed on national television.

Because the speculation seemed so absurd, many journalists felt there was little point in pursuing the implications of Charach's film. Editors thought that the RFK case was one that need never burden their columns, and so any reporter who wanted to follow it up had the utmost difficulty in getting a story into print. Nonetheless, after the Charach film, there were a number of people both on the West and East Coasts who felt that serious questions required answers, and that the investigation should be reopened.

Although the origin of these questions can be attributed to Charach's film, the present uneasiness arises from two lines of inquiry.

In the hope of clarifying these inquiries, we have gone over the testimony of the grand jury hearing and the trial, and examined the autopsy and ballistic evidence developed by the original prosecution and by forensic experts brought into the investigation at later dates. We have talked to the original prosecutors and defense attorneys, to scientists who were consulted and those who were not. As we shall see, it is valid to propose that a number of questions remain unresolved.

Leaving aside all conspiracy theories and concentrating on material evidence of what took place in the Ambassador Hotel pantry, the doubts and the evidence that encourage them arise from these contradictions: the autopsy shows that Kennedy died from a wound in the head, the trajectory being back to front, right to left, and upward. But Sirhan was ahead of Kennedy in his path to the kitchen, and therefore his wounds are not compatible with Sirhan's position. The autopsy also shows that Kennedy was shot at virtually point-blank range. Yet eyewitnesses say that the muzzle of Sirhan's gun was never closer than two feet. Finally, all eight bullets fired by Sirhan should match in characteristics with each other and with the gun that fired them. Yet some ballistic experts claim that the bullets cannot be matched to each other nor to the test bullets introduced at the trial nor to Sirhan's gun. Although evidence can be found to support the official accounting for the position of Kennedy's wounds, the problems arising out of the gun and the bullets are not so easily settled.

The autopsy on Robert Kennedy's body was carried out over a period of six hours in the early morning of June 6, 1968. It was performed by Dr. Thomas Noguchi, the county coroner, along with two assistants and in the presence of at least a dozen people, among them U.S. government pathologists from Washington who had flown to Los Angeles expressly to witness the autopsy. Noguchi found that Kennedy had been hit by three bullets. One had struck his head just behind his right ear and fragmented in the right-hand side of his brain. This was the bullet that killed him. Another had entered the back of the right armpit and exited in the front of the right shoulder. This bullet had left no fragments and was listed in the police accounting as having been "lost somewhere in the ceiling interspace." The third bullet, entering within half an inch of the second one, traveled along the muscle structure of the back and lodged at the base of his neck.

Noguchi retrieved this third bullet, the only one of those striking Kennedy that remained in good enough condition for constructive forensic examination, scratched his initials on its base and handed it over to the police. Noguchi also found that a fourth bullet had passed through Kennedy's right shoulder pad, without actually touching his body.

In the course of his autopsy Noguchi came to certain conclusions regarding the distance of the muzzle of the weapon from Kennedy's body when the shots were fired. He discovered a phenomenon he later described as "very distinct paper-like stapling, as we call it, powder tattooing on the surface of the right ear," confirming the back-to-front trajectory, as "there was no powder in the front of the ear, no powder on the side." At the grand jury hearing he said that the position of the tattooing indicated that the muzzle distance was "very, very close." "Do you have an opinion," he was asked, "as to the maximum distance the gun could have been from the Senator?" "Allowing a variation," Noguchi replied, "I don't think it will be more than two or three inches from the right ear." On June 11, Noguchi organized a test firing with LAPD officers of an Iver Johnson .22 revolver acquired from the LAPD property office on June 10. This gun, the same type used by Sirhan, was used to observe the tattooing pattern on a hog's ear. The observation substantiated the autopsy's conclusion that the shots were almost contact wounds. This conclusion was buttressed by the opinion of DeWayne Wolfer, the LAPD officer who conducted a series of chemical tests on Kennedy's jacket, conducted the test firing with Noguchi, and gave evidence in the trial of Sirhan that the maximum distance would be six inches. That is, Wolfer was allowing for all conceivable errors. During the same examination, he said that he believed that the gun had been fired against Kennedy's head at a range of one inch.

Such conclusions, by both Noguchi and Wolfer, raised some serious contradictions with the eyewitness recollections of people who saw the shooting take place.[1]

The eyewitnesses, many of them standing next to each other, saw—or remembered they saw—very different things. Against the recollections of the assistant maître d'hôtel, who says that he was holding Kennedy's hand and leading him along—toward Sirhan—one can place the recollections of at least four other people who testified that Kennedy was turning to his left at the time Sirhan fired in order to shake hands with one of the waiters. Frank J. Burns, a friend of Kennedy's, was standing off Kennedy's right shoulder when the shots were fired, and he testified at Sirhan's trial that Kennedy had turned "almost ninety degrees" at the time and therefore was not facing Sirhan's gun muzzle but indeed presenting his right and hinder side to it. It is difficult to find witnesses—apart from the assistant maître d'hôtel—who directly contradict his recollections and those of many others, such as Edward Minasian, Martin Petrusky, Jesus Perez, and Vincent DiPierro, all employed in the Ambassador's kitchen.

It is, however, impossible to find witnesses who directly corroborate the autopsy evidence that the gun was practically touch-

[1] At the trial the prosecution bypassed the dilemma, arguing that the eyewitnesses who testified for the government must have been mistaken.

David Fitts, prosecuting attorney: "With reference to the circumstances of the shooting, Your Honor, Your Honor has heard Karl Ueker and any number of witnesses who attempted to describe what happened; one witness has put the muzzle of the revolver some three or four feet from the Senator's head; others have it at varying ranges. The only way we can clear up whatever ambiguity there may be there and to show the truth is by the testimony of this witness [Wolfer], who, on the basis of the powder tattooing, and the experiments he performed with respect thereto, will testify that the muzzle range with respect to the Senator's head was about one inch."

Grant Cooper, the defense counsel, agreed with this position.

ing Kennedy's head. Their estimates vary wildly. Pete Hamill, the columnist, put Sirhan seven feet from Kennedy. Juan Romero, a busboy who had just shaken hands with Kennedy, estimated "approximately one yard." Valerie Schulte, a college student, said at the trial that "Sirhan's arm and gun" were "approximately five yards from me, approximately three yards, something like that, from the Senator." Edward Minasian, who was walking about a yard in front of Kennedy, thought that the barrel of Sirhan's gun was "approximately three feet" from Kennedy. The closest to Kennedy that one can place the gun muzzle, going on these recollections, is about two feet—a distance calculated from one recollection that Sirhan was "three or four" feet away from Kennedy. Taken together with the evidence of autopsy, this presents a problem. Defenders of the official story merely say that witnesses cannot be relied on, which, as anyone familiar with investigations knows, is entirely true. At the time of Sirhan's trial, no one worried about such inconsistencies because no one—including the defense attorneys—thought there was the slightest doubt that Sirhan had fired all the shots. Sirhan's defense rested on insanity-plea questions of "diminished capacity" rather than on the possibility of persuading the jury that there were reasonable doubts about the physical evidence. Sirhan's chief defense attorney, Grant Cooper, subsequently said that he wished he had raised these questions at the trial. At the time it simply never entered his mind to do so.

The prosecution seems to have been more sensible of the problem. On May 13, 1974, one member of the Los Angeles County Board of Supervisors, Baxter Ward, held a public hearing on the problems arising out of the ballistic evidence in Kennedy's assassination. Ward has long been one of the doubters of the official version, and his office has been engaged for some time in amassing as much evidence as possible to confirm his suspicions. At the hearing, Dr. Noguchi was asked if the district attorney's office had been aware of the discrepancy between the testimony of their witnesses and the implications of his findings.

"I do not know," Noguchi answered, "whether they knew or not. One of the deputy district attorneys approached me after I testified in grand jury. . . . He said, 'Tom, are you sure three inches?' He offered that if I misunderstood—if I misstated—this is time now to correct it. . . . He was surprised that there was such a distance we were talking about."

None of the foregoing doubts would have arisen if all the bullets fired in the pantry could be identified as having come from the same gun. But it is the problem of identifying the bullets that creates the most troubling difficulties, difficulties which, to this day, have not been settled and which more than anything else have fostered uneasiness among those who have examined the circumstances of the assassination.

Sirhan's gun was taken from him by Rafer Johnson, who turned it over to an officer in the LAPD. In the grand jury hearings on June 7, DeWayne Wolfer testified briefly that he had examined the "near-perfect" bullet taken from Kennedy's neck and that it had been fired from Sirhan's gun. He had established this, he said, by test-firing Sirhan's gun into a water tank, thus being able to retrieve the slugs unharmed. He had brought "some of the test shots"—four—along to the grand jury and was able to testify that microscopic comparison showed the four bullets to agree in characteristics with the bullet taken from Kennedy's neck, thus showing that the latter bullet came from Sirhan's gun.

As we shall see, it sometimes becomes difficult to keep up with the vagaries of Wolfer's ballistic evidence; even his statement before the grand jury about the four bullets was later contradicted in remarks he made under oath on September 20, 1971, to an attorney who had challenged his professional credentials in this and other cases. In these later statements, Wolfer suggested that the four bullets he had brought to the grand jury didn't prove his point as well as three other bullets that he had left in his laboratory. On June 11, Wolfer performed further tests with another Iver Johnson .22. These tests, conducted in the company of Noguchi and other witnesses, were the ones having to do with the hog's ear.

It is unclear why Wolfer could not have used Sirhan's Iver Johnson .22. At the trial Wolfer said that it was not "available," even though the grand jury hearings had been concluded at the time of his testing and he could have got the gun by court order. Whatever the reasons, Wolfer used for his testing an Iver

Johnson he withdrew from the LAPD property division on June 10, 1968. It bore the serial number H18602. The serial number of Sirhan's gun was H53725. The LAPD said it destroyed the test gun in July 1969.

This test gun has caused many confusions and uncertainties. Among the exhibits at the trial was an envelope, labeled "Exhibit 55," which, according to Wolfer, contained "three of the test shots that I took from people's number six, the weapon [Sirhan's], and this was from the water recovery tank, and that would be three test shots I used for comparison purposes."

No one at the trial bothered to examine this envelope. We must remember the mental disposition of the defending attorneys. As Grant Cooper later explained, "there was no question" in his mind "but that Sirhan was the one that fired the fatal shots that killed Kennedy. Not only did we have the testimony of the witnesses but the conversations I had with Sirhan myself." Some scrutiny of the evidence at the trial would have raised one immediate problem. The envelope alleged to contain the three bullets from Sirhan's gun (test-fired into the water tank the day after the assassination) was quite clearly marked as containing bullets fired from the gun which Wolfer used on the hog on June 11.

This leaves a variety of possibilities. Either Wolfer put the test bullets from the Sirhan gun in the exhibit envelope and then made a mistake and wrote the wrong serial number on the outside; or he simply sent the wrong bullets along to the trial. It is hard to ascribe very sinister motives to the mislabeling, since any vigilant counsel would have noticed it. But the fact remains that at the trial—as at the grand jury—nobody introduced any evidence which scientifically, or even demonstrably, linked Sirhan's gun to the bullets and fragments that made up the other relevant exhibits.

The observation that the envelope had been mislabeled, or contained the wrong bullets, was made by William Harper, an expert in the study of technical and forensic investigation of firearms. A man of considerable reputation in the field, he had for seven years been a consultant to the Pasadena Police Department, and during a period of thirty-five years had handled more than 300 cases for both defense and prosecution in state and federal courts. In his professional capacity, Harper had often disagreed with Wolfer over the years and had warned Grant Cooper not to take Wolfer's statements on trust. Cooper introduced Harper to Theodore Charach in the summer of 1970. Charach had pointed out various anomalies in the case to Cooper, who suggested that he communicate his doubts to Harper. In November 1970 Harper went to the county clerk's office to examine the evidence. The normal apparatus for assessing and comparing bullets is a "comparison microscope." This is a heavy piece of equipment, difficult to drag around, and so Harper used a Balliscan camera which he had developed with the help of Marshall Houts, a writer on medical and legal topics. The camera takes a series of photographs of a cylindrical object rotated in front of it. The resultant images are then blown up and used for comparison purposes. Harper made several visits to the clerk's office, and in December 1970 he swore out an affidavit outlining his conclusions. He mentioned the mistake in the numbering of the exhibits, but he also raised far more serious doubts.

His affidavit reads in part: "From the general circumstances of the shooting, the only reasonable assumption is that the bullet removed from victim Weisel [one of those wounded in the pantry] was in fact fired from the Sirhan gun. This bullet is in near-perfect condition. I have, therefore, chosen it as a 'test' bullet from the Sirhan gun and compared it with the bullet removed from the Senator's neck. . . . My examination disclosed no individual characteristics establishing that Exhibit 47 [the bullet from Kennedy's neck] and Exhibit 54 [the bullet from Weisel] had been fired by the same gun. In fact, my examinations disclosed that bullet Exhibit 47 has a rifling angle of approximately 23 minutes [14 percent] greater than the rifling angle of bullet Exhibit 54. It is, therefore, my opinion that bullets 47 and 54 could not have been fired from the same gun."

More simply, Harper had said this: Bullet A was fired from a different gun than Bullet B. Furthermore, there is no evidence connecting either bullet with Sirhan's gun, apart from Wolfer's sworn testimony to the grand jury and the stipulations of counsel at the trial. Harper's affidavit was made public in the spring of 1971. As could be expected, it provoked a series of attacks and counterattacks. An attorney acting on Harper's behalf attempted to block Wolfer's appointment as chief forensic chemist in charge of the LAPD crime laboratory, charging incompetence in the Sirhan case and others. This move failed. The district attorney of Los Angeles County, Joseph P. Busch, countered by saying that "serious questions" had been raised about the handling of the exhibits in the county clerk's office. These questions were serious enough, he said, to warrant a grand jury investigation into the clerk's handling of the exhibits. Meanwhile, all investigative activity should be suspended. The grand jury duly reported that it had reservations "about the present integrity of the ballistics exhibits." Finally, in the fall of 1971, a board of inquiry dismissed all the questions raised by Charach, Harper, and others. Among other things, it found that Harper's contention was "based on the rifling angle of one bullet being 23 minutes greater than that of a second bullet. When the meaning of 23 minutes of difference is analyzed its importance is questionable."

Matters had reached this impasse at about the time that Charach's film was being released. Vague intimations of ballistic anomalies were reaching a generally somnolent public and receiving—apart from spotty coverage of Charach's film—little public debate.

On April 26, 1974, William Lystrup, medical photographer at the Los Angeles County coroner's office went to the county clerk's office armed with another Balliscan camera and rephotographed the Kennedy and Weisel bullets. He had been dispatched on this mission by Baxter Ward, the inquisitive Los Angeles County supervisor. A former anchorman for KHJ-TV in Los Angeles, Ward was campaigning for the governorship of California, and he decided, in the midst of the spring primary campaign, to hold a public hearing on the Kennedy assassination.

Convened on May 13, [1974], the hearing was attended by, among others, Thomas Noguchi, who confirmed his autopsy report and said that a few weeks earlier he had reexamined the bullet from Kennedy's neck and found the initials he had scratched on it during the autopsy on the night after the shooting. Also at the hearing were two additional experts in forensic ballistics—Herbert MacDonell and Lowell Bradford. MacDonell has a high reputation in the world of forensic investigation; he has appeared in many criminal cases and has developed some widely used techniques in the field of forensic science.

. In an affidavit MacDonell agreed with Harper on the rifling angle variations and added another point—the difference in cannelures. A cannelure is any groove that runs around a bullet or cartridge case: cannelures are sometimes described as "knurled grooves." MacDonell's affidavit stated that the bullet from Kennedy's neck had one cannelure and the bullet from Weisel two cannelures. To expound a piece of news that might seem unexciting to a layman, MacDonell explained that all eight cartridge cases taken from the Sirhan gun were said to be manufactured by OMARK-C.C. 1. So far as MacDonell had been able to determine, all bullets manufactured by this firm have two cannelures. MacDonell found that the location of the cannelures on the Weisel bullet was close enough to the position of regular OMARK-C.C. 1 manufacture. He concluded that, since the Kennedy bullet had only one cannelure, "it could not have been part of one of the cartridges taken from the Sirhan revolver." MacDonell also noticed "a lack of agreement between any of the identifiable characteristics that appear on the two bullets." He concluded that the Kennedy and Weisel bullets could not have been fired from the same weapon and, furthermore, that the bullet taken from Kennedy's neck could not have been fired from Sirhan's gun.

Harper was ill and could not attend the hearing, but an affidavit confirming his previous conclusions was read into the record. Evidence was heard from Lowell Bradford, the director of a crime laboratory and a former employee of the state Department of Justice laboratory in Sacramento. Both Bradford and MacDonell agreed that the new set of Balliscan photographs matched those taken by Harper. Bradford could not find a rifling angle difference between the Kennedy and Weisel bullets, but he agreed with MacDonell on the difference in cannelures. Both Bradford and MacDonell called for a refiring of the Sirhan revolver in a test presided over by a panel of forensic experts. Both agreed that a comparison of the new test bullets with the

Kennedy and Weisel bullets would be the only way to resolve the problems. Ward's motion that the county supervisors propose an official reexamination of the evidence was defeated 3-2.

All speculation about the presence of a second gunman in the pantry of the Ambassador Hotel arises from two questions: the discrepancies of eyewitness testimony and autopsy reports, and the problems of reconciling the Kennedy and Weisel bullets with each other and with Sirhan's gun.

To surmise that another person could have placed a gun within three inches of Kennedy's head and pulled the trigger without being observed by anyone requires a leap of the imagination so enormous that such a possibility could only be forced on us by absolute contradictions in the material evidence. Despite the anomalies that now seem self-evident, the absolute contradictions have not yet been conclusively proved.

The most direct way of discovering whether such contradictions do exist is to conduct a test firing of the gun, together with a review of all the ballistic evidence by a panel of experts. This is now being called for by various concerned people, including Grant Cooper, Sirhan's former attorney; Paul Schrade, who was himself wounded in the pantry; and many others. The district attorney's office has adamantly opposed such an undertaking. In the spring of 1973, Busch insisted that "a refiring of what we absolutely know to be the murder weapon . . . would only give some sort of backhanded credence to sensationalists who are trying to raise some question about the validity of Sirhan working alone."

In fact it appears that the DA's office has been following the debate about the evidence with keen attention. We have seen documents circulated throughout the DA's office which attest to extensive research into Charach's investigation and into other assassination theories.

Since this is so, why won't the DA's office go ahead with the business of firing the gun, examining the bullets, and getting the whole matter resolved? There are, of course, the reasons that Busch publicly adduces, but there are other reasons that are not so obvious. Not everyone feels total confidence in the validity of conclusions established by forensic science. In the words of one detective, "forensic science is a lot softer than forensic scientists would care to let on." Different schools of forensic experts have different methods of evaluating evidence. Wolfer, for example, turned down Noguchi's proposal, immediately after the shooting, to have a neutron activation analysis (NAA) done on the various bullet fragments. This technique involves bombarding metal fragments with neutrons, then measuring and comparing the effects of radioactivity to establish whether the fragments came from the same manufacturer.

At Ward's hearing, Dr. Vincent Guinn, a leading authority on NAA, said this test could still be done. It is entirely possible to find—as we did—forensic experts less confident that neutron tests are absolutely "conclusive." Wolfer appears to have thought that Guinn's NAA test would be so sensitive that results would vary within a single bullet and comparisons would be impossible between different bullets—an opinion hotly disputed by Guinn. Following this line of the absolute uncertainty principle, there are those in the DA's office who believe that a test firing of the gun would not solve anything; they hold that the act of refiring would sufficiently alter the characteristics of the barrel, and hence the bullet, to make satisfactory comparison impossible. MacDonell's answer to this is "Hogwash." The firing of 1,000 rounds from a high-powered rifle, he says, could make alterations, but certainly not a few test firings from Sirhan's revolver. Furthermore, he says that the gun need not necessarily be refired. There is a process called swaging in which soft lead is pushed through the gun barrel, thus displaying characteristics sufficient for forensic purposes.

The district attorney's office has one final position: that the time and place for a refiring of the weapon and comparison of the bullets will come whenever Sirhan's present attorney files a motion for a retrial. Then, says Busch, the reexamination of the evidence—in the framework of a proper court procedure—could take place. Either way, Busch and the DA's office have the situation firmly under control. On the one hand they say that only "assassination freaks" are raising any questions about the shooting. On the other hand, the DA's office indicates that the art of forensic evidence leaves something to be desired and from this position announces that when a motion for retrial is filed, the examination can take place.

And so we come back to where we began. Six years after the assassination of Robert Kennedy, the one shooting that almost everyone believed to have been satisfactorily resolved, the circumstances still attract serious questioning from lawyers, journalists, and politicians across the country who now feel some doubt about the case, even if they are not quite sure why. These doubts will grow and feed on themselves. Hints about a cover-up will become assertions that one exists. This painfully familiar process can be averted by a decision that the DA or the attorney general of California should be sensible enough to make: to establish a panel of forensic experts, organize an independent examination of the relevant bullets and other physical evidence, and examine Sirhan's gun. As Grant Cooper says: "My approach to the DA would be this: 'Look, the biggest feather in your cap would be to show how honest you are. Take the credit for it.' No one likes to be horsewhipped into doing things!"

The world of assassination theory is dense with non sequiturs, misunderstood evidence, wild claims. In this case, excluding the *theoretical* possibilities of Sirhan having been a member of a conspiracy, it is not too difficult to settle speculation about what actually happened in the pantry of the Ambassador Hotel. It takes a candid acceptance by the DA's office of the existence of doubt and a candid effort to dispel that doubt. Given the massive uncertainties of evidence and what that evidence means, one test firing might exorcise at least one of the ghosts of the Sixties.

Postscript

On August 14, 1975, Superior Court Judge Robert A. Wenke ordered a reexamination of the evidence relating to Sirhan's gun, in response to a petition filed by former aide Paul Schrade, CBS and others. A panel of seven experts, acceptable to all parties, was appointed to conduct the reexamination, which began in late September.

The Los Angeles Times *reported the panel's conclusions October 7, 1975. According to the* Times's *report, the panel* found "no substantive or demonstrable evidence that more than one gun was used to fire any of the bullets examined." The panel concluded that the RFK neck bullet did have two cannelures, not one. However, the panel also found that the bullets they examined —one from RFK and others from victims Irwin Stroll, Ira Goldstein and William Weisel—lacked sufficient individual characteristics to permit the panel to conclude that they were fired from Sirhan's gun. The experts did conclude that these bullets "had similar characteristics of .22-caliber long-rifle bullets manufactured by Cascade Cartridges, Inc. of Lewiston, Idaho."—Eds.

FROM DALLAS TO WATERGATE: THE POLITICS OF ASSASSINATION

INTRODUCTION

The next selections move into the areas of context and consequences of the assassinations. The last two essays on policy argue that the assassination of John F. Kennedy led directly to increased electronic surveillance of American citizens (see also Warren Report, Recommendations, supra pp. 46–48, and Richard M. Nixon's August 22, 1973, press conference, supra, p. 304), and was rapidly followed by the resolution of hitherto deliberately ambiguous promises to the Saigon government. Readers are cautioned against drawing the inference that unspecified sinister forces plotted the assassination in order to bring about these consequences. The point is rather that these were the consequences whether they were intended or not—even if the assassination were the act of a demented lone assassin. Unfortunately, this area has attracted far less interest than the mysteries of the assassinations themselves, and it cries out for further exploration.

The first essay in this section argues by analogy from Watergate that we may learn more from studying the Dallas cover-up than from examining the crimes themselves. One of the most frequent objections to the belief that President Kennedy's death was the work of a conspiracy is the simple argument that too many people would appear to be implicated—including the Dallas authorities, the federal investigative agencies, the Warren Commission and all its staff. The argument goes that everyone from Earl Warren on down must have been in collusion with the conspiracy if they kept its secrets. But in the wake of Watergate we have learned to distinguish the cover-up from the crime. We now know that those who collude in the concealment of truth may falsely believe that they are merely keeping a different secret—particularly in the vaguely defined region of "national security." We know, too, of the large and sometimes overlapping networks of intelligence agencies and organized crime where secrecy is a way of life. In retrospect, the Dallas cover-up can be seen to involve many of these elements. The mere hint of an informant relationship between Oswald and the FBI raised "national security" problems—not the proposition that the FBI had plotted the assassination, but the more general embarrassment of any links between the agency and the assumed demented leftist. Jack Ruby's friends in the Dallas police department and the Chicago underworld posed similar embarrassments—prompting evasive testimony from the FBI and others who had secrets to keep which were unrelated to the assassination.

If indeed Lyndon Johnson suspected that Castro's Cuba was somehow implicated in the assassination (see above, pp. 302–303), what "national security" interests made him reluctant to probe the relationship? The charitable explanation is the desire to preserve the lofty ideals of international détente—symbolized by the first nuclear test-ban treaty signed in the summer of 1963. Another factor may have been the fear of uncovering CIA assassination plots directed against Castro—at least one of which was even more embarrassing because it involved the proposed use of Mafia hit-men.

The Ervin Committee's investigations revealed the Nixon White House concern about the CIA's Cuban scenarios—first when Jack Anderson wrote of an assassination plan in a 1971 column, later when it was feared that investigation of E. Howard Hunt and his Watergate burglars would lead straight back to the CIA's plots against Castro. When Richard Nixon ordered the curtailment of the FBI's Watergate investigation June 23, 1972, he alluded to "the Cuba thing" and "the whole Bay of Pigs thing" in the following fateful transcript:

. . . just say [unintelligible] very bad to have this fellow Hunt, ah, he knows too damned much, if he was involved—you happen to know *that? If it gets out that this is all involved, the Cuba thing, it would be a fiasco. It would make the CIA look bad, it's going to make Hunt look bad, and it is likely to blow the whole Bay of Pigs thing which we think would be very unfortunate—both for CIA and for the country, at this time, and for American foreign policy. Just tell him to lay off.*

Five days later CIA Director Richard Helms instructed the FBI to "desist from expanding this investigation into other areas which may well, eventually, run afoul of our operations." (House Judiciary Committee, Statement of Information, II, p. 459)

The Watergate experience demonstrates, if nothing else, how "the Cuba thing" constituted such a murky area of intrigue and covert operations that those who entered it had little hope of eliciting full and straightforward disclosures about practically anything. Howard Hunt's own memoir of the Bay of Pigs expedition shows, even in the brief excerpts reprinted here, the subtle combination of illusion and reality: acknowledging that the assassination of Castro was proposed, denying that it was ever attempted. Hunt's description of Oswald the Castroite by now only adds to the mystery—pulling the alleged assassin deeper into the web of fabrication and cover stories. The selection from Hunt's biographer Tad Szulc makes clear that the assassination plots against Castro did not end with the Bay of Pigs in 1961.

It should be emphasized that only the minutest fraction of the estimated six hundred thousand Cuban exiles in this country became involved in assassinations of any description. Moreover, plots against Castro—whose relevance to the Kennedy assassination remains speculative—involved other segments of American society, notably the CIA and its allies in the U.S. intelligence community, the Howard Hughes organization, and high-level Chicago and Las Vegas representatives of organized crime. There are also other relevant intrigues from this era, such as the FBI's COINTELPRO program against the Socialist Workers Party and other groups.

---

* See also Victor S. Navasky, *Kennedy Justice* (New York: Atheneum, 1971) and Taylor Branch and George Crile III, "The Kennedy Vendetta" (*Harper's*, August 1975).

The fact remains that several who collaborated in the CIA's anti-Castro operations (notably Frank Sturgis and Cubans close to Howard Hunt's protégé Manuel Artime) are named in Warren Commission documents as sources of mutually corroborating stories (all later discredited) linking Oswald to Castro's intelligence network. Oswald himself repeatedly established contacts with Cubans, in New Orleans (with representatives of the CIA's "Cuban Revolutionary Council"), in Mexico, allegedly in Dallas and Los Angeles (19 H 534, 8 H 242), and even in the Soviet Union (5 H 406-7, 16 H 152, contrast R 271). Jack Ruby also was interested in Cuba.

Horace Sutton's account of the Miami Cuban community completes the picture of a milieu which appears recurrently in the dramas of Dallas and Watergate: from the Odio episode (see pp. 101 and 458) to the man in Mexico (see pp. 450–459). The point is not to accuse the Cuban exiles of plotting the assassination of President Kennedy, but simply to illuminate one of the dark regions whose very existence as a network of intrigue and secrets inhibited the Warren Commission's investigation and made a large contribution to the ensuing cover-up.

This section of our book also asks the readers to indulge their imaginations: Gore Vidal reads Arthur Bremer's diary and asks whether it was ghost-written by a mediocre novelist and sometime spy as pre-planned evidence of yet another lone, demented assassin. A bit whimsical and far-fetched perhaps—but also a reminder of how few questions have really been asked about still one more political shooting which has profoundly influenced all of our lives.

FROM DALLAS TO WATERGATE—THE LONGEST COVER-UP
Peter Dale Scott

Ramparts / *November 1973*

The discovery of the Watergate break-in on June 17, 1972, has led slowly but irreversibly to wider revelations about the government's use of crime, past and present. At first glance, it might seem the burglars' long record of covert activities would have made such revelations inevitable. Most of those arrested in the Democratic National Committee offices had been employed by the CIA in anti-Castro activities, and one of them—Eugenio Martinez—was still on a CIA retainer. Another, Frank Sturgis *alias* Fiorini, had defied President Kennedy's ban on U.S.-based raids against Cuba, and continued them with the support of former Havana casino operators with strong links to organized crime. His activities immediately before and after the Kennedy assassination had made Sturgis suspicious in the eyes of some private assassination buffs, long before Watergate made him a public figure.

E. Howard Hunt, the man chosen by Nixon's re-election team to mastermind the Watergate break-in, had served as political officer in the CIA's Bay of Pigs operation, which Richard Nixon had almost single-handedly pressed on the Eisenhower Administration, and for which Nixon was the White House Action Officer. In connection with the Bay of Pigs, Hunt had proposed the assassination of Castro to his CIA superiors, and, according to some sources, continued to propose similar assassination projects, the latest of these against the President of Panama in 1971.

Yet the Watergate cover-up almost succeeded—not despite the exotic records of the defendants, but precisely because of them. Complicity in their past crimes, such as the burglary against Dan Ellsberg's psychiatrist—and who knows what others —left the Nixon Administration with little alternative but to obstruct justice in the case of the Watergate Seven. By 1972 the chain leading from crime to cover-up to new crime was becoming a major preoccupation at the White House. But the establishment consensus necessary for a successful cover-up had been so eroded during the past ten years that the cold warriors could no longer keep their conspiracies secure.

In my opinion it is no coincidence that the key figures in Watergate—Liddy, Hunt, Sturgis, Krogh, Caulfield—had been drawn from the conspiratorial world of government narcotics enforcement, a shady realm in which the operations of organized crime, counterrevolution, and government intelligence have traditionally overlapped. Nor is it a coincidence that one of these men—Watergate burglar Frank Sturgis—played a minor role in the cover-up of the Dallas assassination ten years ago. On the contrary, I believe that a full exposure of the Watergate conspiracy will help us to understand what happened in Dallas, and also to understand the covert forces which later mired America in a criminal war in Southeast Asia. Conversely, an analysis of the cover-up in Dallas will do much to illuminate Watergate and its ramifications, including that Miami demi-monde of exiles, Teamster investments, and Syndicate real estate deals with which Nixon and his friend Bebe Rebozo have been involved.

I hope to show that what makes this Miami connection so dangerous, and what links the scandal of Watergate to the assassination in Dallas, is the increasingly ominous symbiosis between U.S. intelligence networks and the forces of organized crime.

COVER-UP IN DALLAS

The experience of the Ervin Committee suggests a new approach to the Kennedy assassination: to focus on the cover-up rather than on the crime itself. Although many vital records of the Watergate break-in were successfully destroyed, the cover-up actions themselves became new evidence of an on-going conspiracy. Thus the Ervin Committee has learned more about the mechanics of the cover-up than of the original break-in. In Dallas, too, the actual circumstances of the three shootings—of Kennedy, Oswald and Officer Tippit—have been largely obliterated. But if we focus only on the ensuing Dallas cover-up, the evidence of conspiracy, and the identity of some of the principals, are unmistakable—as is the central presence of criminal and intelligence networks also evident in the politics of Watergate and Vietnam.

The Watergate investigations revealed that many men in government will conspire against the law when two justifications are offered—whether or not these justifications are credible or are actually believed. The first is the possibility of a national security threat (as when Ellsberg's revelation of the Pentagon Papers was alleged to have threatened current truce negotiations, or to have involved a leak to the Soviet Embassy). The second is the alleged involvement of a governmental intelligence network or operation (as when on May 22, 1973, Nixon justified his participation in the cover-up by explaining that he had believed, erroneously, that the CIA was implicated).

The second justification flows from the first. E. Howard Hunt was no fool when he used a CIA Minox camera to photograph G. Gordon Liddy in front of the office building of Ellsberg's psychiatrist. Although the photograph was irrelevant to the ensuing burglary, by implying CIA involvement it insured that Hunt and Liddy would be protected by an Administration cover-up—and that, if the cover-up ever collapsed, it could be credited to national security instead of political expediency. By the same logic it was not through oversight, but through foresight, that Bernard Barker had CIA-veteran Hunt's name and White House phone number in his notebook at the time of the break-in (*New York Times*, June 24, 1972, p. 24), and that Frank Sturgis was allegedly "carrying a false passport prepared by the CIA at Hunt's request" (*NYT*, January 14, 1973, p. 38).

In Dallas, allegations both of a security threat and an intelligence involvement were available to justify federal intervention into the investigation, and thus also to justify a massive *ex post facto* cover-up. Following the assassination, a large number of rumors linked Oswald (and sometimes Ruby) in a left-wing conspiracy extending to Castro's Cuba and possibly the Soviet Union. Some of these rumors seemed to be backed by evidence; one, interestingly enough, was "corroborated" by Frank Sturgis.

The Secret Service in Dallas intercepted a letter to Oswald, postmarked Havana, November 28, 1963, and signed by Pedro Charles. The letter indicated that "Oswald had been paid by Charles to carry out an unidentified mission which involved accurate shooting" (CE 2763, 26 H 148). Meanwhile the FBI possessed a letter from Havana to Robert Kennedy, "written by one Mario del Rosario Molina [which] alleged that Lee Harvey Oswald assassinated President Kennedy at the direction of Pedro Charles, a Cuban agent. . . . According to the writer, Oswald met with Charles in Miami, Florida, several months ago [i.e. in early 1963] and was paid $7,000 by Charles" (26 H 148).

By now this story seems absurd: the elaborate FBI chronology of Oswald's movements gave no indication that he ever visited Miami. But at the time the letters arrived, a reporter in the Miami area named James Buchanan was publishing stories (attributed to Frank Sturgis alias Fiorini) that Oswald *had* been in Miami and also had been in contact with Cuban intelligence (CD 59.2-3, CD 395.2; cf. CD 1020). Later reports from James Buchanan's brother Jerry placed Oswald in Miami in March 1963 (CD 1020.7). These concatenating pieces of misinformation from Miami and Havana suggest, in retrospect, a conspiracy to mislead.

The stories today are much less important than Buchanan's sources for them, all of whom came from two Miami-based anti-Castro groups. The first group (CD 49.26), the DRE (Student Revolutionary Directorate), was Cuban, and the CIA used it to infiltrate Cuba in connection with the Bay of Pigs; the DRE was named in Oswald's notebook (16 H 67), since Oswald had been in contact with them in New Orleans (R 728), and perhaps in Dallas (CD 205.646). The second, American, group —which included both James Buchanan and his brother Jerry— was the International Anti-Communist Brigade. It was a small band of mercenaries headed by a named source of Buchanan's articles—Frank Sturgis alias Fiorini, the future burglar of Watergate.

Sturgis, like the DRE, had been employed by the CIA in connection with the Bay of Pigs invasion. But after the Cuban Missile Crisis of 1962, Kennedy had begun to crack down on anti-Castro raids launched from the continental United States. Jerry Buchanan had been arrested by the British in the Bahamas in April 1963, on board a boat formerly used in CIA missions, and now being used (without presidential authorization) for an intended raid against a Soviet tanker (*NYT*, April 2, 1963, pp. 1, 9; April 3, 1963, p. 3). In September, the Federal Government had issued "strong warnings" to six Americans for their anti-Castro activities, including Frank Fiorini (Sturgis) and Alexander Rorke, the owner of Jerry Buchanan's boat (*NYT*, Sept. 16, 1963, p. 39). As for James Buchanan, the Brigade's secretary and propaganda director, Sturgis allegedly broke with him in December 1963 because of his "excessive" attacks on the FBI and the CIA, "even going so far as to describe former President John F. Kennedy as a communist" (CD 1020.6).

Similar anti-Kennedy sentiments were allegedly expressed by Carlos Bringuier, Oswald's contact with the DRE in New Orleans, and a right-winger who later headed up the Cuban-Americans for Nixon-Agnew. Another witness told the Warren Commission that Bringuier, because "the United States didn't help to overthrow Castro . . . hates the United States almost as much as he hates Russia" (11 H 353). Because these sentiments were so widely held among Cuban exiles, many students of the Dallas assassination have theorized that a group of anti-Castro terrorists (Cuban and/or American) may have killed Kennedy in revenge for having been abandoned by the CIA in 1963.

MURDER, INCORPORATED

According to an article in the July 1973 issue of *The Atlantic*, former President Lyndon Johnson also had doubts about the findings of the Warren Commission despite his public support of its "lone assassin" hypothesis. Interviewed not long before his death, Johnson expressed his belief that the assassination in Dallas had been part of a conspiracy. . . . Johnson said that *when he had taken office* he found that "we had been operating a damned Murder Inc. in the Caribbean." A year or so before Kennedy's death a CIA-backed assassination team had been picked up in Havana. Johnson speculated that Dallas had been a retaliation for this thwarted attempt (p. 39). [Emphasis added.]

Johnson's recollection is corroborated by E. Howard Hunt in his memoir on the Bay of Pigs. Hunt admits to having personally proposed an attempt to assassinate Castro. And although he claims that nothing came of his proposal, this is not true. The CIA's assassins nearly succeeded, but were caught and executed in Havana on the day of the Bay of Pigs invasion.

Another detail suppressed by Hunt is that the CIA's assassination plan involved giving the legal green light (and other aid) to a Cuban conspiracy against Castro sponsored by Las Vegas mobster Johnny Roselli and his organized crime allies in gambling —who wanted back their old Havana casinos. A detailed account of the assassination attempt by Andrew St. George—himself a one-time U.S. intelligence agent—suppresses the Mafia angle but confirms that this attempt was but one of a series, in which a prominent role was played by Frank Sturgis' co-conspirator, Alexander Rorke (*Parade*, April 12, 1964, p. 4). In fact Rorke, according to St. George, died in an assassination attempt when his plane crashed in the Caribbean in September 1963 (cf. CD 1020.29). Rorke's 1963 attorney, Hans Tanner, had already published an account of his own assassination attempt in July 1961. His book gave several informed details about the International Anti-Communist Brigade of Frank Sturgis, which he considered to be "financed by dispossessed hotel and gambling room owners who operated under Batista" (Hans Tanner, *Counter-Revolutionary Agent*, G. T. Foulis, 1962, p. 127).

Hunt is said by an authoritative source to have been the CIA's contact for an assassination conspiracy against Castro in 1966, involving Rolando Cubela Secades, who confessed after being captured in Havana. Cubela, a former military leader of the DRE in Batista days, admitted that he had planned, with help from the

CIA and Bay of Pigs leader Manuel Artime, "to shoot Premier Castro with a high-powered telescopic rifle and later share in top posts of a counter-revolutionary regime with Mr. Artime" (*NYT*, March 6, 1966, p. 25). These facts help explain why Artime—for whose child Hunt is a godfather—organized a defense fund for the Watergate burglars, whom he has since continued to visit regularly in prison (*NYT*, July 9, 1973, p. 25, cf. June 19, 1972, p. 20). The same facts may also help us to understand what was being covered up in Dallas.

Bernard Barker testified that he carried out two break-ins for Hunt in the expectation that this would eventually help to depose Castro. He also claimed that up to ten minutes before the Ellsberg break-in he knew only that he was working on a case involving espionage by a Soviet embassy. Such exploitation of anti-Castro militants had long ago been offered as an hypothesis for the Dallas assassination. According to this theory, evidence involving Oswald in a left-wing conspiracy had in fact been planted by militant anti-Communists, to make a case for a retaliatory U.S. invasion of Cuba. This would, for example, explain the oddly self-incriminating letter from "Pedro Charles," which the FBI quickly exposed as fraudulent, having been written on the same typewriter as the second warning letter from Havana (26 H 148).

According to a more sophisticated version of this hypothesis (involving a "two-tier conspiracy"), the clumsy fraud was *meant* to be exposed. Having first served as a pretext to engage the services of anti-Castro Cubans, its ultimate intention was to justify not an invasion but a massive federal de-bunking of all traces of conspiracy—the false and also the true.

We know at any rate that the direct result of such stories was to justify the creation of the Warren Commission. As Lyndon Johnson wrote in his memoirs, *The Vantage Point*:

We were aware of stories that Castro . . . only lately accusing us of sending CIA agents into the country to assassinate him, was the perpetrator of the Oswald assassination plot. These rumors were another compelling reason that a thorough study had to be made of the Dallas tragedy at once. Out of the nation's suspicions, out of the nation's need for facts, the Warren Commission was born (p. 26).

THE OSWALD NEXUS

As the Commission's investigative arm, the FBI, with little other legal authorization, proceeded to expose Buchanan's stories of conspiracy, and others like them. For demonstrating that Oswald was not a Castro agent, but "acted alone," the FBI and the Warren Commission drew applause not only from liberals but even from left-wing critics such as I. F. Stone. Yet in their efforts to establish the "lone assassin" hypotheses for Oswald and Ruby, both the FBI and the Warren Commission were guilty of covering up much evidence to the contrary.

A seemingly minor but significant example is the cover-up of Oswald's relationship (still unclear) to the FBI. On January 24, 1964, the Warren Commission first heard from Dallas District Attorney Henry Wade and Texas Attorney General Waggoner Carr of a rumor that Oswald had been an FBI informant since September 1962. Wade's evidence included hearsay that the name, phone and license-plate number of FBI agent Hosty (who was responsible for surveillance of pro- and anti-Castro Cubans) were in Oswald's address book (just as Hunt's phone was in Barker's), and also that Oswald had a government voucher for $200 at the time of his arrest (5 H 242). The first piece of hearsay turned out to be true (16 H 64), but the Commission did not learn this easily: the FBI had supplied it with an itemized list of names in Oswald's notebook, from which Hosty's had been omitted (5 H 112).

You will look in vain for any of this information in the Warren Report. Instead, the Commission concluded from the sworn testimony of two CIA and five FBI officials, "corroborated by the Commission's independent review of the Bureau files," that "there was absolutely no type of informant or undercover relationship between an agency of the U.S. Government and Lee Harvey Oswald" (R 327). In fact, Chief Justice Warren declined on security grounds to inspect the FBI file on Oswald noting that others "would also demand . . . to see it, and if it is security matters we can't let them see it" (5 H 13). According to the Commission lawyer in charge of this matter, no "independent review" was ever made of the file (Edward Epstein, *Inquest*, New York: Viking, 1966, p. 38).

In any case, the question of Oswald's FBI links is only one part of the puzzle. There is considerably more evidence to indicate Oswald's involvement with U.S. intelligence—evidence that is obscured rather than laid to rest by the Commission Report.

Let us look at a few of the instances in which this "intelligence angle" was covered up. Oswald's mother, trying vainly to convince the Commission her son was "an agent of the government" (1 H 142, cf. 1 H 191), cited his "special work" in the Philippines (apparently in connection with the CIA military intervention in Indonesia) and in the Taiwan crisis (1 H 233, cf. 22 H 723). The Warren Report, without directly refuting this last claim, implied that Oswald had only been in Taiwan for a day or so around September 30, 1958 (R 684); it relied on Oswald's personnel file, and a related Pentagon memo, which placed Oswald's Marine Air Group 11 in Atsugi, Japan (23 H 796, cf. 19 H 658). In reality, MAG-11 had moved from Atsugi to Taiwan, in response to the Quemoy crisis, for an extended period beginning September 8 (Department of Defense Annual Report, 1958-59, pp. 228-29).

This change of status is noted in Oswald's pay records, which only reached the Commission nine days before its report went to press (26 H 709, 715). The pay records also show, in contradiction to the personnel file, that on returning to Atsugi (the base for CIA U-2 and covert commando operations in the Far East), Oswald left MAG-11 (now in Taiwan) and was attached to its replacement MAG-13 (26 H 715). That Oswald's personnel file could put him in one unit, while his pay records put him in another, suggests that Oswald, at least in 1958-59, was engaged in some kind of activity so sensitive that some of his records were altered to conceal it.

There are also discrepancies with regard to Oswald's "hardship discharge" from active duty in September 1959 to support his mother. The Warren Report cites affidavits that Mrs. Oswald "had been injured at work in December 1958, and was unable to support herself" (R 688). In fact, both Mrs. Oswald's regular doctor (CD 5.298) and an Industrial Accident Board denied that she had suffered a loss of wage-earning capacity. Nevertheless, Oswald received his release with an ease and rapidity that surprised some of his colleagues (8 H 257).

In Oswald's group at Santa Ana, Calif., where a "secret clearance . . . was a minimum requirement" (8 H 298, cf. 232), the basic function was "to train both enlisted [men] and officers for later assignment overseas" (8 H 290). The swift handling of Oswald's release suggests that it was a cover: Oswald was being "sheep-dipped," just as U-2 pilot Gary Powers before him had been "released" from the Air Force for assignment to a covert intelligence role. Oswald's immediate application for a passport on September 4 "to attend the Albert Schweitzer College in Switzerland and the University of Turku in Finland" (22 H 78) suggests that that role concerned his "defection" in October to the Soviet Union.

Here, too, the Warren Commission chose to overlook discrepancies. How was the trip paid for? The Report blandly repeats Oswald's own story that he had saved $1,500 from his Marine Corps salary (R 256), ignoring the fact that his only known bank account contained a total of $203 (22 H 180). How did Oswald fly to Finland from London Airport, where his passport was stamped "Embarked 10 Oct. 1959" (18 H 162)? If he had taken the only commercial flight, he would have arrived too late to register before midnight (as claimed) at his Helsinki Hotel (26 H 32). The Report's solution was to conclude that Oswald had departed from London October 9, ignoring both the evidence of the conflicting date stamp and the possibility that his flight was not a commercial one at all (R 690, cf. Sylvia Meagher, *Accessories after the Fact*, New York: Bobbs-Merrill, 1967, p. 331).

The desire of U.S. intelligence agencies to interview even casual visitors to the Soviet Union is well known. In June 1962, Lee Harvey Oswald was a returning Marine defector who had once served at a CIA base and had told the U.S. Embassy in Moscow of his intention to pass information to Soviet officials (18 H 98). For two years he had worked in a sensitive Soviet factory and was now married to the niece of a colonel in Soviet intelligence. Yet the Report tells us that the returning Oswalds were met in New York City, not by the FBI or CIA, but by "Spas T. Raikin, a representative of the Traveler's Aid Society" (R 713).

The FBI interviews did not point out that Spas T. Raikin was also the Secretary-General of the American Friends of the Anti-

Bolshevik Bloc of Nations, a small but vigorous group of right-wing revanchiste East Europeans in direct touch with the FBI and Army Intelligence—and also with the Gehlen spy organization in West Germany, the Kuomintang in Taiwan, the mother of Madame Nhu, right-wing Cubans like Oswald's DRE contact Carlos Bringuier, and other elements of a shadowy "World Anti-Communist League." This WACL had contacts with U.S. anti-communists in New Orleans, in the building with the Camp St. address used by Oswald on his pro-Castro literature, and also by the CIA's Cuban Revolutionary Council of which Bringuier had once been press secretary. As I have indicated in my book, *The War Conspiracy*, Mr. Raikin's personal correspondents in Taiwan (the Asian Peoples' Anti-Communist League) were intelligence agents involved in the Kuomintang's narcotics traffic—a fact dramatically illustrated by the 1971 arrest in Paris of the Chief Laotian Delegate to the APACL, whose suitcase containing 60 kilos of highgrade heroin would have been worth $13.5 million on the streets of New York.

Unfortunately, there has not been space to show the ways in which many if not most of the Commission's staff, like most of the FBI agents involved, did attempt an honest and thorough investigation. I have focused narrowly on some of the indications that there was a cover-up where security and intelligence matters were involved. And, as we have learned from the Watergate and "plumbers" break-ins, the cover-up of an intelligence matter can become a priority, thereby protecting perpetrators of crimes which have no intelligence justification.

THE RUBY CONNECTION

Jack Ruby, the second "lone assassin," was a more difficult subject for a cover-up; his personal and business ties with the police and underworld in Dallas were widely known, and there is evidence they extended considerably beyond Texas. Nevertheless, the Commission went to great lengths to argue that Ruby, like Oswald, "acted independently" (R 373), and in particular to downplay his close links to the Dallas police and also to organized crime. According to a brief and unconsciously humorous section

of the Report, "the evidence indicates that Ruby was keenly interested in policemen and their work" (R 800). Nothing is said of
the testimony of Detective Eberhardt, a veteran of the Special
Services Bureau (SSB), "that he regarded Jack Ruby as a source
of information in connection with his investigatory activities"
(13 H 183)—i.e., as a police informant, specifically in the area of
narcotics.

A word must be interpolated here about the SSB of the Dallas
Police. Like similar "Special Units" in other police forces across
the country (all of which work with one another), the Dallas
SSB had a consolidated responsibility, in collaboration with the
FBI and other agencies, for investigating subversive activities
(allegedly the world of Lee Harvey Oswald), and also organized
crime (the world of Jack Ruby). It also had responsibility for
the area of vice, and particularly for supervising night-clubs such
as Jack Ruby's. Thus SSB Vice Chief Gilmore, a "close friend" of
Ruby (23 H 78, 25 H 290), was said to visit his clubs "every
night they are open" (23 H 207). SSB also had a Narcotics Unit.
Last but not least, the SSB was given the responsibility of protective intelligence for the visits of important government officials—
such as President Kennedy—who visited Dallas (5 H 48).

Ruby's status as a high-level police informant would explain
the repeated stories, from sources inside and outside Dallas,
"that Ruby is the payoff man for the Dallas Police Department"
(CD 4.529) and "had the 'fix' with the county authorities" (23
H 372). One of these reports is particularly credible, inasmuch as
it was received by the FBI seven years before the assassination.
According to a Mrs. James Breen, who with her husband acted "as
informants for the Federal Narcotics Bureau," her husband "had
made connection with large narcotics setup operating between
Mexico, Texas and the East. . . . In some fashion James got the
okay to operate through Jack Ruby of Dallas" (23 H 369).

The Warren Report discounted the even more numerous stories
(one of them from a former Dallas County Sheriff) that Ruby was
linked to organized crime. Commission Exhibit 1268 (22 H 372)
is a typical example of the FBI's and Commission's reluctance to
explore more deeply Ruby's underworld connections. In it a Dave
Yaras (unidentified) "claims 'Sparky' " [i.e. Ruby] "knew Lenny
Patrick 'like he knows him' but was 'positively on his own and

not outfit connected.' " Yaras further described " 'Sparky' as a 'romeo' who was most successful in picking up girls." In the Report only the trivial part of this testimony remains: "one friend regarded him as a 'Romeo,' who was quite successful in attracting young women" (R 792).

We must turn to the Kefauver and McClellan Crime Hearings to learn (in answer to the obvious question not asked by the FBI) that the link between Yaras and Patrick (and hence, inferentially, Ruby) was intimate. Both men were top Syndicate gambling figures on Chicago's Jewish West Side. They had been arrested and indicted together for the syndicate murder in 1946 of wire service king James Ragen, an indictment dropped after the murder of a key witness. The police captain most active in the investigation was himself subsequently murdered, right after he reported to the Kefauver Committee (through his lawyer Luis Kutner) that he had a "hot new witness who will . . . name Leonard Patrick, Dave Yaras, and Willie Block as the killers" (*Newsweek*, October 9, 1950, p. 37). In 1963 news stories that Luis Kutner had intervened for Ruby with the Kefauver Committee, also noted (correctly, it would appear), that Ruby was "linked" to Dave Yaras, Lennie Patrick and Willie Block (*Washington Post*, November 26, 1963, A6).

Dave Yaras himself should have particularly interested the Warren Commission, since the McClellan Committee's counsel, Robert F. Kennedy, had charged him with the same connections later attributed to Ruby: corrupt Teamster interests, and "some gambling in Cuba" (McClellan Hearings, pp. 7416, 12522). Yet it asked no questions about Yaras and instead misspelled his name (as Yeres) when Ruby's sister began spontaneously to reminisce about him and Patrick (14 H 444).

This studied disinterest in Ruby's alleged Teamster connections appears to have been systematic. The Commission asked no questions about Ruby's two telephone calls in November 1963 with Barney Baker (25 H 244), a convicted Teamster hoodlum who phoned Dave Yaras on the eve of the assassination (25 H 295). Nor about Ruby's call to top Teamster bondsman Irwin Weiner (25 H 246)—an organized crime associate of narcotics overlord Sam Battaglia. When Ruby himself began to talk about his phone call to Dusty Miller, head of the Teamsters Southern

Conference (25 H 244), this was transcribed in the Warren Hearings as a call to "Deutsch I. Maylor" (5 H 200).

It is of course quite possible that all these calls were innocent, but the Commission did not bother to find out. None of those called were witnesses, and their names will not be found in the Report. Instead the Report claims that Ruby's friendships with criminals "throughout his life . . . were limited largely to professional gamblers," and adds, even more astonishingly, that "there is no credible evidence that Ruby, himself, gambled on other than a social basis" (R 370). The Commission had received numerous disinterested reports to the contrary (e.g. 23 H 48, 23 H 363, CD 360.115). One of these, from a south Texas businessman, recalled Ruby saying in 1960 that "he had recently been to Cuba, as he and some associates were trying to get some gambling concessions at a casino there but it did not work out" (22 H 858).

The Commission knew that Ruby in fact had visited Cuba in 1959, probably twice. Its Report mentions the eight-day August 1959 trip on one page (R 802), the two-day September trip (22 H 859) on another (R 370), and treats the two trips as one: "Ruby traveled to Havana as a guest of a close friend and known gambler, Lewis J. McWillie. Both Ruby and McWillie state the trip was purely social" (R 370). This covers up several facts which were known to the Commission: a 1959 police report called McWillie (whom Ruby "idolized," 5 H 201) a "gambler and murderer" (23 H 166); he was a former employee of big-time gambler Benny Binion, the power behind the Delois Green gang who was now in Las Vegas (23 H 163, CD 1193.249); in 1959 he was manager of the Tropicana Casino in Havana, a syndicate operation (23 H 166); both in Havana (The Capri) and in Las Vegas (The Thunderbird), McWillie worked at casinos where a cut went to top Syndicate financier Meyer Lansky.

Today this story of a Ruby involvement in Havana gambling has a renewed interest, for in 1959 Castro's supervisor of gambling concessions is said to have been Watergate burglar Frank Sturgis *alias* Fiorini, a gun-runner to Castro before the overthrow of Batista. The owner of the Havana Tropicana (where McWillie worked and Ruby visited) was Norman Rothman, a gun-runner to Castro who in 1959 was indicted on other charges with *mafioso* Samuel Mannarino (another Havana gun-runner and casino operator) and Giuseppe Cotroni, identified in the Senate Narcotics Hearings (p. 1002) as "head of the largest and most notorious narcotics syndicate on the North American continent."

OVERLAPPING CONSPIRACIES

In this dark area of gun-running to Cuba, the careers of Sturgis, of Ruby, and of Oswald begin to overlap. First-hand accounts linked Ruby himself to Cuban gun-running (14 H 330-64), and to Robert McKeown, arrested in 1958 for gun-running with his friend, former Cuban President Carlos Prio Socarras. (Prio Socarras helped organize the Cuban exile demonstrations at the party conventions in 1972, when his Miami office was only two doors away from Bernard Barker's.) And Carlos Bringuier claimed he suspected Oswald of trying to infiltrate—as an informant either for Castro or for the FBI—the Louisiana training camp of the Christian Democratic Movement, a Miami-based exile group close to the DRE, which the Kennedy Administration was cracking down on in late 1963 (10 H 35, 43). Bringuier noted that five days before Oswald's first contact with him, the FBI had raided an illicit arms depot one mile from the camp. These arms were stashed in the home of one of the McLaney brothers, prominent casino operators in Las Vegas, the Bahamas, and in pre-Castro Havana.

Since 1963, U.S. narcotics officials have referred to the existence in Miami of a small but tightly organized "Cuban Mafia" in narcotics, "for the most part previously little-known underworld members employed and trained in pre-Castro Cuba by the American Mafia, which then controlled gambling in Havana" (*NYT*, February 1, 1970, p. 57). Certain U.S. business interests collaborated for decades with the narcotics-linked American Mafia in Cuba—as they did with similar criminal networks in China and later in Vietnam—for the Mafia supplied the necessary local intelligence, cash and muscle against the threat of Communist take-over. Some of those Cuban-Americans recruited by the CIA (presumably from the Cuban-American Mafia) are now suspected by federal and city authorities to be "involved in everything from narcotics trafficking to extortion rackets and bombings" (*NYT Magazine*, June 3, 1973, p. 46).

And behind the bureaucratic screens of "security" and "intelligence" there appear signs of a more sinister overlapping of conspiracies: in the gun-running and gambling background of Frank Sturgis and his allies, and the common responsibility for narcotics intelligence of E. Howard Hunt and John Caulfield in the White House, G. Gordon Liddy in the Treasury Department, and Egil Krogh (supervisor of the White House "plumbers") as Director in 1972 of the Cabinet Committee on International Narcotics Control.

The gray alliance in pre-Castro Cuba between business, intelligence and Mafia led to a central role in the post-war heroin traffic of the Havana connection, which later became the Miami connection. This Miami connection is typified by Bebe Rebozo's business associate "Big Al" Polizzi, who was named in the 1964 Senate Narcotics Hearings as "one of the most influential figures of the underworld in the United States" and "associated with international narcotic traffickers . . . and illicit gambling activities" (p. 1049). Polizzi and Rebozo collaborated in the construction of a Miami shopping center, where Rebozo also employed a former Mayor of Havana under Batista who headed up "Cubans for Nixon" in 1968. In addition, Polizzi and the Rebozo family have been recorded as signing legal petitions in support of each other, in 1952 and again in 1965 (*Newsday*, October 7, 1971; *Village Voice*, Aug. 31-Sept. 6, 1973).

Another piece in the puzzle is provided by the Keyes Realty Company, a Miami business with underworld connections, which has helped both Rebozo and Nixon in various land deals, including the Winter White House. Keyes Realty and its lawyers were named in the Kefauver Crime Hearings (Part 1, p. 716) for their role on behalf of organized crime in bribing Dade County's Sheriff Sullivan to run Miami as a wide-open gambling town. In 1948, Keyes Realty, and its lawyers, with the help of a wealthy Cuban banker called Agustin Batista (no relation to the dictator), collaborated in the transfer of southern Key Biscayne to a shadowy Cuban investment group (the Ansan Corp.) in which an Internal Revenue investigator suspected the presence of funds belonging "to Luciano or other underworld characters" (IRS Report of Feb. 20, 1948, cited by Jeff Gerth in the November-December *Sundance*, p. 38). The visible partners were former Cuban President Prio's investment ally and Education Minister Jose Aleman, who had defrauded his government of tens of millions of dollars (*NYT*, March 26, 1950, p. 92), his wife Elena Santiero, daughter of Luciano's Cuban attorney, and Batista's Finance Minister and investment ally, Anselmo Alliegro.

Later control of this Key Biscayne real estate passed to men near Hoffa and the Teamsters' Pension Fund, and Meyer Lansky's conduit, the Miami National Bank. In 1967, some of this land was sold at bargain rates to Nixon and Rebozo, by a man named Donald Berg; after Nixon became President, the Secret Service advised him to stop associating with Berg because of his background. Nixon delayed registering the purchase of one lot for four years, until the final payment had been made on a mortgage to Arthur Desser, associate of both Jimmy Hoffa and Meyer Lansky.

Recently, Nixon's links with Desser, Keyes Realty *et al.* have been less prominent. But one of the Watergate burglars, Eugenio Martinez, was a vice-president of Keyes Realty until 1971, when he and Bernard Barker set up their own realty office, Ameritas, in the same office building. Some of Barker's real estate ventures, according to Jack Anderson's column (June 26, 1972), have involved Bebe Rebozo. Funds for the Watergate operation were channeled through Barker's bank account in a Cuban-owned Miami bank, Republic National, whose president had formerly worked for Agustin Batista's bank in Cuba. (The first president of this bank had earlier chaired the board of the Miami National Bank and another director was from the law firm of Keyes Realty.)

In 1961, Agustin Batista and his brother Laureano, leader of the Cuban Christian Democratic Movement (CDM), employed Sturgis' friend Hans Tanner in the CDM's "Project 26"—yet another effort to assassinate Castro (Tanner, p. 143). Tanner's account also describes how Nixon himself, out cruising in the Miami River, shouted "Good luck" to a boatload of CDM guerrillas training, supposedly in secrecy, for their diversionary role in the Bay of Pigs (p. 2). In 1965, Nixon intervened legally on behalf on the CDM's imprisoned political leader, Mario Garcia Kohly, who had been arrested by the Kennedy Administration for his anti-Castro activities in October 1963 (William Turner, *Power on the Right*, Ramparts Press, 1971, p. 156).

The Ervin Committee has yet to call Hunt and Sturgis as witnesses, to hear about their alleged illegal activities over the last decade. Some Congressional committee should learn more about these men's Cuban activities, such as those which in September 1963 brought strong U.S. government warnings to Sturgis and death to his friend Rorke. It is almost certain that a full inquiry in this direction would uncover past alliances between intelligence networks and organized crime for mutually advantageous operations including the attempts to assassinate Fidel Castro. And the disturbing evidence of a cover-up in Dallas suggests that such assassination efforts have not all been aimed abroad.

The Ervin Committee did of course subsequently question E. Howard Hunt. It also heard Bernard Barker testify as to his own background in narcotics intelligence. Barker added that his friend Felipe de Diego, another of Hunt's Cuban "plumbers," was a veteran of the CIA's "Operation 40" (Hearings, pp. 375, 378). "Operation 40" was, according to Tad Szulc and Karl E. Meyer's The Cuban Invasion *(New York: Ballantine, 1962, pp. 92, 95), a Bay of Pigs offshoot which allegedly included professional killers recruited for assassinating Artime's opponents within the Bay of Pigs Brigade. The group was recently dissolved, after some of its members were arrested as major narcotics traffickers inside the United States (The New York Times, January 5, 1975, p. 4).*

After the publication of this article in Ramparts *(November 1973), the Ervin Committee staff, in the course of investigating funds transmitted from Howard Hughes to Bebe Rebozo, took unpublished testimony in executive session from Frank Sturgis. In this investigation it also heard from Robert Maheu, chief of Hughes's Las Vegas operations, and from John Roselli, the reputed capomafioso from Chicago in Las Vegas with whom Maheu reportedly dealt in the CIA's project to assassinate Castro. This testimony also remains unpublished.*

More recently, Frank Sturgis has claimed in an interview to have been associated with the assassination squad in "Operation 40." See Michael Canfield and A. J. Weberman, Coup D'Etat in America *(New York: Third Press, 1975).—P.D.S.*

ATTEMPTS TO ASSASSINATE CASTRO
Jack Anderson

January 18 and 19, 1971

In January 1971 Jack Anderson laid out a chilling story that the rest of the press would not pick up until well after Watergate. The CIA, he wrote, had recruited organized crime figure John Roselli, with investigator Robert Maheu as go-between, for a series of plots to assassinate Fidel Castro between 1961 and 1963. Then Anderson raised what he called an ugly question "that high officials would rather keep buried. . . . Could the plot against Castro have backfired against President Kennedy?"

Jack Anderson was proven correct on at least one point: someone wanted the ugly question buried. This part of his column was edited out in at least one newspaper, and the edited version is the one reprinted in the Senate Watergate Hearings (p. 9913). Thanks to the alertness of the Watergate Committee staff, we know also that the Anderson columns caused a flurry of investigative memos inside the Nixon White House. One of these, from former New York policeman Jack Caulfield to John Dean, reported that "Maheu's covert activities . . . with CIA . . . are only generally known here," but warned that "Maheu's controversial activities . . . might well shake loose Republican skeletons from the closet" (p. 9755). Caulfield, though highly evasive, later conceded to the Watergate Committee staff that this memo referred to "the subject matter of the Jack Anderson column" (p. 9723). The Caulfield memo of February 1, 1971, more than a year before Watergate, seems strangely prophetic.

"Six CIA Attempts to Kill Castro Failed—Plot Hushed" and "Were Trujillo, Diem, CIA Targets Too" by Jack Anderson. Reprinted from *Forum*, January 18, 1971, and from the Miami *Herald*, January 19, 1971, by permission of United Feature Syndicate.

SIX CIA ATTEMPTS TO KILL
CASTRO FAILED—PLOT HUSHED

Locked in the darkest recesses of the Central Intelligence Agency is the story of six assassination attempts against Cuba's Fidel Castro.

For 10 years, only a few key people have known the terrible secret. They have sworn never to talk. Yet we have learned the details from sources whose credentials are beyond question.

The plot to knock off Castro began as part of the Bay of Pigs operation. The intent was to eliminate the Cuban dictator before the motley invaders landed on the island. Their arrival was expected to touch off a general uprising, which the Communist militia would have had more trouble putting down without the charismatic Castro to lead them.

After the first attempt failed, five more assassination teams were sent to Cuba. The last team reportedly made it to a rooftop within shooting distance of Castro before members were apprehended. This happened around the last of February or first of March, 1963.

Nine months later, President Kennedy was gunned down in Dallas by Lee Harvey Oswald, a fanatic who previously had agitated for Castro in New Orleans and had made a mysterious trip to the Cuban Embassy in Mexico City.

Among those privy to the CIA conspiracy, there is still a nagging suspicion—unsupported by the Warren Commission's findings—that Castro became aware of the U.S. plot upon his life and somehow recruited Oswald to retaliate against President Kennedy.

To set up the Castro assassination, the CIA enlisted Robert Maheu, a former FBI agent with shadowy contacts, who had handled other undercover assignments for the CIA out of his Washington public relations office. He later moved to Las Vegas to head up billionaire Howard Hughes's Nevada operations.

Maheu recruited John Roselli, a ruggedly handsome gambler with contacts in both the American and Cuban underworlds, to arrange the assassination. The dapper, hawk-faced Roselli, formerly married to movie actress June Lang, was a power in the movie industry until his conviction with racketeer Willie Bioff in a million-dollar Hollywood labor shakedown.

The CIA assigned two of its most trusted operatives, William Harvey and James "Big Jim" O'Connell, to the hush-hush murder mission. Using phony names, they accompanied Roselli on trips to Miami to line up the assassination teams.

The full story reads like the script of a James Bond movie, complete with secret trysts at glittering Miami Beach hotels and midnight powerboat dashes to secret landing spots on the Cuban coast. Once, Roselli's boat was shot out from under him.

For the first try, the CIA furnished Roselli with special poison capsules to slip into Castro's food. The poison was supposed to take three days to act. By the time Castro died, his system would throw off all traces of the poison, so he would appear to be the victim of a natural if mysterious ailment.

Roselli arranged with a Cuban, related to one of Castro's chefs, to plant the deadly pellets in the dictator's food. On March 13, 1961, Roselli delivered the capsules to his contact at Miami Beach's glamorous Fontainebleau Hotel.

A couple weeks later, just about the right time for the plot to have been carried out, a report out of Havana said Castro was ill. But he recovered before the Bay of Pigs invasion on April 17, 1961.

The Cuban who had sneaked the poison into Havana was never seen again. The CIA, unsure whether the plotters had failed or the poison simply hadn't been strong enough, decided to try again with a more powerful dose. Roselli arranged for triple-strength capsules to be slipped into Castro's food several weeks after the Bay of Pigs. But once again, the plot failed and the conspirators disappeared.

Four more attempts were made on Castro's life, using Cuban assassination teams equipped with high-powered rifles, explosives and two-way radios. At intervals in the dark of night, Roselli personally delivered the teams in twin powerboats to the Cuban shores. . . .

The principals in the CIA conspiracy, sworn to deep secrecy, refused to comment on the caper. We got an admission out of Maheu only that he had handled special jobs for the CIA, but he refused to discuss them. Roselli responded with a flat "no comment."

My associate Les Whitten located Harvey, who left the CIA about two years ago, in Indianapolis. Asked about Roselli, Harvey said he had a high regard for him. . . .

We got an admission from "Big Jim" O'Connell, who is still with the CIA, that he had met Roselli through Maheu. But when we asked about Roselli's CIA mission, O'Connell also clammed up.

Finally we spoke to John McCone, who headed the CIA at the time of the assassination attempts. He acknowledged the idea had been discussed inside the CIA but insisted it had been "rejected immediately." He vigorously denied that the CIA had ever participated in any plot on Castro's life. Asked whether the attempts could have been made without his knowledge, he replied: "It could not have happened."

We have complete confidence, however, in our sources.

WERE TRUJILLO, DIEM, CIA TARGETS TOO?

WASHINGTON — The plot to kill Cuban dictator Fidel Castro, hidden for 10 years from the public, raises some ugly questions that high officials would rather keep buried deep inside the Central Intelligence Agency.

1—Has the CIA tried to assassinate any other leaders? John McCone, who headed the CIA during the six attempts to knock off Castro, denied emphatically that the CIA has tried to kill anyone. But ex-Senator George Smathers, one of John F. Kennedy's closest friends, told us the late President suspected that the CIA had arranged the shootings of the Dominican Republic's Rafael Trujillo in 1961 and South Vietnam's Ngo Dinh Diem in 1963.

[2—Did President Kennedy personally sanction the plot against Castro? The preparations to assassinate the Cuban dictator began during the last months of the Eisenhower administration as part of the Bay of Pigs scheme. All six attempts, however, were made during 1961–63 when Kennedy occupied the White House. Smathers told us he once spoke to the late President about assassinating Castro. Kennedy merely rolled back his eyes, recalled Smathers, as if to indicate the idea was too wild to discuss. Subsequently, Kennedy told Smathers of his suspicion that the CIA may have been behind the Trujillo and Diem assassinations.

3—Did the late Robert Kennedy know about the assassination attempts? After the Bay of Pigs fiasco, President Kennedy swore to friends he would like "to splinter the CIA in a thousand pieces and scatter it to the winds." He put his brother Robert in charge of the CIA with instructions to shake it up. The CIA made five attempts on Castro's life after the Bay of Pigs while Robert Kennedy was riding herd on the agency.

4—Could the plot against Castro have backfired against President Kennedy? The late President was murdered nine months after the last assassination team was caught on a Havana rooftop with high-powered rifles. Presumably, they were subjected to fiendish tortures until they told all they knew. None of the assassination teams, however, had direct knowledge of the CIA involvement. The CIA instigators had represented themselves as oilmen seeking revenge against Castro for his seizure of oil holdings.]*

The last surviving brother, Senator Ted Kennedy, could give us no insight. His brothers had never spoken to him about any assassination attempts against Castro, he said. He was aware, he volunteered, only that Senator Smathers had talked to the late President about eliminating Castro.

Smathers told us that President Kennedy seemed "horrified" at the idea of political assassinations. "I remember him saying,"

---

* These bracketed paragraphs were edited out of the newspaper reproduced as an Ervin Committee exhibit.—Eds.

recalled Smathers, "that the CIA frequently did things he didn't know about, and he was unhappy about it. He complained that the CIA was almost autonomous.

"He told me he believed the CIA had arranged to have Diem and Trujillo bumped off. He was pretty well shocked about that. He thought it was a stupid thing to do, and he wanted to get control of what the CIA was doing."

But McCone, disagreeing vigorously, told us that "no plot was authorized or implemented" to assassinate Castro, Trujillo, Diem or anyone else.

"During those days of tension, there was a wide spectrum of plans ranging from one extreme to another," McCone admitted. "Whenever this subject (assassinating Castro) was brought up— and it was—it was rejected immediately on two grounds. First, it would not be condoned by anybody. Second, it wouldn't have achieved anything."

There was also talk in high places, McCone acknowledged, of supporting a coup to oust Diem. The former CIA director said he had argued against this at a secret session with both Kennedy brothers. He had contended that there was no one strong enough to take Diem's place and that a coup, therefore, would bring "political upheaval."

"I told the President and Bobby together," recalled McCone, "that if I were running a baseball team and had only one pitcher, I wouldn't take him out of the game."

The November, 1963, coup caught the U.S. completely by surprise, he said. While the plotters were moving on the palace, he said, then-Ambassador Henry Cabot Lodge was visiting Diem. Admiral Ulysses Sharp, then our Pacific commander, had also been present, but had left early to go to the airport.

McCone said President Diem escaped through a tunnel but was caught in nearby Cholon and "shot in a station wagon."

OSWALD AND CASTRO
E. Howard Hunt

Give Us This Day / *1973*

In the morning I flew back to Tampa and took a connecting flight to Washington where I prepared a report of my impressions. When it came to recommendations related to the project, I listed four:

1. Assassinate Castro *before* or coincident with the invasion (a task for Cuban patriots);

2. Destroy the Cuban radio and television transmitters before or coincident with the invasion;

3. Destroy the island's microwave relay system just before the invasion begins;

4. Discard any thought of a popular uprising against Castro until the issue has already been militarily decided.

My arguments were based on my belief that without Castro to inspire them the Rebel Army and *milicia* would collapse in leaderless confusion. Without radio and television to inform the country, Castro's heirs would be unable to rally mass support, and lacking east-west communications, Raúl Castro, as Minister of Defense, would not be able to order his troops to the attack.

Barnes and Bissell read my report, pondered the recommendations and said that it would weigh in the final planning. (As the months wore on I was to ask Barnes repeatedly about action on my principal recommendation only to be told it was "in the hands of a special group." So far as I have been able to determine no coherent plan was ever developed within CIA to assassinate Castro, though it was the heart's desire of many exile groups.) . . .

Time has eroded American awareness of what the exile expedition was supposed to accomplish, and the responsibility for its failure has been buried under tons of newsprint, books, and magazines. The cumulative theme of this folklore was that President John F. Kennedy, misled by CIA, State, and Defense advisers, gave qualified authorization to the Bay of Pigs landing; and that when the ill-conceived expedition seemed on the point of failure, he judiciously refused to increase the stakes lest he plunge the world into World War III.

The death of Jack Ruby and worldwide controversy over William Manchester's book for a time focused public attention on events surrounding the assassination of John Fitzgerald Kennedy. Once again it became fashionable to hold the city of Dallas collectively responsible for his murder. Still, and let this not be forgotten, Lee Harvey Oswald was a partisan of Fidel Castro, and an admitted Marxist who made desperate efforts to join the Red Revolution in Havana. In the end he was an activist for the Fair Play for Cuba Committee.

But for Castro and the Bay of Pigs disaster there would have been no such "committee." And perhaps no assassin named Lee Harvey Oswald....

CUBA ON OUR MIND
Tad Szulc

Esquire / *February 1974*

In November, 1961, seven months after the fiasco of the Bay of Pigs invasion of Cuba, President John F. Kennedy invited me to the Oval Office at the White House for a private conversation about future United States policies toward Premier Fidel Castro.

"Cuba on Our Mind" by Tad Szulc. Reprinted from *Esquire*, February 1974. Copyright © 1974 by Tad Szulc. Reprinted by permission of the author and his agent, Brandt & Brandt.

I had covered the April invasion from Miami as a correspondent for the New York *Times* and I had been highly critical in print of the whole enterprise. Now, the President said, he would welcome some constructive ideas. We chatted for a while about Cuba, then Kennedy leaned forward in his rocking chair and hurled a question at me:

"What would you think if I ordered Castro to be assassinated?"

I believe this is a virtually verbatim quotation of his words (one doesn't make notes at a private meeting with the President) and I remember being completely taken aback. I also recall blurting out a long sentence to the effect that I was against political assassination as a matter of principle and that, anyway, I doubted this would solve the Cuban problem for the U.S.

Kennedy leaned back in his chair, smiled, and said that he had been testing me because he was under great pressure from advisers in the Intelligence community (whom he did not name) to have Castro killed, but that he himself violently opposed it on the grounds that for moral reasons the United States should never be party to political assassinations. "I'm glad you feel the same way," he said.

This is the first time I am publicly recounting this conversation (the only other person present in the Oval Office was Richard N. Goodwin, then a Presidential assistant) because it stands out in my mind as an extraordinary example of the obsessive frustration and involvements with Cuba and Cubans that for well over a decade have permeated the United States government on the most senior levels. Nothing quite comparable has ever occurred between Americans and any other nation, near or far. The powerful United States and the little island ninety miles from home in the blue Caribbean have never been able to let go of each other. They have been set together as if in a Greek tragedy in which doom always seems impending.

To be sure, Kennedy vetoed the Castro assassination idea in 1961 after having taken full responsibility in April for the Bay of Pigs invasion. I cannot say to what extent he knew, that November, about a scheme elaborated by Military Intelligence officers soon after the Bay of Pigs (and of which I was vaguely aware at the time) to kill Castro and his brother Raúl, the

Deputy Premier and Defense Minister, using Cuban marksmen who were to be infiltrated into Cuba from the United States Naval base at Guantanamo on the island's southeastern coast. Perhaps this is what he had in mind when he talked to me.

Hearing Kennedy's rejection of assassination plots proposed to him by the Washington Intelligence community, I naturally assumed that no such thing would ever happen. In fact the Eisenhower Administration turned down in 1960 the recommendation of a C.I.A. operative to kill Castro.

But as I was to learn much later, the Central Intelligence Agency, presumably acting with President Lyndon Johnson's authority (unless it was another do-it-yourself undertaking), set in motion in late 1964 and 1965 a new secret plan to combine Castro's assassination with a second invasion of the island by Cuban exiles from bases located this time in Costa Rica and Nicaragua. Some infiltrators were to be trained in the Dominican Republic. (Guatemala had been the site of training in 1960 and 1961.)

The new invasion was to be on a smaller scale than the Bay of Pigs. The scenario was to bring ashore some 750 armed Cubans at the crucial moment when Castro would be dead and inevitable chaos had developed. It was an incredibly wild scheme because the resolution of the 1962 Cuban missile crisis, which brought the U.S. and the Soviet Union to the brink of nuclear confrontation, was based in part on Washington's commitment to let Castro be.

The existence of the assassination plot, hatched by the C.I.A. in Paris and Madrid, was disclosed by the Cuban government in March, 1966, after the designated gunman—a bearded Cuban physician and former Cuban Revolutionary Army major named Rolando Cubela—was arrested in Havana following investigations by Castro's counterintelligence agents, who had become suspicious of him.

Actually, the whole assassination-invasion plan had to be canceled when a rebellion unexpectedly erupted in the Dominican Republic in April, 1965, and President Johnson, fearful of "another Cuba," sent U.S. troops to invade that country. The Cuban scheme could not be pursued, and Cubela and his associates were left high and dry in Havana to be finally captured in

February, 1966, along with a small arsenal of weapons, including an FAL automatic rifle equipped with telescopic sights and a silencer provided by the C.I.A. for Castro's planned assassination. Cubela was sentenced to death, but Castro commuted the sentence to a lengthy prison term.

Cuban revelations in 1966 about the Cubela plot had little international impact at the time. But, to the best of my knowledge, the plans for the simultaneous second invasion—known by the code name of "Second Naval Guerrilla"—have never been publicly revealed. I doubt that even Castro had learned much about them inasmuch as Cubela's knowledge was apparently confined only to his end of the broader plan.

The Central American camps were disbanded late in May, 1965, when the Dominican crisis convinced Washington that this was not a propitious time for a new Cuban adventure. Besides, we were already deeply involved in Vietnam. The blueprints for the "Second Naval Guerrilla" were probably quietly filed away in the archives of the C.I.A.'s clandestine-operations division. My information, based on recent interviews with men who participated in this project, is that during a period of about six months in 1964 and 1965, the C.I.A. disbursed $750,000 monthly for the operation and that some $2,000,000 in these funds remains unaccounted for. Subsequently, there were mysterious shoot-outs and deaths among Miami Cubans involved in the stillborn invasion.

Also in 1964, idle Cuban pilots, veterans of the Bay of Pigs, were sent to the Congo by the C.I.A. as mercenaries to fly B-26 bombers on combat missions for the U.S.-backed Congolese government then fighting a leftist rebellion. The Cubans, under contract to CARAMAR (a C.I.A. dummy corporation whose initials stood for Caribbean Marine Aero Corporation), complained at the time that they were ordered to strafe and bomb villages and civilians. Nowadays, some of these pilots are in serious trouble with the law in Florida. One of them is serving an eleven-year prison sentence in Miami for traffic in cocaine and others are said to have acquired nasty criminal records. Another one has been recently charged with a killing in Miami.

And, of course, the whole tortured story has continued. We find that the same cast of characters, ranging from gung-ho

Florida C.I.A. operatives to gullible or corruptible Miami Cubans and Cuban-Americans, reappeared on the scene in 1971 and 1972 as key personages in the Watergate affair. They were picked from the pool of naïvely patriotic, restless and unstable Cubans who are the heritage left by the C.I.A. in Miami.

In almost every case there was the irrepressible presence of the C.I.A. veteran E. Howard Hunt Jr., the political coordinator of the Bay of Pigs under the *nom de guerre* of "Eduardo" and the man who first recommended Castro's murder in 1960 and then helped to plan the 1965 assassination; James W. McCord Jr., associated with the 1961 invasion, the second landing operation, and the use of Cuban pilots in the Congo; and Bernard L. Barker (code name: "Macho"), who was Hunt's aide in 1961, and his teams of Cuban exiles first recruited for combat on Cuba's beaches and later for dirty work in the Watergate scandals. Eugenio Martinez, one of the Watergate raiders, was still on a C.I.A. retainer when the break-in occurred. Barker and his Miami commandos claimed Hunt had assured them that subversion against the Nixon Administration's opponents and the President's reelection would hasten the "liberation" of Cuba from Castro's rule. . . .

BREMER, WALLACE AND HUNT
Gore Vidal

The New York Review of Books / *December 13, 1973*

Now for the shooting of George Wallace. It is not unnatural to suspect the White House burglars of having a hand in the shooting. But suspicion is not evidence and there is no evidence that H. H. [Howard Hunt] was involved. Besides, a good CIA man

Excerpted from "The Art and Arts of E. Howard Hunt." Reprinted from *The New York Review of Books*, December 13, 1973, by permission of the author.

would no doubt have preferred the poison capsule to a gunshot—slipping ole George the sort of slow but lethal dose that Castro's powerful gut rejected. In an AP story this summer,[1] former CIA official Miles Copeland is reported to have said that "senior agency officials are convinced Senator Edmund Muskie's damaging breakdown during the presidential campaign last year was caused by convicted Watergate conspirator E. Howard Hunt or his henchman spiking his drink with a sophisticated form of LSD."

When Wallace ran for president in 1968, he got 13 percent of the vote; and Nixon nearly lost to Humphrey. In May, 1972, 17 percent favored Wallace for president in the Harris Poll. Wallace had walked off with the Michigan Democratic primary. Were he to continue his campaign for president as an independent or as a Democrat in states where he was not filed under his own party, he could have swung the election to the Democrats, or at least denied Nixon a majority and sent the election to the House.

"This entire strategy of ours," Robert Finch said in March, 1972, "depends on whether George Wallace makes a run on his own." For four years Nixon had done everything possible to keep Wallace from running; and failed. "With Wallace apparently stronger in the primaries in 1972 than he had been before," Theodore White observed, "with the needle sticking at 43 percent of the vote for Nixon, the President was still vulnerable—until, of course, May 15 and the shooting. Then it was all over."[2]

Wallace was shot by the now familiar lone assassin—a demented (as usual) busboy named Arthur Bremer. Then on June 21, 1973, the headline in the *New York Post* was "Hunt Tells of Orders to Raid Bremer's Flat."

According to the story by Bob Woodward and Carl Bernstein, H. H. told the Senate investigators that an hour after Wallace was shot, Colson ordered him to fly to Milwaukee and burglarize the flat of Arthur H. Bremer, the would-be assassin—in order to connect Bremer somehow with the commies? Characteristically, the television senators let that one slip by them. As one might expect, Colson denied ordering H. H. to Milwaukee for any pur-

[1] AP Dispatch, London, August 17, 1973.
[2] *The Making of the President, 1972* (Atheneum, 1973), p. 238.

pose. Colson did say that he had talked to H. H. about the shooting. Colson also said that he had been having dinner with the President that evening. Woodward's and Bernstein's "White House source" said, "The President became deeply upset and voiced concern that the attempt on Wallace's life might have been made by someone with ties to the Republican Party or the Nixon campaign." This, Nixon intuited, might cost him the election.[3]

May 15, 1972. Arthur H. Bremer shot George Wallace, governor of Alabama, at Laurel, Maryland, and was easily identified as the gunman and taken into custody. Nearby in a rented car, the police found Bremer's diary (odd that in the post-Gutenberg age Oswald, Sirhan, and Bremer should have all committed to paper their *pensées*).

According to the diary, Bremer had tried to kill Nixon in Canada but failed to get close enough. He then decided to kill George Wallace. The absence of any logical motive is now familiar to most Americans, who are quite at home with the batty killer who acts alone in order to be on television, to be forever entwined with the golden legend of the hero he has gunned down. In a nation that worships psychopaths, the Oswald-Bremer-Sirhan-Ray figure is to the general illness what Robin Hood was to a greener, saner world.

Bremer's diary is a fascinating work of art. From what we know of the twenty-two-year-old author he did not have a literary turn of mind (among his effects were comic books, some porno). He was a television baby, and a dull one. Politics had no interest for him. Yet suddenly for reasons he never gives us—he decides to kill the President and starts to keep a diary on April 4, 1972.

According to Mr. Szulc, in March, 1972, H. H. visited Dita ("call me Mother") Beard in Denver. Wearing a red wig and a voice modulator, H. H. persuaded Dita to denounce as a forgery the memo she had written linking ITT's pay-off to the Republican party with the government's subsequent dropping of the

[3] *New York Post*, June 21, 1973, reprinting a *Washington Post* story.

best part of its antitrust suit against the conglomerate. In May, H. H. was installing the first set of bugs at the Democratic head-quarters. His movements between April 4 and May 15 might be usefully examined—not to mention those of G. Gordon Liddy, et al.

For someone who is supposed to be nearly illiterate there are startling literary references and flourishes in the Bremer diary. The second entry contains "You heard of *'One Day in the Life of Ivan Dynisovich'*? Yesterday was my day." The misspelling of Denisovich is not bad at all. Considering the fact that the name is a hard one for English-speaking people to get straight, it is something of a miracle that Bremer could sound the four sylla-bles of the name correctly in his head. Perhaps he had the book in front of him but if he had, he would not have got the one letter wrong.

The same entry produces more mysteries. "Wallace got his big votes from Republicans who didn't have any choice of candi-dates on their own ballot. Had only about $1055 when I left." This is the first and only mention of politics until page 45 when he describes his square clothes and haircut as "just a disguise to get close to Nixon."

One reference to Wallace at the beginning; then another one to Nixon a dozen pages later. Also, where did the $1,055 come from? Finally, a minor psychological point—Bremer refers to some weeds as "taller than me 5'6"." I doubt if a neurotic twenty-two-year-old would want to remind himself on the page that he is only 5'6" tall. When people talk to themselves they seldom say anything so obvious. On the other hand, authors like this sort of detail.

Popular paperback fiction requires a fuck scene no later than a dozen pages into the narrative. The author of the diary gives us a good one. Bremer goes to a massage parlor in New York (he has told the diary that he is a virgin—would he? Perhaps) where he is given an unsatisfying hand-job. The scene is nicely done and the author writes correctly and lucidly until, suddenly, a block occurs and he can't spell anything right—as if the author suddenly remembers that he is meant to be illiterate.

One of these blocks occurs toward the end of the massage scene when the girl tells Bremer that she likes to go to "wo-gees."

This is too cute to be believed. Every red-blooded American boy, virgin or not, knows the word "orgy." Furthermore, Bremer has been wandering around porno bookstores on 42nd Street and the word "orgy" occurs almost as often in his favored texts as "turgid." More to the point, when an illiterate is forced to guess at the spelling of a word he will render it phonetically. I cannot imagine that the girl said anything that sounded like "wo-gee." It is as if the author had suddenly recalled the eponymous hard-hat hero of the film *Joe* (1970) where all the hippies got shot so satisfyingly and the "g" in orgy was pronounced hard. On this page, as though to emphasize Bremer's illiteracy, we get "spair" for "spare," "enphasis" for "emphasis," and "rememmber." Yet on the same page the diarist has no trouble spelling "anticipation," "response," "advances."

The author of the diary gives us a good many random little facts—seat numbers of airplanes, prices of meals. He does not like "hairy hippies." A dislike he shares with H. H. He also strikes oddly jarring literary notes. On his arrival in New York, he tells us that he forgot his guns which the captain then turned over to him, causing the diarist to remark "Irony abounds." A phrase one doubts that the actual Arthur Bremer would have used. As word and quality, irony is not part of America's demotic speech or style. Later, crossing the Great Lakes, he declares "Call me Ismal." Had he read *Moby Dick*? Unlikely. Had he seen the movie on the Late Show? Possibly. But I doubt that the phrase on the sound track would have stayed in his head.

The diary tells us how Bremer tried to kill Nixon. The spelling gets worse and worse as Bremer becomes "thruorly pissed off." Yet suddenly he writes, "This will be one of the most closely read pages since the Scrolls in those caves." A late April entry records, "Had bad pain in my left temple & just in front & about it." He is now going mad as all the lone killers do, and refers to "writting a *War & Peace*."

More sinister: "saw 'Clockwork Orange' and thought about getting Wallace all thru the picture—fantasing my self as the Alek on the screen. . . ." This is a low blow at highbrow sex'n'violence books and flicks. It is also—again—avant-garde. Only recently has a debate begun in England whether or not the film *Clock-*

work Orange may have caused unbalanced youths to commit crimes (clever youths now tell the Court with tears in their eyes that it was the movie that made them bash the nice old man and the Court is thrilled). The author anticipated that ploy all right —and no matter who wrote the diary we are dealing with a true author. One who writes, "Like a novelist who knows not how his book will end—I have written this journal—what a shocking surprise that my inner character shall steal the climax and destroy the author and save the anti-hero from assasination!" Only one misspelling in that purple patch. But "as I said before, I Am A Hamlet." It is not irony that abounds so much in these pages as literature.

May 8, Bremer is reading *"R.F.K. Must Die!"* by Robert Blair Kaiser. Like his predecessor he wants to be noticed and then die because "suicide is a birth right." But Wallace did not die and Bremer did not die. He is now at a prison in Baltimore, awaiting a second trial. If he lives to be re-examined, one wonders if he will tell us what company he kept during the spring of 1972, and whether or not a nice man helped him to write his diary, as a document for the ages like the scrolls in those caves. (Although H. H. is a self-admitted forger of state papers I do not think that he actually had a hand in writing Bremer's diary on the ground that the journal is a brilliant if flawed job of work, and beyond H. H.'s known literary competence.)

Lack of originality has marked the current Administration's general style (as opposed to the vivid originality of its substance; witness, the first magistrate's relentless attempts to subvert the Constitution). Whatever PR has worked in the past is tried again. Goof? Then take the blame yourself—just like JFK after the Bay of Pigs. Caught with your hand in the till? Checkers time on the tube and the pulling of heart strings.

Want to assassinate a rival? Then how about the Dallas scenario? One slips into a reverie. Why not set up Bremer as a crazy who wants to shoot Nixon (that will avert suspicion)? But have him fail to kill Nixon just as Oswald was said to have failed to kill *his* first target General Walker. In midstream have Bremer —like Oswald—shift to a different quarry. To the real quarry. Make Bremer, unlike Oswald, apolitical. Too heavy an identifi-

cation with the Democrats might backfire. Then oh, genius!—
let's help him to write a diary to get the story across. (Inciden-
tally, the creation of phony documents and memoirs is a major
industry of our secret police forces. When the one-man terror of
the Southeast Asian seas Lieutenant Commander Marcus Aure-
lius Arnheiter was relieved of his command, the Pentagon put
him to work writing the "memoirs" of a fictitious Soviet subma-
rine commander who had defected to the Free World.)[4]

The White House's reaction to the Watergate burglary was
the first clue that something terrible has gone wrong with us.
The elaborate and disastrous cover-up was out of all proportion
to what was, in effect, a small crime the Administration could
have lived with. I suspect that our rulers' state of panic came
from the fear that other horrors would come to light—as indeed
they have. But have the horrors ceased? Is there something that
our rulers know that we don't? Is it possible that during the dark
night of our empire's defeat in Cuba and Asia the American story
shifted from cheerful familiar farce to Jacobean tragedy—to murder, chaos?

[4] See *The Arnheiter Affair* by Neil Sheehan (Random House, 1971).

THE CURIOUS INTRIGUES
OF CUBAN MIAMI
Horace Sutton

Saturday Review/World / *September 11, 1973*

The very circumstances that drove the Miami Cubans to emi-
grate welded them into a fierce anti-Communist force, eager to
perform any service, go to any length, undertake any mission

that would strike a blow against international communism. A Cuban émigré, now an American citizen and vice-president of a local bank, calls Dade County "the number-one stronghold of radical anti-communism in the United States today."

The abortive invasion that ended in the disaster at the Bay of Pigs turned the new arrivals away from the Democratic party of President Kennedy, who had denied them air cover, and into the arms of the Republicans. Although the Bay of Pigs invasion was hatched during the Eisenhower regime, promoted strongly by Richard M. Nixon even after his defeat in 1960, it was Kennedy, the inheritor of the adventure, who drew the enmity of the Cuban exiles. However simplistic the equation, the hatred smolders to this day.

The specter of a Democratic White House inhabited by Humphrey, Muskie, Jackson, or, worst of all, McGovern, any of whom might have moved toward easing the tension between Havana and Washington, loomed ominously before the 1972 elections; and the Miami Cubans were eager to help in any way to keep the Democrats out of power.

After the Pentagon papers were published, President Nixon created a Special Investigations Unit "to stop security leaks and investigate other sensitive security matters." As John Ehrlichman was later to testify before the Ervin committee, the White House felt the FBI was not properly motivated to do its job. Charles Colson, then a White House special counsel, brought in Everette Howard Hunt, Jr., whom he had met at a Brown University party. A prolific author, Hunt had written forty-six books, many of them based on his two decades with CIA in Europe and Latin America.

In the years immediately following the Castro takeover in Cuba, and for some time to follow, the Cuban colony was heavily influenced by the CIA. A prime conduit between the Cubans and The Agency was E. Howard Hunt. A Cuban who in those days was responsible for recruiting some of the leaders of the expeditionary force recalls now that "Eduardo," as Hunt was called, "was well known and very popular. He was the link with the powerful force that represented possible victory over Castro. When Eduardo called somebody, it was important, and it was reliable."

Colson says he submitted Hunt's name to Ehrlichman, and Ehrlichman hired him. Ehrlichman places the blame for Hunt on Colson. No matter who was responsible for his employment, Hunt, once hired, asked Colson if he could reestablish some of his old connections at The Agency. Colson called Ehrlichman, who then allegedly called Gen. Robert E. Cushman, Jr., at the time deputy director of the CIA, to introduce Hunt. Cushman recalls the conversation, but Ehrlichman has no recollection of the call. Whichever, Hunt embarked on a year of cloak-and-dagger services shadowing Senator Kennedy, altering President Kennedy's classified cables concerning the Diem overthrow in Vietnam, placing taps on phones of those suspected of leaking information to the newspapers, and, finally, organizing the break-in at the office of Dr. Lewis J. Fielding, the Beverly Hills psychiatrist who was then treating Dr. Daniel Ellsberg.

Hunt was chosen for this task because it was important that no one with a clear White House connection be associated with the mission. To form a team, Hunt turned first to Bernard Barker, who had been first assistant in the Bay of Pigs. Barker functioned as the financial funnel from the CIA to the Miami Cubans.

The Agency, or "The Company," as the CIA was called in the Cuban colony, supplied the funds, the training, and the psychological motivation to bind the Cuban exiles into a strike force. Although there was no open sponsorship following the Cuban missile crisis in 1962, the hard-line anticommunism of the Cubans was considered a useful tactical asset, and there was American support for it, however modified, until 1969. Even now there are some intellectual Cubans who aver that The Agency is keeping the lid on further activism. The result has been frustration in the Cuban community, and it mounted with the appearance of George McGovern and his statement that he might seek a negotiated settlement with Castro. Reinaldo Pico, a Cuban who demonstrated at J. Edgar Hoover's funeral, was to tell *The Miami Herald*'s Roberto Fabricio, "Barker was our contact for CIA work for Cuba—and every time I would see him on the street I would ask if something was working, and for a few years he would just say no. Suddenly, last year, he said that Eduardo was in touch, and that at last we could work for Cuba."

Barker was born in Havana in 1917 of an American father and a Cuban mother. His grandfather, a Tennessee potato farmer, had gone to Cuba with Teddy Roosevelt's Rough Riders and had stayed there after the war.

A U.S. veteran of World War II, Barker returned to Cuba and worked in Batista's secret police, with, he has said, "the consent and cooperation of the FBI." After Castro, he moved to Miami, worked in a store, managed a fighter, ultimately studied for a real estate license, and opened his own real estate office. Among his associates were Miguel A. Suarez, a prominent lawyer who headed Senator Gurney's election committee three years ago, and Guillermo Alonso Pujol y Bermudez, son of a former vice-president of Cuba in the regime of Carlos Prio. Guillermo's father, Alonso Pujol, a wealthy expatriate, lives now in Caracas. His other son, Jorge Alonso Pujol y Bermudez, a veteran of the Bay of Pigs who had been ransomed from Castro for $100,000 by his father, was caught in a narcotics sweep in Miami three years ago. Arrested with Alonso was Juan Restoy, a member of the Cuban legislature under Batista. Restoy escaped from jail with Mario Escandar, who had a long history of drug arrests. Escandar gave himself up, drew twelve years, a sentence that was later thrown out because authorization for the wire intercept that had to be signed personally by Attorney General John Mitchell, was actually signed, in Mitchell's absence, by his designee. Juan Restoy, who had a reputation as a smuggler in Cuba, was killed in a shoot-out with federal narcotics agents, two of whom he wounded. Alonso was convicted and sentenced to seven years, but he was later released and placed on probation. He was represented by Miguel Suarez.

While in Miami, for a Bay of Pigs reunion in the spring of 1971, Hunt looked up Barker; and the two of them, with their wives, held their own reunion at a Cuban restaurant. That summer Hunt flew to Miami and looked up Barker again. This time he asked Barker to join him in a "national security organization," which, Hunt said, "was above both the CIA and the FBI." Barker was to say later that he was impressed by Hunt's White House position, which might one day prove important in the ultimate liberation of Cuba. He signed on with Hunt and brought in two Cuban members of his real estate firm, Eugenio Martinez and Felipe DeDiego, both confirmed Castro fighters. According to Barker, Martinez had participated in 300 "infiltrations" into Cuba, while DeDiego took part in a raid inside Cuba to capture some Castro documents. It was later to be revealed that Martinez had been on the CIA payroll at $100 a month to screen newly arrived Cuban émigrés for information that might prove useful to Washington. According to Ambassador Richard Helms, former director of The Agency, Barker, Hunt, McCord, and Sturgis all had CIA connections, and it might have been that Mrs. Hunt was so connected, too.

With these credentials in the murky arts, Barker, Martinez, and DeDiego flew from Miami to Los Angeles early in September 1971 and broke into Dr. Fielding's office. Barker says they found nothing on Ellsberg, but DeDiego testified that he had held the Ellsberg file while Martinez made pictures. Hunt, meanwhile, kept a surveillance at Dr. Fielding's house to ensure that the psychiatrist would not make a midnight visit to his office and interrupt his agents.

The Cuban team returned to Miami, and Hunt went to Washington, where he kept in active touch with Barker, using a secret phone in the Special Investigations Unit located in Room 16 in the basement of the Executive Office Building adjacent to the White House. This was the office of the so-called Plumbers. Bills for the calls were sent to the home of a twenty-three-year-old secretary named Kathy Chenow, who took them to an Ehrlichman aide for approval.

The Miami-Cuban connection developed by Hunt proved useful. Money raised in Texas (some of it already laundered in Mexico) and in Minnesota came in to former Secretary of Commerce Maurice Stans, who gave it to Gordon Liddy for further laundering. Five checks, totaling $114,000, were sent to Bernard Barker, who, over a three-week period, converted them to cash in Miami's Republic National Bank in Little Havana. The Nixon campaign fund got $111,500, $2500 having been extracted for expenses.

By now Hunt had moved over to work for the Committee to Re-Elect the President, and, soon, so did his Miami-Cuban connections. Shortly after the famed Key Biscayne strategy meeting in March 1972, at which, according to Jeb Stuart Magruder's testimony to the Watergate committee, John Mitchell, then attorney general, approved plans to maintain a surveillance on the Democrats, reservations for a suite of rooms were made in the Fontainebleau Hotel in Miami Beach, which was to be headquarters for the Democrats during their convention.

Peculiarly enough, the reservations, booked to coincide with the Democratic convention, were made by an executive at the Miami Beach First National Bank who said he needed them for a friend named Edward Hamilton. The head of Miami First National is Frank Smathers, Jr., the brother of former Sen. George Smathers, who first introduced Richard Nixon to Key Biscayne, sold him his house there, and is now his neighbor.

Edward Hamilton is an alias that was used by Frank Sturgis (as well as by Hunt). Sturgis, an American soldier of fortune who also goes under the name of Frank Fiorini, has been active on both sides of the Cuban controversy. He joined Castro in the Sierra Maestra, flew missions for him, was captured and beaten by Batista's police and released. Two weeks later he was flying to Mexico with Castro's air force chief, Maj. Pedro Diaz Lanz, to buy arms that were to be smuggled to Castro forces still in the mountains. Later, he and Major Diaz defected, and Fiorini claimed he had really been working undercover against the Castro government the whole time. Nonetheless, he was stripped of his American citizenship. It was through Senator Smathers's efforts that Fiorini got his citizenship back. At that point he assumed the name of Frank Sturgis. In May 1961, one month after the disaster at the Bay of Pigs, Fiorini showed up on the cover of *Parade*, the Sunday magazine insert, heralding a story on him by Jack Anderson, of all people. Entitled "We Will Finish the Job," the account told of Fiorini's daring exploits harassing Castro by boat and plane.

Fiorini-Sturgis was to surface again in 1968 when he led a group called the Secret Army Organization on an aborted thrust at Cuba. This time he left with an American task force from a Yucatán port to rendezvous with Cuban exiles sailing aboard another boat. The raid would have put forty men ashore in Cuba; but their craft came a cropper on coral reefs, and they ended up in jail in British Honduras. At the time Fiorini-Sturgis said that the Secret Army Organization was an anti-Communist movement that had bases in Mexico.

It was not the first time armed secret groups of Americans and Cubans, banded together for anti-Communist or anti-Castro adventures, had been captured. In August 1963 a heavy cache of arms, all ostensibly for use in an attack against Castro, was found hidden in a cottage on Lake Pontchartrain, Louisiana, that belonged to Mrs. William Julius McLaney. The accounts of the discovery in the New Orleans newspapers listed no arrests by the FBI. Mrs. McLaney, whose husband was described as the operator of a race-horse feed business, said that at the request of friends in Cuba she had lent the house to a newly arrived Cuban refugee. William McLaney's brother, Michael J. McLaney, described as having been in the tourist business in Cuba, actually had operated Havana casinos [. . .] during the Batista years. Even after Castro came out of the hills (and the casinos were under the aegis, for a short time, of Frank Fiorini), McLaney took over the tables in Havana's Nacional Hotel from the Cleveland Syndicate. (Later, McLaney was invited to leave the Bahamas, where he was endeavoring to work out an arrangement with Lynden Pindling's PLP. He is now operating the casino in Haiti.) [Meyer] Lansky is said to have had a $1 million price on Castro's head, and McLaney, remembering those cushy days in Cuba, is reported to have once said, "If it weren't for Castro, Caesars Palace [one of the largest hotels and casino operations in Las Vegas] would have been built in Havana."

The Lake Pontchartrain cache included more than a ton of dynamite, bomb casings, striker assemblies, primer cord, and blasting caps—enough to start a small war. The FBI announced no arrests to the newspapers, but in fact, eleven arrests were made, including a number of Cuban exiles and several Americans, among them Richard Lauchli, Jr., known as one of the founding fathers of the Minutemen.

Some, possibly far-out, theories, advanced by those at variance with the findings of the Warren report, have suggested that one or more of the allegedly anti-Castro build-ups in Central America after the Bay of Pigs were really a camouflage for the assassination attempt on President Kennedy. Kennedy's failure to provide air cover for the Bay of Pigs, his enforcement of the neutrality act, his alleged curtailment of the CIA, the liberal swing of his administration, all produced dissidents on the hard Right, many of them with means, many with the desire to encourage a force that would destroy him.

The CIA, the exiled Cubans, the radical Right, and the Mob had a mutual interest in getting Cuba back. Frequently their efforts were interwoven. As the clock ticked toward the 1972 political campaigns, the Miami Cubans were put on alert for new adventures. Hunt flew often to consult with Barker in Miami, telling him on one visit to commence training his men so they would be in top physical condition. In the interests of anticommunism and of a Republican victory, they were to be used as *agents provocateurs*, street ruffians, and burglars.

Eugenio Martinez, a veteran of the Ellsberg break-in, asked a onetime CIA operative named Pablo Fernandez to enlist the aid of ten young persons who could assume the role of hippies. They were to march on McGovern's headquarters during the Democratic convention, rioting and relieving themselves in public. Fernandez had to turn it down even though it paid a reputed $700 a week. The Cuban, who made $800 a month as a clerk, had already signed on with a special investigator of the Miami police department to foment an overt action at the convention by offering machine guns to the Vietnam Veterans Against the War, who were encamped nearby. "We were hoping for the overt act necessary to produce a charge of conspiracy," Maj. Adam Klimkowski of the City of Miami Police Department was later to say.

The Martinez idea, intended to embarrass McGovern, fell through, but other plans were to be carried out. As Barker and his force prepared to leave for Washington to begin a series of covert operations that was to end with Watergate, J. Edgar Hoover died in the capital.

To handle the demonstrations and counterdemonstrations that were to be staged by the political intelligence group, Barker drew on the services of Reinaldo Pico, Frank Sturgis (Fiorini), Eugenio Martinez, Felipe DeDiego, and an expert locksmith named Virgilio Gonzalez. Pablo Fernandez did accompany the band to help start fights at the Hoover funeral. At the Capitol the next night, in a protest meeting unrelated to the Hoover death, antiwar protesters, including Daniel Ellsberg, were intoning the names of the Vietnam dead. The demonstrators were set upon by the Cuban group; Pico and Sturgis pummeled the pacifists. Both men were arrested. After a quiet aside to the police by an unidentified onlooker, Pico and Sturgis were released.

It was to be a busy spring. Jack Anderson wrote a piece suggesting that Sturgis and Martinez may have been implicated in the May 13 break-in at the Chilean embassy. Late in May the Cuban team was to launch the first of three assaults on Democratic headquarters at the Watergate. The first was unsuccessful. During the second one they placed taps on some of the phones and took photographs of documents that later were to be developed in Rich's photo shop in Miami. Barker insisted he had been told by Hunt to search for documents that would indicate contributions to the Democrats from Castro Cuba or from leftist organizations.

On June 16 the assault team, pared down to Barker, Martinez, Sturgis, and Gonzalez, once more left Miami for Washington, this time to meet their Armageddon. The capture of the Watergate burglars in the capital that night, Sturgis-Fiorini included, created a flurry at the Fontainebleau in Miami Beach. The man from the Smathers bank arrived at the hotel and asked that the reservations that had been made in the name of Edward Hamilton, the Sturgis-Fiorini alias, be changed to the name of Edward Failor. When Mr. Failor arrived, he filed nightly intelligence reports to Clark McGregor, the Nixon campaign manager, and when he left, his bill was sent to the Committee to Re-Elect the President.

The capture of the Watergate burglars set off a chain of firecrackers in Miami. *The Miami Herald* ran a full-page story under an eight-column streamer headline that read, "Spy Thriller Spins Web to Miami." Among the tidbits gleaned was the news that the FBI had traced a portion of the $6300 seized from the Watergate burglars to the Republic National Bank of Miami. The arrested men had registered as employees of Ameritas, a Florida real estate company established a few years earlier by Miguel Suarez, an avid Nixon supporter, a onetime Gurney campaign manager in the Latin community, and a friend of Barker's since they both worked at a Cuban clinic some years ago. . . .

Actually, requests for reservations at the Watergate for the break-in team had been made on the Ameritas letterhead. Suarez holds that the stationery was used either by Barker or Barker's wife, but that one of the burglars "had interests in Ameritas."

Barker's daughter recalls knowing Sturgis since she was a child. When captured in Washington, Sturgis was found to be carrying a full set of fake identification papers, including a Mexican visa made out to Edward Hamilton, the name in which the Committee to Re-Elect the President originally had engaged rooms at the Fontainebleau. Jack Anderson arrived at the bail hearing and asked that Sturgis be released in his custody.

On June 18, one day after the break-in, Leo Zani, then press aide to Sen. Edward Gurney (later to be singled out by John Dean as "Nixon's only sure friend" on the Watergate committee), phoned *The Miami News* with a good story. The *News* was invited to have its reporter inspect the voting rolls in Dade County, where they would discover that the Watergate burglars had registered as Democrats. Zani suggested that in truth the burglars were double agents whose mission had really been to embarrass the Republicans. Martinez had registered as a Democrat in 1971 and Frank Sturgis in 1962. In any case Zani was to call up later in the day. He had been to the Committee to Re-Elect the President and had returned with the theory that the burglars were in the employ of Jack Anderson, who had been a constant gadfly to the administration. "We know that Sturgis is Anderson's tie with the Cuban committee. . . . Somebody finked. Everything is ready-made. Talk about double agents," the Gurney press aide said, "Martinez and Fiorini [Sturgis] were double agents. The others did not know they were being used. That is why they are not getting out of jail."

Ronald Ziegler, the President's own press aide, offered no theories, only disdain. He called it "a third-rate burglary." But if the principals were already cutting away from those who had been caught—as governments traditionally disown spies who have been captured—the Cubans among them were hailed as heroes by Miami's exiled community. Appearing on a William Buckley television show with E. Howard Hunt, Attorney Mario Lazo declared, "These men are heroes who believed they were fighting communism. We should give them a medal instead of throwing them in jail." A fourteen-man "Committee of Help" was formed by Miami Cubans, and five accounts were opened at the Bank of Miami. One was under the name of "The Miami Watergate Defendants' Fund," while the others were opened separately for Barker, Martinez, Gonzalez, and Sturgis. The fund totaled nearly $6000.

Besides Mario Lazo, the committee included Manuel F. Artime, who had been the leader of the Bay of Pigs. Artime has said that he owed his life to Barker, who had smuggled him out of Cuba with the help of the anti-Castro underground. Throughout 1960, during the CIA build-up for the Bay of Pigs, Artime and Hunt had an apartment together in Miami, and Artime is the godfather of one of Hunt's children. While denying prior knowledge of the Watergate break-in, Artime admitted he met Hunt in 1971, when Hunt told him he was working for the White House. At that time Hunt tried to enlist him, along with other Cubans, in an investigation of illicit drug movements in Panama. During one of Hunt's Miami visits, Artime also met G. Gordon Liddy. Frank Sturgis said, after his capture at the Watergate, that in 1971 he had joined Hunt in an investigation of the drug traffic that was entering the United States from Mexico, Paraguay, and Panama. (Some reports suggested that the Plumbers unit even had been involved in an assassination attempt on Brig. Gen. Omar Torrijos Herrera, the military ruler of Panama who has been hostile to the United States.)

The tie-in between this group and drug investigation, as far-fetched as it may appear on first look, becomes apparent when one looks back to the Plumbers, whose formation the President authorized a week after the Pentagon Papers were published. John Ehrlichman was assigned to supervise the unit, which, in the President's words, was "to stop security leaks and *to investigate other sensitive matters*," working on what was called "the heavy stuff." Ehrlichman gave the job to Egil Krogh, Jr., who set up shop in the basement of the Executive Office Building, to which, by the middle of August 1971, Hunt was reporting. The unit was augmented by G. Gordon Liddy, newly fired from the Treasury Department for fighting the gun-control position adopted by the administration. At Treasury, where he worked with Eugene Rossides, an assistant secretary, Liddy held a specific narcotics responsibility. He was charged with creating ideas and programs during the national narcotics crisis in 1970. Krogh, too, had been similarly occupied. As Ehrlichman's assistant in domestic affairs, Krogh had the responsibility of narcotics control, overseeing the work of such agencies as the Bureau of Narcotics and Dangerous Drugs, Customs, and other special-action groups. He was also active in the Cabinet committee for international narcotics control. Krogh knew Liddy at Treasury, and it is not inconceivable to consider that once in command of a freewheeling unit formed at presidential command, with Cubans enlisted for action work in the field, Krogh, with Liddy, might have entertained clandestine antidrug forays no matter whose territory they invaded.

While Artime was never recruited for any of this work, he was visited by Hunt's wife, Dorothy, later killed in a plane crash in Chicago, who assured him that the captured Cubans would not endure legal difficulties in Washington and that money would be delivered to the aid fund. After Mrs. Hunt's death, Artime visited Hunt in Washington and, according to some sources, was given $12,000 in cash. Later, Artime said, he found $9000 stuffed in envelopes and placed in his mailbox. He said the money was distributed to the families of the Cubans.

After the Bay of Pigs, Artime was the mastermind of a second operation for which arms and ammunition were bought in Europe. A few hundred men were recruited, and the expedition was mounted in Costa Rica and Nicaragua. Artime, who is in the export and import trade and deals in meat, is said to be involved with President Anastasio Somoza Debayle of Nicaragua. He was also one of the lessees in Centro Comercial Cubano, the shopping center that Charles "Bebe" Rebozo had built and for which he was able to obtain financing through the Small Business Administration.

An American born of Cuban parents, Rebozo had gotten a start as the operator of gas stations in Florida. When controls were placed on tires during World War II, Rebozo made his first real money by expanding into the tire-recapping business. By coincidence, one of the government officials working in the legal section of the tire-rationing part of OPA was Richard Nixon, then a young lawyer fresh from Duke University. It was a period of Nixon's career he never advertises in his official biographies.

Although some have tried to put Nixon in Florida in the Forties, the accepted meeting between Nixon and Rebozo is said to have occurred in 1951 when George Smathers, then Florida senator, suggested that Nixon, tired from a hard campaign, recuperate in the Florida sun. He put him in touch with Rebozo, who took him deep-sea fishing.

As the Cubans began to flow into Miami after Castro, Rebozo made connections with the community, joining a Cuban group known as El Centro, for which the shopping center was named, and agreeing to take a position as co-chairman of the city's inter-American committee. One of Rebozo's links to the Cuban community was Dr. Edgardo Buttari, former mayor of Havana, who, in 1968, headed the Cubans for Nixon. Rebozo brought Buttari into the Centro shopping center to organize the merchants, each of whom was eligible for a loan of up to $25,000 from the Office of Economic Opportunity.

To build the Centro, Rebozo and his partner, C. V. W. Trice, Jr., employed the Polizzi Construction Company, operated by "Big Al" . . . Polizzi, a Cleveland underworld figure [. . .] Polizzi told the Kefauver committee investigating crime in America in 1950 that he had retired from less savory ventures and was pursuing a straight career; but as late as 1964, according to an investigation by *Newsday*, the Federal Bureau of Narcotics continued to consider him one of the underworld.

Rebozo and Trice sold El Centro to a Canadian group a year later, making a $200,000 profit. Buttari was able to get his citizenship with dispatch and obtained a job with HEW in Miami that pays him $26,898 a year. However, even after the sale, Rebozo maintained an interest in a coin laundry for which space had been set aside in the center and which had not opened. One José Alonso had secured a lease from Buttari to operate this laundry and had obtained a $25,000 loan from OEO to run it. But in 1969 Congressman Wright Patman, the Democrat from Texas who was chairman of the House Committee on Banking and Currency, objected strenuously to the Rebozo loan from SBA for the Centro project, and at that time Alonso decided not to accept his OEO loan. It turned out that Alonso, a refugee from Castro's Cuba, was the manager of Wash Well, Inc., a chain of coin laundries owned by Rebozo. Indeed, Alonso was paying Rebozo rent for an apartment behind one of the Wash Well stores. Once Centro was sold, Alonso's title to the laundry disappeared, along with his request for the loan, and the place opened for customers with Rebozo as owner. "Mr. Rebozo decided he was going to own it," Alonso was later to say.

It was Rebozo, along with Smathers, who was instrumental in helping to form the presidential compound at Key Biscayne. Smathers had bought a ranch house there in 1967, leased it to Nixon during and following the 1968 campaign, and sold it to the President-elect in December of that year. The house next door has been Rebozo's residence for many years. However, Smathers's other neighbor had been Manuel Arca, Jr., a Cuban exile. Arca had lived in the house for ten years, his first permanent home since Castro took away his Cuban house and installed his brother, Raul, in it.

Stating that he was acting as Nixon's agent, Rebozo asked Arca to sell his Biscayne house in order to ensure presidential privacy. The house was sold at a loss to Arca, with Rebozo handling all the details. "The President of the United States wanted it. What else could I do?" Arca said. "Besides, it was an honor. I was very glad and happy to sell it to him," he added.

Through the years such Cuban accommodation had been a great aid to Nixon, who was friendly with the late Fulgencio Batista and with a number of other wealthy Cubans. Carlos Prio, the president of Cuba who was ousted by Batista, is a multimillionaire with interests in sugar and real estate in Puerto Rico. His home is in Miami, and he was an active pro-Nixon placard carrier during the Miami conventions. Another staunch supporter is Nicholas Arroyo, who became Batista's ambassador to Washington. When Castro assumed power, Arroyo, who had once maintained a successful architectural office with his wife, remained in Washington. His investments include sugar in Ecuador and Central America and real estate in Washington and Virginia. Some Cuban sources in Miami put his wealth at $10 million.

Much of the land on Key Biscayne, the island a few minutes from Miami where Rebozo first began to seed his own fortune and where Nixon has accrued profits from his own real estate investments, was developed early by the late José Manuel Aleman, who had been minister of education and, in the words of one informed Miami Cuban, "owned three or four other ministries," one of which was the national treasury.

A senator under Carlos Prio, Aleman spent most of his time in Miami. Before his death he built Miami Stadium, which he willed to his son, José Aleman, who is also represented by Miguel Suarez. The senior Aleman owned Cape Florida, which was to become the state park on the south end of Key Biscayne. Ironically, Cape Florida is such a popular retreat for hundreds of Cuban exiles and their families that park officials often close the gates by 11:00 A.M. Sunday morning. The traffic jam on Key Biscayne at departure time on Sunday afternoons often lasts until evening.

Some perceptive members of the Miami Cuban community see this clannishness as acute introversion. "Instead of mingling with the American community, it has formed an autonomous economy," says one Cuban former editor. "It is creating its own ghetto, feeding on social events that recall the old days in Havana when social position was based on membership in one of the big clubs." . . .

THE KENNEDY ASSASSINATION AND THE VIETNAM WAR
Peter Dale Scott

Pentagon Papers Volume 5: Critical Essays / 1972

It was the received wisdom of American commentators in the first months of Lyndon Johnson's presidency that the assassination of President Kennedy would have little impact on U. S. policies, domestic or foreign. President Johnson's first speech to Congress on November 27, 1963—"Let us continue . . ."—and his retention of Kennedy's top advisers both served to underline this appearance of continuity.

In retrospect, it has become clear that in at least one area of U. S. policy planning—Vietnam—this appearance was illusory. On November 20, 1963, the Kennedy administration had publicly announced plans to withdraw between 1000 and 1300 troops from Vietnam by the year's end. The Johnson administration not only quietly canceled these plans but also replaced them with high-level planning for covert escalation and expansion of the war into North Vietnam.

One of the Pentagon Papers published in 1971 attributes this abrupt reversal of direction to a perception, new in December 1963, of how close the Saigon regime was to collapse. Peter Dale Scott, in his researches into the Pentagon Papers, has reached a different and more disturbing conclusion. Scott argues that the reversal was in fact authorized by a secret National Security Action Memorandum—NSAM 273—at an unofficial emergency meeting on November 24, 1963, only two days after President Kennedy's assassination. As Scott reconstructed the text of NSAM 273 from partial quotations and references, it represented a departure from past policy in at least five respects:

1. An assertion, for the first time, that the "central objective" of the United States was to assist South Vietnam "to win"—rather than simply to "help" South Vietnam.

2. A quiet cancellation of the November 20th plans to withdraw troops, disguised by a public reaffirmation of a previously announced "objective" with respect to withdrawal.

3. Authorization of planning for a coherent program of covert activities in 1964 and for exploring the feasibility of initiating a wider war against North Vietnam.

4. An order to "all senior officers of the government" to avoid any criticism of U. S. Vietnam policy.

5. A directive to the State Department to develop a "case" which would demonstrate Hanoi's control of the Vietcong.

Scott's analysis recognizes that some of these bureaucratic shifts of language were subtle and that their result was to initiate, rather than fulfill, a reversal of policy. He argues, however, that the consequences of the November 24th NSAM, while more symbolic than practical, were well understood, and that they ended a major

*debate over escalation versus phased disengagement which had
for some weeks caused divisions in both Washington and Saigon.
Portions of Scott's analysis follow.—Eds.*

With respect to events in November 1963, the bias and deception of the original Pentagon documents are considerably reinforced in the Pentagon studies commissioned by Robert
McNamara. Nowhere is this deception more apparent than in the
careful editing and censorship of the Report of a Honolulu Conference on November 20, 1963, and of National Security Action
Memorandum 273, which was approved four days later. Study
after study is carefully edited so as to create a false illusion of
continuity between the last two days of President Kennedy's presidency and the first two days of President Johnson's. The narrow
division of the studies into topics, as well as periods, allows some
studies to focus on the "optimism"[1] which led to plans for
withdrawal on November 20 and 24, 1963; and others on the
"deterioration" and "gravity"[2] which at the same meetings led
to plans for carrying the war north. These incompatible pictures
of continuous "optimism" or "deterioration" are supported generally by selective censorship, and occasionally by downright
misrepresentation:

. . . National Security Action Memorandum 273, approved 26 November 1963. The immediate cause for NSAM 273 was the assassination
of President Kennedy four days earlier; newly-installed President Johnson needed to reaffirm or modify the policy lines pursued by his
predecessor. President Johnson quickly chose to reaffirm the Kennedy
policies. . . .

Emphasis should be placed, the document stated, on the Mekong
Delta area, but not only in military terms. Political, economic, social,
educational, and informational activities must also be pushed: "We

[1] *Pentagon Papers* (Washington: Government Printing Office, 1972), hereafter
cited as USG ed., IV.C.1, pp. ii, 2; *Pentagon Papers* (Boston: Beacon Press, 1971),
hereafter cited as Gravel ed., III:2, 17.
[2] USG ed., IV.B.5, pp. viii, 67; Gravel ed., II:207, 275-276. Leslie Gelb, Director of
the Pentagon Study Task Force and author of the study summaries, himself talks in
one study summary of "optimism" (III:2); and in another of "gravity" and "deterioration" (II:207).

should seek to turn the tide not only of battle but of belief. . . ." Military operations should be initiated, under close political control, up to within fifty kilometers inside of Laos. *U.S. assistance programs should be maintained at levels at least equal to those under the Diem government so that the new GVN would not be tempted to regard the U.S. as seeking to disengage.*

The same document also revalidated the planned phased withdrawal of U.S. forces announced publicly in broad terms by President Kennedy shortly before his death: "The *objective* of the United States with respect to withdrawal of U.S. military personnel remains as stated in the White House statement of October 2, 1963."

No new programs were proposed or endorsed, no increases in the level or nature of U.S. assistance suggested or foreseen. . . . The emphasis was on persuading the new government in Saigon to do well those things which the fallen government was considered to have done poorly. . . . *NSAM 273 had,* as described above, *limited cross-border operations to an area 50 kilometers within Laos.*[3]

The reader is invited to check the veracity of this account of NSAM 273 against the text, as reconstructed from various sources, in our Appendix A. If the author of this study is not a deliberate and foolish liar, then some superior had denied him access to the second and more important page of NSAM 273, which "authorized planning for specific covert operations, graduated in intensity, against the DRV," i.e., North Vietnam.[4] As we shall see, this covert operations planning soon set the stage for a new kind of war, not only through the celebrated 34A Operations which contributed to the Tonkin Gulf incidents, but also through the military's accompanying observations, as early as December 1963, that "only air attacks" against North Vietnam would achieve these operations' "stated objective."[5] Leslie Gelb, the Director of the Pentagon Study Task Force and the

[3] USG ed., IV.B.3, pp. 37-38; Gravel ed., II:457-59; emphasis added.

[4] USG ed., IV.C.2.a, p. viii; Gravel ed., III:117; cf. Pentagon Papers (New York Times/Bantam), p. 233. Another study on Phased Withdrawal (IV.B.4, p. 26; Gravel ed., II:191) apparently quotes directly from a close paraphrase of NSAM 273 (2), not from the document itself. Yet the second page of NSAM 273 was, as we shall see, a vital document in closing off Kennedy's plans for a phased withdrawal of U.S. forces.

[5] USG ed., IV.C.2.a, p. ix; Gravel ed., III:117.

author of the various and mutually contradictory Study Summaries notes that, with this planning, "A firebreak had been crossed, and the U.S. had embarked on a program that was recognized as holding little promise of achieving its stated objectives, at least in its early stages."[6] We shall argue in a moment that these crucial and controversial "stated objectives," proposed in CINCPAC's OPLAN 34–63 of September 9, 1963, were rejected by Kennedy in October 1963, and first authorized by the first paragraph of NSAM 273.

The Pentagon studies, supposedly disinterested reports to the Secretary of Defense, systematically mislead with respect to NSAM 273, which McNamara himself had helped to draft. Their lack of *bona fides* is illustrated by the general phenomenon that (as can be seen from our Appendix A), banal or misleading paragraphs (like 2, 3, and 5) are quoted verbatim, sometimes over and over, whereas those preparing for an expanded war are either omitted or else referred to obliquely. The *only* study to quote a part of the paragraph dealing with North Vietnam does so from subordinate instructions: it fails to note that this language was authorized in NSAM 273.[7]

And study after study suggests (as did press reports at the time) that the effect of NSAM 273, paragraph 2, was to perpetuate what Mr. Gelb ill-advisedly calls "the public White House promise in October" to withdraw 1,000 U.S. troops.[8] In fact the public White House statement on October 2 was no promise, but a personal estimate attributed to McNamara and Taylor. As we shall see, Kennedy's decision on October 5 to implement this withdrawal (a plan authorized by NSAM 263 of October 11), was not made public until the Honolulu Conference of November 20, when an Accelerated Withdrawal Program (about which Mr. Gelb is silent) was also approved.[9] NSAM 273 was in fact

[6] USG ed., IV.C.2.a, p. i; Gravel ed., III:106.

[7] USG ed., IV.C.2.a, p. 2; Gravel ed., III:150-151; cf. Stavins *et al.*, pp. 93-94.

[8] USG ed., IV.B.4, p. v; Gravel ed., II:163.

[9] *NYT*, November 21, 1963, pp. 1, 8; Richard P. Stebbins, *The United States in World Affairs, 1963* (New York: Harper and Row, for the Council on Foreign Relations, 1964), p. 193: "In a meeting at Honolulu on November 20, the principal U.S. authorities concerned with the war could still detect enough evidence of improvement to justify the repatriation of a certain number of specialized troops." Jim Bishop (*The Day Kennedy Was Shot*, New York: Funk and Wagnalls, 1968, p. 107) goes further: "They may also have discussed how best to extricate the U.S. from

approved on Sunday, November 24, and its misleading opening paragraphs (including the meaningless reaffirmation of the "objectives" of the October 2 withdrawal statement) were leaked to selected correspondents.[10] Mr. Gelb, who should know better, pretends that NSAM 273 "was intended primarily to endorse the policies pursued by President Kennedy and to ratify provisional decisions reached [on November 20] in Honolulu."[11] In fact the secret effect of NSAM 273's sixth paragraph (which unlike the second was not leaked to the press) was to *annul* the NSAM 263 withdrawal decision announced four days earlier at Honolulu, and also the Accelerated Withdrawal Program: "both military and economic programs, it was emphasized, should be maintained at levels as high as those in the time of the Diem regime."[12]

The source of this change is not hard to pinpoint. Of the eight people known to have participated in the November 24 reversal of the November 20 withdrawal decisions, five took part in both meetings.[13] Of the three new officials present, the chief was Lyndon Johnson, in his second full day and first business meeting as President of the United States.[14] The importance of this second meeting, like that of the document it approved, is indicated by its deviousness. One can only conclude that NSAM 273(2)'s public reaffirmation of an October 2 withdrawal "objective," coupled with 273(6)'s secret annulment of an October 5 withdrawal plan, was deliberately deceitful. The result of the misrepresentations in the Pentagon studies and Mr. Gelb's summaries is, in other words, to perpetuate a deception dating back to NSAM 273 itself.

Saigon; in fact it was a probable topic and the President may have asked the military for a timetable of withdrawal." Cf. USG ed., IV.B.4, p. d; Gravel ed., II:170: "20 Nov. 63 . . . officials agreed that the Accelerated Plan (speed-up of force withdrawal by six months directed by McNamara in October) should be maintained."

[10] *NYT*, November 25, 1963, p. 5; Washington *Post*, November 25, 1963, A2. See Appendix B.

[11] USG ed., IV.C.1, p. ii; Gravel ed., III:2.

[12] USG ed., IV.C.1, p. 3; Gravel ed., III:18.

[13] Rusk, McNamara, Lodge, McGeorge Bundy, and apparently McCone. McCone was not known earlier to have been a participant in the Honolulu Conference, but he is so identified by USG ed., IV.B.4, p. 25 (Gravel ed., II:190).

[14] It would appear that the only other new faces were Averell Harriman (who represented State in the interdepartmental "303 Committee" for covert operations) and George Ball.

This deception, I suspect, involved far more than the symbolic but highly sensitive issue of the 1,000-man withdrawal. One study, after calling NSAM 273 a "generally sanguine" "don't-rock-the-boat document," concedes that it contained "an unusual Presidential exhortation": "The President expects that all senior officers of the government will move energetically to insure full unity of support for establishing U.S. policy in South Vietnam."[15] In other words, the same document which covertly changed Kennedy's withdrawal plans ordered all senior officials not to contest or criticize this change. This order had a special impact on one senior official: Robert Kennedy, an important member of the National Security Council (under President Kennedy) who was not present when NSAM 273 was rushed through the forty-five minute "briefing session" on Sunday, November 24. It does not appear that Robert Kennedy, then paralyzed by the shock of his brother's murder, was even invited to the meeting. Chester Cooper records that Lyndon Johnson's first National Security Council meeting was not convened until Thursday, December 5.[16]

NSAM 273. PARAGRAPH 1: THE CENTRAL OBJECTIVE

While noting that the "stated objectives" of the new covert operations plan against North Vietnam were unlikely to be fulfilled by the OPLAN itself, Mr. Gelb, like the rest of the Pentagon Study Authors, fails to inform us what these "stated objectives" were. The answer lies in the "central objective" defined by the first paragraph of NSAM 273:

[15] USG ed., IV.C.1, pp. 1-3; Gravel ed., III:17-18.

[16] Chester Cooper, The Lost Crusade: America in Vietnam (New York: Dodd Mead, 1970), p. 222. Cooper should know, for he was then a White House aide to McGeorge Bundy, Special Assistant to the President for National Security Affairs. If he is right, then Pentagon study references to an NSC meeting on November 26 (USG ed., IV.B.4, p. 26; Gravel ed., II:191) are wrong—naïve deductions from NSAM 273's misleading title.

It remains *the central objective* of the United States in South Vietnam *to assist* the people and Government of that country *to win* their contest against the externally directed and supported communist conspiracy. The test of all U.S. decisions and actions in this area should be the effectiveness of their contribution *to this purpose*.[17]

To understand this bureaucratic prose we must place it in context. Ever since Kennedy came to power, but increasingly since the Diem crisis and assassination, there had arisen serious bureaucratic disagreement as to whether the U.S. commitment in Vietnam was limited and political ("to assist") or open-ended and military ("to win"). By its use of the word "win," NSAM 273, among other things, ended a brief period of indecision and division, when indecision itself was favoring the proponents of a limited (and political) strategy, over those whose preference was unlimited (and military) .[18]

In this conflict the seemingly innocuous word "objective" had come, in the Aesopian double-talk of bureaucratic politics, to be the test of a commitment. As early as May 1961, when President Kennedy was backing off from a major commitment in Laos, he had willingly agreed with the Pentagon that "The U.S. objective and concept of operations" was "to prevent Communist domination of South Vietnam."[19] In November 1961, however, Taylor, McNamara, and Rusk attempted to strengthen this language, by recommending that "We now take the decision to commit ourselves to the objective of preventing the fall of South Vietnam to Communism."[20] McNamara had earlier concluded that this "commitment . . . to the clear objective" was the "basic issue," adding that it should be accompanied by a "warning" of

[17] Lyndon Baines Johnson, *The Vantage Point* (New York: Holt, Rinehart & Winston, 1971), p. 45. Cf. USG ed., IV.C.1, pp. 46-47, which for "objective" reads "object."

[18] Some disgruntled officials told the *New York Times* that as late as the Honolulu Conference on November 20, two days before the assassination, "there had been a concentration on 'something besides winning the war'" (*NYT*, November 25, 1963, p. 5).

[19] NSAM 52 of May 11, 1961, in Pentagon Papers (NYT/Bantam), p. 126.

[20] Rusk-McNamara memorandum of November 11, 1961, in Pentagon Papers (NYT/Bantam) , p. 152; Gravel ed., II:113.

"punitive retaliation against North Vietnam." Without this commitment, he added, "We do not believe major U.S. forces should be introduced in South Vietnam."[21]

Despite this advice, Kennedy, after much thought, accepted all of the recommendations for introducing U.S. units, *except* for the "commitment to the objective" which was the first recommendation of all. NSAM 111 of November 22, 1961, which became the basic document for Kennedy Vietnam policy, was issued without this first recommendation.[22] Instead he sent a letter to Diem on December 14, 1961, in which "the U.S. officially described the limited and somewhat ambiguous extent of its commitment: . . . 'our primary purpose is to help your people. . . . We shall seek to persuade the Communists to give up their attempts of force and subversion.' "[23] One compensatory phrase of this letter ("the campaign . . . supported and directed from the outside") became (as we shall see) a rallying point for the disappointed hawks in the Pentagon; and was elevated to new prominence in NSAM 273(1)'s definition of a Communist "conspiracy." It would appear that Kennedy, in his basic policy documents after 1961, avoided any use of the word "objective" that might be equated to a "commitment." The issue was not academic: as presented by Taylor in November 1961, this commitment would have been open-ended, "to deal with any escalation the communists might choose to impose."[24]

In October 1963, Taylor and McNamara tried once again: by proposing to link the withdrawal announcement about 1,000 men to a clearly defined and public policy "objective" of defeating communism. Once again Kennedy, by subtle changes of language, declined to go along. His refusal is the more interesting when we see that the word and the sense he rejected in October 1963 (which would have made the military "objective" the *overrid-*

[21] McNamara memorandum of November 8, 1961, commenting on Taylor Report of November 3, 1961; Pentagon Papers (NYT/Bantam), pp. 148-149; Gravel ed., II: 108-109.

[22] Pentagon Papers (NYT/Bantam), pp. 107, 152; Gravel ed., II:110, 113, 117.

[23] G. M. Kahin and J. W. Lewis, *The United States in Vietnam* (New York: Delta, 1967), p. 129; letter in Department of State, *Bulletin*, January 1, 1962, p. 13; Gravel ed., II:805-806.

[24] Pentagon Papers (NYT/Bantam), p. 148.

ing one) are explicitly sanctioned by Johnson's first policy document, NSAM 273. (See table p. 416.)

A paraphrase of NSAM 273's seemingly innocuous first page was leaked at the time by someone highly-placed in the White House to the Washington *Post* and the *New York Times* (see Appendix B). As printed in the *Times* by E. W. Kenworthy this paraphrase went so far as to use the very words, "overriding objective," which Kennedy had earlier rejected.[25] This tribute to the words' symbolic importance is underlined by the distortion of NSAM 273, paragraph 1, in the Pentagon Papers, so that the controversial words "central objective" never once appear.[26] Yet at least two separate studies understand the "objective" to constitute a "commitment": "NSAM 273 reaffirms the U.S. commitment to defeat the VC in South Vietnam."[27] This particular clue to the importance of NSAM 273 in generating a policy commitment is all the more interesting, in that the Government edition of the Pentagon Papers has suppressed the page on which it appears.

. . . The full text of NSAM 273 of November 26, 1963, remains unknown. In all three editions of the Pentagon Papers there are no complete documents between the five cables of October 30 and McNamara's memorandum of December 21; the 600 pages of documents from the Kennedy Administration end on October 30. It is unlikely that this striking lacuna is accidental. We do, however, get an ominous picture of NSAM 273's implications from General Maxwell Taylor's memorandum of January 22, 1964:

National Security Action Memorandum No. 273 makes clear the resolve of the President to ensure victory over the externally directed and supported communist insurgency in South Vietnam. . . . The Joint

[25] *NYT*, November 25, 1963, pp. 1, 5: "President Johnson reaffirmed today the policy objectives of his predecessor regarding South Vietnam. . . . The adoption of all measures should be determined by their potential contribution to this overriding objective."

[26] In one case the disputed "objective" is misquoted as "object" (USG ed., IV.C.1, p. 46; Gravel ed., III:50). In another, it is paraphrased as "purpose" (USG ed., IV.B.5, p. 67; Gravel ed., II:276). In all other studies this sentence is ignored.

[27] USG ed., IV.B.5, p. xxxiv (suppressed); Gravel ed., II:223. Cf. USG ed., IV.B.3, p. 37; Gravel ed., II:457: "that the U.S. reaffirm its commitment."

PROPOSED STATEMENT OCT. 2, 1963 (McNamara-Taylor)	ACTUAL STATEMENT OCT. 2, 1963 (White House– Kennedy)	NSAM 273 (SECRET) NOV. 26, 1963 (White House– Johnson)
The security of South Vietnam *remains vital to United States security.* For this reason we adhere to *the overriding objective of denying* this country to Communism and of suppressing the Viet Cong insurgency as promptly as possible.	The security of South Vietnam *is a major interest of the United States as other free nations.* We will adhere to *our policy of working with the people and Government of South Vietnam to deny* this country to communism and to suppress the *externally stimulated and supported insurgency* of the Viet Cong as promptly as possible. *Effective performance* in this undertaking is the *central objective* of our policy in South Vietnam.	It remains the *central objective* of the United States in South Vietnam to assist the people and Government of that country *to win* their contest against the externally *directed* and supported communist *conspiracy. The test of all U.S. decisions and actions in this area should be the effectiveness of their contributions to this purpose.*[30]
Although we are deeply concerned by repressive practices, *effective performance* in the conduct of the war should be the *determining factor* in our relations with the GVN.[28]	While such practices have not yet significantly affected the war effort, they could do so in the future.	
	It remains the *policy* of the United States, in South Vietnam *as in other parts of the world,* to support the efforts of the people of that country to defeat aggression and to build a peaceful and free society.[29]	

[28] McNamara-Taylor Report of October 2, 1963, in Pentagon Papers (NYT/Bantam), p. 213; Gravel ed., II:753.

[29] Gravel ed., II:188.

[30] L. B. Johnson, *The Vantage Point*, p. 45.

Chiefs of Staff are convinced that, in keeping with the guidance in NSAM 273, the United States must make plain to the enemy our determination to see the Vietnam campaign through to a favorable conclusion. To do this, we must prepare for whatever level of activity may be required and, being prepared, must then proceed to take actions as necessary to achieve our purposes surely and promptly.[31]

The Joint Chiefs urged the President to end "self-imposed restrictions," to go beyond planning to the implementation of covert 34A operations against the North and Laos, and in addition to "conduct aerial bombing of key North Vietnam targets."

It was not only the military who drew such open-ended conclusions from the apparently "limited" wording of NSAM 273. As a State Department official told one Congressional committee in February 1964, "the basic policy is set that we are going to stay in Vietnam in a support function as long as needed to win the war."[32] McNamara himself told another committee that the United States had a commitment to win, rather than "support":

The survival of an independent government in South Vietnam is so important . . . that I can conceive of no alternative other than to take all necessary measures within our capability to prevent a Communist victory.[33]

All of this, like the text of NSAM 273 itself, corroborates the first-hand account of the November 24 meeting reported some years ago by Tom Wicker. According to that account Johnson's commitment, a message to the Saigon government, was not made lightly or optimistically. The issue was clearly understood, if not the ultimate consequences:

Lodge . . . gave the President his opinion that hard decisions would be necessary to save South Vietnam. "Unfortunately, Mr. President," the

[31] Pentagon Papers (NYT/Bantam), pp. 274-275.

[32] U.S. Cong., House, Committee on Foreign Affairs, *Winning the Cold War: the U.S. Ideological Offensive, Hearings*, 88th Cong., 2nd Sess. (Feb. 20, 1964), statement by Robert Manning, Assistant Secretary of State for Public Affairs, p. 811.

[33] U.S. Cong., House, Committee on Appropriations, *Department of Defense Appropriations for 1965, Hearings*, 88th Cong., 2nd Sess. (Washington: G.P.O., 1964), Part IV, p. 12; cf. pp. 103-104, 117-118.

Ambassador said, "you will have to make them." The new President, as recalled by one who was present, scarcely hesitated. "I am not going to lose Vietnam," he said. "I am not going to be the President who saw Southeast Asia go the way China went." . . . His instructions to Lodge were firm. The Ambassador was to return to Saigon and inform the new government there that the new government in Washington intended to stand by previous commitments and continue its help against the Communists. In effect, he told Lodge to assure Big Minh that Saigon "can count on us." That was a pledge. . . . All that would follow . . . had been determined in that hour of political decision in the old Executive Office Building, while . . . Oswald gasped away his miserable life in Parkland Hospital.[34]

The new President's decisions to expand the war by bombing and to send U.S. troops would come many months later. But he had already satisfied the "military" faction's demand for an unambiguous commitment, and ordered their "political" opponents to silence.

NSAM 273(2) AND 273(6): THE DOUBLETALK ABOUT "WITHDRAWAL"

The Joint Chiefs of Staff had consistently and persistently advised their civilian overseers (e.g., on May 10, 1961 and January 13, 1962) that for what they construed as the "unalterable objectives" of victory a decision should be made to deploy additional U.S. forces, including combat troops if necessary.[35] They were opposed from the outset by the proponents of a more political "counterinsurgency" concept, such as Roger Hilsman. But in April 1962 Ambassador Galbraith in New Delhi proposed to President Kennedy a different kind of (in his words) "political solution." Harriman, he suggested, should tell the Russians

---

[34] Tom Wicker, *JFK and LBJ: The Influence of Personality Upon Politics* (New York: William Morrow: 1968), pp. 205-206. Cf. I. F. Stone, *New York Review of Books*, March 28, 1968, p. 11; Marvin Kalb and Elie Abel, *Roots of Involvement* (New York: Norton, 1971), p. 153: "Lyndon Johnson, President less than forty-eight hours, had just made a major decision on Vietnam and a worrisome one."

[35] JCSM-33-62 of 13 Jan. 1962; Gravel ed., II:663-666.

of our determination not to let the Viet Cong overthrow the present government. . . . The Soviets should be asked to ascertain whether Hanoi can and will call off the Viet Cong activity in return for *phased American withdrawal*, liberalization in the trade relations between the two parts of the country and general and non-specific agreement to talk about reunification after some period of tranquillity.[36]

It is of course highly unusual for ambassadors to report directly to presidents outside of "channels." Contrary to usual practice the memorandum did not come up through Secretary Rusk's office; the White House later referred the memorandum for the comments of the Secretary of Defense (and the Joint Chiefs), but *not* of the Secretary of State. The very existence of such an unusual memorandum and procedure demonstrates that President Kennedy was personally interested in at least keeping his "political" options open. This was the second occasion on which Kennedy had used the former Harvard professor as an independent "watchdog" to evaluate skeptically the Rusk-McNamara consensus of his own bureaucracy; and there are rumors that Professor Galbraith (who for some unexplained reason saw President Johnson on November 23, 1963) continued to play this role in late 1963, after his return to Harvard.[36a] Another such independent "watchdog" was Kennedy's White House assistant, Michael Forrestal.

The response of the Joint Chiefs to Galbraith's "political solution" was predictably chilly. They argued that it would constitute "disengagement from what is by now a well-known commitment," and recalled that in the published letter of December 14, 1961 to Diem, President Kennedy had written that "we are prepared to help" against a campaign "supported and directed from outside."[37] In their view this language affirmed "support . . . to whatever extent may be necessary," but their particular exegesis, which Kennedy declined to endorse in October 1963, did not become official until Johnson's NSAM 273(1).

On the contrary, for one reason or another, the Defense Department began in mid-1962 "a formal planning and budgetary process" for precisely what Galbraith had contemplated, a "phased

[36] Memorandum for the President of April 4, 1962; USG ed., V.B.4, pp. 461-462; Gravel ed., II:671, emphasis added.
[36a] Galbraith since denied going in 1963 [P.D.S.]
[37] USG ed., V.B.4, p. 464; Gravel ed., II:671-672.

withdrawal of U.S. forces from Vietnam."[38] Pentagon Paper
IV.B.4, which studies this process, ignores the Galbraith memorandum entirely; and refers instead to what Leslie Gelb calls
"the euphoria and optimism of July 1962."[39] Assuredly there
were military professions of optimism, in secret as well as public
documents.[40] These professions of optimism do not, however,
explain why in 1963 the actual level of U.S. military personnel
continued to rise, from 9,865 at New Year's[41] (with projected
highs at that time of 11,600 in Fiscal Year 1963, 12,200 in February 1964, and 12,200 in February 1965) to unanticipated levels of
14,000 in June and 16,500 on October.[42] About these troop
increases, which Diem apparently opposed,[43] the Pentagon
Papers are silent.

By mid-1963, with the aggravating political crisis in Vietnam,
the pressure to move ahead with withdrawal plans was increasing.
This increased pressure was motivated not by military "euphoria"
(if indeed it ever had been) but by political dissatisfaction. A
State Department telegram from Rusk to Lodge on August 29,
1963, expresses the opinion that U.S. political pressures on Diem
would otherwise be futile:

Unless such talk included a real *sanction* such as a threatened *withdrawal* of our support, it is unlikely that it would be taken seriously
by a man who may feel that we are inescapably *committed* to an anti-
Communist Vietnam.[44]

[38] USG ed., IV.B.4, p. i; Gravel ed., II:160.

[39] *Ibid.*

[40] Arthur Sylvester, the Pentagon press spokesman, reported after a Honolulu
Conference in May 1963 the hopes of officials that U.S. forces could be reduced "in
one to three years" (*NYT*, May 8, 1963, p. 10; Cooper, *The Lost Crusade*, p. 208).

[41] U.S. Congress, House, Committee on Appropriations, *Department of Defense
Appropriations for 1967, Hearings*, 89th Cong., 2nd Sess., Washington: G.P.O., 1966,
Part 1, p. 378.

[42] Projected levels in January 1963 from USG ed., IV.B.4, p. 10; Gravel ed.,
II:179, cf. p. 163 (Gelb).

[43] Cooper, *The Lost Crusade*, p. 207; *NYT*, April 27, 1963. Cooper also tells us
that he "was sent to Vietnam in the spring [of] 1963 to search for the answer to 'Can
we win with Diem?' The very phrasing of the question implied more anxiety about
developments in Vietnam that official statements were currently admitting" (p. 202).

[44] State 272 of August 29, 1963 to Lodge, USG ed., V.B.4, p. 538; Gravel ed.,
II:738; emphasis added.

Pentagon Paper IV.B.4 ignores this telegram as well; yet even it (in marked contrast to Leslie Gelb's "Summary and Analysis" of it) admits that

Part of the motivation behind the stress placed on U.S. force withdrawal, and particularly the seemingly arbitrary desire to effect the 1,000-man withdrawal by the end of 1963, apparently was as a signal to influence both the North Vietnamese and the South Vietnamese and set the stage for possible later steps that would help bring the insurgency to an end.[45]

At the time of Galbraith's proposal for talks about phased U.S. withdrawal between Harriman and the Russians, Harriman was Chairman of the American delegation to the then deadlocked Geneva Conference on Laos, which very shortly afterwards reconvened for the rapid conclusion of the 1962 Geneva Agreements. Relevant events in that development include a sudden U.S. troop buildup in Thailand in May, the agreement among the three Laotian factions to form a coalition government on June 11, and Khrushchev's message the next day hailing the coalition agreement as a "pivotal event" in Southeast Asia and good augury for the solution of "other international problems which now divide states and create tension."[46] The signing of the Geneva Accords on July 23 was accompanied by a partial withdrawal of U.S. troops in Thailand, as well as by a considerable exacerbation of Thai-U.S. relations, to the extent that Thailand, infuriated by lack of support in its border dispute with Cambodia, declared a temporary boycott of SEATO.[47]

The 1962 Geneva Agreements on Laos were marked by an unusual American willingness to "trust" the other side.[48] Chester Cooper confirms that their value lay in

[45] USG ed., IV.B.4, p. 23; Gravel ed., II:189.

[46] *NYT*, June 13, 1962, p. 3.

[47] Richard P. Stebbins, *The United States in World Affairs 1962* (New York: Harper and Row, for the Council on Foreign Relations, 1963), pp. 197-200.

[48] Stebbins [1962], p. 199: "This was not the kind of ironclad arrangement on which the United States had been insisting in relation to such matters as disarmament, nuclear testing, or Berlin."

a private deal worked out between the leaders of the American and Soviet delegations—the "Harriman-Pushkin Agreement." In essence the Russians agreed to use their influence on the Pathet Lao, Peking, and Hanoi to assure compliance with the terms agreed on at the Conference. In exchange for this, the British agreed to assure compliance by the non-Communists.[49]

He also confirms that, before Harriman and Kennedy could terminate U.S. support for the CIA's protégé in Laos, Phoumi Nosavan, "some key officials in our Mission there . . . had to be replaced."[50] The U.S. *Foreign Service List* shows that the officials recalled from Vientiane in the summer of 1962 include both of the resident military attachés and also the CIA Station Chief, Gordon L. Jorgensen.[51] In late 1964 Jorgensen returned to Saigon, to become, as the Pentagon Papers reveal, the Saigon CIA Station Chief. [Gravel ed., II:539]

This purge of right-wing elements in the U.S. Mission failed to prevent immediate and conspicuous violation of the Agreements by Thai-based elements of the U.S. Air Force through jet overflights of Laos. These same overflights, according to Hilsman, had been prohibited by Kennedy, on Harriman's urging, at a National Security Council meeting. In late October 1963 Pathet Lao Radio began to complain of stepped-up intrusions by U.S. jet aircraft, as well as of a new military offensive by Phoumi's troops (about which we shall say more later).[52]

According to Kenneth O'Donnell, President Kennedy had himself (like Galbraith) abandoned hopes for a military solution as early as the spring of 1963. O'Donnell allegedly heard from Kennedy then "that he had made up his mind that after his re-election he would take the risk of unpopularity and make a complete withdrawal of American forces from Vietnam . . . in

[49] Cooper, p. 190.

[50] Cooper, p. 189.

[51] Hilsman, pp. 152-153; Scott, *The War Conspiracy,* pp. 33-35.

[52] FBIS *Daily Report,* October 24, 1963, PPP3; October 28, 1963, PPP4; October 31, 1963, PPP4. About the same time State Department officials began to refer to "intelligence reports" of increased North Vietnamese activity in Laos, including the movement of trucks; but it is not clear whether these intelligence sources were on the ground or in the air (*NYT,* October 27, 1963, p. 27; October 30, 1963, p. 1).

1965."[53] Whether the President had so unreservedly and so early adopted the Galbraith perspective is debatable; there is, however, no questioning that after the Buddhist crisis in August the prospect of accelerated or total withdrawal was openly contemplated by members of the bureaucracy's "political" faction, including the President's brother.

How profoundly this issue had come to divide "political" and "military" interpreters of Administration policy is indicated by General Krulak's minutes of a meeting in the State Department on August 31, 1963:

Mr. Kattenburg stated . . . it was the belief of Ambassador Lodge that, if we undertake to live with this repressive regime . . . we are going to be thrown out of the country in six months. He stated that at this juncture it would be better for us to make the decision to get out honorably. . . . Secretary Rusk commented that Kattenburg's recital was largely speculative; that it would be far better for us to start on the *firm basis of two things—that we will not pull out of Vietnam until the war is won, and that we will not run a coup.* Mr. McNamara expressed agreement with this view. Mr. Rusk . . . then asked the Vice President if he had any contribution to make. The Vice President stated that he agreed with Secretary Rusk's conclusions completely; that he had great reservations himself with respect to a coup, particularly so because he had never really seen a genuine alternative to Diem. He stated that from both a practical and a political viewpoint, it would be a *disaster to pull out*; that we should stop playing cops and robbers and . . . once again go about *winning the war.*[54]

At this meeting (which the President did not attend) the only opposition to this powerful Rusk-McNamara-Johnson consensus was expressed by two more junior State Department officials with OSS and CIA backgrounds: Paul Kattenburg (whom Rusk inter-

[53] Kenneth O'Donnell; "LBJ and the Kennedys," *Life* (August 7, 1970), p. 51; *NYT*, August 3, 1970, p. 16. O'Donnell's claim is corroborated by his correct reference (the first I have noted in print) to the existence of an authorized plan in NSAM 263 of October 11: "The President's order to reduce the American personnel in Vietnam by 1,000 men before the end of 1963 was still in effect on the day that he went to Texas" (p. 52).

[54] *Pentagon Papers* (NYT/Bantam), pp. 204-205; USG ed., V.B.4. pp. 541-543; Gravel ed., II:742-743, emphasis added.

rupted at one heated point) and Roger Hilsman. One week later, however, Robert Kennedy, who was the President's chief trouble-shooter in CIA, Vietnam, and counterinsurgency affairs, himself questioned Secretary Rusk's "firm basis" and entertained the solution which Johnson had called a "disaster":

The first and fundamental question, he felt, was what we were doing in Vietnam. As he understood it, we were there to help the people resisting a Communist take-over. The first question was whether a Communist take-over could be successfully resisted with any government. If it could not, *now was the time to get out of Vietnam entirely*, rather than waiting. If the answer was that it could, but not with a Diem-Nhu government as it was now constituted, we owed it to the people resisting Communism in Vietnam to give Lodge enough *sanctions* to bring changes that would permit successful resistance.[55]

One way or another, in other words, withdrawal was the key to a "political" solution.

These reports show Robert Kennedy virtually isolated (save for the support of middle-echelon State officials like Hilsman and Kattenburg) against a strong Rusk-McNamara bureaucratic consensus (supported by Lyndon Johnson). Yet in October and November both points of Mr. Rusk's "firm basis" were undermined by the White House: unconditional plans for an initial troop withdrawal were announced on November 20; and the United States, by carefully meditated personnel changes and selective aid cuts, gave signals to dissident generals in Saigon that it *would* tolerate a coup. The first clear signal was the unusually publicized removal on October 5 of the CIA station chief in Saigon, John Richardson, because of his close identification with Diem's brother Ngo Dinh Nhu. And, as Leslie Gelb notes, "In October we cut off aid to Diem in a direct rebuff, giving a green light to the generals."[56]

[55] Hilsman, p. 501, emphasis added.
[56] USG ed., IV.B.5, p. viii; Gravel ed., II:207. Cf. Chester Cooper, *The Lost Crusade* (New York: Dodd Mead, 1970), p. 220: "The removal of Nhu's prime American contact, the curtailment of funds for Nhu's Special Forces, and, most importantly, the cutting off of import aid must have convinced the generals that they could proceed without fear of subsequent American sanctions."

But this brief political trend, publicly announced as late as November 20, was checked and reversed by the new President at his first substantive policy meeting on November 24. As he himself reports,

I told Lodge and the others that I had serious misgivings. . . . Congressional demands for our withdrawal from Vietnam were becoming louder and more insistent. I thought we had been mistaken in our failure to support Diem. . . . I told Lodge that I had not been happy with what I read about our Mission's operations in Vietnam earlier in the year. There had been too much internal dissension. I wanted him to develop a strong team. . . . In the next few months we sent Lodge a new deputy, a new CIA chief, a new director of the U.S. Information Agency (USIA) operations, and replacements for other key posts in the U.S. Embassy.[57]

In other words, Richardson's replacement (presumably Frederick W. Flott) was himself replaced (by Peer de Silva, an Army Intelligence veteran). Others who were purged included the number two Embassy official, William Trueheart, a former State intelligence officer, and John W. Mecklin, the USIA director: both Trueheart and Mecklin were prominent, along with Kattenburg and Hilsman, in the "get Diem" faction. This purge of the Embassy was accompanied by the replacement, on January 7, 1964, of Paul Kattenburg as Chairman of the Vietnam Inter-Department Working Group, and soon after by the resignation of Roger Hilsman.[58] The State Department's *Foreign Service List* failed to reflect the rapidity with which this secret purge was effected.[59]

Above all NSAM 273 sent a new signal to the confused Saigon

[57] Johnson, *The Vantage Point*, p. 44.

[58] Kattenburg had been named Chairman on August 4, 1963, the same day that Frederick Flott assumed his duties in Saigon. Mecklin's replacement, Barry Zorthian, assumed duties in Saigon on February 2, 1964.

[59] For the purposes of the April 1964 State Department *Foreign Service List* de Silva remained attached to Hong Kong, and both Richardson and Flott were still in Saigon. In fact de Silva was functioning as Saigon CAS station chief by February 9 (USG ed., IV.C.1, p. 33). Trueheart did not surface in Washington until May; his replacement, David Nes, officially joined the Saigon Embassy on January 19, but was already in Saigon during the McNamara visit of mid-December 1963 (USG ed., IV.C.8 [alias IV.C.11], p. 59; Gravel ed., III:494).

generals, to replace the "political" signals of October and November. For the first time (as we shall see) they were told to go ahead with a "graduated" or escalating program of clandestine military operations against North Vietnam.[60] On January 16 these 34A Operations were authorized to begin on February 1. In Saigon as in Washington, a brief interlude of government by politically minded moderates gave way to a new "military" phase. On January 30, Nguyen Khanh ousted the Saigon junta headed by Duong van Minh, on the grounds that some of its members were "paving the way for neutralism and thus selling out the country."[61] According to the Pentagon Papers Khanh notified his American adviser, Col. Jasper Wilson, of the forthcoming coup; but in a recent interview Khanh has claimed Wilson told him of the American-organized coup less than twenty-four hours in advance. [62]

Lyndon Johnson, like other observers, discounts the novelty of NSAM 273, by referring back to President Kennedy's firm statements in two TV interviews of early September. In one of these Kennedy had said, "I don't agree with those who say we should withdraw." In the other, he had argued against any cut in U.S. aid to South Vietnam: "I don't think we think that would be helpful at this time. . . . You might have a situation which could bring about a collapse."[63] From these two statements Ralph Stavins has also concluded that "had John F. Kennedy lived, he would not have pulled out of Southeast Asia and would have taken any steps necessary to avoid an ignominious defeat at the hands of the Viet Cong."[64]

But Kennedy had clearly shifted between early September 1963 (when he had pulled back from encouraging a reluctant Saigon coup) and late November (after he had given the signals for one). The TV interviews soon proved to be poor indicators of his future policy: by mid-October Kennedy was making significant aid cuts, as requested by dissident generals in Saigon, in order to weaken

---

[60] USG ed., IV, B.5, p. 67.

[61] Franz Schurmann, Peter Dale Scott, Reginald Zelnik, *The Politics of Escalation* (New York: Fawcett, 1966), p. 26.

[62] USG ed., IV.C.1, p. 35; Gravel ed., III:37; *Stern* (January 1970).

[63] Lyndon Baines Johnson, *The Vantage Point*, p. 61.

[64] Ralph Stavins et al., *Washington Plans on Aggressive War*, p. 81.

Diem's position, and above all to remove from Saigon the CIA-trained Special Forces which Diem and Nhu relied on as a private guard.[65] And on October 2 the White House statement had announced that

Secretary McNamara and General Taylor reported their judgment that the major part of the U.S. military task can be completed by the end of 1965, though there may be a continuing requirement for a limited number of U.S. training personnel. They reported that by the end of this year, the U.S. program for training Vietnamese should have progressed to the point where 1,000 U.S. military personnel assigned to South Viet-Nam can be withdrawn.[66]

This language constituted a personal "judgment" rather than an authorized "plan" (or, as Mr. Gelb calls it, a "public . . . promise"). The distinction was recognized by the secret McNamara-Taylor memorandum of October 2 which proposed it. McNamara and Taylor, moreover, recommended an announcement as "consistent" with a program whose inspiration was explicitly political:

an application of selective short-term *pressures*, principally economic, and the conditioning of long-term aid on the satisfactory performance by the Diem government in meeting military and political objectives which *in the aggregate equate to* the requirements of final victory.[67]

The memo called for the Defense Department "to announce in the very near future presently prepared plans [as opposed to intentions] to withdraw 1,000 U.S. military personnel."[68] This recommendation was approved by the President on October 5, and incorporated in NSAM 263 of October 11, but with the proviso that "no *formal* announcement be made of the *implementation* of plans to withdraw 1,000 U.S. military personnel by the end of 1963."[69]

Instead the President began to leak the NSAM 263 plans informally. In his press conference of October 31, on the eve of the

[65] A White House message on September 17 had authorized Lodge to hold up any aid program if this would give him useful leverage in dealing with Diem (CAP Message 63516; USG ed., V.B.4, II, p. 545; Gravel ed., II:743).

[66] *Public Papers of the Presidents,* John F. Kennedy: 1963 (Washington: G.P.O., 1964), pp. 759-760; Gravel ed., II:188.

[67] USG ed., V.B.4, Book II, pp. 555, 573; Gravel ed., II:766; emphasis added.

[68] *Loc. cit.,* p. 555.

[69] *Loc. cit.,* p. 578; cf. IV.B.4, p. d.

coup against Diem, the President answered an informed question about "any speedup in the withdrawal from Vietnam" by speculating that "the first contingent would be 250 men who are not involved in what might be called front-line operations."[70] A fortnight later he was more specific, in the context of a clearly political formulation of U.S. policy objectives:

That is our object, to bring Americans home, permit the South Vietnamese to maintain themselves as a free and independent country, and permit democratic forces within the country to operate. . . . We are going to bring back several hundred before the end of the year. But on the question of the exact number, I thought we would wait until the meeting of November 20th.[71]

The November 20 meeting was an extraordinary all-agency Honolulu Conference of some 45 to 60 senior Administration officials, called in response to the President's demand for a "full-scale review" of U.S. policy in Southeast Asia, following the overthrow of Diem.[72] This all-agency Conference, like the follow-up "Special Meeting" of June 1964, is apparently to be distinguished from the regular SecDef Honolulu Conferences, such as the Seventh in May 1963 and the Eighth in March 1964.[73] It was extraordinary in its size and high-level participation (McNamara, Rusk, McCone, McGeorge Bundy, Lodge, Taylor, Harkins), yet Robert Kennedy, the President's Vietnam trouble-shooter, did not attend: on November 20 he celebrated his birthday at home in Washington. (The only Cabinet members left in Washington were Attorney General Robert Kennedy, HEW Secretary Celebrezze, and the new Postmaster General John Gronouski. Because of a coincident Cabinet trip to Japan, Dillon of Treasury, Hodges of Commerce, Wirtz of Labor, Freeman of Agriculture, and Udall of the Interior were also in Honolulu during this period.)[74]

[70] *Public Papers*, p. 828.

[71] Press Conference of November 14, 1963; *Public Papers*, pp. 846, 852.

[72] USG ed., IV.B.4, p. 24; Johnson, *The Vantage Point*, p. 62; *NYT*, November 21, 1963, p. 8; Weintal and Bartlett, p. 71.

[73] USG ed., IV.B.4, pp. a, e; Gravel ed., II:166, 171.

[74] William Manchester, *The Death of a President: November 20-25, 1963* (New York: Harper and Row, 1967) , pp. 101, 158.

As the President's questioner of October 31 was apparently aware, the issue was no longer whether 1,000 men would be withdrawn (with a Military Assistance Program reduction in Fiscal 1965 of $27 million), but whether the withdrawal program might not be *accelerated* by six months, with a corresponding MAP aid reduction of $33 million in Fiscal 1965.[75] Planning for this second "Accelerated Plan" had been stepped up after the October 5 decision which authorized the first.[76] The issue was an urgent one, since the Fiscal 1965 budget would have to be presented to Congress in January.

The chronology of Pentagon Paper IV.B.4, on Phased Withdrawal of U.S. Forces, tells us that on November 20, two days before the assassination, the Honolulu Conference secretly "agreed that the Accelerated Plan (speed-up of force withdrawal by six months directed by McNamara in October) should be maintained."[77] In addition the Honolulu Conference issued a press release which, according to the *New York Times*, "reaffirmed the United States *plan* to bring home about 1,000 of

[75] USG ed., IV.B.4, p. 29; Cf. pp. 14-16; cf. Gravel ed., II:180–192. Another study (USG ed., IV.C.1, p. 15) quotes different figures, but confirms that a reduction in the Fiscal '65 support level was agreed to at Honolulu.

[76] USG ed., IV.B.4, p. 23.

[77] USG ed., IV.B.4, p. d; Gravel ed., II:170. The text of the same study corroborates this very unclearly (IV.B.4, p. 25; II:190), but the text is strangely self-contradictory at this point and may even have been editorially tampered with. In comparing Honolulu to NSAM 273, the Study assures us of total continuity: "Universally operative was a desire to avoid change of any kind during the critical interregnum period." Yet the same Study gives us at least one clear indication of change. McNamara on November 20 "made it clear that he thought the proposed CINCPAC MAP [Military Assistance Program] could be cut back" (p. 25; II:190); yet McNamara on November 23, in a written memorandum to the new President, "said that . . . the U.S. must be prepared to raise planned MAP levels" (p. 26; II:191; the Chronology adds that "funding well above current MAP plans was envisaged"). The study itself, very circumspectly, calls this "a hint that something might be different," only ten lines after speaking of the "universally operative . . . desire to avoid change of any kind."

What is most striking is that this Study of Phased Withdrawal makes no reference whatsoever to NSAM 273(6), which emphasized that "both military and economic programs . . . should be maintained at levels as high as those in the time of the Diem regime" (USG ed., IV.C.1, p. 3; Gravel ed., III:18). Yet the Study refers to McNamara's memorandum of November 23, which apparently inspired this directive. Mr. Gelb's summary chooses to skip from October 2 to December 21, and is silent about the Accelerated Withdrawal Plan.

its 16,500 troops from South Vietnam by January 1."[78] Thus
the language of NSAM 273 of November 26, by going back to the
status quo ante October 5, was itself misleading, as is the careful
selection from it in the Pentagon Study. By reverting to the
informal "objective" of October 2, NSAM 273(2) tacitly effaced
both the formalized plans of NSAM 263 (October 5 and 11)
announced on November 20, and *also* the Accelerated Plan discussed and apparently agreed to on the same day. NSAM 273(6),
according to most citations of it, would have explicitly "maintained
both military and economic programs . . . at levels as high as
those . . . of the Diem regime."[79]

Most volumes of the Pentagon Papers attribute the letter and
spirit of NSAM 273 to a misplaced military "optimism."[80]
But President Johnson's memoirs confirm the spirit of urgency
and "serious misgivings" which others have attributed to the
unscheduled Sunday meeting which approved it.[81] President
Kennedy had envisaged no formal meetings on that Sunday:
instead he would have met Lodge privately for lunch at his
private Virginia estate (or, according to William Manchester, at
Camp David).[82] But President Johnson, while still in Dallas
on November 22, "felt a national security meeting was essential
at the earliest possible moment"; and arranged to have it set up
"for that same evening."[83]

Johnson, it is true, tells us that his "first exposure to the details
of the problem of Vietnam came forty-eight hours after I had

---

[78] *NYT*, November 21, 1963, p. 8, emphasis added. Cf. USG ed., IV.B.5, p. 67:
"An uninformative press release . . . pointedly reiterated the plan to withdraw 1,000
U.S. troops." Inasmuch as this was the first formal revelation of the plan the press
release does not deserve to be called "uninformative." I have been unable to locate
anywhere the text of the press release.

[79] Pentagon Study IV.C.1, p. 2; Gravel ed., III:18, in Appendix A. Cf. USG ed.,
IV.C.9.a, p. 2; Gravel ed., II:304.

[80] USG ed., IV.B.3, p. 37; IV.C.1, p. ii.

[81] Johnson, p. 43; cf. 22: "South Vietnam gave me real cause for concern."
Chester Cooper (*The Lost Crusade*, New York, Dodd, Mead, 1970) also writes of the
"growing concern" and "the worries that were submitted" in this memorandum; cf.
I. F. Stone, *New York Review of Books*, March 28, 1968, p. 11.

[82] Johnson writes that Lodge "had flown to Washington a few days earlier for
scheduled conferences with President Kennedy, Secretary of State Dean Rusk, and
other administration officials" (p. 43). But Rusk, if he had not been turned back by
the assassination, would have been in Japan.

[83] Johnson, p. 16.

taken the oath of office,"[84] i.e., on Sunday, November 24. But Pentagon Study IV.B.4 and the *New York Times* make it clear that on Saturday morning, for fifty minutes, the President and McNamara discussed a memorandum of some four or five typewritten pages:

In that memo, Mr. McNamara said that the new South Vietnamese government was confronted by serious financial problems, and that the U.S. must be prepared to raise planned MAP levels.[85]

The Chronology adds to this information the statement that "funding well above current MAP plans was envisaged."[86]

The true significance of the symbolic 1,000-man withdrawal was as a political signal; and politics explains why NSAM 263 was overridden. As we have seen, another Pentagon study admits that

The seemingly arbitrary desire to effect the 1,000-man reduction by the end of 1963, apparently was as a signal to influence both the North Vietnamese and the South Vietnamese and set the stage for possible later steps that would bring the insurgency to an end. . . .[87]

NSAM 273, PARAGRAPH 7(?): GRADUATED COVERT MILITARY OPERATIONS

All of this suggests that the Pentagon Studies misrepresent NSAM 273 systematically. Although it is of course possible that NSAM 273 had already been censored before it was submitted to some or all of the authors of the Pentagon Papers, it is striking that different studies use different fragments of evidence to arrive (by incompatible narratives) at the same false picture of con-

[84] Johnson, p. 43.

[85] USG ed., IV.B.4, p. 26; *NYT*, November 24, 1963; p. 7: "The only word overheard was 'billions,' spoken by McNamara."

[86] USG ed., IV.B.4, p. d; Gravel ed., II:170. A page in another Pentagon study, suppressed from the Government volumes but preserved in the Gravel edition, claims, perhaps mistakenly, that Lodge first met with the President in Washington on Friday, November 22, the day of the assassination itself. Gravel ed., II:223 (suppressed page following USG ed., IV.B.5, p. xxxiii); cf. IV.B.5, p. 67.

[87] USG ed., IV.B.4, p. 23; Gravel ed., II:189.

tinuity between November 20 and 24. One study (IV.B.3, p. 37) suggests that these were "no new programs" proposed either at the Honolulu Conference or in NSAM 273, because of the "cautious optimism" on both occasions. Another (IV.C.2.a, pp. 1-2) speaks of a "different . . . new course of action" in early 1964— the 34A covert operations—that flowed from a decision "made" at the Honolulu Conference under Kennedy and ratified on November 26 under Johnson:

The covert program was spawned in May of 1963, when the JCS directed CINCPAC to prepare a plan for GVN "hit and run" operations against NVN. These operations were to be "non-attributable" and carried out "with U.S. military material, training and advisory assistance." 4/ Approved by the JCS on 9 September as CINCPAC OPLAN 34-63, the plan was discussed during the Vietnam policy conference at Honolulu, 20 November 1963. Here a decision was made to develop a combined COMUSMACV-CAS, Saigon plan for a 12-month program of covert operations. Instructions forwarded by the JCS on 26 November specifically requested provision for: " (1) harassment; (2) diversion; (3) political pressure; (4) capture of prisoners; 5) physical destruction; (6) acquisition of intelligence; (7) generation of intelligence; and (8) diversion of DRV resources." Further, that the plan provide for "selected actions of graduated scope and intensity to include commando type coastal raids." 5/ To this guidance was added that given by President Johnson to the effect that "planning should include . . . estimates of such factors as: (1) resulting damage to NVN; (2) the plausibility of denial; (3) possible NVN retaliation; and (4) other international reaction." 6/ The MACV-CAS plan, designated OPLAN 34A, and providing for "a spectrum of capabilities for RVNAF to execute against NVN," was forwarded by CINCPAC on 19 December 1963. 7/ The idea of putting direct pressure on North Vietnam met prompt receptivity on the part of President Johnson.

The density of misrepresentations in this study, and especially this paragraph, suggests conscious deception rather than naïve error. The footnotes have unfortunately been suppressed, so we do not have the citation for the alleged directive of May 1963. The chronology summarizing this Study gives a clue, however, for it reads "11 May 63# NSAM 52# Authorized CIA-sponsored operations against NVN."[88] But the true date of NSAM 52, as the author must have known, was May 11, 1961; and indeed he makes a point of contrasting the sporadic CIA operations, authorized in 1961 and largely suspended in 1962, with the 34A "elaborate program" of *sustained* pressures, under a *military* command, in three planned "graduated" or *escalating* phases, which began in February 1964.

The inclusion in planning of MACV was in keeping with the Kennedy doctrine, enacted after the Bay of Pigs fiasco, that responsibility for "any *large* paramilitary operation wholly or partly covert . . . is properly the primary responsibility of the Department of Defense."[89] Before November 26, 1963, U.S. covert operations in Asia had always (at least in theory) been "secret" and "plausibly deniable"; these were the two criteria set for itself in 1948 by the National Security Council when it first authorized CIA covert operations under its "other functions and duties" clause in the 1947 National Security Act.[90] Throughout 1963 the Kennedy Administration was under considerable pressure, public as well as within its personnel, to go beyond these guidelines, and intervene "frankly" rather than "surreptitiously." In May 1963 this appeal for escalation was publicly joined by William Henderson, an official of Socony Mobil which had a major economic interest in Southeast Asia, to an appeal to move from a "limited" to an "unlimited" commitment in that area.[91]

[88] USG ed., IV.C.2.a, p. viii.

[89] NSAM 57 of 1961, in Gravel ed., II:683.

[90] David Wise and Thomas B. Ross, *The Invisible Government* (New York: Bantam, 1964), pp. 99-100.

[91] William Henderson, "Some Reflections on United States Policy in Southeast Asia," in William Henderson, ed., *Southeast Asia: Problems of United States Policy* (Cambridge, Mass.: M.I.T. Press, 1963), p. 263; cf. pp. 253-254: "We shall ultimately fail to secure the basic objectives of policy in Southeast Asia until our commitment to the region becomes unlimited, which it has not been up till now. This does not mean simply that we must be prepared to fight for Southeast Asia, if necessary, although it certainly means that at a minimum. Beyond this is involved a much greater commitment of our resources. . . ."

[For a more extended analysis of this lobbying, cf. Peter Dale Scott, "The Vietnam War and the CIA-Financial Establishment," in Mark Selden, ed., *Remaking Asia: Essays on the American Uses of Power* (New York: Pantheon, 1974, pp. 125-30).—Eds.]

The covert operations planning authorized by NSAM 273 seems to have been the threshold for at least the first of these policy changes, if not both. In contrast both were wholly incompatible with the Kennedy Administration's last movements toward withdrawal. In May 1963 McNamara had authorized changes in long-range planning "to accomplish a more rapid withdrawal"[92] and on November 20 in Honolulu, as we have seen, the resulting initial withdrawal of 1,000 men was supplemented by the so-called Accelerated Plan.[93] It is hard to imagine, at either date, the same man or men contemplating a new 34A "elaborate program" of acts which threatened war, to coincide with an accelerated withdrawal of U.S. forces.

The next sentence of Study IV.C.2.a tells us that CINCPAC OPLAN 34-63 was "approved by the JCS on 9 September"— this "approval" means only that, at the very height of the paralytic stand-off between the "political" and "military" factions, the Joint Chiefs forwarded one more tendentious "military" alternative for consideration by McNamara and above all by the 303 Committee (about whom the author is silent). One Gravel Pentagon Papers Chronology (III:141) suggests that Kennedy and his White House staff never were consulted by McNamara about OPLAN 34-63.

The same Gravel chronology reports that CIA cross-border operations, radically curtailed after the 1962 Geneva Agreements on Laos, were resumed by November 19, 1963, one day before the Honolulu Conference, even though the first Presidential authorization cited for such renewed operations is Johnson's NSAM 273 of November 26.[94] Kennedy's NSAM 249 of June 25, 1963, in rejecting State's proposals for actions against North Vietnam, had authorized planning for operations against Laos conditional on further consultation; and it had urged review [of] whether "additional U.S. actions should be taken in Laos before any action be directed against North Vietnam."[95]

Although the overall language of NSAM 249 (which refers to an unpublished memorandum) is obscure, this wording seems

[92] USG ed., IV.B.4, p. 12.
[93] USG ed., IV.B.4, pp. 25, d.
[94] Gravel ed., III:141; Stavins, p. 93.
[95] USG ed., V.B.4, p. 525; Gravel ed., II:726.

to indicate that in June 1963 Kennedy had delayed authorization of *any* action against North Vietnam. Yet North Vietnamese and right-wing U.S. sources agree that in this very month of June 1963 covert operations against North Vietnam were resumed by South Vietnamese commandos; these actions had the approval of General Harkins in Saigon, but not (according to the U.S. sources) of President Kennedy.[96] The same sources, further corroborated by the Pentagon Papers, both linked these raids to increased military cooperation between South Vietnam and the Chinese Nationalists, whose own commandos began turning up in North Vietnam in increasing numbers.[97]

It has also been suggested that KMT influences, and their sympathizers in Thailand and the CIA, were behind the right-wing political assassinations and military offensive which in 1963 led to a resumption of fighting in Laos, "with new American supplies

[96] Robert S. Allen and Paul Scott, "Diem's War Not Limited Enough," Peoria *Journal-Star*, September 18, 1963, reprinted in *Congressional Record*, October 1, 1963, p. A6155: "Since Diem—under a plan prepared by his brother, Ngo Dinh Nhu—began sending guerrillas into North Vietnam in June, powerful forces within the administration have clamored for the President to curb the strong anti-Communist leader. . . . General Paul D. Harkins, head of the U.S. Military Assistance Command in Saigon, who favors the initiative by Diem's forces, violently disagreed . . . but President Kennedy accepted the diplomatic rather than the military view." Cf. Radio Hanoi, FBIS *Daily Report*, October 22, 1963, JJJ13; April 8, 1964, JJJ4.

[97] Allen and Scott, *loc cit.*: "Diem also notified the White House that he was opening talks with a representative of Chiang-Kai-shek on his offer to send Chinese Nationalist troops to South Vietnam from Formosa for both training and combat purposes. This . . . so infuriated President Kennedy that he authorized an undercover effort to curb control of military operations of the South Vietnam President by ousting Nhu . . . and to organize a military junta to run the war"; Hanoi Radio, November 10, 1963 (FBIS *Daily Report*, November 14, 1963, JJJ2): "The 47 U.S.-Chiang commandos captured in Hai Ninh declared that before intruding into the DRV to seek their way into China, they had been sent to South Vietnam and received assistance from the Ngo Dinh Diem authorities." Cf. USG ed., IV.C.9.b, p. vii (censored); Gravel ed., II:289-290: "GVN taste for foreign adventure showed up in small, irritating ways. . . . In 1967, we discovered that GVN had brought in Chinese Nationalists disguised as Nungs, to engage in operations in Laos." Hilsman (p. 461) relates that in January 1963 Nhu discussed with him "a strategy to defeat world Communism for once and for all—by having the United States lure Communist China into a war in Laos, which was 'an ideal theater and battleground.' " Bernard Fall confirmed that in Washington, also, one faction believed "that the Vietnam affair could be transformed into a 'golden opportunity' to 'solve' the Red Chinese problem as well" (*Vietnam Witness 1953-1966* [New York: Praeger, 1966] p. 103; cf. Hilsman, p. 311; Scott, *The War Conspiracy*, pp. 21-23, 208).

and full U.S. political support."[98] This autumn 1963 military offensive in Laos coincided with escalation of activities against Prince Sihanouk in Cambodia by the CIA-supported Khmer Serei in South Vietnam. After two infiltrating Khmer Serei agents had been captured and had publicly confessed, Cambodia on November 19 severed all military and economic ties with the United States, and one month later broke off diplomatic relations.[99]

All of these disturbing events suggest that, in late 1963, covert operations were beginning to escape the political limitations, both internal and international (e.g., the Harriman-Pushkin agreement), established during the course of the Kennedy Administration. During the months of September and October many established newspapers, including the *New York Times*, began to complain about the CIA's arrogation of power; and this concern was echoed in Congress by Senator Mansfield.[100] The evi-

---

[98] D. Gareth Porter, in Nina S. Adams and Alfred W. McCoy, eds., *Laos: War and Revolution* (New York: Harper and Row, 1970), p. 198. An Air America plane shot down in September 1963 carried an American pilot along with both Thai and KMT troops, like so many other Air America planes in this period. The political assassinations of April 1963, which led to a resumption of fighting, have been frequently attributed to a CIA-trained assassination team recruited by Vientiane Security Chief Siho Lamphoutacoul, who was half Chinese (Scott, *The War Conspiracy*, p. 36). After Siho's coup of April 19, 1964, which ended Laotian neutralism and led rapidly to the U.S. air war, the *New York Times* noted that "In 1963 he attended the general staff training school in Taiwan and came under the influence of the son of Generalissimo Chiang Kai-shek, General Chiang Ching-kuo, who had learned secret police methods in Moscow and was the director of the Chinese Nationalist security services" (*NYT*, April 27, 1964, p. 4).

[99] *NYT*, November 20, 1963, p. 1: The two prisoners "said they had conducted activities against the Cambodian Government in a fortified hamlet in neighboring South Vietnam under control of U.S. military advisers. They said Radio Free Cambodia transmitters had been set up in such villages. One prisoner said he had been supplied with a transmitter by U.S. officials." For U.S. corroboration of CIA involvement in Khmer Serei operations, cf. Scott, *The War Conspiracy*, pp. 158-159.

[100] A *New York Times* editorial (October 6, 1963, IV, 8) noting "long-voiced charges that our intelligence organization too often tends to 'make' policy," added that "there is an inevitable tendency for some of its personnel to assume the functions of kingmakers," in answer to its question "Is the Central Intelligence Agency a state within a state?" Cf. Washington *Daily News*, October 2, 1963, reprinted in *Congressional Record*, October 1963, p. 18602: "If the United States ever experiences a 'Seven Days in May' it will come from the CIA, and not the Pentagon, one U.S. official commented caustically. . . . People . . . are beginning to fear the CIA is becoming a third force, coequal with President Diem's regime and the U.S. government and answerable to neither."

dence now published in the Pentagon Papers, including Kennedy's NSAM 249 of June and the Gravel chronology's testimony to the resumption of crossborder operations, also suggests that covert operations may have been escalated in defiance of the President's secret directives.

If this chronology is correct, then Pentagon Study IV.C.2.a's efforts to show continuity between the Kennedy and Johnson regimes suggest instead that President Kennedy had lost control of covert planning and operations. OPLAN 34–63, which "apparently . . . was not forwarded to the White House"[101]

was discussed during the Vietnam policy conference at Honolulu, 20 November 1963. Here a decision was made to develop a combined COMUSMACV-CAS, Saigon plan for a 12-month program of covert operations.

That NSAM 273's innovations were hatched at Honolulu is suggested also by the Honolulu press communiqué, which, anticipating NSAM 273(1), spoke of "an encouraging outlook for the *principal objective* of joint U.S.-Vietnamese policy in South Vietnam." In Pentagon Study IV.B.4, this anticipatory quotation is completed by language reminiscent of Kennedy's in early 1961 "—the successful prosecution of the war against the Viet Cong communists."[102] But at the Honolulu press conference the same key phrase was pointedly (and presciently) glossed by Defense and State spokesmen Arthur Sylvester and Robert C. Manning, in language which Kennedy had never used or authorized, to mean "the successful promotion of the war against the *North Vietnam* Communists."[103]

Study IV.C.2.a's implication that the escalation planning decision was made officially by the Honolulu Conference (rather than at it without Kennedy's authorization) is hard to reconcile with the other Studies' references to the Conference's "optimism" and projections of withdrawal. The author gives no footnote for these crucial sentences; and in contrast to his own Chronol-

[101] Gravel ed., III: 141.
[102] USG ed., IV.B.4, p. 25; Gravel ed., III:190.
[103] Washington *Post*, November 21, 1963, A 19; San Francisco *Chronicle*, November 21, 1963, p. 13; emphasis added.

ogy he does not even mention NSAM 273. His next citation is to the JCS directive on November 26 (which, we learn from his own Chronology and Stavins, repeats that of NSAM 273 itself);[104] but this citation clearly begs the question of what official decision, if any, was reached on November 20. What is left of interest in the author's paragraph is the speedy authorization by the infant Johnson Administration, and the personal guidance added to the new JCS directives by the new President himself.

NSAM 273, it seems clear, was an important document in the history of the 1964 escalations, as well as in the reversal of President Kennedy's late and ill-fated program of "Vietnamization" by 1965. The systematic censorship and distortion of NSAM 273 in 1963 and again in 1971, by the Pentagon study and later by the *New York Times*, raises serious questions about the *bona fides* of the Pentagon study. . . . It also suggests that the Kennedy assassination was itself an important, perhaps a crucial, event in the history of the Indochina war. . . .

[104] Stavins *et al.*, pp. 93-94; cf. USG ed., IV.C.2.a, p. viii: "NSAM 273 Authorized planning for specific covert operations, graduated in intensity, against the DRV."

APPENDIX A

NSAM 273 of November 26, 1963: a partial reconstruction of the text

IV.C.1, pp. 46–47; = Gr. III:50; Johnson, p. 45	TO: [All the senior officers of the government responsible for foreign affairs and military policy]
ªobject, IV.C.1	1. It remains the central objectiveª of the United States in South Vietnam to assist the people and Government of that country to win their contest against the externally directed and supported communist conspiracy. The test of all U.S. decisions and actions in

ᵇ*overriding objective,* *NYT,* Nov. 25, 1963, p. 5

this area should be the effectiveness of their contribution to this purpose.ᵇ

IV.C.1, p. 2; = Gr. III:18. IV.B.3, p. 37; = Gr. II:276 ᶜ*objectives,* IV.B.2, p. 26; IV.B.5, p. 67. *objective,* IV.B.3, p. 37

[2.] The objectivesᶜ of the United States with respect to the withdrawal of U.S. military personnel remain as stated in the White House statement of October 2, 1963.

IV.C.1, p. 3; = Gr. III:19

3. It is a major interest of the United States government that the present provisional government of South Vietnam should be assisted in consolidating itself in holding and developing increased public support . . . [*NYT:* for programs directed toward winning the war].

IV.C.1, p. 2; = Gr. III:18; Johnson, p. 45; IV.B.5, p. 67

[4.] The President expects that all senior officers of the government will move energetically to insure the full unity of support for established U.S. policy in South Vietnam. Both in Washington and in the field, it is essential that the government be unified. It is of particular importance that express or implied criticism of officers of other branches be assiduously avoided in all contacts with the Vietnamese government and with the press.

IV.C.1, p. 3; = Gr. III:18; IV.B.5, p. 67

5. We should concentrate our efforts, and insofar as possible we should persuade the government of South Vietnam to concentrate its effort, on the critical situation in the Mekong Delta. This concentration should include not only military but economic, social, educational and informational effort. We should seek to turn the tide not only of battle but of belief, and we should seek to increase not only the controlled hamlets but the productivity of this area, especially where the proceeds can be held for the advantage of anti-Communist forces.

IV.B.5, p. 67; = Gr. II:276
IV.C.1, p. 2; = Gr. III:18

[6.] [Economic and military aid to the new regime should be maintained at the same levels as during Diem's rule.]

[6.] [Both military and economic programs, it was emphasized, should be maintained at levels as high as those in the time of the Diem regime.]

Cooper, p. 224

[Johnson . . . stressed that all military and economic programs were to be kept at the levels maintained during the Diem regime.]

IV.B.3, p. 37; = Gr. II:458

[U.S. assistance programs should be maintained at levels at least equal to those under the Diem government so that the new CVN would not be tempted to regard the U.S. as seeking to disengage.]

IV.C.2.a, p. viii; = Gr. III:117

[7?] [NSAM 273 Authorized planning for specific covert operations, graduated in intensity, against the DRV.]

Stavins, pp. 94–95
Stavins, p. 93; = Gr. III:141; cf. IV.C.2.a, p. 2

[NSAM 273 authorized Krulak to form a committee and develop a coherent program of covert activities to be conducted during 1964, while the rest of the national security apparatus explored the feasibility of initiating a wider war against the North. . . . This NSAM provided that] . . . planning should include different levels of possible increased activity, and in each instance there should be estimates of such factors as:

    a. Resulting damage to NVN;
    b. The plausibility of denial;
    c. Possible NVN retaliation;
    d. Other international reaction.

IV.B.5, p. xxxiv (suppressed) ; = Gr. II:223

[Clandestine operations against the North and into Laos are authorized.]

IV.B.5, p. 67; = Gr. II:276

[And in conclusion, plans were requested for clandestine operations by the GVN against the North and also for operations up to 50 kilometers into Laos.]

Gr. III:141	[8?] [The directive also called for a plan, to be submitted for approval, for military operations] "up to a line up to 50 km. inside Laos, together with political plans for minimizing the international hazards of such an enterprise" (NSAM 273) .
V.B.3, p. 37; = Gr. II:458	[Military operations should be initiated, under close political control, up to within fifty kilometers inside of Laos.]
IV.B.5, p. 67; = Gr. II:276; = NYT/Bantam, p. 233	[9?] [As a justification for such measures, State was directed to develop a strong, documented case] "to demonstrate to the world the degree to which the Viet Cong is controlled, sustained, and supplied from Hanoi, through Laos and other channels."
Johnson, p. 45	[The NSAM also assigned various specific actions to the appropriate department or agency of government.]

APPENDIX B

Clues to the existence on November 24, 1963, of a White House paraphrase of NSAM 273 (paragraphs 1 to 4) for press purposes.

Both the *New York Times*[1] and Washington Post,[2] referring in customary terms to a White House source or sources, printed paraphrases of NSAM 273's first (i.e., more innocuous and misleading) page, and these paraphrases share certain divergences from the official text. These shared divergences suggest the existence of an intermediary written archetype, a background paper for the use of certain preferred correspondents. (The *Times* paraphrase was printed in a story by E. W. Kenworthy, who later helped write and edit the New York Times/Bantam Pentagon Papers.)

[1] *NYT*, November 25, 1963, p. 5.
[2] Washington *Post*, November 25, 1963, A2.

SAMPLE DIVERGENCES:

NSAM 273(1)	It remains the central objective of the United States
Washington Post	central point of United States policy remains
New York Times	central point of United States policy remains

NSAM 273(1)	contribution to this purpose
Washington Post	directed toward that objective
New York Times	contribution to this overriding objective

NSAM 273(4)	senior officers . . . move . . . to insure the full unity of support
Washington Post	all Government agencies . . . complete unity of purpose
New York Times	All agencies . . . full unity of purpose

The press reports of this paraphrase suggest that the closing words of NSAM 273(3), as quoted in USG ed., IV.C.3 (p. 3), may have been suppressed; and that the increased "public support" referred to was not in fact political but military:

NYT, November 25, 1963, p. 5: "development of public support for programs directed toward winning the war."

San Francisco *Chronicle* (AP and UPI), November 25, 1963, p. 5: "to develop public support for its policies aimed at winning the war against the Communist Viet Cong."

Los Angeles *Times*, November 25, 1963, p. 6: "development of programs to oppose the Viet Cong."

AP, as quoted by Peking Radio, November 25, 1963 (FBIS *Daily Report*, November 26, 1963, BBB4): "consolidate its position and win public support for the policy mapped out by it, in order to win the war against the Vietnamese Communists."

NSAM 273(3), as quoted in USG ed., IV.C.1, p. 3: "the present provisional government of South Vietnam should be assisted in consolidating itself in holding and developing increased public support."

ASSASSINATIONS AND DOMESTIC SURVEILLANCE
Peter Dale Scott

1975

Events since the Kennedy assassination have alerted us to the possibility of illicit collaboration between members of Army Intelligence and the Secret Service. In 1970 the Washington *Star* reported that "plainclothes military intelligence agents played a questionable—and still secret—surveillance role at the 1968 national conventions" in Chicago, where the Secret Service admitted borrowing agents from the Illinois-based 113th Intelligence Group (Washington *Star*, Dec. 2, 1970, A-8). These borrowed "security" forces conducted extensive domestic intelligence operations, and there were rumors of provocations as well. In 1972 there were similar rumors about the 1972 party conventions and the 111th Intelligence Group in Miami, where one provocateur (Pablo Fernandez) was said to be a former CIA agent working with Watergate burglar E. Howard Hunt (*Nation*, October 1, 1973, p. 297; *Saturday Review-World*, September 11, 1973, p. 28 [supra, pp. 392–406]). What we know from these later disturbances suggests that it is now common practice for the Secret Service, whose local offices are scantily staffed, to augment their staff for special events with auxiliary personnel from military Intelligence and other sources.

Quite by accident, we know that the Dallas Secret Service recruited thirty men from the Fort Worth Chamber of Commerce Sports Committee (of whom the informant at least was a former Army Air Force Intelligence officer) to "assist the Secret Service at the breakfast for President Kennedy" on November 22 (18 H 691). In Dallas, where Adlai Stevenson had been attacked only one month earlier, one would have expected the Secret Service, which gave "special attention" to this event (2 H 108), to recruit even more such auxiliaries. Yet the reports and testimony of

Winston Lawson and other Secret Service agents are silent on this score. Meanwhile the FBI reported that its offer of assistance had been declined (17 H 821). The Warren Commission, faced with reports and rumors of unexplained additional "Secret Service" on the grassy knoll (6 H 196), with Deputy Chief George Lumpkin (4 H 162), behind the Texas School Book Depository (6 H 312), in front of the TSBD (19 H 524, 20 H 443) and even at the Tippit killing (3 H 332, cf. 12 H 202, 24 H 204, 12 H 45) asked no questions and learned nothing.

Political constraints made it difficult for the Warren Commission, which had questionable constitutional authority and no independent investigative staff, to pursue the documentary indications of a possible conspiracy linking Army Intelligence and the local Dallas police to the Secret Service. Thus one might exculpate the Warren Commission for not having asked more questions of high-level witnesses, such as Washington Secret Service Inspector Thomas J. Kelley. It was Kelley who ratified the strange and possibly illegal arrangements under which the Secret Service, after being telephoned by Peter Gregory himself, sequestered Marina Oswald for thirty-six hours from other investigative agencies and brought in Gregory as her interpreter (2 H 344, CD 5.292, CD 87, SS 533.1-2 cf.; 20 H 445). Kelley himself had attended four interviews with Oswald but was not questioned about them (7 H 403); he was questioned only about his later role in the controversial official "reenactment" of the assassination, concerning which conflicting testimony had been received (5 H 130).

Considering the Warren Commission's difficulties in the face of so many unanswered questions about the role of the Secret Service, the failure to pursue these questions is less surprising than the Warren Commission's controversial recommendations that the Secret Service's domestic surveillance responsibilities be radically *increased* (R 25-26). Somewhat illogically, the Warren Report concluded both "that Oswald acted alone" (R 22), like most American assassins (R 463), and also that the Secret Service, FBI, and CIA, should coordinate more closely the surveillance of "organized groups" (R 463). In particular it recommended that the Secret Service acquire a computerized data bank compatible with that already developed by the CIA (R 464-65, cf. 5 H 125, 472-75, 577-79).

Thanks to Senator Ervin's investigation into federal data banks, in the wake of the Army Intelligence espionage scandals of 1970, we know that these recommendations were eventually implemented, under the direction of the same Thomas J. Kelley, who by now was assistant director of the Secret Service for Protective Intelligence (*The New York Times*, June 28, 1970, p. 42, reprinted in *Federal Data Banks Hearings*, p. 1669). The Warren Commission's recommendation was by 1970 "widely cited in the government as the authority for citizen surveillance" by any agency, including the controversial Army Intelligence program (loc. cit., p. 1668).

Federal domestic surveillance increased after November 22, 1963, even before this recommendation; and it increased again after the Watts and Detroit riots. For Army Intelligence "the big build-up in information gathering, however, did not come until after the shooting of the Rev. Martin Luther King, Jr. in April 1968" (Washington *Star*, Dec. 6, 1970, reprinted in *Federal Data Banks Hearings*, p. 1728). Army Intelligence agents were assigned to spy at the 1968 political conventions because the Secret Service "had been handed the job of protecting presidential candidates after the June 5, 1968, assassination of Senator Robert F. Kennedy—and didn't have enough men of its own" (Washington *Star*, December 2, 1970, reprinted in *Federal Data Banks Hearings*, p. 1752). The termination of these Army Intelligence programs, after their disclosure in 1970, led directly to the Huston Plan and the succeeding series of White House intelligence operations, which climaxed with the so-called "plumbers" unit of Watergate burglar E. Howard Hunt. Once again Thomas J. Kelley was the Secret Service participant in at least one of these clandestine White House units (*Watergate Hearings*, p. 3401).

Of all these increases in domestic surveillance policy, perhaps the sharpest and most questionable were those granted the Secret Service by Public Law 90-331 on June 6, 1968. Although this measure was publicly debated and passed in response to Senator Robert Kennedy's death that same day, it had in fact been proposed by President Johnson two weeks earlier, and had already been discussed at a secret Senate subcommittee hearing on May 27, 1968. Under PL 90-331 the Secret Service can request assistance from any other federal department or agency. This vague provision was later used to cloak the secret expansion of the White House budget under Nixon (some say to $100 million a year) and to justify such extraordinary expenditures as the $17 million of public funds spent on Nixon's San Clemente estate.

This rapid glance at the post-assassination increase in domestic surveillance operations does not tell us anything about who committed those assassinations. It does however refute the absurd but frequently encountered hypothesis that assassinations have had no impact on the structure of U. S. government. Not only have assassinations (or attempts at assassination) had a very direct bearing on the outcome of the last three presidential elections, they have also helped inaugurate a new era of domestic intelligence operations which, as one Nixon official conceded, "would have been unthinkable, and frankly, unattainable from Congress in a different climate" (*Federal Data Banks Hearings*, p. 1668).

Thus the failure of the Warren Commission to establish the true facts about the John F. Kennedy assassination, and the subsequent failure of Congress to rectify that deficiency, have a direct bearing on America's current political crisis and erosion of congressional power. I have tried to suggest that, on the grounds of the documentary evidence alone there exists a case for the reopening of an official investigation of what happened in Dallas, one which this time will not be left in the hands of federal and local agencies which ought more properly to have been themselves under suspicion. It would appear to be a matter of practical urgency, not just of historical curiosity, to challenge the Warren Commission's dubious mandate for what became an unprecedented program of political espionage. Once again, as so often in history, the key to a more open and rational future would appear to lie in a better understanding of our past.

Unpublished manuscript. © 1975 Peter Dale Scott.

THE ROCKEFELLER
COMMISSION AND
ITS UNANSWERED
QUESTIONS

INTRODUCTION

The CIA came through Watergate relatively unscathed, but it was embroiled in its own scandal within a few months of President Richard Nixon's resignation. The New York Times *published a series of reports that the agency had engaged in massive illegal domestic operations. To investigate these charges, President Gerald Ford appointed a commission headed by Vice-President Nelson Rockefeller. The Commission's report, released in June 1975, includes a short chapter on the John F. Kennedy assassination, which is reprinted below.*

Various factors (such as the viewing of the Zapruder film on national television) led the Commission to report on the Kennedy assassination, and President Ford (who had served on the Warren Commission) indicated his approval of the new investigation at an April 3, 1975, press conference (see above, p.305). The question of CIA assassination plots against foreign leaders quickly became the most sensitive area of the Rockefeller Commission's concerns, and helped to revive speculation about assassinations in the United States. Another area of great public concern was the residue of unanswered questions from the Watergate affair, notably those surrounding the activities of E. Howard Hunt and his associates. Finally, the presence of former Warren Commission staff lawyer David W. Belin as executive director of the Rockefeller Commission probably influenced the Commission's ill-advised attempt to shore up the Warren Report. It has also been reported that Belin was influential in persuading

*the Commission to investigate assassination plots against Cuban
Premier Fidel Castro.*

*Although public interest was undoubtedly heightened by
extensive media coverage of allegations that Hunt and his long-
time associate Frank (Fiorini) Sturgis were at the scene of the
Kennedy assassination, it is regrettable that these charges
became the focus of the Rockefeller Commission's treatment of
the assassination.*

*We are including two pieces which were submitted to the
Commission in early April 1975. In both cases, Executive Director Belin responded by asking the authors about Lee Oswald's
connection with the killing of Police Officer J. D. Tippit. The
content of both pieces was ignored by the Commission, at least
in its published report. For the historical record, we also include
Dr. Cyril Wecht's response to the report, indicating that the
thrust of his testimony on the medical evidence was distorted.*

THE CIA AND THE MAN WHO WAS NOT OSWALD
Bernard Fensterwald and George O'Toole

The New York Review of Books / *April 3, 1975*

Six weeks before the assassination of President Kennedy on
November 22, 1963, the Central Intelligence Agency sent the
following teletype message to the Federal Bureau of Investigation and the Departments of State and the Navy:

Subject: Lee Henry OSWALD

1. On 1 October 1963 a reliable and sensitive source in Mexico reported that an American male, who identified himself as Lee OSWALD, contacted the Soviet Embassy in Mexico City inquiring whether the Embassy had received any news concerning a telegram which had been sent to Washington. The American was described as approximately 35 years old, with an athletic build, about six feet tall, with a receding hairline.

2. It is believed that OSWALD may be identical to Lee Henry OSWALD, born on 18 October 1939 in New Orleans, Louisiana. A former U.S. Marine who defected to the Soviet Union in October 1959 and later made arrangement through the United States Embassy in Moscow to return to the United States with his Russian-born wife, Marina Nikolaevna Pusakova, and their child.

3. The information in paragraph one is being disseminated to your representatives in Mexico City. Any further information received on this subject will be furnished you. This information is being made available to the Immigration and Naturalization Service.[1]

Was the Lee *Henry* Oswald of the CIA message Lee Harvey Oswald? Yes, according to Richard Helms, then chief of the Agency's Clandestine Services. In a March 1964 memorandum to J. Lee Rankin, general counsel to the Warren Commission, Helms explained that "OSWALD'S middle name was erroneously given as 'Henry' in the subject line and in paragraph two of the dissemination. . . . The maiden surname of Mrs. OSWALD was mistakenly listed as 'PUSAKOVA.' "[2]

But Lee Harvey Oswald was not "approximately 35 years old, with an athletic build"; he was twenty-three years old and slender.[3] Apparently the CIA was concerned about the discrepancy, for on October 23 it sent the following message to the Department of the Navy:

Subject: Lee Henry OSWALD

Reference is made to CIA Out Teletype No. 74673 [the earlier message], dated 10 October 1963, regarding possible presence of subject in

[1] Warren Commission Document 631, The National Archives, Washington, D.C.

[2] Ibid. Her correct maiden name was Prusakova.

[3] *Report of the President's Commission on the Assassination of President Kennedy* (US Government Printing Office, 1964), p. 144. (Hereafter, *Report.*)

Mexico City. It is requested that you forward to this office as soon as possible two copies of the most recent photograph you have of subject. We will forward them to our representative in Mexico, who will attempt to determine if the Lee OSWALD in Mexico City and subject are the same individual.[4]

Since Oswald had served in the Marine Corps, which comes under the administration of the Navy, his personnel records would have included his photograph.

What the Agency did not say in this cable is that it had in its possession a photograph of the man who had apparently "identified himself" as Oswald. The man in the CIA photo was not Lee Harvey Oswald; he was, just as the Agency's "reliable and sensitive source" had described him, approximately thirty-five years old, with an athletic build and a receding hairline.

According to a memorandum by Helms, the CIA never received the Navy's pictures of Oswald and only concluded after the assassination that two different people were involved.[5] Meanwhile, the photograph was delivered to the FBI on November 22, 1963.[6]

One can only guess at the confusion caused by the picture. The FBI needed no Navy photograph to establish that the mystery man was not Oswald—Lee Harvey Oswald was sitting handcuffed in a third-floor office of the Dallas police headquarters. The next day Special Agent Bardwell D. Odum was dispatched with the photograph to the motel where Oswald's wife and mother were hidden. He showed the picture to Mrs. Marguerite Oswald, mother of the accused assassin. Mrs. Oswald looked at the photo and told Odum she didn't recognize the man.[7] The following day, however, shortly after her son was murdered in the basement of Dallas City Hall, Mrs. Oswald erroneously identified the mystery man. She told the press the FBI had shown her a picture of Jack Ruby the night before.

[4] Commission Document 631, op cit.

[5] Ibid.

[6] Hearings Before the President's Commission on the Assassination of President Kennedy (US Government Printing Office, 1964), Vol. 11, p. 469 (hereafter, Hearings).

[7] Ibid., p. 468.

Mrs. Oswald's mistake was understandable—the mystery man bore a superficial resemblance to Jack Ruby, and in her recollection of a brief glance at the photograph, two faces became one. But the misidentification made it necessary for the Warren Commission to refer, however obliquely, to the affair of the mystery man. In the twenty-six volumes of published testimony and evidence supplementary to the Warren Report, the Commission printed the picture that was shown to Mrs. Oswald.[8] The Warren Report contains a very brief account of the incident.

According to the Report, the CIA had provided the FBI with a photograph of "a man who, it was thought at the time, might have been associated with Oswald."[9] The Report quoted an affidavit by Richard Helms that "the original photograph had been taken by the CIA outside of the United States sometime between July 1, 1963 and November 22, 1963."[10]

The Commission's explanation is both inaccurate and misleading. The implication that the CIA thought the mystery man was "associated with Oswald" only masks the true situation. On the basis of its own evidence, the Agency must have concluded either that the mystery man was impersonating Oswald or that an unlikely chain of errors had accidentally linked both the man in the photograph and the man who "contacted" the Soviet Embassy to Lee Harvey Oswald.

The truth was further obscured by the Report's reference to the Helms affidavit, which described the circumstances in which the mystery man was photographed only in the most vague and general terms. The affidavit was dated August 7, 1964.[11] However, the Commission never mentioned in its Report or in its twenty-six supplementary volumes that it had obtained an earlier affidavit from Helms on July 22, 1964 in which he was much more specific.[12] "The original photograph," Helms testified, "was taken in Mexico City on October 4, 1963."[13] (This earlier Helms affi-

8 Ibid., Odum Exhibit 1.
9 *Report*, p. 364.
10 Ibid., pp. 364-365.
11 *Hearings*, Vol. 11, p. 469.
12 Commission Document 1287, The National Archives, Washington, D.C.
13 Ibid.

davit was released in 1967 through the efforts of Paul Hoch, a private researcher.)

There is no available record that Richard Helms ever told the Warren Commission exactly where in Mexico City the mystery man was photographed, but the circumstances in which the photograph was given to the Commission offer a very plausible suggestion. The CIA required the FBI to crop out the background in the photo before handing it over to the Commission.[14] The obvious conclusion is that the photograph was taken by a hidden surveillance camera, and the CIA wished to avoid disclosing its location. According to knowledgeable former employees of the CIA, the Soviet and Cuban embassies, among others in Mexico City, were under constant photographic surveillance at the time. It seems likely then that the man who, according to the CIA, "identified himself as Lee Oswald" was photographed leaving the Mexico City embassy of the Soviet Union or of some other communist country.

The first public hint that the mystery man may have been impersonating Oswald came in 1966, with the publication of Edward Jay Epstein's *Inquest*, a scholarly study of the Warren Commission.[15] Epstein interviewed one of the Commission's legal staff who recalled the incident. He said he had asked Raymond G. Rocca, the Agency's liaison with the Commission,[16] about the photograph. The lawyer later received word from the Agency that the mystery man was thought to be Oswald at the time the photograph was given to the FBI. Why, he asked, did the Agency mistake someone so dissimilar in appearance for Lee Harvey Oswald? The CIA said they would check further and call him back. The lawyer told Epstein that they never called him back and the Warren Report contains no explanation of the Agency's mistake.[17]

---

[14] *Hearings*, Vol. 11, p. 469.

[15] Edward Jay Epstein, *Inquest: The Warren Commission and the Establishment of Truth* (Viking, 1966).

[16] Mr. Rocca, deputy chief of the CIA's Counterintelligence Staff, was one of the four senior Agency officials who resigned last December in the wake of *The New York Times*'s revelations of illegal domestic operations by the CIA's Clandestine Services.

[17] Epstein, *Inquest*, p. 94.

Another piece of the puzzle fell into place early in 1971, when the National Archives released a previously classified memorandum about the mystery man from Richard Helms to the Commission's general counsel, J. Lee Rankin.[18] Dated March 24, 1964, the memo informed Rankin:

On 22 and 23 November, immediately following the assassination of President Kennedy, three cabled reports were received from [deleted] in Mexico City relative to photographs of an unidentified man who visited the Cuban and Soviet Embassies in that city during October and November 1963. . . .[19]

On the basis of these cables, Helms went on to say, the CIA had sent several reports to the Secret Service. Attached to the Helms memorandum were paraphrases of these reports.[20] Two dealt with the mystery man:

Message to the Protective Research Staff, The Secret Service, delivered by hand on 23 November 1963, at 1030 hours.

Through sources available to it, the CIA [deleted] had come into possession of a photograph of an unidentified person thought to have visited the Cuban Embassy in mid-October. This individual, it was believed at the time, might be identical with Lee Harvey OSWALD.[21]

and,

Message to the Protective Research Staff, The Secret Service, delivered by hand on 23 November 1963, at 1030 hours.

CIA Headquarters was informed [deleted] on 23 November that several photographs of a person known to frequent the Soviet Embassy in Mexico City, and who might be identical with Lee Harvey OSWALD, had been forwarded to Washington by the hand of a United States official returning to this country.[22]

---

[18] Commission Document 674, The National Archives, Washington, D.C.
[19] Ibid.
[20] Ibid.
[21] Ibid.
[22] Ibid.

Helms's covering memorandum affirmed that "the subject of the photographs mentioned in these reports is not Lee Harvey OSWALD."[23]

Several photographs, then, of a mysterious stranger who kept being confused with Lee Harvey Oswald, and who had visited *both* the Soviet and Cuban embassies. Was it the same mystery man whose picture had been shown to Mrs. Oswald? Or was it yet another Oswald Doppelgänger?

Firm evidence of the existence of additional photographs of the unidentified man mentioned in the Warren Report was turned up by Robert Smith, a private researcher. In 1972 Smith, then research director for the Committee to Investigate Assassinations, was poring over some recently declassified Warren Commission documents when he found reference to the mystery photo *and two other views of the same person.*[24] Smith called his discovery to the attention of one of the authors, Bernard Fensterwald, who instituted a suit under the Freedom of Information Act for release of the two pictures. The government yielded and turned over the photographs to Fensterwald and Smith.

The two new views of the mystery man were taken at a different time from the first picture. In the first picture, the one published in the Warren Commission volumes, he is wearing a long-sleeved dark shirt and appears empty-handed; in the two new photos he is wearing a short-sleeved white shirt and is carrying some kind of bag or pouch. The new photos also show him holding a small, passport-sized booklet and what appears to be a wallet. As in the first photograph, the backgrounds of the two new photos have been cropped out. Whoever he was, he managed to be photographed, apparently by the CIA's hidden surveillance cameras, on at least two separate occasions. And neither of the new photographs reveals any resemblance between the mystery man and Lee Harvey Oswald.

The Warren Commission concluded that Oswald had been in Mexico in late September and early October 1963. Records of Mexican Customs and Immigration, bus lines, and a Mexico

[23] Ibid.
[24] Commsision Document 566, The National Archives, Washington, D.C., pp. 3-4.

City hotel indicate that Oswald entered Mexico at Nuevo Laredo on the U.S. border on September 26, traveled by bus to Mexico City, arriving there the next morning, and returned to the United States on October 3.[25] Passengers on the bus to Mexico City remembered Oswald, but there is almost no eyewitness testimony to support the Commission's reconstruction of Oswald's movements after he arrived in that city.[26] The Commission's finding that Oswald made repeated visits to both the Soviet and Cuban embassies rests heavily upon the affidavit of one witness, a Mexican woman who worked at the Cuban Embassy.[27]

Silvia Tirado de Duran was secretary to the Cuban Consul in Mexico City. In a sworn statement[28] she gave to the deputy director of Mexican Federal Security on November 23, 1963, she said that Oswald had visited the Cuban Embassy in late September to apply for a visa to visit Cuba during a planned trip to the Soviet Union. Mrs. Duran recalled a heated exchange between Oswald and the Consul when the Cuban official told him his request could not be granted immediately. She remembered making a "semiofficial" phone call to the Soviet Embassy to try to speed up action on Oswald's application. She identified the Lee Harvey Oswald who visited the Cuban Embassy as the accused assassin whose photograph appeared in the Mexican newspapers on November 23.[29]

Apparently the Warren Commission staff did not interview Silvia Duran, but instead relied solely on her affidavit. Whether any attempt to talk to her was made is not recorded in any available document. However, according to the Commission files,

---

[25] *Report*, p. 299.

[26] Ibid., pp. 733-736.

[27] Ibid., p. 734. Two other witnesses told the FBI they saw Oswald at the Cuban Embassy. A Mexican private detective who had visited the embassy on October 1, 1963, identified Oswald from newspaper photographs as someone he had seen leaving the embassy on that date in the company of a Cuban. The detective was shown other photos of Oswald and failed to identify him, and the FBI seems to have concluded that he was mistaken (Commission Document 566). The Warren Report does not offer the detective's testimony as evidence of Oswald's visit. Another witness who claimed to have seen Oswald at the Cuban Embassy retracted his testimony after failing to pass a polygraph examination (*Report*, p. 308).

[28] Commission Document 776a, The National Archives, Washington, D.C.

[29] Ibid., p. 5.

a Mexican newspaper reporter tried to interview her in April 1964. Her husband would not permit the man to speak with her, saying "she had suffered a nervous breakdown following her interrogation by the Mexican authorities and had been prohibited by her physician . . . from discussing the Oswald matter further."[30] If this report is correct, the interrogation of Silvia Duran may have been a more emotional interview than one would conclude from the report forwarded by the Mexican police. The report gives the impression that the police were routinely collecting information about Oswald's Mexican trip for the American authorities. One question that arises is whether Duran's statement was given voluntarily, and, if not, whether her identification of Oswald as the visitor to the embassy is valid.

The Warren Commission may have omitted a full exploration of this question because it had collateral evidence of Oswald's visit to the Cuban Embassy. There were, for example, Oswald's application for a Cuban visa, bearing his photograph and signature,[31] and a letter reportedly written by Oswald to the Soviet Embassy in Washington, referring to his visit to the Cuban Embassy.[32] The address book found among Oswald's possessions, moreover, contained Duran's name and telephone number. But the only credible eyewitness testimony that Oswald in fact visited the embassy is the statement of Silvia Duran.

When viewed in the light of the recently disclosed evidence suggesting that someone might have visited the embassy impersonating Oswald, the Commission's failure to settle completely the question of the three misidentified photos seems extraordinary. It is probable that the CIA did in fact supply an explanation of the photographs that was enough to satisfy the Commission at the time. If so, that explanation remains a part of the classified Warren Commission documents not available to the public.

Raymond Rocca (who, until his recent resignation, was the Agency's action officer for all post-Warren Report inquiries about the matter) told one of the authors that the CIA could not iden-

---

[30] Commission Document 963, The National Archives, Washington, D.C., p. 16.
[31] *Hearings*, Commission Exhibit 2564.
[32] Ibid., Commission Exhibit 15.

tify the mystery man. If this is so, we may wonder how the Agency could have offered a satisfactory explanation of the incident to the Commission. Until additional documents bearing on this matter are declassified, the conclusion that Oswald really visited the Cuban Embassy must remain in some doubt. But even if he did, the question whether someone was nevertheless trying to impersonate him remains a crucial one.

If someone posing as Oswald visited the Soviet and Cuban embassies in the early autumn of 1963, what implications might be drawn from this discovery? One obvious interpretation is that someone sought to counterfeit a fresh connection between the man who was soon to become the accused presidential assassin and the governments of those two communist countries. But it is not necessary to speculate further. If someone were trying to impersonate Oswald eight weeks before the assassination, the Warren Commission's theory of a lone assassin, unconnected with any conspiracy, is seriously undermined and the case should be reopened.

There could be, of course, an innocent explanation of how the CIA came to misidentify the mystery man as Lee Harvey Oswald. Oswald may actually have visited the Cuban and Soviet embassies. If this were the case, then somewhere in the CIA's files there should be photographs of the real Lee Harvey Oswald departing from the Soviet and Cuban embassies in Mexico City. If those photographs exist, their publication would help to settle the question. If they don't, the CIA should now explain why not. In either case, it should also disclose what it knows about the man it wrongly identified as Oswald on two separate occasions. It should explain why it believes that this man was not impersonating Oswald. All these matters should be clarified both by the CIA itself and by the congressional committees that are about to investigate its activities.

CIA ACTIVITIES AND THE WARREN COMMISSION INVESTIGATION
Paul L. Hoch

March 24, 1975

I. INTRODUCTION

A. FEDERAL INTELLIGENCE AGENCIES AND THE KENNEDY ASSASSINATION

Even before the disclosures of the last three months, there were ample reasons for an investigation of improper activities by the CIA and the FBI in the case of Lee Harvey Oswald, and of the extent of the cooperation between these agencies and the Warren Commission.

After the assassination, allegations were promptly made that Oswald had been an informant or employee of some intelligence agency (and that therefore the Secret Service had not been warned about him). Even though the Warren Commission took these reports very seriously, it failed to properly investigate either this specific charge or the exact nature of the relationships between Oswald and the CIA, the FBI and military intelligence.

The bulk of the Commission's investigation was done through various federal agencies, notably the FBI. Thus these agencies were in large part responsible for the cover-up of much of what the Commission was supposed to be reporting for the American people. It is clear, for example, that the FBI misled the Warren Commission about the extent of its files on Oswald, and also in other ways discouraged the Commission from examining the implications of some of the Bureau's intelligence-gathering methods—e.g., the interception of several of Oswald's letters to left-wing political groups. Hoover sidetracked the Commission's investigation of the allegation that Oswald had been an FBI informant, and went through semantic contortions to deny the fact that Jack Ruby had apparently been a Potential Criminal Informant for the FBI.

B. The Utility of a Study of the Records

The Oswald case provides an unusual opportunity to check the practices and records of one intelligence agency against the files kept by other agencies. A great deal of information has been published by the Warren Commission, made available in the National Archives, or preserved there but not released. This includes the purportedly complete files on Oswald of the CIA, the State Department, and the Defense Department (including the Office of Naval Intelligence), as well as a list of the FBI Headquarters file. There is, however, evidence that those files are not complete, and suggestions that sensitive or improper activities, domestic and foreign, were not fully recorded in the appropriate files. An analysis of the flow of records in this case could provide a "control" study useful in other cases. This would be particularly helpful if credible allegations of improper CIA activities are not supported by the records made available to the investigating committees.

The available evidence on the FBI's relationship with, and files on, Oswald will be analyzed in a book I am writing. This memo concentrates on the CIA, with emphasis on specific questions relevant to domestic CIA activities, possible CIA nondisclosure to the Warren Commission, and possible links between the assassination and CIA attempts to kill Fidel Castro. Copies of available documents which are cited can be obtained from me. Where possible, I have specified known but unavailable records which might be relevant.

I have deliberately excluded certain extremely implausible allegations for which the purported evidence is weak. Charges have even been made that the CIA or the FBI was responsible for the assassination. Despite the lack of evidence or logical support for many of these allegations, they are, I think, a matter of substantial public concern. A serious attempt to answer specific questions which have been raised seems appropriate. I am concerned that bad evidence tends to drive out good evidence; the necessary rebuttal of some of the wilder allegations must not become an excuse for avoiding more complicated, but more plausible, charges.

Consideration should be given to the possibility of disinformation being used by some intelligence agency to focus attention away from less sensational but more serious charges. Within the past year someone has gone to the trouble of putting together and making available to some Warren Report critics a false FBI document relating to purported connections between Jack Ruby and the federal government.[1] Also, statements have been made about a purported anti-Kennedy National Security Council memo which (if it exists at all) may well be the result of a disinformation effort.[2]

II. THE CIA AND LEE HARVEY OSWALD

A. QUESTIONS ABOUT DOMESTIC CIA INTELLIGENCE GATHERING

The first three of these questions may not be very significant in the assassination investigation, but they might lead to new information about the extent of certain questionable CIA activities.

1. Government Knowledge of Letter Sent to Oswald in Russia

Did the CIA intercept a letter and money order which Oswald's mother sent to him shortly after he defected to Russia? If, as the record suggests, this did happen, why do the FBI and CIA files given to the Commission not fully reflect this?

The first known FBI report relating to Oswald starts with the statement that Mrs. Marguerite Oswald "is reported to have purchased 'foreign money transfer No. 142,688' at the First National Bank of Fort Worth, Texas, on 1/22/60 by means of which she

[1] This false document says that Ruby was "performing information functions" for Nixon and HUAC in 1947. In fact, Ruby did try to contact the Kefauver Crime Committee in that year, possibly to act as an informant; that was suppressed by the FBI and not explored by the Warren Commission.

[2] *New York Times* [hereinafter "NYT"], Feb. 3, 1975, p. 14.

sent the sum of $25 to her son, Lee Harvey Oswald, in care of Hotel Metropole, Moscow, Russia."[3] The FBI told the Warren Commission that "we determined on January 25, 1960, that Mrs. Marguerite C. Oswald had transmitted the sum of $25" to Oswald at the Metropole Hotel;[4] this prompted interviews of Mrs. Oswald and her other son.

It seems atypical that the contemporary FBI report gives no indication of the origin of that information; that omission may indicate a particularly sensitive source. The recently disclosed CIA project of "selective" interception of mail from the U.S. to Russia and China may have been involved. The CIA has claimed that this program was in operation in 1960 in only one city.[5]

It is also quite possible that the FBI got its information about this private transaction from the bank. The money order was purchased on a Friday, and the FBI learned of it on Monday— which seems a bit fast for a mail interception.

The CIA file on Oswald given to the Commission contains no information on this other than the FBI report.[6] The relevant FBI file was not given to or listed for the Commission.[7] The FBI should be asked specifically about their source for this report.

2. CIA Attention to Oswald's Political Activities

In the summer of 1963, Oswald engaged in various legal political activities in New Orleans on behalf of the Fair Play for Cuba Committee. He distributed literature on the street several times, once being arrested after getting into a scuffle, and participated in a radio debate.

[3] CE [i.e., Warren Commission Exhibit] 821 (17H700 [i.e., Hearings Before the President's Commission on the Assassination of President Kennedy, Vol. 17, page 700]).

[4] CE 834, question #1 (17H789-790).

[5] NYT Jan. 16, 1975, p. 31. In 1960 the CIA intercepted a letter sent to the Soviet Union by Bella Abzug in connection with her legal work in an estate case. (NYT, March 8, 1975, p. 11)

[6] CD [i.e., Warren Commission Document (in the National Archives)] 692, part (a). (See section II.D infra.)

[7] That is, the file entitled "Funds Transmitted to Residents of Russia," as distinguished from the file entitled "Oswald."

The FBI sent the CIA copies of six reports entitled "Lee Harvey Oswald" or "Funds Transmitted to Residents of Russia," including four after his return to the U.S. in 1962. This seems proper, since as a former resident of Russia he was of interest to the CIA. It may be more significant, in terms of the extent of CIA attention to domestic dissent, that the FBI also sent the CIA a report entitled "Fair Play for Cuba Committee—New Orleans Division." In fact, this report dealt only with Oswald and "A. J. Hidell," later determined to be his alias.[8]

An attempt should be made to understand the dissemination of that report inside the Agency—that is, to see whether it was processed not only as a report on Oswald but as a report on a politically active group. That might lead to a better understanding of the CIA's handling of such information on other groups.

It should be determined whether any CIA personnel (employees or informants) were aware of Oswald's activities in New Orleans. The Warren Report says that the CIA "took note of his Fair Play for Cuba Committee activities in New Orleans."[9] There is no footnote for that statement; it may refer only to the presence of the FBI report on the FPCC in Oswald's CIA file, but that should be checked.

3. Computerized File Entries for Oswald and Others

In the CIA file, the "CS copy" of the FBI report on the New Orleans FPCC is stamped "Index," and handwritten notations indicate that two of the names mentioned were indexed in a standardized (presumably computerized) form. One was Oswald; the other was Carlos Bringuier, an anti-Castro Cuban citizen living in New Orleans.[10]

Apparently these men were indexed to record their connections with the FPCC and the DRE (Revolutionary Student Directorate, possibly a CIA-supported group) respectively. This is in itself of no particular significance in connection with the assassination, but an explanation may shed some light on the CIA's file-building procedures.

[8] CD 692, part (a), item 4.
[9] WR [i.e., Report of the President's Commission on the Assassination of President Kennedy] 326.
[10] CD 692, part (a), item 4, pp. 1-2.

4. The 544 Camp Street Connection

The most provocative link between Oswald's activities in New Orleans and the CIA is his use of the address 544 Camp Street on some of his pro-Castro literature. One office in that building had previously been occupied by one of the two principal offices of the Cuban Revolutionary Council, a front organization established by the CIA (reportedly through E. Howard Hunt) in connection with the Bay of Pigs invasion. It is apparently true, as the Warren Report noted,[11] that the CRC had left 544 Camp Street some time earlier, and that Oswald himself never actually rented an office there. However, at the time of the assassination, another office at 544 Camp was occupied by Guy Banister, a former FBI agent who was still active in intelligence work, especially Cuban activities. The Banister connection was never pursued by the Warren Commission.

The 544 Camp connection was extensively publicized at the time of Jim Garrison's "investigation." Numerous reports surfaced of witnesses who could link Oswald with David Ferrie and others who hung around Banister's office. Unfortunately many of these reports come from sources who must be considered unreliable, and who might have had reasons of their own for exaggerating this link. The most promising source of hard evidence on this matter would be a close study of the pre-assassination FBI and CIA records.

From a document not given to the Warren Commission but released to me under the Freedom of Information Act, it can be firmly established that the FBI knew before the assassination about Oswald's use of 544 Camp Street as an address for the Fair Play for Cuba Committee. This fact was not mentioned in the appropriate contemporaneous reports, and was apparently not checked out at the time, even though FBI field offices had been specifically asked to be on the alert for FPCC activities, and the FBI did check out other similar leads (such as the Post Office Box on some of Oswald's literature, and the alias A. J. Hidell).

After the assassination, the FBI hid from the Commission the fact that it had known about Oswald's use of 544 Camp Street earlier, and suppressed the link to Banister by giving his address

11 WR 408; see also WR 290.

(531 Lafayette Street) without indicating that it was the same corner building as 544 Camp Street. Even the limited amount of documentary evidence which has not been kept from the Warren Commission and the public strongly suggests that the FBI was keeping hands off Oswald's activities, quite plausibly because the Bureau believed that he was not in fact a pro-Castro activist but was working for Banister or for some official intelligence agency.

5. Allegations That Oswald Was a CIA Informant

The Commission heard, and was concerned about, allegations that Oswald had been a CIA or FBI informant.[12] The Commission's rebuttal rested largely on affidavits provided by CIA Director John McCone and J. Edgar Hoover.[13] However, the members of the Commission had been told in secret session by Allen Dulles that the CIA would generally not admit someone had been an informant or agent, even under oath, except at the specific direction of the President.[14] This fact, which was apparently not passed on to the Commission's working staff, makes the CIA's pro forma denial totally worthless.

An attempt to resolve this matter now should include interrogation of the appropriate lower-level CIA personnel. One should also try to specify and evaluate the specific situations in which Oswald might have been approached by the CIA. One obvious possibility was on his return from Russia. From the existing record, he was not debriefed by the CIA, which in itself seems odd.[15] Unlike another defector who returned at about the same time, Oswald was not questioned by the Senate Internal Security Subcommittee.[16] (Oswald was met on his return by a case worker

[12] See, for example, a memo to the files from General Counsel J. Lee Rankin, undated but approximately January 24-27, 1964, entitled "Rumors that Oswald was an undercover agent." The reported CIA informant number, 110669, was apparently not checked out. For the Commission's reaction to these rumors, see "Whitewash IV—JFK Assassination Transcript," written and published by Harold Weisberg.

[13] WR 325-7.

[14] Washington Post, Nov. 22, 1974, p. 3; Commission executive session transcript for Jan. 27, 1964, p. 153-4 (reprinted in Weisberg book, note 12).

[15] The CIA also denied having interviewed Oswald in Moscow. See CD 528.

[16] The other defector was Robert Edward Webster. See NYT, 5/25/62, p. 5.

for the Travelers Aid Society, who was also an official of an "anti-Bolshevik" organization with strong intelligence connections.[17] The extent of the CIA's routine coverage of people returning from Russia is not known, but it was extensive enough to net a photograph taken by a tourist in Minsk which (after the assassination) was found to show Oswald. The question is, therefore, not just whether the CIA ever contacted Oswald, but if not why not.

In 1962, Oswald prepared (and had typed) a manuscript about his life in Russia which was full of the kind of details which might logically be of interest to the CIA. The Warren Report's brief account avoids the evidence that Oswald did not keep all of the material which was typed for him.[18] Inquiries should be made to see whether the CIA got any of it, perhaps under circumstances which would not have led to its being filed under his name.

Considerable publicity, for which there is no substantial direct evidence, has been given to allegations that Oswald was a CIA informant. It should be noted that it is more likely that he had an informant relationship with someone else, notably the FBI, but also perhaps military intelligence or some nonofficial intelligence organization. I have studied in detail how the FBI failed to adequately rebut the claim that Oswald was an informant, and how the Warren Commission responded to Hoover's obvious displeasure at being investigated by failing to press for satisfactory explanations.

For example, the FBI omitted from their original listing of Oswald's address book the name of one of the Bureau's Special Agents; the record strongly suggests that the FBI lied to conceal the fact that the relevant page of that listing was retyped. Also, the FBI submitted affidavits from several agents denying that Oswald was an informant. These agents were supposedly all of those who were in a position to recruit him or know of his service. Some of the affidavits were revised before being given to the Commission, allegedly with no material alteration of the substance, but the originals are withheld. Also, no affidavits were provided from the two New Orleans agents who had the most

---

17 WR 713; Peter Dale Scott, *Ramparts*, November 1973, p. 17.
18 WR 700, but compare 8H330-343 and CE 92.

contact with the Oswald case.[19] An examination of the circumstances under which these affidavits were prepared might be productive. Another peculiar FBI explanation which the Commission never challenged was Hoover's statement that the FBI interview of Oswald when he was in custody after the assassination was not only to gather facts or admissions about the shooting, but was also aimed at obtaining "any information he might have been able to furnish of a security nature."[20] This cryptic language suggests that Oswald had been considered a potential source of internal security information. These examples are by no means the only or even the strongest indications that the FBI had something in their relationship with Oswald that they thought necessary to hide from the Warren Commission.

B. Unanswered Questions About the CIA and the Assassination

This section covers a number of questions about the intelligence agencies (primarily the CIA) and the assassination which were not satisfactorily resolved by the Warren Commission. (They are presented here in summary form. Further details and the available documentation, which comes largely from the Commission's records, can be provided by the author.) Whether or not these questions fall within the mandate of the Rockefeller and Church investigations, they do need to be answered. There is no doubt that a new investigation of the Kennedy assassination should explore these issues, among others. The focus here is on problems for which a study of the documentary record is likely to be productive, so this memo goes into only a small fraction of the defects in the Commission's case against Lee Harvey Oswald.

1. Photographs of Possible Oswald Impostor in Mexico City

In October 1963 the CIA learned of Oswald's visit to the Russian Embassy in Mexico City. Several photographs were obtained, presumably from a Mexican police surveillance camera at the

[19] Milton Kaack and Warren C. DeBrueys. Compare CE 825 with CE 826 and CD 692 (a) 4.
[20] CE 835 (17H816).

Embassy, of a still-unidentified Embassy visitor who does not physically resemble Oswald. This man was identified as Oswald in a CIA telegram to the FBI before the assassination. The explanation of the mix-up in identification, if that is what it was, was not released by the Warren Commission. Some CIA explanation, true or not, is presumably in the withheld documents at the Archives. It may also be that the unidentified man was an associate of Oswald, or an impostor.[21]

2. Intercepted Conversations By or About Oswald in Mexico

An FBI report on Oswald in Mexico strongly suggests that the CIA intercepted at least two phone calls between the Cuban and Russian Embassies in which Oswald was discussed. During one phone call Oswald was apparently on the phone himself.[22] The CIA also had detailed knowledge of Oswald's conversation with a guard at the Soviet Embassy, including the fact that he spoke broken Russian; this conversation may also have been bugged.[23] A recording of these calls would be important evidence as to whether an impostor was making some of these contacts on Oswald's behalf. The CIA has declined to tell me whether any such recorded conversations now exist, or to release any relevant records to me.

3. Did E. Howard Hunt Know of Oswald's Activities Before the Assassination?

It has been reported that E. Howard Hunt was the CIA's acting station chief in Mexico City during August and September 1963, which might overlap with Oswald's visit starting in late September.[24] Hunt has reportedly denied to the Rockefeller Commission that he met Oswald at that time.[25] It should be determined whether Hunt had any knowledge of Oswald's activities, whether

---

[21] See the article by Fensterwald and O'Toole in the *New York Review of Books*, April 3, 1975, and the Warren Commission records cited therein.

[22] CD 1084D, pp. 4-5.

[23] CD 1084D, pp. 5-6; also see draft memo of April 1, 1964, by Coleman and Slawson, p. 3.

[24] Tad Szulc, *Compulsive Spy*, pp. 96-97.

[25] NYT, Mar. 8, 1975, p. 11.

or not he met him. This requires an examination of contemporaneous CIA records relating to Oswald, and an understanding of the flow of communications within the CIA station. A number of the internal CIA communications were turned over to the Warren Commission (and are still withheld);[26] however, they may not include all the information needed to determine who in the CIA station had substantial contact with the Oswald case.

4. The Handling of the Story of "D"

An attempt should be made to understand what role CIA personnel might have played in building up, disseminating and then denigrating a report that Oswald had received money to kill Kennedy from someone at the Cuban Embassy in Mexico City.[27] The circumstances suggest that someone with intelligence connections was eager to push the idea that the Cuban government was behind the Kennedy assassination.

The immediate source of the story was Gilberto Alvarado Ugarte, a Nicaraguan who said he was trying to get to Cuba on a penetration mission for the Nicaraguan Secret Service. After a few days he reportedly retracted his story, saying that he had made it up to get the U.S. to take action against Castro; then he withdrew this retraction. He ultimately took a lie-detector test which showed he was lying; he then said that the lie detector must be correct. This kind of retraction suggests that Alvarado had told the story as an agent who later did not know whose orders to follow.

At first this story was treated with considerable respect. The CIA communications (which went to the White House as well as the FBI, the State Department and the Secret Service) show that the agency was taking the allegation quite seriously. Alvarado was said to be of questionable reliability but not wholly discredited; the CIA described him as a "very serious person who speaks with conviction."[28]

It is known that President Johnson was concerned about a Castro plot when he set up the Warren Commission, and that he did not

---

26 Some are presumably in part (g) of CD 692, for example.

27 WR 307-8; also CD 1084E, section IX.

28 CD 1000. Some passages are still withheld.

accept all the conclusions of the Warren Report; it has been reported that he specifically believed that the assassination was a retaliatory act by the Cuban Communists.[29] That is, the apparent effect of the story of "D,"—which may have been intended—was to impress upon President Johnson (and thus ultimately on the Warren Commission) the potential threat of an international incident posed by the reports that Castro was behind the assassination, and (by extension) by any alternative to the lone-assassin hypothesis.

The Warren Report concluded that Alvarado was lying about having seen Oswald, but did not explore the possible implications of a planted false story. It is plausible that a major conscious or subconscious motivation for a cover-up was a desire to avoid allegations of conspiracy such as this one, which were thought to be untrue but which might lead to very serious problems. Some observers have recognized a pattern of anti-Castro allegations arising from intelligence-related sources, including Watergate burglar Frank Sturgis.[30]

5. Correlation of Various Agency Files and Actions Concerning Oswald

The files of the FBI, State Department and the Marines on Oswald before the assassination reflect various peculiar actions which might be explained not only by Oswald's being an agent of the agency which was acting oddly, but by a belief that he was working for someone else. Such an evaluation, of course, would probably never be written down; it would be detectable only through resulting agency actions or omissions.

As far as I know, the Warren Commission never did the required kind of detailed comparative study of the intelligence agency files. Considerable attention was given to the most striking anomalies in the State Department file, notably the Department's efforts to facilitate Oswald's return from Russia, and the ease with which he got a new passport in late 1963. Even in the case of the State Department, however, the Commission did not get into all

---

[29] *Time,* Feb. 10, 1975, p. 16: *The Vantage Point,* pp. 26-7 (paperback edition); *Atlantic,* July 1973, p. 39.
[30] Peter Dale Scott, *Ramparts,* Nov. 1973, p. 13.

the major questions about the evaluation of Oswald. For example, the Commission examined the reasons why the Passport Office did not react to the CIA telegram about Oswald's visit to the Russian Embassy, but failed to explore the reaction of others, primarily the Office of Security, for whom the telegram was more relevant.

The relatively sparse CIA file does not reflect any such strikingly peculiar actions. However, close study of the CIA file by an expert might reveal whether they did anything odd in the Oswald case. It is quite possible, for example, that someone in the CIA recognized that his defection and return might have been a mission for (e.g.) military intelligence, and that the Agency therefore kept away from his case, making no attempt to question him about his stay in Russia.

6. Possible Unusual CIA Interest in Defectors

In 1960, the year after Oswald's move to Russia, the CIA and the State Department exchanged some correspondence relating to defectors in general. The purpose of this study, which included compiling statistics and making lists of Americans who had defected, is not clear. Although this material was given to the Warren Commission, apparently no explanation was asked for or provided.

There have been rumors that Otto Otepka, who worked on this project and with Oswald's file while he was head of the State Department's Office of Security, was suspicious of the way the Oswald case was handled. He should be given the opportunity to present any relevant information he might have.

7. Possible CIA Contact with Oswald Through Alexis Davison

Oswald's notebook contained the name and address of a Russian living in Atlanta who was identified as the mother of the U.S. Embassy Doctor, Alexis Davison. Davison had routinely examined Oswald's wife when the couple was preparing to return to the U.S. in 1962. Davison gave no persuasive explanation of why he gave his mother's address to the Oswalds, suggesting only an understanding that they could look her up if they happened to be in Atlanta. Davison told the Secret Service he did not remember the Oswalds, but later recalled the contact quite clearly for the

FBI and said he did not recall giving his mother's address to any other people who were going back to the U.S.[31]

In December 1962, Davison was charged by the USSR with receiving information from the American spy Oleg Penkovsky. Evidently, in addition to his official duties as a medical doctor and an Assistant Air Attaché, Davison was engaged in very sensitive intelligence work. It should be determined whether he had any contact with Oswald in that capacity, or reported to any intelligence agency about him.

8. Report of Dallas CIA Agent Familiar with Oswald

George DeMohrenschildt, a man with many hints of intelligence connections in his own background who helped the Oswald family in Dallas, testified that before doing so he asked one or more of his friends if that would be okay. One person whom he said he may have asked about Oswald was J. Walton Moore, who he thought was an FBI agent.[32] Moore was probably in fact with the CIA: he interviewed DeMohrenschildt at length in 1957 after his trip to Yugoslavia. He did have an office in a government building and was listed as an "employee, U.S. government"; the FBI told DeMohrenschildt that Moore was not with the FBI.[33]

The Warren Commission seems not to have been interested in this or other reports that the government had indicated that Oswald was not someone who had to be avoided.[34] An attempt should be made to identify Moore's employer, determine what he knew about Oswald, and what he may have told DeMohrenschildt or anyone else.

9. Alleged Presence of CIA Agent at Parkland Hospital

Within an hour of the assassination, a CIA agent presented his credentials to a Secret Service agent at Parkland Hospital and said that he would be "available." It is not clear what he might have been expected to do. A short time later an unknown FBI

[31] CD 87, SS 569; CD 235; CD 409, p. 3; CD 1115-XIII-103; Wise & Ross, *Invisible Government*, p. 268 (paperback edition).

[32] 9H235-6; CD 555, p. 76.

[33] CD 555, p. 76.

[34] See, e.g., *Whitewash II* by Harold Weisberg, Ch. 6; CD 950.

agent had to be forcibly restrained from entering the emergency room.[35] Apparently the Commission did not investigate either of these occurrences. As far as I know the CIA was not asked what action they may have taken in Dallas or in Washington after Kennedy was shot or after Oswald was arrested.

10. Questionable Records of Oswald's Security Clearance

One of the peculiarities in Oswald's military records which is suggestive of an intelligence connection has to do with his security clearance. The personnel file which was given to the Commission by the Marine Corps reflected only that Oswald had been given a Confidential clearance. However, persuasive testimony indicated that Oswald (like the other men in his unit) must have been cleared at least for Secret information. When the Commission staff asked about this discrepancy, the Marine Corps said, in effect, that if Oswald was doing Secret work then he must have had Secret clearance.[36] The Commission apparently did not press for a proper answer or otherwise resolve this problem.

Irregularities of this kind at least raise the possibility that Oswald had been "sheep dipped"—that is, that he was formally discharged from the Marines while actually continuing government employment for some sort of intelligence work. There is firm evidence that the Department of Defense was not telling the truth when it claimed that it had given the Warren Commission all of its records on Oswald. His pay records, for example, were submitted months after that claim. There is solid documentary evidence of other omissions. There are also hints of further missing records: the FBI was told soon after the assassination that the CIC and CID files at the California base where Oswald had served in 1959 had nothing on Oswald; some of the California Marine Corps files had been forwarded to Washington.[37] These files might be expected to contain the records of any investigation for a high-level clearance.

---

35 18H795-6.
36 CE 1961; Rankin letter of 5/19/64 to Folsom.
37 CD 33, pp. 1-2.

11. Alleged Photo of Hunt and Sturgis in Dallas

The Rockefeller Commission is reportedly checking out and rebutting the allegation that E. Howard Hunt and Frank Sturgis (also known as Fiorini) appear in the photographs of several men apparently picked up by the Dallas police immediately after the assassination. These photographs represent an authentic unresolved mystery, it is true; however, the men pictured have been "positively identified," on previous occasions, as other "suspects" in the assassination.

Aside from the absence of any striking similarity in appearance, it is inherently most unlikely that a professional intelligence operative like Hunt (who got a wig just to interview Dita Beard) would get himself photographed without a disguise at the scene of an assassination if he had anything to do with it.

While such allegations should be seriously checked out, they should not be allowed to distract attention from more plausible but less spectacular evidence of improper CIA activities in connection with Oswald or the assassination investigation. To allow that to happen would be to invite disinformation efforts by the Agency and its friends.

C. STATEMENT BY JAMES ANGLETON

It is quite possible that a CIA investigation of the assassination of President Kennedy was among the domestic activities which recently caused concern within the Agency. At the time of his resignation as head of the CIA's Counterintelligence Division, James Angleton was quoted as making the following remarks when Seymour Hersh asked about alleged CIA wrongdoing and his domestic activities: "A mansion has many rooms and there were many things going on during the period of the [anti-war (NYT addition)] bombings. I'm not privy to who struck John."[38]

From the context of Angleton's statement, it is impossible to decide what he may have been referring to. "Who struck John" may be a literary reference or cliché which is not familiar to me.

---

[38] NYT, Dec. 25, 1974, p. 1.

It may have been a reference to some other John—e.g., Mitchell. Also, it is conceivable that "Who Struck John" was some sort of code name for a CIA study of the Kennedy assassination.

Angleton should be asked to explain that statement, and whether he is aware of any CIA investigations of Oswald or the assassination, particularly any which may have reached conclusions different from the Warren Commission's. Regardless of what Angleton now says he meant by his comment, an intended reference to John Kennedy seems as likely as any other explanation.*

D. Availability of Documentary Material

Warren Commission Document [CD] 692 purports to be an exact copy of the CIA's pre-assassination dossier on Oswald. Of the material predating Oswald's October 1963 trip to Mexico, almost all has been released; most is information from other agencies. A good part of the Mexico material is still withheld.[39]

A number of other Commission Documents and internal memoranda deal with the CIA's pre- and post-assassination investigations. Some of the withheld CD's would be very interesting: e.g., CD 935, a Top Secret CIA memo dealing in part with the reaction of the Cuban Intelligence Service to the assassination.[40] Enough of the CIA material submitted to the Commission has been released to provide a basis for the formulation of appropriately specific questions.

Certainly most of the still withheld material should be released at this time. However, overemphasis on the material at the

---

* It now appears that "who struck John" is CIA jargon for "the details." In congressional testimony on an unrelated matter, a high CIA official used this phrase and then, presumably realizing that its meaning was unclear, translated it: "He merely accepted the information. We did not go into who struck John, about any details." This testimony, by Paul F. Gaynor, chief of the Security Research Staff, was taken on February 26, 1974 (long before Angleton's remark) but was not published until later. We do not know whether this usage began before or after the Kennedy assassination. In any case, it now appears that Angleton's comment was not an overt reference to Kennedy, although it may have been a Freudian slip or even intended to draw attention to the JFK case.—Eds.

39 E.g., CD 692 (g).
40 Lists of withheld CD's and CIA CD's are available from the author.

Archives should be avoided. Erroneous claims are frequently made that many of the Warren Commission files have been locked up for seventy-five years from the date of the assassination. In fact, there is no such fixed-term withholding. All of the withheld material is reviewed every five years, and in addition is subject to agency and judicial review under the Freedom of Information Act when a request is made by any citizen. Some of the withheld material might even remain withheld for more than seventy-five years. In fact, an extraordinary amount of investigative material (largely raw data in FBI reports) has been released or published. This was done to some degree over the objection of the FBI.

It is probable that the most sensitive material in government files on Oswald never reached the Warren Commission. I am sure that was the case with the FBI files, only a small fraction of which were given to the Commission.

In response to my Freedom of Information Act requests, the CIA has told me that they "are highly in favor of declassifying everything possible in connection with the records of the Warren Commission. The most convincing motive for us to do this is our firm belief that all the information so declassified would merely go to support the conclusions of the Warren Commission and dispel any possible confusion or suspicion that the continued classification may have raised."[41] (This motive has been balanced against the protection of classified information and intelligence sources and methods.) I expect that this is a sincere opinion, at least as it applies to the CIA material in the Archives. (The following section examines the indications that the CIA did not make a full disclosure to the Commission.) Of course, even the currently available material invalidates many of the Commission's conclusions.

Because of these facts, the demand for release of the Warren Commission's records should be only a part of the demand for full disclosure. At the very least, the CIA should be asked about files other than CD 692 in which there is any reference to Lee Harvey Oswald or to members of his family.

[41] Letter of Dec. 14, 1971, from L. K. White to the author.

III. THE CIA AND THE INVESTIGATION OF THE ASSASSINATION

A. POSSIBILITY THAT INFORMATION WAS WITHHELD FROM THE COMMISSION

1. False CIA Statement to the FBI on November 22, 1963

On the day of the assassination, an FBI agent from the Washington field office interviewed Birch D. O'Neal of the CIA for the purpose of obtaining "any information" in the CIA files on Oswald. According to the FBI's report, he "learned there is nothing in CIA file [sic] regarding Oswald other than material furnished to CIA by the FBI and the Department of State."[42] That was certainly untrue, most conspicuously with regard to the important CIA-originated material about Oswald's trip to Mexico.[43]

The possibility that the FBI misrecorded the CIA statement must be acknowledged. The Bureau's headquarters file included some CIA-created records, so the Bureau should have known that the CIA claim was wrong when they reported it to the Warren Commission. Whatever O'Neal's exact statement about the CIA file was, it seems clear that the CIA did not want to immediately reveal to the FBI the full extent of their coverage of Oswald, and the serious problems raised (e.g., by the photographs of the visitor to the Russian Embassy).

The significance of this FBI report is not primarily that material was withheld from the FBI, since some of it had been turned over previously and more apparently was forwarded quite soon; it is that at least once the CIA made a false statement about the extent of their Oswald file.

2. Topics on Which Disclosure May Have Been Limited

(a) Marina Oswald

The FBI told the Warren Commission that their case on Lee Harvey Oswald was returned to active status in March 1963 as a

---

[42] CD 49, p. 22.
[43] See p. 468–9 supra.

result of information obtained during an investigation relating to his wife Marina. FBI agent Hosty testified that it was the FBI's practice to interview immigrants from Communist countries "on a selective basis," and that Marina Oswald had been selected.[44] The results of this FBI practice would seem naturally and properly to be of interest to the CIA. However, the CIA file on Lee Oswald does not give any indication of CIA interest in Marina specifically. There is no apparent reference to any effort by or with the FBI relating to Russian immigrants. (The routine transmittal slips for the FBI reports on Lee Oswald do not refer to the FBI's case on Marina.)

The CIA should be asked to produce any records it has on Marina Oswald. The Agency should be asked if they ever contacted her as a potential informant or otherwise, directly or indirectly. She may well have been known to the CIA through Russians in Dallas, some of whom had links to CIA-supported groups and might well have been reporting to the CIA on the activities of the Russian community.

(b)   Oswald's contacts with Albert Schweitzer College

When Oswald left the U.S. in 1959, he had indicated on his passport application that he intended to attend Albert Schweitzer College. This is a small Unitarian-affiliated school in Switzerland specializing in advanced studies in philosophy and the liberal arts.[45] Oswald had indeed been accepted by that school, despite the apparent absence of the proper references and background. When he failed to show up, an investigation was undertaken by the FBI through its Legal Attaché in Paris, perhaps in part at the request of Oswald's mother through her Congressman.[46] Since the relevant FBI records have not been made available, I do not know whether any of them were sent to the CIA, but that would have been appropriate. It should be determined whether there was any FBI-CIA liaison on this matter (and if not, why not); and, if so, why there is no record of it in the CIA file on Oswald, CD 692.

[44] 4H441.
[45] WR 688.
[46] 1H213; CD 120, p. 4-5; CE 834, items 13, 15-18, 20.

The CIA, the FBI and ONI should also be asked if there was any intelligence interest in Schweitzer College, or any direct or indirect government support. That might explain Oswald's peculiar contacts with the College. If the CIA evaluated this matter in documents provided to the Warren Commission, they should be made public.

(c)   The unidentified man photographed in Mexico City

(See section II.B.1 *supra*.) I am confident that the CIA ultimately did provide an explanation of this "mistake" which was good enough to satisfy the Warren Commission. However, there are strong indications that the CIA was not candid with the Commission at first. The Commission first learned about the photo because it had been shown to Marguerite Oswald shortly after the assassination. However, as late as March 12 the Commission was asking the CIA about Oswald's activities in Mexico and about the photograph apparently without knowing that these matters were related.[47] The CIA had evidently not yet replied to a letter which had been sent a month previously asking for an explanation of the photograph.

3.   *CIA Assertions of Full Disclosure*

CIA Director McCone and Deputy Director Helms testified that the substance of all relevant pre-assassination information had been supplied to the Commission.[48] CD 692 was described in a covering memo as "an exact reproduction of the Agency's official dossier on Lee Harvey Oswald," but it included only a summary of some of the pre-assassination internal CIA messages about Oswald.[49] A Commission staff member went to Langley and saw a computerized printout on Oswald, which he described as including no document which the Commission had not been given in full or in paraphrase.[50]

The CIA should be asked to list (and, if possible, to release) all records not in the "official dossier" which mentioned Oswald.

---

[47] Memo of 3/12/64, Slawson to the files, p. 7 (also p. 8); Coleman memo 3/26/64.
[48] 5H122.
[49] Slawson memo of 3/12/64, p. 8.
[50] Stern memo of 3/27/64 to Rankin; 5H122.

Specifically, since some records had Oswald's middle name as "Henry," the extent of their search involving variant names should be examined.

B. Key Persons in the CIA–Warren Commission Investigation

Raymond Rocca, who recently resigned from the Counter-intelligence Division, was the CIA's liaison with the Warren Commission. Arthur Dooley, who retired in 1973, was apparently one of the CIA men most involved in the investigation.

According to a Commission memo, Richard Helms was one of the two men at a meeting on March 12, 1964, who would have known whether Oswald had been a CIA informant.[51] The name of the second man has been withheld. He should be identified and both should be questioned.

It might be particularly useful to ask the following people from the Warren Commission staff about the issues raised in this memo, and about the degree of CIA cooperation with the Commission.

W. David Slawson, now at the U.S.C. Law School, was the junior lawyer who apparently had the most extensive dealings with the CIA. His area of investigation was Oswald's foreign activities. *The New York Times* has reported that he recently said that the investigation should be reopened.[52]

William T. Coleman, now Secretary of Transportation, was the senior lawyer in the same area.

Wesley J. Liebeler, now with the federal government in Washington, was reportedly involved in the investigation of the unidentified-man photo, and was reportedly unable to get a satisfactory explanation from the CIA for their misidentification of the man as Oswald.[53]

Samuel A. Stern, now with Wilmer, Cutler and Pickering in Washington, examined the CIA evaluation of Oswald, particularly from the viewpoint of liaison with the Secret Service and

[51] Slawson memo of 3/12/64, p. 8.
[52] NYT, Feb. 23, 1975, p. 32.
[53] Epstein, *Inquest*, pp. 93-95 (hardcover edition).

procedures for presidential protection. He was also involved with investigating the allegations that Oswald was an FBI or CIA informant.

C.   THE CIA'S OWN INVESTIGATION OF THE ASSASSINATION

1.   CIA Capability for an Independent Investigation

The CIA, of course, openly worked with the Warren Commission in areas involving foreign activities. In addition, the Agency was given the ability to assess much of the evidence in other areas. At the Commission's request, the FBI sent the CIA not only material with foreign aspects, but also reports on possible subversive activities by Oswald in the U.S.; the FBI also forwarded to the CIA all the major investigative reports coming out of the Dallas office.[54] The Secret Service was also asked to send the CIA a number of its reports, including all interviews of Marina Oswald.[55]

On occasion during the life of the Commission, the CIA actively suggested further investigation. For example, one Agency memo said it was of considerable importance to investigate the report that Oswald had attempted suicide in Russia, and that if necessary his body should be exhumed to see if he really did have a scar on his wrist.[56]

The Warren Commission, constrained by (among other things) the need to make a public report within a reasonable time, did not even adequately pursue all the important leads in the material the FBI did submit. The CIA was not so constrained.

2.   Unknown CIA Conclusions

The CIA interest in the assassination continued after the Warren Commission finished its work. For example, more than two months after the Warren Report came out, the CIA asked for a copy of the Zapruder film of the shooting. According to the FBI,

[54] Rankin letter to Hoover, 1/31/64; Hoover letter to Rankin, Feb. 5, 1964.
[55] Rankin letters to J. Rowley (USSS), Jan. 31 and Feb. 7, 1964.
[56] Helms memo to Papich (FBI), Feb. 18, 1964.

it was requested "for training purposes."[57] Presumably this means for training photoanalysts.

The FBI-Commission study of this film was superficial. Most notably, the Warren Report failed to mention, much less explain, the fact that Kennedy was driven forcefully backward by the fatal shot (which, according to the Commission, came from behind him). Contrary to expectations, a target does sometimes recoil back toward the gun.[58] It would be interesting to know whether the CIA came up with this explanation. In any case, the Agency should reveal what use it made of, and what conclusions it reached from, the Zapruder film.[59]

Agency officials testified in May 1964 that they had found no evidence causing them to conclude that there had been a conspiracy, but that the case would never be considered closed.[60] The CIA should be asked to produce their internal reports on the assassination, particularly any which reached conclusions or post-dated the Warren Report.

3. CIA Activities Related to Critics of the Warren Report

It would be perfectly proper if the CIA has investigated charges made by the critics alleging foreign involvement in the assassination. Such investigative reports should be made public.

CIA coverage of the critics may have included the dissemination of false reports to draw attention away from serious questions which involved the Agency. Other researchers who have been more active in the investigation than I could no doubt provide details about some of the suspicious incidents and persons.

Jim Garrison charged that the CIA was involved in the assassination and also hindered his investigation. Since the former charge has received wide attention, despite Garrison's lack of

[57] Hoover letter to Rankin, Feb. 4, 1964 (Weisberg, *Photographic Whitewash*, p. 143.)

[58] This has been confirmed by an experiment I helped another investigator [Luis Alvarez] perform.

[59] My request for this information under the Freedom of Information Act is pending.

[60] 5H123-4.

substantiating evidence, the CIA should be asked to explain its links with any of the principals in the Garrison matter. This should include suspects, peripheral figures associated with them, investigators, and some of the witnesses and their attorneys; CIA connections with David Ferrie and Guy Banister should be given special attention.[61] If it is true, as Victor Marchetti has reportedly said, that Clay Shaw had been a CIA contact in connection with his foreign trade activities and the CIA was concerned about keeping this fact secret, that might explain some of the strong opposition to Garrison (although it would not add to Garrison's flimsy case that Shaw conspired to kill Kennedy).

The extent of CIA efforts to disseminate derogatory information about the critics should be examined. The Agency did give the Warren Commission a 1937 Gestapo memo on Joachim Joesten, the author of one of the first critical books on the assassination.[62] Information that Joesten had been a member of the German Communist Party, taken from the same memo, was later introduced into the *Congressional Record* in a report (allegedly written by the CIA) which claimed that his criticism of the Warren Report was part of a "Communist bloc defamation campaign."[63] The Agency should also be asked if it intercepted the mail of, or otherwise interfered with, any of the critics of the Warren Report, in the United States or abroad.

IV. POSSIBLE LINK BETWEEN THE KENNEDY ASSASSINATION AND CIA ANTI-CASTRO ACTIVITIES

A. SUMMARY OF THE FACTUAL BASIS FOR AN INQUIRY

The considerable attention recently given to the possibility of a connection between the CIA and the Kennedy assassination has been largely based on two very provocative and undoubtedly significant facts. The first is that the CIA tried to kill Fidel Castro, working on occasion through the Mafia. This CIA plot

---

[61] See, for example, Jim Squires' article in the *Chicago Tribune*, 3/16/75, p. 1.
[62] CD 1532, still withheld.
[63] Cong. Rec. 9/28/65, p. 25393; Marchetti & Marks, *The CIA and the Cult of Intelligence*, p. 339 (paperback edition).

was reportedly the basis for fears that Castro had retaliated against Kennedy. The second is one of the major unresolved questions of Watergate: E. Howard Hunt's apparently sensational knowledge about "the whole Bay of Pigs thing" which led President Nixon to cut off the investigation. Since the basic facts of the Bay of Pigs are hardly secret, and Hunt has admitted proposing the assassination of Castro in connection with that operation, it is reasonable to speculate that "the whole Bay of Pigs thing" was a reference to knowledge of such a plot or its consequences, or to the related Howard Hughes-CIA link.

These matters undoubtedly should be given major attention by those who are now investigating the CIA. I would like to suggest that they should be studied with the perspective provided by a third fact: a definite link between a man representing himself as "Leon Oswald" (perhaps Lee Harvey Oswald himself) and one of the assassination attempts against Castro.

B. LINK BETWEEN "OSWALD" AND A PLOT TO KILL CASTRO

1. Summary of the Sylvia Odio Incident

An episode which caused the Warren Commission staff a great deal of concern was reported by Sylvia Odio, a Cuban active in the anti-Castro movement. She identified Lee Harvey Oswald as one of three men who had visited her home in Dallas about two months before the assassination. Odio said that this man was introduced to her as "Leon Oswald" and was described as an American ex-Marine—"great, kind of nuts"—who thought that President Kennedy should have been shot after the Bay of Pigs "because he was the one who was holding the freedom of Cuba."[64] The men themselves linked attempts against Kennedy and Castro, saying that Leon Oswald "could do anything like getting underground in Cuba, like killing Castro."[65] These men said they were seeking Odio's help in their anti-Castro activities and persuasively claimed to be friends of her father, who was imprisoned in Cuba. Odio's veracity was strengthened by the way her story came out,

---

[64] 11H372. For a general discussion, see WR 321-4 and Meagher, *Accessories after the Fact*, pp. 376-387.

[65] 11H377.

and by the fact that it tied Oswald to a movement with which she sympathized (specifically the relatively moderate JURE group, headed by Manolo Ray).[66]

This incident is important whether or not the real Oswald was involved. An attempt to impersonate Oswald in such a situation would establish a conspiracy not only against Kennedy but against Oswald.[67] The Commission staff recognized the significance of Odio's story. David Slawson called her "the most significant witness linking Oswald to anti-Castro Cubans."[68] Assistant Counsel Burt Griffin said that "the most reasonable situations under which Oswald might have had conspirators . . . derive from his efforts to infiltrate the anti-Castro Cubans and to obtain a visa to Cuba"; he said that the Warren Report "should explore at length the allegations made by Sylvia Odio."[69] Just ten days before the Warren Report came out, Wesley Liebeler wrote that "Odio may well be right" and that "the Commission will look bad if it turns out she is."[70]

The Commission's investigation never really got beyond a search (reasonably successful) for evidence that Oswald himself was not one of Odio's visitors. At the last minute, three anti-Castro activists were tentatively identified as the visitors, but later interviews seem to have invalidated that hypothesis.[71]

2. *Connection Between Odio and an Attempt to Kill Castro*

Sylvia Odio's father, with whom her visitors claimed to be well acquainted, was generally described as a "political prisoner."[72] The fact is that he was arrested by the Cuban government *because of his involvement in an attempt to kill Castro.* The senior Odios had harbored one of the assassins after this attempt on Castro failed.

These facts are established by a combination of investigative

[66] On Odio's veracity, see e.g., Meagher (note 64), p. 380.

[67] There were other incidents where someone might have been impersonating Oswald. David Slawson has said that "the interposition of an impostor, if that happened, is a political act." (Ref. 52) See also p. 468 supra.

[68] Hubert and Griffin memo of April 7, 1964 to Rankin.

[69] Griffin memo of August 20, 1964 to Willens.

[70] Liebeler memo of September 14, 1964 to Willens.

[71] Meagher (note 64), p. 387; compare WR 324 and CD 1553.

[72] WR 322.

reports submitted to the Warren Commission and press reports which appeared before the Kennedy assassination. I am not mentioning the name of the man arrested with Mr. Odio in this memo, because I think an investigation should be conducted before this material is made public. (I do not know anything other than what is in public sources.)[73]

Because this assassination attempt occurred reasonably close in time to the Bay of Pigs, it is reasonable to suspect that the CIA was directly involved in it. In any case, the CIA must have learned the details of the plot, if only after it happened. It is clearly important that Agency records and witnesses be probed to learn as much as possible about this link between the Kennedy assassination and an action of the kind the CIA was mounting against Castro.

C. Press Reports Interpreting CIA Actions Against Castro

Alleged CIA attempts to kill foreign leaders, notably Castro, have received a great deal of attention lately.[74] The latest reports make explicit what was strongly suggested earlier: that the publication of the stories about possible retaliation by Castro was in itself an act with political significance and consequences. Given the information in the previous section, it is important to examine these reports while keeping in mind the possibility that the CIA had an interest in diverting attention from this particular link between its activities and the Kennedy case.

Jack Anderson reported in 1967 that "President Johnson is sitting on a political H-bomb—an unconfirmed report that Senator Robert Kennedy may have approved an assassination plot which then possibly backfired against his late brother."[75] Anderson said that a plot against Castro was considered while Robert Kennedy was "riding herd on the Agency" after the Bay of Pigs. "Insiders" told Anderson that for the plot to "reach the high level it did," it must have been taken up with Kennedy; one source "insisted" that Robert Kennedy played a key role in the plan-

[73] I will be glad to send this material to serious investigators. Copies have already been given to several researchers.

[74] E.g., NYT, March 10, 1975, p. 1.

[75] Drew Pearson column of March 3, 1967 in (e.g.) the S.F. *Chronicle*. Apparently this column did not appear in the Washington *Post* except for a very short version on March 7, 1967.

ning. Anderson also cited John Kennedy's disillusionment with the CIA, and a report that Castro "with characteristic fury" launched a counterplot; he said that the FBI told President Johnson that Cuban leaders had hoped for Kennedy's death.[76] Anderson suggested that Robert Kennedy's "morose" behavior after the assassination might have been due to the "terrible thought that he had helped put into motion forces that indirectly may have brought about his brother's martyrdom."

In 1971, Anderson expanded his story, reporting that there were six CIA attempts to kill Castro, occurring between March 1961 and March 1963. All six were reportedly carried out through John Roselli, a man with strong links to organized crime.[77] These columns repeated the suggestion that the plots might have backfired against Kennedy when Castro learned of them.[78]

The Anderson columns did not go into the possibility—rather, the probability—that there were other CIA attempts against Castro.[79] Nor did they raise the possibility that a plot had backfired when the Kennedys or the CIA tried to call it off, and the resentful gunmen turned against the United States. There is at least as much political logic to this hypothesis as to the alternate version. It is known that some anti-Castro Cubans resented President Kennedy's lack of support in 1962–63, typified by the well-publicized raid on an anti-Castro training camp near New Orleans in summer 1963[80] and by the reported withdrawal of support for a second invasion around the time of the Missile Crisis.[81] If Castro had decided to retaliate against Kennedy, it is most unlikely that he would have used Oswald, whose pro-Castro activities were a matter of record in CIA and FBI files, and were also known to the public (because of his radio appearances) and to the anti-Castro Cuban community. Surely the Cuban government had agents in the U.S. with solid anti-Castro covers.

[76] This may be a reference to CD 1359, a still-withheld Top Secret letter of 6/17/64 from Hoover to Rankin, re statements by Castro on the assassination.

[77] The first two attempts involved poison capsules, and the other four involved teams with rifles and explosives who were taken to Cuba by Roselli.

[78] Jack Anderson columns of Jan. 18, Jan. 19, and Feb. 23, 1971.

[79] For other attempts against Castro, see Szulc, *Esquire*, Feb. '74, pp. 90, 91, and Scott, *Ramparts*, Nov. '73, pp. 14-15, 54.

[80] New Orleans *Times-Picayune*, August 1, 1963, p. 1.

[81] E.g., NYT, 4/19/63, p. 14; 4/21/63, p. 26; 5/1/63, p. 11.

It is reasonable to assume that the original Anderson report was based on information given to him by the CIA. This conclusion is supported not only by his citations of "top officials" as sources, but by information provided to me by a moderately reliable source suggesting that Anderson thought the story had been given to him with the approval of the Director of the CIA. Whoever the source, I can only speculate about his intentions. There may have been a desire to affect the strained relationship between President Johnson and Robert Kennedy, or there may have been reasons related to Kennedy's continuing passive endorsement of the Warren Report in the face of strong public concern about the assassination. Even if the only true part of the 1967 report was that some elements in the U.S. Government had planned to kill Castro, it may have been leaked for the purpose of persuading Robert Kennedy to continue his silence about his brother's death. It should be noted that the CIA has apparently not chosen to leak information about the anti-Castro assassination attempt which is linked to the Odio incident.

It has just recently been revealed that Robert Kennedy was "outraged" by the 1967 Anderson column. He told two of his assistants that he had stopped, not started, the plot against Castro.[82] (It appears that he was referring to an attempt using the Mafia, presumably Roselli.) One news report indicated that one of the Kennedy aides had emphasized that Robert Kennedy learned of the CIA-Mafia link before his brother became President, thus implying that Castro could not have retaliated against the Kennedys because of it.[83] Obviously the extent and chronology of all CIA attempts against Castro must be cleared up.

D. POSSIBLE RELEVANT KNOWLEDGE OUTSIDE THE CIA

1. Basis for E. Howard Hunt's Blackmail of President Nixon

As many observers have noticed, President Nixon's reactions to Hunt's demands for money seem to be based on a fear that he would divulge information on something even more damaging

---

[82] NYT, Mar. 10, 1975, p. 1.
[83] This was a national TV network news report; the text is not available to me now.

than Watergate. On June 23, 1972, Nixon told Haldeman to have the CIA cut off the FBI investigation on the grounds that it might open up "the whole Bay of Pigs thing." That was presumably related to the long-time CIA links of Hunt and some of the men on his team.

Of course, many details of the CIA's involvement in the Bay of Pigs have been known for years. Whether or not Nixon's fear in that area was genuine, he must have had some reason to believe that the CIA and the FBI would have some idea of what he was referring to. It is quite plausible that "the whole Bay of Pigs thing" was a euphemism for CIA assassination attempts against Castro which had grown out of the Bay of Pigs operation. It seems essential to find out what all of the involved parties —Nixon, Haldeman, Helms and the FBI—thought (or now think) this meant.

2. Hunt and Assassination Attempts Against Castro

Hunt chose to bring up the matter of assassination attempts against Castro in his book. He said that he had proposed such an attempt in connection with his work on the Bay of Pigs. He recommended, evidently in writing, that Castro be killed before or at the time of the invasion. Hunt was told that his recommendation was "in the hands of a special group." Perhaps choosing his words to conceal or hint at what he knew, rather than to reveal it, he wrote: "So far as I have been able to determine no coherent plan was ever developed within CIA to assassinate Castro, though it was the heart's desire of many exile groups."[84]

3. White House Concern

In the process of unraveling the stories about the CIA attempts against Castro, it might be helpful to explain the White House reaction to the 1971 Anderson columns. In the Senate Watergate Committee hearings, where this was touched on, there is some indication that these columns touched off a minor flurry of activity.[85] Since the purpose of the Watergate break-in has never

---

[84] Hunt, *Give Us This Day*, pp. 38-39.
[85] Senate Watergate Committee Hearings, pp. 9723, 9749-55.

been publicly clarified, and there has been much speculation that Larry O'Brien's knowledge of Howard Hughes' activities was somehow involved, it may be relevant that Anderson did specify that the CIA had recruited Roselli through Robert Maheu, a top Hughes aide.[86]

4. The Warren Commission

The CIA apparently never volunteered to the Warren Commission any information about the Odio family link to an assassination attempt against Castro. That link should have been established the first time the CIA ran the name of Sylvia Odio through their files. If the link was not noticed within the government earlier, it may be relevant that shortly after the 1971 Anderson columns appeared, I sent him the details in my possession, in the hope that he would pursue the matter; he eventually decided not to, but he may well have checked out some of the details with his CIA contacts.

It is reasonable to assume that by now the CIA has done an internal investigation of possible Agency links to the Odio visitors. Any such report, whether or not it was given to the Warren Commission, should be made public.

E. Unanswered Questions in This Area

As indicated above, there are many aspects of the CIA's actions against Castro which should be examined. One of the many possible sources is Victor Marchetti, whose book contains a footnote commenting on these CIA activities, and noting a published report that President Johnson thought that Kennedy had been killed in retaliation. The related section of the text was deleted by the CIA before publication; it should be made public now.[87]

Various sources should be asked about the indications that the CIA leaked information about the Roselli plots to Jack Anderson. The observations of Robert Kennedy's aides Peter Edelman and Adam Walinsky should be made part of the formal public record.

---

[86] Anderson column, Jan. 18, 1971 (S.F. *Chronicle*, p. 39).
[87] Marchetti & Marks (ref. 63), p. 290 (paperback edition).

There are many aspects of the Odio matter which should be investigated. Many people named in relevant documents were not thoroughly questioned by the FBI or the Warren Commission. First, the activities of the three men who the Warren Report suggested were Odio's visitors should be closely examined; they should be asked to provide any relevant information.

One of these men, Loran Hall, came to the attention of the FBI on the day after the assassination, when it was reported that he had retrieved a pawned rifle; presumably the FBI's source suspected Hall of complicity in the death of Kennedy. It is not clear why the FBI then dropped the matter quickly and reported it to the Warren Commission inadequately and only after a long delay.

A friend of Sylvia Odio insisted that she had told her that anti-Castro Cubans in New Orleans had warned some Dallas Cubans before the assassination that Oswald was thought to be a double agent trying to infiltrate anti-Castro groups; Odio emphatically denied having said this.[88] Some of the New Orleans Cubans who had encountered Oswald, including Odio's uncle, were associated with the CIA-sponsored Cuban Revolutionary Council.

The most important new topic for investigation is the attempt to kill Castro which led to the arrest of Sylvia Odio's father. The degree of CIA sponsorship or knowledge of it must be determined.

The whole story of links between Cuban activities (pro- and anti-Castro), Oswald and the assassination is a complicated one. The most significant evidence might emerge from some of the clues that were too complex to attract the attention of the Warren Commission. The Odio incident and its ramifications (some of which were not known to the Commission) can properly be explored without a formal recognition of the overall inadequacies of the Commission's work. It is to be hoped that some members of the Commission staff will be willing to admit that their work was at least incomplete, and will endorse a reopening of the entire investigation.

[88] CD 1546, p. 179; CE 3147, p. 5.

Particularly relevant here are two examples of leads which were not obvious but which should have been checked out by the Commission (and should be checked out now). The first story involves a lawyer from the firm that in mid-1963 defended Chicago syndicate figure Sam Giancana against FBI harassment. (Giancana has been named as a Mafia leader who may have aided the CIA in spying against Castro.)[89] On the day after the assassination, this lawyer sent a telegram to Oswald offering his services if Oswald had not been able to obtain counsel. I am convinced that this gesture was made on proper civil-libertarian grounds, in response to the apparent violation of Oswald's rights in the absence of an attorney. The law firm involved had a good reputation for civil rights work. This lawyer should be given the chance to answer for the record any suspicions that might be raised by his firm's prior representation of Giancana.

The second story might turn out to be a new and valuable clue to the identity, purposes and organizational links of the men who visited Sylvia Odio. There was an anti-Castro Cuban in Dallas who apparently resembled Oswald so much that a gas station operator who saw him a few days before the assassination later told the FBI that he thought he had seen Oswald. The FBI was told by an informant that this man was "violently" anti-Kennedy; he denied that. He was the president of the Dallas branch of the anti-Castro organization which was headed by one of the principals in the attempt on Castro's life which had led to the arrest of Odio's parents. The Dallas group held meetings at 3126 Hollandale [Street]; the Warren Commission received but did not resolve an allegation reported to a Dallas Deputy Sheriff that Oswald had attended meetings of a Cuban group at "3128 Harlendale."[90] This man [Manuel Rodriguez Orcarberro—Eds] is named in several Warren Commission records, but as far as I know, the staff never took note of the apparent resemblance to Oswald, and never checked out the possibility that he had been the "Leon Oswald" who visited Sylvia Odio or that he had otherwise been involved in a conspiracy.

[89] NYT, Mar. 10, 1975, p. 1.
[90] 19H534.

POSTSCRIPT: WARREN COMMISSION STAFF SPECULATION ABOUT THE ODIO INCIDENT

After this memo was written, I received from the National Archives a formerly withheld internal Commission memo in which the Odio incident is discussed at some length. This undated memo was written by William Coleman and David Slawson at roughly the midpoint of the investigation, to present to the Commission members the evidence pertaining to foreign involvement in the assassination. This discussion of the Odio incident reflects the kind of reasonable speculation and intelligent critical analysis which is so conspicuously missing from most of the final report.

This analysis sounds as if it were written by one of the more knowledgeable critics of the Warren Report. After summarizing the known facts in the Odio case, Coleman and Slawson wrote:

The evidence here *could* lead to an anti-Castro Cuban involvement in the assassination on some sort of basis as this: Oswald could have become known to the Cubans as being strongly pro-Castro. He made no secret of his sympathies, and so the anti-Castro Cubans must have realized that the law-enforcement authorities were also aware of Oswald's feelings, and that therefore, if he got into trouble, the public would also learn of them. The anti-Cuban [sic] group may even have believed the fiction Oswald tried to create that he had organized some sort of large active Fair Play For Cuba group in New Orleans. Second, someone in the anti-Castro organization might have been keen enough to sense that Oswald had a penchant for violence that might easily be aroused. This was evident, for example, when he laughed at the Cubans and told them it would be easy to kill Kennedy after the Bay of Pigs. On these facts, it is possible that some sort of deception was used to encourage Oswald to kill the President when he came to Dallas. Perhaps "double agents" were even used to persuade Oswald that pro-Castro Cubans would help in the assassination or in the getaway afterward. The motive of this would of course be the expectation that after the President was killed, Oswald would be caught or at least his identity ascertained, the law-enforcement authorities and the public would then blame the assassination on the Castro government, and the call for its forceful overthrow would be irresistible. A "second Bay of Pigs Invasion" would begin, this time, hopefully, to end successfully.

The memo's next sentence calls for the comment that speculation which seemed "wild" eleven years ago may not be so wild today:

The foregoing is probably only a wild speculation, but the facts that we already know are certainly sufficient to warrant additional investigation.

The Commission's additional investigation was not adequate, and facts known now but not known to Coleman and Slawson in 1964 make additional investigation even more necessary.

Unpublished manuscript. © 1975 Paul L. Hoch.

ALLEGATIONS CONCERNING THE ASSASSINATION OF PRESIDENT KENNEDY

Report of the Commission on CIA Activities Within the United States   /   June 6, 1975

COMMISSION ON CIA ACTIVITIES WITHIN THE UNITED STATES

VICE PRESIDENT NELSON A. ROCKEFELLER, *Chairman*

Counsel

MARVIN L. GRAY, Jr.   JAMES N. ROETHE
GEORGE A. MANFREDI   JAMES B. WEIDNER

Special Counsel   Staff Members

RONALD J. GREENE   R. MASON CARGILL
                       PETER R. CLAPPER
                       TIMOTHY S. HARDY

Special Counsel to   Counsel to
the Vice President   the Vice President

SOL NEIL CORBIN   PETER J. WALLISON

Allegations have been made that the CIA participated in the
assassination of President John F. Kennedy in Dallas, Texas, on
November 22, 1963. Two different theories have been advanced
in support of those allegations. One theory is that E. Howard
Hunt and Frank Sturgis, on behalf of the CIA, personally participated in the assassination. The other is that the CIA had connections with Lee Harvey Oswald or Jack Ruby, or both of them,
and that those connections somehow led to the assassination.
The Commission staff has investigated these allegations.

Neither the staff nor the Commission undertook a full review
of the Report of the Warren Commission. Such a task would
have been outside the scope of the Executive Order establishing
this Commission, and would have diverted the time of the Commission from its proper function. The investigation was limited
to determining whether there was any credible evidence pointing to CIA involvement in the assassination of President Kennedy.

A. THE THEORY THAT HUNT AND STURGIS PARTICIPATED IN THE ASSASSINATION

The first of the theories involves charges that E. Howard Hunt
and Frank Sturgis, both convicted of burglarizing the Democratic National Committee headquarters at the Watergate in

1972, were CIA employees or agents at the time of the assassination of the President in 1963. It is further alleged that they were together in Dallas on the day of the assassination and that shortly after the assassination they were found in a railroad boxcar situated behind the "grassy knoll," an area located to the right front of the Presidential car at the time of the assassination.

Under this theory, Hunt and Sturgis were allegedly in Dallas on November 22, 1963, and were taken into custody by the police, but were mysteriously released without being booked, photographed or fingerprinted by the police—although they were allegedly photographed by press photographers while they were being accompanied to the Dallas County Sheriff's office.

It is further contended that the persons shown in these press photographs bear "striking resemblances" to photographs taken of Hunt and Sturgis in 1972. Portions of two amateur motion picture films of the assassination (Zapruder and Nix) are alleged to reveal the presence of several riflemen in the area of the grassy knoll.

The Hunt-Sturgis theory also rests on the assumption that at least one of the shots that struck President Kennedy was fired from the area of the grassy knoll, where Hunt and Sturgis were alleged to be present. The direction from which the shots came is claimed to be shown by the backward and leftward movement of President Kennedy's body almost immediately after being struck by that bullet. Taken together, these purported facts are cited as the basis for a possible conclusion that CIA personnel participated in the assassination of President Kennedy, and, at least inferentially, that the CIA itself was involved.

The Commission staff investigated the several elements of this theory to the extent deemed necessary to assess fairly the allegation of CIA participation in the assassination. The findings of that investigation follow.

FINDINGS

1. The Allegation That Hunt and Sturgis Were CIA Employees or Agents in 1963

E. Howard Hunt was an employee of the CIA in November 1963. He had been an employee of the CIA for many years before that, and he continued to be associated with the CIA until his retirement in 1970. Throughout 1963 he was assigned to duty in Washington, D.C., performing work relating to propaganda operations in foreign countries. His duties included travel to several other cities in the United States, but not to any place in the South or Southwest. He lived with his family in the Washington, D.C., metropolitan area throughout that year, and his children attended school there.

Frank Sturgis was not an employee or agent of the CIA either in 1963 or at any other time. He so testified under oath himself, and a search of CIA records failed to discover any evidence that he had ever been employed by the CIA or had ever served it as an agent, informant or other operative. Sturgis testified that he had been engaged in various "adventures" relating to Cuba which he believed to have been organized and financed by the CIA. He testified that he had given information, directly and indirectly, to federal government officials, who, he believed, were acting for the CIA. He further testified, however, that at no time did he engage in any activity having to do with the assassination of President Kennedy, on behalf of the CIA or otherwise.

2. *The Allegation That Hunt and Sturgis Were Together in Dallas on the Day of the Assassination*

Hunt and Sturgis testified under oath to members of the Commission staff. They both denied that they were in Dallas on the day of the assassination. Hunt testified that he was in the Washington, D.C., metropolitan area throughout that day, and his testimony was supported by two of his children[1] and a former domestic employee of the Hunt family. Sturgis testified that he was in Miami, Florida, throughout the day of the assassination, and his testimony was supported by that of his wife and a nephew of his wife. The nephew, who was then living with the Sturgis family, is now a practicing attorney in the Midwest.

With the exception of the domestic employee of the Hunt

---

[1] A son who was nine years old at the time could not recall whether his parents were present or absent that day; the fourth (and youngest) Hunt child was not born then. Mrs. Hunt is now deceased.

family, all witnesses directly supporting the presence of Hunt and Sturgis in Washington, D.C., and Miami, Florida, on the day of the assassination are family members or relatives. Less weight can be assigned to the testimony of such interested witnesses if there is substantial evidence to the contrary. In the absence of substantial conflicting evidence, however, the testimony of family members cannot be disregarded.

Hunt testifies that he had never met Frank Sturgis before they were introduced by Bernard Barker in Miami in 1972. Sturgis testified to the same effect, except that he did not recall whether the introduction had taken place in late 1971 or early 1972. Sturgis further testified that while he had often heard of "Eduardo," a CIA political officer who had been active in the work of the Cuban Revolutionary Council in Miami prior to the Bay of Pigs operation in April 1961, he had never met him and did not know until 1971 or 1972 that "Eduardo" was E. Howard Hunt. Sturgis had also been active in anti-Castro groups in the Miami area before, during and after Hunt's assignment on the political aspects of the Bay of Pigs project in 1960 and early 1961.

Other testimony linked Hunt to Sturgis at a date earlier than 1971. One witness asserted that Sturgis is a pseudonym; that his name is Frank Fiorini; and that he took the name Sturgis from a fictional character (Hank Sturgis) in a novel written by Hunt in 1949. (*Bimini Run*). Sturgis testified that his name at birth was Frank Angelo Fiorini; that his mother's maiden name was Mary Vena; that his father's name was Angelo Anthony Fiorini; that his parents were divorced when he was a child; that his mother subsequently remarried a man named Ralph Sturgis; and that at his mother's urging he legally changed his name in Norfolk, Virginia, sometime in the 1950's, to take the last name of his stepfather.

A search of the relevant court records disclosed that a petition was filed on September 23, 1952, in the Circuit Court of the City of Norfolk (Virginia) pursuant to which a Frank Angelo Fiorino petitioned to change his name to Frank Anthony Sturgis. The petition recited that his mother had divorced his father about 15 years previously and had married one Ralph Sturgis, that he had been living with his mother all of his life, that his mother was known as Mary Sturgis, and that his stepfather also desired him to change his name to Sturgis. An order of the Court was entered on September 23, 1952 (the same date as the petition) changing his name to Frank Anthony Sturgis. The order appears in the records of the Circuit Court of the City of Norfolk, Virginia. In the petition and the order relating to the change of name, *Fiorini* was misspelled as *Fiorino*.

In the light of this documentary evidence, no weight can be given to the claim that Sturgis took his present name from a character in a Hunt novel—or that the name change was associated in any way with Sturgis' knowing Hunt before 1971 or 1972.

The personnel, payroll and travel records of the CIA were checked with respect to E. Howard Hunt. Daily attendance records for the period are no longer available because they are destroyed in the ordinary course of the Agency's records disposal system three years after completion of the audit for each year. What records remain, including annual leave, sick leave, and travel records, disclose that Hunt had no out-of-town travel associated with his employment in the month of November 1963. He used no annual leave and eleven hours of sick leave in the two-week pay period ending November 23, 1963. The exact date or dates on which the sick leave was taken could not be ascertained. There is some indication, however, that some of these eleven hours of sick leave may have been taken by Hunt on November 22, 1963. He testified that, on the afternoon of that day, he was in the company of his wife and family in the Washington, D.C., area, rather than at his employment duties. That was a Friday, and therefore a working day for employees at the CIA. Hunt could not recall whether he was on duty with the CIA on the morning of that day.

Because Sturgis was never an agent or employee of the CIA, the Agency has no personnel, payroll, leave or travel records relating to him.

In examining the charge that Hunt and Sturgis were together in Dallas on the day of the assassination, the investigators were handicapped by the fact that the allegation was first made in 1974, more than ten years after the assassination. Evidence which might have been available at an earlier time was no longer available. Contacts with relatives, friends, neighbors or fellow employees (who might have known of the whereabouts of Hunt and Sturgis on that particular day) could not be recalled. Some of these persons are now dead. Finally, records which might have been the source of relevant information no longer exist.

It cannot be determined with certainty where Hunt and Sturgis actually were on the day of the assassination. However, no credible evidence was found which would contradict their testimony that they were in Washington, D.C., and Miami, Florida, respectively.

3. *The Allegation That Hunt and Sturgis Were Found Near the Scene of the Assassination and Taken to the Dallas County Sheriff's Office*

This allegation is based upon a purported resemblance between Hunt and Sturgis, on the one hand, and two persons who were briefly taken into custody in Dallas following the assassination.

The shooting of President Kennedy occurred at about 12:30 p.m., Dallas time, on November 22, 1963, while the Presidential motorcade was passing Dealey Plaza as it headed generally westward on Elm Street. Witnesses to the shooting gave the police varying accounts of where they thought the shots had come from. On the basis of the sound of the shots, some believed that they had come from the Texas School Book Depository building (TSBD), which was behind and slightly to the right of President Kennedy when he was hit. Others thought the shots had come from other directions. Law enforcement officials understandably conducted a widespread search for evidence relating to the assassination.

Several hours after the shooting, officers of the Dallas Police Department checked all railroad freight cars situated on tracks anywhere in the vicinity of Dealey Plaza. About six or eight persons, referred to as "derelicts," were found in or near the freight cars. These persons were taken either to the nearby Dallas County Sheriff's office, or to the Dallas Police Department, for questioning. All were released without any arrest record being made, or any fingerprinting or photographing being done by the authorities.

Among the six or eight "derelicts" found in the vicinity of the freight cars were three men who, according to the arresting officers, were found in a boxcar about one-half mile *south* of the scene of the assassination. They were taken to the Sheriff's office by the Dallas police officers, who walked northward along the railroad tracks to a point west of the Texas School Book Depository, then north to Houston Street and back south to the Sheriff's office. This somewhat circuitous route was actually the most convenient one available, according to the Dallas policemen. As the police and the "derelicts" passed the TSBD building and headed for the Sheriff's office, they were photographed by several press photographers on the scene. Copies of five of the photographs showing the "derelicts" were submitted to the Commission's staff as evidence.

A witness who volunteered his testimony stated on the basis of hearsay that the three "derelicts" in question were found in a boxcar situated to the near *northwest* of the assassination scene, which would have been to the right front of the Presidential car at the time of the shooting. Between the area in which that boxcar was claimed by this witness to be located and that part of Elm Street where the assassination occurred was a "grassy knoll."

It was alleged by other witnesses (who were associated with the first witness and who also volunteered testimony) that a bullet fired from the area of that "grassy knoll" struck President Kennedy in the head. It was also claimed by the same witnesses that one of the three photographed "derelicts" bears a "striking" facial resemblance to E. Howard Hunt and that another of them bears a "striking" facial resemblance to Frank Sturgis. Finally, it was alleged that if those two "derelicts" were, in fact, Hunt and Sturgis, and if the President was in fact struck by a bullet fired from his right front, the CIA would be shown to be implicated in the killing of President Kennedy.

The photographs of the "derelicts" in Dallas have been compared with numerous known photographs of Hunt and Sturgis taken both before and after November 22, 1963. Even to non-experts it appeared that there was, at best, only a superficial resemblance between the Dallas "derelicts" and Hunt and Sturgis. The "derelict" allegedly resembling Hunt appeared to be substantially older and smaller than Hunt. The "derelict" allegedly resembling Sturgis appeared to be thinner than Sturgis and to have facial features and hair markedly different from those of Sturgis.

The witnesses who testified to the "striking resemblance" between the "derelicts" and Hunt and Sturgis were not shown to have any qualifications in photo identification beyond that possessed by the average layman. Their testimony appears to have been based on a comparison of the 1963 photographs of the "derelicts" with a single 1972 photograph of Sturgis and two 1972 photographs of Hunt.

Over fifty photographs taken of Hunt and Sturgis both before and after November 22, 1963, were submitted to the FBI photographic laboratory for a comparison with all known photographs of the "derelicts." (The FBI assembled a complete set of all photographs of the "derelicts" taken by the three photographers known to have photographed them.) The comparison was made by FBI Agent Lyndal L. Shaneyfelt, a nationally-recognized expert in photo identification and photo analysis.

The report of Agent Shaneyfelt, embodied in a Report of the FBI Laboratory, dated April 21, 1975, and signed by Clarence M. Kelley, Director of the FBI, concluded that "neither E. Howard Hunt nor Frank Sturgis appear as any of the three 'derelicts' arrested in Dallas, Texas, as shown in the photographs submitted."

With respect to Hunt, it was found that he had a much younger appearance, a smooth and tightly contoured chin, and a more angular or pointed chin, compared with the "derelict" in question. The latter was much older, had a chin with protruding pouches and a more bulbous nose.

With respect to Sturgis, even more distinguishing characteristics were observed. Sturgis looked like a Latin, whereas the "derelict" had the general appearance of a Nordic. Sturgis had very black, wavy hair—and the "derelict" had light or blond and straighter hair. Sturgis had a rather round face with square chin lines; the "derelict" had an oval face with a more rounded chin. Sturgis and the "derelict" had markedly different ratios between the length of their noses and the height of their foreheads. They also had different ear and nose contours.

Hunt is approximately five feet nine inches tall, and Sturgis is approximately five feet eleven inches tall. The FBI laboratory made an on-site study in Dallas, using the cameras with which the photographs of the "derelicts" were originally taken; it concluded from the study that the "derelict" allegedly resembling Hunt was about five feet, seven inches tall, and that the "derelict" allegedly resembling Sturgis was about six feet two inches tall, with a one inch margin for error in each direction. The difference between the height of the two "derelicts" was therefore about seven inches, while the difference between Hunt's height and that of Sturgis is only about two inches.

The photographs of the "derelicts" in Dallas have been displayed in various newspapers in the United States, on national television programs, and in the April 28, 1975, issue of *Newsweek* magazine. But no witnesses have provided testimony that either of the "derelicts" was personally known to be Hunt or Sturgis—and no qualified expert was offered to make such an identification.

4. The Allegation That President Kennedy Was Struck in the Head by a Bullet Fired From His Right Front

The witnesses who presented evidence they believed sufficient to implicate the CIA in the assassination of President Kennedy placed much stress upon the movements of the President's body associated with the head wound that killed the President. Particular attention was called to the Zapruder film, and especially Frame 312 and the succeeding frames of that film. It was urged that the movements of the President's head and body immediately following the head wound evidenced in Frame 313 established that the President was struck by a bullet fired from the right front of the Presidential car—the direction of the grassy knoll and the freight car in which "Hunt" and "Sturgis" were allegedly found.

By Frame 312 of the Zapruder film, President Kennedy had already been wounded by a bullet which had struck him in the region of his neck. His body is shown to be facing generally toward the front of the Presidential car. He is leaning toward the left. His head is turned somewhat toward the left front, and it is facing downward toward the floor in the rear portion of the car. His chin appears to be close to his chest.

At Frame 313 of the Zapruder film, the President has been struck by the bullet that killed him, and his head has moved forward noticeably. At Frame 314 (which is about 1/18 of a second later) his head is already moving backward. Succeeding frames of the film show a rapid backward movement of the President's head and upper body, and at the same time his head and body are shown to be turning toward his left. Still later frames show the President's body collapsing onto the back seat of the car.

The evidence presented to the Warren Commission revealed that the speed of the Zapruder motion picture camera was 18.3 frames per second. If the film is projected at that speed, the forward movement of the President's head from Frame 312 to Frame 313 is not readily perceived. On the other hand, such forward movement is evident upon careful measurement of still projections of the relevant frames. It is very short, both in distance and duration. The backward movement and the turning of the President's head toward the left are rapid, pronounced and readily apparent during a running of the film at either normal or slow speed.

It was claimed that the movement of the President's head and body backward and to the left is consistent only with a shot having come from the right front of the Presidential car—that is, from the direction of the grassy knoll.

Medical and ballistics experts were consulted. Also considered were (1) the autopsy report on the body of President Kennedy, and (2) the report of a panel of medical experts who, in February 1968, at the request of Attorney General Ramsey Clark, reviewed the autopsy report and the autopsy photographs, x-ray films, motion picture films of the assassination, the clothing worn by President Kennedy and other relevant materials.

The autopsy report of James J. Humes, M.D., J. Thornton Boswell, M.D., and Pierre A. Finck, M.D., described the President's head wound as follows:

The fatal wound [sic] entered the skull above and to the right of the external occipital protuberance. A portion of the projectile traversed the cranial cavity in a posterior-anterior direction (see lateral skull roentgenograms) depositing minute particles along its path. A portion of the projectile made its exit through the parietal bone on the right carrying with it portions of the cerebrum, skull and scalp. The two wounds of the skull combined with the force of the missile produced extensive fragmentation of the skull, laceration of the superior sagittal sinus, and of the right cerebral hemisphere.

In February 1968, a panel of physicians met in Washington, D.C., at the request of Attorney General Ramsey Clark, to examine the autopsy report, the autopsy photographs and x-rays, the Zapruder, Nix and Muchmore motion picture films of the assassination, and various other evidence pertaining to the death of President Kennedy. Each of the four physicians constituting the panel had been nominated by a prominent person who was not in the employment of the federal government. They were:

William H. Carnes, M.D., Professor of Pathology, University of Utah, Salt Lake City, Utah; Member of Medical Examiner's Commission, State of Utah. Nominated by Dr. J. E. Wallace Sterling, President of Stanford University.

Russell S. Fisher, M.D., Professor of Forensic Pathology, University of Maryland; and Chief Medical Examiner of the State of Maryland, Baltimore, Maryland. Nominated by Dr. Oscar B. Hunter, Jr., President of the College of American Pathologists.

Russell H. Morgan, M.D., Professor of Radiology, School of Medicine, and Professor of Radiological Science, School of Hygiene and Public Health, The Johns Hopkins University, Baltimore, Maryland. Nominated by Dr. Lincoln Gordon, President of The Johns Hopkins University.

Alan R. Moritz, M.D., Professor of Pathology, Case Western Reserve University, Cleveland, Ohio; and former Professor of Forensic Medicine, Harvard University. Nominated by Dr. John A. Hannah, President of Michigan State University.

After reviewing the autopsy photographs, and making their findings concerning them, the Panel said in its report:

These findings indicate that the back of the head was struck by a single bullet traveling at high velocity, the major portion of which passed through the right cerebral hemisphere, and which produced an explosive type of fragmentation of the skull and laceration of the scalp. The appearance of the entrance wound in the scalp is consistent with its having been produced by a bullet similar to that of Exhibit 399.[2]

After a review of the autopsy x-rays, the Panel's report states:

The foregoing observations indicate that the decedent's head was struck from behind by a single projectile. It entered the occipital region 25 mm. to the right of the midline and 100 mm. above the external occipital protuberance. The projectile fragmented on entering the skull, one major section leaving a trail of fine metallic debris as it passed forward and laterally to explosively fracture the right frontal and parietal bones as it emerged from the head.

The Panel discussed its findings as follows:

The decedent was wounded by two bullets both of which entered his body from behind.

One bullet struck the back of the decedent's head well above the external occipital protuberance. Based upon the observation that he was leaning forward with his head turned obliquely to the left when this bullet struck, the photographs and x-rays indicate that it came from a site above and slightly to his right.

The absence of metallic fragments in the left cerebral hemisphere or below the level of the frontal fosse on the right side together with the absence of any holes in the skull to the left of the midline or in its base and the absence of any penetrating injury of the left hemisphere eliminate with reasonable certainty the possibility of a projectile having passed through the head in any direction other than from back to front as described in preceding sections of this report.

[2] CE 399 was Warren Commission Exhibit 399, a nearly whole bullet found in Parkland Memorial Hospital in Dallas on the day of the assassination. It was established by ballistics experts as having been fired by the rifle found on the sixth floor of the TSBD building and found by the Warren Commission to have belonged to Lee Harvey Oswald. The Warren Commission determined that bullet passed through President Kennedy's neck and then struck Governor Connally, who was sitting directly in front of President Kennedy, and who was taken to Parkland Hospital.

Certain other evidence relating to the source of the bullets that struck President Kennedy was noted. This included the following:

a. The bullet fragments found in the Presidential car which were large enough to bear ballistics marks were determined by the FBI to have been fired by the Oswald rifle found on the sixth floor of the Texas School Book Depository building, and not from any other weapon. CE 399 was also fired from that rifle.

b. No physical evidence, such as a rifle, shell casings, bullets, or damage to the Presidential car, was ever found which would support a theory that one or more shots were fired from a direction other than from behind and above the President.

c. Most eyewitnesses testified that three shots were fired. Three shell casings were found near the window at the southeast corner of the sixth floor of the Texas School Book Depository building, and all of them were determined by the FBI to have been fired by the Oswald rifle to the exclusion of any other weapon. That window was also the one in which a man firing was seen by witnesses who testified before the Warren Commission. The Oswald rifle was found on the sixth floor of the TSBD building within an hour after the assassination.

d. No witness at the scene was found who saw any other assassin, or who saw anyone firing, or disposing of a weapon in any other location. Three TSBD employees testified before the Warren Commission that they had been watching the motorcade from open windows near the southeast corner of the fifth floor of the TSBD building. One of them testified that he heard not only the three shots, but also the sound above him of a rifle bolt in action and the sound of empty shells hitting the floor. All three of them testified that "debris" fell down from above them at the time of the shots, and that they talked to each other at that time about the shots having come from above them.

e. A shot fired from the direct front of the Presidential car can be ruled out. Such a bullet would have had to pass through the windshield of the car unless fired from above the overpass just ahead of the Presidential car. There were no holes in the windshield, and the overpass was guarded by two policemen in the presence of some fifteen railroad employees. None of them saw or heard any shooting take place from the overpass.

Nonetheless, a re-examination was made of the question whether the movements of the President's head and body following the fatal shot are consistent with the President being struck from (a) the rear, (b) the right front, or (c) both the rear and the right front. The Zapruder, Nix and Muchmore films, a set of all relevant color slides of the Zapruder film, the autopsy photographs and x-rays, the President's clothing and back brace, the bullet and bullet fragments recovered, and various other materials, were reviewed at the request of the Commission staff by a panel of experts consisting of:

Lieutenant Colonel Robert R. McMeekin, MC, USA; Chief, Division of Aerospace Pathology, Armed Forces Institute of Pathology, Washington, D.C.
Richard Lindenberg, M.D., Director of Neuropathology & Legal Medicine, Department of Mental Health, State of Maryland, Baltimore, Maryland.
Werner U. Spitz, M.D., Chief Medical Examiner, Wayne County, Detroit, Michigan.
Fred J. Hodges, III, M.D., Professor of Radiology, The Johns Hopkins School of Medicine, Baltimore, Maryland.
Alfred G. Olivier, V.M.D., Director, Department of Biophysics, Biomedical Laboratories, Edgewood Arsenal, Aberdeen Proving Grounds, Maryland.[3]

The Panel members separately submitted their respective conclusions. They were unanimous in finding that the President was struck by only two bullets, both of which were fired from the rear, and that there is no medical evidence to support a contention that the President was struck by any bullet coming from any other direction.

They were also unanimous in finding that the violent back-

[3] Dr. McMeekin is a forensic pathologist who has done extensive studies in the field of accident reconstruction, utilizing computer-assisted analysis of the reactions of human body components to the application of various forces. Dr. Lindenberg is a prominent authority in the field of neuropathology, i.e., the pathology of the brain and nervous system. Dr. Spitz is a forensic pathologist who has had extensive experience with gunshot wounds and is an editor of a textbook on forensic pathology. Dr. Hodges is a specialist in radiology and surgery associated with the brain and nervous system. In 1973-1974 he served as President of the American Society of Neuroradiology. Dr. Olivier has conducted numerous experiments to study the effects on animals and humans of penetrating wounds from high velocity bullets. Drs. Spitz, Lindenberg and Hodges hold faculty positions in the Medical Schools of Wayne State University, the University of Maryland, and The Johns Hopkins University, respectively.

ward and leftward motion of the President's upper body following the head shot was not caused by the impact of a bullet
coming from the front or right front.

Drs. Spitz, Lindenberg and Hodges reported that such a
motion would be caused by a violent straightening and stiffening
of the entire body as a result of a seizure-like neuromuscular
reaction to major damage inflicted to nerve centers in the brain.

Dr. Olivier reported that experiments which have been conducted at Edgewood Arsenal disclosed that goats shot through
the brain evidenced just such a violent neuromuscular reaction.
There was a convulsive stiffening and extension of their legs to
front and rear, commencing forty milliseconds (1/25 of a second) after the bullet entered the brain. In the past two decades,
Dr. Olivier and his associates have conducted extensive tests on
the effects of high velocity bullets fired into live animals, using
high speed photography to record the results.

Dr. Olivier reported that the violent motions of the President's
body following the head shot could not possibly have been
caused by the *impact* of the bullet. He attributed the popular
misconception on this subject to the dramatic effects employed
in television and motion picture productions. The *impact* of such
a bullet, he explained, can cause some immediate movement of
the *head* in the direction of the bullet, but it would not produce
any significant movement of the *body*. He also explained that a
head wound such as that sustained by President Kennedy produces an "explosion" of tissue at the area where the bullet exits
from the head, causing a "jet effect" which almost instantly
moves the head back in the direction from which the bullet
came.

Drs. Olivier and McMeekin, utilizing enlargement of the film
and an accurate measuring device, made measurements of the
movement of the President's head associated with the head shot.
They found that in the interval between Zapruder Frames 312
and 313, the President's head moved forward significantly; at
Frame 314 (1/18 of a second later) it was already moving backward and it continued to move backward in the succeeding
frames.

Dr. Olivier was of the opinion that the start of the backward movement resulted from both a neuromuscular reaction and a "jet effect" from the explosion at the right front of the head where the bullet exited. Thereafter, the violent backward and leftward movement of the upper body, he believes, was a continuing result of the neuromuscular reaction. Dr. McMeekin's report to the Commission contained no reference to the subject of a "jet effect."

Dr. Olivier credited Dr. Luis Alvarez with originating studies into the "jet effect" produced by high velocity bullets fired into the head. Dr. Alvarez is a Nobel Prize-winning physicist at the Lawrence Berkeley Laboratories, University of California at Berkeley. An article describing his experiments is soon to be published.

Dr. John K. Lattimer of New York and Dr. Cyril H. Wecht of Pittsburgh were also interviewed. Each of them has studied in detail the autopsy photographs, x-rays, and other materials, as well as the motion pictures of the assassination, and has published the results of his findings.

Dr. Lattimer testified that there was no medical evidence to support a theory that the President had been hit by a bullet from any direction other than from the rear and above. The medical evidence showed that the President had not been hit from the front or right front. Had a second and nearly simultaneous bullet from the front or right front hit the President's head after Frame 313 of the Zapruder film, it would either have encountered no skull (in which case it would have passed through the brain and exited elsewhere) or it would have struck the skull. In either case, it would have left evidence which would be revealed by the autopsy photographs and x-rays.

Dr. Lattimer also testified that he has performed experiments to test both the damage effects of a bullet fired into the rear of the head (in the precise area where the President was hit) and the principle of the "jet effect." He utilized a Mannlicher-Carcano 6.5 millimeter rifle of the same model as the one found by the Warren Commission to belong to Lee Harvey Oswald, and ammunition from the same manufacturer and lot number as that found to have been used by Oswald. The results, he said, confirmed both the head injuries shown in the autopsy photographs and x-rays and the principle of the "jet-effect." Dr. Lattimer presented to the Commission staff as evidence a motion picture film and still photographs showing the results of his experiments.

Dr. Wecht testified that the available evidence all points to the President being struck only by two bullets coming from his rear, and that no support can be found for theories which postulate gunmen to the front or right front of the Presidential car.

In a 1974 article written by Dr. Wecht and an associate, an article which was made an exhibit to his testimony, Dr. Wecht stated that "if any other bullet struck the President's head, whether before, after, or simultaneously with the known shot, there is no evidence for it in the available autopsy materials." He testified that on the autopsy photographs of the back of the President's head, there was something above the hairline which he could not identify at all, and he thought it was possible that this was an exit wound. He stated that the other autopsy photographs and the autopsy x-rays provided no support to that possibility, but he thought it was possible that the physicians who performed the autopsy could have missed finding such a wound.

Dr. Wecht said that there was some question about the backward and leftward movement of the President's head and upper body after Frame 313, but he also said that a neuromuscular reaction could occur within about one-tenth of a second.

The Commission staff also interviewed by telephone Dr. E. Forrest Chapman of Michigan, the only other physician who is known to have studied the autopsy photographs and x-rays. Dr. Chapman declared that if there were any assassins firing at the President from the grassy knoll, "they must have been very poor shots because they didn't hit anything."

No witness who urged the view that the Zapruder and other motion picture films proved that President Kennedy was struck by a bullet fired from his right front was shown to possess any professional or other special qualifications on the subject.

On the basis of the investigation conducted by its staff, the Commission believes that there is no evidence to support the claim that President Kennedy was struck by a bullet fired from either the grassy knoll or any other position to his front, right front or right side, and that the motions of the President's head and body, following the shot that struck him in the head, are fully consistent with that shot having come from a point to his rear, above him and slightly to his right.

5. *The Allegation That Assassins (Allegedly Including "Hunt" and "Sturgis") Are Revealed by the Zapruder and Nix Films To Be Present in the Area of the Grassy Knoll*

In further support of his contention that shots were fired at President Kennedy from the grassy knoll—and inferentially by "Hunt" and "Sturgis"—a witness called attention to certain frames of motion picture films taken at the time of the assassination. He asserted that these frames, including Frames 413 and 454–478 of the Zapruder film, reveal the presence of other "assassins" bearing rifles in the area of the grassy knoll.

The Zapruder and Nix films have been carefully reviewed. Frames alleged to reveal the presence of assassins in the area of the grassy knoll have received particularly close attention, together with those frames immediately preceding them and immediately following them. In addition, the Commission has had the benefit of a study of these films by the photographic laboratory of the FBI, and a report on that study.

The Commission staff members who reviewed the films were of the opinion that the images allegedly representing assassins are far too vague to be identifiable even as human beings. For example, Zapruder Frames 412, 413, and 414, which have tree foliage in the foreground, show combinations of light and shadow along their lower margins which are varyingly shaped somewhat in the form of a rain hat or a German army helmet of World War II vintage. In Frames 411 and 415, however, the contours of the shadows are markedly different and bear no resemblance to a human head—with or without a rain hat or helmet.

Since each frame of the film is only about 1/18 of a second removed in time from its adjacent frame, it was not believed reasonable to postulate that an assassin's head would come into view, and then disappear, directly in front of the Zapruder camera, in the space of about ¼ of a second (the elapsed time between Frames 411 and 415), or that the shape of a head would change so rapidly and markedly.

The conclusion was that the alleged assassin's head was merely the momentary image produced by sunlight, shadows, and leaves within or beyond the foliage. The same was true of the "rifle" allegedly in evidence in Frame 413. Even to make out the rough image of a rifle in that frame required imagination—and in the adjacent frames, it is nowhere in evidence.

From the extensive photographic work done in connection with the Warren Commission investigation, the FBI has a substantial library of both its own photographs and copies of the photographs and motion pictures of others taken at the assassination scene.

The place where Abraham Zapruder was standing when he took his famous motion picture has been established. (He was standing on a concrete wall elevated approximately four feet, two inches above the ground to his front.) Based upon an analysis of the direction in which the Zapruder camera was facing at Frame 413, the FBI Laboratory was able to identify from other photographs the exact tree shown in that frame. With the aid of reports from the FBI Laboratory, it was concluded that: (1) The tree was between 6 feet and 6½ feet high; (2) it was barren of any branches or leaves to height of about 4 feet to 4½ feet above the ground; (3) its foliage was about 2 feet high and 4 feet wide; (4) the near side of its foliage was about five feet directly in front of Mr. Zapruder's legs; (5) its trunk was only a few inches in diameter; (6) only the top of the tree came within view of the Zapruder camera; (7) it was the only tree in the immediate vicinity; (8) a human head (even without a helmet) 5 feet in front of Mr. Zapruder would have occupied about one-half of the total area of Frame 413 (many times as much as is occupied by the image of the alleged assassin's head); and (9) it is not reasonable to postulate an assassin in or behind that tree.

An assassin would be unlikely to hide himself behind the barren trunk of a tree only a few inches in diameter, with only his head and shoulders behind the foliage, and with his whole person almost within arm's length in front of a spectator taking movies of the motorcade. Neither would such an assassin go unseen and undiscovered, able to make his escape over open ground with a rifle in hand, again unseen by anyone among the numerous motorcade police, spectators and Secret Service personnel present.

A clear photograph of the tree in question, taken on May 24, 1964 (about six months after the assassination), was made a part of the FBI Laboratory Report. It was marked to show the place where Zapruder was standing as he took his motion picture.

The FBI photography laboratory was also able to identify the tree in question on some of the frames of the Nix film, which was also being taken at the time of the assassination. An examination of those frames of the Nix film reveals that there was nobody in or behind that tree. Also made a part of the FBI Laboratory Report was a series of frames from the Nix film, with the tree in question, Mr. Zapruder, and the alleged positions of "assassins" separately marked.

A similar examination was made by the FBI photography laboratory of other frames of the Zapruder and Nix films alleged to reveal assassins in the area of the grassy knoll. Frames 454 through 478 of the Zapruder film were found to reveal no formation "identifiable as a human being or an assassin with a rifle or other weapon." With respect to the Nix film, the FBI reported that "no figure of a human being could be found in the area" of another alleged rifleman, which was determined to be "approximately nineteen feet to the right of where Mr. Zapruder was standing and clearly visible to him." The FBI concluded that the configuration described as a rifleman was actually produced by some "clump type shrubbery" in the background.

On the basis of its staff investigation, the Commission believes that there is no credible basis in fact for the claim that any of the known motion pictures relating to the assassination of President Kennedy reveals the presence of an assassin or assassins in the area of the grassy knoll.

B. THE THEORY THAT THE CIA HAD RELATIONSHIPS WITH LEE HARVEY OSWALD AND JACK RUBY

The second theory advanced in support of allegations of CIA participation in the assassination of President Kennedy is that various links existed between the CIA, Oswald and Ruby. Lee Harvey Oswald was found by the Warren Commission to be the person who assassinated the President. Jack Ruby shot and killed Oswald two days after the President's assassination.

There is no credible evidence that either Lee Harvey Oswald or Jack Ruby was ever employed by the CIA or ever acted for the CIA in any capacity whatever, either directly or indirectly.

Testimony was offered purporting to show CIA relationships with Oswald and Ruby. It was stated, for example, that E. Howard Hunt, as an employee of the CIA, engaged in political activity with elements of the anti-Castro Cuban community in the United States on behalf of the CIA prior to the Bay of Pigs operation in April 1961. In connection with those duties, it was further alleged that Hunt was instrumental in organizing the Cuban Revolutionary Council and that the Cuban Revolutionary Council had an office in New Orleans. Finally, it was claimed that Lee Harvey Oswald lived in New Orleans from April to September 1963, and that a pamphlet prepared and distributed by Oswald on behalf of the Fair Play for Cuba Committee during that period indicated that the office of the Fair Play for Cuba Committee was situated in a building which was also the address of the New Orleans office of the Cuban Revolutionary Council.[4]

It was therefore implied that Hunt *could* have had contact with Lee Harvey Oswald in New Orleans during the spring or summer of 1963. No evidence was presented that Hunt ever met

---

[4] Each of these statements is substantially true, but many other relevant facts disclosed in the Warren Commission Report are omitted. It is not mentioned, for example, that Oswald made up the Fair Play for Cuba Committee pamphlets; that the address he stamped on the pamphlets was never an office of that Committee; that he fabricated a non-existent New Orleans Chapter of the Committee, a non-existent President of that Committee, and a non-existent office for it; that the building in question was a *former office*, rather than a current office, of an anti-Castro organization when Oswald made up his pamphlets; and that Oswald had tried to infiltrate the anti-Castro organization.

Oswald, or that he was ever in New Orleans in 1963, or that he had any contact with any New Orleans office of the Cuban Revolutionary Council.

Hunt's employment record with the CIA indicated that he had no duties involving contacts with Cuban exile elements or organizations inside or outside the United States after the early months of 1961. This was more than two years before Oswald went to New Orleans in April 1963 and more than a year before Oswald returned to the United States from the Soviet Union, where he had lived for almost three years.

An example of the testimony relating to an alleged relationship between the CIA and Jack Ruby consisted of a statement that Frank Sturgis was engaged in a series of revolutionary activities among Cuban exiles in the United States in the 1950's and 1960's and that the CIA also sponsored and organized anti-Castro activities among Cuban exiles in the United States in 1959 and the early 1960's.

It was further stated that someone once reported to the FBI that Jack Ruby had engaged in supplying arms to persons in Cuba in the early 1950's in association with a former Cuban President, Carlos Prio, and that Frank Sturgis also had connections with Carlos Prio during the 1950's and 1960's.

In addition, it was alleged that Frank Sturgis was at one time (before he escaped from Cuba in June 1959) a director of gambling and gaming establishments in Havana for the Castro government, and that in August or September, 1959, Jack Ruby made a trip to Havana at the invitation of a friend who had interests in gambling establishments in Cuba and the United States.

Moreover, both Sturgis and Ruby were alleged to have had connections with underground figures who had interests in the United States and Cuba.

From this group of allegations, the witness inferred that Sturgis and Ruby *could* have met and known each other—although no actual evidence was presented to show that Ruby or Sturgis ever met each other.

Even if the individual items contained in the foregoing recitations were assumed to be true, it was concluded that the inferences drawn must be considered farfetched speculation insofar as they purport to show a connection between the CIA and either Oswald or Ruby.

Even in the absence of denials by living persons that such connections existed, no weight could be assigned to such testimony. Moreover, Sturgis was never an employee or agent of the CIA.

A witness, a telephone caller, and a mail correspondent tendered additional information of the same nature. None of it was more than a strained effort to draw inferences of conspiracy from facts which would not fairly support the inferences. A CIA involvement in the assassination was implied by the witness, for example, from the fact that the Mayor of Dallas at that time was a brother of a CIA official who had been involved in the planning of the Bay of Pigs operation in Cuba several years previously, and from the fact that President Kennedy reportedly blamed the CIA for the Bay of Pigs failure.

The same witness testified that E. Howard Hunt was Acting Chief of a CIA station in Mexico City in 1963, implying that he *could* have had contact with Oswald when Oswald visited Mexico City in September 1963. Hunt's service in Mexico City, however, was twelve years earlier—in 1950 and 1951—and his only other CIA duty in Mexico covered only a few weeks in 1960. At no time was he ever the Chief, or Acting Chief, of a CIA station in Mexico City.

Hunt and Sturgis categorically denied that they had ever met or known Oswald or Ruby. They further denied that they ever had any connection whatever with either Oswald or Ruby.

Conclusions

Numerous allegations have been made that the CIA participated in the assassination of President John F. Kennedy. The Commission staff investigated these allegations. On the basis of the staff's investigation, the Commission concluded there was no credible evidence of any CIA involvement.

TESTIMONY DISTORTED
Cyril H. Wecht

June 12, 1975

The report of the Rockefeller Commission seriously misrepresents my testimony in connection with the medical and scientific evidence in the assassination of President Kennedy.

The Commission is perpetrating a fraud upon the public by seizing on and publicizing a secondary aspect of my testimony, while ignoring the primary part. Moreover, the Commission has refused to make my testimony available to the public, and even refuses to provide me with a copy of it for my own use.

On May 7, 1975, I testified by deposition for approximately five and a half hours to the effect that the Warren Report's principal conclusion, namely that the President was assassinated by a lone gunman, was wrong and absolutely irreconcilable with the medical and scientific evidence in the case. In certain technical papers that I have previously published on the case, it is true that I have stated that the available evidence, assuming it to be valid, gives no support to theories which postulate gunmen to the front or right-front of the presidential car, and quite likely, I may have reiterated that statement in the course of my deposition to the Rockefeller Commission. I must emphasize that I have never myself advocated that President Kennedy was shot from the Grassy Knoll or similar forward locations, so that this statement in no way represents a change from my previous views.

However, the crux and the primary thrust of my testimony, as well as of the papers I have published, is that the Warren Commission's single-bullet theory is wrong, and that the available medical, physical and photographic evidence all point to the fact that the assassination was carried out by two gunmen. The fact that both gunmen were located to the rear of the President, which after all includes half of the earth's surface, in no way diminishes the impact of that conclusion. Neither does such a conclusion have any bearing at all, pro or con, or the question of

CIA involvement in the assassination, and I have never claimed otherwise.

For the Commission to seize on a purely secondary aspect of my views, namely that I see no evidence for gunmen in front of the President, to bolster its claims that the Warren Report is correct, and that the CIA was not involved, is so absurd a *non sequitur* as to suggest that the Commission or its staff deliberately sought to misrepresent my testimony.

Representatives of the Commission have repeatedly asserted to me that the Commission's purposes in examining the JFK assassination have been restricted to the question of possible CIA involvement. In the report just issued, we find, in the section on this subject, that the Commission went well beyond that point, discussing evidentiary aspects of the case which suggest that Lee Harvey Oswald was the sole assassin, and citing various medical experts to bolster that claim. It is in this context that reference is made to a selected portion of my own testimony, as though I had concurred in the lone-assassin finding.

Obviously, it is a distortion to suggest, on the basis of a selected portion of my testimony, that I concur with the Commission's implied defense of the Warren Report when the great bulk of my testimony was directly to the opposite effect. Nor can the Commission justify its neglect of my other testimony on the ground that it lay outside its purposes of investigating only the question of CIA involvement, when, in fact, its report went considerably beyond that question.

Finally, I am outraged that the Commission refuses to make my testimony available to the public, and refuses even to make a copy available to me. For that reason, I am asking the Senate Committee chaired by Senator Church to investigate this aspect of the Commission's operations, and I have offered my cooperation in obtaining the release of such material.

Press release. © 1975 Cyril H. Wecht. Reprinted by permission.

EVIDENCE IGNORED
Paul L. Hoch

June 17, 1975

The Rockefeller Commission has apparently ignored evidence alleging a link between Lee Harvey Oswald and a specific plot to kill Fidel Castro. A memo* I sent to the Commission included new evidence relating to a visit by Oswald—or an impersonator—to Mrs. Sylvia Odio, a Dallas anti-Castro Cuban, about two months before the assassination of President Kennedy. "Oswald," in the company of two anti-Castro Cubans, reportedly told Mrs. Odio that Kennedy should have been shot. These two men were apparently friends of Mrs. Odio's father, who was in prison in Cuba specifically because of his role in an assassination attempt against Fidel Castro. (He had harbored one of the leaders of the plot, whose name is known.) This fact was apparently not known to the Warren Commission staff members, who took the Odio incident seriously, speculated that it might have reflected a conspiracy, and never successfully explained it.

I also pointed out to the Rockefeller Commission that the Warren Commission failed to check out reports about an apparent Oswald look-alike in Dallas, Manuel Rodriguez Orcarberro, who was affiliated with the same anti-Castro group as Odio's father's co-conspirators against Castro.

Executive Director David Belin told me that Commission Counsel Robert Olsen would be in touch with me about my memo, but Olsen never did contact me. Belin's only other response was to ask whether I agreed that Oswald shot Kennedy and Dallas Police Officer J. D. Tippit!

The Rockefeller Commission Report contains no reference to the information I provided. It is silent on the theory that a plot

---

* See "CIA Activities and the Warren Commission Investigation" earlier in this volume.

against Castro somehow backfired against Kennedy, either because of resentment when it was called off or (less plausibly) through retaliation by Castro. It was reported that the Commission was looking into this widely publicized theory.

The Commission purportedly limited its investigation of the Kennedy assassination to allegations that the CIA was involved, on the grounds that a broader review would be outside the scope of the mandate to investigate domestic CIA activities. The Report conspicuously fails to comment on one charge that is clearly within the mandate: that the CIA withheld information from the Warren Commission. It was widely believed that the Commission would cover this topic. Former Warren Commission staff lawyers David Slawson and Richard Mosk wrote in the Los Angeles *Times* of May 11 that "Currently, for example, the news media has reported that the White House Commission on the CIA is investigating the allegation that the CIA may not have fully disclosed all *relevant* information to the Warren Commission in an effort to cover up its own involvement with an assassination attempt on Castro. [My emphasis.] Such an issue should be investigated and apparently it is." (Since the CIA was reportedly involved in several attempts to kill Castro, and presumably knew of others, it probably has information in its files that is relevant to the Odio incident and was not given to the Warren Commission.)

It is possible that material on this aspect of the Kennedy assassination is in the file on CIA plots against foreign leaders which was omitted from the Report and given to President Ford and the Church Committee. (There is, however, no indication in the Rockefeller Report or in the press that any Kennedy assassination material was included.) I have asked Mr. Belin whether my memo was passed on; there has been no answer.

The only possible reference to my memo in the Rockefeller Report is the statement that "A witness, a telephone caller, and a mail correspondent tendered additional information of the same nature. None of it was more than a strained effort to draw inferences of conspiracy from facts which would not fairly support the inferences." I have asked Mr. Belin and a Commission member (who also received the memo) if I am the mail correspondent whose work was dismissed in that fashion, and so far have received no answer.

Other allegations of CIA withholding from the Warren Commission do not relate to Castro assassination plots and thus should have been covered by the Rockefeller Report. (The Report has chapters on the CIA and the Watergate cover-up, and on relationships with other agencies, where the Warren Commission issue could have been dealt with, but was not.) I provided documentary evidence that the CIA falsely told the FBI on the day of the assassination that there was no CIA-originated material in the Oswald file. Daniel Schorr has reported that the CIA was reluctant to provide information from Soviet defector Yuri Nosenko because the Agency suspected he was a plant. I also discussed in detail the indications that the CIA may have withheld material on Oswald's contacts with Albert Schweitzer College, Agency files on Marina Oswald, and an unidentified man photographed in Mexico and mistakenly identified as Oswald. (An article by Bernard Fensterwald and George O'Toole on the Mexico photos was submitted to the Commission and ignored in the Report.)

The Rockefeller Commission chose to restrict its inquiry into the Kennedy assassination in a way that allowed it to focus on some of the most sensational and (by and large) easily rebuttable charges. Almost all of Chapter 19 is devoted to the highly implausible theory that the CIA, through E. Howard Hunt and Frank Sturgis, was responsible for the assassination. The claim that Hunt and Sturgis are the well-known "tramps" photographed shortly after the assassination has been rejected by most of the responsible critics. I told the Commission that "the necessary rebuttal of some of the wilder allegations must not become an excuse for avoiding more complicated, but more plausible, charges." The Commission eagerly used that excuse.

The brief discussion of the CIA's relationship with Oswald and Ruby improperly concentrates on rebutting the claim that Oswald knew Hunt or Ruby knew Sturgis. There is no reference to newly disclosed evidence that the members of the Warren Commission knew that the CIA would have denied an informant relationship with Oswald if one existed. There is no discussion of the questions I and others raised about domestic CIA intelligence gathering in the Oswald case, several apparent peculiarities in the CIA's handling of Oswald, possible CIA investigation of the assassination after the Warren Report was issued, and possible improper interest in Warren Report critics.

A PETITION TO CONGRESS TO INVESTIGATE THE JOHN KENNEDY ASSASSINATION AND COVER-UP

ASSASSINATION INFORMATION BUREAU
1975

WHEREAS:	the Warren Commission's verdict that President John Kennedy was killed by Lee Harvey Oswald, acting alone, has not stood the test of adversary investigation, and yet official voices still maintain it;
WHEREAS:	individual citizens, working with only their persistence, courage and common sense against official indifference, hostility and outright sabotage, have nevertheless proved to reasonable people that the assassination of the President is an unsolved crime;
WHEREAS:	a government that fails to properly investigate the assassination of its elected leader cannot pretend to be democratic;
THEREFORE:	We the undersigned petition the Congress to investigate the facts of the assassination of President John F. Kennedy in 1963 and the continuing cover-up.
	In particular, we petition the committees of Congress now examining the conduct of the Central Intelligence Agency, the Federal Bureau of Investigation, and other governmental, police and investigating authorities to investigate that cover-up and any other part that such police and investigating authorities may have played relative to the facts surrounding the assassination of John F. Kennedy.

[A.I.B., 63 Inman St., Cambridge, Ma. 02139]

FOR FURTHER REFERENCE

In addition to the AIB, whose conferences and lecture tours have done much to generate and focus revived interest in the assassinations, the following groups are currently active:

Committee to Investigate Assassinations (headed by Bernard Fensterwald), 927 15th Street, NW, Washington, D.C. 20005
Citizens Commission of Inquiry (headed by Mark Lane), 103 2nd Street, NE, Washington, D.C. 20002
Committee to Investigate Political Assassinations, 11926 Santa Monica Boulevard, Los Angeles, California 90025
Campaign for Democratic Freedoms (headed by Don Freed), P.O. Box 9662, Marina Del Rey, California 90291
The Fifth Estate, P.O. Box 647, Washington, D.C. 20044

In this anthology, we have unfortunately been constrained to omit a large amount of important and informative material from many books and articles. Some of the books mentioned herein contain valuable bibliographies. Readers are also referred to "The Assassination of John Fitzgerald Kennedy: An annotated bibliography," by David R. Wrone (*Wisconsin Magazine of History*, Autumn 1972) and "American Political Assassinations: A bibliography of works published 1963–1970 . . ." compiled by the Committee to Investigate Assassinations.

Bibliographic Citations for Contents, in Order of Appearance

Johnson, Lyndon Baines, *The Vantage Point* (New York: Holt, Rinehart and Winston, 1971), pp. 25–27.

Report of the President's Commission on the Assassination of President Kennedy (Washington: Government Printing Office, 1964), pp. 1–27.

Lane, Mark, "A Defense Brief for Lee Harvey Oswald," *National Guardian*, December 19, 1963.

Meagher, Sylvia, *Accessories after the Fact* (Indianapolis and New York: Bobbs-Merrill, 1967), pp. 253–282.

Roffman, Howard, *Presumed Guilty* (Rutherford, N.J.: Fairleigh Dickinson University Press, 1975), pp. 201–203, 213–224.

Meagher, Sylvia, op. cit., pp. 376–387.

Weisberg, Harold, *Frame-Up* (New York: Outerbridge and Dienstfrey, 1971), pp. 468–481.

Hoch, Paul L., "Ford, Jaworski and the National Security Cover-Up," unpublished manuscript, 1974.

Lesar, James, "Freedom Is Secrecy," in Harold Weisberg and James Lesar, *Whitewash IV* (Frederick, Md.: Harold Weisberg, 1974), pp. 172–177.

O'Toole, George, "Lee Harvey Oswald Was Innocent," *Penthouse*, April 1975, pp. 45ff.

Meagher, Sylvia, op. cit., pp. 27–35.

Lifton, David S. and David Welsh, "The Case for Three Assassins," *Ramparts*, January 1967.

Lifton, David S., "A Note on the Fatal Shot, As Depicted on the Zapruder Film," unpublished manuscript, 1975.

Thompson, Josiah, *Six Seconds in Dallas* (New York: Bernard Geis Associates, 1967), pp. 142–165.

Wecht, Cyril H., "Pathologist's View of JFK Autopsy: An Unsolved Case," *Modern Medicine*, November 27, 1972, pp. 28–32.

Wecht, Cyril H. and Robert P. Smith, "The Medical Evidence in the Assassination of President John F. Kennedy," *Forensic Science*, 3 (1974), pp. 124–128.

Meagher, Sylvia, "The Curious Testimony of Mr. Givens," *Texas Observer*, August 13, 1971, pp. 11–12.

Belin, David W., "Truth Was My Only Goal," *Texas Observer*, August 13, 1971, pp. 13–15.

Belin, David W., "The Warren Commission Was Right," *The New York Times*, November 22, 1971.

Policoff, Jerry, "The Media and the Murder of John Kennedy," *New Times*, August 8, 1973, pp. 29–36.

Slawson, W. David, and Richard M. Mosk, "Kennedy Conspiracy Discounted," *Los Angeles Times*, May 11, 1975.

Turner, William, "The Garrison Commission," *Ramparts*, January 1968, pp. 46–52.

Noyes, Peter, *Legacy of Doubt*, (New York: Pinnacle Books, 1973), pp. 104–114.

Meagher, Sylvia, *Accessories*, pp. 456–457.

Chastain, Wayne, "Ray Says Guilty Plea Coerced," Pacific News Service, October 20, 1974.

Weisberg, Harold, *Frame-Up*, pp. 451–454.

Kaiser, Robert Blair, "*R.F.K. Must Die!*" (New York: E. P. Dutton, 1970), pp. 530–539.

Langman, Betsy, and Alexander Cockburn, "Sirhan's Gun," *Harper's*, January 1975.

Scott, Peter Dale, "From Dallas to Watergate," *Ramparts*, November 1973, pp. 12–18, 53–54.

Anderson, Jack, columns of January 18 and 19, 1971, United Feature Syndicate.

Hunt, E. Howard, *Give Us This Day* (New Rochelle, New York: Arlington House, 1973), pp. 14–15, 38–39.

Szulc, Tad, "Cuba on Our Mind," *Esquire*, February 1974, pp. 90–91.

Vidal, Gore, "The Art and Arts of E. Howard Hunt," *New York Review of Books*, December 13, 1973, pp. 17–18.

Sutton, Horace, "The Curious Intrigues of Cuban Miami," *Saturday Review/World*, September 11, 1973, pp. 24–30.

Scott, Peter Dale, "Vietnamization and the Drama of the Pentagon Papers," in Noam Chomsky and Howard Zinn, eds., *Pentagon Papers Volume 5: Critical Essays* (Boston: Beacon Press, 1972), pp. 211–247.

Scott, Peter Dale, "Assassinations and Domestic Surveillance," unpublished manuscript, 1975.

Fensterwald, Bernard, and George O' Toole, "The CIA and the Man Who Was Not Oswald," *New York Review of Books*, April 3, 1975, pp. 24–25.

Hoch, Paul L., "CIA Activities and the Warren Commission Investigation," unpublished memorandum, March 24, 1975.

Report of the Commission on CIA Activities Within the United States, (Washington: Government Printing Office, 1975), pp. 251–269.

Wecht, Cyril H., press release, June 12, 1975.

Hoch, Paul L., press release, June 17, 1975.

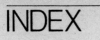

INDEX

(Contributors are indicated by pages in italics)

Rocca, Raymond G., 454, 458, 481

Rockefeller Commission, 211, 265, 270, 305, 449–523

Rockefeller, Nelson, 449, 495

Rodriguez Orcarberro, Manuel, 493, 521

Roetke, James N., 496

Roffman, Howard, 5, *93*

Rolland, Chuck, 281

Romero, Juan, 341

Rorke, Alexander, 361–2, 374

Roselli, John, 362, 374–5, 377–8, 488–9, 491

Rossides, Eugene, 402

Rostow, Eugene, 11

Rothman, Norman, 370

Rowland, Arnold, 207–8

Rowley, James J., 219

Ruby, Jack, xiii, 3, 11, 36, 37, 40–2, 53, 56, 67, 75–6, 113–4, 131, 146, 337, 354, 356, 360, 364, 367–71 382, 452–3, 461–2, 496, 516–8, 523

Rusk, Dean, 11, 411fn., 413, 419–20, 423–4, 428, 430fn

Russell, Richard, 13–14, 138, 171

Russo, Perry Raymond, 287, 296

St. George, Andrew, 362

St. Louis *Post-Dispatch*, 182–4

Salandria, Vincent J., 178, 209, 212

Salisbury, Harrison, 264–6

Sandlin, Det. Sgt., 329

Santiero, Elena, 373

Saturday Evening Post, 264, 296

Sawyer, J. Herbert, 24, 245, 248

Schacht, Hjalmar, 293

Schauer, Richard, 335

Schlei, Norbert A., 130

Schlesinger, Arthur M., Jr., 112, 264

Schlumberger Well Co., 284

Schorr, Daniel, 523

Schrade, Paul, 347, 349

Schulte, Valerie, 341

Schwarzer, William W., 495

Scobey, Alfredda, 14

Scoggins, William W., 23, 56, 58, 84, 252, 260

Scott, Peter Dale, *357, 406, 407–8, 443*

"Second Naval Guerrilla," 385

Secret Service, 16, 34, 43–8, 113, 118, 126, 128, 136, 140, 152, 157, 177, 179, 183–4, 199, 245, 247, 270, 282, 287, 294, 360, 373, 443–6, 455, 460, 470, 472–3, 481–2, 515

Seymour, William, 103–6, 111, 115

Shaffer, Charles N., Jr., 14

Shaneyfelt, Lyndal L., 171, 503

Shannon, Edgar F., Jr., 495

Sharp, Ulysses, 380

Shaw, Clay, 8–9, 268, 284–5, 287, 290, 292, 294–7, 299–300, 484

Shaw, Raymond, 331–2

Shaw, Robert R., 173, 175–6, 223

Sheehan, Joseph and Margaret, 329

Shelley, William, 195, 246

Shelton, Robert, 130

Sihanouk, Prince, 436

MARK LANE is the author of *Rush to Judgment* and now heads the Citizens Commission of Inquiry in Washington, D.C.

SYLVIA MEAGHER compiled the definitive subject index to the Warren Report and the twenty-six volumes of Warren Commission hearings and is the author of *Accessories after the Fact.*

HOWARD ROFFMAN is the author of *Presumed Guilty* and is writing a book on the origins of the Cold War.

HAROLD WEISBERG is the author of six books on the John F. Kennedy assassination (*Whitewash I & II, Photographic Whitewash, White-Wash IV, Oswald in New Orleans* and *Post-Mortem*) and one on the Martin Luther King assassination (*Frame-Up*).

JAMES H. LESAR served on the James Earl Ray defense team, has handled a number of important suits under the Freedom of Information Act, and now practices law in Washington, D.C.

GEORGE O'TOOLE, former chief of the CIA's Problems Analysis Branch, is the author of *The Assassination Tapes.*

DAVID S. LIFTON, a long-time student of the Warren Report, is writing a book on the John F. Kennedy assassination.

DAVID WELSH directed the investigation of the John F. Kennedy assassination and its aftermath for *Ramparts* magazine.

JOSIAH THOMPSON teaches philosophy at Haverford College and is the author of *Six Seconds in Dallas*.

CYRIL H. WECHT, the coroner of Allegheny County in Pennsylvania, is director of the Institute of Forensic Sciences at the Duquesne University School of Law in Pittsburgh.

ROBERT P. SMITH, formerly in charge of research at the Committee to Investigate Assassinations, is associated with the Coroner's Office of Allegheny County in Pittsburgh, Pennsylvania.

DAVID W. BELIN served as assistant counsel to the Warren Commission and executive director of the Rockefeller Commission.

JERRY POLICOFF is a researcher who has specialized in media coverage of the assassinations of the Kennedy brothers and Martin Luther King.

W. DAVID SLAWSON served as assistant counsel to the Warren Commission and is now professor of law at the University of Southern California.

RICHARD M. MOSK served on the staff of the Warren Commission and now practices law in Los Angeles.

WILLIAM W. TURNER, a former FBI agent, was an investigator for Jim Garrison in New Orleans and is the author of *Hoover's FBI* and *Power on the Right*.

PETER NOYES, a journalist, is the author of *Legacy of Doubt*.

WAYNE CHASTAIN, a Memphis attorney, has written several articles on the Martin Luther King assassination.

ROBERT BLAIR KAISER, is the author of *R.F.K. Must Die!* and *Pope, Council and World*.

BETSY LANGMAN is writing a book on the assassination of Robert F. Kennedy.

ALEXANDER COCKBURN is a columnist for the *Village Voice*.

E. HOWARD HUNT, a former CIA agent, is the author of *Give Us This Day* and many works of fiction.

TAD SZULC, a former correspondent for *The New York Times*, is the author of *Compulsive Spy*, a biography of E. Howard Hunt.

GORE VIDAL is the author of *Burr* and other novels.

HORACE SUTTON is editorial director of *Saturday Review*.

BERNARD FENSTERWALD served as chief counsel to Senator Edward Long's investigation of government wiretapping and is now director of the Committee to Investigate Assassinations in Washington, D.C.

ABOUT THE EDITORS

PETER DALE SCOTT was born in 1929 in Montreal, Canada. A former Canadian diplomat with a Ph.D. in political science, he now teaches English at the University of California, Berkeley. In addition to poetry and translations of poetry, he has published on topics ranging from medieval literature to the origins of the Vietnam War. While writing a book-length study of the latter (*The War Conspiracy*, 1972), he discovered important shifts in U.S. Vietnam policy that followed within forty-eight hours of the assassination of President John F. Kennedy. Since 1972 he has continued to research and publish on the political context of the Kennedy assassination.

PAUL L. HOCH, born in 1942, received a Ph.D. in elementary-particle physics from the University of California, Berkeley. Since 1965 he has worked with many of the Warren Report critics whose work appears in this book. He is completing a study of the Warren Commission's investigation of the relationship between the FBI and Lee Harvey Oswald (and has been trying without much success to obtain the release of the FBI's Oswald files).

RUSSELL STETLER was born in Philadelphia in 1945. A former aide to Bertrand Russell, he now writes for the West Coast news service Internews. His political journalism has been widely published. He is the author of *The Battle of Bogside* (1970), a critique of an official investigation of the effects of riot-control technology in Northern Ireland. He has also edited collections on Vietnam (1970) and the Arab-Israeli conflict (1972).